THE LITERATURE OF ARCHITECTURE

DON GIFFORD is a Professor of English at Williams College, where he has taught for the past fifteen years. He was educated at The Principia College in Illinois, at Cambridge University, and at Harvard University. During World War II he drove an ambulance in the American Field Service before serving in the Army of the United States. After the war Mr. Gifford tried his hand at writing novels and working on commercial films before he settled down to teach, first at Mills College of Education in New York and subsequently at Williams. His teaching career has occasionally been interrupted by periods of work as a consultant to various industries on the process of invention.

The Literature *of* Architecture

THE EVOLUTION OF ARCHITECTURAL THEORY
AND PRACTICE IN NINETEENTH-CENTURY AMERICA

Edited by

Don Gifford

New York / E. P. DUTTON & CO., INC. / 1966

A Dutton  *Paperback*

Acknowledgments

Grateful acknowledgment is made to the following for permission
to quote from copyright material:

Robert Mills: "The Progress of Architecture in Virginia" and "The
Architectural Works of Robert Mills." Reprinted from *Robert
Mills, Architect of the Washington Monument* by H. M. Pierce
Gallagher by permission of the Columbia University Press.
Copyright, 1935, by the Columbia University Press.

Ralph Waldo Emerson: "Letter to Margaret Fuller" and "Letter
to Horatio Greenough." Reprinted from *The Letters of Ralph
Waldo Emerson,* ed. Ralph L. Rusk, by permission of the Ralph
Waldo Emerson Memorial Association and the Columbia Uni-
versity Press. Copyright, 1939, by the Columbia University
Press.

Horatio Greenough: "Letter to R. W. Emerson." Reprinted from
"Ralph Waldo Emerson and Horatio Greenough" by Nathalia
Wright in the *Harvard Library Bulletin,* Winter, 1958, by per-
mission of the President and Fellows of Harvard College.

Henry David Thoreau: Excerpt reprinted from *The Journal of*

Contents

List of Illustrations

ACKNOWLEDGMENTS

The starred (*) illustrations have been provided by Sandak, Inc., from the survey of the Arts of the United States conducted under a grant from the Carnegie Corporation. Colored slides from the survey collection are available from Sandak, Inc., 4 East Forty-eighth Street, New York, N.Y. The remainder of the illustrations, unless otherwise acknowledged, have been prepared specifically for this volume.

Illustration 7 is reproduced with the permission of the Maryland Historical Society, Baltimore, Maryland.

Illustration 15 is reproduced with the permission of the New Haven Colony Historical Society, New Haven, Connecticut.

Illustration 18 is reproduced with the permission of the New York Historical Society, New York, N.Y.

Illustrations 29 and 37 are reproduced with the permission of the Frank Lloyd Wright Foundation and through the courtesy of the Horizon Press in New York City.

Illustrations 39–42 are reproduced with the permission of the *Chicago Tribune*, Chicago, Illinois.

Acknowledgments

This anthology has evolved from a ten-year cooperative experiment with a course in American Art and Literature that was established as part of a coordinated study of several phases of the American past in The American Studies Program for Executives at Williams College. The course in art and literature as originally conceived was designed and taught by three of us: Professors William H. Pierson, Jr., and Whitney S. Stoddard of the Department of Art, and myself from the Department of English at Williams College. As designed, the course alternated individual lectures on art, architecture, and literature with panel discussions in which we related (and discriminated among) aspects of the three arts in their cultural contexts. From its outset the course was an exciting voyage of discovery for each of us. It was the sort of interdisciplinary study that is one of the values of a liberal-arts approach, an educational value we all too often have to forego in favor of economy and of the demands of our individual disciplines.

After the first year of the course Professor Pierson withdrew from direct participation under the pressure of other commitments, notably to the Carnegie Foundation's survey of the arts of the United States, a survey from which many of the illustrations for this volume have been drawn. The continuing association and dialogue with Professor Stoddard has led me deeper into an interest in "the very compound nature of architecture," a nature that makes architecture, among other things, a fascinating reflector of aesthetic experience in nineteenth-century America. Professor Stoddard's guidance and concern and Professor Pierson's advice have been central in the apprenticeship that has led to this book; and yet I hardly intend this as a subtle transfer of responsibility from myself to my colleagues. The student's responsibilities are and remain his own; if he is well taught (and I have been), he should be that much the better prepared to go it alone.

Since the anthology is interdisciplinary, ranging not only beyond my own field but also beyond the field of architecture, the process of editing has been, in part, a brain-picking expedition; many of my colleagues and friends have helped me with instruction and references; to list them all would be to make these acknowledgments read like the list of courses of instruction in a college catalogue.

For the information on that elusive character William E. Bell, I should like to thank J. Ray Beffel of the Ottawa, Illinois, *Daily Republican-Times*. I am indebted to Mrs. Ruth Vollmer of New York and to Mrs. Lily Boecher of Stockbridge, Massachusetts, for their translations from the German; to Miss Juanita Terry, Reference Librarian at Williams College, for her assistance; and particularly to Mrs. Nancy MacFadyen of the Williams College Library staff, whose patient pursuit of many of the relatively rare documents excerpted for this anthology has literally made the anthology possible.

D. G.

Introduction

Nineteenth-century man in the Western world seems, in retrospect, to have been involved in a multidirectional search for new "forms" among what struck him as a bewildering variety of alternatives. Science, technology, religion, the economic structure, and the political and social order, all were undergoing radical and disruptive change. The search for form in this world of change appears to us a century later to have been profoundly ambiguous: buoyed up by the assurance of a brave new world just over the horizon of progress, and haunted by the sense of a world in violent disintegration where, in Matthew Arnold's phrase, old forms were "dead," new forms "powerless to be born." But for all its ambiguity, the nineteenth-century search for form produced an impressive variety of creative efforts. One field that reflects this variety of search with all its false starts, its self-contradictions, and its creative promise is the field of architecture. Architecture, combining as it does technology, economics, and aesthetics, is a peculiarly sensitive reflector of the ideas-complex of the nineteenth century.

The central focus of this anthology is on the various and conflicting attitudes, both theoretical and practical, that characterized the field of architecture in nineteenth-century America and that resolved into the watchword phrase "Form follows function" and the ideal of an "organic architecture" at the end of the century. The anthology is divided into five parts. Part I, "Prologue in Europe (1750–1825)" and Part V, "Reaction in America and Epilogue in Europe (1893–1920)" provide a frame for Parts II, III, and IV, which concentrate on the American scene: II, "The Confluence of Ideas (1820–1865)"; III, "The New Technology (1820–1880)"; and IV, "Coordination of Theory and Practice (1880–1910)." Spelling, punctuation, and typography have been made consistent with modern American usage. Errors of fact, where detectable, or of orthography, especially in some of the earlier authors, have been corrected. Ellipses indicate omission of irrelevant material.

The objectives of this anthology are several. It seeks to reflect in its selections the variety, confusion, and evolution of attitudes that reached a climax in the work of Louis Sullivan and Frank Lloyd Wright at the end of the nineteenth century. In this sense the anthology seeks to reflect developments in a period of architectural history. The anthology also seeks to present a microcosm for a study in the history of ideas and in the history of culture—an example of how a complex but identifiable concept was imported from Europe, how it underwent sea changes and transformations in this country, and how subsequently it was exported to Europe before World War I, only to be reimported, ironically enough, as "modern architecture" in the 1930's. Architecture involves delimited concepts with comparatively well-focused history, theory, criticism, and practice—as against the concepts that cluster around "nature," "the soul," "man," "society," and so on; consequently, a study of architectural concepts offers the student of culture or the student of ideas a glimpse of direction in the flux of ideas and attitudes, not unlike the glimpse of direction that dye poured into the current of a stream affords.

The limitations of this anthology are also several. It does not attempt to trace all the beginnings of the variety of architectural and critical ideas that were abroad in the nineteenth century. Arbitrarily, eighteenth-century figures such as Marc-Antoine Laugier and Carlo Lodoli have been treated as a beginning, which, of course, they weren't. This anthology also treats the American experience partially *in vacuo,* pretending, for the sake of economy and some clarity, that the importation of ideas was complete by the 1830's; the selection thus by-passes what was a lively American interest in parallel European developments, in the ideas of the English theologian Edward Lacy Garbett; of the English critic John Ruskin; of the Scotch architectural historian James Fergusson; and of the French architect Eugène Viollet-le-Duc. Another anthology could helpfully trace these parallel and yet quite different developments in European theory, but the present anthology could not so complicate itself and remain portable.

One final limitation: The anthology ends with the emergence of the twentieth-century point of view in Sullivan and Wright, and with the initial impact of their ideas and practices in the first two decades of this century. This end point may give the impression that a single point of view was born in the period 1890–1910, when what was born has proved to be quite as various as the multifaceted nineteenth-century past from which it derived.

A note of caution: Many of the selections in this book repeat the same general ideas, but it would be a mistake to assume communication among all these writers. The ideal of an "organic" architecture in which "form follows function" seems to have been approached simultaneously by a number of individuals, working from a variety of different points of view and using at times deceptively similar vocabularies. It seems to have been an ideal that was "in the air," felt in general as a "bent of the mind" rather than as an ideal adopted from one dramatic and powerful announcement. Even if we ask: Who defined this ideal in the first place? there is no very clear answer; and the search for the sole originator could well distract us from the generative flux created by the many originators who gave the ideal its flesh and its various expressions. Perhaps we too carelessly assume that an idea is first generated, then articulated and published, and finally adopted and applied—when what really happens is like a soup mix with all three steps interconfused by a multitude of cooks. Similarly, in the history of technology we carelessly assume that first a need arises, then the problem is formulated, and finally the solution is invented, when quite often the solution is invented before the problem is clearly understood and before the need has arisen.

Historians of nineteenth-century architecture stress the sense of a century divided against itself. On the one hand theory called for an architecture that would be both useful and beautiful, organic in its forms; on the other hand architectural practice indulged in a series of revivals (Greek, Gothic, Tuscan Villa, Elizabethan, Romanesque, Queen Anne, and so on) in which buildings as various as cowsheds and cathedrals were given the same "picturesque" forms. The irony is that, as divergent as these two approaches seem, at the core they both derive from the Romantic Movement and both reflect essentially literary and "poetic" attitudes toward the experience of architecture. The Romantic ideal of "organic form" received its initial definition and emphasis in literary criticism, from Coleridge's distinction between the organic form of Shakespeare's plays ("innate, it shapes, as it develops itself from within") and the "mechanic" form of lesser drama ("when on any given material we impress a predetermined form not necessarily arising out of the properties of the material.")

Parallel with the Romantic desire for organic form were the Romantic sympathies that rediscovered and re-evaluated periods of the past. The Romantics downgraded the Romans as materialists and upgraded the Greeks as idealists. Byron and Keats saw in Greek art the democratic ideal in its earliest and fullest flower; and the Greek war of independence against the Turks in the 1820's excited the Romantic imagination not only with the ideal of political liberty but also with visions of a Periclean rebirth. The Greek "revival" was particularly appealing to Americans who saw the United States as democratic Greece, as against the imperial Rome of England, and who saw in the Greek struggle for independence a repetition of the American struggle in a classic setting. Romantic attitudes subsequently shifted, qualifying the early Romantics' devotion to things Greek and finding in Gothic architecture images of the mystery and excitement of deep spiritual and moral impulse—the natural, emotional, and organic, as against the cold reason of the Enlightenment that had condemned the Middle Ages as barbaric, as the creation of the Goths.

The Greek and Gothic revivals in architecture were essentially attempts to give present experience added dimension and meaning. Thus the revivals were of particular importance to America with its superabundance of the new and its foreshortened past. On this level the revivals became an attempt to create a past, to fill a gap in the American's sense of his country's history, just as Washington Irving tried to transpose the history of New Netherland into comic legend, just as Cooper tried to make Natty Bumpo's frontier into something like Scott's Middle Ages. The revivals were also more important here than abroad because there was simply more building in America as territory expanded and as the population grew, exploded, from 5 million in 1800 to 31 million in 1860 and 76 million in 1900. The revivals were not only attempts to create a sense of history; they were also attempts to excite an emotional response to architecture by literary and picturesque reference to idealized historical periods. The ideal of an organic form was similarly expressive in its aim, intended to excite an intuitive and emotional response that transcended the rational and mechanical.

The revival approach underwent a series of changes in the nineteenth century. It began with Greek revival in the 1820's, Gothic in the 1840's, and then, rapidly, Tuscan Villa, Elizabethan, Romanesque, Queen Anne, and, in the early twentieth century, Renaissance and Georgian. Each revival was subject to a wide variety of interpretation by its practitioners: from painstakingly honest replication of monuments of the past to eclectic combination of any and all the bits and pieces from the grab bag of architectural history. Superficially, revivalism appears to be at odds with functionalism and organicism, but the high point in the history of the revivals is the work of Henry Hobson Richardson. The vitality of Richardson's Romanesque forms impressed, among others, Louis Sullivan, as a great architectural breakthrough in the 1880's; thus Richardson stands as the most successful practitioner of the revivalist approach, and yet the vigor and strength of his architectural forms and his forthright use of materials excite the functional-organic idealist. Revivalism, of course, declined into decadence in the conspicuous-consumption classicism of the World Columbian Exposition (Chicago, 1893) and in the Gothicism of the Woolworth Building (1913).

The ideal of organic form, innate, developing from a spiritual or ideational withinness, has also undergone its metamorphoses. Initially, following Coleridge, "organic" implied a necessary relation between the imaginative idea within and the outward material form. But the word "organic" suggests a variety of possibilities: that an architectural form should be like a natural organism, that the interrelation of parts to each other and to the whole should be "natural," that the relation of a building to its occupants and their pursuits should be natural and plastic, that the relation of a building to its site and to the natural world should be in organic continuum. All this variety crops up in nineteenth-century speculation, and has hardly been clarified into more

than a suggestive ideal, even by Frank Lloyd Wright, its
great twentieth-century exponent.

The ideal of organic form is further complicated when it is
interrelated with ideals of fitness and utility: that a building's
forms should fit and not disguise the uses for which the
building is intended. This complication is compounded by
the wide-ranging definitions of "use," and consequently of
"fitness." "Use" can be defined in terms of crass utility; it
can also be defined, following Emerson's suggestion, in terms
of the aesthetic, moral, and intellectual usefulness of beauty.
The key words have thus been subject to a variety of inter-
pretations and meanings. This is also true of the watchword
phrase "Form follows function." The phrase occurs first in a
letter from Horatio Greenough to Emerson (1852) and again
in the table of contents, though not in the text, of Leopold
Eidletz's *The Nature and Function of Art* (1881); finally,
of course, it became Sullivan's and the twentieth century's
watchword. But as a phrase, it presents the same definition
problems: Does "function" mean sheer utility or does it
include expressive, moral, and aesthetic overtones? Does form
mean the visual and decorative or does it mean structural
pattern or does it refer to the inclusive shapes of spaces
and masses? Nineteenth- and twentieth-century answers to
these questions have ranged widely, and continue to range
widely, between the possible extremes. Not that this variety
is good or bad but that it should render the student of
architectural theory humble and wary.

Perhaps the most complex of these tangles of definition
centers on the words "nature" and "natural"—words that
repeatedly are associated with the organic and the functional.
As Frank Lloyd Wright put it:

Integration, or even the word "organic" itself, means that
nothing is of value except as it is naturally related to the whole in
the direction of some living purpose.

It makes a great deal of difference whether nature ("naturally") in this context is considered as a system of balanced
and rationally describable laws, as the Abbé Laugier assumed
in 1752; or whether it is "essences unchanged by man," essences essentially benign and with which man is capable of
intuitive harmony, as Emerson declared in 1836; or whether

nature is "power," as Sullivan felt in the 1890's; or whether nature is regarded ecologically as comprising "all the requirements and characteristics of live organisms," as Richard Neutra remarked in 1954. This variety of possible meanings requires an alert attention to contexts and a willingness to assume that emphasis has shifted profoundly even if the theory appears constant in its expression from Greenough in 1852 to our own time.

The ideals of organicism, functionalism, and revivalism appear to be opposed on the surface, but they are difficult to separate either in their inception or in their development. When they are arbitrarily separated and treated as opposites among which the critic has to choose, the critic finds himself in trouble. If he chooses functionalism, he is required to downgrade the sensitive Greek and Gothic buildings of architects such as Town and Davis, and he is also embarrassed into having to rationalize Richardson's use of Romanesque forms and Sullivan's florid, curvilinear decoration. The clearest way out of this embarrassment is to regard revivalism, functionalism, and organicism as the interrelated and interdependent points of view that historically they were.

Another way of focusing this sense of the nineteenth century as a century divided against itself is to point up the opposition between technology and art. In architecture this opposition is reflected as a split between the architect as engineer and the architect as decorator. The opposition seems to be a real and apparent one, but it needs to be qualified, though perhaps not so severely as the oppositions among revivalism, functionalism, and organicism. In the nineteenth century the opposition between technology and art appears to have been less obvious to its practitioners than it is to us. Ithiel Town (1784–1844) made a fortune from the technological invention of the Town Lattice Truss (1820); but he was also a careful and sensitive designer of Greek and Gothic revival buildings. Samuel F. B. Morse (1791–1872), who is important to us as the inventor of the telegraph, was important to himself and to his contemporaries as a professional and successful easel painter. Horatio Greenough, whose vigorous call for a "new architecture" has appealed to some historians as the origin of modern architectural theory, performed somewhat differently in his role as professional sculptor. When he was commissioned to do a statue of George Washington for the Rotunda of the Capitol in Washington, D.C., he produced a figure, naked to the waist, in the attitude of Phidias's lost statue of Zeus; he produced in sculpture precisely what he seemed to have been inveighing against in architecture. Upon its arrival in Washington from Florence where it was carved, Greenough's sculpture proved too large for the doors of the Rotunda; the jambs had to be removed; and when it was in place, it was visually distorted by inadequate lighting, and the floor threatened to sag—all this from a man who was arguing eloquently for organic interrelation of form and function, beauty and use.

The mid-nineteenth-century individual could apparently combine in himself the opposed impulses of art and technology, just as an Emerson could alternate between "Concord and Boston, the dear old spiritual world and even the dear old devil not far off." Or just as a Thoreau or an Audubon could combine in himself the poet of nature with the scientific naturalist, dedicated to precise observation. The opposition between art and technology, while dramatically apparent in retrospect, was not nearly so apparent to the nineteenth-century individual living in the midst of that opposition. Technological change not only alters man's capacity to arrange his environment; it also alters his capacity to organize the fields of his perception. There have clearly been times in history when one capacity has outstripped the other—as the technological explosion of the period 1820–1860 radically expanded the capacity to change the environment, and simultaneously confused the capacity to organize the fields of perception. The rapid implementation of the railroad and the telegraph in this period, for example, faced the individual not just with a new mechanical ability to move and to send messages but also with a profound change in the space-time in terms of which he was to perceive. In 1820 it took days to deliver a message from Boston to New York; in 1860 it was a matter of hours by railroad or seconds by telegraph. This change meant, in effect, that the hand could do things which the eye had not been trained to synthesize into a coherent perceptual world. The awareness of the disparity between hand and eye became sharper *after* the impact of change (by the 1890's) than it was at the actual time of the change, even though by 1900 the eye had begun to catch up with what the hand had already done. In this sense the disparity is a twentieth-century concern for which we have found in the readily apparent disparities of the nineteenth-century world a convenient vocabulary of historical example. The irony is that the twentieth century continues to change the environment with the hand at a rate far beyond the eye's informed capacity to envision a coherent world. This imbalance is not necessarily good or bad in itself, but an awareness of it should make us cautious about the ways in which we depict (and often ridicule) the imbalances of the past.

Twentieth-century definitions of what architecture ought to be seem to have established a broad base of agreement, but they are still none too clear. For all this century's self-consciousness about the necessity for clarity in definition, architects, critics, and commentators continue to create and to enjoy a soup mix not unlike that of the nineteenth century. We postulate functionalism as a generally accepted "ideal for the architect, yardstick for the critic"; at the same time we are none too clear about what we mean by "function." We can, for example, treat the two words "functional" and "organic" as interchangeable expressions of the same ideal. "Organic" as a word partially lends itself to this interchange, reinforced as it is by the emphasis, in evolutionary biology, on the ways in which organisms are fitted for their functions. But the two words do not interchangeably mean the same thing, and our tendency to mix them serves to obscure a deeply rooted potential conflict between the assumption that form is abstract, a formal imposition on what is essentially chaos, and the assumption that form is relative, an outgrowth of what is essentially an underlying order. This conflict, once in the open, could become an important source of creative dialogue and energy, and to obscure it may well be to hamper ourselves in conformity to fixed but unclarified definitions instead of freeing ourselves to create and clarify new points of departure.

Another ideal that we regard as having a sort of universal validity in the twentieth century is the ideal that the beautiful should be useful, the useful, beautiful. But this is hardly a new ideal; its roots are intertwined with the roots of Western civilization. The newness resides not in the ideal itself but in our altered sense of the relationships it involves. Whether we vote for use as primary or beauty as primary makes little difference in face of the way the ideal has changed in the last two centuries. The development of modern technology has had three effects on the development of architcture: (1) It has changed systems and materials of construction; (2) it has changed the needs for and uses of architectural structures; (3) it has profoundly altered our sense of the beautiful and the useful and their interrelation. Of these three, the first two can be measured and documented. The third is elusive, difficult to measure and document. But it is this third effect that teases the mind because it suggests a profound alteration in our ways of thinking, and it suggests the circle questions: To what extent has the growth of technology effected an alteration of human thought and perception? and, To what extent has an alteration of thought and perception caused the growth of technology? The circle is, of course, unbreakable, a chicken-and-egg series; but within this circle there may be suggestive keys to the riddles: What are beauty and use, form and function, organic and abstract? and, What are or should be their interrelations?

DON GIFFORD

Williams College
Williamstown, Mass.

Part I: Prologue in Europe (1750-1825)

1. Introduction

The eighteenth century is usually characterized as an "Age of Reason," a century of preoccupation with rational analysis and with criticism. This characterization can be quite useful, but it can also trap us into regarding the eighteenth-century mind as narrowly dedicated to a sort of mental conformity, when in fact the century was impressive in the variety and wealth of the theoretical speculation that it produced. Speculation in aesthetic theory, and specifically in architectural theory, was particularly rich and various. There were countless attempts to discover and establish "rational principles," that is, principles that would be absolute and universally reproducible in practice. It was assumed that rational principles once achieved would be recognized and held in common by "all educated men" and that the principles applied would dictate good design and sound critical evaluation. The analogy to Newton's laws of motion would hold: universal recognition of Newton's principles was assumed to be inevitable; the principles could be applied in the practice of classical mechanics; and critically, analytically, they could be assumed to provide a coherent and sound evaluation of the systems of the universe.

The Italian architect Andrea Palladio (1518-1580), in his theory and through his practice, was regarded in the eighteenth century as the spokesman for Renaissance authority. He asserted:

Architecture (as all the other arts) being grounded upon Rules taken from imitation of Nature, admits of nothing that is contrary or foreign to that Order which Nature has prescrib'd to all things [in translation, London, 1742].

In accord with Palladio's dictum, the hinge of eighteenth-century speculative attempts to achieve a rational architecture was "Nature," and the shifting emphases of eighteenth-century architectural theory reflect shifting concepts of "Nature." The seventeenth-century Puritan assumed that "Nature" was "Order," and could regard reading in "the Book of Nature" as second in importance only to reading in the Bible. He regarded nature, from an essentially medieval point of view, as a system of hieroglyphs, "a mappe and shadowe of the spirituall estate of the soules of men," established by God for the moral instruction of mankind. The Puritan's secular Renaissance counterpart also assumed that nature was order, a system of symmetries, balances, and regularities established for the mathematical, rational instruction of mankind. As opposed as these two views seem to be, they both regarded nature as primarily "measure," "rule," "order," and in the eighteenth century they existed side by side in counterpoint, fusing in a variety of different ways.

Eighteenth-century architectural theoreticians could regard an architecture "in accordance with nature" as an architecture that reflected on the one hand moral order and on the other hand mathematical clarity and simplicity. One fusion of these two approaches occurred in the mid-century reaction against the forms of Baroque (circa 1550–1750) and Rococo (circa 1700–1750) architecture. The vitality of Baroque offended the partisans of moral order with what appeared an excessive, counter-Renaissance appeal to sensory response; and it offended the partisans of mathematical clarity and simplicity with its florid, curvilinear animation of spaces and masses and its disguise of structure. The mannered elaborations of the Rococo (a secular extension of the Baroque?) was attacked for similar offenses. As a corollary to this reaction from mid-century on, there was increasing interest in, and praise of, Greek architecture. Theoreticians saw it (as Pope saw Greek poetry) as "Nature still, but Nature methodiz'd"—nature and classical authority in combination. In contrast to Greek architecture, they regarded Gothic (and Baroque), in Berkeley's phrase, as "fantastical . . . for the most part founded neither in nature nor in reason, necessity or use." The double parallels (nature-reason, nature-necessity; necessity-use, reason-use) suggest the theoretical framework behind the evaluation "fantastical." It is ironic that the Romantic view of architecture when it emerged at the beginning of the nineteenth century would also call for an architecture in accord with nature, but would regard nature not as symmetries, balances, and regularities designed for mathematical-rational instruction, but as vital motion, flow, process, and growth designed to inspire the imagination and intuition; and this shift in the concept of nature would lead the nineteenth-century critic to rehabilitate the spiritual and emotional aspiration of Gothic architecture and to downgrade the cold rationality of Greek.

Although concepts of nature are basic, it would be misleading to argue that they were all-determinant. Architectural theory was also concerned with other problems and definitions: concepts of beauty, of utility and use, of proportion and fitness and their interrelations. These concepts were also subject to shifting and ambiguous emphasis. Beauty, for example, could be defined in absolute terms (as inherent by principle) and in relative terms (as dependent on the eye of the beholder). If beauty were regarded as absolute, then it would follow that architecture should consist in the determination and application of rule, mathematically established proportions, and so on; if relative, then architecture must concern itself with variations in customs, climate, materials, and so on. Sir Christopher Wren (1632–1723) made this distinction, and opted for what was to become a typical eighteenth-century resolution of the implied ambiguity:

There are two causes of Beauty, natural and customary. Natural is from geometry, consisting in Uniformity (that is Equality) and Proportion. Customary Beauty is begotten by the use of our senses to those objects which are usually pleasing to us from other causes, as Familiarity or particular Inclination breeds a Love to things not in themselves lovely . . . but always the true test is natural or geometrical Beauty.

In the course of the century this emphasis on the primacy of "natural," absolute beauty was modified and complicated by the growing interest in "antiquities" (archaeology) and by the emergence of modern attitudes toward history. From the

Renaissance until the middle of the eighteenth century the "classical" architecture known to Western Europe was largely Roman, and except in literature, little distinction was made between Greek and Roman art. Shortly after mid-century a succession of archaeological publications on Greek architecture made descriptive and analytic materials available for the first time. But the assumption that Greek architecture, like Greek literature, was a model of absolute beauty, "Nature methodiz'd," had predated familiarity with or knowledge of Greek buildings; and basically the assumption was, and tended to remain, literary rather than architectural. Archaeology thus helped to strengthen the interlink between "nature" and the authority of classical models and to reinforce the emphasis on absolute beauty. At the same time concepts of history as an open-ended or cyclical process began to emerge; and these new concepts combined with archaeological discovery to complicate and subtilize attitudes toward the historical past, and tended to reinforce the view that beauty was "custom"— relative to a place, a time, a climate, and a culture.

Concepts of utility and use reflect much the same ambiguity that invests concepts of beauty. Rational analysis logically came to the conclusion that *use* was primary in architectural design; but use was variously regarded as concern with the human functions to be housed, with moral values, with the symbolic function of monuments, and so on. Furthermore, rational analysis could as readily lead away from an emphasis on utility and use toward a preoccupation with fitness and proportion, with arbitrary geometrical patterns and balances. In effect, rational analysis led in contradictory directions just as the assumption that nature was rule and order established potentially contradictory principles.

The second half of the eighteenth century produced a richly speculative groundwork for the evolution of architectural theory in the nineteenth century. Not that this groundwork was a single theory or even a coordinated complex, but a sort of upwelling of interest in architectural theory and of reaction against the mannered "decadence" of Baroque-Rococo architectural practices. Simultaneously in France, Italy, Germany, and England critical reaction began to emphasize the need for a "new architecture," and to propound principles for its guidance. This upwelling had not one but many sources, and many personal and national variations, not all of them interrelated; but the many had in common one assumption: that conscious adherence to rationally developed principles would give birth to the new architecture.

In France a central figure in this revolution was Marc-Antoine Laugier (1713–1769), a Jesuit priest whose *Essai sur l'architecture* (1753) was a thorough and radical rejection of the fashionable Rococo in favor of new architectural principles. Laugier argued for "that which is natural and true, wherein all is reduced to simple rules and executed according to great principles." To derive these rules and principles, he speculatively traced the origins of architecture to the primitive hut, following much the same pattern of reasoning that was leading Jean-Jacques Rousseau (1712–1778) to speculate about and to idealize primitive man in a state of nature—in contrast to the inequalities and decadences of civilized society. Laugier saw in his imaginary reconstruction of the primitive hut those "simple rules" for architecture that Rousseau was to parallel with political and social rules derived from an imaginary reconstruction of primitive society. Laugier's approach, like Rousseau's, was psychological and introspective as well as historical and evolutionary. Laugier examined his own reactions to architecture in the attempt to determine what his approvals had in common and what his rejections had in common. His idealization of the natural and primitive thus provided a historical rationalization of the critical principles he had established by psychological analysis of the impact of architecture.

This psychological-historical approach led Laugier to reject useless and unnecessary ornament, and it led him to the attempt "to distinguish between the parts which are essential to the composition of a work of architecture and those which necessity has introduced and caprice added to them." His conclusion was founded on what he called "our little rustic hut":

. . . in every architectural order only the column, the entablature and the pediment could form an essential part of its composition. If each of these three parts is suitably placed and suitably formed, nothing else need be added to make the work perfect.

Laugier, unlike many of his contemporaries, rejected elaborate mathematical attempts to determine proportions on the analogy of music. He argued that proportion was to be achieved by "that obscure path" where "only taste and experience can guide the architect." Rules, he felt, should not be based on what is or what has been but on what ought to be. His approach led him finally in the direction of a qualified historical relativism: the classical orders were fitted to a time, place, and environment, but their fitness was only relatively, never absolutely, appropriate; therefore, while he regarded the classical orders as having their perfections, he did not accept them as models for contemporary practice, but as examples of attempts at the perfect architecture that "ought to be."

Laugier himself functioned as critic, theoretician, and consultant. His influence was largely through his theories and writings rather than by architectural example. His ideas, somewhat modified, were carried into the early nineteenth century in the work of the French "revolutionary architects," Étienne-Louis Boulée (1728–1799), Claude-Nicolas Ledoux (1736–1806), and Jean-Jacques Lequeu (1757–circa 1825). Boulée and Ledoux were caught up in the humanitarian idealism and utopianism of the early impulse of the French Revolution. They designed not only actual buildings but also imaginary and "way-out" structures that, particularly in Ledoux's folio *L'Architecture* (1804), were attempts to project what Ledoux called "a dramatic enthusiasm for the medium" of architecture, characterized by a daring emphasis on pure geometric forms. Boulée attempted to combine an emphasis on basic geometric forms with the "picturesque" (the "picturesque" was to be of central importance in nineteenth-century architectural practice). Lequeu was extravagantly romantic, and aimed at a theatrical rather than architectural expressiveness that was also to appeal strongly to the essentially literary preoccupation of nineteenth-century architecture.

Laugier's influence was also perpetuated by the English architect and teacher Sir John Soane (1753–1837). Soane regarded Laugier's *Essai* (translated, London, 1755) as a basic text, and apparently distributed it among his students. Soane's emphasis was on *"Solidity in Construction, Convenience in Distribution, and Beauty in Characteristic Decoration"* (*Lectures on Architecture*, circa 1809). He resolved the potential opposition between "natural" and "customary" beauty in much the same way Wren had resolved it a hundred years earlier: by regarding natural beauty as primary, customary beauty as necessary but tributary. Soane's theory was in a sense a practitioner's synthesis of the theoreticians' conflicting speculations. Historically he was of key importance in establishing Greek-revival architecture in England and in America. Thus Laugier's ideas, modified toward conservatism by Soane's British pragmatism, and modified toward radical utopianism in France, helped to condition architectural theory and practice in the opening decades of the nineteenth century.

In Italy the need for a "new architecture" was preached by the Venetian Franciscan Carlo Lodoli (1690–1761). Lodoli's revolutionary approach parallels Laugier's in its reaction against the "falsehood" of eighteenth-century architectural practice. But Lodoli's analysis leads him to the articulation of somewhat different principles: (1) ". . . only that shall show that has a definite function and which derives from the strictest necessity"; and, (2) "Architecture must conform to the nature of the materials." No writings of Lodoli's remained after his death, nor was he a practicing architect; consequently his influence was largely perpetrated through his teaching and through the excitement he aroused in his pupils. The mark of Lodoli's followers, the *rigoristi* (the rigorous ones, or the purists), can be detected in nineteenth-century Italian discussions and speculations about the arts, and one can postulate an influence on Americans who studied and worked in Italy, among them Washington Allston and Horatio Greenough.

Architectural theory in eighteenth-century Germany was dominated by a concern with philosophical aesthetics (G. E. Lessing, 1729–1781) and by researches in "antiquities" (Johann Winckelmann, 1717–1768). Central in the development of German theory is Goethe's *On German Architecture* (1773). Like Laugier in France and Lodoli in Italy, Goethe attacked what he regarded as the dishonesty of Baroque and Rococo architecture; but, though Geothe essentially shared Laugier's and Lodoli's premises, he found the primitive emphasis of Laugier's "great principles" uncongenial. (He apparently did not know Lodoli's theories.) Goethe, at the opening of his essay, describes the psychological impact of Strasbourg Cathedral, and records what, in effect, was his "conversion" to Gothic. He notes that he had shared the fashionable rejection of Gothic as "barbarous," and then remarks:

With what unexpected emotions did the sight surprise me when
I actually saw it! An impression of grandeur and unity filled my
soul, which, because it consisted of a thousand harmonizing details,
I could taste and enjoy, but by no means understand and explain.
. . . Hard it is for the mind of man when his brother's work is so
elevated that he can only bow down and pray. . . .

This experience of Gothic he found the more stimulating
because it appealed to both reason and emotion: ". . . my
power unfolded itself both to enjoy it and to understand it
at once," and because in Gothic architecture he found the
same order and harmony "as in the works of eternal nature."
Not unlike Laugier's, Goethe's approach combines psychological analysis of his own reactions with an analysis of
nature-history. In effect, Goethe synthesized in himself the
emphases of eighteenth-century neoclassicism, and anticipated
the emphases of nineteenth-century Romanticism.

Goethe's influence on architectural theory was in large part
a function of his stature as the leading European man of
letters of his time, and it was also a function of the seminal
role German letters played in the evolution of the Romantic
Movement. Interest in German letters and German philosophy
was particularly strong among the American Romantics
(Emerson and the New England Transcendentalists), and
American architectural theory reflects this interest. Goethe's
suggestion of a synthesis of theory and history was developed
by Georg Moller in the essay included in this anthology, an
essay Goethe praised when it was published in 1819. Moller's
essay is essentially eclectic in that it combines various aspects
of eighteenth-century theory (and archaeology) with nineteenth-century attitudes and responses. It can be regarded not
only as an essay in itself but also as a pivotal document that
sums up the past (1750–1819) and looks forward into the
nineteenth century as future. In this sense Moller's essay can
stand in this anthology as a metaphor for European back-
grounds to nineteenth-century American architectural theory.

2

Georg Moller, AN ESSAY / ON THE / ORIGIN AND PROGRESS / OF / GOTHIC ARCHITECTURE / TRACED IN AND DEDUCED FROM THE / ANCIENT EDIFICES OF GERMANY, / WITH REFERENCES TO THOSE OF ENGLAND, ETC. / FROM THE / EIGHTH TO THE SIXTEENTH CENTURIES (London, 1824), pp. xi–xvi, 1–81.

Georg Moller (1784–1852) was a German architect, architectural critic, and historian. He designed the ducal palace of Hesse at Wiesbaden, the theatre at Mainz, and various buildings in Darmstadt, notably the classical Ludwigskirche (1822–1827). In the course of his historical investigations he discovered the original designs of Cologne Cathedral, and the towers were finished in accordance with his published facsimile. In addition to the *Essay*, his most important publications were *Denkmaler Deutscher Baukunst* (1815–1851) and *Beitrage zu der Lehre von den Konstrucktionen* (1833–1841). The *Essay* was first published in Darmstadt in 1819, and was apparently well known in England, where it appeared in two versions, the 1824 one quoted here, reprinted in 1836 as pages 1–48 of *Moller's Memorials of German Gothic Architecture; with Additional Notes and Illustrations from Stieglitz, etc.*, by W. H. Leeds.

Moller's *Essay* came to Emerson's attention in the early 1850's; it is tempting to speculate an agency on Greenough's part, since Emerson's one published remark on Moller occurs at the right time (roughly 1852) and has a Greenough flavor:

Moller, in his Essay on Architecture, taught that the building which was fitted accurately to answer its end would turn out to be beautiful though beauty had not been intended.*

But there is no evidence that Greenough knew of Moller, and Emerson's acquaintance with Moller's "teachings" could as probably have been the result of Goethe's praise or of the general American interest in the English publisher John Weale's series, "Architectural Library." Emerson's mention of Moller's *Essay* is enough, however, to ensure that it was noted and read in this country.

Introduction

There is no study more instructive nor worthy of a thinking being than the history of the human race. Its gradual development, its apparent sinking at some periods, and the improvements generally attendant upon its misfortunes fill the mind with an awful veneration and humble adoration of divine Providence.

This history, however, does not merely consist in a barren enumeration of names, nor in the narrative of perpetually recurring wars, nor of all the sufferings and crimes which rapine and ambition have entailed upon mankind; but rather of the more tranquil picture of manners, religion, civil constitution, commerce, and arts and sciences. The history of architecture constitutes an essential part of this picture. By affording us the most animated and most instructive notions of the individuality, knowledge, and power of their authors, the works of architecture offer to those who consider them with attention the most interesting, and, in some periods, the only remaining documents of earlier times. The comparison of the Temple of Minerva, at Athens, with the petty, tasteless pagan temples in Japan and China establishes the relation of the ancient Greeks to the Japanese and Chinese in a more lively and more unquestionable manner than the most diffuse dissertation. This historical importance of the works of architecture has been frequently acknowledged, and the ancient architectural monuments belonging to foreign nations have

* From "Fate" in *The Conduct of Life*, 1860.

generally been described with care and delineated by learned antiquaries and artists, so that their knowledge may be considered as the common property of all civilized nations. But is it not surprising that the edifices of our country (Germany), which, independent of their value as works of art, ought to attract our attention by their magnitude, and the resistance which their durability has opposed for so many ages to the influences of the weather, and to the destructive fury of men, are so totally unknown? How happens it that young architects measure and delineate over and over again the ruins of Rome, which have been so often drawn and engraved, before they have obtained even a mere superficial knowledge of the works of their forefathers, with which they are surrounded at home? It is because its works are unknown that the history of German architecture still opposes very considerable difficulties to the inquirer, and considered singly, it is often impossible to explain the striking singularities with which it abounds. Correct notions can be obtained only through the means of an accurate and complete knowledge of the most ancient monuments of the art, up to its improvement and over-refinement. Within the last centuries, however, many of these buildings of earlier times have perished, partly through the desolating wars of which Germany has been the theatre, and partly from other causes; and many of those that are still extant are threatened with a similar fate.

It is therefore the duty of all intelligent patriotic architects to use their utmost efforts that our ancient buildings, and, above all, the edifices of the earliest periods, which are every day becoming more scarce, should be made fully known, and their knowledge preserved through faithful admeasurements and correct delineations. Strongly impressed with this idea, and desirous of saving whatever is yet to be saved, I have studied them, as much as time and circumstances would allow, and offer these fragments as additions to the materials necessary for a correct history of the civilization of Germany. I have attempted to arrange them in chronological order, and submit the results of my researches concerning the improvement of German architecture to the examination of the learned. Independent of this view of the subject, historians will be enabled, by my quotations of the sources of my information and delineations of the objects themselves, to draw their own conclusions from my observations.

An Essay

CHAPTER I / ON THE AGE OF THE BUILDINGS OF THE MIDDLE
   AGE, THEIR DIFFERENT STYLES OF ARCHITECTURE, AND THEIR
   MERITS

To fix the age of ancient buildings is the first indispensable requisite in the history of architecture, since it is the only way of obtaining a correct view of its progress. But the great number of contradictory hypotheses which have been hitherto advanced on the origin and improvement of ancient architecture in general, and on the churches of the Middle Age in particular, are evident proofs that to ascertain the age of an ancient edifice is usually attended with considerable difficulties.

On a perusal of the accounts of the erection of ancient buildings, we frequently discover that the assigned period of their foundation does not agree with the style of their architecture, which is either of an earlier or more recent period. In all the descriptions of the Strasbourg Minster, for instance, it is stated that the nave of this church was built by Bishop Werner in the year 1015, and finished in thirteen years. On this evidence, the identity of the nave supposed to have been built by Bishop Werner with the existing nave of the cathedral of Strasbourg has been assumed as unquestionable, though the style of its architecture clearly belongs to the thirteenth century. And this fully corresponds with a statement of Schade, which has, I suspect, been hitherto overlooked. He says: "The church, which is now called the minster, was finished only in the year 1275," (page 13); and when he speaks (page 15) of the great fire of the minster in the year 1298, he says: "The fire consumed all the woodwork of the minster, particularly the covering (the roof), which at that time was not vaulted. The heat was so great that much of the stonework was cracked. It therefore became necessary to build anew, and to repair at a great expense the parts which were damaged by the conflagration, and the whole was made much more beautiful than it had formerly been. It was at this time that the upper windows with their ornaments were executed." Similar errors are so frequent, and repeatedly made, that a few observations on the principles to be adopted in such inquiries will not be deemed unimportant.

There are two species of proof of the historical truth of statements concerning the history of any art; one *direct*, from documents, the other *indirect*, from arguments. Whenever the authors of the former were contemporary, when they were notoriously in a situation to know the truth, and it cannot be presumed that they made their statements on light grounds, or that in a given case they could have a particular bias to deviate from truth, the evidence of such contemporary, well-informed, and impartial historians has very great weight. Among the documents of this kind, inscriptions hold the first rank, although they are frequently of much later date than the events which they record: many tombs on which inscriptions or epitaphs are found have been erected a long time, and frequently some centuries after the death of the individuals whose memory they were intended to perpetuate; as is the case, for instance, with the tomb of King Dagobert of France, and with the monument erected by the Emperor Charles IV at Engern, in Westphalia, to the memory of Wittekind, Duke of Saxony. The examination of the sources whence we derive our information, therefore, requires particular caution.

Later writers who advance assertions upon the authority of others are worthy of belief only so far as they were able to draw from the right sources, and were endowed with a correct judgment and capable of sound criticism. Certain it is, however, that the historians of the Middle Age, who were wont to take upon trust, and publish with boldness, the most ridiculous legendary tales as undoubted facts, are by no means calculated to inspire us with much confidence. I know, from my own experience, that those which unfortunately are often the only statements extant have no greater value than popular traditions. But even when a statement has been found altogether worthy of belief, another difficulty arises, from the circumstance of most of the ancient buildings having undergone a great many alterations, and consisting of parts whose different periods and styles of architecture are manifest; nay, frequently not a vestige of the original building remains. A document concerning the erection of an edifice may therefore be perfectly genuine, and yet the uncertainty whether the work to which the document refers be really the identical building or another, and whether the statement relates to the whole edifice, or only to some of its parts, is not removed. In such a case, nothing but the strictest inquiry of scholars as well as artists of sound judgment, capable of judging how far the statements are worthy of belief, can guard us against errors; and the historian is entitled to our thanks who, instead of copying unauthenticated matter, directs our attention to the uncertainty in which the objects of his research are enveloped.

In order to judge correctly of the internal credibility of statements concerning the history of architecture, the buildings to which they refer must not be considered singly, but in connection with earlier, contemporary, and later works. But above all, the history of the art is never to be separated from the history of the nation, whose fate it shares alike in its progress and in its decay. Architecture, whose application, more than that of any other art, depends on outward contingencies, develops itself but slowly and gradually. The creations of the greatest genius are constantly modified by the influence of the time to which he belongs, so that the best and most perfect work can only be considered as the result of the progressive improvement of several generations; and an accurate comparison of a series of architectural works combined with a diligent study of history, points out the only safe road on which the development of the different styles of architecture is to be pursued. After the principal periods of the improvement of the art have thus been carefully and critically fixed, a proper place is more easily assigned to some special, though anomalous, works.

With regard to the names of the several styles of architecture which appeared in Europe after the decay of Roman architecture, and continued till the sixteenth century, when they were superseded by the modern Greco-Roman art, they were all for a long time comprised under the general name of Gothic architecture. This epithet was afterward applied to the pointed-arch style, which predominated in the thirteenth century. At present it is well known that the appellation of Gothic architecture is not a suitable one: but as those of Byzantine, Saxon, and German architecture, by which it has been attempted to supersede it, are neither generally received, nor sufficiently distinct, I shall content myself with designating the different styles of architecture by the century and the country in which they flourished. In respect, however, of the question to whom the merit of the invention and of the improvement of the art is to be ascribed, the following more architectural than historical observations may perhaps be of some importance in the inquiry.

The forms of buildings are far from being arbitrary and accidental in their origin. The climate, the building materials, and the character of the nation exercise a very essential influence on them, and cause those diversified appearances which vary as much as the physiognomy of countries and the situation of nations. Whatever is produced by these causes is singular in its kind, and in harmony with itself. Every species of architecture, on the contrary, which, owing its origin to foreign nations, to a different climate, and different circumstances, is transferred to other people and other countries retains the character of unsuitableness and unconnectedness, until some artist of eminent talents successfully appropriates it to his own use, and forms out of it a new, national, and consistent style of building. If this be admitted, that nation undoubtedly has the merit of a particular style of architecture, whose edifices

1. Correspond with the climate, with the style of construction adapted to the materials, and with the sentiments and manners of the nation and of the times; *and*

2. Constitute in their principal forms, and in their several parts and ornaments, a whole in harmony with itself, which excludes or rejects every thing foreign and unsuitable.

These principles, which, without a view to any particular school, may be applied alike in forming a judgment of the works of all ages and all nations . . . are a sure guard against any partial over- or underrating, and will hereafter serve to regulate our examination of the several hypotheses concerning the architecture of the Middle Age.

CHAPTER II / ON THE ROMANO-GRECIAN STYLE OF ARCHITEC-
       TURE, FROM THE INTRODUCTION OF CHRISTIANITY AS THE
       RELIGION OF THE STATE IN THE ROMAN EMPIRE, TO THE
       EIGHTH CENTURY, AND ON ITS INFLUENCE UPON THE ARCHI-
       TECTURE OF THE REST OF EUROPE

To form a correct notion of this style of architecture it will be necessary to consider the forms of earlier buildings.

The edifices of Egypt are distinguished by their uncommon durability. They have no inclined roofs; their covering consists of very large and thick stone plates, disposed horizontally; and the strength of their columns, the proximity of these columns, as well as the horizontal direction of the roofs and openings, are natural consequences of this kind of construction.

The Grecian buildings, which also are very durable, display, moreover, the most beautiful proportions. They had timber roofs covered with tiles of burnt clay, or of marble. Large edifices had flat timber coverings; but smaller ones, like the outward colonnades, are covered with stone: hence the Grecian columns, which, compared to the Egyptian, have no heavy burden to support, are more slender than the latter. The use of timber coverings, and the necessity of employing large stone masses, is the cause (as in the Egyptian architecture) of the horizontal covering of the inner rooms and colonnades, as well as of the doors and windows. Vaulted roofs and arched doors and windows were not in use. Both the Egyptian and the Grecian edifices, whilst they are suitable to the climate, the building materials at hand, and the purpose for which they were erected, possess at the same time the greatest harmony in their forms. They are free from inconsistency and disagreement.

Colonies of Greeks diffused their civilization through lower Italy. The temples of Paestum in Magna Graecia, at present the Kingdom of Naples, belong to the best works of Grecian architecture. This species of art flourished also at Rome: but, whatever the beauty of the plan and of the construction of the buildings peculiar to the Romans, of their basilicas, their amphitheatres, bridges, aqueducts, streets, and baths, yet the Roman temples, which are imitations of the Grecian ones, though more splendid and more extensive, have not that simplicity of form nor that purity of style which characterize the Grecian edifices. The Etrurians in middle Italy, judging of them by their works, were a highly civilized people. They practiced architecture with the most distinguished success, and, like the Egyptians and Greeks, they were not only acquainted with the art of constructing buildings of large blocks of freestone without the aid of mortar, but also erected the most durable vaults.[*]

---

[*] The Cloaca Maxima, that admirable common sewer to carry off the dirt and filth of Rome, was built by the Tarquinians, and may be regarded as the work of Etrurian architects.[†]

[†] Unless otherwise indicated, all footnotes are Moller's.—ED.

The Romans, situated in the center between Magna Graecia and Etruria, and more addicted to war than to the arts, adopted both the Grecian and Etrurian architecture, and employed both vaults and colonnades in their buildings. The remains of Maecenas's villa at Tivoli, the Pantheon, and many similar works, excite astonishment by their magnitude, and delight the beholder by their excellent and ingenious construction of the large vaults which have been preserved unimpaired. To harmonize with the vaulted roofs, wherever they occurred, the openings of doors and windows were likewise provided with vaulted coverings; but columns, unable to support the pressure of large vaults, lost, through the introduction of the latter, their principal destination. Having been retained as ornaments in vaulted buildings, they were employed in situations *disengaged* from the walls, as in the interior of the Pantheon; or half *engaged* with the walls, as in Maecenas's villa, in the theatre of Marcellus, and in the Colosseum. This combination of vaults with columns and horizontal architraves, parts totally heterogeneous at their origin, affords, in my opinion, a very simple solution of the riddle which the specimens of later Roman and Byzantine architecture, as well as those of the Middle Age up to the latter half of the twelfth century, offer throughout the different countries of Europe by the frequent disharmony of their forms and construction. To solve this, a number of hypotheses have been invented. If, as in the Temple of Peace, enormous cross vaults could, though but in appearance, be rested on columns and their friezes, there was no reason why, in smaller distances, they might not likewise be connected by arches, instead of horizontal architraves. And as columns were already in most cases considered as mere decorations, requisite for effect, and might be omitted without prejudice to the stability of the building, the Romans did not scruple to introduce them even in places where they were to serve merely as ornaments without any apparent object.

In this stage of decline was the Roman architecture anterior to the invasion of the barbarians, under Diocletian, the last emperor before the introduction of the Christian religion. In the baths of this monarch at Rome we find large groined vaulting on columns, counterpoised by flying buttresses in the exterior, which were subsequently so much improved in larger churches. In his palace at Spalatro, the colonnades of the courtyards are connected by means of arches resting directly upon the columns, and over the Porta Aurea (Golden Gate), the principal entrance of the palace, there are rows of lesser columns also connected by arches, as decorations. All this shows that the decline of the empire was also attended by the decay of the arts and that this decay was brought on by the Romans themselves, a long time before the invasion of foreign nations.

When Constantine removed the seat of the Roman Empire to Byzantium, and Christianity became the only religion of the state, it seemed likely that architecture should have derived a new splendor from the extensive buildings which the emperors erected to embellish their new residence.*

I do not know whether any of the edifices that were then built at Byzantium are still in existence: but when we observe how the buildings at Rome, particularly the Triumphal Arch of Constantine, as far as it was renovated at that time, are constructed, we are soon sensible to what extent unfortunate Rome had already declined. The decay of the arts and the decline of the general prosperity, introduced, after Constantine's time, the custom of pulling down old buildings to erect new ones with their materials. It is evident that the columns and parts of the old buildings thus applied could not possibly suit the new edifices. A total neglect of exact proportions was the natural consequence of this ruinous practice. The style of building probably underwent less alteration in dwelling houses and strongholds, or fortresses, on which the existence of empires depended in those times more than in ours. The walls and towers of the palace at Spalatro, and many other edifices of that period, still manifest considerable stability; and the frequently tottering Empire of the East was often indebted for its preservation, during eleven centuries, to the solidity and height of the walls and towers of Byzantium. But the style of building edifices for public worship was much more extensively altered.

The temples, which at their origin had never been destined to receive large congregations in their interior, were either not sufficiently roomy to serve as churches or they were at first regarded as having been profaned by the worship of the heathen gods. Their place was supplied by basilicas, partly with flat timber roofs, as was generally the case, and partly

* See Gibbon's *History of the Decline and Fall of the Roman Empire*.

vaulted. Churches were rarely built on a circular or polygonal plan, after the model of the Pantheon or of the Temple of Minerva Medica. The want, in these round churches, of a chancel, of vaulted aisles on each side of the nave, and of a portico frequently induced the architects to erect in the middle of the building four transepts of equal dimensions in the shape of a Greek cross, which style of building appears to have been in great favor, particularly in the Greek Empire. The church of St. Sophia at Constantinople; those of St. Vitale at Ravenna, and of St. Constance and St. Agnes at Rome, as well as the cathedral of St. Mark at Venice, although it was built at a later period, but entirely in the Grecian style, and the cathedral of Pisa, are evidences of this combination of domes and circular churches with colonnades and the shape of basilicas.

The practice of filling the voids of large and small arched openings with columns, which, though they do not contribute to the solidity of the building, yet seem essential supporters, and frequently give the whole a light and at the same time rich appearance, was introduced by the Byzantines. The first example of it, is, however, found in the Pantheon at Rome. This practice is particularly characteristic, and appears of great importance in the architecture of the following centuries.

All the buildings which, from Constantine down to the ninth century, were erected within the limits of the former Roman Empire bear witness to the corrupted Roman architecture of Diocletian's age, with the additional alterations which the use of churches, the custom of building with old materials, and the continually sinking state of the empire and of the nation, necessarily introduced. The irruption of the Goths and other barbarians who inundated the provinces of the Roman Empire did not probably introduce any material alteration in the state of the art, except that of hastening its fall. I cannot possibly accede to the opinion of those connoisseurs who ascribe an individual and peculiar style of architecture to the Goths and Lombards in Italy and Spain, to the Franks in Gaul, and to the Saxons in England. On examining their works, it will be found that the Roman architecture of the fifth and sixth centuries, with some few modifications, prevailed in these countries; and the circumstance is easily explained. The conquerors did not exterminate the old inhabitants, but left to them exclusively, at least in the first periods of their invasion, the practice of those arts of peace upon which the rude warrior looked with contempt. And, even at a later time, the intimate connection with Rome, which the clergy, then the only civilized part of the nation, entertained, and the unceasing and generally continued use of the Latin language in the divine service, gave considerable influence to Roman arts and sciences. This must have been so much the more the case from the constant obligation of all free men to devote themselves to war; whereby the practice of the arts was left almost exclusively to the clergy. The taste for fine proportions was almost entirely lost in these barbarous ages, and architecture became little less than a mere slavish imitation of earlier forms. Yet it appears that the art of preparing mortar, and the selection of building materials, as well as the knowledge of solid construction in their structures, for which the ancient Romans were so eminent, were fortunately preserved.

It will be proper to mention here a passage in the epistles of Cassiodorus, the senator and chancellor of Theodoric, the Gothic king who reigned in Italy from the years 493 to 525, in which he describes the state of architecture in his time. Tiraboschi quotes it in his *History of the Sciences in Italy* (third volume, page 68). Speaking of the then existing works which excited his admiration, Cassiodorus gives a particular description of the very great lightness and elegance of columns in the following terms: "Quid dicamus columnarum junceam proceritatem? Moles illas sublimissimas fabricarum quasi quibusdam erectis hastilibus contineri et substantiae qualitate concavis canalibus excavatas, ut magis ipsas aestimes fuisse transfusas; alias ceris judices factum, quod metallis durissimis videas expolitum."* This passage, if clearly and correctly translated, and confirmed by the architectural monuments of that time, would be of immense interest to the history of architecture. I do not know of any building, from the time of Theodoric down even to the tenth century, to which this description seems to apply. The basement of the palace, which is supposed to have been built by Theodoric at Terracina, is entirely in the Roman style. The church of St. Apollonaris at

---

* What should we say about the reedlike height of the columns? Should we say that these very tall structural masses are, as it were, held in place like some upright spear shafts, and hollowed out in concave channels so that one would think they had been poured out; at other times one would think they had been made from wax, but one can see that they are made from hard materials.—Cassiodorus, *Opera*, Venetiis, MDCCXXIX, page 103. Editor's translation.

Ravenna is a common basilica, like the many that have been erected before and after, and the front of the convent of the Franciscan friars in the same town, which is said to have been the entrance to the palace, bears the greatest resemblance to the Porta Aurea of Diocletian at Spalatro. All these buildings are very far from being in a light or daring style; they are, on the contrary, extremely heavy. One Aloysius, and the well-known Boetius, a native of Rome and a Roman senator, whose skill and knowledge are frequently praised by Cassiodorus, are mentioned as the principal architects of Theodoric; and this is a strong confirmation of the Goths having no peculiar style of architecture, but that their edifices were built by Romans, and in the Roman style. Even all the buildings erected in Europe at a later period, from the seventh to the tenth century, as, for instance, the south gate of the cathedral at Mentz, have, it is true, pillars in recesses, but of a very heavy, antiquated form, not agreeing in the least with the description of Cassiodorus. The gates of St. Leonard's Church at Mentz, on the contrary, and those of the church at Gelnhausen, as well as many other works which were erected toward the end of the twelfth or in the beginning of the thirteenth century (consequently full six hundred years after the reign of the Goths in Italy), appear so completely to correspond with that description that one could fancy Cassiodorus had these buildings before his eyes. His description therefore seems to possess few criteria of inward credibility, and must continue unintelligible until the buildings still extant in Italy, of the time of Theodoric, are more accurately and more critically examined and described than they have hitherto been. But were it even demonstrable that architecture had been at that time such as the quoted passage of Cassiodorus seems to describe it, yet the art could not be ascribed, as Tiraboschi seems to do, to the Goths, who, as warlike nomads, only invaded Italy in Theodoric's time—and to whose reign Narses, the general of the Greek Empire, had put an end in the year 552, their sway having lasted only fifty-nine years—but rather to the Byzantine Romans, among whom we must search for all that was preserved of arts and sciences.

The Lombards, who in the year 568 overran Italy after the Goths, and whose reign continued to the year 774, were in the habit of building much, and appear to have quickly attained a higher degree of civilization than the Goths. The twenty-fourth plate of D'Agincourt's *History of Architecture* exhibits the church of St. Julia, near Bergamo, that of St. Michael at Pavia, and the round church of St. Thomas at Bergamo, which are ascribed to the Lombards. As far as it is possible to judge from these plates, which are on a very small scale; and admitting what, however, still requires proof, that the delineated buildings are really the original churches erected by the Lombards, the same remark will apply here which was made above, respecting the edifices built under the sway of the Goths. The Lombards, a rude invading people, adopted the civilized manners of the conquered, as well as their architecture. Considering the very imperfect knowledge of which we are hitherto in possession of the style of building of the Lombards, it is certainly erroneous to ascribe to them, as but lately has been done, even down to the eleventh century, and after they had already left the scene for three hundred years, any material influence upon the architecture of the west and north of Europe. Still more erroneous is it to give the appellation of Lombardic to the style of church building which prevailed in France and Germany during the Middle Ages.

CHAPTER III / ON THE STYLE OF BUILDING IN GERMANY
    WHICH PREVAILED FROM THE EIGHTH TO THE FIFTEENTH
    CENTURY

On comparing the ancient churches of Germany with each other, we discover in their style of building two leading differences, all others being mere gradations or combinations of them. The *first,* and earliest, is foreign, and came from the south; it is by no means rude, having been originally a highly finished style of building, but it latterly degenerated. The buildings of this kind are distinguished by forms and decorations either Roman or imitated from the Romans, but especially by flat, or at least not very high roofs, by semi-circular arches and vaults, and by the great solidity of their construction.* The *second* and more modern style of building still retains the semicircle, but begins to substitute for the

* Of this style are the portico at Lorsch, the cathedrals at Spire, Worms, Mentz, Aix-la-Chapelle, the convent churches at Paulinzell near Rudolstadt, at Schwarzach near Rastadt, at Ilbenstadt in Wetteravia.

southern flat gable end that of the high roofed, which is more suitable for a northern climate.* To harmonize with the shape of the roof, the forms of the towers are pyramidal, and the windows and vaults in the pointed-arch style,† whilst all the minor ornaments still preserve the semicircle form. It was only at a later period that the decorations, and all the minor and subordinate parts of the main building, assumed the shape of the pointed arch.‡ Of this latter style are the grandest works or architecture which Germany possesses, works which will remain an object of admiration for ages to come.

These are the chief features in the church architecture of Germany, observable in ancient buildings. They show how a northern peculiar style was gradually formed out of the foreign southern one, and they are by no means in contradiction to history, although we are still ignorant of the many causes which may have influenced the improvement of the art.

Prior to the sway of the Romans in Germany, and in those parts which they did not occupy, architecture was undoubtedly very rude. Although the want of precise information leaves us in uncertainty about its state, yet the picture which Tacitus draws of the Germans of his time shows how little they cultivated the arts in general. The southern provinces of Germany, however, and the countries on the Rhine, being governed and reclaimed by the Romans, received an earlier and more extensive civilization; and Roman architecture flourished therein, as is evident from the numerous remains of buildings of that period. When Christianity prevailed in the Roman Empire, churches also were erected in Germany, as appears from ancient documents; especially in Austria, Bavaria, and on the Rhine. I am not, however, acquainted with any remains in Germany of that more ancient species of Roman Christian churches with which Italy abounds. After the lapse of ages of devastation, the authenticated history of our country begins only with the reign of Charles the Great; with whom, not a Gaul, but by birth and descent a German, commences the series of our architectonic documents. It is well known that in his court, as in that of the

---

* Of the style that still retains the semicircle, but has in this age high gable roofs, are the west side of the cathedral at Worms, the St. Paul's Church in the same place, the western tower of the church at Gelnhausen, and others.

† See the churches at Gelnhausen and Limbourg.

‡ See the church at Oppenheim.

earlier kings of the Franks, whatever related to science and art was of Roman origin. Architecture—which, more than any other art depends on the influence of religion; the temple being with many nations its only, and among all, its highest object—became a necessary art, through the diffusion of the Christian religion; and was practiced in the way it had been applied to the buildings requisite for public worship in the Greco-Roman Empire, since the reign of Constantine. The cathedral of Aix-la-Chapelle, and the portico of the ancient convent of Lorsch, near Worms, on the road called the Bergstrasse, are, as far as I can judge, the only buildings of the time of Charles the Great extant in Germany. The latter is in a very corrupt Roman style; such as we perceive after the fall of the empire in buildings, sarcophagi, and paintings.*

This disparity which is observable between the civilization of Italy and Germany existed also between the several provinces of Germany itself. On the Rhine, and in the south of Germany, cities arose when these countries belonged to the Roman Empire; and in such cities flourished the arts of peace, and the Christian religion; whilst the north and east of Germany were still uncivilized and addicted to paganism. The introduction of Christianity among the Germans, and their gradual civilization, proceeded, with very few exceptions,† from the southern and western parts of Germany. History also teaches us that the clergy themselves directed, at that time, the building of churches and convents. Under these circumstances, the influence of the ancient paganism of the Germans upon the style of church building, which D'Agincourt and several other historians assert, appears to me neither probable nor historically proved; religious ceremonies and church buildings were introduced at that period from abroad, and did not proceed from, nor were they improved by, the Germans, who were split into many

* This view of the first development of German architecture which Professor Fiorillo drew from documents, and which he gives in the introduction to his excellent history of the arts of design, was impressed upon the author from his examination of the ancient buildings themselves. A long residence in Italy, where he examined with particular attention the edifices of the times of the decline of the Roman Empire still remaining, enabled him to compare the ancient buildings of Germany with those of Italy, and thus to arrive at safe and steady conclusions.

† Christianity is said to have been propagated in the northeast of Germany by missionaries from Byzantium. It would be of high interest if churches should still be discovered which attested this fact, as is the case, for instance, with several churches in Russia.

separate nations, or tribes, without any common tie. Hence, the buildings of those countries that were first civilized, and from whence the arts passed into other places, are of the highest importance in the ancient history of German architecture; and it is in the south and west of Germany that the farther improvement of the art must so much the more be sought for, as all external circumstances were there more favorable to its success.

I have no knowledge of any buildings of the ninth century. In the tenth and eleventh century, several important churches were built in Germany, as the cathedrals of Spire, Worms, Mentz, and many others, which are still in existence, and astonish us by their solidity and magnificence. The leading form of these churches, as of those which were built at the same period in England, France, and Italy, is, in imitation of the basilicas, a long parallelogram with side naves, a strongly marked cross nave, which represents the arms of the cross, on whose intersection there is frequently a louvre. The chancel ends with a semicircle on the plan, and the whole has very thick walls, with comparatively small openings, and without any tall or aspiring pillars. In the drawings of these buildings, we find in all the windows, gates, and arched aisles the pure semicircle. The nave is high; the covering frequently consists of groined vaulting; but raised in the shape of cupolas, and often with flat timber coverings: on the exterior, the gable is usually of little inclination, and in the upper part of the building there are rows of small pillars in the wall. The horizontal line still predominates generally on the whole exterior, contrary to the style of building of the thirteenth century, in which all the parts of the building seem to aim at rising still higher. The profiles of the parts and ornaments are almost all, without exception, of antique origin; and several, as for instance the continually recurring attic base, are perfectly correct in their forms. From what has been stated, it is evident that the invention of this style of church building can by no means be claimed by the Germans; though there are in the composition, as well as in the parts as in the *tout ensemble,* many individual peculiarities in these buildings, the attentive examination of which fills us with a high respect for the taste and technical ability of their builders.

The difference between these German churches and the

Roman basilicas consists in the almost general covering of
the interior with vaulting. The consequence of this was that
it became necessary to substitute pillars for the isolated
columns which supported the flat wooden roofs and which
were too weak to bear vaults, or to connect the pillars with
the columns. Yet there are still a few churches found which,
together with the flat covering, preserve those ranks of
isolated columns of the ancient basilica; as, for instance,
a church at Ratisbon, and the convent churches at Paulinzell
and Schwarzach. Although the columns which were introduced as ornaments of the pillars were originally in imitation
of the Roman series of arches, they were soon justly altered.
The isolated column was proportioned to its height and to the
load which it was intended to carry. But the column, which
is used as an ornament of the pillar, has nothing in common
with the destination of the isolated column; it only forms
part of the pillar. D'Agincourt labors under a misapprehension when, on comparing the columns, he separates the light
staffs in the pillars of the churches of the Middle Age from
the columns, in order to show their disproportion as columns.
They are one and the same with the pillars, which bear, in
general, a very beautiful and exact proportion with their load
and the height of the vaults. Even in this originally foreign
style of church building, the German architects appear to
have had the merit of having divested it of everything that
could have reminded one of the heterogeneous timber construction and horizontal covering, and of having treated
it as a pure and consistent stone construction applied to
vaults. To have left out under the vaults the friezes and
cornices, which had no object in such a situation, appears,
therefore, no matter of reproach, but was, on the contrary,
perfectly in character.

Toward the latter end of the twelfth and in the beginning
of the thirteenth century, important deviations from this
ancient style of church building were introduced. The high
northern roof took the place of the flat southern gable, and
the introduction of this high pitched gable brought along
with it the use of the pointed arch, instead of the semi-
circular one, in order to introduce more harmony with the
other parts of the building. When the roof and the vaults
were thus raised, it was proper that the inferior part of the
building should also receive a comparatively greater height;

hence, all the proportions of the columns, capitals, vaults, towers, and so on, became slenderer toward the latter end of the century, and the flat pilaster spreads more outward, and rises as a flying buttress. After all the essential parts of the building had thus been altered in their forms and proportions, the details and decorations of the earlier style of building were yet retained for some time. The edifices of this period, though possessed of many beauties, are yet full of anomalies. Circular and pointed arches, rising pillars and vaults, intersected by horizontal cornices, form the most disagreeable combinations. The crisis which marks every transition into another state, and which throughout nature in general is momentarily discordant and disagreeable, bears visibly the same character here. This heterogeneous combination of the ancient southern style of building with the new one, which, in the main, agreed better with the climate, lasted but a short time. The sound sense of the German architects was not long in discovering that such heterogeneous parts could not be employed without disturbing all proportions; perhaps they were also influenced by a wish to introduce some peculiar style of their own in lieu of the old one. The buildings abovementioned show, in a very interesting manner, how the architect resolved gradually to replace all the subordinate parts of the ancient style by others more corresponding with the leading forms that were now adopted. In the year 1235, when the church of the Teutonic Order of Knights was begun at Marburg, and soon after finished in the same style up to the western gate or porch, the alteration of this style of building appears to have been perfectly accomplished. The high gable and the pointed arch prevail throughout, and each of the individual parts is in perfect harmony with the whole. This church, besides being constructed and finished in a masterly, skillful, and workmanlike manner, is distinguished by the greatest simplicity and elegance, the happy combination of which is not easily met with in such perfection. After this appropriate, peculiar, and rational style of building, which in its leading forms corresponds with the climate and building materials, and in its parts with the *whole,* had been thus improved, we behold it quickly brought to the highest perfection in many admirable architectural works. As early as the year 1248, they began to build the cathedral of Cologne upon its present plan, and in the year

1276 the porch of the minster at Strasbourg, under the direction of Erwin von Steinbach; two structures which, though unfinished, will be the admiration of all ages, from the boldness of their design, the beauty and elegance of their parts, and the excellence of their execution. This new style of building prevailed almost at the same time in all the countries of Europe, and we find its influence upon all the churches built in this and the following century. To analyze the principles on which this style was formed is not within the scope of this essay, and can never be successfully attempted before the principal edifices built in this style have been more accurately examined and considered. The great impression which these churches, particularly their interior, make upon the mind of every unprejudiced person, on that of the intelligent and well informed, as well as that of the uncultivated and ignorant, is truly wonderful; they combine the simplicity and majesty of the groves of the forest with the richness and beauty of its flowers and leaves; all is variety, greatness, and sublimity. The golden age of this style continues from the middle of the thirteenth to the latter end of the fourteenth century. The desire to produce something new and still more beautiful, as it had caused the decline of the ancient Roman, and afterward, in the seventeenth century, that of the Italian style of architecture, occasioned likewise the decay of the German style of church building. To a severe regularity of forms succeeded arbitrary petty decorations; and whereas the best examples of the thirteenth century are ornamented with fruits and flowers, the edifices of the fifteenth were themselves frequently in the form of plants, a freak which seems to overstep the bounds of architecture. This style of building, having outlived its prosperity, was the more easily superseded in the sixteenth century by a more modern Italian style.

As the question has of late been frequently started—"Whether the style of architecture of the thirteenth century and its forms might not be applied and used in our times," it may not be improper to discuss it in this place. The art which produced the Strasbourg Minster, the cathedral of Cologne, and other masterpieces is splendid and sublime—but it was the result of its time. The condition of public and private life at that period, the relation of the respective states and individual cities to each other, the situation of commerce, and, above all, the religious zeal which every-where animated every order of persons, exerted a powerful influence on the origin and improvement of this style of building. The great architects of the Strasbourg Minster, of the cathedral of Cologne, and of all the most distinguished buildings with which we are acquainted, were adapted to their own age; they and their works are only the result of the time in which they lived. We may admire and imitate these works, but we cannot produce the like, because the circumstances under which that style of building arose are now no longer the same.* If we attempt to apply their detail, their windows, gates, and ornaments, and so on, to the edifices of the present day, we shall produce an incongruous and absurd composition, because the parts are not homogeneous with the whole; and the disproportions and incongruity would be so much the more striking as the originals from which they are borrowed are grand and splendid.

But though it seems unadvisable again to introduce the style of building of the thirteenth century, yet a more inti-mate acquaintance with it is both instructive and useful. It has already been observed how much architectural works are calculated to inform us respecting the earlier civil and ecclesiastical situation of nations, and how these documents of stone afford, to those who can read them, the most lively picture of centuries that are lapsed; but, even independent of this high interest in the eyes of the philosophical historian, they offer an abundant harvest to artists and friends and patrons of the arts. Very few Greeks and Romans have carried technical ability and a strictly correct calculation of the proportions between strength and burden so far as the architects of the churches of the thirteenth century. The boldness and lightness of their structures will long continue unrivaled. Not only were the buildings of these great masters erected with the smallest possible expenditure of building materials,† and are still in excellent condition, but the ar-

* The case is very different with the Grecian style of building, which we are still in the habit of applying daily. Fancy and religion predominate in the German architecture, but the Grecian is the result of an enlightened understanding and of a correct sense of the beautiful. It strictly limits itself to what is absolutely necessary, to which it strives to impart the most beautiful forms; and on this account it will never cease to be capable of application to our purposes.

† The vaults of many very large churches are only from nine to ten inches thick, and the outer walls, though more than sixty feet high, are frequently but two feet thick.

rangement of the whole, and the proportions of the parts also, are so well calculated that their edifices appear much larger than they are in reality, whilst it is exactly the reverse with most of the works built in the antique style, and particularly with St. Peter's Church. As the greatest art consists in producing the grandest effects with the smallest means, the churches of the thirteenth century are, in this respect, highly instructive to the thinking artist. To these advantages, as connected with the study of the architecture of the Middle Age, must be added another no less important. By these we learn that harmony, beauty, and propriety are not limited to one style of building nor the authority of great names,* but that every work of art is to be judged only by the laws of inherent perfection; and that every building which appears discordant in its parts and unsuitable to its purpose is bad, whether it be called Gothic, Grecian, or Roman. That all artists may be convinced of this truth is much to be desired, for there is not a science or art in which ancient custom and the adoption of antiquated pretended rules are so frequently connected with a total neglect of the eternal rules of the human understanding, as architecture.

The neglect of the architectural works of Germany has lately, however, been succeeded by a more correct estimation of their merits, which are daily more appreciated. Since such eminent men as Goethe, Herder, and George Forster have so loudly proclaimed the veneration in which they hold those masterpieces, the attention of the public has at least been awakened. By their publications of ancient architectural works, and their historical researches, Messrs. Boisserée, Büsching, Costenoble, Fiorillo, Frick, Hundeshagen, Quaglio, Stieglitz, and many others† have already acquired just claims to the gratitude of an enlightened public, and we may confidently look for more important publications at their hands. But as the number of ancient buildings, which

* Several of the ancient writers on architecture are of opinion that every building is good only as it approximates the Roman or Greek style of architecture. This proposition is pretty nearly as correct as if we should say—"The rose is a beautiful flower, the lily is not like the rose, consequently the lily is ugly."

† The restoration of the magnificent castle of Marienburg, in Prussia, which was proposed by and is now under the direction of President Von Schoen, by means of voluntary contributions, deserves to be mentioned here as a distinguished instance of a proper estimation of the monuments of art extant in our country.

either have remained unknown or are only imperfectly known, is so very considerable, and as many of them are perishing from year to year, it is very much to be wished that the governments of the several German states would publish historical and critical catalogues of the remarkable ancient buildings in their respective dominions, in which the bad should be carefully separated from whatever is worthy of being preserved. Independent of affording correct information of the buildings still existing, these works would thus be placed under the safeguard of the public eye, and the fear of public disgrace would put a stop to the vandalism of ignorant subordinate magistrates who, in many places, do not scruple to consider and use such ancient buildings as excellent stone quarries.*

* The Grand Duke of Hesse Darmstadt, to whose enlightened mind nothing that can promote the arts and sciences is foreign, issued a proclamation in 1818 whose object was to preserve the antiquities extant in the Grand Duchy, and to make them more generally known. As the editor does not know any other country which has similar regulations, he thinks that the contents of this proclamation will not be deemed uninteresting. It runs thus:

"Louis, by the grace of God Grand Duke of Hesse, &c. &c. Considering that the monuments of ancient architecture still existing are among the most important and most interesting documents of history, and afford instructive views of the early manners, civilization, and civil constitution of the nation, thus rendering their preservation highly desirable, we have decreed as follows:

"1. Our Board of Works is to procure correct catalogues of all the remains of ancient architecture which, either in a historical point of view or as works of art, are worthy of being preserved, and to have their present situation described, and the other monuments of art extant in the same, as paintings, statues, &c. particularly mentioned.

"2. The said Board is to invite the learned of every province, who are best acquainted with its history, to cooperate in the historical preparation of such catalogues, for which purpose the requisite documents are to be communicated to them out of the archives.

"3. The principal of these buildings, or those which are in the most ruinous state, are to be delineated, and the designs, together with the descriptions, to be deposited in our Museum.

"4. The Board of Works is to submit to our approbation the list of the buildings deemed worthy to be preserved or delineated, to correspond respecting their repairs with the requisite authorities, and to make the requisite proposals to us on the subject.

"5. If it should be thought proper to make alterations in any of these buildings, or to pull them down, it is to be done only under the cognizance of the said Board, and with our approval in the requisite cases.

"6. If in digging, or on other occasions, relics of antiquity should be discovered, our public functionaries are to take care that they be carefully preserved; and notice of their discovery is to be immediately sent to the Board of Works or to the Managers of the Museum.

"7. All public functionaries are enjoined carefully to watch over the preservation of all the monuments recorded in the aforesaid catalogues, for which purpose the latter are to be printed and communicated to them.

[Signed]   Louis

"Darmstadt, January 22nd, 1818"

CHAPTER IV / A COMPARISON OF SOME BUILDINGS OF THE
STYLE OF THE THIRTEENTH CENTURY, IN DIFFERENT COUN-
TRIES OF EUROPE, AND ON THE SEVERAL HYPOTHESES CON-
CERNING THE FIRST USE OF THIS STYLE OF ARCHITECTURE

The annexed chronological series of buildings from the
eighth to the sixteenth century exhibits the gradual development of the different styles of building which have successively prevailed in Germany, without having recourse to any
hypothesis concerning their invention. But as very dissimilar
conjectures have been advanced respecting their origin, and
especially respecting the pointed-arch style, which, as has
been already observed, prevailed over almost the whole of
Europe, a short examination of these conjectures may be of
some interest. According to these different hypotheses the
invention of that style of building is derived:

1. From the holy groves or thickets of the ancient
Celtic nations.

2. From huts made with the entwined twigs of trees.

3. From the structure of the framing in wooden buildings.

4. From the pyramids of Egypt.

5. From the imitation of pointed arches generated by the
intersection of semicircles.

The *first* opinion, according to which the slender pillars
and bold vaults of the churches of the thirteenth century are
supposed to be an imitation of the holy groves or thickets in
which the ancient Celtic nations worshiped the Divinity, is
ingenious and pleasing, but has no historical foundation.
The most ancient churches have no trace of this similarity;
it is only in the fourteenth and fifteenth centuries, consequently seven hundred years after the old religion of the
country had ceased, that the introduction of vaults entwined
with ribs, which have been compared to twigs of trees, had
existence.

The *second* hypothesis, according to which this style of
building is supposed to be an imitation of huts made with
the entwined twigs of trees, and which an Englishman, Sir
James Hall, has lately endeavored to support with many examples, is not better founded, and inadmissible on the grounds

before stated. It is only the latest and corrupt buildings of the fifteenth and sixteenth centuries that display this imitation of twigs.

The *third* hypothesis supposes that the structure of the timberwork in wooden buildings was the origin of the pointed arch style. An attentive examination of the buildings of the thirteenth century shows that the ancient style of church building presupposes above all the art of erecting vaults, and is therefore grounded entirely on stone constructions. But the later pointed-arch style is derived from that more ancient style of architecture; and although its forms differ from those of the latter, yet they all refer to the vault and arch. Stone, therefore, is likewise with this style of building the materials used in the construction of churches, and it was merely the framing of the roofs which was of wood, and the workmanship of the carpenter. The old timber dwelling or guild houses of the fifteenth or sixteenth century bear no resemblance to the style of church building of the Middle Age; their forms, on the contrary, are very suitably and intelligently adapted to structures of carpentry. It is the principal advantage of a consistent and improved style of architecture that the forms of buildings and of their separate parts should be conformable to the building materials used in their construction, and that wood is not to represent freestone, nor freestone to represent wood. The editor has, in several parts of Germany, met with wooden houses, in which individual parts, the house doors, for instance, were in the pointed-arch style; but this imitation of stone construction will ever remain inappropriate.*

Mr. Murphy, the editor of the celebrated work on the convent of Batalha, in Portugal, and the buildings of the Moors in Spain, derives the pointed-arch style from the pyramids of Egypt, and argues in this manner: "The pyramids of the Egyptians are tombs; the dead are buried in churches,

---

* It will be proper on this occasion to say something about what is called *masking*, in which many architects delight. They fancy they have performed something very ingenious if the exterior of a stable or a warehouse looks like a dwelling house, or a wooden building prettily plastered over and painted resembles freestone. After the mortar has fallen down in the course of a few years, the miserable deception is discovered. The wooden houses of our ancient towns, or the peasants' cottages in Tyrol and in Switzerland, which display at once their wooden structure, are far more pleasing, and are even much more solid than these plastered dwelling houses. True taste rejects all false appearances. Every building ought to have the proper exterior suitable to its destination and to the materials with which it is constructed.

and on their towers are pyramidal forms; consequently, the
pyramids of the towers indicate that there are graves in
churches; and as the pyramidal form constitutes the essence
of the pointed-arch style, and the pyramids of the towers are
imitations of the Egyptian pyramids, the pointed arch is
derived from the latter." But the burying of the dead in
churches was a mere secondary, subordinate object, not their
principal destination. Hence it could not be the intention to
designate churches on their outside as tombs; and the most
ancient churches and those of the south rarely have pointed
steeples: their towers generally end in roofs of very little
or no elevation. Neither are the tombs of the Middle Age
in the form of pyramids or obelisks; this ornament, on the
contrary, is very modern. The points of towers are nothing
but a high roof, and whenever the church had such a roof, it
could not be omitted in the higher tower; an imitation of
the Egyptian pyramid, therefore, is entirely out of the
question.

The *fifth* hypothesis is that of Mr. Milner, to whom we are
indebted for several valuable works on the architecture of
the Middle Age. After ably refuting with much learning and
sound criticism several hypotheses of other writers, he fancies
he discovers the origin of the pointed-arch style, and of the
architecture of the Middle Age in general, in an imitation of
the intersecting semicircular arches used as ornaments in the
ancient English style of building. But this explanation likewise appears unsatisfactory.

The question is not who invented the pointed arch; this,
like every other mathematical figure, had long been known.
The only question is how this pointed arch happened to
prevail in the style of building of the thirteenth century:
*Ornaments, as unessential parts, are conformably in every
style of building to the essential main parts of buildings: but
never are the main parts conformably, vice versa, to the
ornaments.* It is not to be supposed that all the highly characteristic forms of a style of building, which was so generally
diffused and so consistently contrived, should have been
borrowed from an accidental and unessential decoration of
the cornices. Experience also is in our favor, since we
observe, in all the buildings of the time in which the older
style of building passed over to the pointed-arch style, how
changes were first introduced in the main forms, gables and

roofs, later in the vaults and windows, and still later in the unessential parts and ornaments. Thus, for instance, the small arched decoration which so frequently appears in cornices and cinctures or bands is still in the semicircular form in the church of Gelnhausen, whilst the gables and windows are thus early pointed.

The foregoing observations show the groundlessness of the several hypotheses mentioned; but the solution of the question whether the pointed-arch style belongs to one single nation exclusively, and to which, is attended with greater difficulties. If the hypotheses on the origin of the pointed-arch style are various, opinions are not less divided on the present question, and the invention of this style has been ascribed to the Goths, the Lombards, the Saracens or Arabs, to the Spaniards, the Italians, the French, the English, and the Germans.

It has been shown in the second chapter that the Goths or Lombards were not the inventors of the architecture which takes their name, nor of any other style of building, and that the ancient paganism of the northern nations had no influence upon the style of church building.

The Arabs, who appeared as conquerors from the year of our Lord 610, and who, besides the countries which they conquered in Asia and Africa, possessed themselves in the year 713 of the greatest part of Spain and Portugal, erected in the latter countries some very considerable buildings, which are partly yet existing, and impress us with high notions of their knowledge of the arts, and of their magnificence. But a careful examination of their buildings shows that there is nothing in them that has the most distant resemblance to what is called the Gothic style. In the Arabian buildings the arches are in the shape of a horseshoe; the columns are all low; they stand single, and are never connected in pillars; the windows are small, the roofs flat, and the horizontal is the prevailing form in the whole composition of their buildings. In the ancient churches of the thirteenth century, the arches, on the contrary, are pointed, the pillars high, and composed of several columns; the windows large, the roofs and gables high. The more the two styles of building are compared, the more one is astonished that the Arabs could ever have been thought of as the inventors of a style of building so different from their own. It is true that many Arabian capitals, whose form is square at the top and joins the round column below, bear some resemblance to many capitals in the buildings of the Middle Age; but columns are also met with in Arabian buildings with Corinthian and Roman capitals, and yet we do not regard these as an invention of the Arabs. These occurrences are easily explained when we consider that the Arabs, originally a nation of herdsmen, could not have any architecture whatever, and that it was only after they became stationary in the countries which they had conquered, and from nomads became an agricultural people, that they formed a particular style of building for themselves. And as all the new possessions of the Arabs had formerly belonged to the vast Roman Empire, it is very easy to conceive that they must have adopted in their style of building much that they found in the structures of the earlier or later Christian Roman times.

The question about the influence of Arabian architecture is thus easily solved; but the solution of the question which of the people of Europe first introduced or improved the pointed-arch style is not so easy, for we find this style of building almost contemporary in all parts of Europe. A comparison of the churches built in different countries will facilitate the solution, if we attend to the principles stated in the first chapter, according to which that style of building alone can lay claim to being national *which in its forms corresponds with the climate and building materials of the country, and constitutes at the same time a consistent, intelligent whole, excluding everything heterogeneous.*

The cathedral of Orvieto in Italy, which is supposed to be the work of Nicolas of Pisa, who lived about the year 1240, has throughout, with exception of that in the front, rose windows, and exhibits in the front the style of building of the thirteenth century. But behind the pointed gables of the front there are flat roofs, so that the gables stand quite free above them. A glance at the dwelling houses of that town shows that flat roofs are indigenous in Italy; and we may therefore justly conclude that the whole style of building which has high gables is foreign there, and comes from a northern country. And just as the high gables on the flat Italian roofs belong to a northern country, so the flat gable on the high German roof has evidently been transplanted into Germany from a southern country.

The church of Batalha in Portugal affords another instance

of the use of the pointed-arch style in southern countries. The roof of the church is quite flat, covered with large stone slabs, and suitable to the climate; the whole form of the building, the pyramids, and the small pointed gables with which the aspiring pillars are ornamented, are, however, discordant with the horizontal termination of the nave of the church, and clearly show that the high gable roof is essential in this style of building, and that, consequently, its origin can be sought for in a northern climate only.

It has been seen in the preceding chapter that the pointed-arch style of the thirteenth century arose out of the more ancient Christian Roman style. If this and the foregoing observations be admitted, we shall be obliged to look for its origin in a country *which has a northern climate, and in which that ancient style of building prevailed;* consequently, in the north of France, in England, or in Germany.

The French churches of the Middle Age, some of which are considerable, are but little known by drawings; the editor, therefore, can refer here only to the cathedral of Paris. The main form of the front gate, which is said to have been built in the reign of King Philip Augustus, has, upon the whole, no high aspiring proportions; on the contrary, the horizontal line which prevails in the composition, and the flat roofs of the towers, correspond infinitely more with the ancient Christian Roman style than with the architecture of the Middle Age, from which the details alone of the ornaments appear to be borrowed.

Among the more ancient English churches none is more celebrated than York Minster, which was built toward the latter end of the thirteenth, and in the beginning of the fourteenth century. As the English lay such positive claims to the merit of having invented and improved the pointed-arch style of the thirteenth century, a closer examination of this church will not be deemed superfluous. Its main forms, the low gable roof, and the flat towers, evidently belong to an originally southern style of building. The whole ornamental system, on the contrary, is of northern origin, and stands in evident contradiction to these leading forms. The pointed gable which crowns the middle window, and is repeated in all the ornaments of the edifice, does not harmonize with the flat gable of the roof. The flat roofs of the towers correspond as little with the other parts of the building; they should necessarily have terminated in pyramids, as all the smaller towers of the aspiring pillars have the pyramidal form. All this shows the incongruous combination of two completely heterogeneous styles of building, and prejudices us so much the less in behalf of the originality of the English ecclesiastical architecture, as at the time when the York Minster was built the German churches already displayed the completest development of the art.

Lastly, let us examine the German style of church building, and particularly the minsters of Strasbourg and Freiburg, and the church at Oppenheim, which were all built in the second half of the thirteenth and in the beginning of the fourteenth century. The main forms, as well as the whole system of their ornaments, are in perfect harmony in these churches, and rest upon the pointed gable, the pyramid, and the pointed arch. The smallest tower which crowns the aspiring pillars displays, in the manner in which it is filled up, the form of the ornamented windows; above these, the pointed gables, and then the pyramid; and thus it repeats on a small scale the figure of the whole. A similar harmony of forms reigns in all the best German churches, from the thirteenth to the fifteenth century.

Having compared these different architectural works, and recollecting the principles laid down in the first chapter, the scholar and the connoisseur will now be enabled to judge which of the nations of Europe displays the greatest harmony and peculiarity in their buildings, and may most confidently claim the merit of the invention and improvement of the architecture of the thirteenth century.

Part II: The Confluence of Ideas (1820–1865)

1. Introduction

The architectural legacy that early nineteenth-century America inherited from its seventeenth- and eighteenth-century colonial past was essentially a matter of practice rather than of theory, and colonial practices in architecture had been largely an extension of practices in the European parent countries. England, of course, became dominant among these parent countries as its control of the colonial seaboard expanded. In the seventeenth century the New England Puritans and the settlers in Virginia, once out of the temporary hut phase, had moved rapidly to build as their middle-class English contemporaries were building. Their attempt was to reproduce in this country the physical dimensions and patterns of the settled English environment. The settlements John Eliot established in New England for the "praying Indians" are a direct, and to us almost comic, attempt to reproduce a conventional English environment: the Indians were converted not only to congregationalism (in their own language) but also to modest English lower-middle-class housing, clothing, tools, farming practices, community organization, and so on.

Colonial American architecture, and particularly that of New England, has been assessed as an original departure by some critics and historians, but this assessment is valid only in a very minimal sense. Comparisons in architectural history are sometimes hampered (as they appear to have been in this case) by the nature of the monuments the historian selects as characteristic of a period and a culture. If the historian selects, for example, the Duke of Devonshire's Chatsworth (1687–

1706) as characteristic of the architecture of its time in England, and then selects the Parson Capen House (1683) in Topsfield, Massachusetts, as characteristic of the architecture of New England, the generalization that "there is a radically different architecture in America" would hold, but the contrast between the duke's seat and a parson's contemporary house would hold in England as well, and the fair comparison (between the two 1683 parsons) would reveal that the New England house is first country cousin to its English counterpart.

Whatever there was of the original in colonial architecture was hardly the result of a conscious effort at a new departure, but a function of various necessities. The available materials were somewhat different than those available in England; there was a surplus of wood; there was no glass industry, and imported glass was expensive; brick and stone, which could have been available, were used sparingly because they required skilled labor and were slower modes of construction. Central among the necessities that conditioned colonial architecture was economy: there was a great deal of building to be done in a short time and with a short supply of skilled labor. Farms, villages, and towns could not be inherited; they had to be built; and those who built them then had to turn to other pursuits. Weather conditions also played their part as necessities, but only gradually did architectural forms along the eastern seaboard begin to vary and reflect conditions of climate that were so sharply different from each other and from those of England. Much as we might like to discover the reflection of Yankee ingenuity in colonial architecture, the Yankee seems to have expended his ingenuity in the effort to conform to the architectural practices of the mother country as he knew them through architectural handbooks. This attempt to conform resulted in a fascinating evolution of handtools for woodworking and in the evolution of building techniques that could utilize semiskilled labor.

Jefferson complained of a tendency to mannered overdecoration among his contemporaries, but there was no reaction against the Baroque-Rococo in eighteenth-century America comparable to the reaction in Europe, largely because the colonies had been and continued to be dominated by middle-class Protestant attitudes and because those attitudes had from the late sixteenth century rejected, at times

• 1.   Charles Bulfinch, First Church of Christ (Old Meeting House)
.. (1816–1817), Lancaster, Massachusetts.

quite violently, the florid, sensory emphasis of "the papist
arts." Mutterings in New England diaries about decorative
opulence in the homes of the rich appear to have been reflections of political and economic jealousies rather than of an
aesthetic point of view. While the Puritans were not the
repressed and unemotional stick figures caricature has rendered them, they were deeply suspicious of aesthetic experience—as a mode of approach to men's souls that the devil
might easily use to his advantage, and as an uneconomical
waste of time and productive energy. To this suspicion the
Puritans coupled the insistence that the arts (and particularly
literature) prove their usefulness both in terms of immediate
utility and in the crusade to convert man and reform his
society.

The nineteenth century's legacy from the American past
included the middle-class Protestant suspicion that aesthetic
experience was wasteful and/or subversive, the habit of relying on architectural handbooks for design ideas, a wide dissemination of the basic skills of carpentry, and an improved
set of woodworking tools. The eighteenth century had attempted to build modern England in America, and had
blushed occasionally for the Cousin Jonathan nature of its
provincial efforts. The nineteenth century, charged at the
outset with the competitive chauvinism of a new nation, made
self-conscious demands for a truly American expression in
literature and the arts, an expression that would vie with the
arts in Europe. "America," the orator Edward Everett proclaimed in 1824 "will become a utopian playground for the
intellect." And, he argued, as the arts and letters of democratic Greece outshone the productions of all the autocratic
states from Rome to Georgian England, so the arts and letters
of democratic America. . . . The net result of this self-
consciousness was a cyclical alternation between cultural
braggadocio and a cultural inferiority complex.

Architectural practice in the opening decades of the nineteenth century (in the Federal style and in the restrained
departures of Charles Bulfinch [1763–1844], Thomas Jefferson, and Samuel McIntire [1757–1811], and others) continued to evolve from the provincial Georgian forms that had
dominated eighteenth century public architecture. Jefferson
self-consciously looked to Roman and French prototypes as
a way of freeing himself from Georgian forms with their

2. William Strickland, Second Bank of the United States, later Customs House, (1812–1824), Philadelphia, Pennsylvania.

English associations. In retrospect it seems to have been the classical revival, not Jefferson's Roman as much as the Greek, which America first made its own, not only on the large scale of public buildings, such as William Strickland's Second Bank of the United States (1818–1824), but also on the small scale of anonymous and provincial buildings (see illustrations 2, 3, and 4). A variety of influences combined to establish the Greek revival. The plan and development of Washington, D.C., announced a revival of classical forms as the American and Republican mode. The cultural inferiority complex could be assuaged with Greek forms that could be regarded as having an inherent cultural dignity. The geometrical simplicity of Greek forms appealed to middle-class prejudice as economical, modest, and morally pure, though the interior distribution of space in Greek-revival houses represents no real departure from eighteenth-century practices. There were also romantic or sentimental overtones, deriving from an idealization of the Periclean Age and from the habit of associating the contemporary Greek war against the Turks with the American Revolution.

The revival point of view also had corollary appeals. Professional architects in the early nineteenth century (Strickland, for example) were not only "architects" in our sense of the word; they were also civil engineers capable of the design of waterworks, canals, bridges, and so forth. Many architects and builders, among them Ithiel Town (see pages 298 ff.), were accomplished technological inventors. The "art" in architecture tended to be modification and refinement of accepted forms; the creative tended to be technological and innovative. It could be argued that the architect's acceptance of revival forms provided him with ready-made vocabularies that in turn freed him for his concentration on technology. Jacob Bigelow in *Elements of Technology* (Boston, 1829) overstated the case for this emphasis on technology; he argued that his time was carrying technology toward "perfection":

The imitative arts were carried in antiquity to the most signal perfection. Their sculpture has been the admiration of subsequent ages, and their architecture has now furnished models which we strive to imitate, but do not pretend to excel.

Bigelow's remarks are also a bald statement of the historical and cultural inferiority that haunted his contemporaries—as though the new consciousness of history with its eclectic emphasis had transformed the historical past so that it overawed the present.

Eventually, though not initially, the basic rationalization of the revival point of view was to derive from Romantic idealism; not that revivalism was caused by Romantic idealism but that the two evolved together and became inseparably intertwined. On one level Romantic idealism attempted to resolve what eighteenth-century rational psychology had come to regard as a discontinuity within the individual between the outer, objective, self and the inner, subjective, self. The attempt at resolution postulated as an ideal state an organic continuity between outer, objective, rational "surfaces" and the inner, subjective, complex of imagination-intuition-emotion. Ideally the "surfaces" would become symbols, outgrowths of inner, intuitive, impulse—so that the inner motion would speak through the surfaces; and so, conversely, things, as Emerson put it, would "speak to the imagination." Basic to this conception of an ideal organic continuum was the assumption that the inner impulsion could be "translated," that is, that it could not only become conscious but that it could also be expressed and realized in words. This assumption was not asserted but was simply "there" as a corollary to the asserted ideal. From the ideal itself, Emerson, Greenough, and others derived their strictures against "imitation" and in favor of an organic architecture, useful as well as beautiful and honest to its materials; they postulated an architecture (as well as a poetry, art, morality, and philosophy) that from its inner spiritual-imaginative core would "speak" through its surfaces to the perceiving surfaces of the beholder's mind and thence to the beholder's imagination or core. The architectural ideal they postulated can easily be equated with that postulated by Sullivan and Wright, provided we overlook the mid-nineteenth-century emphasis on "language" as a metaphor for architectural experience, and in fact for all aesthetic experience (see A. J. Downing, pages 214 ff. and Emerson, page 99).

This tendency to emphasize the verbal and literary, and to regard art as "translation," can be seen in the painting and sculpture of the period as well as in the architecture. Painting and sculpture strive to "speak," and use anecdotal, associational, and descriptive devices that a twentieth-century

3. Anonymous, Greek Revival House (circa 1850), Eastham, Cape Cod, Massachusetts.

critic would regard as properly the devices of literature. It would not be accurate to argue that the emphasis on "language" dictated revivalism, but it is equally inaccurate to argue that, for example, Greenough's approach dictated an architecture like Sullivan's or Wright's; what Greenough's approach seemed to him to dictate can be seen in his projection of the Cooper Monument (see page 160). When Emerson remarked that things must "speak to the imagination," he could easily have been understood as arguing for the revivals —in the sense that Greek-revival forms could be associated through a sort of literary imagining with the democratic splendors of Greek culture, and a church in Gothic style could be regarded as a statement that the "sea of faith" for this congregation "was at its full." Gothic could also be regarded, on a more generalized level, as natural and organic because it reflected, as Jarves remarked, "freedom of hand and thought," and because it was, unlike the Greek, not geometrically confined. By mid-century this *literary* approach had been popularized into a sentimental cliché. If a house achieved the "picturesque," it was assumed that it would improve its inhabitants, enhancing their lives with the new dimensions of a history that was a collection of sentimental ideals. Catherine E. Beecher and Harriet Beecher Stowe thus illustrate "A Christian House" in their book (pages 275 ff.) as a Gothic cottage because the exterior would then both reflect and influence the Christian lives of its inhabitants. Similarly, Downing's remark that the fireplace had "the genial expression of *soul* in its ruddy blaze" could reflect the popular sentimental emphasis on the hearth as the heart and image of moral refinement in the home.

For all its protestations of inferiority in the face of the architectural past, the nineteenth-century-revival point of view, once popularized, had admixtures of a profound and self-assured superiority—not only in its regard for the new technology but also in its outspoken assumption of the moral superiority of its country and its age. Edward Everett, paralleling democratic America and democratic Greece in 1824, would with one hand give the Greeks the laurel for creative enterprise and take it away with the other hand because the Greeks were pagan, "crude and barbarous," and lacking in moral refinement. It was overtly assumed that democratic America was rapidly approaching a pinnacle of Christian

4. Anonymous, Congregational Church (1838), Madison, Connecticut.

moral refinement that in combination with America's inevitable intellectual achievement would surpass the glory that was Greece. This blatant optimism was, of course, severely attacked by nineteenth-century critics, but it remained a dominant mode of nineteenth-century sentiment; and the optimism could be reinforced by regarding the radical technological improvement of the time as a direct metaphor for moral refinement. In these terms the Beecher sisters could invent a house consistently "useful" on all levels, from the utilitarian emphasis on domestic technology and economics to "poetic" emphasis on the home as moral and spiritual symbol.

The critical attacks on blatant moral and aesthetic optimism, as mounted variously by Emerson, Greenough, Thoreau, Vaux, and Jarves, also enjoy one assumption in common: that it is possible, as Thoreau put it, to wake one's neighbors up, to educate them; in short, it is possible through literary effort to accomplish the aesthetic education of democratic America. Here again the revival architecture that appealed to the sentimental optimist could be regarded by the critic in slightly more refined terms as a useful instrument in the effort to achieve aesthetic literacy.

The selections that follow do not develop a line of argument, but a climate of ideas and opinion—a confluence from a variety of points of view: professional, critical, and theoretical, popular and sentimental. Architectural practice in this period continued in a dual emphasis: on usefulness, utility, and economy, and on revival forms that were valued for what was regarded as their higher usefulness—educational, aesthetic, moral, and spiritual.

Thomas Jefferson, from "Query XV," NOTES ON
THE STATE OF VIRGINIA in THE WRITINGS OF
THOMAS JEFFERSON (New York, 1894),
Vol. III, pp. 257–259; "Letter to the Trustees
for the Lottery of East Tennessee College,"
The Complete Jefferson (New York, 1943),
pp. 1063–1064.

Thomas Jefferson (1743–1826), the third President of
the United States, has been much praised as an architect,
particularly for the originality of the designs of Monticello
and of the University of Virginia at Charlottesville (see illustration 5). On one level these designs represent a mild
departure from the modified Renaissance forms of Georgian
(and Federal) architecture in favor of classical Roman and
contemporary French precedents. The core of Jefferson's
originality is in the way he conceptualized and programmed
functions within architectural spaces. The Roman details of
Jefferson's buildings are in conformity rather than at variance
with the decorative conventions of his time; but his grasp of
the human implications of an architectural plan appeals to the
modern critic as radically perceptive and creative. Jefferson's
architectural influence made itself felt not only through
example and political influence but also through the careers
of his protégés, the architects Benjamin Latrobe (see pages
85 ff., and illustration 7) and Robert Mills (see pages 80 ff.
and illustration 6).

5. Thomas Jefferson, University of Virginia (1817–1826), Charlottesville, Virginia. Entire complex as it appeared in 1853 after addition of Robert Mills's Rotunda Annex (at left).

From "Query XV,"
Notes on the State of Virginia (1782)

The private buildings are very rarely constructed of stone or brick, much the greatest proportion being of scantling and boards, plastered with lime. It is impossible to devise things more ugly, uncomfortable, and happily more perishable. There are two or three plans, on one of which, according to its size, most of the houses in the state are built. The poorest people build huts of logs, laid horizontally in pens, stopping the interstices with mud. These are warmer in winter, and cooler in summer, than the more expensive constructions of scantling and plank. The wealthy are attentive to the raising of vegetables, but very little so to fruits. The poorer people attend to neither, living principally on milk and animal diet. This is the more inexcusable, as the climate requires indispensably a free use of vegetable food, for health as well as comfort, and is very friendly to the raising of fruits. The only public buildings worthy mention are the Capitol, the Palace, the College, and the Hospital for Lunatics, all of them in Williamsburg,* heretofore the seat of our government. The Capitol is a light and airy structure, with a portico in front of two orders, the lower of which, being Doric, is tolerably just in its proportions and ornaments, save only that the inter-colonnations are too large. The upper is Ionic, much too small for that on which it is mounted, its ornaments not proper to the order, nor proportioned within themselves. It is crowned with a pediment, which is too high for its span. Yet, on the whole, it is the most pleasing piece of architecture we have. The Palace is not handsome without, but it is spacious and commodious within, is prettily situated, and with the grounds annexed to it, is capable of being made an elegant seat. The College and Hospital are rude, misshapen piles, which, but that they have roofs, would be taken for brick kilns. There are no other public buildings but churches and courthouses, in which no attempts are made at elegance.

* The twentieth-century reconstruction of Williamsburg is not necessarily accurate enough to present a dependable frame of reference for Jefferson's critical comments.

Indeed, it would not be easy to execute such an attempt, as a workman could scarcely be found here capable of drawing an order. The genius of architecture seems to have shed its maledictions over this land. Buildings are often erected, by individuals, at considerable expense. To give these symmetry and taste would not increase their cost. It would only change the arrangement of the materials, the form and combination of the members. This would often cost less than the burthen of barbarous ornaments with which these buildings are sometimes charged. But the first principles of the art are unknown, and there exists scarcely a model among us sufficiently chaste to give an idea of them. Architecture being one of the fine arts, and as such within the department of a professor of the college, according to the new arrangement, perhaps a spark may fall on some young subjects of natural taste, kindle up their genius, and produce a reformation in this elegant and useful art. But all we shall do in this way will produce no permanent improvement to our country, while the unhappy prejudice prevails that houses of brick or stone are less wholesome than those of wood. A dew is often observed on the walls of the former in rainy weather, and the most obvious solution is that the rain has penetrated through these walls. The following facts, however, are sufficient to prove the error of this solution. 1. This dew on the walls appears when there is no rain, if the state of the atmosphere be moist. 2. It appears on the partition as well as the exterior walls. 3. So, also, on pavements of brick or stone. 4. It is more copious in proportion as the walls are thicker; the reverse of which ought to be the case, if this hypothesis were just. If cold water be poured into a vessel of stone or glass, a dew forms instantly on the outside: but if it be poured into a vessel of wood, there is no such appearance. It is not supposed, in the first case, that the water has exuded through the glass, but that it is precipitated from the circumambient air; as the humid particles of vapor, passing from the boiler of an alembic through its refrigerant, are precipitated from the air, in which they were suspended, on the internal surface of the refrigerant. Walls of brick or stone act as the refrigerant in this instance. They are sufficiently cold to condense and precipitate the moisture suspended in the air of the room, when it is heavily charged therewith. But walls of wood are not so. The question then is whether air in which this moisture is left floating, or that which is deprived of it, be most wholesome? In both cases, the remedy is easy. A little fire kindled in the room, whenever the air is damp, prevents the precipitation on the walls: and this practice, found healthy in the warmest as well as coldest seasons, is as necessary in a wooden as in a stone or a brick house. I do not mean to say that the rain never penetrates through walls of brick. On the contrary, I have seen instances of it. But with us it is only through the northern and eastern walls of the house, after a northeasterly storm, these being the only ones which continue long enough to force through the walls. This, however, happens too rarely to give a just character of unwholesomeness to such houses. In a house the walls of which are of well-burned brick and good mortar, I have seen the rain penetrate through but twice in a dozen or fifteen years. The inhabitants of Europe, who dwell chiefly in houses of stone or brick, are surely as healthy as those of Virginia. These houses have the advantage, too, of being warmer in winter and cooler in summer than those of wood; of being cheaper in their first construction, where lime is convenient, and infinitely more durable. The latter consideration renders it of great importance to eradicate this prejudice from the minds of our countrymen. A country whose buildings are of wood can never increase in its improvements to any considerable degree. Their duration is highly estimated at fifty years. Every half century then our country becomes a *tabula rasa,* whereon we have to set out anew, as in the first moment of seating it. Whereas when buildings are of durable materials, every new edifice is an actual and permanent acquisition to the state, adding to its value as well as to its ornament.

Letter to the Trustees for the Lottery of East Tennessee College, May 6, 1810

I consider the common plan followed in this country, but not in others, of making one large and expensive building as unfortunately erroneous. It is infinitely better to erect a small and separate lodge for each separate professorship, with only a hall below for his class, and two chambers above for himself; joining these lodges by barracks for a certain portion of the students, opening into a covered way to give a dry communication between all the schools. The whole of these arranged around an open square of grass and trees would make it, what it should be in fact, an academical village, instead of a large and common den of noise, of filth, and of fetid air. It would afford that quiet retirement so friendly to study, and lessen the dangers of fire, infection, and tumult. Every professor would be the police officer of the students adjacent to his own lodge, which should include those of his own class of preference, and might be at the head of their table, if, as I suppose, it can be reconciled with the necessary economy to dine them in smaller and separate parties rather than in a large and common mess. Those separate buildings, too, might be erected successively and occasionally, as the number of professorships and students should be increased or the funds become competent.

I pray you to pardon me if I have stepped aside into the province of counsel; but much observation and reflection on these institutions have long convinced me that the large and crowded buildings in which youths are pent up are equally unfriendly to health, to study, to manners, morals, and order.

3

Robert Mills, "The Progress of Architecture in Virginia," and "The Architectural Works of Robert Mills" from H. M. Pierce Gallagher, ROBERT MILLS / ARCHITECT OF THE WASHINGTON MONUMENT (New York, 1935), pp. 155–158, 168–171.

Robert Mills (1781–1855) was, by his own assertion, "the first native American who directed his studies to architecture as a profession." As a young man he was sponsored and encouraged by Thomas Jefferson, and he worked (1802–1808) in the office of Benjamin Latrobe, the English architect and engineer who had emigrated to America in 1791. Mills climaxed his career as "architect of the General Government" of the United States (1836–1852); in that office he designed the Treasury Building, (see illustration 6), the General Post Office, the Patent Office Building, and the Washington Monument. Mills's designs, strongly flavored as they are by Greek forms, suggest architectural conformity, but his theory and his preoccupation with engineering argue a substrate of originality.

6. Robert Mills, Treasury Building (1836–1842), Washington, D.C.

The Progress of Architecture in Virginia

AN ESSAY BY ROBERT MILLS

[The MS was never finished. The original is in the possession of the Dimitry family.]

The introduction of architecture into this state received, we may say, its first impulse from the untiring industry and zeal of Thomas Jefferson, whose immortal name is associated with the political and literary prosperity of this country. The Capitol at Richmond might be regarded as almost the first architectural public work erected in Virginia, and we are indebted to Mr. Jefferson for the model of this building—which model is still preserved in the State Library in the Capitol. In its general features there is little difference in design between it and the model of the building as executed. The particular difference consists in the omission of the attic windows and in the substitution of a high basement story—a change which comports better with our ideas of utility, and convenience of access to the rooms and for office purposes. I may here add a word on the character of architecture adapted to the wants of our country: utility first, ornament secondly.

I have always deprecated the servile copying of the buildings of antiquity; we have the same principles and materials to work upon that the ancients had, and we should adapt these materials to the habits and customs of our people as they did to theirs. There is no objection to the use of orders in columns as established by the ancients, for the proportions of these are founded upon nature and where we are applying them to the same purposes as their architects did we should follow their proportions rigidly. I have regretted to see American architects and artists taking European, Asiatic, and Egyptian examples for their models. We have the same natural models which the ancients had when they formed their buildings, their statues, and so on, and shall we go to the copy and not to the original for our models? To illustrate: Benjamin West, when at the instance of his friends and patrons went to Europe to pursue his studies, was taken to the Vatican by enthusiastic friends to be surprised with the first vision of that *chef d'œuvre* of art the Apollo Belvedere, kept from the vulgar gaze to be looked on only by the lovers of art. West was introduced to the alumni of the place as the young American who had come out from the wilds of his native country to study the glorious arts, and desirous of seeing the grand statue. He was received with enthusiastic interest and favor by these gentlemen, who were delighted with the opportunity of witnessing the effect which this splendid work of art would have upon an unsophisticated, though gifted, son of the forest in love with the fine arts. He was conducted into the sanctum sanctorum, but the statue was veiled by a curtain with the view of taking the young artist by surprise. As the curtain rose, the countenance of young West was intently watched by the anxious amateurs present, but no expression of surprise was observed in that countenance, no manifestation of enthusiastic delight when the whole figure of the Apollo burst upon his vision. . . . What a disappointment was here! What is the cause of this indifference? was the exclamation. Certainly he is no artist; he has not even the feelings of an artist, and by such remarks he was about to be condemned by his peers as devoid of common taste, when the friend of the young man begged the gentlemen to suspend their decision until Mr. West had explained himself. His friend therefore informed Mr. West of the disappointment of these gentlemen in that he had manifested no surprise, pleasure, nor even approval of the work, and wished him to explain his position. West modestly remarked that he had often witnessed in real life the action of the figure before him among the Mohawk Indians in his country, and that he saw nothing more to admire save the skill of the artist. The explanation was perfectly satisfactory to the company and it was the highest compliment, they declared, to the artist of the Apollo, as it proved his close observation of nature, and they decreed that the young American surpassed his contemporaries in judgment, taste, and artistic tact. It is a remarkable fact that American artists have born off the palm, even in Europe, because they have followed nature in their models; the realities were the only models they had, and hence their success. Our artists, therefore, should never forget the original models of their country, neither the customs nor manners of their people, when they execute works of art either for their gov-

ernment or for their fellow citizens. Examples of the failure
of these artistic works to give satisfaction to the public are
unfortunately too numerous; the colossal statue of Washington
within the eastern enclosure of the Capitol at Washington—a
splendid work*—has failed to meet public approval, not only
from the costume used but the sitting attitude of the figure.
Canova's Washington† at the Capitol of North Carolina, the
pride of this artist, was a failure from the same cause, its
costume, which was *outré*, out of character with our customs.
Chantry's [Chantrey] Washington,‡ at Boston, comes under
the same ban, but let the American visit the Capitol at Richmond and view the statue of Washington (Houdon's),§ and all
other statues fall into the shade before this beautiful and
correct representation of the father of his country. This last
statue is approved by the million, where but a few admire the
others named, and I say to our artists: Study your country's
tastes and requirements, and make classic ground *here* for
your art. Go not to the Old World for your examples. We
have entered a new era in the history of the world; it is our
destiny to lead, not to be led. Our vast country is before us
and our motto Excelsior. The importance of the subject must
plead for this digression.

The architectural order of the Capitol at Richmond is
Roman, as economy had to enter into the execution of this
building, inferior materials utilized in its construction; the
details, however, are kept up remarkably well in both exterior
and interior. The dimensions on the plan are 70 by 150 feet;
its principal façade is to the south, and presents a hexagonal
portico; two intercolumniations in depth surmounted by a
pediment. The ground, or basement, story is occupied by the
state offices. On the second, or principal, floor are the two
halls of Legislature, the Senate on the south, the House on
the north, and the hall between is occupied by the grand
staircase and vestibule; the center by an open galleried hall in
the middle of which stands the marble statue of Washington,

---

* Horatio Greenough, "George Washington," marble (1833–1841); see
illustration 8.

† Antonio Canova (1757–1822), an Italian sculptor whose imaginary
Washington is represented in an armor and attitude appropriate to Julius
Caesar.

‡ Sir Francis Legatt Chantrey (1781–1842), an English sculptor.

§ Jean Antoine Houdon (1741–1828), a French sculptor who portrayed
Washington from life in 1785 and in contemporary eighteenth-century
costume. Houdon was the only one of these sculptors who saw Washington
in the flesh.

which presents him in the costume of the time and is considered a correct likeness of the man. The accompaniments are argicultural and represent him as the farmer. The whole presents a very natural appearance, being of the exact height of the man. It was erected by the state, and on the pedestal is the following inscription: "George Washington, the General Assembly of the Commonwealth of Virginia have caused this statue to be erected as a monument of affection and gratitude to George Washington who, uniting to the endowments of the hero the virtues of the patriot, and exerting both in establishing the liberty of his country, has rendered his name dear to her fellow citizens and given the world an immortal example of true glory. Done in the year of Christ, 1788, and in the year of the commonwealth, the 12th." The artist that executed this statue was Houdon, a celebrated French sculptor who came over for the purpose. The head of this statue has been considered so much like Washington that it has been the standard head to all the other statues ordered subsequently of this great man. An iron railing surrounds the whole group, and the Hall, as before observed, is surrounded by a gallery. It extends up to the roof and is lighted through an aperture there. The third floor is occupied by the office of the Governor of Virginia and his counsel, the Secretary of State, and the State Library. All the rooms within are furnished in heavy Roman Palladian style, and have a venerable antique appearance. The erection of this building commenced the introduction of some attention to the public and domestic architecture of Virginia, but as there were no architects in the country at that time, there were many defects in their design. The location of this building is on a high eminence, and commands an extensive prospect. I remember the impression it made on my mind when first I came in view of it coming from the south. It gave me an idea of the position of those Greek temples which are the admiration of the world.

In 1791 Benjamin Henry Latrobe, Esq. [27 years old], an eminent English architect and engineer, came from England to reside in Virginia. This gentleman was the son of the sculptor of the great Zenzendorf (the founder of the Moravian sect of Christians). Mr. Latrobe was led to Virginia by the expectation of inheriting a large patrimonial estate there belonging to his father, but was disappointed in its value. About this period the penitentiary system was introduced into Virginia, and Mr. Latrobe was employed to design and super-

7. Benjamin Henry Latrobe, Bank of Pennsylvania (1799–1801), Philadelphia, Pennsylvania.

intend its erection. This building was designed upon architectural principles; it was the best constructed and arranged prison then extant in the Union. In 1791, Mr. Latrobe was called to Philadelphia to design and erect the Bank of Pennsylvania—a beautiful marble structure of the temple form after that of Theseus in Athens. Virginia thus lost the personal and professional services of one of the first of architects in any country. This gentleman was afterward engaged upon the Delaware and Chesapeake Canal and as an architect of the Capitol at Washington, at which time I entered his office as a student under the advice and recommendation of Mr. Jefferson, then President of the United States. I had been previously pursuing my studies in the office of the architect of the President's house [James Hoban], and as there were no architectural works to be had, Mr. Jefferson kindly offered me the use of his library, where I found several works, all of Roman character, principally Palladio, of whom Mr. Jefferson was a great admirer. During this period I made some plans and elevations for his mansion at Monticello according to his view of interior arrangement, which were of the French character. He was . . .

[pp. 155–158]

The Architectural Works of Robert Mills (consisting principally of buildings of a public character executed in various parts of the United States)

BY ROBERT MILLS

[This is a copy of what was apparently a merest scribbled outline of an intended paper (or book) under the title given. The original is in the possession of Moïse Goldstein, Esq., of New Orleans.]

INTRODUCTION

The author, having the honor of being the first native American who directed his studies to architecture as a profession, may have some claim to the favorable mention of his fellow citizens, and having acted as a pioneer in the cause, his more enlightened brethren of the profession will be less severe in their criticisms than they would otherwise be on these, his original efforts.

The author is altogether American in his views—his studies having never been out of the United States and consequently had very little advantage of and from a personal examination of the celebrated works of antiquity, or of more modern date, except that which is to be found in books, and even these were few and difficult to procure at the time he was a student, as architecture was then in its infancy in this country and no invitation was held out for the importation of works of art.

Fortunately for the author, Mr. Jefferson, then President of the United States (befriended him), to whose library he had the honor of having access, where he found some few works of eminent Roman architects but no Grecian writers.

Mr. Jefferson was an amateur and a great admirer of architecture. He was therefore much gratified to find an American turning his attention to its study, and he gave him every encouragement in the pursuit of his profession. Through his recommendation and advice, the author entered into the office of that celebrated architect and engineer Benjamin H. Latrobe, whom Mr. Jefferson had lately appointed Surveyor of the Public Buildings. With this gentleman, the author pursued and completed his studies and practiced in both branches of his profession, as Mr. Latrobe was, at this time, acting engineer of the Chesapeake and Delaware Canal.

The talents of this gentleman were of the first order; his style was purely Greek, and for the first time in this country was it introduced by him in the Bank of Pennsylvania—a building much admired for its chasteness of design and execution.

It was fortunate that this style was so early introduced into our country, both on the ground of economy and of correct taste, as it exactly suited the character of our political institutions and pecuniary means. Mr. Jefferson was a Roman in his views of architecture, as evidenced in Monticello House, his late residence, which was designed by him, and for the execution of which he furnished with his own hands all the detail drawings.

The example and influence of Mr. Jefferson at first operated in favor of the introduction of the Roman style into the country, and it required all the talents and good taste of such a man as Mr. Latrobe to correct it by introducing a better. The natural good taste and the unprejudiced eye of our citizens required only a few examples of the Greek style to convince them of its superiority over the Roman for public structures, and its simplicity recommended its introduction into their private dwellings.

During this period also, Europe, which for centuries had adapted the Roman and mixed style, began to emerge out of its prejudices, and the light which had been thrown upon the Greek architecture by such men as Stewart* caused it to be early substituted in their place. Since then it has been universally approved throughout civilized Europe, and in our own country we now find the simple and chaste style of the Grecian buildings generally adopted.

The author has contributed his mite in this important work, and has acted as a pioneer in the undertaking. He had many and great difficulties to contend against which those who may succeed him in the profession will never be subject to. In a new country like ours, where everything had to be done and little means to accomplish it with, it will readily be seen that the architect would receive little encouragement and the value of his labors be little appreciated. The increasing prosperity of the Union, the wealth and good taste of our citizens are every day aiding the cause of the fine arts, and we may anticipate the time when the United States will rival the most enlightened country of the Old World, if not in the splendor, yet in the magnitude, utility, and good taste of its public works.

The nature of our public institutions, the independent character of our people, their liberal education, and the wide field for successful enterprise opened in the various pursuits of life all tend to enlarge the mind and give the most exalted views on every subject of art and science. Taken in the aggregate, there is not a more liberal and enlightened people on the face of the globe than the people of the United States.

The professional labors of the author are distributed in various parts of the Union. The principal part of the designs found in his work were executed in Philadelphia, Baltimore,

---

* "Stewart" was James Stuart (1713–1788), an English painter and architect, nicknamed "the Athenian" for his leading role in creating *Antiquities of Athens Measured and Delineated* . . . (London, 1762).

Washington, Richmond, Charleston, Columbia, Camden, and other towns of South Carolina, Augusta, Georgia, New Orleans, Mobile, and so on.

Utility and economy will be found to have entered into most of the studies of the author, and little sacrificed to display; at the same time his endeavors were to produce as much harmony and beauty of arrangement as practicable. The principle assumed and acted upon was that beauty is founded upon order, and that convenience and utility were constituent parts. In the cases of private buildings it is of special importance that convenience, utility, and economy should be associated, and the author was generally successful in developing these. European works of architecture were, some years ago, very deficient in plans for private houses, and those laid down were both unsuitable and wanting in economy and convenience. The author experienced no aid in this important . . . , and was obliged to refer to his own resources for assistance. The subject of domestic economy in the arrangement of private houses has since undergone considerable improvement, particularly in France, and many useful hints now are to be gathered from French works on architecture; but the author has made it a rule never to consult books when he had to design a building. His considerations were—first, the object of the building; second, the means appropriated for its construction; third, the situation it was to occupy; these served as guides in forming the outline of his plan. Books are useful to the student, but when he enters upon the practice of his profession, he should lay them aside and consult them only upon doubtful points, or in matters of detail or as mere studies, not to copy buildings from.

The science of architecture is perhaps the most difficult, important, and interesting of all branches of study, where it is intended to form the groundwork of practice. There is no other profession that embraces so wide a field of research and practical operation. Some idea may be formed of the nature of these researches when the requisites to constitute an accomplished architect are taken into consideration. The student, after going through the usual collegiate course, will find himself on the threshold of the temple. Besides having an intimate acquaintance with the different styles of building, ancient and modern, and a thorough knowledge of the five orders (as they are termed), which necessarily demand an acquaintance with drawing, he must study the infinite detail which makes up the endless variety of parts constituting the higher class of structure. There is not a mechanic art, from the laborer who excavates the foundation to the highest artisan who decorates the interior of the building, but should acquire such knowledge as would enable him to give direction and judge whether the work executed is done in proper manner. There is scarcely a science but is embraced in greater or less degree in this profession: mathematics, natural philosophy, chemistry, geology, botany, natural history, jurisprudence, and theology. In short, to be an accomplished architect is to be not only an accomplished scholar but an accomplished artist and mechanic. There is not a more fascinating study in the whole range of the liberal professions than that of architecture, even considered in the light of study only; but when its utility is examined, and that it offers one of the most honorable pursuits, it cannot be too highly commended to our youth. If it constituted a part of liberal education, we should see a better taste and a more attractive character of buildings adopted in our country. Until our citizens can distinguish between the crude drawings of the illiterate artist and the designs of the regular-bred architect, it is not to be expected that a judicious selection of plans would always be made. It is all-important, therefore, that architecture should constitute one of the sciences taught in our colleges and academies.

[pp. 168–171]

4

Ralph Waldo Emerson, "III, Beauty" from NATURE (1836); "Thoughts on Art," THE DIAL, Vol. I, No. III, pp. 367–378 (Boston, January, 1841); from "Self-Reliance" in ESSAYS, FIRST SERIES (Boston, 1841); from "Art" in ESSAYS, FIRST SERIES; from "Beauty" in THE CONDUCT OF LIFE (Boston, 1860), pp. 253–259, 266–270; from THE LETTERS OF RALPH WALDO EMERSON, ed. Ralph L. Rusk (New York, 1939), Vol. III, pp. 121–122; Vol. IV, pp. 271–272; from HARVARD LIBRARY BULLETIN (Cambridge, Winter 1958), Vol. XII, No. 1, pp. 98–100.

R. W. Emerson (1803–1882) occupied a central position in, and exerted a variety of influences upon, the evolution of aesthetic and architectural theory in nineteenth-century America. Emerson's stance as philosopher-essayist was essentially eclectic and suggestive rather than systematic and definitive; as he put it, he intended to accomplish "a sort of farmer's almanac of mental moods." Emerson's stance accounts in part for his capacity to respond in dialogue, as with Horatio Greenough; and it also accounts for the ways in which Emerson's statements excited a variety of specific ideas in individuals as sharply different as Thoreau and Andrew Carnegie. As initially stated in "Beauty" (*Nature,* 1836) and in "Thoughts on Art" (1841), Emerson's aesthetic was to retain its general outlines throughout his career; so much so that he republished, with minor revisions, "Thoughts on Art" as the essay "Art" in *Society and Solitude* (1870). In this light, the meetings with Greenough (in Florence, 1833 —in Washington, 1843—and in Concord-Boston, 1852) do not seem to have influenced Emerson to alter his theory. He affirmed Greenough's theories as "original and magnificent" in 1852; yet at the same time Emerson appears to have regarded them as specific extensions and confirmations of the general and flexible position he himself had developed by 1841. Greenough's conversation in 1833 had focused not on "form and function" but on his theory that art should be a cooperative, noncompetitive enterprise—as Emerson put it in *English Traits* (1856), Greenough had argued that "art would never prosper until we left our shy jealous ways and worked in society." This phase of Greenough's thought took its final shape in his 1843 essay "Remarks on American Art," and did not change materially in the nine years that remained of his life. Emerson did not read this essay or "American Architecture" (also 1843, see pages 141 ff.) until 1852, when Greenough called them to his attention. By that time Greenough's preoccupation with "form and function" had overshadowed his earlier interest in the cooperative nature of artistic creation.

1836   Beauty

A nobler want of man is served by nature, namely, the love of Beauty.

The ancient Greeks called the world κόσμος,* beauty. Such is the constitution of all things, or such the plastic power of the human eye, that the primary forms, as the sky, the mountain, the tree, the animal, gave us a delight *in and for themselves;* a pleasure arising from outline, color, motion, and grouping. This seems partly owing to the eye itself. The eye is the best of artists. By the mutual action of its structure and of the laws of light, perspective is produced, which integrates every mass of objects, of what character soever, into a well-colored and shaded globe, so that where the particular

* Cosmos, universe, order, harmony.

objects are mean and unaffecting, the landscape which they compose is round and symmetrical. And as the eye is the best composer, so light is the first of painters. There is no object so foul that intense light will not make beautiful. And the stimulus it affords to the sense and a sort of infinitude which it hath, like space and time, make all matter gay. Even the corpse has its own beauty. But besides this general grace diffused over nature, almost all the individual forms are agreeable to the eye, as is proved by our endless imitations of some of them, as the acorn, the grape, the pine cone, the wheatear, the egg, the wings and forms of most birds, the lion's claw, the serpent, the butterfly, seashells, flames, clouds, buds, leaves, and the forms of many trees, as the palm.

For better consideration, we may distribute the aspects of Beauty in a threefold manner.

1. First, the simple perception of natural forms is a delight. The influence of the forms and actions in nature is so needful to man that, in its lowest functions, it seems to lie on the confines of commodity and beauty. To the body and mind which have been cramped by noxious work or company, nature is medicinal and restores their tone. The tradesman, the attorney comes out of the din and craft of the street and sees the sky and the woods, and is a man again. In their eternal calm, he finds himself. The health of the eye seems to demand a horizon. We are never tired, so long as we can see far enough.

But in other hours, Nature satisfies by its loveliness, and without any mixture of corporeal benefit. I see the spectacle of morning from the hilltop over against my house, from daybreak to sunrise, with emotions which an angel might share. The long slender bars of cloud float like fishes in the sea of crimson light. From the earth, as a shore, I look out into that silent sea. I seem to partake its rapid transformations; the active enchantment reaches my dust, and I dilate and conspire with the morning wind. How does Nature deify us with a few and cheap elements. Give me health and a day, and I will make the pomp of emperors ridiculous. The dawn is my Assyria; the sunset and moonrise my Paphos, and unimaginable realms of faerie; broad noon shall be my England of the senses and the understanding; the night shall be my Germany of mystic philosophy and dreams.

Not less excellent, except for our less susceptibility in the afternoon, was the charm, last evening, of a January sunset. The western clouds divided and subdivided themselves into pink flakes modulated with tints of unspeakable softness, and the air had so much life and sweetness that it was a pain to come within doors. What was it that nature would say? Was there no meaning in the live repose of the valley behind the mill, and which Homer or Shakespeare could not re-form for me in words? The leafless trees become spires of flame in the sunset, with the blue east for their background, and the stars of the dead calices of flowers, and every withered stem and stubble rimed with frost, contribute something to the mute music.

The inhabitants of cities suppose that the country landscape is pleasant only half the year. I please myself with the graces of the winter scenery, and believe that we are as much touched by it as by the genial influences of summer. To the attentive eye, each moment of the year has its own beauty, and in the same field, it beholds, every hour, a picture which was never seen before, and which shall never be seen again. The heavens change every moment, and reflect their glory or gloom on the plains beneath. The state of the crop in the surrounding farms alters the expression of the earth from week to week. The succession of native plants in the pastures and roadsides, which makes the silent clock by which time tells the summer hours, will make even the divisions of the day sensible to a keen observer. The tribes of birds and insects, like the plants punctual to their time, follow each other, and the year has room for all. By watercourses, the variety is greater. In July, the blue pontederia or pickerel weed blooms in large beds in the shallow parts of our pleasant river, and swarms with yellow butterflies in continual motion. Art cannot rival this pomp of purple and gold. Indeed the river is a perpetual gala and boasts each month a new ornament.

But this beauty of Nature which is seen and felt as beauty is the least part. The shows of day, the dewy morning, the rainbow, mountains, orchards in blossom, stars, moonlight, shadows in still water, and the like, if too eagerly hunted, become shows merely, and mock us with their unreality. Go out of the house to see the moon, and 'tis mere tinsel; it will not please as when its light shines upon your necessary journey. The beauty that shimmers in the yellow afternoons of

October, who ever could clutch it? Go forth to find it, and it is gone; 'tis only a mirage as you look from the windows of diligence.

2. The presence of a higher, namely, of the spiritual element is essential to its perfection. The high and divine beauty which can be loved without effeminacy is that which is found in combination with the human will. Beauty is the mark God sets upon virtue. Every natural action is graceful. Every heroic act is also decent, and causes the place and the bystanders to shine. We are taught by great actions that the universe is the property of every individual in it. Every rational creature has all nature for his dowry and estate. It is his, if he will. He may divest himself of it; he may creep into a corner, and abdicate his kingdom, as most men do, but he is entitled to the world by his constitution. In proportion to the energy of his thought and will, he takes up the world into himself. "All those things for which men plow, build, or sail obey virtue," said Sallust. "The winds and waves," said Gibbon, "are always on the side of the ablest navigators." So are the sun and moon and all the stars of heaven. When a noble act is done— perchance in a scene of great natural beauty; when Leonidas and his three hundred martyrs consume one day in dying, and the sun and moon come each and look at them once in the steep defile of Thermopylae; when Arnold Winkelried, in the high Alps, under the shadow of the avalanche, gathers in his side a sheaf of Austrian spears to break the line for his comrades; are not these heroes entitled to add the beauty of the scene to the beauty of the deed? When the bark of Columbus nears the shore of America—before it the beach lined with savages, fleeing out of all their huts of cane; the sea behind; and the purple mountains of the Indian Archipelago around, can we separate the man from the living picture? Does not the New World clothe his form with her palm groves and savannahs as fit drapery? Ever does natural beauty steal in like air, and envelop great actions. When Sir Harry Vane was dragged up the Tower hill, sitting on a sled, to suffer death as the champion of the English laws, one of the multitude cried out to him, "You never sate on so glorious a seat!" Charles II, to intimidate the citizens of London, caused the patriot Lord Russell to be drawn in an open coach through the principal streets of the city on his way to the scaffold. "But," his biographer says, "the multitude imagined

they saw liberty and virtue sitting by his side." In private places, among sordid objects, an act of truth or heroism seems at once to draw to itself the sky as its temple, the sun as its candle. Nature stretches out her arms to embrace man, only let his thoughts be of equal greatness. Willingly does she follow his steps with the rose and the violet, and bend her lines of grandeur and grace to the decoration of her darling child. Only let his thoughts be of equal scope, and the frame will suit the picture. A virtuous man is in unison with her works, and makes the central figure of the visible sphere. Homer, Pindar, Socrates, Phocion associate themselves fitly in our memory with the geography and climate of Greece. The visible heavens and earth sympathize with Jesus. And in common life whosoever has seen a person of powerful character and happy genius will have remarked how easily he took all things along with him—the persons, the opinions, and the day, and nature became ancillary to a man.

3. There is still another aspect under which the beauty of the world may be viewed, namely, as it becomes an object of the intellect. Beside the relation of things to virtue, they have a relation to thought. The intellect searches out the absolute order of things as they stand in the mind of God, and without the colors of affection. The intellectual and the active powers seem to succeed each other, and the exclusive activity of the one generates the exclusive activity of the other. There is something unfriendly in each to the other, but they are like the alternate periods of feeding and working in animals; each prepares and will be followed by the other. Therefore does beauty, which, in relation to actions, as we have seen, comes unsought, and comes because it is unsought, remain for the apprehension and pursuit of the intellect; and then again, in its turn, of the active power. Nothing divine dies. All good is eternally reproductive. The beauty of nature re-forms itself in the mind, and not for barren contemplation, but for new creation.

All men are in some degree impressed by the face of the world; some men even to delight. This love of beauty is Taste. Others have the same love in such excess, that, not content with admiring, they seek to embody it in new forms. The creation of beauty is Art.

The production of a work of art throws a light upon the mystery of humanity. A work of art is an abstract or epitome of the world. It is the result or expression of nature, in miniature. For although the works of nature are innumerable and all different, the result or the expression of them all is similar and single. Nature is a sea of forms radically alike and even unique. A leaf, a sunbeam, a landscape, the ocean make an analogous impression on the mind. What is common to them all—that perfectness and harmony—is beauty. The standard of beauty is the entire circuit of natural forms—the totality of nature; which the Italians expressed by defining beauty *"il più nell' uno."** Nothing is quite beautiful alone; nothing but is beautiful in the whole. A single object is only so far beautiful as it suggests this universal grace. The poet, the painter, the sculptor, the musician, the architect seek each to concentrate this radiance of the world on one point, and each in his several work to satisfy the love of beauty which stimulates him to produce. Thus is Art a nature passed through the alembic of man. Thus in art does Nature work through the will of a man filled with the beauty of her first works.

The world thus exists to the soul to satisfy the desire of beauty. This element I call an ultimate end. No reason can be asked or given why the soul seeks beauty. Beauty, in its largest and profoundest sense, is one expression for the universe. God is the all-fair. Truth, and goodness, and beauty are but different faces of the same All. But beauty in nature is not ultimate. It is the herald of inward and eternal beauty, and is not alone a solid and satisfactory good. It must stand as a part, and not as yet the last or highest expression of the final cause of Nature.

1841   *Thoughts on Art*

Every department of life at the present day—trade, politics, letters, science, religion—seem to feel, and to labor to express, the identity of their law. They are rays of one sun; they translate each into a new language the sense of the other. They are sublime when seen as emanations of a necessity contradistinguished from the vulgar fate by being instant and alive, and dissolving man, as well as his works, in its flowing

* The many in the one.

beneficence. This influence is conspicuously visible in the principles and history of art.

On one side, in primary communication with absolute truth, through thought and instinct, the human mind tends by an equal necessity, on the other side, to the publication and embodiment of its thought—modified and dwarfed by the impurity and untruth which, in all our experience, injures the wonderful medium through which it passes. The child not only suffers but cries; not only hungers but eats. The man not only thinks but speaks and acts. Every thought that arises in the mind, in its rising, aims to pass out of the mind into act; just as every plant, in the moment of germination, struggles up to light. Thought is the seed of action; but action is as much its second form as thought is its first. It rises in thought to the end that it may be uttered and acted. The more profound the thought, the more burdensome. Always in proportion to the death of its sense does it knock importunately at the gates of the soul, to be spoken, to be done. What is in will out. It struggles to the birth. Speech is a great pleasure, and action a great pleasure; they cannot be forborne.

The utterance of thought and emotion in speech and action may be conscious or unconscious. The sucking child is an unconscious actor. A man in an ecstasy of fear or anger is an unconscious actor. A large part of our habitual actions are unconsciously done, and most of our necessary words are unconsciously said.

The conscious utterance of thought, by speech or action, to any end, is art. From the first imitative babble of a child to the despotism of eloquence; from his first pile of toys or chip bridge to the masonry of Eddystone Lighthouse or the Erie Canal; from the tattooing of the Owhvhees to the Vatican Gallery; from the simplest expedient of private prudence to the American Constitution; from its first to its last works, art is the spirit's voluntary use and combination of things to serve its end. The will distinguishes it as spiritual action. Relatively to themselves, the bee, the bird, the beaver have no art, for what they do they do instinctively; but relatively to the Supreme Being, they have. And the same is true of all unconscious action; relatively to the doer, it is instinct; relatively to the First Cause, it is art. In this sense, recognizing the Spirit which informs Nature, Plato rightly said, "Those things which are said to be done by Nature are indeed done by divine art." Art, universally, is the spirit creative. It was defined by Aristotle, "The reason of the thing, without the matter," as he defined the art of shipbuilding to be, "All of the ship but the wood."

If we follow the popular distinction of works according to their aim, we should say, the Spirit, in its creation, aims at use or at beauty, and hence art divides itself into the useful and the fine arts.

The useful arts comprehend not only those that lie next to instinct, as agriculture, building, weaving, and so on, but also navigation, practical chemistry, and the construction of all the grand and delicate tools and instruments by which man serves himself; as language; the watch; the ship; the decimal cipher; and also the sciences, so far as they are made serviceable to political economy.

The moment we begin to reflect on the pleasure we receive from a ship, a railroad, a drydock; or from a picture, a dramatic representation, a statue, a poem, we find that they have not a quite simple, but a blended origin. We find that the question What is art? leads us directly to another, Who is the artist? and the solution of this is the key to the history of art.

I hasten to state the principle which prescribes, through different means, its firm law to the useful and the beautiful arts. The law is this. The universal soul is the alone creator of the useful and the beautiful; therefore to make anything useful or beautiful, the individual must be submitted to the universal mind.

In the first place, let us consider this in reference to the useful arts. Here the omnipotent agent is Nature; all human acts are satellites to her orb. Nature is the representative of the universal mind, and the law becomes this—that art must be a complement to nature, strictly subsidiary. It was said, in allusion to the great structures of the ancient Romans, the aqueducts and bridges—that their "Art was a Nature working to municipal ends." That is a true account of all just works of useful art. Smeaton built Eddystone Lighthouse on the model of an oak tree, as being the form in nature best designed to resist a constant assailing force. Dollond formed his achromatic telescope on the model of the human eye. Duhamel built a bridge by letting in a piece of stronger timber for the middle of the under surface, getting his hint from the structure of the shinbone.

The first and last lesson of the useful arts is that Nature tyrannizes over our works. They must be conformed to her law, or they will be ground to powder by her omnipresent activity. Nothing droll, nothing whimsical will endure. Nature is ever interfering with art. You cannot build your house or pagoda as you will, but as you must. There is a quick bound set to our caprice. The leaning tower can only lean so far. The veranda or pagoda roof can curve upward only to a certain point. The slope of your roof is determined by the weight of snow. It is only within narrow limits that the discretion of the architect may range. Gravity, wind, sun, rain, the size of men and animals, and such like, have more to say than he. It is the law of fluids that prescribes the shape of the boat—keel, rudder, and bows—and, in the finer fluid above, the form and tackle of the sails. Man seems to have no option about his tools, but merely the necessity to learn from Nature what will fit best, as if he were fitting a screw or a door. Beneath a necessity thus almighty, what is artificial in man's life seems insignificant. He seems to take his task so minutely from intimations of Nature that his works become as it were hers, and he is no longer free.

But if we work within this limit, she yields us all her strength. All powerful action is performed by bringing the forces of nature to bear upon our objects. We do not grind corn or lift the loom by our own strength, but we build a mill in such a position as to set the north wind to play upon our instrument, or the elastic force of steam, or the ebb and flow of the sea. So in our handiwork we do few things by muscular force, but we place ourselves in such attitudes as to bring the force of gravity, that is, the weight of the planet, to bear upon the spade or the ax we wield. What is it that gives force to the blow of the ax or crowbar? Is it the muscles of the laborer's arm, or is it the attraction of the whole globe below it, on the ax or bar? In short, in all our operations we seek not to use our own, but to bring a quite infinite force to bear.

Let us now consider this law as it affects the works that have beauty for their end, that is, the productions of the fine arts.

Here again the prominent fact is subordination of man. His art is the least part of his work of art. A great deduction is to be made before we can know his proper contribution to it.

Music, eloquence, poetry, painting, sculpture, architecture. This is a rough enumeration of the fine arts. I omit rhetoric, which only respects the form of eloquence and poetry. Architecture and eloquence are mixed arts, whose end is sometimes beauty and sometimes use.

It will be seen that in each of these arts there is much which is not spiritual. Each has a material basis, and in each the creating intellect is crippled in some degree by the stuff on which it works. The basis of poetry is language, which is material only on one side. It is a demigod. But being applied primarily to the common necessities of man, it is not new created by the poet for his own ends.

The basis of music is the qualities of the air and the vibrations of sonorous bodies. The pulsation of a stretched string or wire gives the ear the pleasure of sweet sound before yet the musician has enhanced this pleasure by concords and combinations.

Eloquence, as far as it is a fine art, is modified how much by the material organization of the orator, the tone of the voice, the physical strength, the play of the eye and countenance! All this is so much deduction from the purely spiritual pleasure. All this is so much deduction from the merit of art, and is the attribute of Nature.

In painting, bright colors stimulate the eye before yet they are harmonized into a landscape. In sculpture and in architecture, the material, as marble or granite; and in architecture, the mass—are sources of great pleasure, quite independent of the artificial arrangement. The art resides in the model, in the plan, for it is on that the genius of the artist is expended, not on the statue or the temple. Just as much better as is the polished statue of dazzling marble than the clay model; or as much more impressive as is the granite cathedral or pyramid than the ground plan or profile of them on paper, so much more beauty owe they to Nature than to art.

There is a still larger deduction to be made from the genius of the artist in favor of Nature than I have yet specified.

A jumble of musical sounds on a viol or a flute, in which the rhythm of the tune is played without one of the notes being right, gives pleasure to the unskillful ear. A very coarse imitation of the human form on canvas or in waxwork—a very coarse sketch in colors of a landscape, in which imitation is all that is attempted—these things give to unpracticed eyes, to the uncultured, who do not ask a fine spiritual delight, almost as much pleasure as a statue of Canova or a picture of Titian.

And in the statue of Canova or the picture of Titian, these give the great part of the pleasure; they are the basis on which the fine spirit rears a higher delight, but to which these are indispensable.

Another deduction from the genius of the artist is what is conventional in his art, of which there is much in every work of art. Thus how much is there that is not original in every particular building, in every statue, in every tune, in every painting, in every poem, in every harangue. Whatever is national or usual; as the usage of building all Roman churches in the form of a cross, the prescribed distribution of parts of a theatre, the custom of draping a statue in classical costume. Yet who will deny that the merely conventional part of the performance contributes much to its effect?

One consideration more exhausts, I believe, all the deductions from the genius of the artist in any given work.

This is the adventitious. Thus the pleasure that a noble temple gives us is only in part owing to the temple. It is exalted by the beauty of sunlight, by the play of the clouds, by the landscape around it, by its grouping with the houses and trees and towers in its vicinity. The pleasure of eloquence is in greatest part owing often to the stimulus of the occasion which produces it; to the magic of sympathy, which exhalts the feeling of each, by radiating on him the feeling of all.

The effect of music belongs how much to the place, as the church or the moonlight walk, or to the company, or, if on the stage, to what went before in the play, or to the expectation of what shall come after.

In poetry, "It is tradition more than invention helps the poet to a good fable." The adventitious beauty of poetry may be felt in the greater delight which a verse gives in happy quotation than in the poem.

It is a curious proof of our conviction that the artist does not feel himself to be the parent of his work and is as much surprised at the effect as we, that we are so unwilling to impute our best sense of any work of art to the author. The very highest praise we can attribute to any writer, painter, sculptor, builder, is that he actually possessed the thought or feeling with which he has inspired us. We hesitate at doing

Spenser so great an honor as to think that he intended by his allegory the sense we affix to it. We grudge to Homer the wise human circumspection his commentators ascribe to him. Even Shakespeare, of whom we can believe everything, we think indebted to Goethe and to Coleridge for the wisdom they detect in his Hamlet and Antony. Especially have we this infirmity of faith in contemporary genius. We fear that Allston and Greenough did not foresee and design all the effect they produce on us.

Our arts are happy hits. We are like the musician on the lake, whose melody is sweeter than he knows, or like a traveler, surprised by a mountain echo, whose trivial word returns to him in romantic thunders.

In view of these facts, I say that the power of Nature predominates over the human will in all works of even the fine arts, in all that respects their material and external circumstances. Nature paints the best part of the picture; carves the best part of the statue; builds the best part of the house; and speaks the best part of the oration. For all the advantages to which I have adverted are such as the artist did not consciously produce. He relied on their aid, he put himself in the way to receive aid from some of them, but he saw that his planting and his watering waited for the sunlight of nature, or was vain.

Let us proceed to the consideration of the great law stated in the beginning of this essay, as it affects the purely spiritual part of a work of art.

As in useful art, so far as it is useful, the work must be strictly subordinated to the laws of nature, so as to become a sort of continuation, and in no wise a contradiction of nature; so in art that aims at beauty as an end, must the parts be subordinated to ideal nature, and everything individual abstracted, so that it shall be the production of the universal soul.

The artist, who is to produce a work which is to be admired, not by his friends or his townspeople or his contemporaries, but by all men; and which is to be more beautiful to the eye in proportion to its culture, must disindividualize himself, and be a man of no party and no manner and no age, but one through whom the soul of all men circulates, as the common air through his lungs. He must work in the spirit in which we conceive a prophet to speak; or an angel of the Lord to act; that is, he is not to speak his own words or do his own works or think his own thoughts, but he is to be an organ through which the universal mind acts.

In speaking of the useful arts, I pointed to the fact that we do not dig or grind or hew by our muscular strength, but by bringing the weight of the planet to bear on the spade, ax, or bar. Precisely analogous to this, in the fine arts, is the manner of our intellectual work. We aim to hinder our individuality from acting. So much as we can shove aside our egotism, our prejudice, and will, and bring the omniscience of reason upon the subject before us, so perfect is the work. The wonders of Shakespeare are things which he saw whilst he stood aside, and then returned to record them. The poet aims at getting observations without aim; to subject to thought things seen without (voluntary) thought.

In eloquence, the great triumphs of the art are when the orator is lifted above himself; when consciously he makes himself the mere tongue of the occasion and the hour, and says what cannot but be said. Hence the French phrase *l'abandon* to describe the self-surrender of the orator. Not his will, but the principle on which he is horsed, the great connection and crisis of events thunder in the ear of the crowd.

In poetry, where every word is free, every word is necessary. Good poetry could not have been otherwise written than it is. The first time you hear it, it sounds rather as if copied out of some invisible tablet in the eternal mind than as if arbitrarily composed by the poet. The feeling of all great poets has accorded with this. They found the verse, not made it. The muse brought it to them.

In sculpture, did ever anybody call the Apollo a fancy piece? Or say of the Laocoön how it might be made different? A masterpiece of art has in the mind a fixed place in the chain of being, as much as a plant or a crystal.

The whole language of men, especially of artists, in reference to this subject, points at the belief that every work of art, in proportion to its excellence, partakes of the precision of fate; no room was there for choice; no play for fancy; for the moment, or in the successive moments, when that form was seen, the iron lids of Reason were unclosed, which ordinarily are heavy with slumber: that the individual mind became for the moment the vent of the mind of humanity.

There is but one Reason. The mind that made the world is not one mind, but *the* mind. Every man is an inlet to the same, and to all of the same. And every work of art is a more or less pure manifestation of the same. Therefore we arrive at this conclusion, which I offer as a confirmation of the whole view: That the delight which a work of art affords seems to arise from our recognizing in it the mind that formed Nature again in active operation.

It differs from the works of Nature in this, that they are organically reproductive. This is not: but spiritually it is prolific by its powerful action on the intellects of men.

In confirmation of this view, let me refer to the fact that a study of admirable works of art always sharpens the perceptions of the beauty of Nature; that a certain analogy reigns throughout the wonders of both; that the contemplation of a work of great art draws us into a state of mind which may be called religious. It conspires with all exalted sentiments.

Proceeding from absolute mind, whose nature is goodness as much as truth, they are always attuned to moral nature. If the earth and sea conspire with virtue more than vice—so do the masterpieces of art. The galleries of ancient sculpture in Naples and Rome strike no deeper conviction into the mind than the contrast of the purity, the severity, expressed in these fine old heads, with the frivolity and grossness of the mob that exhibits, and the mob that gazes at them. These are the countenances of the firstborn, the face of man in the morning of the world. No mark is on these lofty features of sloth or luxury or meanness, and they surprise you with a moral admonition, as they speak of nothing around you, but remind you of the fragrant thoughts and the purest resolutions of your youth.

Herein is the explanation of the analogies which exist in all the arts. They are the reappearance of one mind, working in many materials to many temporary ends. Raphael paints wisdom; Handel sings it, Phidias carves it, Shakespeare writes it, Wren builds it, Columbus sails it, Luther preaches it, Washington arms it, Watt mechanizes it. Painting was called "silent poetry"; and poetry "speaking painting." The laws of each art are convertible into the laws of every other.

Herein we have an explanation of the necessity that reigns in all the kingdom of art.

Arising out of eternal reason, one and perfect, whatever

is beautiful rests on the foundation of the necessary. Nothing is arbitrary, nothing is insulated in beauty. It depends forever on the necessary and the useful. The plumage of the bird, the mimic plumage of the insect, has a reason for its rich colors in the constitution of the animal. Fitness is so inseparable an accompaniment of beauty that it has been taken for it. The most perfect form to answer an end is so far beautiful. In the mind of the artist, could we enter there, we should see the sufficient reason for the last flourish and tendril of his work, just as every tint and spine in the seashell pre-exists in the secreting organs of the fish. We feel, in seeing a noble building, which rhymes well, as we do in hearing a perfect song, that it is spiritually organic, that is, had a necessity in nature for being, was one of the possible forms in the Divine mind, and is now only discovered and executed by the artist, not arbitrarily composed by him.

And so every genuine work of art has as much reason for being as the earth and the sun. The gayest charm of beauty has a root in the constitution of things. The Iliad of Homer, the songs of David, the odes of Pindar, the tragedies of Aeschylus, the Doric temples, the Gothic cathedrals, the plays of Shakespeare were all made, not for sport, but in grave earnest, in tears, and smiles of suffering and loving men.

Viewed from this point, the history of art becomes intelligible, and, moreover, one of the most agreeable studies in the world. We see how each work of art sprang irresistibly from necessity, and, moreover, took its form from the broad hint of Nature. Beautiful in this wise is the obvious origin of all the known orders of architecture, namely, that they were the idealizing of the primitive abodes of each people. Thus the Doric temple still presents the semblance of the wooden cabin in which the Dorians dwelt. The Chinese pagoda is plainly a Tartar tent. The Indian and Egyptian temples still betray the mounds and subterranean houses of their forefathers. The Gothic church plainly originated in a rude adaptation of forest trees, with their boughs on, to a festal or solemn edifice, as the bands around the cleft pillars still indicate the green withes that tied them. No one can walk in a pine barren, in one of the paths which the woodcutters make for their teams, without being struck with the architectural appearance of the grove, especially in winter, when the bareness of all other trees shows the low arch of the

Saxons. In the woods, in a winter afternoon, one will see as readily the origin of the stained-glass window with which the Gothic cathedrals are adorned, in the colors of the western sky, seen through the bare and crossing branches of the forest. Nor, I think, can any lover of nature enter the old piles of Oxford and the English cathedrals without feeling that the forest overpowered the mind of the builder, with its ferns, its spikes of flowers, its locust, its oak, its pine, its fir, its spruce. The cathedral is a blossoming in stone, subdued by the insatiable demand of harmony in man. The mountain of granite blooms into an eternal flower, with the lightness and delicate finish, as well as aerial proportions and perspective of vegetable beauty.

There was no willfulness in the savages in this perpetuating of their first rude abodes. The first form in which they built a house would be the first form of their public and religious edifice also. This form becomes immediately sacred in the eyes of their children, and the more so as more traditions cluster around it, and is, therefore, imitated with more splendor in each succeeding generation.

In like manner, it has been remarked by Goethe that the granite breaks into parallelopipeds, which, broken in two, one part would be an obelisk; that in Upper Egypt the inhabitants would naturally mark a memorable spot by setting up so conspicuous a stone. Again, he suggested we may see in any stone wall, on a fragment of rock, the projecting veins of harder stone which have resisted the action of frost and water, which has decomposed the rest. This appearance certainly gave the hint of the hieroglyphics inscribed on their obelisk. The amphitheatre of the old Romans—anyone may see its origin who looks at the crowd running together to see any fight, sickness, or odd appearance in the street. The first comers gather round in a circle; those behind stand on tiptoe; and further back they climb on fences or windowsills, and so make a cup of which the object of attention occupies the hollow area. The architect put benches in this order, and enclosed the cup with a wall, and behold a coliseum.

It would be easy to show of very many fine things in the world, in the customs of nations, the etiquette of courts, the constitution of governments, the origin in very simple local necessities. Heraldry, for example, and the ceremonies of a coronation are a splendid burlesque of the occurrences that might befall a dragoon and his footboy. The College of Cardinals were originally the parish priests of Rome. The leaning towers originated from the civil discords which induced every lord to build a tower. Then it became a point of family pride—and for pride a leaning tower was built.

This strict dependence of art upon material and ideal nature, this adamantine necessity which it underlies, has made all its past, and may foreshow its future history. It never was in the power of any man, or any community, to call the arts into being. They come to serve his actual wants, never to please his fancy. These arts have their origin always in some enthusiasm, as love, patriotism, or religion. Who carved marble? The believing men, who wished to symbolize their gods to the waiting Greeks.

The Gothic cathedrals were built when the builder and the priest and the people were overpowered by their faith. Love and fear laid every stone. The Madonnas of Raphael and Titian were made to be worshipped. Tragedy was instituted for the like purpose, and the miracles of music—all sprang out of some genuine enthusiasm, and never out of dilettantism and holidays. But now they languish, because their purpose is merely exhibition. Who cares, who knows what works of art our government has ordered to be made for the Capitol? They are a mere flourish to please the eye of persons who have associations with books and galleries. But in Greece, the Demos of Athens divided into political factions upon the merits of Phidias.

In this country, at this time, other interests than religion and patriotism are predominant, and the arts, the daughters of enthusiasm, do not flourish. The genuine offspring of our ruling passions we behold. Popular institutions, the school, the reading room, the post office, the exchange, the insurance company, and an immense harvest of economical inventions are the fruit of the equality and the boundless liberty of lucrative callings. These are superficial wants; and their fruits are these superficial institutions. But as far as they accelerate the end of political freedom and national education, they are preparing the soil of man for fairer flowers and fruits in another age. For beauty, truth, and goodness are not obsolete; they spring eternal in the breast of man; they are as indigenous in Massachusetts as in Tuscany or the Isles of Greece. And that Eternal Spirit, whose triple face they are, molds from them forever, for this mortal child, images to remind him of the Infinite and Fair.

1841   From "Self-Reliance"

It is for want of self-culture that the idol of traveling, the idol of Italy, of England, of Egypt, remains for all educated Americans. They who made England, Italy, or Greece venerable in the imagination did so not by rambling round creation as a moth round a lamp, but by sticking fast where they were, like an axis of the earth. In manly hours, we feel that duty is our place, and that the merry men of circumstance should follow as they may. The soul is no traveler: the wise man stays at home with the soul, and when his necessities, his duties, on any occasion call him from his house, or into foreign lands, he is at home still, and is not gadding abroad from himself, and shall make men sensible by the expression of his countenance that he goes the missionary of wisdom and virtue, and visits cities and men like a sovereign, and not like an interloper or a valet.

I have no churlish objection to the circumnavigation of the globe, for the purposes of art, of study, and benevolence, so that the man is first domesticated, or does not go abroad with the hope of finding somewhat greater than he knows. He who travels to be amused, or to get somewhat which he does not carry, travels away from himself, and grows old even in youth among old things. In Thebes, in Palmyra, his will and mind have become old and dilapidated as they. He carries ruins to ruins.

Traveling is a fool's paradise. We owe to our first journeys the discovery that place is nothing. At home I dream that at Naples, at Rome, I can be intoxicated with beauty, and lose my sadness. I pack my trunk, embrace my friends, embark on the sea, and at last wake up in Naples, and there beside me is the stern Fact, the sad self, unrelenting, identical, that I fled from. I seek the Vatican, and the palaces. I affect to be intoxicated with sights and suggestions, but I am not intoxicated. My giant goes with me wherever I go.

But the rage of traveling is itself only a symptom of a deeper unsoundness affecting the whole intellectual action.

The intellect is vagabond, and the universal system of education fosters restlessness. Our minds travel when our bodies are forced to stay at home. We imitate; and what is imitation but the traveling of the mind? Our houses are built with foreign taste; our shelves are garnished with foreign ornaments; our opinions, our tastes, our whole minds lean, and follow the Past and the Distant, as the eyes of a maid follow her mistress. The soul created the arts wherever they have flourished. It was in his own mind that the artist sought his model. It was an application of his own thought to the thing to be done and the conditions to be observed. And why need we copy the Doric or the Gothic model? Beauty, convenience, grandeur of thought, and quaint expression are as near to us as to any, and if the American artist will study with hope and love the precise thing to be done by him, considering the climate, the soil, the length of the day, the wants of the people, the habit and form of the government, he will create a house in which all these will find themselves fitted, and taste and sentiment will be satisfied also.

Insist on yourself; never imitate. Your own gift you can present every moment with the cumulative force of a whole life's cultivation; but of the adopted talent of another you have only an extemporaneous, half-possession. That which each can do best, none but his Maker can teach him. No man yet knows what it is, nor can, till that person has exhibited it. Where is the master who could have taught Shakespeare? Where is the master who could have instructed Franklin or Washington or Bacon or Newton? Every great man is an unique. The Scipionism of Scipio is precisely that part he could not borrow. If anybody will tell me whom the great man imitates in the original crisis when he performs a great act, I will tell him who else than himself can teach him. Shakespeare will never be made by the study of Shakespeare. Do that which is assigned thee, and thou canst not hope too much or dare too much. There is at this moment, there is for me an utterance bare and grand as that of the colossal chisel of Phidias or trowel of the Egyptians, or the pen of Moses or Dante, but different from all these. Not possibly will the soul all rich, all eloquent, with thousand-cloven tongue, deign to repeat itself; but if I can hear what these patriarchs say, surely I can reply to them in the same pitch of voice: for the ear and the tongue are two organs of one nature. Dwell up there in the simple and noble regions of thy life, obey thy heart, and thou shalt reproduce the Foreworld again.

1841   From "Art"

Yet when we have said all our fine things about the arts, we must end with a frank confession that the arts, as we know them, are but initial. Our best praise is given to what they aimed and promised, not to the actual result. He has conceived meanly of the resources of man who believes that the best age of production is past. The real value of the Iliad, or the Transfiguration, is as signs of power; billows or ripples they are of the great stream of tendency; tokens of the everlasting effort to produce, which even in its worst estate, the soul betrays. Art has not yet come to its maturity if it do not put itself abreast with the most potent influences of the world, if it is not practical and moral, if it do not stand in connection with the conscience, if it do not make the poor and uncultivated feel that it addresses them with a voice of lofty cheer. There is higher work for Art than the arts. They are abortive births of an imperfect or vitiated instinct. Art is the need to create; but in its essence, immense and universal, it is impatient of working with lame or tied hands, and of making cripples and monsters, such as all pictures and statues are. Nothing less than the creation of man and nature is its end. A man should find in it an outlet for his whole energy. He may paint and carve only as long as he can do that. Art should exhilarate, and throw down the walls of circumstance on every side, awakening in the beholder the same sense of universal relation and power which the work evinced in the artist, and its highest effect is to make new artists.

Already History is old enough to witness the old age and disappearance of particular arts. The art of sculpture is long ago perished to any real effect. It was originally a useful art, a mode of writing, a savage's record of gratitude or devotion, and among a people possessed of a wonderful perception of form, this childish carving was refined to the utmost splendor of effect. But it is the game of a rude and youthful people, and not the manly labor of a wise and spiritual nation. Under an oak tree loaded with leaves and nuts, under a sky full of

eternal eyes, I stand in a thoroughfare; but in the works of
our plastic arts, and especially of sculpture, creation is driven
into a corner. I cannot hide from myself that there is a
certain appearance of paltriness, as of toys, and the trum-
pery of a theatre, in sculpture. Nature transcends all
our moods of thought, and its secret we do not yet
find. But the gallery stands at the mercy of our moods, and
there is a moment when it becomes frivolous. I do not wonder
that Newton, with an attention habitually engaged on the
path of planets and suns, should have wondered what the
Earl of Pembroke found to admire in "stone dolls." Sculpture
may serve to teach the pupil how deep is the secret of form,
how purely the spirit can translate its meanings into that
eloquent dialect. But the statue will look cold and false before
that new activity which needs to roll through all things, and
is impatient of counterfeits, and things not alive. Picture and
sculpture are the celebrations and festivities of form. But true
art is never fixed, but always flowing. The sweetest music is
not in the oratorio, but in the human voice when it speaks
from its instant life, tones of tenderness, truth, or courage.
The oratorio has already lost its relation to the morning, to
the sun, and the earth, but that persuading voice is in tune
with these. All works of art should not be detached, but
extempore performances. A great man is a new statue in every
attitude and action. A beautiful woman is a picture which
drives all beholders nobly mad. Life may be lyric or epic, as
well as a poem or a romance.

A true announcement of the law of creation, if a man were
found worthy to declare it, would carry art up into the kingdom of nature, and destroy its separate and contrasted existence. The fountains of invention and beauty in modern
society are all but dried up. A popular novel, a theatre, or a
ballroom makes us feel that we are all paupers in the almshouse of this world, without dignity, without skill, or industry.
Art is as poor and low. The old tragic Necessity, which lowers
on the brows even of the Venuses and the Cupids of the
antique, and furnishes the sole apology for the intrusion of
such anomalous figures into nature—namely, that they were
inevitable; that the artist was drunk with a passion for form
which he could not resist, and which vented itself in these fine
extravagancies—no longer dignifies the chisel or the pencil.
But the artist, and the connoisseur, now seek in art the exhibi-

tion of their talent, or an asylum from the evils of life. Men
are not well pleased with the figure they make in their own
imagination, and they flee to art, and convey their better sense
in an oratorio, a statue, or a picture. Art makes the same
effort which a sensual prosperity makes, namely, to detach the
beautiful from the useful, to do up the work as unavoidable,
and hating it, pass on to enjoyment. These solaces and com-
pensations, this division of beauty from use, the laws of nature
do not permit. As soon as beauty is sought, not from religion
and love, but for pleasure, it degrades the seeker. High beauty
is no longer attainable by him in canvas or in stone, in sound,
or in lyrical construction; an effeminate prudent, sickly beauty,
which is not beauty, is all that can be formed; for the hand
can never execute anything higher than the character can
inspire.

The art that thus separates is itself first separated. Art must
not be a superficial talent, but must begin farther back in man.
Now men do not see nature to be beautiful, and they go to
make a statue which shall be. They abhor men as tasteless,
dull, and inconvertible, and console themselves with color
bags, and blocks of marble. They reject life as prosaic, and
create a death which they call poetic. They dispatch the day's
weary chores, and fly to voluptuous reveries. They eat and
drink, that they may afterward execute the ideal. Thus is art
vilified; the name conveys to the mind its secondary and bad
senses; it stands in the imagination as somewhat contrary to
nature, and struck with death from the first. Would it not
be better to begin higher up—to serve the ideal before they
eat and drink; to serve the ideal in eating and drinking, in
drawing the breath, and in the functions of life? Beauty must
come back to the useful arts, and the distinction between the
fine and the useful arts be forgotten. If history were truly
told, if life were nobly spent, it would be no longer easy or
possible to distinguish the one from the other. In nature, all
is useful, all is beautiful. It is therefore beautiful because it
is alive, moving, reproductive; it is therefore useful because
it is symmetrical and fair. Beauty will not come at the call
of a legislature, nor will it repeat in England or America its
history in Greece. It will come, as always, unannounced, and
spring up between the feet of brave and earnest men. It is in
vain that we look for genius to reiterate its miracles in the
old arts; it is its instinct to find beauty and holiness in new

and necessary facts, in the field and roadside, in the shop and mill. Proceeding from a religious heart, it will raise to a divine use the railroad, the insurance office, the joint stock company, our law, our primary assemblies, our commerce, the galvanic battery, the electric jar, the prism, and the chemist's retort, in which we seek now only an economical use. Is not the selfish, and even cruel aspect which belongs to our great mechanical works, to mills, railways, and machinery, the effect of the mercenary impulses which these works obey? When its errands are noble and adequate, a steamboat bridging the Atlantic between Old and New England, and arriving at its ports with the punctuality of a planet, is a step of man into harmony with nature. The boat at St. Petersburg, which plies along the Lena by magnetism, needs little to make it sublime. When science is learned in love, and its powers are wielded by love, they will appear the supplements and continuations of the material creation.

1860 From "Beauty"

The question of Beauty takes us out of surfaces, to thinking of the foundations of things. Goethe said, "The beautiful is a manifestation of secret laws of Nature, which, but for this appearance, had been forever concealed from us." And the working of this deep instinct makes all the excitement—much of it superficial and absurd enough—about works of art which leads armies of vain travelers every year to Italy, Greece, and Egypt. Every man values every acquisition he makes in the science of beauty, above his possessions. The most useful man in the most useful world, so long as only commodity was served, would remain unsatisfied. But as fast as he sees beauty, life acquires a very high value.

I am warned by the ill fate of many philosophers not to attempt a definition of beauty. I will rather enumerate a few of its qualities. We ascribe beauty to that which is simple; which has no superfluous parts; which exactly answers its end; which stands related to all things; which is the mean of many extremes. It is the most enduring quality, and the most ascending quality. We say, love is blind, and the figure of Cupid is drawn with a bandage round his eyes. Blind: yes, because he does not see what he does not like; but the sharpest-sighted hunter in the universe is Love, for finding what he seeks, and only that; and the mythologists tell us that Vulcan was painted lame, and Cupid blind, to call attention to the fact that one was all limbs, and the other, all eyes. In the true mythology, Love is an immortal child, and Beauty leads him as a guide: nor can we express a deeper sense than when we say, Beauty is the pilot of the young soul.

Beyond their sensuous delight, the forms and colors of nature have a new charm for us in our perception, that not one ornament was added for ornament, but is a sign of some better health, or more excellent action. Elegance of form in bird or beast, or in the human figure, marks some excellence of structure: or beauty is only an invitation from what belongs to us. 'Tis a law of botany that in plants the same virtues follow the same forms. It is a rule of largest application, true in a plant, true in a loaf of bread, that in the construction of any fabric or organism, any real increase of fitness to its end is an increase of beauty.

The lesson taught by the study of Greek and of Gothic art, of antique and of Pre-Raphaelite painting, was worth all the research—namely, that all beauty must be organic; that outside embellishment is deformity. It is the soundness of the bones that ultimates itself in a peach-bloom complexion: health of constitution that makes the sparkle and the power of the eye. 'Tis the adjustment of the size and of the joining of the sockets of the skeleton that gives grace of outline and the finer grace of movement. The cat and the deer cannot move or sit inelegantly. The dancing master can never teach a badly built man to walk well. The tint of the flower proceeds from its root, and the lusters of the seashell begin with its existence. Hence our taste in building rejects paint, and all shifts, and shows the original grain of the wood: refuses pilasters and columns that support nothing, and allows the real supporters of the house honestly to show themselves. Every necessary or organic action pleases the beholder. A man leading a horse to water, a farmer sowing seed, the labors of haymakers in the field, the carpenter building a ship, the smith at his forge, or, whatever useful labor, is becoming to the wise eye. But if it is done to be seen, it is mean. How beautiful are ships on the sea! but ships in the theatre—or ships kept for picturesque effect on Virginia Water, by George

IV, and men hired to stand in fitting costumes at a penny an hour! What a difference in effect between a battalion of troops marching to action, and one of our independent companies on a holiday! In the midst of a military show, and a festal procession gay with banners, I saw a boy seize an old tin pan that lay rusting under a wall, and poising it on the top of a stick, he set it turning, and made it describe the most elegant imaginable curves, and drew away attention from the decorated procession by this startling beauty.

Another text from the mythologists. The Greeks fabled that Venus was born of the foam of the sea. Nothing interests us which is stark or bounded, but only what streams with life, what is an act or endeavor to reach somewhat beyond. The pleasure a palace or a temple gives the eye is that an order and method have been communicated to stones, so that they speak and geometrize, become tender or sublime with expression. Beauty is the moment of transition, as if the form were just ready to flow into other forms. Any fixedness, heaping, or concentration on one feature—a long nose, a sharp chin, a humpback—is the reverse of the flowing, and therefore deformed. Beautiful as is the symmetry of any form, if the form can move, we seek a more excellent symmetry. The interruption of equilibrium stimulates the eye to desire the restoration of symmetry, and to watch the steps through which it is attained. This is the charm of running water, sea waves, the flight of birds, and the locomotion of animals. This is the theory of dancing, to recover continually in changes the lost equilibrium, not by abrupt and angular, but by gradual and curving movements. I have been told by persons of experience in matters of taste, that the fashions follow a law of gradation, and are never arbitrary. The new mode is always only a step onward in the same direction as the last mode; and a cultivated eye is prepared for and predicts the new fashion. This fact suggests the reason of all mistakes and offense in our own modes. It is necessary in music, when you strike a discord to let down the ear by an intermediate note or two to the accord again: and many a good experiment, born of good sense, and destined to succeed, fails only because it is offensively sudden. I suppose the Parisian milliner who dresses the world from her imperious boudoir will know how to reconcile the Bloomer costume to the eye of mankind, and make it triumphant over Punch himself, by interposing the just gradations. I need not

say how wide the same law ranges; and how much it can be
hoped to effect. All that is a little harshly claimed by progressive parties may easily come to be conceded without question,
if this rule be observed. Thus the circumstances may be easily
imagined in which woman may speak, vote, argue causes,
legislate, and drive a coach, and all the most naturally in the
world, if only it come by degrees. To this streaming or flowing belongs the beauty that all circular movement has; as, the
circulation of waters, the circulation of the blood, the periodi-
cal motion of planets, the annual wave of vegetation, the
action and reaction of Nature: and, if we follow it out, this
demand in our thought for an ever-onward action is the argument for the immortality.

One more text from the mythologists is to the same
purpose—*Beauty rides on a lion*. Beauty rests on necessities.
The line of beauty is the result of perfect economy. The cell
of the bee is built at that angle which gives the most strength
with the least wax; the bone or the quill of the bird gives the
most alar strength, with the least weight. "It is the purgation
of superfluities," said Michelangelo. There is not a particle to
spare in natural structures. There is a compelling reason in
the uses of the plant, for every novelty of color or form: and
our art saves material by more skillful arrangement, and
reaches beauty by taking every superfluous ounce that can be
spared from a wall, and keeping all its strength in the poetry
of columns. In rhetoric, this art of omission is a chief secret
of power, and, in general, it is proof of high culture to say
the greatest matters in the simplest way.

But the sovereign attribute remains to be noted. Things are
pretty, graceful, rich, elegant, handsome, but, until they speak
to the imagination, not yet beautiful. This is the reason why
beauty is still escaping out of all analysis. It is not yet possessed; it cannot be handled. Proclus says, "It swims on the
light of forms." It is properly not in the form, but in the mind.
It instantly deserts possession, and flies to an object in the
horizon. If I could put my hand on the north star, would it be
as beautiful? The sea is lovely, but when we bathe in it the
beauty forsakes all the near water. For the imagination and
senses cannot be gratified at the same time. Wordsworth
rightly speaks of "a light that never was on sea or land,"
meaning that it was supplied by the observer, and the Welsh
bard warns his countrywomen that "half of their charms with

Cadwallon shall die." The new virtue which constitutes a thing beautiful is a certain cosmical quality, or a power to suggest relation to the whole world, and so lift the object out of a pitiful individuality. Every natural feature—sea, sky, rainbow, flowers, musical tone—has in it somewhat which is not private, but universal, speaks of that central benefit which is the soul of Nature, and thereby is beautiful. And, in chosen men and women, I find somewhat in form, speech, and manners which is not of their person and family, but of a humane, catholic, and spiritual character, and we love them as the sky. They have a largeness of suggestion, and their face and manners carry a certain grandeur, like time and justice.

The feat of the imagination is in showing the convertibility of every thing into every other thing. Facts which had never before left their stark common sense suddenly figure as Eleusinian mysteries. My boots and chair and candlestick are fairies in disguise, meteors and constellations. All the facts in nature are nouns of the intellect, and make the grammar of the eternal language. Every word has a double, treble, or centuple use and meaning. What! has my stove and pepperpot a false bottom! I cry you mercy, good shoebox! I did not know you were a jewel case. Chaff and dust begin to sparkle, and are clothed about with immortality. And there is a joy in perceiving the representative or symbolic character of a fact, which no bare fact or event can ever give. There are no days in life so memorable as those which vibrated to some stroke of the imagination.

The poets are quite right in decking their mistresses with the spoils of the landscape, flower gardens, gems, rainbows, flushes of morning, and stars of night, since all beauty points at identity, and whatsoever thing does not express to me the sea and sky, day and night, is somewhat forbidden and wrong. Into every beautiful object there enters somewhat immeasurable and divine, and just as much into form bounded by outlines, like mountains on the horizon, as into tones of music or depths of space. Polarized light showed the secret architecture of bodies; and when the *second sight* of the mind is opened, now one color or form or gesture, and now another, has a pungency, as if a more interior ray had been emitted, disclosing its deep holdings in the frame of things.

The laws of this translation we do not know, or why one feature or gesture enchants, why one word or syllable intoxi-

cates, but the fact is familiar that the fine touch of the eye, or
a grace of manners, or a phrase of poetry, plants wings at our
shoulders; as if the Divinity, in his approaches, lifts away
mountains of obstruction, and deigns to draw a truer line,
which the mind knows and owns. This is that haughty force
of beauty, *"vis superba formae,"* which the poets praise—
under calm and precise outline, the immeasurable and divine:
Beauty hiding all wisdom and power in its calm sky.

All high beauty has a moral element in it, and I find the
antique sculpture as ethical as Marcus Antoninus: and the
beauty ever in proportion to the depth of thought. Gross and
obscure natures, however decorated, seem impure shambles;
but character gives splendor to youth, and awe to wrinkled
skin and gray hairs. An adorer of truth we cannot choose but
obey, and the woman who has shared with us the moral sentiment—her locks must appear to us sublime. Thus there is a
climbing scale of culture, from the first agreeable sensation
which a sparkling gem or a scarlet stain affords the eye, up
through fair outlines and details of the landscape, features of
the human face and form, signs and tokens of thought and
character in manners, up to the ineffable mysteries of the
intellect. Wherever we begin, thither our steps tend: an ascent
from the joy of a horse in his trappings, up to the perception
of Newton, that the globe on which we ride is only a larger
apple falling from a larger tree; up to the perception of Plato,
that globe and universe are rude and early expressions of an
all-dissolving Unity—the first stair on the scale to the temple
of the Mind.

Letter: *Emerson to Margaret Fuller*

WASHINGTON, 13 January, 1843

DEAR MARGARET,

You shall have a word from your friend escaped from his
village to the Capitol, if only that he may s'orienter in the
fine place. I came hither day before yesterday from Baltimore,
& fell instantly & softly on the kind offices of two or three
young men who have shown me the best things. The Capitol
deserves its name & singularly pleases by its mass—in this

8. Horatio Greenough, "George Washington" (1833–1841),
marble, Smithsonian Institution.

country where we never have the satisfaction of seeing large buildings; satisfies too, by its commanding position, & fine entrances. The interior passages are inconveniently small from the doors to the Rotunda & from thence to the legislative chambers, but the Rotunda I admire. Night before last I went thither to see the Washington, which Greenough was endeavoring to show by torch light. It was his private experiment merely to see if it were practicable to show it so, for now in the daylight it is a statue in a cave. The experiment did not turn out well: a sufficiently powerful light could not be shed on the whole of so great a figure but it must be shown part by part by removing the light—which is not easy, as there are no fixtures to which the sconce could be attached excepting a standing pole which had been erected & rigged for the purpose. The statue is simple & grand, nobly draped below & nobler nude above, the right Washington head in its plain strength pretty well adhered to, the left arm resigning his sheathed sword, the right arm uplifted. Ill lighted as it is, I suppose this uplifted arm will not please, will not seem sufficiently motivated. Greenough wishes to light the face that we may see the reason of the action. It happened that night that our sconce did not succeed very well for it soon set on fire the wooden case which held the lamps & was let down rapidly lamps melting & exploding & brilliant balls of light falling on the floor By the time it was fairly down it was a brilliant bonfire & it was necessary in order not to fill the rotunda (picture hung) with smoke to drag it out of the doors on to the piazza where it drew together a rabble from all parts.— Afterward with a humbler contrivance the details of the figure which are of great beauty were successively brought out.—But the two hours I spent here were very pleasant. I sat on the stone floor in all parts of this grand area & watched the statue with its great limbs & the colossal shadows of the five or six persons who were moving about; the great height above, & the moonlight looking in at the skylight and the resonance of every word & footstep and the electric air of this place, the political center of the continent made it a very fanciful & exhilarating spot—John C. Calhoun was one of the company. Greenough talks very well about his work. He is not confident he says that he has translated the public sentiment of this country for Washington into marble, but he is very sure of his own diligence & that what has been in his

mind must sooner or later appear. I told him I had rather
have it in this Rotunda, in the worst light, than anywhere else
in the best: The genius of the place is omnipotent here; but
he wishes a separate structure. But I have not written you
what I would; I have been driven to the wall here with many
sights & much company, & shall, I hope, have the more to tell
you hereafter. I go to Baltimore Saturday P.M. Yours WALDO

Letter: Horatio Greenough to Emerson

WASHINGTON D.C. Dec. 28th '51

R. W. EMERSON ESQR

My Dear Sir—I ask permission to occupy your attention
for a moment—I am unwilling to invade your leisure—But
I find the men who are capable of such investigation as I
require, are so busy in holding each other's hands and watching each others eyes, that I cant effect a lodgment of my
whim-wham—I broached a theory 10 years since (1843) in
the *Democratic Review**—a theory of structure—My occupations since that time have prevented my doing more than to
confirm myself in that theory and to ripen it. I find this
country in such want of an application, practical, immediate
and thorough-going of that theory—I find also in the ships—
the carriages and engines, a partial illustration of the doctrine
and a *glorious* foretaste of what structure can be in this
country in 10 years time—if men of science and speech will
come to the rescue of a population struggling amid gewgaws
and extravagance after a *beauty* which will never obey other
than the call of genius—The men are not wanting—if they
can be made to see the soundness of the basis. Here is my
theory of structure A scientific arrangement of spaces and
forms to functions and to site—An emphasis of features proportioned to their *gradated* importance in function—Color
and ornament to be decided and arranged and varied by
strictly organic laws—having a distinct reason for each de-

* "American Architecture" in *The United States Magazine, and Democratic Review* (New York, August, 1843), Vol. XIII, No. LXII, pp. 206–210. Greenough republished this article, unchanged, as Chapter IX in *The Travels, Observations, and Experience of a Yankee Stonecutter* (New York, 1852), pp. 131–146. The essay is included in this anthology, pp. 141 ff.

cision—The entire and immediate banishment of all make-shift and make believe—

Now I wish you to hear me read what I have prepared on this subject and I beg you in the interim to reflect that this godlike human body has no ornament for the same reason that men do not gild gold—That the painted flowers are tinted to enable them to take their respective doses of sunlight, and that even the mottled and pearly shells are stained for the myriads of the deep—not to charm the idle eye as they are here & there one tossed in ruin on the shore.

This theory is too lovely not to be hated by those who are not loving and strong—It is a true theory—and will do for all structure from a bedstead to a cathedral what the Doric law did for the Parthenon—It will produce harmony—for all machines have a family likeness & are blood relations—It will not be monotonous for the wants on which it will wait are varied It will be expressive—for a guillotine and a rocking chair both speak English—It will be as much more beautiful than what we now possess as a naked Apollo is more beautiful than a tattooed and feathered and blanketed savage—

I wish to strike a blow for this style now because the aesthetical world abhors a vacuum, and ours is fast sucking in hostile elements I mean the excremental corruptions of foreign and hostile systems.—Pray let me know if I can find you at Concord when I come to Boston Will you favor me with a few words addressed to care of Henry Greenough Cambridge Mass—I had a letter from Landor not long since but missed seeing him in London by a strange chance—I found your "representative men" in the hands of a *dame* du Palais at Vienna in '48 and have learned that she has been exiled—having made herself politically obnoxious—

Very respectfully yours
H GREENOUGH
Sculptor

Letter: Emerson to Greenough

CONCORD
MASS.   7 January, 1852

MY DEAR SIR,

Your letter which reached me a little indirectly two days ago was the happiest omen of the new year & should have been acknowledged at once if it had not found me on a working day & inextricably engaged. It was a beam of sunlight however & happiest-timed. For I was just now reading Garbetts little Essay*—Garbett, Ruskins scholar, and I find the pupil a better teacher than the master—then I had read the "Seven Lamps" & the "Stones," and I was proud to find that the doctrine they urge with so much energy, you had been teaching long already. I am to go to Boston tomorrow, & shall find the *Democratic Review* of 1843 (which I have never seen) without delay. But the doctrine is not one of time, but of genius. Genius is forever simple—white light, & burns up frauds. And though we know this assuredly, yet every act & word betraying it does not less give us a shock of joy. Well, joy, & the largest fullest unfolding to your theory! which I shall faithfully attend. I understand you to promise me some written or spoken details, which I am erect to hear. If you come to Boston before February, I shall hold you bound to me in Concord for the earliest day you can spare. On the first of February, I believe I am to migrate, for a week or two, into Western New York, & into the city of N.Y: but I shall immediately afterward be at home again. I often recall quite the most magnanimous theory of art & artists, I have ever chanced to hear from one of themselves, namely, a day dream (or, shall I not say, a night *vigil*) you gave me on this head in Florence.

It will be my pleasure to recall it to you, when I see you. Prosperity!

Yours faithfully
R. W. EMERSON

* Edward Lacy Garbett (1817–1887), English theologian whose *Rudimentary Treatise on the Principles of Design in Architecture as Deducible from Nature and Exemplified in the Works of the Greek and Gothic Architects* was published by John Weale in his "Architectural Library" in 1850. Moller's *Essay* had been published in this same series in 1836.

5

Horatio Greenough (pseudonym Horace Bender), THE / TRAVELS, OBSERVATIONS, / AND EXPERIENCE OF A / YANKEE STONECUTTER (New York, 1852), "Aesthetics at Washington" from Chapter I, and Chapters IX, XIII, and "Relative and Independent Beauty," which appears as a separate essay following Chapter XVI, pp. 13–33; 131–146, 158–177, 197–213. Chapter IX, "American Architecture," was first published in THE UNITED STATES MAGAZINE, AND DEMOCRATIC REVIEW (New York, August, 1843), Vol. XIII, No. LXII, pp. 206–210. See Greenough's letter to Emerson, pp. 123–124 in this anthology.

Horatio Greenough (1805–1852) was born in Boston and educated at Harvard where he came under the influence of the American Romantic painter Washington Allston (1779–1843). Allston, a friend of Coleridge and of Emerson, seems to have been a key figure in the articulation of the Romantic concept of "organic form," but his influence was largely a function of his brilliance as a conversationalist, and is thus difficult to trace. Greenough's career as sculptor was essentially an expatriate one; he worked in studios first in Rome and later in Florence. Greenough and his friend Hiran Powers (1805–1873) were regarded by their con-

9. Horatio Greenough, "The Rescue" (1837), marble, The Capitol, Washington, D.C.

temporaries as the foremost American sculptors of the
1840's and 1850's. Greenough's twentieth-century reputation rests instead on his essays, primarily on the four
essays included in this anthology. His practice as sculptor
strikes the twentieth-century critic as sharply opposed to his
preachments as essayist on architecture and aesthetics. (See
illustrations 8 and 9.) Greenough's approach to sculpture
was essentially pictorial and anecdotal; he attempted to
transmute spatial and visual experience into literary and
descriptive experience; that is, he attempted to fulfill the
Romantic ideal of "inner meaning" by "telling a story";
thus, "The Rescue" is a "story in stone," and George Washington as Phidias's lost statue of Zeus is an attempt to
articulate the literary significance of Washington, "[to trans-
late] the public sentiment of this country for Washington
into marble" (see page 122). Emerson was aware of this
disparity between theory and practice in Greenough; in a
letter to Carlyle, Emerson remarked that he was a sculptor
"whose tongue was far cunninger in talk than his chisel
to carve." The scatter-shot essays included in *The Travels*
. . . show an analogous disparity between radical aesthetics
on the one hand and an illiberal approach to politics and
personalities on the other.

CHAPTER I / AESTHETICS AT WASHINGTON

An American citizen who has gone abroad to study a
refined art presents himself before his fellow countrymen at
disadvantage. To the uninitiated, his very departure from
these shores is an accusation of the fatherland. If he sail away
to strike the whale on the Pacific, or load his hold with
the precious teeth, and gums, and sands of Africa, it is well;
but to live for years among Italians, Frenchmen, and
Germans, for the sake of breathing the air of high art,
ancient and modern, this is shrewdly thought by the many
to show a lack of genius, whose boast it is to create, and
we are often asked triumphantly if nature is not to be
found here on this continent. They who thus reason and
thus feel, are not aware of the peculiar position of the aspirant
to artistic activity in these States. They see that lawyers and

statesmen, divines, physicians, mechanics, all are here developed, are said to be home grown, nay, often also self-made. They forget that all the elements of our civilization have been imported. They forget that our schools and colleges, our libraries and churches are filled with the most material proof that Greek and Roman thought is even now modifying and guiding our intellectual development. A moment's attention will enable them to perceive that the American student of art only seeks to effect for his own department of knowledge a like transfer of rudimental science, and at this late day, make the form of our culture harmonious with its essential and distinctive character.

We are still imbued, deeply imbued, with the stern disregard of everything not materially indispensable, which was generated by ages of colonial, and border, and semisavage life. We have imported writings on art in abundance, and there is scarcely a scholar in the land who cannot wield the terms of dilettantism as glibly as e'er a European professor; but unfortunately for us, the appreciation of an aesthetical theory without substantial art is as difficult as to follow a geometric demonstration without a diagram. It is sterile and impotent, as is all faith without works.

If the arts of design could have simply remained in a negative state, like seeds buried in autumn, to await the action of a more genial season, we should be justified in postponing, even now, their cultivation. But like the *Bourgeois gentilhomme,* who talked prose from his boyhood, without being aware of it, we have been compelled, both to design and to adorn, and our efforts, from their nature, must remain monuments of chaotic disorder in all that relates to aesthetics. In a word, we have negative quantities to deal with, before we can rise to zero. I do not mean to say that the beautiful has not been sought and found among us. I wish, and I hope, to show that we have done more in a right direction than has been appreciated, much in a wrong direction that must be examined and gotten rid of.

I am sensible of the disadvantage under which I labor, in speaking of matters to which I have devoted my attention for many years. I regret that I have no such right to sympathy and to support as that set forth by the author of a recent work when he says: "I have no qualifications for a critic in art, and make no pretensions to the character. I

write only for the great multitude, as ill instructed in this
sphere as I cheerfully admit myself." When the writer of
that profession shall have learned what the main qualifications for a critic on art really are, I cannot believe that he
will cheerfully renounce them; and far as I am from a
personal acquaintance with the great multitude, I cannot
believe that one "as ill instructed as themselves" is the exact
person whom they would depute to deal with matters which,
to say the least of them, require some training.

It is the great multitude that has decided the rank of the
statesmen, the poets, and the artists of the world. It is the
great multitude for whom all really great things are done
and said and suffered. The great multitude desires the best
of everything, and in the long run is the best judge of it. I
have said this much in relation to the aesthetical observations of this writer, because, though I generally sympathize
with his views, and often admire the expression of them,
I look upon the ground he here takes, as one too often
taken—in itself untenable, and apt to mislead by an exaggerated expression of modesty. Substantially, it is analogous
to the conduct of one who should commence by declaring
that all men are free and equal, and go on to give orders to
the right and left as to valets. Fain would I also lay claim
to the title of self-made man; indeed, I graduated at Harvard,
in 182–, which they who knew the school will allow was near
enough self-making to satisy any reasonable ambition. But
since then I have been beholden to very many for light as
for assistance.

If there were in our character or in our institutions aught
that is at war with art in the abstract, I for one would be
silent, preferring the humblest labor, if any labor deserve
the name of humble, to the development of an influence
adverse to American freedom. I speak of art now, because
I think I see that it is a want—a want widely felt, deeply
felt—an intellectual want, a social want, an economical
want—and that to a degree which few seem to suspect. I
believe that these States need art as a visible exponent of their
civilization.* They call for it as a salvation from merely

* In the speech of Mr. Smith, of Alabama, in explanation of a resolution
offered by him in relation to Kossuth, I find the following passage: "I will
make another observation, and that is in reference to the idea of establishing
republican governments in Europe. New governments there are constantly
rising and falling and they have been trying to establish republican govern-

material luxury and sensual enjoyment; they require it as the guide and ornament of inevitable structure and manufacture.

Joyfully have the governing men of England, France, and Germany beheld in the United States that policy which has denied all national education, except for the purposes of war and trade. Joyfully have they seen the individual States equally blind to the swift coming requirements of this people; and they have founded and perfected schools of design, of which the abler pupils are employed in illustrating the national history; the lower talents fill the factory, the foundry, and the atelier, to fashion fabrics for ourselves. From Boston to New Orleans no house, no tavern, no bar-room, I had almost said, that does not give proof, by the tawdry spawn of European manufacture, of our tribute to their *savoir faire,* and their appreciation of our taste. But what, it will be asked, has the development of art to do with manufactures? High art stands in relation to manufactures, and all the so-called lower trades, where high literature stands in relation to social and to civil life. Ask how much of the fruit of high culture and mental training reaches the public through the forum, the pulpit, and the diurnal press, and you will have the measure of the influence of pure art on structure and manufacture in all their branches. Who in England urged this matter upon the attention of Parliament, until the best models of Greece and Italy were placed within reach of every manufacturing population? The Board of Trade. That body caused to be translated from

ments for the last thousand years; have they ever succeeded? and why not? Because of their antiquities and their monuments, breathing, smacking, and smelling of nobility and royalty, and because half of the people are magnates."

I take note of this remark, because I believe there is good, solid truth in it. "Quoi si je pourrai fripponner quelque chose pour étayer mon pauvre petit livre!" (Oh, that I could pilfer something to shore up my poor little book.)

I should have placed the magnates first in the list of obstacles to republican progress, but I will not quarrel about precedence. The statesmen may be allowed to settle this matter.

I rejoice to find that American legislators have found out the value and significance of monuments, and of antiquities in their political influence. May we not expect that our civilization and our institutions will obtain this support from Congress? I hope, in a subsequent paper, to urge this matter more fully. I will now merely state that there stands in the studio of Mr. Powers, at Florence, a statue of America, which is not only a beautiful work of art, but which "breathes, smacks, and smells" of republicanism and Union. If placed conspicuously, by Mr. Walter, in one of the new wings of the Capitol, it would be a monument of Union. The sooner it is done, the sooner it will become an "antiquity."

foreign languages, and illustrated by elaborate drawings, the most approved works of Munich, Berlin, and Paris. They have ransacked, at great cost, the medieval magnificence of Italy, to find new forms, and add a grace to the products of their looms, their potteries, and their foundries. Does any statesman fancy that these governments have been invaded by a sudden love of the sublime and beautiful? I believe that they who watch our markets and our remittances will agree with me that their object is to keep the national mints of America at work for themselves; and that the beautiful must, to some extent, be cultivated here, if we would avoid a chronic and sometimes an acute tightness of the money market. The statistics of our annual importation of wares, which owe their preference solely to design, will throw a light on this question that will command the attention of the most thrifty and parsimonious of our legislators.

In founding a school of art, we have an obstacle to surmount, viz: a puritanical intolerance thereof. The first work of sculpture by an American hand exhibited in this country, executed for the illustrious Cooper,* was a group of children. The artist was rebuked and mortified by loud complaints of their nudity. Those infantine forms roused an outcry of censure which seemed to have exhausted the source whence it sprang, since all the harlot dancers who have found an El Dorado in these Atlantic cities have failed to reawaken it. I say seemed to have exhausted it—but only seemed—for the same purblind squeamishness which gazed without alarm at the lascivious Fandango awoke with a roar at the colossal nakedness of Washington's manly breast. This fact will show how easy it is to condemn what is intrinsically pure and innocent, to say the least; how difficult to repress what is clearly bad and vicious. They who speculate upon the corrupt tastes of a public, when they have learned that genteel comedy is neglected, that tragedy is a bore, that galleries of painting and statuary are unknown in a large

---

* James Fenimore Cooper (1789–1851) befriended and encouraged Greenough; Cooper's novel *Home as Found* (1838) contains a discussion of domestic architecture in which Greenough's criticisms of unnecessary ornament are presented in inconclusive form by one of the characters. The sculpture, by Greenough himself, was "The Chanting Cherubs" (1829–1831), two cherubs taken from a Raphael painting, "Madonna del Baldacchino." There were complaints, but they were not "loud"; the general reception of the sculpture in America was apathetic rather than responsive.

and wealthy community, such speculators take their Bayaderes thither as to a sure market. They know that a certain duration of abstinence, voluntary or forced, makes garbage tolerable, and ditch water a luxury. I do not venture to hope that even high art will abolish "cakes and ale," but I trust before many years are elapsed no *useé** Terpsichore of Paris or Vienna will be able to show half a million as a measure of our appetite for "ginger."

I wish not to be misunderstood for a moment as recommending a Smithsonian school, with a hierarchy of dignitaries in art. I have elsewhere stated my conviction that such a system is hostile to artistic progress. I desire to see working normal schools of structure and ornament, organized simply but effectively, and constantly occupied in designing for the manufacturers, and for all mechanics who need aesthetical guidance in their operations—schools where emulation shall be kindled by well-considered stimuli, and where all that is vitally important in building or ornament shall be thoroughly taught and constantly practiced. I know not how far the limit of congressional action may admit the founding of such schools by the central government. Should it be impossible to interest Congress in the matter, I am not without hope that some, at least, of the state legislatures may effect it; and, failing this resource, I hope that associated individuals will combine for this object. I cannot but believe that a report, called for by Congress, on the amount of goods imported, which owe the favor they find here to design, would show the importance of such schools in an economical point of view. I believe that such a report would show that the schools which we refuse to support here we support abroad, and that we are heavily taxed for them.

It surely cannot be asking too much that the seat of government, where the national structures rise, and are yearly increasing in number and importance, should present a specimen of what the country can afford in material and workmanship, in design and ornament. If this were resolved on, a stimulus would be given to exertion, while the constant experience here acquired would soon perfect a school of architectural design.

* Worn out.

The defects of the stone of which the Capitol was built could have been no secret to Mr. Bulfinch.* Had there existed a board or a school or any other responsible depository of architectural experience, we should not have witnessed the deplorable recurrence to the same quarries for the construction of the Patent Office and the Treasury buildings.† The outlay in paint alone, to which recourse has been had in order to sheathe this friable material, would have maintained a school, which would have saved us from the blunder, not to mention the great advantage we should have derived from its designs and its pupils. Had the amount expended in white lead been invested, a fund would have now accumulated sufficient to reface them all with marble. I am convinced that true economy would at this moment order the Potomac stone, wherever it has been used, to be immediately replaced by a better material.

Setting aside, however, the question of economy, and looking at the question of propriety, can anything be more absurd than to expend millions upon noble pieces of masonry, and then to smear them with lead—thereby reducing them to a level with the meanest shingle palace? Stone among building materials, standing where gold stands among metals, to paint stone is like covering gold with tinfoil. So far has this been carried, that even in the Rotunda, where no conceivable motive could exist for the vandalism, the entire masonry has been painted, and that too of various tints, so that I will venture to affirm that many carry away the idea that the whole is but a piece of carpenter's work. The treatment of the Treasury buildings, where the granite basement has been painted of one color, the columns of a second, and the wall behind them of a third, where even the lampposts have been daubed with divers tints, like a barber's pole, is noticed with priceless naïveté in an important public document as a *neat* piece of work. What shall we say of the balustrades, where massive iron bars have been driven

---

* Charles Bulfinch (1763–1844) was a Boston architect who, in 1818, succeeded the English-American Benjamin Latrobe (1764–1820) as architect of the Capitol. Bulfinch designed and built the Rotunda after plans suggested by Latrobe. The western approaches and the portico, completed by 1830, were original with Bulfinch. The defects of the stone were apparently not the fault of Bulfinch or the other architects, but of influential Congressmen.
† These two buildings were designed by Robert Mills, who is quoted in this anthology, pp. 80 ff.

bodily into the columns, as though a column in a first class building, might be treated like a blind wall in the basest structure? and that, too, without a shadow of need. What shall we say of the iron railings that obtrude upon the eye about the blockings of the Patent Office, and veil with their inharmonious blackness the organization of that building? What of the one slender chimney of red brick, which peers over the broken profile of the marble Post Office? Will any adept in the science of construction explain why the gas light which is seen at the eastern entrance of the Capitol was made to hang with so many feet of tiny pipe, and then secured by shabby wires driven into the columns? Would any person conversant with the proprieties of building tolerate such a slovenly arrangement in a private house? or in a private stable, if columns formed a feature of that stable? Do not such absurd and ignorant malpractices look as if a barbarous race had undertaken to enjoy the magnificence of a conquered people, and not known how to set about it? Does any one fancy that the uninstructed multitude does not feel these incongruities? It is not so. As well may you hope to sin against grammar in your speeches, and against decency and self-respect in your dress or deportment, and expect that it will pass unobserved.

The effect produced by the grounds and shrubbery in the neighborhood of the Capitol deserve a moment's attention. There is somewhat in flower beds and fancy gardening, with corbeilles of ephemeral plants, so out of all keeping with the character and functions of this edifice, as to give the spectator a painful sense that the idea of the adaptation of grounds to buildings has never recurred to those whose duty it was to look after these matters. Trees and verdure are beautiful, and flowers still more so, but they are impertinent adjuncts to the Capitol of the United States, and where they veil and obstruct the view of the façade, as at the Post Office, are insufferable. The creeping vines that have been led over the arches which support the platform in rear of the Naval monument are a grosser instance of misguided search after the picturesque. If these arches are properly constructed, the vines are impertinent, for they hide their articulation. Whether well or ill built, the proximity of these vines is a destructive element, uselessly added to the inevitable wear of the weather. Further, if the principle which guided their introduction here be a sound one, logical sequence and harmony call for their appearance in other, like situations.

The recent appointment of a gentleman of approved taste* to superintend the arrangement of the public grounds gives well-founded reasons to hope that these, and the like unsightly anomalies, will disappear; and that all, at least within his department, will be made in harmony with the character and purposes of the chief edifice of the country.

The position of the group of Columbus and the Indian girl† is anomalous and absurd. Anomalous, because it invades the front view of the portico, chokes the façade, and hides another statue by the same artist. Absurd, because it treats the building as somewhat on which to mount into conspicuous view, not as a noble and important vase which it is called humbly to adorn and illustrate. The statue of Washington‡ is surrounded by dwarf cypress and clumps of rose bush. These are impertinent and ridiculous—impertinent because they hide the pedestal and obstruct the view of the inscription, thus overlaying the intention of the monument, and that for the mere display of ephemeral vegetation, a phenomenon, however attractive, not here in place—ridiculous, because they seem as if intended in some way to help and eke out the sculpture; which, when a statue of this class requires it, must be done by replacing it with something worthy to stand alone. The grass within the railing, if cut close, destroys the monumental effect, by the exhibition of frequent care, if neglected, offends by its rank growth and decay. The railings which have been placed about the statues of the Capitol accuse a want of respect in the public for the public property. They accuse it without remedying it; for in spite of their protection, perhaps because of it, the statues of Columbus and of Washington have received more injury in the few years that they have been so guarded than many figures wrought before the birth of Christ have suffered in coming to us through the so-called Dark Ages. I have several times seen boys at play on the portico of the Capitol; which, if

* A. J. Downing, see pp. 198 ff. in this anthology.

† This sculpture by the Italian Luigi Persico (1791–1860) was one of two marble groups designed to be placed on the blockings of the steps of the east front of the Capitol; the other group was Greenough's "The Rescue."

‡ Greenough's statue of Washington was designed for and placed in the Rotunda of the Capitol in 1841; in 1843 it was moved outside; and finally in 1908 it was moved into the Smithsonian Institution, where it now stands.

right, makes it wrong there to place costly sculptures. If I protest against iron railings around statuary, it is because I believe they avail not for their object. I trust to the intelligence of the many to do justice to artistic efforts made for their sake. In the end, I believe the people will be the best guardians of public works here, as they have proved themselves elsewhere. Four lamps have been placed around the statue of Washington; by night they light only the feet of the figure, by day they exactly obstruct two of the principal views of it. I doubt not that the person* who so placed these lights meant to do the statue a service. He probably never heard of "the eight views" of a statue. These ever-jarring principles of magnificence and economy—laying out millions for dignity and denying the thousands necessary to ensure care, intelligence, and taste, in their conservation and exposition—produce a certain compound pretension and meanness of effect, highly to be deprecated in great public works. I say highly to be deprecated, for, however, they who have given no attention to art and its influences may be surprised at the assertion—such a chaos cannot be daily seen with impunity. What at first shocked soon becomes familiar, and the susceptibility to healthy impressions from the display of order, harmony, logical dependence, and adaptation are weakened, if not destroyed, in the observer.

I have mentioned some flagrant instances of the want of care or of knowledge on the part of those to whom the national buildings have been entrusted. This strain of remark might be continued until we had passed in review almost every detail of the structure and ornaments of the public works. It is an ungrateful task. Enough has been said to show that the evident intention of Congress to render these buildings and grounds worthy of the nation, both in their construction and maintenance, has thus far been very imperfectly effected. I will now state what I believe to be the reason why so much outlay has produced so unsatisfactory a result. First: I believe that the absence of any clear and distinct ideas of what is becoming, dignified, and proper in the premises lies at the root of the evil. For this, no one is to blame. The wants of this people have called—imperatively called—the active and able men of the country to

---

* Robert Hills, see pp. 80 ff. in this anthology.

pursuits far removed from an investigation of the beautiful, either in theory or in practice. These minds have been engaged in laying the foundations, broad and deep, of a mighty empire. They have reared the walls—they have distributed the blessed light and blessing air throughout the vast structure. They have tamed the forest, subdued the wilderness, and spread the benign influence of the gospel and of education from the Atlantic to the Pacific Ocean. They have left to later days and men of other mold the task of throwing around the pillars of the state the garlands of a refined artistic culture. Had they been men intent upon the questions that occupy us now, they had been as unfit for the task imposed on them as the land was unprepared for their labors. But untutored as they were in the mysteries of art, an instinct, great, noble, and unerring, guided their decision in respect to the visible attributes of this metropolis. The selection of this site, the ground plan of this city, show the outline of a master,* and years must elapse ere any school which we can found will be capable of worthily filling it. Secondly: I believe that the heterogeneous and chaotic character of these buildings and grounds arises from an ill-judged interference with technical design and arrangement on the part of men in authority, whether in the legislative or executive branches of government. Since our institutions carry with them, as a necessary consequence, a frequent change in the *personnel* of government, it is clear that if each succeeding wave of deputed authority is to leave the impress of its taste and its will upon the public structures, these must ere long be but a patchwork of as many whims, fancies, and artistic dogmas as have found favor in the eyes of the temporary occupants of place, unless some standard can be established which all will recognize—a consummation not now to be hoped for. I believe that this country is alone in referring matters of art to legislative committees. In England committees supervise and report, and Parliament criticizes and condemns, but the artist is not interfered with, in his own province. The law maxim is held good in that case. I have been told that the invention of the *alto relievo* upon the tympanum was due to Mr. Adams. If so, it was an unhappy

---

* The site plan of Washington, D.C., was developed by the French military engineer Pierre Charles L'Enfant (1754–1825), and the American civil engineer Andrew Ellicott (1754–1820).

exertion of his great powers. Sculpture, when it adorns buildings, is subordinate to them; and when the sculptor invades the tympanum he must fill it, or he produces a meager and mean effect. Mr. Adams knew all of art that books and much observation could teach him, but he could not, of course, be aware of the many proprieties violated in that invention. The work has another defect as sculpture. It is the translation of rhetoric into stone—a feat often fatal to the rhetoric, always fatal to the stone.

As a most honorable contrast to ever conflicting claims of private taste and whim to get utterance in the public works, I feel pleasure and pride in observing the course adopted by the architect* who has been honored with the task of adding the wings of the Capitol. That architect, trained in the severest school of ancient art, had he been called on for a new building would surely have attempted something very different from the actual Capitol. Called to enlarge it, he has sought to divest himself of every prepossession that would interfere with its harmony as a whole. He has approached his task with reverence. He has sought to keep company with his predecessor. This is not only honorable and just as regards Latrobe, but can take nothing from his own well-earned reputation. Speaking now and in view of the mere model, I doubt if it be even in his power so widely to extend the façade, without painfully isolating the cupola, and leaving the present edifice too low, too wanting in mass and weight, to characterize a center. Avoiding this defect, he will triumph over a great obstacle. What the architect has here decided in reference to the original design of the Capitol seems worthy of all emulation on the part of such as, by the vicissitudes of office, may have charge of the national buildings.

In all remarks upon important public edifices, there is a two-fold subject under contemplation. First: The organic structure of the works. Second: Their monumental character. To plant a building firmly on the ground—to give it the light that may, the air that must be needed—to apportion the spaces for convenience—decide their size—and model their shapes for their functions—these acts organize a building. No college of architects is a quorum to judge this part of

* Thomas Ustick Walter (1804–1887) was an American architect who designed not only the wings but also the cast-iron dome of the Capitol (1851–1865).

the task. The occupants alone can say if they have been well served—time alone can stamp any building as solid. The monumental character of a building has reference to its site—to its adaptation in size and form to that site. It has reference also to the external expression of the inward functions of the building—to the adaptation of its features and their gradation to its dignity and importance, and it relates, moreover, to that just distinction which taste always requires between external breadth and interior detail.

To ascertain what the organic requirements of a building like the Capitol are, is, in itself, a most laborious task. To meet them requires all the science we possess. Have we not seen the House of Lords, in spite of all the experience and the knowledge brought to bear upon the vast outlay that reared it, pronounced a gewgaw by the men who were obliged to work therein? Discomfort and annoyance soon find utterance! Decoration and magnificence in such cases, like the velvet and gilding of a ship's cabin, seen with seasick eyes, aggravate our discontent. Nor is a defective arrangement merely uncomfortable; it may prove costly beyond all belief. I have been assured by one of the chief officers of a department, that one-half of the employees of his section of the administration were required only by the blundering and ignorant arrangement of the edifice. To say that such oversights are inevitable is an unjust accusation of the art. When those who are called to the task of lodging one of the departments of the Government shall make organization the basis of their design, instead of a predetermined front, which often deserves to have the inverted commas of quotation affixed to it, we shall hear no such complaints as I have above related.

The men who have reduced locomotion to its simplest elements, in the trotting wagon and the yacht *America,* are nearer to Athens at this moment than they who would bend the Greek temple to every use. I contend for Greek principles, not Greek things. If a flat sail goes nearest the wind, a bellying sail, though picturesque, must be given up. The slender harness, and tall gaunt wheels, are not only effective; they are beautiful for they respect the beauty of a horse, and do not uselessly task him. The English span is a good one, but they lug along more pretension than beauty; they are stopped in their way to claim respect for wealth and station; they are stopped for this, and, therefore, easily passed by those who care not to seem, but are. To prefer housings to horseflesh, and trappings to men, is alike worthy of a savage.

[pp. 13–33]

CHAPTER IX / AMERICAN ARCHITECTURE

We have heard the learned in matters relating to art express the opinion that these United States are destined to form a new style of architecture. Remembering that a vast population, rich in material and guided by the experience, the precepts, and the models of the Old World, was about to erect durable structures for every function of civilized life, we also cherished the hope that such a combination would speedily be formed.

We forgot that though the country was young, yet the people were old, that as Americans we have no childhood, no half-fabulous, legendary wealth, no misty, cloud-enveloped background. We forgot that we had not unity of religious belief, nor unity of origin; that our territory, extending from the white bear to the alligator, made our occupations dissimilar, our character and tastes various. We forgot that the Republic had leaped full-grown and armed to the teeth from the brain of her parent, and that a hammer had been the instrument of delivery. We forgot that reason had been the dry nurse of the giant offspring, and had fed her from the beginning with the stout bread and meat of fact; that every wry face the bantling ever made had been daguerreotyped, and all her words and deeds printed and labeled away in the pigeonholes of official bureaus.

Reason can dissect, but cannot originate; she can adopt, but cannot create; she can modify, but cannot find. Give her but a cockboat, and she will elaborate a line-of-battle ship; give her but a beam with its wooden tooth, and she turns out the patent plow. She is not young, and when her friends insist upon the phenomena of youth, then is she least attractive. She can initiate the flush of the young cheek, but where is the flash of the young eye? She buys the teeth—alas! she cannot buy the breath of childhood. The puny cathedral of

Broadway,* like an elephant dwindled to the size of a dog, measures her yearning for Gothic sublimity, while the roar of the Astor House, and the mammoth vase of the great reservoir, shows how she works when she feels at home, and is in earnest.

The mind of this country has never been seriously applied to the subject of building. Intently engaged in matters of more pressing importance, we have been content to receive our notions of architecture as we have received the fashion of our garments, and the form of our entertainments, from Europe. In our eagerness to appropriate we have neglected to adapt, to distinguish—nay, to understand. We have built small Gothic temples of wood, and have omitted all ornaments for economy, unmindful that size, material, and ornament are the elements of effect in that style of building. Captivated by the classic symmetry of the Athenian models, we have sought to bring the Parthenon into our streets, to make the temple of Theseus work in our towns. We have shorn them of their lateral colonnades, let them down from their dignified platform, pierced their walls for light, and, instead of the storied relief and the eloquent statue which enriched the frieze, and graced the pediment, we have made our chimney tops to peer over the broken profile, and tell by their rising smoke of the traffic and desecration of the interior. Still the model may be recognized, some of the architectural features are entire; like the captive king stripped alike of arms and purple, and drudging amid the Helots of a capital, the Greek temple as seen among us claims pity for its degraded majesty, and attests the barbarian force which has abused its nature, and been blind to its qualities.

If we trace architecture from its perfection, in the days of Pericles, to its manifest decay in the reign of Constantine, we shall find that one of the surest symptoms of decline was the adoption of admired forms and models for purposes not contemplated in their invention. The forum became a temple, the tribunal became a temple, the theatre was turned into a church; nay, the column, that organized member, that subordinate part, set up for itself, usurped unity, and was a monument! The great principles of architecture being once abandoned, correctness gave way to novelty; economy and vainglory associated produced meanness and pretension.

* Richard Upjohn's Trinity Church (1846). See illustration 10.

10. Richard Upjohn, Trinity Church (1846), New York City.
Photographed in 1902. The Empire Building is at the far right.

Sculpture, too, had waned. The degenerate workmen could no longer match the fragments they sought to mingle, nor copy the originals they only hoped to repeat. The moldering remains of better days frowned contempt upon such impotent efforts, till, in the gradual coming of darkness, ignorance became content, and insensibility ceased to compare.

We say that the mind of this country has never been seriously applied to architecture. True it is that the commonwealth, with that desire of public magnificence which has ever been a leading feature of democracy, has called from the vasty deep of the past the spirits of the Greek, the Roman, and the Gothic styles; but they would not come when she did call to them! The vast cathedral with its ever open portals, towering high above the courts of kings, inviting all men to its cool and fragrant twilight, where the voice of the organ stirs the blood, and the dim-seen visions of saints and martyrs bleed and die upon the canvas amid the echoes of hymning voices and the clouds of frankincense, this architectural embodying of the divine and blessed words "come to me, ye who labor and are heavy laden, and I will give you rest!" demands a sacrifice of what we hold dearest. Its cornerstone must be laid upon the right to judge the claims of the church. The style of Greek architecture as seen in the Greek temple demands the aid of sculpture, insists upon every feature of its original organization, loses its harmony if a note be dropped in the execution, and when so modified as to serve for a customhouse or a bank departs from its original beauty and propriety as widely as the crippled gelding of a hackney coach differs from the bounding and neighing wild horse of the desert. Even where, in the fervor of our faith in shapes, we have sternly adhered to the dictum of another age, and have actually succeeded in securing the entire exterior which echoes the forms of Athens, the pile stands a stranger among us! and receives a respect akin to what we should feel for a fellow citizen in the garb of Greece. It is a make-believe! It is not the real thing! We see the marble capitals; we trace the acanthus leaves of a celebrated model—incredulous *odi*! It is not a temple.

The number and variety of our experiments in building show the dissatisfaction of the public taste with what has been hitherto achieved; the expense at which they have been made proves how strong is the yearning after excellence;

the talents and acquirements of the artists whose services have been engaged in them are such as to convince us that the fault lies in the system, not in the men. Is it possible that out of this chaos order can arise? that of these conflicting dialects and jargons a language can be born? When shall we have done with experiments? What refuge is there from the absurdities that have successively usurped the name and functions of architecture? Is it not better to go on with consistency and uniformity in imitation of an admired model than incur the disgrace of other failures? In answering these questions let us remember with humility that all salutary changes are the work of many and of time; but let us encourage experiment at the risk of license rather than submit to an iron rule that begins by sacrificing reason, dignity, and comfort. Let us consult nature, and in the assurance that she will disclose a mine, richer than was ever dreamed of by the Greeks, in art as well as in philosophy. Let us regard as ingratitude to the author of nature the despondent idleness that sits down while one want is unprovided for, one worthy object unattained.

If, as the first step in our search after the great principles of construction, we but observe the skeletons and skins of animals, through all the varieties of beast and bird, of fish and insect, are we not as forcibly struck by their variety as by their beauty? There is no arbitrary law of proportion, no unbending model of form. There is scarce a part of the animal organization which we do not find elongated or shortened, increased, diminished, or suppressed, as the wants of the genus or species dictate, as their exposure or their work may require. The neck of the swan and that of the eagle, however different in character and proportion, equally charm the eye and satisfy the reason. We approve the length of the same member in grazing animals, its shortness in beasts of prey. The horse's shanks are thin, and we admire them; the greyhound's chest is deep, and we cry, beautiful! It is neither the presence nor the absence of this or that part or shape or color that wins our eye in natural objects; it is the consistency and harmony of the parts juxtaposed, the subordination of details to masses, and of masses to the whole.

The law of adaptation is the fundamental law of nature in all structure. So unflinchingly does she modify a type in accordance with a new position, that some philosophers have declared a variety of appearance to be the object aimed at; so entirely does she limit the modification to the demands of necessity, that adherence to one original plan seems, to limited intelligence, to be carried to the very verge of caprice. The domination of arbitrary rules of taste has produced the very counterpart of the wisdom thus displayed in every object around us; we tie up the camel leopard to the rack; we shave the lion, and call him a dog; we strive to bind the unicorn with his band in the furrow, and to make him harrow the valleys after us!

When the savage of the South Sea islands shapes his war club, his first thought is of its use. His first efforts pare the long shaft, and mold the convenient handle; then the heavier end takes gradually the edge that cuts, while it retains the weight that stuns. His idler hour divides its surface by lines and curves, or embosses it with figures that have pleased his eye or are linked with his superstition. We admire its effective shape, its Etruscan-like quaintness, its graceful form and subtle outline, yet we neglect the lesson it might teach. If we compare the form of a newly invented machine with the perfected type of the same instrument, we observe, as we trace it through the phases of improvement, how weight is shaken off where strength is less needed, how functions are made to approach without impeding each other, how the straight becomes curved, and the curve is straightened, till the straggling and cumbersome machine becomes the compact, effective, and beautiful engine.

So instinctive is the perception of organic beauty in the human eye, that we cannot withhold our admiration even from the organs of destruction. There is majesty in the royal paw of the lion, music in the motion of the brinded tiger; we accord our praise to the sword and the dagger, and shudder our approval of the frightful aptitude of the ghastly guillotine.

Conceiving destruction to be a normal element of the system of nature equally with production, we have used the word "beauty" in connection with it. We have no objection to exchange it for the word "character," as indicating the mere adaptation of forms to functions, and would gladly substitute the actual pretensions of our architecture to the former, could we hope to secure the latter.

Let us now turn to a structure of our own, one which from its nature and uses commands us to reject authority, and we shall find the result of the manly use of plain good sense so like that of taste and genius too, as scarce to require a distinctive title. Observe a ship at sea! Mark the majestic form of her hull as she rushes through the water, observe the graceful bend of her body, the gentle transition from round to flat, the grasp of her keel, the leap of her bows, the symmetry and rich tracery of her spars and rigging, and those grand wind muscles, her sails! Behold an organization second only to that of an animal, obedient as the horse, swift as the stag, and bearing the burden of a thousand camels from pole to pole! What Academy of Design, what research of connoisseurship, what imitation of the Greeks produced this marvel of construction? Here is the result of the study of man upon the great deep, where Nature spake of the laws of building, not in the feather and in the flower, but in winds and waves, and he bent all his mind to hear and to obey. Could we carry into our civil architecture the responsibilities that weigh upon our shipbuilding, we should ere long have edifices as superior to the Parthenon for the purposes that we require, as the *Constitution* or the *Pennsylvania* is to the galley of the Argonauts. Could our blunders on *terra firma* be put to the same dread test that those of shipbuilders are, little would be now left to say on this subject.

Instead of forcing the functions of every sort of building into one general form, adopting an outward shape for the sake of the eye or of association, without reference to the inner distribution, let us begin from the heart as a nucleus and work outward. The most convenient size and arrangement of the rooms that are to constitute the building being fixed, the access of the light that may, of the air that must, be wanted, being provided for, we have the skeleton of our building. Nay, we have all excepting the dress. The connection and order of parts, juxtaposed for convenience, cannot fail to speak of their relation and uses. As a group of idlers on the quay, if they grasp a rope to haul a vessel to the pier, are united in harmonious action by the cord they seize, as the slowly yielding mass forms a thorough bass to their livelier movement, so the unflinching adaptation of a building to its position and use gives, as a sure product of that adaptation, character and expression.

What a field of study would be opened by the adoption in civil architecture of those laws of apportionment, distribution, and connection which we have thus hinted at? No longer could the mere tyro huddle together a crowd of ill-arranged, ill-lighted and stifled rooms, and masking the chaos with the sneaking copy of a Greek façade, usurp the name of architect. If this anatomic connection and proportion has been attained in ships, in machines, and, in spite of false principles, in such buildings as make a departure from it fatal, as in bridges and in scaffolding, why should we fear its immediate use in all construction! As its first result, the bank would have the physiognomy of a bank, the church would be recognized as such, nor would the billiard room and the chapel wear the same uniform of columns and pediment. The African king standing in mock majesty with his legs and feet bare, and his body clothed in a cast coat of the Prince Regent, is an object whose ridiculous effect defies all power of face. Is not the Greek temple jammed in between the brick shops of Wall Street or Cornhill, covered with lettered signs, and finished by groups of moneychangers and apple women, a parallel even for his African majesty?

We have before us a letter in which Mr. Jefferson recommends the model of the Maison Carrée for the State House at Richmond. Was he aware that the Maison Carrée is but a fragment, and that too, of a Roman temple? He was. It is beautiful! is the answer. An English society erected in Hyde Park a cast in bronze of the colossal Achilles of the Quirinal, and changing the head, transformed it into a monument to Wellington. But where is the distinction between the personal prowess, the invulnerable body, the heaven-shielded safety of the hero of the Iliad, and the complex of qualities which makes the modern general? The statue is beautiful! is the answer. If such reasoning is to hold, why not translate one of Pindar's odes in memory of Washington, or set up in Carolina a colossal Osiris in honor of General Greene?

The monuments of Egypt and of Greece are sublime as expressions of their power and their feeling. The modern nation that appropriates them displays only wealth in so doing. The possession of means, not accompanied by the sense of propriety or feeling for the true, can do no more for a nation than it can for an individual. The want of an illustrious ancestry may be compensated, fully compensated;

but the purloining of the coat of arms of a defunct family is intolerable. That such a monument as we have described should have been erected in London while Chantry flourished, when Flaxman's fame was cherished by the few, and Bailey and Behnes were already known, is an instructive fact. That the illustrator of the Greek poets, and of the Lord's Prayer, should in the meanwhile have been preparing designs for George the Fourth's silversmiths is not less so.*

The edifices in whose construction the principles of architecture are developed may be classed as organic, formed to meet the wants of their occupants, or monumental, addressed to the sympathies, the faith, or the taste of a people. These two great classes of buildings, embracing almost every variety of structure, though occasionally joined and mixed in the same edifice, have their separate rules, as they have a distinct abstract nature. In the former class, the laws of structure and apportionment, depending on definite wants, obey a demonstrable rule. They may be called machines, each individual of which must be formed with reference to the abstract type of its species. The individuals of the latter class, bound by no other laws than those of the sentiment which inspires them, and the sympathies to which they are addressed, occupy the positions and assume the forms best calculated to render their parent feeling. No limits can be put to their variety; their size and richness have always been proportioned to the means of the people who have erected them.

If from what has been thus far said it shall have appeared that we regard the Greek masters as aught less than the true apostles of correct taste in building, we have been misunderstood. We believe firmly and fully that they can teach us; but let us learn principles, not copy shapes; let us imitate them like men, and not ape them like monkeys. Remembering what a school of art it was that perfected their system of ornament, let us rather adhere to that system in enriching what we invent than substitute novelty for propriety. After observing the innovations of the ancient Romans, and of the modern Italian masters in this department, we cannot but recur to the Horatian precept—

---

* John Flaxman (1755–1826), William Behnes (1795–1864), and Edward Hodges Baily, "Bailey" (1788–1867) were reputable English sculptors. The "illustrator" was the Finden Brothers, Edward Francis (1791–1857) and William (1787–1852).

exemplaria Græca
Nocturna versate manu, versate diurna!*

To conclude. The fundamental laws of building found at the basis of every style of architecture must be the basis of ours. The adaptation of the forms and magnitude of structures to the climate they are exposed to, and the offices for which they are intended, teaches us to study our own varied wants in these respects. The harmony of their ornaments with the nature that they embellished and the institutions from which they sprang calls on us to do the like justice to our country, our government, and our faith. As a Christian preacher may give weight to truth, and add persuasion to proof by studying the models of pagan writers, so the American builder, by a truly philosophic investigation of ancient art, will learn of the Greeks to be American.

The system of building we have hinted at cannot be formed in a day. It requires all the science of any country to ascertain and fix the proportions and arrangement of the members of a great building, to plant it safely on the soil, to defend it from the elements, to add the grace and poetry of ornament to its frame. Each of these requisites to a good building requires a special study and a lifetime. Whether we are destined soon to see so noble a fruit may be doubted; but we can, at least, break the ground and throw in the seed.

We are fully aware that many regard all matters of taste as matters of pure caprice and fashion. We are aware that many think our architecture already perfect; but we have chosen, during this sultry weather, to exercise a truly American right—the right of talking. This privilege, thank God! is unquestioned—from Miller, who, robbing Béranger, translates into fanatical prose, "Finissons en! le monde est assez vieux!"† to Brisbane, who declares that the same world has yet to begin, and waits a subscription of two hundred thousand dollars in order to start. Each man is free to present his notions on any subject. We have also talked, firm in the belief that the development of a nation's taste in art depends on a thousand deep-seated influences beyond the ken

---

* Night and day peruse the Greek models—from Horace, *Ars Poetica*, *Epistles*, Book III, #3, lines 268–269.
† Let us be done with it! the world is old enough!

of the ignorant present; firm in the belief that freedom and knowledge will bear the fruit of refinement and beauty, we have yet dared to utter a few words of discontent, a few crude thoughts of what might be, and we feel the better for it. We promised ourselves nothing more than that satisfaction which Major Downing attributes to every man "who has had his say, and then cleared out," and we already perceive pleasingly what he meant by it.

[pp. 131–146]

CHAPTER XIII / THE COOPER MONUMENT

It is useless to regret that discussions of principle involve, to a certain extent, persons also. If this were not, on the whole, a good arrangement, principles would have been furnished with a better lodging. I take it that passions and interests are the great movers and steadiers of the social world, and that principles, like the bread on Sir John Falstaff's score, are an unconscionably small item.

The working forces and restraints are like the furnaces and engines, the lock up and lock out of the mint at Philadelphia,* all very effective for their objects. A showy front masks all these things and adorns Chestnut Street by the maimed quotation of a passage of Greek eloquence, relating to something else. A huge brick chimney rises in the rear, talks English, and warns you that the façade is to be taken with some grains of allowance.

The domain of taste is eminently one of free discussion. In most civilized countries, the individual is restrained by the magistracy from offending the public eye, by unsightly or ill-timed exhibitions of any very peculiar dogma of his own, because it is thought that the harm thus done to the public is not compensated by the gratification of the unit. Still, he is allowed to maintain his theory by any means short of an invasion of the public sense of propriety.

I have occasion to say a few words in relation to structure and ornament. I wish to speak of the monument proposed to

* The mint was designed by the American architect William Strickland (1788–1854).

be erected to Fenimore Cooper,* and before I touch upon
that monument, I must ask attention to some reflections and
observations of a general character.

One unaccustomed to tracing the influence of associated
ideas of example, and of authority, would naturally suppose
that each climate, each creed and form of government, would
stamp its character readily and indelibly upon the structures of
a thinking population. It is not so. It is only by degrees that
leisure and wealth find means to adapt forms elsewhere invented to new situations and new wants.

When civilization gradually develops an indigenous type,
the complex result still carries the visible germ whence it
sprung. The harmony of the Chinese structures indicates a
oneness of origin and modification. The sign manual of the
sultan is but the old mark pompously flourished. There is a
blood relationship between the pipe of the North American
savage and the temples of Central America.

In the architecture of Greece, of Italy, and of the more
recent civilizations on the other hand, we remark a struggle
between an indigenous type, born of the soil and of the earlier
wants of a people, and an imported theory which, standing
upon a higher artistic ground, captivates the eye and wins
the approval of dawning taste. If my limits permitted, it were
not amiss to trace this conquest of refinement, and to follow
it out also in relation to literature, and to dress, and to amusements. The least effort of memory will suggest numerous inva-
sions of artistic theory upon primitive expedients, conflicts
between the home-grown habit which has possession, and
exotic theory which seeks it.

There is one feature in all the great developments of architecture which is worthy to occupy us for a moment. They are
all fruits of a dominating creed. If we consider how vast was
the outlay they required, we shall not wonder that religion
alone has thus far been able to unite in a manner to wield
them, the motives and the means for grand and consistent
systems of structure. The magnificence of the Romans, the
splendor of Venice and Genoa, like the ambitious efforts of

* The monument to Cooper was suggested by Greenough in 1851, and
coincidentally by a committee in New York City under the leadership of
Washington Irving. The design was to have been Greenough's, but the project
foundered over the question of expenses.

France, England, and Germany in more recent days, had a certain taint of dilettantism in their origin, which, aiming to combine inconsistent qualities, and that for a comparatively low motive, carried through all their happiest combinations the original sin of impotence, and gave, as a result, bombast instead of eloquence, fritter instead of richness, baldness for simplicity, carving in lieu of sculpture. The laws of expression are such that the various combinations which have sought to lodge modern functions, in buildings composed of ancient elements, developed and perfected for other objects, betray, in spite of all the skill that has been brought to bear upon them, their bastard origin. In literature, the same struggle between the ancient form so dear to scholars, and the modern thought which was outgrowing it, was long and obstinate. In literature the battle has been won by the modern thought. The models of Greece are not less prized for this. We seek them diligently; we ponder them with delight and instruction. We assimilate all of their principles that is true and beautiful, and we learn of them to belong to our day and to our nation, as they to theirs.

In all structure that from its nature is purely scientific, in fortifications, in bridges, in shipbuilding, we have been emancipated from authority by the stern organic requirements of the works. The modern wants spurned the traditional formula in these structures, as the modern life outgrew the literary molds of Athens. In all these structures, character has taken the place of dilettantism, and if we have yet to fight for sound doctrine in all structure, it is only because a doctrine which has possession must be expelled, inch by inch, however unsound its foundation.

The developments of structure in the animal kingdom are worthy of all our attention, if we would arrive at sound principles in building. The most striking feature in the higher animal organizations is the adherence to one abstract type. The forms of the fish and the lizard, the shape of the horse, and the lion, and the camelopard are so nearly framed after one type, that the adherence thereto seems carried to the verge of risk. The next most striking feature is the modification of the parts, which, if contemplated independently of the exposure and the functions whose demands are thus met, seems carried to the verge of caprice. I believe few persons not conversant with natural history ever looked through a collection of birds, or fish, or insects without feeling that they were the result of Omnipotence at play, for mere variety's sake.

If there be any principle of structure more plainly inculcated in the works of the Creator than all others, it is the principle of unflinching adaptation of forms to functions. I believe that colors also, so far as we have discovered their chemical causes and affinities, are not less organic in relation to the forms they invest than are those forms themselves.

If I find the length of the vertebrae of the neck in grazing quadrupeds increased so as to bring the incisors to the grass, if I find the vertebrae shortened in beasts of prey in order to enable the brute to bear away his victim, if I find the wading birds on stilts, the strictly aquatic birds with paddles, if, in pushing still further the investigation, I find color arrayed either for disguise or aggression, I feel justified in taking the ground that organization is the primal law of structure, and I suppose it, even where my imperfect light cannot trace it, unless embellishment can be demonstrated. Since the tints as well as the forms of plants and flowers are shown to have an organic significance and value, I take it for granted that tints have a like character in the mysteriously clouded and pearly shell, where they mock my ken. I cannot believe that the myriads are furnished at the depths of the ocean with the complicated glands and absorbents to nourish those dyes in order that the hundreds may charm my idle eye as they are tossed in disorganized ruin upon the beach.

Let us dwell for a moment upon the forms of several of the higher types of animal structure. Behold the eagle as he sits on the lonely cliff, towering high in the air, carry in your mind the proportions and lines of the dove, and mark how the finger of God has, by the mere variation of diameters, converted the type of meekness into the most expressive symbol of majesty. His eye, instead of rushing, as it were, out of his head to see the danger behind him, looks steadfastly forward from its deep cavern, knowing no danger but that which it pilots. The structure of his brow allows him to fly upward with his eyes in shade. In his beak and his talons we see at once the belligerent, in the vast expanse of his sailing pinions the patent of his prerogative. *Dei Gratia Raptor!** Whence the beauty and majesty of the bird? It is the oneness of his func-

* Ravisher by the Grace of God.

tion that gives him his grandeur; it is transcendental mechanism alone that begets his beauty. Observe the lion as he stands! Mark the ponderous predominance of his anterior extremities —his lithe loins, the lever of his hock—the awful breadth of his jaws and the depth of his chest. His mane is a cuirass, and when the thunder of his voice is added to the glitter of his snarling jaws, man alone with all his means of defense stands self-possessed before him. In this structure again are beheld, as in that of the eagle, the most terrible expression of power and dominion, and we find that it is here also the result of transcendental mechanism. The form of the hare might well be the type of swiftness for him who never saw the greyhound. The greyhound overtakes him, and it is not possible in organization that this result should obtain, without the promise and announcement of it, in the lengths and diameters of this breed of dogs.

Let us now turn to the human frame—the most beautiful organization of earth, the exponent and minister of the highest being we immediately know. This stupendous form, towering as a lighthouse, commanding by its posture a wide horizon, standing in relation to the brutes where the spire stands in relation to the lowly colonnades of Greece and Egypt, touching earth with only one half the soles of its feet—it tells of majesty and dominion by that upreared spine, of duty by those unencumbered hands. Where is the ornament of this frame? It is all beauty; its motion is grace; no combination of harmony ever equaled, for expression and variety, its poised and stately gait; its voice is music; no cunning mixture of wood and metal ever did more than feebly imitate its tone of command or its warble of love. The savage who envies or admires the special attributes of beasts maims unconsciously his own perfection to assume their tints, their feathers, or their claws; we turn from him with horror and gaze with joy on the naked Apollo.

I have dwelt a moment on these examples of expression and of beauty, that I may draw from them a principle in art, a principle which, if it has been often illustrated by brilliant results, we constantly see neglected, overlooked, forgotten— a principle which I hope the examples I have given have prepared you to accept at once, and unhesitatingly. It is this—in art, as in nature the soul, the purpose of a work will never fail to be proclaimed in that work in proportion to the subordination of the parts to the whole, of the whole to the function. If you will trace the ship through its various stages of improvement, from the dugout canoe and the old galley to the latest type of the sloop-of-war, you will remark that every advance in performance has been an advance in expression, in grace, in beauty, or grandeur, according to the functions of the craft. This artistic gain, effected by pure science in some respects, in others by mere empirical watching of functions where the elements of the structure were put to severe tests, calls loudly upon the artist to keenly watch traditional dogmas, and to see how far analogous rules may guide his own operations. You will remark also, that after mechanical power had triumphed over the earlier obstacles, embellishment began to encumber and hamper ships, and that their actual approximation to beauty has been effected, first, by strict adaptation of forms to functions, second, by the gradual elimination of all that is irrelevant and impertinent. The old chairs were formidable by their weight, puzzled you by their carving, and often contained too much else to contain convenience and comfort. The most beautiful chairs invite you by a promise of ease, and they keep that promise; they bear neither flowers nor dragons, nor idle displays of the turner's caprice. By keeping within their province they are able to fill it well. Organization has a language of its own, and so expressive is that language, that a makeshift or make-believe can scarce fail of detection. The swan, the goose, the duck, when they walk toward the water, are awkward; when they hasten toward it, are ludicrous. Their feet are paddles and their legs are organized mainly to move those paddles in the water; they, therefore, paddle on land, or, as we say, waddle. It is only when their breasts are launched into the pond that their necks assume the expression of ease and grace. A serpent, upon a smooth hard road, has a similar awkward expression of impotence; the grass or pebbles or water, as he meets either, affords him his *sine qua non*, and he is instantly confident, alert, effective.

If I err not, we should learn from these and the like examples, which will meet us wherever we look for them, that God's world has a distinct formula for every function, and that we shall seek in vain to borrow shapes; we must make the shapes, and can only effect this by mastering the principles.

It is a confirmation of the doctrine of strict adaptation that

I find in the purer Doric temple. The sculptures which adorned certain spaces in those temples had an organic relation to the functions of the edifice; they took possession of the worshiper as he approached, lifted him out of everyday life, and prepared him for the presence of the divinity within. The world has never seen plastic art developed so highly as by the men who translated into marble in the tympanum and the metope, the theogony and the exploits of the heroes. Why, then, those columns uncarved? Why, then, those lines of cornice unbroken by foliages, unadorned by flowers? Why that matchless symmetry of every member, that music of gradation, without the tracery of the Gothic detail, without the endless caprices of arabesque? Because those sculptures *spake*, and speech asks a groundwork of silence and not of babble, though it were of green fields.

I am not about to deny the special beauties and value of any of the great types of building. Each has its meaning and expression. I am desirous now of analyzing that majestic and eloquent simplicity of the Greek temple, because, though I truly believe that it is hopeless to transplant its forms with any other result than an expression of impotent dilettantism, still I believe that its principles will be found to be those of all structure of the highest order.

When I gaze upon the stately and beautiful Parthenon, I do not wonder at the greediness of the moderns to appropriate it. I do wonder at the obtuseness which allowed them to persevere in trying to make it work in the towns. It seems like the enthusiasm of him who should squander much money to transfer an Arabian stallion from his desert home that as a blindfolded gelding he might turn his mill. The lines in which Byron paints the fate of the butterfly that has fallen into the clutches of its childish admirer would apply not unaptly to the Greek temple at the mercy of a sensible building committee, wisely determined to have their money's worth.

When high art declined, carving and embellishment invaded the simple organization. As the South Sea islanders have added a variety to the human form by tattooing, so the cunning artisans of Greece undertook to go beyond perfection. Many rhetoricians and skilled grammarians refined upon the elements of the language of structure. They all spake, and demigods, and heroes, and the gods themselves, went away and were silent.

If we compare the simpler form of the Greek temple with the ornate and carved specimens which followed it, we shall be convinced, whatever the subtlety, however exquisite the taste that long presided over those refinements, that they were the beginning of the end, and that the turning point was the first introduction of a fanciful, not demonstrable, embellishment, and for this simple reason, that embellishment being arbitrary, there is no check upon it; you begin with acanthus leaves, but the appetite for sauces, or rather the need of them, increases as the palate gets jaded. You want jasper and porphyry and serpentine and giallo antico at last. Nay, you are tired of Aristides the Just, and of straight columns; they must be spiral, and by degrees you find yourself in the midst of barbaric pomp, whose means must be slavery; nothing less will supply its waste, whose enjoyment is satiety, whose result is corruption.

It was a day of danger for the development of taste in this land, the day when Englishmen perceived that France was laying them under contribution by her artistic skill in manufacture. They organized reprisals upon ourselves, and in lieu of truly artistic combinations they have overwhelmed us with embellishment, arbitrary, capricious, setting at defiance all principle, meretricious dyes and tints, catchpenny novelties of form, steam-woven fineries and plastic ornaments, struck with the die or pressed into molds. In even an ordinary house we look around in vain for a quiet and sober resting place for the eye; we see nought but flowers, flourishes the "remissance" of Louis Quatorze gingerbread embellishment. We seek in vain for aught else. Our own manufacturers have caught the furor, and our foundries pour forth a mass of ill-digested and crowded embellishment which, one would suppose, addressed to the sympathies of savages or of the colored population, if the utter absence of all else in the market were not too striking to allow such a conclusion.

I do not suppose it is possible to check such a tide as that which sets all this corruption toward our shore. I am aware of the economical sagacity of the English, and how fully they understand the market, but I hope that we are not so thoroughly *asphixiés* by the atmosphere they have created as to follow their lead in our own creation of a higher order. I remark with joy that almost all the more important efforts of this land tend, with an instinct and a vigor born of the institutions, toward simple and effective organization, and they never fail, whenever they toss overboard the English dictum and work from their own inspirations, to surpass the British, and there, too, where the world thought them safe from competition.

I would fain beg any architect who allows fashion to invade the domain of principles to compare the American vehicles and ships with those of England, and he will see that the mechanics of the United States have already outstripped the artists, and have by the results of their bold and unflinching adaptation entered the true track, and hold up the light for all who operate for American wants, be they what they will.

In the American trotting wagon I see the old-fashioned and pompous coach dealt with as the old-fashioned palatial display must yet be dealt with in this land. In vain shall we endeavor to hug the associations connected with the old form. The redundant must be pared down, the superfluous dropped, the necessary itself reduced to its simplest expression, and then we shall find, whatever the organization may be, that beauty was waiting for us, though perhaps veiled, until our task was fully accomplished.

Far be it from me to pretend that the style pointed out by our mechanics is what is sometimes miscalled an economical, a cheap style. No! It is the dearest of all styles! It costs the thought of men, much, very much thought, untiring investigation, ceaseless experiment. Its simplicity is not the simplicity of emptiness or of poverty; its simplicity is that of justness, I had almost said, of Justice. Your steam artisan would fill your town with crude plagiarisms, *calqués* upon the thefts from Pompeii or modern Venice, while the true student is determining the form and proportions of one article.

Far be it from me to promise any man that when he has perfected the type of any artistic product, he shall reap the fruit of his labor in fame or money. He must not hope it. Fame and money are to be had in plenty; not in going against the current but in going with it. It is not difficult to conceive that the same state of the popular taste which makes the corrupted style please, will render the reformed style tasteless. It is not possible to put artistic products to a test analogous to that which tries the ship and the carriage, but by a lapse of time. True it is that society always reserves a certain number of minds and of eyes unpoisoned by the vogue of the hour, and in the sympathy of these must the artist often find his chief reward in life.

It is with great reluctance, nay, with grief, that I have undertaken to speak of this monument to Cooper. Accustomed to express my conception in the language of form, and of addressing the mind and the imagination of the constituency by means of substantial art, I feel painfully the impotence of my language to express my feeling as well as my meaning.

I propose for this monument a parallelogram of 24 by 48 feet, enclosing a room of about 20 feet high, equally lighted throughout from above. I propose to raise this building upon 3 high steps which will quite surround it. At the corners of these steps I propose to erect on pedestals four figures illustrating four of Cooper's most striking creations of character. The external frieze I propose to decorate with designs embodying national traits described by the poet, and in the interior I propose to call upon four of the ablest painters of the country to make visible a certain number of his most effective descriptions. The colossal bronze portrait of Cooper will ornament the extremity of this room opposite the entrance. I propose that in form this building shall be an example of symmetry and effective masonry, and that all its parts shall be specimens of what can be afforded by the country now. I propose to exclude from the entire work all ornament, except the graceful modification of the necessary elements and the pictorial and sculptural illustrations I have enumerated.

I count upon the soul of this building to impress itself on the body, and if, as I believe, its purpose is great and noble, let no man fear that greatness and nobility will not get utterance through the hands of those who rear and illustrate it, even as the leaden types arrange themselves now at the command of the long-buried Shakespeare.

I propose that a large and thoroughly digested model of the entire work be prepared before anything farther be attempted.

I do not deny that for the sum of money which this work will absorb, a vast pile of Gothic fritter or other European claptrap could be erected, which would fill all the papers of the land with hyperbolical eulogium and self-gratulation.

I do not deny that when all is effected that I propose to attempt, the spectator must bring to the view of the work a warm love of the first American novelist, a keen relish for the simple, the fervid, the true, or he will go away as they go who enticed by the hope of a feast only get a sermon.

I believe, notwithstanding, that this work would have several desirable results. It could scarce fail to develop and improve highly the artists employed on it, who, unless this or other similar works be commanded, must continue the expectants of private patronage or caprice, and as such, too often accept tasks calculated rather to belittle than to expand and develop their faculties. In art swimming is only learned in the water.

I believe that as a type of structure, this work could scarce fail to influence in the most wholesome manner the structures of the country, by showing in practice what a few sound and pure maxims will do for any building.

I feel confident that as a homage to a man who has been a great national benefactor and a literary hero, it would command the respect of all beholders. By degrees the public would learn to understand its language, and when that has been accomplished a great step will have been made in this branch of culture.

I have stated my views in regard to this monument in a general manner; to go farther into detail it would be necessary to have elaborated the design, and to have performed all but the material execution thereof, a labor of many months, and requiring somewhat of expense in experiment.

I cannot close without expressing my regret that a building has not already been prepared, and does not already preserve a public testimonial to other illustrious sons of New York, to which this monument of Cooper would have been a noble addition. I believe that since the fire which destroyed the old Exchange annihilated the statue of Hamilton, nothing worthy of the state or the man remains to record visibly his fame. Fulton's statue, or even bust if it exist, has not been seen by me. The fate of the statue of Hamilton, that of Washington's statue at Raleigh, the destruction of the library at Washington, of the Academy of Fine Arts of Philadelphia, of the antiquities of Central America at New York, the burning of the Panorama of Athens at Cambridge, are all examples of our habitual reliance upon combustible material, against all principles of true and wise economy, and warnings not to be slighted in the face of the statistics of conflagration and the new, saddening element of voluntary and malicious incendiarism now beginning to be developed in these States.

I am fully aware that the great calls made upon the means of citizens by amusements of an expensive character, by feasts and dances that vie with the royal follies of the Old World, and embellishments domestic and personal, which like the triumphs of Rome, represent the achievements and the whims of the known world, leave but scanty resources available for purposes like that I propose, but I have still thought it best to speak of what might be, believing that such an object would be a decoration of the city, a stimulus to youth, matter for pleasing study and instruction for the leisure of the citizens, and as permanent and connected with the national glory, a beginning of that fund of artistic wealth by which we measure the minds of nations whose conquests are past, and whose policy has suffered the fate of all things here below.

[pp. 158–177]

RELATIVE AND INDEPENDENT BEAUTY

There are threads of relation which lead me from my specialty to the specialties of other men. Following this *commune quoddam vinculum,** I lay my artistic dogma at the feet of science; I test it by the traditional lore of handicraft; I seek a confirmation of these my inductions, or a contradiction and refutation of them; I utter these inductions as they occur to myself; I illustrate them by what they spontaneously suggest; I let them lead me as a child.

Persons whose light I have sought have been worried and fretted at the form, the body of my utterance. Since this soul, if soul it be, took the form of this body, I have received it as it came. If I seek another form, another dress than that with which my thought was born, shall I not disjoin that which is one? Shall I not disguise what I seek to decorate? I have seen that there is in the body and the dress an indication of the quantum and quality of the mind, and therefore doth it seem honest that I seek no other dress than mine own. I also know by heart some lines and propor-

* Certain common bond or tie.

tions of the work of able penmen. The *lucidus ordo** of
another mind is not displayed before me as pearls before
swine. I love to bear in my bosom a nosegay plucked in
classic ground: it sweetens me to myself. I respect too much
the glory of Schiller and Winkelmann, of Goethe and Hegel,
to dare purloin their vesture for my crudities. The partial
development of my mind makes the dress and garb of imper-
fection proper for me. My notion of art is not a somewhat
set forth for sale, that I should show it to advantage, or
soldier in uniform anxious to pass muster, but rather a poor
babe whom I strip before the faculty, that they may council
and advise—peradventure bid me to despair.

Bodies are so varied by climate, and so changed by work,
that it is rash to condemn them until impotence is demonstrated. The cameleopard was long declared a monster born
of fancy, a nightmare of traveler's brain; but when the
giraffe stood browsing in the treetops before us, we felt that
we had been hasty. God's taste is as far away from our taste
as his ways are beyond our ways. I know full well that
without dress and ornament, there are places whence one
is expelled. I am too proud to seek admittance in disguise.
I had rather remain in the street than get in by virtue of
borrowed coat. That which is partial and fractional, may
yet be sound and good as far as it goes.

In the hope that some persons, studious of art, may be
curious to see how I develop the formula I have set up, I
proceed. When I defined beauty as the promise of function,
action as the presence of function, character as the record
of function, I arbitrarily divided that which is essentially one.
I considered the phases through which organized intention
passes to completeness, as if they were distinct entities.
Beauty, being the promise of function, must be mainly present
before the phase of action; but so long as there is yet a
promise of function there is beauty, proportioned to its
relation with action or with character. There is somewhat of
character at the close of the first epoch of the organic life,
as there is somewhat of beauty at the commencement of the
last, but they are less apparent and present rather to the
reason than to sensuous tests.

If the normal development of organized life be from

* Clear order.

beauty to action, from action to character, the progress is a progress upward as well as forward; and action will be higher than beauty, even as the summer is higher than the spring; and character will be higher than action, even as autumn is the résumé and result of spring and summer. If this be true, the attempt to prolong the phase of beauty into the epoch of action can only be made through nonperformance; and false beauty or embellishment must be the result.

Why is the promise of function made sensuously pleasing? Because the inchoate organic life needs a care and protection beyond its present means of payment. In order that we may respect instinctive action, which is divine, are our eyes charmed by the aspect of infancy, and our hearts obedient to the command of a visible yet impotent volition.

The sensuous charm of promise is so great that the unripe reason seeks to make life a perennial promise; but promise, in the phase of action, receives a new name—that of nonperformance, and is visited with contempt.

The dignity of character is so great that the unripe reason seeks to mark the phase of action with the sensuous livery of character. The ivy is trained up the green wall, and while the promise is still fresh on every line of the building, its function is invaded by the ambition *to seem* to have lived.

Not to promise for ever or to boast at the outset, not to shine and to seem, but to be and to act, is the glory of any coordination of parts for an object.

I have spoken of embellishment as false beauty. I will briefly develop this view of embellishment. Man is an ideal being; standing, himself inchoate and incomplete, amid the concrete manifestations of nature, his first observation recognizes defect, his first action is an effort to complete his being. Not gifted as the brutes with an instinctive sense of completeness, he stands alone as capable of conative action. He studies himself; he disciplines himself. Heautontimoroumenos!* Now, his best efforts at organization falling short of the need that is in his heart, and therefore infinite, he has sought to compensate for the defect in his plan by a charm of execution. Tasting sensuously the effect of a rhythm and harmony in God's world, beyond any adaptation of means to ends that his reason could measure and approve, he has sought to

* Greek, meaning "a man scaring or tormenting himself," Latinized as the title of a play by Terence after the Greek play by Menander.

perfect his own approximation to the essential by crowning it with a wreath of measured and musical, yet nondemonstrable, adjunct. Now, I affirm that, from the ground whereon I stand and whence I think I see him operate, he thus mirrors, but darkly, God's world. By the sense of incompleteness in his plan, he shows the divine yearning that is in him; by the effort to compensate for defect in plan by any makeshift whatever, he forbids, or at least checks, further effort. I understand, therefore, by embellishment, THE INSTINCTIVE EFFORT OF INFANT CIVILIZATION TO DISGUISE ITS INCOMPLETENESS, EVEN AS GOD'S COMPLETENESS IS TO INFANT SCIENCE DISGUISED. The many-sided and full and rich harmony of nature is a many-sided response to the call for many functions; not an aesthetical utterance of the Godhead. In the tree and in the bird, in the shell and in the insect, we see the utterance of him who sayeth YEA, YEA, and NAY, NAY; and, therefore, whatever is assumed as neutral ground, or margin around the essential, will be found to come of evil, or in other words to be incomplete.

I base my opinion of embellishment upon the hypothesis that there is not one truth in religion, another in the mathematics, and a third in physics and in art; but that there is one truth even as one God, and that organization is his utterance. Now, organization obeys his law. It obeys his law by an approximation to the essential, and then there is what we term life; or it obeys his law by falling short of the essential, and then there is disorganization. I have not seen the inorganic attached to the organized but as a symptom of imperfect plan, or of impeded function, or of extinct action.

The normal development of beauty is through action to completeness. The invariable development of embellishment and decoration is more embellishment and more decoration. The *reductio ad absurdum* is palpable enough at last; but where was the first downward step? I maintain that the first downward step was *the introduction of the first inorganic, nonfunctional element, whether of shape or color*. If I be told that such a system as mine would produce *nakedness*, I accept the omen. In nakedness I behold the majesty of the essential, instead of the trappings of pretension. The agendum is not diminished; it is infinitely extended. We shall have grasped with tiny hands the standard of Christ, and borne it into the academy, when we shall call upon the architect and sculptor and painter, to seek to be perfect even as our Father is perfect. The assertion that the human body is other than a fit exponent and symbol of the human being is a falsehood, I believe. I believe it to be false on account of the numerous palpable falsehoods which have been necessary in order to clinch it.

Beauty is the promise of function. Solomon, in all his glory is, therefore, not arrayed as the lily of the field. Solomon's array is the result of the instinctive effort of incompleteness to pass itself for complete. It is pretension. When Solomon shall have appreciated nature and himself, he will reduce his household and adapt his harness, not for pretension, but for performance. The lily is arrayed in heavenly beauty, because it is organized both in shape and color, to dose the germ of future lilies with atmospheric and solar influence.

We now approach the grand conservative trap, the basis of independent beauty. Finding in God's world a sensuous beauty, not organically demonstrated to us, the hierarchies call on us to shut our eyes and kneel to an aesthetical utterance of the divinity. I refuse. Finding here an apparent embellishment, I consider the appearance of embellishment an accusation of ignorance and incompleteness in my science. I confirm my refusal after recalling the fact that science has thus far done nothing else than resolve the lovely on the one hand, the hateful on the other, into utterances of the Godhead —the former being yea, the latter nay. As the good citizen obeys the good law because it is good, and the bad law that its incompleteness be manifest, so does every wrong result from divine elements, accuse the organization, and by pain and woe represent X, or the desired solution. To assert that this or that form or color is beautiful per se is to formulate prematurely; it is to arrogate godship; and once that false step is taken, human-godship or tyranny is inevitable without a change of creed.

The first lispings of science declared that nature abhors a vacuum; there we see humanity expressing its ignorance, by transferring a dark passion to the Godhead which is light and love. This formula could not outlive experiment, which has demonstrated that God's care upholds us with so many pounds to the square inch of pressure on every side, and that the support is variable.

The ancients knew somewhat of steam. They formulated

steam as a devil. The vessels at Pompeii all speak one language—look out for steam! The moderns have looked into
steam, and by wrestling with him have forced him to own
himself an angel—an utterance of love and care.

We are told that we shall know trees by their fruits: even
because of the fruits of refusing to kneel, and of worshipping
with the eyes open, do I proceed to seek that I may find.

Mr. Garbett,* in his learned, amiable treatise on the principles of design in architecture, has dissected the English
house, and found with the light of two words, fallen from Mr.
Emerson, the secret of the inherent ugliness of that structure.
It is the *cruelty* and *selfishness* of a London house, he says
(and I think he proves it, too), which affects us so disagree-
ably as we look upon it. Now, these qualities in a house, like
the blear-eyed stolidity of the habitual sot, are symptoms, not
diseases. Mr. Garbett should see herein the marvelous expression of which bricks and mortar can be made the vehicles. In
vain will he attempt to get by embellishment a denial of
selfishness, so long as selfishness reigns. To medicate symptoms will never at best do more than effect a metastasis—
suppress an eruption; let us believe, rather, that the Englishman's love of home has expelled the selfishness from the
boudoir, the kitchen, and the parlor, nobler organs, and
thrown it out on the skin, the exterior, where it less threatens
life and stands only for X or a desired solution. If I have been
clear in what I have said, it will be apparent that the intention,
the soul of an organization, will get utterance in the organization in proportion to the means at its disposal; in vain shall
you drill the most supple body of him that hates me into a
manifestation of love for me; while my blind and deaf cousin
will soon make me feel, and pleasingly feel, that I was the
man in all the world that he wished to meet.

In seeking, through artistic analysis, a confirmation of my
belief in one God, I offend such hierarchies as maintain that
there be two Gods, the one good and *all*-powerful, the other
evil and somewhat powerful. It is only necessary in order to
demolish the entire structure I have raised, that some advocate
of independent beauty and believer in the devil—for they go
and come together—demonstrate embellishment for the sake
of beauty in a work of the divine hand. Let me be understood;
I cannot accept as a demonstration of embellishment a sensu-

* See note to page 125.

ous beauty not yet organically explained. I throw the *onus probandi** on him who commands me to kneel. I learned this trick in Italy, where the disappointed picture dealer often defied me denying his daub to be a Raphael, to say, then, what it was. No, my friend, I care not whose it is; when I say certainly not a Raphael, I merely mean that I will none of it!

If there be in religion any truth, in morals any beauty, in art any charm, but through fruits, then let them be demonstrated; and the demonstration in regard to morals and faith will work backward and enlighten art.

I have diligently sought, with scalpel and pencil, an embellishment for the sake of beauty, a sacrifice of function to other than destruction. I have not found it. When I, therefore, defy the believer in the devil to show me such an embellishment, I do so humbly. I want help.

It seems to me that a word of caution is necessary before seeking independent beauty. Beauty may be present, yet not be recognized as such. If we lack the sense of the promise of function, beauty for us will not exist. The inhabitants of certain Swiss valleys regard a goiter as ornamental. It is a somewhat superadded to the essential, and they see it under the charm of association. The courtiers of Louis XIV admired the *talon rouge*, and the enormous *perruque*. They were somewhat superadded to the essential, and they saw them under the charm of association; but the educated anatomist in Switzerland sees the goiter as we see it. The educated artist of Louis XIVth's time saw the maiming pretension of his dress as we see it.

The aim of the artist, therefore, should be first to seek the essential; when the essential hath been found, then if ever will be the time to commence embellishment. I will venture to predict that the essential, when found, will be complete. I will venture to predict that completeness will instantly throw off all that is not itself, and will thus command, "Thou shalt have no other Gods beside me." In a word, completeness is the absolute utterance of the Godhead; not the completeness of the Catholic bigot, or of the Quaker, which is a pretended one, gotten by negation of God-given tendencies; but the completeness of the sea, which hath a smile as unspeakable as the darkness of its wrath, the completeness of earth whose every atom is a microcosm, the completeness of the

* Burden of proof.

human body, where all relations are resumed at once and dominated. As the monarch rises out of savage manhood a plumed Czar, embellishing his shortcomings with the sensuous livery of promise; yet entering the phase of developed thought and conscious vigor stands the eagle-eyed and gray-coated Bonaparte—so will every development of real humanity pass through the phase of nondemonstrable embellishment, which is a false completeness to the multiform organization which responds to every call.

I hold the human body, therefore, to be a multiform command. Its capacities are the law and gauge of manhood as connected with earth. I hold the blessings attendant upon obedience to this command, to be the YEA, YEA; the woe consequent upon disobedience, the NAY, NAY, of the Godhead. These God daily speaketh to him whose eyes and ears are open. Other than these I have not heard. When, therefore, the life of man shall have been made to respond to the command which is in his being, giving the catholic result of a sound collective mind in a sound aggregate body, he will organize his human instrument or art for its human purpose, even as he shall have adapted his human life to the divine instrument which was given him. I wish to be clear; the instrument or body being of divine origin, we formulate rashly when we forego it before thoroughly responding to its requirement. That it is in itself no final or complete entity is herein manifest, that it changes. The significance of yesterday, today, and tomorrow is this, that we are in a state of development. Now, the idea of development necessarily supposes incompleteness; now, completeness can know no change. The instrument of body is no haphazard datum given as an approximation, whose shortcomings we are to correct by convention, *arbitrium*,* and whim, but an absolute requirement, and only then responding to the divine intention when its higher nature shall be unfolded by high function, even as the completeness of the brute responds to the requirement of his lower nature.

Internecine war is the law of brute existence. War! The lion lives not by food alone. Behold how he pines and dwindles as he growls over his butcher's meat? 'Tis in the stealthy march, the ferocious bound and deadly grapple, tearing palpitating flesh from writhing bone—a halo of red rain around

* The decision of an arbitrator.

his head—that he finds the completion of his being, in obedience to a word that proceeded out of the mouth of God. Now, the law of brute life is the law of human life, in so far as the brute man is undeveloped in his higher tendencies. They therefore, who having formulated a credo for infant intelligence, and finding domination thereby secured, proceed to organize a *perennial infancy,* that they may enjoy an eternal dominion, will sooner or later see their sheep transformed to tigers; for the law of development, being a divine law, can only be withstood by perishing. If what I have said be true, collective manhood will never allow exceptional development to slumber at the helm or to abuse the whip. Collective manhood calls for development. If exceptional development answer—lo! ye are but wolves. Manhood will reply—then have at you! He who cannot guide must come down. We feel that we cannot remain where we are.

I have followed this train of remark whither it led me. Let us resume. Organization being the passage of intention through function to completeness, the expression of its phases are symptoms only. The same philosophy which has cloaked and crippled and smothered the human body as rebelling against its creator, yet always in vain, because the human body, like the Greek hero, says, strike! But learn, that philosophy has set up a theory of beauty by authority, of beauty independent of other things than its own mysterious harmony with the human soul. Thus, we remark that the human soul, so inclined to evil in the moral world, according to the same philosophy, is sovereign arbiter of beauty in the aesthetical world. The creator, who formed man's soul with a thirst for sin, and his body as a temple of shame, has therefore made his taste infallible! Whose taste! Let us seek through the whole history of arbitrary embellishment to find a resting place. We shall look in vain; for the introduction of the inorganic into the organized is destruction; its development has ever been a *reductio ad absurdum.*

There is no conceivable function which does not obey an absolute law. The approximation to that law in material, in parts, in their form, color, and relations, is the measure of freedom or obedience to God, in life. The attempt to stamp the green fruit, the dawning science, the inchoate life, as final, by such exceptional minds and social achievements as have produced a wish to remain here, and a call for a tabernacle, THESE ARE ATTEMPTS TO DIVIDE MANHOOD WHICH IS ONE. They are attempts to swim away from brute man sinking in the sea of fate. They will ever be put to shame; for the ignorance of the ignorant confounds the wise; for the filth of the filthy befouls the clean; for the poverty of the poor poisons the quiet of the possessor. The brute man clings to the higher man; he loves him even as himself; he cannot be shaken off; he must be assimilated and absorbed.

I call, therefore, upon science in all its branches to arrest the tide of sensuous and arbitrary embellishment, so far as it can do it, not negatively by criticism thereof alone, but positively, by making the instrument a many-sided response to the multiform demands of life. The craving for completeness will then obtain its normal food in results, not the opiate and deadening stimulus of decoration. Then will structure and its dependent sister arts emerge from the stand-still of *ipse dixit,* and, like the ship, the team, the steam engine, proceed through phases of development toward a response to need.

The truth of such doctrine, if truth be in it, must share the fate of other truth, and offend him whose creed is identified with the false; it must meet the indifference of the many who believe that a new truth is born every week for him who can afford to advertise. But it must earn a place in the heart of him who has sought partial truths with success; for truths are all related.

[pp. 197–213]

6

Henry David Thoreau, from THE JOURNAL OF
HENRY DAVID THOREAU, ed. Bradford Torrey
and Francis H. Allen (Boston, 1906), Vol.
III, pp. 181–184; from WALDEN (Boston,
1896), pp. 45–85; from MAINE WOODS, published posthumously, ed. William Ellery
Channing (Boston, 1893), pp. 141, 146,
168–169.

H. D. Thoreau (1817–1862) was regarded in the
nineteenth century as a disciple of Emerson's—the lesser, but
perhaps the more practical, prophet. It was not until the
1890's, and then in the "Chicago Renaissance," that Thoreau's
influence and image began to separate from Emerson's.
Thoreau's emphasis is sharply different from Emerson's;
Thoreau is preoccupied not with "mental moods" but with
the counterpoint between mind and hand: when an idea is
embodied in practice, the embodiment modifies the idea,
which in turn modifies practice in an endless dialogue.
Thoreau's response when faced with Greenough's letter to
Emerson (see pages 123–124) was thus not "cantankerous,"
as some commentators have felt; it was a reassertion of his
argument that ideas were not to be judged as complete in
themselves but in interaction with their embodiment in practice. This 1852 response is not unlike Thoreau's review in
1843 of J. A. Etzler's *The Paradise Within the Reach of All
Men* (1833; see pages 312 ff.): "Etzler has more of the
practical than usually belongs to so bold a schemer, so reso-
lute a dreamer. Yet his success is in theory, and not in practice, and he feeds our faith rather than contents our

understanding." As for the influences of Greenough's theories on Thoreau, they can easily be overrated if Thoreau's arguments are read as aesthetic and architectural. Thoreau's objections to elaboration and ornament are on the grounds that they are "uneconomical," they cost more mental effort than they are worth in terms of their capacity to inform and enlighten. Thoreau's basic concern is with "psychic economy," not only in *Walden* but also as early as the review of Etzler in which he asks: If we want to be utopian in an ultimate sense, "Why may we not finish the outward world for posterity, and leave them leisure to attend to the inner."

From JOURNAL, *January 11, 1852*

What need to travel? There are no sierras equal to the clouds in the sunset sky. And are not these substantial enough? In a low or level country, perchance, the forms of the clouds supply the place of mountains and precipices to the eye, the grosser atmosphere makes a mountainous country in the sky.

The glory of these afternoons, though the sky may be mostly overcast, is in the ineffably clear blue, or else pale greenish-yellow, patches of sky in the west just before sunset. The whole cope of heaven seen at once is never so elysian. Windows to heaven, the heavenward windows of the earth. The end of the day is truly Hesperian.

R[alph] W[aldo] E[merson] showed me yesterday a letter from H. Greenough, the sculptor, on architecture, which he liked very much. Greenough's idea was to make architectural ornaments have a core of truth, a necessity and hence a beauty. All very well, as I told R. W. E., from Greenough's point of view, but only a little better than the common dilettantism. I was afraid I should say hard things if I said more.

We sometimes find ourselves living fast—unprofitably and coarsely even—as we catch ourselves eating our meals in unaccountable haste. But in one sense we cannot live too leisurely. Let me not live as if time was short. Catch the pace of the seasons; have leisure to attend to every phenomenon of nature, and to entertain every thought that comes to you.

Let your life be a leisurely progress through the realms of nature, even in guest quarters.

This reminds me that the old Northman kings did in fact board round a good part of the time, as schoolmasters sometimes with us.

But as for Greenough, I felt as if it was dilettantism, and he was such a reformer in architecture as Channing in social matters. He began at the cornice. It was only how to put a core of truth within the ornaments, that every sugar plum might in fact have an almond or caraway seed in it, and not how the inhabitant, the indweller, might be true and let the ornaments take care of themselves. He seemed to me to lean over the cornice and timidly whisper this half-truth to the rude indwellers, who really knew it more interiorly than he. What of architectural beauty I now see, I know has gradually grown from within outward, out of the character and necessities of the indweller and builder, without even a thought for mere ornament, but an unconscious nobleness and truthfulness of character and life; and whatever additional beauty of this kind is destined to be produced will be preceded and accompanied, aye, created, by a like unconscious beauty of life. One of the most beautiful buildings in this country is a logger's hut in the woods, and equally beautiful will be the citizen's suburban box, when the life of the indweller shall be as simple and as agreeable to the imagination, and there is as little straining after effect in the style of his dwelling. Much it concerns a man, forsooth, how a few sticks are slanted under him or over him, what colors are daubed upon his box! One man says, in his despair, "Take up a handful of the earth at your feet, and paint your house that color!" What an abundance of leisure he must have on his hands! An enterprise to improve the style of cottage architecture! Grow your own house, I say. Build it after an Orphean fashion. When R. W. E. and Greenough have got a few blocks finished and advertised, I will look at them. When they have got my ornaments ready I will wear them. What do you take up a handful of dirt for? Why don't you paint your house with your blood? with your sweat? Thin not the paint with *spirits* of turpentine. There's a deal of nonsense abroad.

The question is not Where did the traveler go? What places did he see?—it would be difficult to choose between places—but Who was the traveler? How did he travel? How genuine an experience did he get? For traveling is, in the main, like as if you stayed at home, and then the question is How do you live and conduct yourself at home? What I mean is that it might be hard to decide whether I would travel to Lake Superior or Labrador or Florida. Perhaps none would be worth the while, if I went by the usual mode. But if I travel in a simple, primitive, original manner, standing in a truer relation to men and nature, travel away from the old and commonplace, get some honest experience of life, if only out of my feet and homesickness, then it becomes less important whither I go or how far. I so see the world from a new and more commanding point of view. Perhaps it is easier to live a true and natural life while traveling—as one can move about less awkwardly than he can stand still.

[Vol. III, pp. 181–184]

From Chapter I, "Economy" in WALDEN *(1854)*

As for a shelter, I will not deny that this is now a necessary of life, though there are instances of men having done without it for long periods in colder countries than this. Samuel Laing* says that "the Laplander in his skin dress, and in a skin bag which he puts over his head and shoulders, will sleep night after night on the snow . . . in a degree of cold which would extinguish the life of one exposed to it in any woollen clothing." He had seen them asleep thus. Yet he adds, "They are not hardier than other people." But, probably, man did not live long on the earth without discovering the convenience which there is in a house, the domestic comforts, which phrase may have originally signified the satisfactions of the house more than of the family; though these must be extremely partial and occasional in those climates where the house is associated in our thoughts with winter or the rainy season chiefly, and two-thirds of the year, except for a parasol, is unnecessary. In our climate, in the summer, it was formerly almost solely a covering at night. In the Indian gazettes a

---

* Samuel Laing (1780–1868), a Scottish writer and traveler whose *Journal of a Residence in Norway* (London, 1836) Thoreau quotes.

wigwam was the symbol of a day's march, and a row of them
cut or painted on the bark of a tree signified that so many
times they had camped. Man was not made so large limbed
and robust but that he must seek to narrow his world, and
wall in a space such as fitted him. He was at first bare and
out of doors; but though this was pleasant enough in serene
and warm weather, by daylight, the rainy season and the
winter, to say nothing of the torrid sun, would perhaps have
nipped his race in the bud if he had not made haste to clothe
himself with the shelter of a house. Adam and Eve, according
to the fable, wore the bower before other clothes. Man wanted
a home, a place of warmth, or comfort, first of physical
warmth, then the warmth of the affections.

We may imagine a time when, in the infancy of the human
race, some enterprising mortal crept into a hollow in a rock
for shelter. Every child begins the world again, to some extent,
and loves to stay outdoors, even in wet and cold. It plays
house, as well as horse, having an instinct for it. Who does
not remember the interest with which, when young, he looked
at shelving rocks or any approach to a cave? It was the
natural yearning of that portion of our most primitive ancestor
which still survived in us. From the cave we have advanced
to roofs of palm leaves, of bark and boughs, of linen woven
and stretched, of grass and straw, of boards and shingles, of
stones and tiles. At last, we know not what it is to live in the
open air, and our lives are domestic in more senses than we
think. From the hearth the field is a great distance. It would
be well, perhaps, if we were to spend more of our days and
nights without any obstruction between us and the celestial
bodies, if the poet did not speak so much from under a roof,
or the saint dwell there so long. Birds do not sing in caves,
nor do doves cherish their innocence in dovecotes.

However, if one designs to construct a dwelling house, it
behooves him to exercise a little Yankee shrewdness, lest after
all he find himself in a workhouse, a labyrinth without a clue,
a museum, an almshouse, a prison, or a splendid mausoleum
instead. Consider first how slight a shelter is absolutely necessary. I have seen Penobscot Indians, in this town, living in
tents of thin cotton cloth, while the snow was nearly a foot
deep around them, and I thought that they would be glad to
have it deeper to keep out the wind. Formerly, when how to
get my living honestly, with freedom left for my proper

pursuits, was a question which vexed me even more than it does now, for unfortunately I am become somewhat callous, I used to see a large box by the railroad, six feet long by three wide, in which the laborers locked up their tools at night; and it suggested to me that every man who was hard pushed might get such a one for a dollar, and, having bored a few auger holes in it, to admit the air at least, get into it when it rained and at night, and hook down the lid, and so have freedom in his love, and in his soul be free. This did not appear the worst, nor by any means a despicable, alternative. You could sit up as late as you pleased, and, whenever you got up, go abroad without any landlord or house-lord dogging you for rent. Many a man is harassed to death to pay the rent of a larger and more luxurious box who would not have frozen to death in such a box as this. I am far from jesting. Economy is a subject which admits of being treated with levity, but it cannot so be disposed of. A comfortable house for a rude and hardy race, that lived mostly out of doors, was once made here almost entirely of such materials as Nature furnished ready to their hands. Gookin, who was superintendent of the Indians subject to the Massachusetts Colony, writing in 1674, says, "The best of their houses are covered very neatly, tight and warm, with barks of trees, slipped from their bodies at those seasons when the sap is up, and made into great flakes, with pressure of weighty timber, when they are green. . . . The meaner sort are covered with mats which they make of a kind of bulrush, and are also indifferently tight and warm, but not so good as the former. . . . Some I have seen, sixty or a hundred feet long and thirty feet broad. . . . I have often lodged in their wigwams, and found them as warm as the best English houses." He adds that they were commonly carpeted and lined within with well-wrought embroidered mats, and were furnished with various utensils. The Indians had advanced so far as to regulate the effect of the wind by a mat suspended over the hole in the roof and moved by a string. Such a lodge was in the first instance constructed in a day or two at most, and taken down and put up in a few hours; and every family owned one, or its apartment in one.

In the savage state every family owns a shelter as good as the best, and sufficient for its coarser and simpler wants; but I think that I speak within bounds when I say that, though the birds of the air have their nests, and the foxes their holes, and the savages their wigwams, in modern civilized society not more than one half the families own a shelter. In the large towns and cities, where civilization especially prevails, the number of those who own a shelter is a very small fraction of the whole. The rest pay an annual tax for this outside garment of all, become indispensable summer and winter, which would buy a village of Indian wigwams, but now helps to keep them poor as long as they live. I do not mean to insist here on the disadvantage of hiring compared with owning, but it is evident that the savage owns his shelter because it costs so little, while the civilized man hires his commonly because he cannot afford to own it; nor can he, in the long run, any better afford to hire. But, answers one, by merely paying this tax the poor civilized man secures an abode which is a palace compared with the savage's. An annual rent of from twenty-five to a hundred dollars (these are the country rates) entitles him to the benefit of the improvements of centuries, spacious apartments, clean paint and paper, Rumford fireplace,* back plastering, Venetian blinds, copper pump, spring lock, a commodious cellar, and many other things. But how happens it that he who is said to enjoy these things is so commonly a *poor* civilized man, while the savage, who has them not, is rich as a savage? If it is asserted that civilization is a real advance in the condition of man—and I think that it is, though only the wise improve their advantages—it must be shown that it has produced better dwellings without making them more costly and the cost of a thing is the amount of what I will call life which is required to be exchanged for it, immediately or in the long run. An average house in this neighborhood costs perhaps eight hundred dollars, and to lay up this sum will take from ten to fifteen years of the laborer's life, even if he is not encumbered with a family—estimating the pecuniary value of every man's labor at one dollar a day, for if some receive more, others receive less—so that he must have spent more than half his life commonly before *his* wigwam will be earned. If we suppose him to pay a rent instead, this is but a doubtful choice of evils. Would the savage have been wise to exchange his wigwam for a palace on these terms?

It may be guessed that I reduce almost the whole advantage

---

* Benjamin Thompson, Count Rumford of Bavaria (1753–1814). See pp. 289 ff.

of holding this superfluous property as a fund in store against the future, so far as the individual is concerned, mainly to the defraying of funeral expenses. But perhaps a man is not required to bury himself. Nevertheless this points to an important distinction between the civilized man and the savage; and, no doubt, they have designs on us for our benefit, in making the life of a civilized people an *institution,* in which the life of the individual is to a great extent absorbed, in order to preserve and perfect that of the race. But I wish to show at what a sacrifice this advantage is at present obtained, and to suggest that we may possibly so live as to secure all the advantage without suffering any of the disadvantage. What mean ye by saying that the poor ye have always with you, or that the fathers have eaten sour grapes, and the children's teeth are set on edge?

"As I live, saith the Lord God, ye shall not have occasion any more to use this proverb in Israel."

"Behold all souls are mine; as the soul of the father, so also the soul of the son is mine: the soul that sinneth it shall die."

When I consider my neighbors, the farmers of Concord, who are at least as well off as the other classes, I find that for the most part they have been toiling twenty, thirty, or forty years, that they may become the real owners of their farms, which commonly they have inherited with encumbrances, or else bought with hired money—and we may regard one-third of that toil as the cost of their houses—but commonly they have not paid for them yet. It is true, the encumbrances sometimes outweigh the value of the farm, so that the farm itself becomes one great encumbrance, and still a man is found to inherit it, being well acquainted with it, as he says. On applying to the assessors, I am surprised to learn that they cannot at once name a dozen in the town who own their farms free and clear. If you would know the history of these homesteads, inquire at the bank where they are mortgaged. The man who has actually paid for his farm with labor on it is so rare that every neighbor can point to him. I doubt if there are three such men in Concord. What has been said of the merchants, that a very large majority, even ninety-seven in a hundred, are sure to fail, is equally true of the farmers. With regard to the merchants, however, one of them says pertinently that a great part of their failures are not genuine pecuniary failures, but merely failures to fulfill their engage-

ments, because it is inconvenient; that is, it is the moral
character that breaks down. But this puts an infinitely worse
face on the matter, and suggests, besides, that probably not
even the other three succeed in saving their souls, but are
perchance bankrupt in a worse sense than they who fail
honestly. Bankruptcy and repudiation are the springboards
from which much of our civilization vaults and turns its
somersets, but the savage stands on the unelastic plank of
famine. Yet the Middlesex Cattle Show goes off here with
éclat annually, as if all the joints of the agricultural machine
were suent.

The farmer is endeavoring to solve the problem of a livelihood by a formula more complicated than the problem itself.
To get his shoestrings he speculates in herds of cattle. With
consummate skill he has set his trap with a hair springe to
catch comfort and independence, and then, as he turned away,
got his own leg into it. This is the reason he is poor; and
for a similar reason we are all poor in respect to a thousand
savage comforts, though surrounded by luxuries. As Chapman
sings—

> The false society of men—
> —for earthly greatness
> All heavenly comforts rarefies to air.

And when the farmer has got his house, he may not be the
richer but the poorer for it, and it be the house that has got
him. As I understand it, that was a valid objection urged by
Momus against the house which Minerva made, that she "had
not made it movable, by which means a bad neighborhood
might be avoided"; and it may still be urged, for our houses
are such unwieldy property that we are often imprisoned
rather than housed in them; and the bad neighborhood to be
avoided is our own scurvy selves. I know one or two families,
at least, in this town, who, for nearly a generation, have been
wishing to sell their houses in the outskirts and move into
the village, but have not been able to accomplish it, and only
death will set them free.

Granted that the *majority* are able at least either to own
or hire the modern house with all its improvements. While
civilization has been improving our houses, it has not equally
improved the men who are to inhabit them. It has created

palaces, but it was not so easy to create noblemen and kings. And *if the civilized man's pursuits are no worthier than the savage's, if he is employed the greater part of his life in obtaining gross necessaries and comforts merely, why should he have a better dwelling than the former?*

But how do the poor *minority* fare? Perhaps it will be found that just in proportion as some have been placed in outward circumstances above the savage, others have been degraded below him. The luxury of one class is counter-balanced by the indigence of another. On the one side is the palace; on the other are the almshouse and "silent poor." The myriads who built the pyramids to be the tombs of the Pharaohs were fed on garlic, and it may be were not decently buried themselves. The mason who finishes the cornice of the palace returns at night perchance to a hut not so good as a wigwam. It is a mistake to suppose that, in a country where the usual evidences of civilization exist, the condition of a very large body of the inhabitants may not be as degraded as that of savages. I refer to the degraded poor, not now to the degraded rich. To know this I should not need to look farther than to the shanties which everywhere border our rail-roads, that last improvement in civilization; where I see in my daily walks human beings living in sties, and all winter with an open door, for the sake of light, without any visible, often imaginable, woodpile, and the forms of both old and young are permanently contracted by the long habit of shrinking from cold and misery, and the development of all their limbs and faculties is checked. It certainly is fair to look at that class by whose labor the works which distinguish this generation are accomplished. Such too, to a greater or less extent, is the condition of the operatives of every denomina-tion in England, which is the great workhouse of the world. Or I could refer you to Ireland, which is marked as one of the white or enlightened spots on the map. Contrast the physical condition of the Irish with that of the North American Indian or the South Sea Islander or any other savage race before it was degraded by contact with the civilized man. Yet I have no doubt that that people's rulers are as wise as the average of civilized rulers. (Their condition only proves what squalid-ness may consist with civilization.) I hardly need refer now to the laborers in our southern states who produce the staple exports of this country, and are themselves a staple production of the South. But to confine myself to those who are said to be in *moderate* circumstances.

Most men appear never to have considered what a house is, and are actually though needlessly poor all their lives because they think that they must have such a one as their neighbors have. As if one were to wear any sort of coat which the tailor might cut out for him, or, gradually leaving off palmleaf hat or cap of woodchuck skin, complain of hard times because he could not afford to buy him a crown! It is possible to invent a house still more convenient and luxurious than we have, which yet all would admit that man could not afford to pay for. Shall we always study to obtain more of these things, and not sometimes to be content with less? Shall the respectable citizen thus gravely teach, by precept and example, the necessity of the young man's providing a certain number of superfluous glow-shoes, and umbrellas, and empty guest chambers for empty guests, before he dies? Why should not our furniture be as simple as the Arab's or the Indian's? When I think of the benefactors of the race, whom we have apotheosized as messengers from heaven, bearers of divine gifts to man, I do not see in my mind any retinue at their heels, any carload of fashionable furniture. Or what if I were to allow—would it not be a singular allowance?—that our furniture should be more complex than the Arab's, in proportion as we are morally and intellectually his superiors! At present our houses are cluttered and defiled with it, and a good housewife would sweep out the greater part into the dust hole, and not leave her morning's work undone. Morning work! By the blushes of Aurora and the music of Memnon, what should be man's *morning work* in this world? I had three pieces of limestone on my desk, but I was terrified to find that they required to be dusted daily, when the furniture of my mind was all undusted still, and I threw them out the window in disgust. How, then, could I have a furnished house? I would rather sit in the open air, for no dust gathers on the grass, unless where man has broken ground.

It is the luxurious and dissipated who set the fashions which the herd so diligently follow. The traveler who stops at the best houses, so called, soon discovers this, for the publicans presume him to be a Sardanapalus, and if he resigned himself to their tender mercies he would soon be completely emasculated. I think that in the railroad car we are inclined to spend more on luxury than on safety and convenience, and it threatens without attaining these to become no better than a modern drawing room, with its divans, and ottomans, and sunshades, and a hundred other Oriental things, which we are taking west with us, invented for the ladies of the harem and the effeminate natives of the Celestial Empire, which Jonathan should be ashamed to know the names of. I would rather sit on a pumpkin and have it all to myself than be crowded on a velvet cushion. I would rather ride on earth in an oxcart, with a free circulation, than go to heaven in the fancy car of an excursion train and breathe a *malaria* all the way.

The very simplicity and nakedness of man's life in the primitive ages imply this advantage, at least, that they left him still but a sojourner in nature. When he was refreshed with food and sleep he contemplated his journey again. He dwelt, as it were, in a tent in this world, and was either threading the valleys or crossing the plains or climbing the mountaintops. But lo! men have become the tools of their tools. The man who independently plucked the fruits when he was hungry is become a farmer; and he who stood under a tree for shelter, a housekeeper. We now no longer camp as for a night, but have settled down on earth and forgotten heaven. We have adopted Christianity merely as an improved method of *agri*-culture. We have built for this world a family mansion, and for the next a family tomb. The best works of art are the expression of man's struggle to free himself from this condition, but the effect of our art is merely to make this low state comfortable and that higher state to be forgotten. There is actually no place in this village for a work of *fine* art, if any had come down to us, to stand, for our lives, our houses and streets, furnish no proper pedestal for it. There is not a nail to hang a picture on, nor a shelf to receive the bust of a hero or a saint. When I consider how our houses are built and paid for, or not paid for, and their internal economy managed and sustained, I wonder that the floor does not give way under the visitor while he is admiring the gewgaws upon the mantelpiece, and let him through into the cellar, to some solid and honest though earthy foundation. I cannot but perceive that this so-called rich and refined life is a thing jumped at, and I do not get on in the enjoyment of the

fine arts which adorn it, my attention being wholly occupied
with the jump; for I remember that the greatest genuine leap,
due to human muscles alone, on record, is that of certain
wandering Arabs, who are said to have cleared twenty-five
feet on level ground. Without factitious support, man is sure
to come to earth again beyond that distance. The first question
which I am tempted to put to the proprietor of such great
impropriety is, Who bolsters you? Are you one of the ninety-
seven who fail or the three who succeed? Answer me these
questions, and then perhaps I may look at your baubles and
find them ornamental. The cart before the horse is neither
beautiful nor useful. Before we can adorn our houses with
beautiful objects the walls must be stripped, and our lives
must be stripped, and beautiful housekeeping and beautiful
living be laid for a foundation; now, a taste for the beautiful
is most cultivated out of doors, where there is no house and
no housekeeper.

Old Johnson, in his *Wonder-Working Providence,* speaking
of the first settlers of this town, with whom he was contemporary, tells us that "they burrow themselves in the earth for
their first shelter under some hillside, and, casting the soil
aloft upon timber, they make a smoky fire against the earth,
at the highest side." They did not "provide them houses,"
says he, "till the earth, by the Lord's blessing, brought forth
bread to feed them," and the first year's crop was so light that
"they were forced to cut their bread very thin for a long
season." The secretary of the Province of New Netherland,
writing in Dutch, in 1650, for the information of those who
wished to take up land there, states more particularly that
"those in New Netherland, and especially in New England,
who have no means to build farm houses at first according
to their wishes, dig a square pit in the ground, cellar fashion,
six or seven feet deep, as long and as broad as they think
proper, case the earth inside with wood all round the wall,
and line the wood with the bark of trees or something else
to prevent the caving in of the earth; floor this cellar with
plank, and wainscot it overhead for a ceiling, raise a roof of
spars clear up, and cover the spars with bark or green sods,
so that they can live dry and warm in these houses with their
entire families for two, three, and four years, it being understood that partitions are run through those cellars which are
adapted to the size of the family. The wealthy and principal
men in New England, in the beginning of the colonies, com-

menced their first dwelling houses in this fashion for two reasons: firstly, in order not to waste time in building, and not to want food the next season; secondly, in order not to discourage poor laboring people whom they brought over in numbers from Fatherland. In the course of three or four years, when the country became adapted to agriculture, they built themselves handsome houses, spending on them several thousands."

In this course which our ancestors took there was a show of prudence at least, as if their principle were to satisfy the more pressing wants first. But are the more pressing wants satisfied now? When I think of acquiring for myself one of our luxurious dwellings, I am deterred, for, so to speak, the country is not yet adapted to *human* culture, and we are still forced to cut our *spiritual* bread far thinner than our forefathers did their wheaten. Not that all architectural ornament is to be neglected even in the rudest periods; but let our houses first be lined with beauty, where they come in contact with our lives, like the tenement of the shellfish, and not overlaid with it. But, alas! I have been inside one or two of them, and know what they are lined with.

Though we are not so degenerate but that we might possibly live in a cave or a wigwam or wear skins today, it certainly is better to accept the advantages, though so dearly bought, which the invention and industry of mankind offer. In such a neighborhood as this, boards and shingles, lime and bricks, are cheaper and more easily obtained than suitable caves, or whole logs, or bark in sufficient quantities, or even well-tempered clay or flat stones. I speak understandingly on this subject, for I have made myself acquainted with it both theoretically and practically. With a little more wit we might use these materials so as to become richer than the richest now are, and make our civilization a blessing. The civilized man is a more experienced and wiser savage. But to make haste to my own experiment.

Near the end of March, 1845, I borrowed an ax and went down to the woods by Walden Pond, nearest to where I intended to build my house, and began to cut down some tall arrowy white pines, still in their youth, for timber. It is difficult to begin without borrowing, but perhaps it is the most generous course thus to permit your fellow men to have an interest in your enterprise. The owner of the ax, as he released his hold on it, said that it was the apple of his eye; but I returned it sharper than I received it. It was a pleasant hillside where I worked, covered with pine woods, through which I looked out on the pond, and a small open field in the woods where pines and hickories were springing up. The ice in the pond was not yet dissolved, though there were some open spaces, and it was all dark colored and saturated with water. There were some slight flurries of snow during the days that I worked there; but for the most part when I came out onto the railroad, on my way home, its yellow sand heap stretched away gleaming in the hazy atmosphere, and the rails shone in the spring sun, and I heard the lark and pewee and other birds already come to commence another year with us. They were pleasant spring days, in which the winter of man's discontent was thawing as well as the earth, and the life that had lain torpid began to stretch itself. One day, when my ax had come off and I had cut a green hickory for a wedge, driving it with a stone, and had placed the whole to soak in a pond hole in order to swell the wood, I saw a striped snake run into the water, and he lay on the bottom, apparently without inconvenience, as long as I stayed there, or more than a quarter of an hour; perhaps because he had not yet fairly come out of the torpid state. It appeared to me that for a like reason men remain in their present low and primitive condition; but if they should feel the influence of the spring of springs arousing them, they would of necessity rise to a higher and more ethereal life. I had previously seen the snakes in frosty mornings in my path with portions of their bodies still numb and inflexible, waiting for the sun to thaw them. On the 1st of April it rained and melted the ice, and in the early part of the day, which was very foggy, I heard a stray goose groping about over the pond and cackling as if lost, or like the spirit of the fog.

So I went on for some days cutting and hewing timber, and also studs and rafters, all with my narrow ax, not having many communicable or scholar-like thoughts, singing to myself—

> Men say they know many things;
> But lo! they have taken wings, —
> The arts and sciences,
> And a thousand appliances;
> The wind that blows
> Is all that anybody knows.

I hewed the main timbers six inches square, most of the studs
on two sides only, and the rafters and floor timbers on one
side, leaving the rest of the bark on, so that they were just
as straight and much stronger than sawed ones. Each stick
was carefully mortised or tenoned by its stump, for I had
borrowed other tools by this time. My days in the woods
were not very long ones; yet I usually carried my dinner of
bread and butter, and read the newspaper in which it was
wrapped, at noon, sitting amid the green pine boughs which
I had cut off, and to my bread was imparted some of their
fragrance, for my hands were covered with a thick coat of
pitch. Before I had done I was more the friend than the foe
of the pine tree, though I had cut down some of them, having
become better acquainted with it. Sometimes a rambler in the
wood was attracted by the sound of my ax, and we chatted
pleasantly over the chips which I had made.

By the middle of April, for I made no haste in my work,
but rather made the most of it, my house was framed and
ready for the raising. I had already bought the shanty of
James Collins, an Irishman who worked on the Fitchburg
Railroad, for boards. James Collins's shanty was considered an
uncommonly fine one. When I called to see it he was not at
home. I walked about the outside, at first unobserved from
within, the window was so deep and high. It was of small
dimensions, with a peaked cottage roof, and not much else
to be seen, the dirt being raised five feet all around as if it
were a compost heap. The roof was the soundest part, though
a good deal warped and made brittle by the sun. Doorsill there
was none, but a perennial passage for the hens under the
door board. Mrs. C. came to the door and asked me to view
it from the inside. The hens were driven in by my approach.
It was dark, and had a dirt floor for the most part, dank,
clammy, and aguish, only here a board and there a board
which would not bear removal. She lighted a lamp to show
me the inside of the roof and the walls, and also that the
board floor extended under the bed, warning me not to step
into the cellar, a sort of dust hole two feet deep. In her own
words, they were "good boards overhead, good boards all
around, and a good window"—of two whole squares originally, only the cat had passed out that way lately. There
were a stove, a bed, and a place to sit, an infant in the house
where it was born, a silk parasol, gilt-framed looking glass,

and a patent new coffee mill nailed to an oak sapling, all told.
The bargain was soon concluded, for James had in the meanwhile returned. I to pay four dollars and twenty-five cents
tonight, he to vacate at five tomorrow morning, selling to
nobody else meanwhile: I to take possession at six. It were
well, he said, to be there early, and anticipate certain in-
distinct but wholly unjust claims on the score of ground rent
and fuel. This he assured me was the only encumbrance. At
six I passed him and his family on the road. One large bundle
held their all—bed, coffee mill, looking glass, hens—all but
the cat; she took to the woods and became a wild cat, and,
as I learned afterward, trod in a trap set for woodchucks, and
so became a dead cat at last.

I took down this dwelling the same morning, drawing the
nails, and removed it to the pond side by small cartloads,
spreading the boards on the grass there to bleach and warp
back again in the sun. One early thrush gave me a note or two
as I drove along the woodland path. I was informed treacher-
ously by a young Patrick that neighbor Seeley, an Irishman,
in the intervals of the carting, transferred the still tolerable,
straight, and drivable nails, staples, and spikes to his pocket,
and then stood when I came back to pass the time of day,
and look freshly up, unconcerned, with spring thoughts, at
the devastation; there being a dearth of work, as he said.
He was there to represent spectatordom, and help make this
seemingly insignificant event one with the removal of the
gods of Troy.

I dug my cellar in the side of a hill sloping to the south,
where a woodchuck had formerly dug his burrow, down
through sumac and blackberry roots, and the lowest stain of
vegetation, six feet square by seven deep, to a fine sand
where potatoes would not freeze in any winter. The sides were
left shelving, and not stoned; but the sun having never shone
on them, the sand still keeps its place. It was but two hours'
work. I took particular pleasure in this breaking of ground,
for in almost all latitudes men dig into the earth for an
equable temperature. Under the most splendid house in the
city is still to be found the cellar where they store their roots
as of old, and long after the superstructure has disappeared
posterity remark its dent in the earth. The house is still but
a sort of porch at the entrance of a burrow.

At length, in the beginning of May, with the help of some

of my acquaintances, rather to improve so good an occasion for neighborliness than from any necessity, I set up the frame of my house. No man was ever more honored in the character of his raisers than I. They are destined, I trust, to assist at the raising of loftier structures one day. I began to occupy my house on the 4th of July, as soon as it was boarded and roofed, for the boards were carefully feather-edged and lapped, so that it was perfectly impervious to rain, but before boarding I laid the foundation of a chimney at one end, bringing two cartloads of stones up the hill from the pond in my arms. I built the chimney after my hoeing in the fall, before a fire became necessary for warmth, doing my cooking in the meanwhile out of doors on the ground, early in the morning: which mode I still think is in some respects more convenient and agreeable than the usual one. When it stormed before my bread was baked, I fixed a few boards over the fire, and sat under them to watch my loaf, and passed some pleasant hours in that way. In those days, when my hands were much employed, I read but little, but the least scraps of paper which lay on the ground, my holder or tablecloth, afforded me as much entertainment, in fact answered the same purpose, as the Iliad.

It would be worth the while to build still more deliberately than I did, considering, for instance, what foundation a door, a window, a cellar, a garret, have in the nature of man, and perchance never raising any superstructure until we found a better reason for it than our temporal necessities even. There is some of the same fitness in a man's building his own house that there is in a bird's building its own nest. Who knows but if men constructed their dwellings with their own hands, and provided food for themselves and families simply and honestly enough, the poetic faculty would be universally developed, as birds universally sing when they are so engaged? But alas! we do like cowbirds and cuckoos, which lay their eggs in nests which other birds have built, and cheer no traveler with their chattering and unmusical notes. Shall we forever resign the pleasure of construction to the carpenter? What does architecture amount to in the experience of the mass of men? I never in all my walks came across a man engaged in so simple and natural an occupation as building his house. We belong to the community. It is not the tailor alone who is the ninth part of a man; it is as much the preacher, and the merchant, and the farmer. Where is this division of labor to end? and what object does it finally serve? No doubt another *may* also think for me; but it is not therefore desirable that he should do so to the exclusion of my thinking for myself.

True, there are architects so called in this country, and I have heard of one at least possessed with the idea of making architectural ornaments have a core of truth, a necessity, and hence a beauty, as if it were a revelation to him. All very well perhaps from his point of view, but only a little better than the common dilettantism. A sentimental reformer in architecture, he began at the cornice, not at the foundation. It was only now to put a core of truth within the ornaments, that every sugar plum in fact might have an almond or caraway seed in it—though I hold that almonds are most wholesome without the sugar—and not how the inhabitant, the indweller, might build truly within and without, and let the ornaments take care of themselves. What reasonable man ever supposed that ornaments were something outward and in the skin merely—that the tortoise got his spotted shell, or the shellfish its mother-o'-pearl tints, by such a contract as the inhabitants of Broadway their Trinity Church? But a man has no more to do with the style of architecture of his house than a tortoise with that of its shell: nor need the soldier be so idle as to try to paint the precise *color* of his virtue on his standard. The enemy will find it out. He may turn pale when the trial comes. This man seemed to me to lean over the cornice, and timidly whisper his half-truth to the rude occupants who really knew it better than he. What of architectural beauty I now see, I know has gradually grown from within outward, out of the necessities and character of the indweller, who is the only builder—out of some unconscious truthfulness, and nobleness, without ever a thought for the appearance; and whatever additional beauty of this kind is destined to be produced will be preceded by a like unconscious beauty of life. The most interesting dwellings in this country, as the painter knows, are the most unpretending, humble log huts and cottages of the poor commonly; it is the life of the inhabitants whose shells they are, and not any peculiarity in their surfaces merely, which makes them *picturesque;* and equally interesting will be the citizen's suburban box, when his life shall be as simple and as agreeable to the imagination, and there is as little straining after effect in the style of his dwelling. A great proportion of architectural ornaments are literally hollow, and a September gale would strip them off, like borrowed plumes, without injury to the substantials. They can do without *architecture* who have no olives nor wines in the cellar. What if an equal ado were made about the ornaments of style in literature, and the architects of our bibles spent as much time about their cornices as the architects of our churches do? So are made the belles lettres and the beaux arts and their professors. Much it concerns a man, forsooth, how a few sticks are slanted over him or under him, and what colors are daubed upon his box. It would signify somewhat, if, in any earnest sense, *he* slanted them and daubed it; but the spirit having departed out of the tenant, it is of a piece with constructing his own coffin—the architecture of the grave, and "carpenter," is but another name for "coffin-maker." One man says, in his despair or indifference to life, take up a handful of the earth at your feet, and paint your house that color. Is he thinking of his last and narrow house? Toss up a copper for it as well. What an abundance of leisure he must have! Why do you take up a handful of dirt? Better paint your house your own complexion; let it turn pale or blush for you. An enterprise to improve the style of cottage architecture! When you have got my ornaments ready I will wear them.

Before winter I built a chimney, and shingled the sides of my house, which were already impervious to rain, with imperfect and sappy shingles made of the first slice of the log, whose edges I was obliged to straighten with a plane.

I have thus a tight shingled and plastered house, ten feet wide by fifteen long, and eight-feet posts, with a garret and a closet, a large window on each side, two trapdoors, one door at the end, and a brick fireplace opposite. The exact cost of my house, paying the usual price for such materials as I used, but not counting the work, all of which was done by myself, was as follows; and I give the details because very few are able to tell exactly what their houses cost, and fewer still, if any, the separate cost of the various materials which compose them:—

Boards	$8 03½,	mostly shanty boards.
Refuse shingles for roof and sides	4 00	
Laths	1 25	
Two second-hand windows with glass	2 43	
One thousand old brick . .	4 00	
Two casks of lime	2 40	That was high.
Hair	0 31	More than I needed.
Mantle-tree iron . . .	0 15	
Nails	3 90	
Hinges and screws	0 14	
Latch	0 10	
Chalk	0 01	
Transportation	1 40	} I carried a good part on my back.
In all	$28 12½	

These are all the materials excepting the timber, stones, and sand, which I claimed by squatter's right. I have also a small woodshed adjoining, made chiefly of the stuff which was left after building the house.

I intend to build me a house which will surpass any on the main street in Concord in grandeur and luxury, as soon as it pleases me as much and will cost me no more than my present one.

I thus found that the student who wishes for a shelter can obtain one for a lifetime at an expense not greater than the rent which he now pays annually. If I seem to boast more than is becoming, my excuse is that I brag for humanity rather than for myself; and my shortcomings and inconsistencies do not affect the truth of my statement. Notwithstanding much cant and hypocrisy—chaff which I find it difficult to separate from my wheat, but for which I am as sorry as any man—I will breathe freely and stretch myself in this respect, it is such a relief to both the moral and physical system; and I am resolved that I will not through humility become the devil's attorney. I will endeavor to speak a good word for the truth. At Cambridge College the mere rent of a student's room, which is only a little larger than my own, is thirty dollars each year, though the corporation had the advantage of building thirty-two side by side and under one roof, and the occupant suffers the inconvenience of many and noisy neighbors, and perhaps a residence in the fourth story. I cannot but think that if we had more true wisdom in these respects, not only less education would be needed, because, forsooth, more would already have been acquired, but the pecuniary expense of getting an education would in a great measure vanish. Those conveniences which the student requires at Cambridge or elsewhere cost him or somebody else ten times as great a sacrifice of life as they would with proper management on both sides. Those things for which the most money is demanded are never the things which the student most wants. Tuition, for instance, is an important item in the term bill, while for the far more valuable education which he gets by associating with the most cultivated of his contemporaries no charge is made. The mode of founding a college is, commonly, to get up a subscription of dollars and cents, and then following blindly the principles of a division of labor to its extreme, a principle which should never be followed but with circumspection—to call in a contractor who makes this a subject of speculation, and he employs Irishmen or other operatives actually to lay the foundations, while the students that are to be are said to be fitting themselves for it; and for these oversights successive generations have to pay. I think that it would be *better than this,* for the students, or those who desire to be benefited by it, even to lay the foundation themselves. The student who secures his coveted leisure and retirement by systematically shirking any labor necessary to man obtains but an ignoble and unprofitable leisure, defrauding himself of the experience which alone can make leisure fruitful. "But," says one, "you do not mean that the students should go to work with their hands instead of their heads?" I do not mean that exactly, but I mean something which he might think a good deal like that; I mean that they should not *play* life, or *study* it merely, while the community supports them at this expensive game, but earnestly *live* it from beginning to end. How could youths better learn to live than by at once trying the experiment of living? Methinks this would exercise their minds as much as mathematics. If I wished a boy to know something about the arts and sciences, for instance, I would not pursue the common course, which is merely to send him into the neighborhood of some professor, where anything is professed and practiced but the art of life—to survey the world through a telescope or a microscope, and never with his natural eye; to study chemistry, and not learn how his bread is made, or mechanics, and not learn how it is earned; to discover new satellites to Neptune, and not detect the motes in his eyes, or to what vagabond he is a satellite himself; or to be devoured by the monsters that swarm all around him, while contemplating the monsters in a drop of vinegar. Which would have advanced the most at the end of a month —the boy who had made his own jackknife from the ore which he had dug and smelted, reading as much as would be necessary for this—or the boy who had attended the lectures on metallurgy at the Institute in the meanwhile, and had received a Rogers' penknife from his father? Which would be most likely to cut his fingers? . . . To my astonishment I was informed on leaving college that I had studied navigation!—why, if I had taken one turn down the harbor I should have known more about it. Even the *poor* student studies and is taught only *political* economy, while that economy of living which is synonymous with philosophy is not even sincerely professed in our colleges. The consequence is, that while he is reading Adam Smith, Ricardo, and Say, he runs his father in debt irretrievably.

As with our colleges, so with a hundred "modern improvements"; there is an illusion about them; there is not always a positive advance. The devil goes on exacting compound interest to the last for his early share and numerous succeeding investments in them. Our inventions are wont to be pretty toys, which distract our attention from serious things. They are but improved means to an unimproved end, an end which it was already but too easy to arrive at; as railroads lead to Boston or New York. We are in great haste to construct a magnetic telegraph from Maine to Texas; but Maine and Texas, it may be, have nothing important to communicate. Either is in such a predicament as the man who was earnest to be introduced to a distinguished deaf woman, but when he was presented, and one end of her ear trumpet was put into his hand, had nothing to say. As if the main object were to talk fast and not to talk sensibly. We are eager to tunnel under the Atlantic and bring the Old World some weeks nearer to the New; but perchance the first news that will leak through into the broad, flapping American ear will be that the Princess Adelaide has the whooping cough. After all, the man whose horse trots a mile in a minute does not carry the most important messages; he is not an evangelist, nor does he come round eating locusts and wild honey. I doubt if Flying Childers ever carried a peck of corn to mill.

[pp. 45–85]

From MAINE WOODS *(1864)*

I lay awake awhile, watching the ascent of the sparks through the firs, and sometimes their descent in half-extinguished cinders on my blanket. They were as interesting as fireworks, going up in endless, successive crowds, each after an explosion, in an eager, serpentine course, some to five or six rods above the treetops before they went out. We do not suspect how much our chimneys have concealed; and now air-tight stoves have come to conceal all the rest. In the course of the night, I got up once or twice and put fresh logs on the fire, making my companions curl up their legs.

[p. 141]

How far men go for the material of their houses! The inhabitants of the most civilized cities, in all ages, send into far, primitive forests, beyond the bounds of their civilization, where the moose and bear and savage dwell, for their pine boards for ordinary use. And, on the other hand, the savage soon receives from cities iron arrow points, hatchets, and guns, to point his savageness with.

[p. 146]

I was interested to see how a pioneer lived on this side of the country. His life is in some respects more adventurous than that of his brother in the West; for he contends with winter as well as the wilderness, and there is a greater interval of time at least between him and the army which is to follow. Here immigration is a tide which may ebb when it has swept away the pines; there it is not a tide, but an inundation, and roads and other improvements come steadily rushing after.

As we approach the log house, a dozen rods from the lake, and considerably elevated above it, the projecting ends of the logs lapping over each other irregularly several feet at the corners gave it a very rich and picturesque look, far removed from the meanness of weatherboards. It was a very spacious, low building, about eighty feet long, with many large apartments. The walls were well clayed between the logs, which were large and round, except on the upper and under sides, and as visible inside as out, successive bulging cheeks gradually lessening upward and tuned to each other with the ax, like Pandean pipes. Probably the musical forest gods had not yet cast them aside; they never do till they are split or the bark is gone. It was a style of architecture not described by Vitruvius, I suspect, though possibly hinted at in the biography of Orpheus; none of your frilled or fluted columns, which have cut such a false swell, and support nothing but a gable end and their builder's pretensions— that is, with the multitude; and as for "ornamentation," one of those words with a dead tail which architects very properly use to describe their flourishes, there were the lichens and mosses and fringes of bark, which nobody troubled himself about. We certainly leave the handsomest paint and clapboards behind in the woods, when we strip off the bark and poison ourselves with white lead in the towns. We get but half the spoils of the forest. For beauty, give me trees with the fur on. This house was designed and constructed with the freedom of stroke of a forester's ax, without other compass and square than Nature uses. Wherever the logs were cut off by a window or door, that is, were not kept in place by alternate overlapping, they were held one upon another by very large pins, driven in diagonally on each side, where branches might have been, and then cut off so close up and down as not to project beyond the bulge of the log, as if the logs clasped each other in their arms. These logs were posts, studs, boards, clapboards, laths, plaster, and nails, all in one. Where the citizen uses a mere sliver or board, the pioneer uses the whole trunk of a tree. The house had large stone chimneys, and was roofed with spruce bark. The windows were imported, all but the casings. One end was a regular logger's camp, for the boarders, with the usual fir floor and log benches. Thus this house was but a slight departure from the hollow tree, which the bear still inhabits —being a hollow made with trees piled up, with a coating of bark like its original.

The cellar was a separate building, like an icehouse, and it answered for a refrigerator at this season, our moose meat being kept there. It was a potato hole with a permanent roof. Each structure and institution here was so primitive that you could at once refer it to its source; but our buildings commonly suggest neither their origin nor their purpose. There was a large, and what farmers would call handsome, barn, part of whose boards had been sawed by a whipsaw; and the sawpit, with its great pile of dust, remained before the house. The long split shingles on a portion of the barn were laid a foot to the weather, suggesting what kind of weather they have there. Grant's barn at Caribou Lake was said to be still larger, the biggest ox nest in the woods, fifty feet by a hundred. Think of a monster barn in that primitive forest lifting its gray back above the tree tops! Man makes very much such a nest for his domestic animals, of withered grass and fodder, as the squirrels and many other wild creatures do for themselves.

[pp. 168–171]

7

A. J. Downing, THE / ARCHITECTURE / OF / COUNTRY HOUSES; / INCLUDING / DESIGNS FOR COTTAGES, FARM-HOUSES, AND VILLAS, / WITH / REMARKS ON INTERIORS, FURNITURE, AND THE BEST MODES OF WARMING / AND VENTILATING (New York, 1850), pp. 1–38; RURAL ESSAYS, ed. George William Curtis (New York, 1853), pp. 205–213.

Andrew Jackson Downing (1815–1852) began his career as a nurseryman and pomologist, developed into a prominent horticulturalist and landscape architect, and, as the author of various books of architectural suggestions, into one of the most important architectural influences of his time. (See illustrations 11 and 12.) He designed the landscaping for the national Capitol, the White House, and the Smithsonian Institution, and he established "free" or "English" landscape gardening in America through his own example and through the careers of his disciples Calvert Vaux (1824–1895, see pages 236 ff.) and Frederick Law Olmsted (1822–1903). Downing's assumption was that good landscaping and good housing should be "fitting, tasteful, and significant" and thus "a powerful means of civilization." Downing's "image" in the minds of his friends and students was "idyllic . . . a kind of pastoral poet," and they regarded his Gothic/Elizabethan home as "his finest work . . . materially beautiful, and spiritually bright with the purest lights of affection." In effect, his contemporaries "read" his works as literature, as the personal creations of a "poet"; this tendency to read for "expressions of the *soul*" was fixed by Downing's premature death: he was drowned while trying to save lives on the burning Hudson River steamboat *Henry Clay*. This "poeticizing" of Downing's career has somewhat obscured his accomplishments as a scientific horticulturist (see his *Fruits and Fruit Trees of America*, 1845).

Country Houses*

SECTION I / *1850* ON THE REAL MEANING OF ARCHITECTURE

Certainly the national taste is not a matter of little moment. Whether another planet shall be discovered beyond Le Verrier's† may or may not affect the happiness of a whole country; but whether a young and progressive people shall develop ideas of beauty, harmony, and moral significance in their daily lives; whether the arts shall be so understood and cultivated as to elevate and dignify the character; whether the country homes of a whole people shall embody such ideas of beauty and truth as shall elevate and purify its feelings—these are questions of no mean or trifling importance.

Now, the real progress which a people makes in any of the fine arts must depend on the public sensibility and the public taste. Sensibility to beauty must exist, and there must be some means afforded of developing and cultivating the taste; for, however instinctive and natural a gift the former may be, a correct taste is only the result of education: the feeling must be guided by the judgment.

While a general ignorance on the subject of architecture among us must be admitted, we must also avow that the liveliest interest in it is now strongly felt on all sides. And this very ignorance is mainly owing to the dry and barren manner in which architects have usually written on the real meaning or philosophy of their art. It would seem that men who work out beautiful thoughts in ponderous stone seldom wield so slight an implement as a pen with grace and power. Why else should nine-tenths of even the educated believe that the whole circle of architecture is comprised of the five Orders;

* Unless otherwise indicated, all footnotes are Downing's.—ED.
† Urbain-Jean-Joseph Le Verrier (1811–1877) was a French astronomer whose mathematical calculations led to the discovery of Neptune in 1846. —ED.

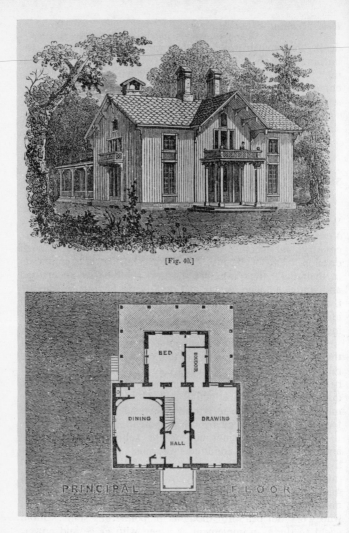

[Fig. 40.]

11. A. J. Downing?, A Cottage in the Bracketed Style, from *Cottage Residences* (1842).

or, at most, that a Greek temple and a Gothic cathedral are the Alpha and Omega of the art? Why should so many of the most intelligent persons imagine that domestic architecture is only perfect when it is similar to that of public edifices; or, at least, when it borrows all its ornaments from such structures?

It is not an easy task to lay bare the principles of an art, compounded thus of the useful and the beautiful; to show how and why it appeals so powerfully to the whole nature of man—to his senses, his heart, and his understanding.

But it is, perhaps, this very compound nature of architecture, this appeal which it makes to the sensation, the sentiment, and the knowledge of man, which has left it in so unsatisfactory a shape to the popular apprehension; which has caused it to be looked upon by some as the mere province of the builder; by others, as the object of enthusiastic admiration, and by the rest as a subject of scientific investigation; until half the world imagines the beauty of an edifice, like genius, to be a happy accident, to be enjoyed when found, but as difficult to seize as the rainbow itself.

It would be a boon to the age if some gifted artist would show the world the secret sources of the influence which architecture wields in all civilized nations. This is as far beyond our province as our ability. Still, we must be indulged in a brief analysis of the elements of interest which architecture possesses for the human mind, and a glance at the partially concealed sources of that power which it exerts over our hearts and understandings.

Something of this kind seems to us to be demanded by the inquiring mind and the expanding taste of our people; and domestic architecture itself, which, amid the louder claims of civil and ecclesiastical art, has been too much neglected, seems to demand a higher consideration in a country where the ease of obtaining a house and land, and the ability of almost every industrious citizen to build his own house, constitute a distinctive feature of national prosperity.

THE USEFUL IN ARCHITECTURE

The senses make the first demand in almost every path in human life. The necessity of shelter from the cold and heat, from sun and shower, leads man at first to *build a habitation*.

What this habitation shall be depends partly on the habits of the man, partly on the climate in which he lives. If he is a shepherd and leads a wandering life, he pitches a tent. If he is a hunter, he builds a rude hut of logs or skins. If he is a tiller of the soil, he constructs a dwelling of timber or stones, or lodges in the caverns of the rocky hillsides.

As a mere animal, man's first necessity is to provide shelter; and, as he is not governed by the constructive instinct of other animals, the clumsiest form which secures him against the inclemency of the seasons often appears sufficient: there is scarcely any design apparent in its arrangement, and the smallest amount of convenience is found in its interior. This is the first, primitive, or savage idea of building. Let us look a step higher in the scale of improvement.

On the eastern borders of Europe is a tribe or nation of the Slavonic people, called the Croats, who may be said to be only upon the verge of civilization. They lead a rude, forest, and agricultural life. They know nothing of the refinements of the rest of Europe. They live in coarse, yet strong and warm houses. But their apartments are as rude as their manners, and their cattle frequently share the same rooms with themselves.

Our third example may be found in any portion of the United States. It is nothing less common than a plain, rectangular house, built of timber from the forest sawmill, with a roof to cover it, windows to light it, and doors to enter it. The heat is kept out by shutters, and the cold by fires burned in chimneys. It is well and strongly built; it affords perfect protection to the physical nature of man; and it serves, so far as a house can serve, all the most imperative wants of the body. It is a warm, comfortable, convenient dwelling.

It is easy to see that in all these grades of man's life, and the dwellings which typify them, only one idea has as yet manifested itself in his architecture—viz., that of utility. In the savage, the half civilized, and the civilized states, the idea of the useful and the convenient differ, but only in degree. It is still what will best serve the body—what will best shelter, lodge, feed, and warm us—which demands the whole attention of the mere builder of houses.

It would be as false to call only this "architecture" as to call the gamut music, or to consider rhymes poetry, and yet it is the framework or skeleton on which architecture grows and wakens into life; without which, indeed, it can no more rise to the dignity of a fine art than perfect language can exist without sounds.

There are also certain principles which belong to *building* (as this useful part of architecture is properly called), which are of the utmost importance, since they may not be in the slightest degree violated without proving more or less destructive to the enjoyment of the finest work.

Many of these are mechanical principles involved in masonry, in carpentry, and other kinds of artisanship, which are sufficiently familiar in their nature to the general reader, and are subjects of technical expertness on the part of those employed in building.

But there are also other principles besides these, which govern the workmen in their labors, and which must always control even him who only aims at the useful in architecture.

The first and most obvious of these rules of utility is that the cost of the building shall not exceed the means of the owner or occupant. Out of a want of practical knowledge in the builder grow, not infrequently, mistakes that are fatal to the use of a house, since, if too much is expended in the whole structure, the owner may be forced to sell it to another, rather than enjoy it himself: if too much is expended on a part, the economy necessary in the remainder may render parts of the house uncomfortable from defects in their construction.

The second rule governs the quality of the materials and workmanship employed in the construction. That the materials should be of the soundest and best quality in the best edifices, and of ample strength and durability for the end in view, even in those of the humblest class, is a rule which may never be for a moment violated by the builder, without injury to the structure. Nature here, as always, must be constantly respected, or she punishes severely all infringements of her laws. A wall that is not perpendicular, a foundation that is not firm, a roof that is not tight, a chimney that smokes, sooner or later, but inevitably, shows the builder's want of comprehension or respect for the laws of gravitation or the atmosphere, and impairs or destroys the usefulness of all architecture.

The last and highest rule of utility is that which involves convenience. In all architecture, adaptation to the end in view is important; in domestic architecture it is a principle which, in its influence on our daily lives, our physical comfort, and enjoyment, is paramount and imperative. Hence, however full of ornament or luxury a house may be, if its apartments do not afford that convenience, comfort, and adaptation to human wants which the habits of those who are to live in it demand, it must always fail to satisfy us, or to merit the approval of the most matter-of-fact critic. Such a house may be compared to a column with well-molded shaft and richly decorated capital, but composed of such flimsy material that it will bear no weight; or, to a person whose education has been that of accomplishments, with a total neglect of solid acquirements.

This practical part of architecture involves, more particularly, what is called the plan of a building—providing apartments for the various wants of domestic and social life, adapting the size of such apartments to their respective uses, and all other points which the progress of modern civilization has made necessary to our comfort and enjoyment withindoors.

The illustrations of these points will be found, to a considerable extent, in the treatment of the various designs which follow. It may be remarked, however, that no absolute rules for guidance can be laid down here. Domestic life varies not only in different countries, but even in different portions of a territory so broad as that of the United States. Even different families have somewhat various habits, and therefore require different accommodations. The ingenuity and talents of the architect must therefore be put in full activity, even to meet the requirements of this humblest platform of his art. And we may add that it is a proof of weakness, rather than strength, to treat with the slightest neglect, this, its wholly utilitarian side. To the majority of mankind the *useful* is the largest satisfaction derived from architecture; and while an able architect will always treat the materials placed in his hands for a new design so as to give something of the expression of beauty even to the simplest forms, he must never imagine that in his art he can largely neglect the useful for the beautiful. As in the Apollo every muscle must be found which enters into the body of the hardiest day laborer, so in all perfect architecture no principle of utility will be found sacrificed to beauty, but only elevated and ennobled by it.

THE BEAUTIFUL IN ARCHITECTURE

We have shown as yet only the useful in architecture. At least, we have endeavored to show how an edifice may combine fitness in all respects, how it may be strong, well built, warm, comfortable, and convenient, and no more. To attain this there is no need of its displaying any appreciable grace, harmony, or beauty; nay, it may be even faulty in its proportions, and unpleasing in effect. Such examples are, in fact, every day before us—buildings which completely answer the useful requirements of man, and yet give not a ray of pleasure or satisfaction to his heart or understanding. And yet there are persons who, because the useful and the beautiful, in some arts, may be most intimately combined, imagine that they are identical. This is the grossest error, of which, if the commonplace buildings we have just quoted are not a sufficient refutation, abundant others may be drawn every day from the works of nature or art.

A head of grain, one of the most useful of vegetable forms, is not so beautiful as a rose; an ass, one of the most useful of animals, is not so beautiful as a gazelle; a cotton mill, one of the most useful of modern structures, is not so beautiful as the temple of Vesta; yet no one thinks of comparing them for utility.

The truth, then, is undeniable that the beautiful is, intrinsically, something quite distinct from the useful. It appeals to a wholly different part of our nature; it requires another portion of our being to receive and enjoy it.

There are many to whose undeveloped natures the useful is sufficient; but there are, also, not a few who yearn, with

an instinct as strong as for life itself, for the manifestation of
a higher attribute of matter—the beautiful.

We have said that the useful in architecture is based wholly
on the physical wants of man; that it is a response to the
demand of our senses.

We may also add that the beautiful is an original instinct
of the sentiment of our nature. It is a worship, by the heart,
of a higher perfection manifested in material forms.

To see, or rather to feel how, in nature, matter is ennobled
by being thus touched by a single thought of beauty, how it
is almost deified by being made to shadow forth, even dimly,
His attributes, constitutes the profound and thrilling satisfaction which we experience in contemplating the external works
of God. To be keenly sensible of the power of even the
imperfect reproduction of such ideas in the various fine arts
—poetry, music, painting, sculpture, architecture, etc.—is
to acknowledge the power of beauty over our feelings in
another and a more personal form.

To desire to surround ourselves with such sources of
enjoyment, rather than to be content with mere utility, is
only to acknowledge the existence of a sentiment which,
next to the religious one, is the purest and noblest part of
our nature.

Looking at the subject before us, it must be admitted that
if it is a step forward in civilization to separate ourselves
from our cattle, rather than share our apartments with them,
like the Croats, it is a much higher step to evince, by the
beauty of our architecture, that our hearts are alive to some
of the highest emotions of which they are capable.

What is beauty in architecture? In order to rid ourselves
of the vague and indefinite meaning which hangs about this
part of our subject, like a thick mist, in the minds of most
persons, let us examine it somewhat closely.

All beauty in architecture seems to us to resolve itself into
two kinds—*absolute* and *relative*.

ABSOLUTE BEAUTY lies in the expression, in material forms,
of those ideas of perfection which are universal in their
application. We find them in nature as well as in art. We find
them in the figures of the heavenly bodies, in the orbits of
planets, in drops of water, in animal forms, in the growth
of trees, in the structures of crystals. This proves not only that
they are divine in their origin, but that they pervade all time

and space. These typical ideas of beauty are PROPORTION, SYMMETRY, VARIETY, HARMONY, and UNITY. They may be called abstract ideas of beauty of form, and apply to all the arts, as well as to everything in nature—to a symphony of Beethoven or a statue by Powers,* as well as to the sublime curve of Niagara or the varied outlines of the Alps.

In order that the uninitiated reader may be able to analyze and understand these universal ideas of beauty, let us look at them, architecturally, a little in detail.

A fundamental idea of the beautiful in architecture is proportion.

PROPORTION, in material objects, is the relation of individual parts to the whole. Mr. Ruskin has cleverly defined it to be "the sensible relation of quantities." In all the arts, it is the realization of the most perfect idea of the height, breadth, outline, and form of the object aimed at, and therefore involves the highest single feeling of pure material beauty.

In architecture, proportion is shown first in the composition of the outline or mass of the entire building. If endowed with this quality, it will neither be too long nor too broad, too low nor too high. It will exhibit to the eye, at a glance, that nice relation of all the parts to each other and to the whole which gives to that whole the stamp of the best, most suitable, and perfect form.

Proportion may be shown in the smallest building as well as in the largest; in a cottage of twenty feet as well as in St. Peter's of ten acres. In the former, however, it is much more simple, as it involves only the height and breadth of a few parts: in the latter, it is evolved by the skillful grouping of many parts. Hence, in large piles of buildings, the central mass is raised up in a domelike or pyramidal form, not only for the sake of making a whole, but also to give that proportion of the whole which great extent and the multiplication of parts render necessary. But proportion does not merely govern the form of the whole mass in architecture; it descends into the smallest details. It demands that the height of a room, of a window, or a door should accord with its breadth and length. The minutest object, the smallest details, are equally capable of expressing it. It applies as well to the form of a

---

* Hiram Powers (1805–1873), an American sculptor who shared with Greenough the rank of "foremost American sculptor" in the second quarter of the nineteenth century.—ED.

cornice, a molding, or an ornament as to the whole outline of the edifice itself.

Proportion, in architecture, has been aptly likened, by a German writer, to time in music—that measure which confers a completeness of form on the entire melody; and though the parallel cannot be carried so closely as to enable us strictly to agree with Madame de Stäel, who called architecture "frozen music," the illustration is scarcely less forcible.

That proportion is one of those qualities of beauty most universally felt, it does not require any argument of ours to prove. The immediate delight which all persons experience in a well-proportioned human figure, a statue, or a Grecian column is well known. That this is quite independent of education, that it requires only sensibility to beauty, is equally true. Hence the want of proportion in a building is felt as a great and irremediable defect, at the first glance, by many who are totally ignorant of architecture as an art; and hence, if absent, it is a fundamental want, for which no decoration, no style, no beauty of parts, however excellent in themselves, can ever wholly compensate.

One would suppose that some definite rules would have been deduced for the production of so fundamental a quality as this in architecture.* But no such rules exist at the present day, and its production seems to depend mainly on the genius of the artist. That education and study of the best examples will aid in the appreciation of it is undoubtedly true; but the many blunders in proportion which the works of modern artists exhibit prove that it is one of the qualities of beauty less vividly felt, and less easily produced, than any other at the present time.

SYMMETRY is that quality of beauty in material objects which may be defined, that balance of *opposite parts* necessary to form an agreeable whole. Thus, in the human figure, it is the joining of the opposite sides, each with its separate limbs, which makes the whole symmetrical: if an arm is wanting, the symmetry is destroyed. In trees, it is seen in the balance of the opposite sides of their heads: if a large limb is cut away, the balance is lost. In architecture, it is the arrangement on each side of a center, of two parts that balance each

* Mr. Hay, of Edinburgh, in his ingenious treatise on beauty of form has endeavored to prove that the Greeks, whose architecture certainly displays the most perfect *proportions*, were possessed of a system of rules which enabled them uniformly to produce it.

other, and that do not make a whole without this center. Hence the superior effect of a building which is a plain cube with a wing on each side over a cube without wings. The wings raise the character of the form from uniformity to symmetry.

This leads us to remark here that regularity and uniformity, two qualities common in architecture, are often classed as distinct elements of beauty in themselves. They may be such, in an artistical point of view, as denoting the presence of art, but they are, in fact, only primary steps toward symmetry, which comprehends them both. A *regular* building in architecture is one in which a given form is repeated at regular distances, such as a square house in which the same windows and doors are repeated at regular intervals, or a long row of houses in a street, in which the same general forms are regularly repeated.

A *uniform* building is one in which the same forms are repeated on all sides; as a cubical house with the same windows all round, or a block formed of two or more houses exactly alike, and placed side by side.

Symmetry involves something more. It asks for a central part which shall connect the two other parts into a whole, and thereby make something involving a more complete idea than regularity and uniformity. Thus Design VI is a symmetrical cottage, from the front of which neither the central part nor the sides can be taken away without destroying the composition as a whole. The difference between this and a regular or a uniform building of the same length is that the latter might be divided into several parts, each of which is equally regular and uniform, and therefore as complete in itself as the whole building.

Symmetry is one of the greatest beauties in all architecture. The author of *Modern Painters** conceives it to be the symbol of *abstract justice;* and certainly, in material forms, when joined to proportion, it conveys at once an idea of completeness of form, which gives universal satisfaction. The Grecian temples owe to these two elements their great and lasting power over the human mind for so many ages; for it is a beauty which may be bestowed on a cottage, a villa, or indeed any kind of building; and as it is one which appeals

* John Ruskin (1819–1900); *Modern Painters* "By a graduate of Oxford" (London, 1846–1860).—ED.

intuitively to every mind, it is never neglected by artists who wish to impress the beautiful upon their works.

Symmetry is quite distinct from proportion. It is only necessary to remember that it is a balance made between opposite parts, and that proportion is the relation between all the parts, to comprehend it more clearly. Thus, a statue may be perfectly symmetrical on all sides, and yet too short or too high in its proportions. The central part of a symmetrical building, like that in Design VI, might be raised or lowered several feet, without injuring the symmetry of the composition, though the proportion would be at once destroyed.

It has been justly said that though symmetry is not the highest quality of beauty, yet no object can be perfectly beautiful without it. Hence, in many beautiful objects, where, from the nature of the structure or purposes, exact or regular symmetry is impossible, a certain balance must be found before they can give full satisfaction. There are, then, in nature and art, two kinds of symmetry; that which is regular, and strikes us at a glance, like that of a poplar or fir tree whose limbs are equal on all sides of the head; and that which is irregular, such as we see in a spreading oak with branches unequal, but forming altogether a head which is equally symmetrical with respect to the trunk.

The strict application of the principle of a regular balance of parts, as it would be deduced from our remarks, would prevent our finding any symmetry in all irregular buildings. But in fact this is not the case. The most irregular building, if composed by an artist of genius, will always evince symmetry; that is to say, it will form an outline, in which there will be a central portion or point which unites two sides into one symmetrical whole; two parts which, if they do not balance each other in exact forms and proportions as in regular symmetry, do balance in the general impression which they make on the eye, in the mass and grouping of the composition. The villas in Designs XXI, XXII, are examples of irregular symmetry, and may be compared with the symmetrical villas in some of the other designs. Any building so irregular as not to show some recognition of this principle of irregular symmetry can never be called beautiful, though it may be strikingly odd or grotesque.

We may remark here that buildings in an irregular style, highly expressive of irregular symmetry, are much more striking in a picturesque point of view, and are therefore preferred by many artists. They are more expressive of character and individuality (in other words, of relative beauty) than of abstract or universal beauty; and while they are, perhaps, not so agreeable to the universal mind, they are far more so to certain mental organizations. We may also add that irregular symmetry can rarely be expressed, with much success, in a small edifice. It requires considerable extent, and the introduction of a variety of parts, to enable one to introduce this quality, in a manner altogether satisfactory, in a dwelling of small size. For this reason those cottages and small villas give the greatest pleasure in which proportion and regular symmetry are the prevailing elements of beauty.

VARIETY, though always a subordinate, is still an essential quality of absolute beauty. As, in nature, it gives richness and interest to landscape, to sky, to the vegetable and animal kingdoms, so, in art, it adds to the interest of the whole by the diversity which it affords in the arrangement, sizes, or forms of the different parts. In architecture, variety is of the greatest value, often preventing simple forms from degenerating into baldness, or plain broad surfaces from being monotonous, by its power in the arrangement or the decoration of details; for it is in the details of regular and symmetrical buildings, such as the cornices, moldings, etc., that variety is chiefly to be introduced. In irregular buildings there may also be variety in the various parts, projections, recesses, towers, etc. A slight difference in the forms, sizes, or decorations of certain parts of a building is sufficient to give it an expression of variety, and by the judicious employment of this quality, every architect is able to increase the beauty of his whole composition. But it should be remembered that in architecture, even more than in the other arts, it must be kept under the control of the judgment, since, if carried to a great length, it leads to confusion, the result of which is always painful and destructive of all beauty. Intricacy, which is a complex sort of variety, is therefore to be avoided in domestic architecture, as likely to become wearisome and perplexing.

HARMONY is an element of beauty little understood, though in the highest degree necessary to our enjoyment of all complicated or elaborate productions. It may be defined as an agreement made in the midst of the variety of forms, sounds, or colors, by some one feeling which pervades the whole and brings all the varied parts into an agreeable relation with each other.

Thus, in landscapes involving the utmost variety of colors and forms, the softening effect of the atmosphere spread over them brings all into harmony: in music, changes of opposite character are brought into harmony by dominant chords: in painting, strong contrasts of colors are introduced, not only without discord, but with a most powerful and agreeable effect, by the introduction of some other tint or some pervading tone that brings the whole into harmony.

In architecture, harmony, in its highest sense, is possible only in buildings of considerable extent, where there is sufficient variety of form and outline in the parts to demand its presence. In simple and regular buildings, when the same forms are repeated with little or no variation throughout, harmony cannot exist, because there is no tendency to confusion or disagreement; and the beauty of harmony is felt only when it so presides over all, like the charm of a golden temper, or the glow of a rich sunset, as to bring every thing it touches under the influence of its magical power for unison.

As a simple example of the production of harmony, we may mention the Ionic column, in which the agreement between the circular lines of the shaft and the straight line of the entablature is brought about by the intermediate, partly straight and partly curved lines of the volutes. In Gothic architecture, the squareheaded door and window heads are made to harmonize with those of pointed form by introducing an arched spandril under the square head. A rosette in the middle of a square ceiling is out of harmony with it; but it may be made to harmonize by surrounding it with a border in which the two forms are ingeniously blended. The façade of a villa in which a round tower is joined to the square angles of straight walls is destitute of harmony; but harmony is made by repeating the same feeling of the beauty of the curve in the arched windows. . . . In Mr. King's villa,* at Newport, . . . the architect has introduced a variety of Italian window forms. The effect would be discordant were it not that the arched or roundheaded window predominates over all, and brings out of this great variety a complete harmony.

Examples of this kind might be multiplied to an endless

* "Kingscote" (1838), designed by Richard Upjohn (1802–1878).—ED.

extent, but we have said enough to suggest how the presence of this predominant feeling gives unity and completeness to a whole composition which, without it, would show only tasteless diversity and discord.

In domestic architecture, the feeling of harmony is more demanded, and more easily evinced in the interiors than in the exteriors of houses—because the interiors show a greater variety of lines, forms, and colors; or in the shape and arrangement of the rooms; or in their architectural decorations and their furniture. Harmony is evinced in all these cases by rejecting all forms, outlines, and colors that do not intrinsically admit of being brought into harmonious agreement with each other. Harmony may pervade an entire mansion, so that all its portions and details exhibit the most complete agreement throughout, or it may be confined to each apartment, extending its influence only over the various objects which enter into its composition. As regularity is the simplest quality of absolute beauty, and the first recognized, even by those of least sensibility to the beautiful, so harmony, being the most complex, is the last recognized, and usually requires some cultivation to lead us to its full perception. We see, every day, buildings in which symmetry and proportion are not wanting; but those in which we find these united to variety, and the whole pervaded by harmony, are comparatively rare.

It by no means follows, however, that SIMPLICITY is without its charms, because harmony, which can only grow out of the display of a greater variety than simple forms admit, involves a higher charm. On the contrary, the pleasure which in a small building we derive from simplicity or chasteness is far greater than that derived from the pretension of harmony, since, in a small cottage, there is no legitimate reason for variety.

It is plain, therefore, that proportion and symmetry are the proper sources of beauty in a cottage of small size, and that we should look for variety and harmony only in private dwellings of a larger size, where there is opportunity for the production of these elements.

UNITY is the highest idea or quality of abstract beauty, for it comprehends, includes, and governs all the others. It is the predominance of one single feeling, one soul, one mind in every portion, so that, whether of the simplest or the most complicated form, the same spirit is recognized throughout the whole.

To understand the value of unity, we may suppose a building finely proportioned, symmetrical, varied, and harmonious, and yet composed of such different and unsuitable materials as to have no unity of substance; or of different though perhaps harmonious kinds of architecture, so as to have no unity of style; or of different hues, so as to have no unity of color; or, in character, partly a cottage, partly a farmhouse, and partly a villa, so as to have no unity of expression. Ideas of beauty, of various kinds, there certainly would be in such buildings, but no unity—nothing to indicate that they sprang from a single comprehensive feeling, or from one wise and consistent mind.

RELATIVE BEAUTY. Having shown the qualities of simple or absolute beauty—the sources of our pleasure in what is commonly called "beauty of form," we turn to the consideration of relative beauty—that beauty which expresses peculiar moral, social, or intellectual ideas, and which is usually termed "beauty of expression."

Relative beauty, in architecture, is the expression of elevated and refined ideas of man's life. In this art, its first and most powerful expressions are those of his public life, or his religious and intellectual nature—in the temple, the church, or the library or gallery of art—all forms of civil architecture. Its secondary expression is confined to the manifestation of his social and moral feelings, in the dwellings which man inhabits; and this is domestic architecture.

We cannot better convey an idea of the beauty of expression of which the grander generic forms or styles of architecture are capable, than by the following brief description by another hand:

In the forms of the Gothic cathedral are embodied *the worshipping principle, the loving reverence for that which is highest, and the sentiment of Christian brotherhood*, or that perception of affiliation which is founded on recognizing in man goodness and truth, and reverencing them in him. This is expressed in the principal lines, which are all vertical [aspiring, tending upward]; in the whole mass falling under, or within the *pyramidal* (the fire, or symbol of love) form; in the pointed character of all the openings, *ogive,* as the French call it, being the ideal line expressive of firmness of base, embracingness of tendency, and upward ascension, as its ultimate aim; and in the clustering and grouping of its multiple parts. Gothic architecture being thus representative rather of the unity of love, than of the diversities of faith, it seems proper that it should be the style used for all ecclesiastical and other purposes having reference to religious life.

But it is not Gothic art, alone, that has developed the form of some principle of life: all architecture is as expressive. In Roman art, we see the ideal of the *state* as fully manifested as is in the Gothic the ideal of the church. Its type-form is the *dome*—the encircling, overspreading dome, whose center is within itself, and which is the binding of all for the perfection of the whole. Hence the propriety of using this style in state houses, capitols, parliament houses, town halls, where this idea is to be expressed.

Again, we have the pure Greek temple as another architectural type. This can also be used in a special way (having its individual expression). It is the most simple, rational, and harmoniously elegant style that can be conceived, for simple halls, for public, oratorical, lecture, and philosophical rooms. Buildings which have but one object, and which require one expression of that object, cannot be built in a style better adapted to convey the single idea of their use, than in the Grecian-temple form. Here, with the single exception of the pediment (which distinctly, by its outline, marked the place as the abode of the gods, and the tympanum, which was always occupied by statues of the highest intelligence, and the representative arrangement of all deities expressive of the perfect subordination of all principles, human and divine, under the supremacy of Almighty Love), every thing falls under the *horizontal line*—the level line of rationality; it is all logical, orderly, syllogistically perfect, as the wisdom of the schools.

In domestic architecture, though the range of expression may at first seem limited, it is not so in fact, for when complete, it ought to be significant of the whole private life of man —his intelligence, his feelings, and his enjoyments.

Indeed, it is from this complexity of feelings and habits that domestic architecture is capable of a great variety of expression. This will not appear singular when we reflect that public buildings, for the most part, are intended for a single and definite use—as a church for public worship, or a town hall for political assemblies; while man's dwelling, in its most complete form, may be regarded as the type of his whole private life. It is true, the private life of many men is simple almost to monotony, but that of others abounds with infinite diversity.

Now, all this variety, in domestic life, is capable of being expressed, and really is expressed, in domestic architecture, especially in country architecture, which is not cramped in its manifestation, but develops itself freely, as a tree expands which is not crowded by neighbors in a forest, but grows in the unrestrained liberty of the open meadow.

If we pass an ill-proportioned dwelling, where the walls and the roof are built only to defend the inmates against cold and heat; the windows intended for nothing but to admit the light and exclude the air; the chimneys constructed only to carry off the smoke; the impression which that house makes upon us at a glance is that of mere utility.

If, on the other hand, the building is well proportioned, if there is a pleasing symmetry in its outward form, and (should it be large) if it display variety, harmony, and unity, we feel that it possesses much absolute beauty—the beauty of a fine form.

If, in addition to this, we observe that it has various marked features, indicating intelligent and cultivated life in its inhabitants; if it plainly shows by its various apartments that it is intended not only for the physical wants of man, but for his moral, social, and intellectual existence; if hospitality smiles in ample parlors: if home virtues dwell in cosy, fireside family rooms; if the love of the beautiful is seen in picture or statue galleries; intellectuality, in well-stocked libraries; and even a dignified love of leisure and repose, in cool and spacious verandas; we feel, at a glance, that here we have reached the highest beauty of which domestic architecture is capable—that of individual expression.

Hence, everything in architecture that can suggest or be made a symbol of social or domestic virtues adds to its beauty, and exalts its character. Every material object that becomes the type of the spiritual, moral, or intellectual nature of man becomes at once beautiful, because it is suggestive of the beautiful in human nature.

There are, doubtless, many persons who rarely analyze their feelings, and who usually see nothing of this beauty of expression in domestic architecture—they see only the fact that a house is a house (more or less costly, and therefore to be admired), a window a window, and a door a door: these are those who pay no attention to expression in nature—a daisy-spangled meadow is to them only a "field," or the most poetical landscape, only a "prospect"—those who never see their friends' characters in their faces, only in the *facts* of their lives. But this no more proves that the expression does not exist in all visible forms than that the earth is not round because common observation tells us it is flat.

More than this, beauty of expression, in architecture as in other arts, and even in nature, requires educated feeling— it is as obscure and imperceptible to the majority of those who have never sought for it, as the beauty of clouds or aerial perspective in landscapes is to the most ignorant plowman in the fields.

We are bound to add here that in all arts other thoughts may be expressed besides those of beauty. Vices may be expressed in architecture as well as virtues; the worst part of our natures as well as the best. A house built only with a view to animal wants, eating and drinking, will express sensuality instead of hospitality. A residence marked by gaudy and garish apartments, intended only to dazzle and impress others with the wealth or importance of the proprietor, will express pride and vanity instead of a real love of what is beautiful for its own sake; and a dwelling in which a large and conspicuous part is kept for show, to delude others into the belief of dignity and grace on our part, while our actual life is one in mean apartments, expresses anything but honest sincerity of character.

It requires the more judgment to guard against the effect of such vicious expression, because it is often coupled with some beauty. A house may be copied after a pure model, and thus possess absolute beauty in the fine symmetry and proportion of its leading forms, and yet be debased in certain parts by the expression of the pride, vanity, egotism, or other bad traits of its possessors.

Yet, after all, this, like all other manifestations of the individual man, while it has a tendency to degrade art, gives us the key to the character of the artist and the possessor. And we often find that the want of virtue and beauty of character in the owner of a house which is beautiful, because designed by other hands (a want which almost certainly shows itself in the details or the furniture), deadens or destroys its beauty by overlaying its fair features with a corrupt or vicious expression.

After these remarks, it will not appear singular to our readers that we believe much of the character of every man may be read in his house. If he has molded its leading features from the foundation, it will give a clue to a large part of his character. If he has only taken it from other hands, it will, in its internal details and use, show at a glance something of the daily thoughts and life of the family that inhabits it.

Admitting the truth of this, it is evident that domestic architecture is perfect only when it is composed so as to express the utmost beauty and truth in the life of the individual. It is not always that a proprietor can design his own house, or even that his architect knows him so completely as to make his work express the individual truly. Hence we seldom see entirely satisfactory architecture, where a beautiful house fully reflects a fine character; but as character always makes its mark, something of this kind always does happen, and in proportion to its completeness does it heighten our pleasure.*

The different *styles* of domestic architecture, as the Roman, the Italian, the Swiss, the Venetian, the rural-Gothic, are nothing more than expressions of national character, which have, through long use, become permanent. Thus, the gay and sunny temperament of the south of Europe is well expressed in the light balconies, the grouped windows, the open arcades, and the statue- and vase-bordered terraces of the Venetian and Italian villas: the homely, yet strong and quaint character of the Swiss, in their broad-roofed, half rude, and curiously constructed cottages: the domestic virtues, the love of home, rural beauty, and seclusion cannot possibly be better expressed than in the English cottage, with its many upward-pointing gables, its intricate tracery, its spacious bay windows, and its walls covered with vines and flowering shrubs.

There are positive and human elements of beauty in these styles which appeal at once to the feelings, but there is, besides, another source of pleasure to most minds, which springs not from the beauty of form or expression in these styles of architecture, but from personal or historical *asso-*

* Hence, also, it is impossible in a series of designs . . . to make any one of them entirely satisfactory, as a residence, to any individual of taste. To do this, the architect must know the man. All that we can do is to offer to the feelings and judgment of our readers a number of designs. If their own character is more or less typified in any one of them, that design will be at once preferred by them.

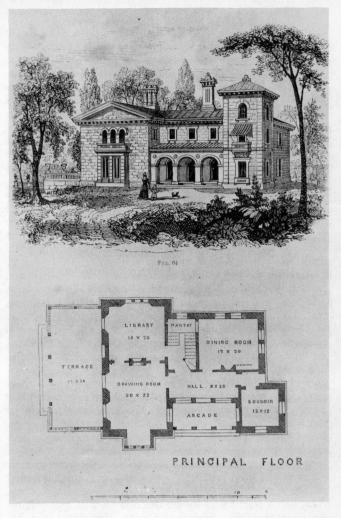

FIG. 64

LIBRARY
18 x 20

PANTRY

DINING ROOM
17 x 20

TERRACE
15 x 35

DRAWING ROOM
20 x 22

HALL 8 x 28

BOUDOIR
12 x 12

ARCADE

PRINCIPAL FLOOR

12. A. J. Downing?, A Villa in the Italian Style, from *Cottage Residences* (1842).

ciations connected with them; and which, by a process half
addressed to the feelings and half to the intellect, makes
them in the highest degree interesting to us. Something too
of novelty and strangeness makes mere *style* in architecture,
like accent in a foreign language, captivating to those whose
love of novelty is stronger than their love of what is
intrinsically beautiful. So far as an admiration of foreign
style in architecture arises from the mere love of novelty,
it is poor and contemptible; so far as it arises from an
admiration of truthful beauty of form or expression, it is
noble and praiseworthy. A villa in the style of a Persian
palace (of which there is an example lately erected in Connecticut), with its Oriental domes and minarets, equally
unmeaning and unsuited to our life or climate, is an example
of the former; as an English cottage, with its beautiful home
expression and its thorough comfort and utility, evinced in
steep roofs to shed the snow, and varied form to accommodate
modern habits, is of the latter.

Architectural style is only exhibited in its severity and
perfection in public buildings of the first class, whose dignity,
grandeur, and importance demand and permit it; such as
the church, the capitol, public institutions, etc. In them we
see, for example, the Gothic or Greek styles, in their greatest
completeness and fullest development. Domestic architecture,
on the contrary, should be less severe, less rigidly scientific,
and it should exhibit more of the freedom and play of feeling
of everyday life. A man may, in public halls, recite a poem
in blank verse, or deliver a studied oration with the utmost
propriety; but he would be justly the object of ridicule if at
the fireside he talked about the weather, his family, or his
friend in the same strain. What familiar conversation, however tasteful and well bred, is to public declamation, domestic
is to civil or ecclesiastical architecture; and we have no more
patience with those architects who give us copies of the temple
of Theseus, with its high, severe colonnades, for dwellings,
than with a friend who should describe his wife and children
to us in the lofty rhythm of Ossian. For this reason the
Italian, Venetian, Swiss, rural-Gothic, and our bracketed
style, all modified and subdued forms of the Gothic and
Greek styles, are the variations of those types most suitable
for domestic architecture.

A word or two may, perhaps, not be out of place here on

the *picturesque,* as distinguished from the beautiful, in architecture. Whatever critics may affirm, we look upon them as distinct in their nature, though often blended together in rural architecture.

The beautiful, in architecture, is the complete embodiment of ideas of beauty in a given material form; an embodiment in which the idea triumphs over the material and brings it into perfect subjection—we might almost say, of repose; where there is neither want of unity, proportion, harmony, nor the right expression.

The picturesque is seen in ideas of beauty manifested with something of rudeness, violence, or difficulty. The effect of the whole is spirited and pleasing, but parts are not balanced, proportions are not perfect, and details are rude. We feel at the first glance at a picturesque object, the idea of power exerted, rather than the idea of beauty which it involves.

As regularity and proportion are fundamental ideas of absolute beauty, the picturesque will be found always to depend upon the opposite conditions of matter—irregularity, and a partial want of proportion and symmetry. Thus the purest Greek architecture, or the finest examples of Palladio, are at once highly symmetrical and beautiful; the varied Italian villa, or the ruder Swiss chalet, highly irregular and picturesque.

As picturesqueness denotes power, it necessarily follows that all architecture in which beauty of expression strongly predominates over pure material beauty must be more or less picturesque. And as force of expression should rightly spring from force of character, so picturesque architecture, where its picturesqueness grows out of strong character in the inhabitant, is the more interesting to most minds: though if the beautiful, as we believe, signifies the perfect balance between a beautiful idea and the material form in which it is conveyed to the eye, a truly beautiful form, so rarely seen, and involving, of course, harmonious expression, whether it be in man, nature, or art, is more perfect and satisfactory than a picturesque one; as, in character, the beauty and symmetry of Washington is more satisfactory than the greater power and lesser balance of Napoleon; or, in nature, a "golden landscape of Arcady" is more perfect than a wild scene in the Hartz Mountains; or, in architecture, a villa of the most exquisite symmetry is more permanently pleasing than one of great irregularity. But this is, perhaps, pursuing the matter further than our readers require. We have gone far enough to show the sources of the two kinds of interest. And no person can harmoniously combine rural architecture and rural scenery unless he understands something, at least, of the nature of both.*

THE TRUE IN ARCHITECTURE

Having considered architecture as addressing the senses and the heart, let us examine what control the knowledge, reason, or judgment of man has over it.

Architecture may be useful, it may be beautiful, and still not altogether satisfactory, unless it is also truthful or significant. The intellect must approve what the senses relish and the heart loves.

Now it by no means follows that truth and beauty are the same thing; though some writers have labored hard to convince themselves of the existence of such a synonym. Artificial flowers or false gems may awaken the same ideas of beauty in the ignorant beholder as if they were real. A house built of lath and plaster may, with good proportions and fair ornaments, raise in us the same emotions of beauty as one built of marble or freestone. But the moment our reason discovers that beauty and truth are at variance, the pleasure is either greatly weakened, or altogether destroyed.

On the other hand, architecture may be full of truth, and yet from the want of proportion, symmetry, harmony, or expression, fall entirely short of real beauty.†

But although beauty and truth are not synonymous in art, all beauty, to be satisfactory, must be based upon truth. This

---

* In the fourth edition of our treatise on landscape gardening, we have endeavored more fully to develop the nature of the picturesque in scenery; and we refer those to that volume, who wish to aim at the production of the most harmonious effects by adapting the house to the scenery where it is to be placed. [See *A Treatise on the Theory and Practice of Landscape Gardening Adapted to North America* (New York, 1849).—ED.]

† And in this respect, architecture more than most other arts. A landscape painter, for instance, though he only copies the truth of nature, cannot fail in producing much beauty, because there is something of beauty in all nature's works; though he will not produce so much beauty as another artist who studies and reproduces only the finest and most beautiful ideas in nature.

is especially true in architecture, which, it must never be forgotten, is not only a beautiful art, but an art the primary condition of which is that it must be useful.

Now, there are three most important truths which all domestic architecture should present, and without which it must always be unsatisfactory. The first is, the *general truth* that the building is intended for a dwelling house; the second, the *local truth* that it is intended for a town or country house; and the third, the *specific truth* that it is intended for a certain kind of country house—as a cottage, farmhouse, or villa.

It may appear singular to one not accustomed to dwell on this subject that it should be necessary to insist on the value of so obvious a truth as that a dwelling house should look like a dwelling house. But, strange to say, men who are blinded by fashion or false taste are as likely to commit this violation of architectural truth as any other. We recall a villa on the banks of the Hudson, built in the form of a Doric temple, all the chimneys of which are studiously collected together in the center of the roof, and are hidden from even a suspicion of their existence by a sort of mask that resembles nothing, unless it be a classic well-curb set on the top of the house. Now, as chimneys, in a northern climate, are particularly expressive of human habitation and domestic life, any concealment of them is a violation of general truth, and one might well be puzzled to know what sort of edifice was intended in the villa in question. So, too, in the neighborhood of some of our cities, we still occasionally see houses which are pretty close imitations of Greek temples; as these buildings have sometimes as much space devoted to porticoes and colonnades as to rooms, one may well be pardoned for doubting exactly for what purpose they were designed.

Every feature, on the other hand, which denotes domestic life becomes a valuable truth in domestic architecture. Windows, doors, and chimneys are the first of these truths, though they are not the highest, as churches, factories, and outbuildings also have windows, doors, and chimneys; and therefore such windows, doors, and chimneys as particularly belong to or distinguish a dwelling house from all other buildings are more valuable truths than those forms that are merely useful without being truthful.

Verandas, piazzas, bay windows, balconies, and so on, are the most valuable general truths in domestic architecture; they

express domestic habitation more strongly because they are
chiefly confined to our own dwellings.*

Local truth in architecture is one which can never be
neglected without greatly injuring the effect of country houses.
And yet, such is the influence of fashion and false taste, and
so little do the majority of citizens trouble themselves to
think on this subject, that nothing is more common in some
parts of the country than to see the cockneyism of three-story
town houses violating the beauty and simplicity of country
life. In our own neighborhood, there is a brick house standing in the midst of gardens and orchard, which has a front
and rear pierced with windows, but only blank wall at the
sides; looking, in fact, precisely as if lifted out of a three-
story row in a well-packed city street, and suddenly dropped
in the midst of a green field in the country, full of wonder
and contempt, like a true cockney, at the strangeness and
dullness of all around it. During a drive on Long Island, last
autumn, we saw with pain and mortification the suburban villa
of a wealthy citizen, a narrow, unmistakable "six-story brick,"
which seemed, in its forlornness and utter want of harmony
with all about it, as if it had strayed out of town, in a fit of
insanity, and had lost the power of getting back again.

To give an expression of local truth to a country house,
it should always show a tendency to *spread out* and extend
itself on the ground, rather than to run up in the air. There
is space enough in the country; and because a citizen has
lived in town, where land is sold by the square foot, and
where, in consequence, he has had to mount four pair of stairs
daily, is surely no reason why he should compel himself to
do the same thing in the country. Indeed, economy in the
first cost of a house (that is to say, the lessened expense of
building two stories under the same roof and over the same
foundation) is the principal reason why most country houses
are not still more ample, extended, and rambling on the
surface than they usually are.

Another exhibition of the want of local truth in many large
country houses is seen in their internal arrangements. Their

* To show the difference between an idea of truth and one of beauty, we may
here remark that mere chimney tops, windows, verandas, and so on, though
in the highest degree valuable as truths, do not become beauties until they are
made beautiful by proportion, or grace of form, or by expressing some feeling
other than that of mere utility. A chimney may be an ugly chimney, and yet
give a truthful expression to a dwelling; or it may be a finely formed chimney,
and thus become a beautiful truth.

plan is, indeed, a hall running directly through the house, with two or four rooms on a floor, and hence the same meagerness, and want of variety and convenience, as in the cramped space of a small town house.

Specific truths, in our rural architecture, are perhaps less frequently neglected than the others. In the majority of cases. the amount of means to be expended prevents builders from making cottages look like villas. Still, there is undoubtedly a great want of perception of the value of specific truth in many cases here; but it arises, partly, from a foolish ambition in those who build cottages and wish to make them appear like villas; and, partly, from an ignorance of what the true beauty of a country cottage consists in—which is not architectural ornament so much as a good form, simplicity of details, and the rural embellishment of vines and foliage.

If all persons building in the country knew how much the beauty and pleasure we derive from rural architecture is enhanced by truthfulness, we should be spared the pain of seeing so many miserable failures in country houses of small dimensions. A cottage (by which we mean a house of small size) will never succeed in an attempt to impose itself upon us as a villa. Nay, it will lose its own peculiar charm, which is as great, in its way, as that of the villa. This throwing away the peculiar beauty and simplicity of a cottage, in endeavoring to imitate the richness and variety of a villa, is as false in taste as for a person of simple and frank character to lay aside his simplicity and frankness to assume the cultivation and polish of a man of the world. The basis for enduring beauty is truthfulness, no less in houses than in morals; and cottages, farmhouses, and villas which aim to be only the best and most agreeable cottages, farmhouses, and villas will be infinitely more acceptable to the senses, feelings, and understanding than those which endeavor to assume a grandeur foreign to their nature and purpose. This we say, too, with the fullest desire that the cottage should contain every comfort and refinement which our happy country, above all others, places within the reach of workingmen; and we say it because, being intelligent workingmen, they ought, more than the same class anywhere else, to feel the value and the dignity of labor, and the superior beauty of a cottage home which is truthful, and aims to be no more than it honestly is, over one that strives to be something which it is not.

In order to assist the reader in judging of truth in domestic architecture, we shall again refer to the significance of expression, form, and decoration in the cottage, farmhouse, and villa in succeeding pages.

A word or two may very properly be said here regarding truthfulness of materials.

The principle which the reason would lay down for the government of the architect, under this head, is the simple and obvious one that the material should *appear* to be what it is. To build a house of wood so exactly in imitation of stone as to lead the spectator to suppose it stone is a paltry artifice, at variance with all truthfulness.

When we employ stone as a building material, let it be clearly expressed: when we employ wood, there should be no less frankness in avowing the material. There is more merit in so using wood as to give to it the utmost expression of which the substance is capable than in endeavoring to make it look like some other material.*

There are certain architectural fictions, with regard to apparent truthfulness of material, which are so well understood as not to deceive, and are not, therefore, reprehensible ones: such as painting the surface of wooden, and cementing or stuccoing the exteriors of brick and stone houses. Protection from the weather demands this, and no one fails to recognize wood or solid walls, though entirely hidden from the eye. And in the case of stuccoed walls, the expression of strength and solidity is very properly conveyed to the eye by marking it off in courses, to denote the bonds and courses of the solid wall beneath, and to take away the mere lath-and-plaster look of a plain stuccoed wall. To mark off in courses a house actually built of lath and stucco, as we have sometimes seen done, is, on the other hand, a downright violation of architectural truth. For the same reason we would prefer to see the stuccoed exterior of a brick wall marked faintly, in small courses, so as to denote that brick is the material of

* Perhaps an exception may be allowed in the case of wooden verandas, and such light additions to buildings of solid materials as we often see added in this country, in districts where the stone is so hard as to be very costly when wrought into small parts, so that wood is often used, but is so painted and sanded as to harmonize with the stone. In this case, we say, the apparent untruthfulness is permissible, for the sake of a principle almost equally important—unity of effect; for nothing is more offensive to the eye than an avowed union of wood and stone in the same building. But, of course, this is a sacrifice to expediency; and the more truthful treatment, viz., making all portions of one material, is the only entirely satisfactory one.

the wall, rather than boldly in large courses, to signify stone. There is no reason why the stucco which only stands for stucco should not have an agreeable color, wholly different from those of the brick and stone put beneath it (because it is only when stone or brick is not altogether satisfactory to the eye that we cover it with stucco); but the principle of truth should lead us to point out, by the lines on the stucco, whether it cover a stone or brick wall.*

There is a glaring want of truthfulness, sometimes practiced in this country by ignorant builders, that deserves condemnation at all times. This is seen in the attempt to express a style of architecture which demands massiveness, weight, and solidity in a material that possesses none of these qualities. We could point to two or three of these imitations of Gothic castles, with towers and battlements built of wood. Nothing can well be more paltry and contemptible. The sugar castles of confectioners and pastry cooks are far more admirable as works of art. If a man is ambitious of attracting attention by his house, and can only afford wood, let him (if he can content himself with nothing appropriate) build a gigantic wigwam of logs and bark, or even a shingle palace, but not attempt mock battlements of pine boards, and strong towers of thin plank. The imposition attempted is more than even the most uneducated person of native sense can possibly bear.

As we shall develop, little by little, our views on these and other points already suggested in our remarks on the different classes of houses and the designs themselves in the succeeding pages, we shall not pursue these introductory remarks further at the present time.

We have, as we trust, already clearly impressed upon the reader the three principal sources of interest in all architecture, and especially in domestic architecture. We have shown how a house may be useful without being beautiful; how it may be useful and beautiful without being satisfactory

---

* Marking off stucco to indicate a stone wall is the common and prevalent mode in this country; though we have never seen brick expressed as we have suggested. This might be most easily and effectually done by pressing a mold, marked with lines, upon the face of the stucco, as soon as it is put on the wall. Patterns of various kinds were thus stamped upon the walls in Moorish architecture, with beautiful effect. The lines would always express that the wall beneath was of brick; but they should be only faintly impressed, and not deeply stamped, and without the mortar lines whitened so as to *imitate* brick.

to the understanding; and how it may be useful, beautiful, and significant or truthful, and thus thereby satisfy us fully and completely—satisfy all the rational desires of the senses, the affections, and the intellect.

If it fall short of this, it is not architecture in the true sense of the word—for as another writer has well observed, every fine art is the art of so treating objects as to give them a moral significance; and unless the architect can stamp both feeling and imagination, as well as utility, upon his work, he cannot truly be called an architect.

[pp. 1–38]

From the third section, "Rural Architecture," in RURAL ESSAYS (1853)

A FEW WORDS ON RURAL ARCHITECTURE

July, 1850

No one pretends that we have, as yet, either a national architecture or national music in America; unless our Yankee clapboard house be taken as a specimen of the first, and "Oh, Susannah" of the second fine art. But there is, on the other hand, perhaps, no country where there is more building or more "musicianing," such as they are, at the present moment. And as a perfect taste in arts is no more to be expected in a young nation, mainly occupied with the practical wants of life, than a knowledge of geometry is in an infant school, we are content with the large promise that we find in the present, and confidently look forward for fulfillment to the future.

In almost every other country, a few landlords own the land, which a great many tenants live upon and cultivate. Hence the general interest in building is confined to a comparatively small class, improvements are made in a solid and substantial way, and but little change takes place from one generation to another in the style of the dwelling and the manner of living.

But in this country we are, comparatively, all landlords. In the country, especially, a large part of the rural population own the land they cultivate, and build their own houses. Hence it is a matter of no little moment to them to avail themselves of every possible improvement in the manner of constructing their dwellings, so as to secure the largest amount of comfort, convenience, and beauty for the moderate sum which an American landholder has to spend. While the rural proprietors of the other continent are often content to live in the same houses, and with the same inconveniences as their forefathers, no one in our time and country, who has any of the national spirit of progress in him, is satisfied unless, in building a new house, he has some of the "modern improvements" in it.

This is a good sign of the times; and when we see it coupled with another, viz., the great desire to make the dwelling agreeable and ornamental as well as comfortable, we think there is abundant reason to hope, so far as the country is concerned, that something like a national taste will come in due time.

What the popular taste in building seems to us to require, just now, is not so much *impulse* as right *direction*. There are numberless persons who have determined, in building their new home in the country, that they "will have something pretty"; but precisely what character it shall have, and whether there is any character, beyond that of a "pretty cottage" or a "splendid house," is not perhaps very clear to their minds.

We do not make this statement to find fault with the condition of things; far from it. We see too much good in the newly awakened taste for the beautiful to criticize severely its want of intelligence as to the exact course it should take to achieve its object—or perhaps its want of definiteness as to what that object is, beyond providing an agreeable home. But we allude to it to show that, with a little direction, the popular taste now awakened in this particular department may develop itself in such a manner as to produce the most satisfactory and beautiful results.

Fifteen years ago there was but one idea relating to a house in the country. It must be a Grecian temple. Whether twenty-feet or two-hundred-feet front, it must have its columns and portico. There might be comfortable rooms behind them or not; that was a matter which the *severe* taste of the classical builder could not stoop to consider. The roof might be so flat that there was no space for comfortable servant's bedrooms, or the attic so hot that the second story was uninhabitable in a midsummer's day. But of what consequence was that, if the portico were copied from the temple of Theseus, or the columns were miniature imitations in wood of those of Jupiter Olympus?

We have made a great step onward in that short fifteen years. There is, to be sure, a *fashion* now in building houses in the country—almost as prevalent and despotic as its pseudoclassical predecessor, but it is a far more rational and sensible one, and though likely to produce the same unsatisfactory effect of all other fashions—that is, to substitute sameness and monotony for tasteful individuality—yet we gladly accept it as the next step onward.

We allude, of course, to the Gothic or English cottage, with steep roofs and high gables—just now the ambition of almost every person building in the country. There are, indeed, few things so beautiful as a cottage of this kind, well designed and tastefully placed. There is nothing, all the world over, so truly rural and so unmistakably country-like as this very cottage, which has been developed in so much perfection in the rural lanes and amidst the picturesque lights and shadows of an English landscape. And for this reason, because it is essentially rural and country-like, we gladly welcome its general naturalization (with the needful variation of the veranda, and so on, demanded by our climate) as the type of most of our country dwellings.

But it is time to enter a protest against the absolute and indiscriminate employment of the Gothic cottage in *every* site and situation in the country—whether appropriate or inappropriate—whether suited to the grounds or the life of those who are to inhabit it, or the contrary.

We have endeavored, in our work on country houses, just issued from the press, to show that rural architecture has more significance and a deeper meaning than merely to afford a "pretty cottage" or a "handsome house" for him who can afford to pay for it. We believe not only that a house may have an absolute beauty of its own, growing out of its architecture, but that it may have a relative beauty, no less interesting, which arises from its expressing the life and occupation of those who build or inhabit it. In other words, we think the home of every family possessed of character may be made to express that character, and will be most beautiful (supposing the character good) when in addition to architectural beauty it unites this significance or individuality.

We have not the space to go into detail on this subject here; and to do so would only be repeating what we have already said in the work in question. But the most casual reader will understand from our suggestion, that if a man's house can be made to express the best traits of his character, it is undeniable that a large source of beauty and interest is always lost by those who copy each other's homes without reflection, even though they may be copying the most faultless *cottage ornée*.

We would have the cottage, the farmhouse, and the larger country house all marked by a somewhat distinctive character of their own, so far as relates to making them complete and individual of their kind; and believing, as we do, that the beauty and force of every true man's life or occupation depend largely on his pursuing it frankly, honestly, and openly, with all the individuality of his character, we would have his house and home help to give significance to and dignify that daily life and occupation by harmonizing with them. For this reason, we think the farmer errs when he copies the filigree work of the retired citizen's cottage, instead of showing that rustic strength and solidity in his house which are its true elements of interest and beauty. For this reason, we think he who builds a simple and modest cottage in the country fails in attaining that which he aims at by copying, as nearly as his means will permit, the parlors, folding doors, and showy furniture of the newest house he has seen in town.

We will not do more at present than throw out these suggestions, in the hope that those about to build in the country will reflect that an entirely satisfactory house is one in which there are not only pretty forms and details, but one which has some *meaning* in its beauty, considered in relation to their own position, character, and daily lives.

MORAL INFLUENCE OF GOOD HOUSES

February, 1848

A very little observation will convince anyone that, in the United States, a new era in domestic architecture is already commenced. A few years ago, and all our houses, with rare exceptions, were built upon the most meager plan. A shelter from the inclemencies of the weather; space enough in which to eat, drink, and sleep; perhaps some excellence of mechanical workmanship in the details—these were the characteristic features of the great mass of our dwelling houses—and especially country houses—a few years ago.

A dwelling house, for a civilized man, built with no higher aspirations than these, we look upon the same feelings that inspire us when we behold the Indian, who guards himself against heat and cold by that primitive, and, as he considers it, sufficient costume—a blanket. An unmeaning pile of wood or stone serves as a shelter to the bodily frame of man; it does the same for the brute animals that serve him; the blanket covers the skin of the savage from the harshness of the elements as the thick shaggy coat protects the beasts he hunts in the forest. But these are only manifestations of the grosser wants of life; and the mind of the civilized and cultivated man as naturally manifests itself in fitting, appropriate, and beautiful forms of habitation and costume as it does in fine and lofty written thought and uttered speech.

Hence, as society advances beyond that condition in which the primary wants of human nature are satisfied, we naturally find that literature and the arts flourish. Along with great orators and inspired poets come fine architecture, and tasteful grounds and gardens.

Let us congratulate ourselves that the new era is fairly commenced in the United States. We by no means wish to be understood, that all our citizens have fairly passed the barrier that separates utter indifference or puerile fancy from good taste. There are, and will be for a long time, a large proportion of houses built without any definite principles of construction, except those of the most downright necessity. But, on the other hand, we are glad to perceive a very considerable sprinkling over the whole country—from the Mississippi to the Kennebec—of houses built in such a manner as to prove at first glance that the ideal of their owners has risen above the platform of mere animal wants: that they perceive the intellectual superiority of a beautiful design over a meaningless and uncouth form; and that a house is to them no longer a comfortable shelter merely, but an expression of the intelligent life of man, in a state of society where the soul, the intellect, and the heart are all awake, and all educated.

There are, perhaps, few persons who have examined fully the effects of a general diffusion of good taste, of well-being, and a love of order and proportion upon the community at large. There are, no doubt, some who look upon fine houses as fostering the pride of the few, and the envy and discontent of the many; and—in some transatlantic countries, where wealth and its avenues are closed to all but a few—not without reason. But, in this country, where integrity and industry are almost always rewarded by more than the means of subsistence, we have firm faith in the *moral* effects of the fine arts. We believe in the bettering influence of beautiful cottages and country houses—in the improvement of human nature necessarily resulting to all *classes* from the possession of lovely gardens and fruitful orchards.

We do not know how we can present any argument of this matter, if it requires one, so good as one of that long-ago distinguished man—Dr. Dwight. He is describing, in his *Travels in America,** the influence of good architecture, as evinced in its effects on the manners and character of the inhabitants in a town in New England:

There is a kind of symmetry in the thoughts, feelings, and efforts of the human mind. Its taste, intelligence, affections, and conduct are so intimately related that no preconcertion can prevent them from being mutually causes and effects. The first thing powerfully operated upon, and, in its turn, proportionately operative, is the taste. The *perception* of beauty and deformity, of refinement and grossness, of decency and vulgarity, of propriety and indecorum, is the first thing which influences man to attempt an escape from a groveling, brutish character; *a character in which morality is chilled, or absolutely frozen.* In most persons, this perception is

---

* Timothy Dwight (1752–1817), president of Yale (1795–1817); the book Downing refers to is *Travels in New England and New York* (1821).—Ed.

awakened by what may be called the *exterior* of society, particularly by the mode of building. Uncouth, mean, ragged, dirty houses, constituting the body of any town, will regularly be accompanied by coarse, groveling manners. The dress, the furniture, the mode of living, and the manners will all correspond with the appearance of the buildings, and will universally be, in every such case, of a vulgar and debased nature. On the inhabitants of such a town, it will be difficult, if not impossible, to work a conviction that intelligence is either necessary or useful. Generally, they will regard both learning and science only with contempt. Of morals, except in the coarsest form, and that which has the least influence on the heart, they will scarcely have any apprehensions. The rights enforced by municipal law they may be compelled to respect, and the corresponding duties they may be necessitated to perform; but the rights and obligations which lie beyond the reach of magistracy, in which the chief duties of morality are found, and from which the chief enjoyments of society spring, will scarcely gain even their passing notice. They may pay their debts, but they will neglect almost every thing of value in the education of their children.

The very fact, that men see good houses built around them will, more than almost anything else, awaken in them a sense of superiority in those by whom such houses are inhabited. The same sense is derived, in the same manner, from handsome dress, furniture, and equipage. The sense of beauty is necessarily accompanied by a perception of the superiority which it possesses over deformity; and is instinctively felt to confer this superiority on those who can call it their own, over those who cannot.

This, I apprehend, is the manner in which coarse society is first started toward improvement; for no objects, but those which are sensible, can make any considerable impression on coarse minds.

The first motive which leads men to build good houses is, no doubt, that of increasing largely their own comfort and happiness. But it is easy to see that, in this country, where so many are able to achieve a home for themselves, he who gives to the public a more beautiful and tasteful model of a habitation than his neighbors is a benefactor to the cause of morality, good order, and the improvement of society where he lives. To place before men reasonable objects of ambition, and to dignify and exalt their aims, cannot but be laudable in the sight of all. And in a country where it is confessedly neither for the benefit of the community at large, nor that of the succeeding generation, to amass and transmit great fortunes, we would encourage a taste for beautiful and appropriate architecture, as a means of promoting public virtue and the general good.

We have said beautiful and *appropriate* architecture—not without desiring that all our readers should feel the value of this latter qualification as fully as we do. Among the many strivings after architectural beauty which we see daily made by our countrymen, there are, of course, some failures, and only now and then examples of perfect success. But the rock on which all novices split—and especially all men who have thought little of the subject, and who are satisfied with a feeble imitation of some great example from other countries— this dangerous rock is *want of fitness,* or *propriety.* Almost the first principle, certainly the grand principle, which an apostle of architectural progress ought to preach in America, is, "Keep in mind PROPRIETY." Do not build your houses like temples, churches, or cathedrals. Let them be, characteristically, dwelling houses. And more than this; always let their individuality of purpose be fairly avowed; let the cottage be a cottage—the farmhouse a farmhouse—the villa a villa, and the mansion a mansion. Do not attempt to build a dwelling upon your farm after the fashion of the town house of your friend, the city merchant; do not attempt to give the modest little cottage the ambitious air of the ornate villa. Be assured that there is, if you will search for it, a peculiar beauty that belongs to each of these classes of dwellings that heightens and adorns it almost magically; while, if it borrows the ornament of the other, it is only debased and falsified in character and expression. The most expensive and elaborate structure, overlaid with costly ornaments, will fail to give a ray of pleasure to the mind of real taste, if it is not appropriate to the purpose in view, or the means or position of its occupant; while the simple farmhouse, rustically and tastefully adorned, and ministering beauty to hearts that answer to the spirit of the beautiful, will weave a spell in the memory not easily forgotten.

[pp. 205–213]

8

Calvert Vaux, VILLAS AND COTTAGES. / A SERIES OF / DESIGNS PREPARED FOR EXECUTION / IN THE / UNITED STATES (New York, 1857), pp. 13–17, 30–37, 39–40.

Calvert Vaux (1824–1895) was born in England and educated there as an architect and landscape gardener; he emigrated to the United States in 1850 through the influence of A. J. Downing, whose partner he subsequently became. After Downing's death, Vaux continued alone until 1857 when he went into partnership in New York City with Frederick Law Olmsted. That partnership made the plans for Central, Riverside, and Morningside parks in New York, for Prospect Park in Brooklyn, and for the New York State Reservation at Niagara Falls. His life was gradually divided between a career as designer and a career as a public official; as landscape architect to the Department of Parks in New York City, he championed the original designs for the Central Park territory, and managed, with considerable political effort, to preserve that territory intact. His writing extends the patterns established by Downing, but he is less analytic and abstract in his attempts to rationalize architectural goals, and his point of view tends to be that of the critical outsider who observes the American scene and councils "education and the diffusion of knowledge" as the social and political basis of a healthy architecture.

From "Preliminary Chapter," VILLAS AND COTTAGES *(1857)*

Although there is a cheering prospect for American architecture in the good time coming, its present appearance is in many ways far from satisfactory. Over the length and breadth of this country are scattered cities and villages by thousands, and public and private edifices innumerable; and yet we may fairly say, There are the buildings, but where is the architecture? There is the matter, but where is the manner? There is the opportunity, but where is the agreeable result? Is it in the churches? A few really creditable specimens may be pointed out, but the large majority are unquestionably deficient in truthful dignity and artistic beauty. Is it in the public buildings? Several fine works of art may at once occur to the mind, and although a floating doubt somewhat questions the Americanism of their expression, still, as they are nobly conceived and do not shrink from the ordeal of the artist's pencil, it is granted that they are successful. Then comes the question of the great majority again. Does the memory linger with pleasure over the reminiscences of a provincial tour, and delight to recall the pleasant impression left on the mind by each elm-shaded town, with its tasteful hall, schoolhouses, library, theatre, museum, banks, baths, courts of justice, and other buildings cheerfully erected and gracefully arranged by its free and enlightened inhabitants—for their own use and pleasure, of course, but with a wise regard for mutual advantage and individual enjoyment, that ensures the sympathy of every passing stranger; the more readily, too, as each discovers that he, even he, has been thought of, and that some study has been expended to give him pleasure? No, this is not the result to be looked for at present. Does the secret of beauty lie in the private buildings, the stores, the warehouses, the mansions, the villas, the hotels, the streets, or the cottages? There are probably as magnificent hotels and stores in the large cities of America as anywhere in the world. Architecture, within the last ten years, has managed to get a genuine foothold in this department of building; it has begun to *pay*, and that is an excellent sign, and one that offers food for reflection and solid encouragement; yet it is the few and not the many, even here, that speak of refinement, and a love of grace, which is as averse to meretricious display as it is to ungainly awkwardness. Among the private residences a great number are excellent; but still the mass are unsatisfactory in form, proportion, color, and light and shade. What is the reason of all this? Why is there comparatively so little beauty in American buildings? Some will say America is a dollar-loving country, without taste for the arts; others, that expense is the obstacle, and that the republican simplicity of America can not afford the luxury of good architecture. The latter of these solutions is clearly incorrect, for it is knowledge, and not money, that is the chief source of every pleasurable emotion that may be caused by a building. Indeed a simple, well-planned structure costs less to execute, for the accommodation obtained, than an ill-planned one; and the fact of its being agreeable and effective, or otherwise, does not depend on any ornament that may be superadded to the useful and necessary forms of which it is composed, but on the arrangement of those forms themselves, so that they may balance each other and suggest the pleasant ideas of harmonious proportion, fitness, and agreeable variety to the eye, and through the eye to the mind. All this is simply a matter of *study before* building, not of additional *cost in* building. The other solution of the problem, that Americans do not appreciate the beautiful, and do not care for it or value it, is a more specious but equally erroneous one. There are, doubtless, many obstructions that have hindered, and do hinder, the development of correct taste in the United States. The spring, however, is by no means dry, although these obstacles prevent its waters from flowing freely; and there is, in fact, no real difficulty that earnestness and ordinary patience may not overcome. One important evidence of a genuine longing for the beautiful may be at once pointed out. Almost every American has an equally unaffected, though not, of course, an equally appreciative, love for "the country." This love appears intuitive, and the possibility of ease and a country place or suburban cottage, large or small, is a vision that gives a zest to the labors of industrious thousands. This one simple fact is of marked importance; it shows that there is an innate homage to the natural in

Origins of philistinism

contradistinction to the artificial—a preference for the works of God to the works of man; and no matter what passing influences may prevent the perfect working of this tendency, there it exists; and with all its town-bred incongruities and frequently absurd shortcomings, it furnishes a valuable proof of inherent good, true, and healthy taste. Moreover, the greater includes the less. An actual love for nature, however crude it may be, speaks clearly of a possible love for art.

Till within a comparatively recent period the fine arts in America have been considered by the great bulk of the population as pomps and vanities so closely connected with superstition, popery, or aristocracy that they must be eschewed accordingly, and the result is not *altogether* undesirable, though it has appeared to retard the advance of refinement and civilization. The awakening spirit of republicanism refused to acknowledge the value of art as it then existed, a tender hothouse plant ministering to the delights of a select few. The democratic element rebelled against this idea *in toto,* and tacitly, but nonetheless practically, demanded of art to thrive in the open air, in all weathers, for the benefit of all, if it was worth anything, and if not, to perish as a troublesome and useless encumbrance. This was a severe course to take, and the effects are everywhere felt. But, after all, it had truth on its side; and candor must allow that no local, partial, class-recognizing advance in art, however individually valuable its examples might have been, could, in reality, have compensated for the disadvantage that would have attended it. Now, every step in advance, slow though it be, is a real step taken by the whole country. When we look at the ruins of old Rome, we say, What a great people! what temples! what mighty works! and undoubtedly Rome was really great *in individuals*; very great in a strong and clever minority, who spent with marked ability the labor of the weak and ignorant majority; but the *plebs,* the unlettered, unthought-of common people, the million, were not great, nor were they taught to be so, and therefore Rome fell.

During the last hundred years there has been a continuous effort to give to the American million the rudiments of self-reliant greatness, to abolish class legislation, and to sink the importance of individuals. *"Aut America aut nullus"*— "America or no *one*," has been, is, and will probably ever be the practical motto. It is not surprising, then, that the advancement in the arts has been somewhat less rapid than the progress in commercial prosperity and political importance. The conditions were new, and, it must be confessed, rather hard. Continuous ease and leisure readily welcome art, while constant action and industry require time to become acquainted with its merits. To the former, it may be a parasite and yet be supported; to the latter, it must be a friend or nothing. The great bulk of money that is laid out on building in the United States belongs to the active workers, and is spent by them and for them. The industrious classes, therefore, decide the national standard of architectural taste.

The question then occurs, How is this universal taste to be improved? There is the sound, healthy material, unprejudiced, open to conviction, with a real though not thoroughly understood desire for what is good and true—there is plenty of prosperity and opportunity, plenty of money and industry, plenty of everything but education and the diffusion of knowledge. . . .

[pp. 13–17]

In America perfect liberty, that absolute essential for healthy life, has been, in due course, talked for, fought for, legislated for, and, in these free States, decidedly realized; and it seems, therefore, scarcely fair now to train all the best men to be lawyers and politicians, because the talent is more wanted somewhere else. The sensation of freedom is nothing more than the felt certainty of noninterference, and, however complete it may be, it can neither supply the will to do anything, nor suggest any deed to be done; it is like light, only perceptible when reflected from an object; it offers a solid rock on which to build, but not one idea for the superstructure adapted to it. In America this rock commands a boundless prospect, and no fitting or enduring edifice can be erected on it that does not include the most liberal manners, the most generous aspirations, the most noble institutions, and the most pure and beautiful arts that unfettered humanity is capable of conceiving. There has not, indeed, been, from the commencement of the world till this moment, an opportunity for the advance of the fine arts so replete with the material of true success as now exists in America; this advance is a question of choice, not time; of purpose, not ability; of direction, not force; there is *capacity* enough spread over all the country, and being wasted daily: it is *conviction* and *will* that are needed.

When the talent and energy that are fostered by American institutions are distributed with tolerable fairness, we shall, among many other things, be justified in expecting to find in every architectural effort, not something so new that it is unintelligible, but some distinctive characteristics that show it to be a genuine American invention. These, however, can hardly be expected to depend much on the employment of really new forms. Webster and Clay were orators of originality, but their words were all old. Their stock in trade is common property in the form of a dictionary, and the boundary lines, over which neither ever ventured to pass, are fairly set forth in a good grammar. Any desire on their part to invent a brand-new language would have been, of course, absurd, and any wish to produce a brand-new style of building is, without doubt, an equally senseless chimera.

All previous experience in architecture is the inherited property of America, and should be taken every advantage of. Each beautiful thought, form, and mode that is not unsuited to the climate and the people ought to be studied, sifted, and tested, its principles elucidated, and itself improved on; but the past should always be looked on as a servant, not as a master.

Individual sentiment and education should be encouraged to act freely in every instance, and by degrees that important fact, a genuine public taste, will be fairly unfolded. The authority of precedents will then be unneeded, for actual ideas, such as "fitness," "unity," "variety," will give the critical standard to the general taste. Every individual of sound mind will then help to improve the national architecture, for each will resolutely refuse to admire any structure that does not seem agreeable to him or her individually, and all will freely insist on a right to call *good* whatever coincides with their untrammeled, but not uncultivated, natural perceptions. Emerson says forcibly on this point, "Why need we copy the Doric or the Gothic model? Beauty, convenience, grandeur of thought, and quaint expression are as near to us as to any, and if the American artist will study with hope and love the precise thing to be done by him, considering the climate, the soil, the length of day, the wants of the people, the habit and form of government, he will create a home in which all these will find themselves fitted, and taste and sentiment will be satisfied also."*

In a country like this, where the printing press accompanies each stride that is made into new localities, and where every step is marked by a building of some sort, it seems inconsistent that there should be but little popular literature on architectural matters; yet such is undoubtedly the fact, and although Americans are certainly diligent readers and energetic builders, their habit of reading has scarcely had so much influence for good on their habit of building as might naturally be expected, when we consider the practical character and universally recurring interest of the subject of domestic architecture.

It has not, certainly, till within the last few years, been an easy matter to place before the public the necessary illustrations in a convenient form, and as mere verbal descriptions of plans or designs are seldom thoroughly intelligible, this difficulty has probably retarded the diffusion of popular architectural information. Now, however, with the present rapid development and general application of the art of wood engraving in the United States, this hindrance no longer exists, and a fair field is open for the free communication of ideas among American architects, and for the profitable interchange of hints and suggestions.

The study of what has been done by other nations, though useful as a help, will never, by itself, lead to much result in America, where the institutions, the needs of the climate, and the habits of the people have a distinctive character that requires special consideration; and this remark applies particularly to rural architecture. Thus the Greek mode, though completely beautiful when contemplated from a proper point of view, has for its leading characteristic a passionless repose that is not heartily sympathized with either by the American atmosphere or the spirit of this locomotive age; and, consequently, no architectural effort imitated from the Greek can help being, to a great extent, a mere lifeless parody. The failure is generally very conspicuous, but even in the least unsatisfactory instances some absurd incon-

* From "Self-Reliance," in *Essays, First Series* (Boston, 1841), quoted p. 111 in this anthology.

sistency is sure to assert itself. Common sense will insist on chimneys and verandas, and the pure classic outline in due course suffers grievous mutilation, being thus punished for its intrusion into a locality where it had no business to be attempted.

Styles like the Chinese or Moorish assist us but little, though each exhibits isolated features that deserve careful examination. The Moorish, for example, shows what magical effects may be produced by light, recessed arcades, and gives some good suggestions for verandas. The Chinese again, with its trellises and balconies, is interesting in detail; but neither of these phases of architectural taste is of comprehensive value. They are very deficient in compactness and completeness of plan, and in artistic design they depend too much for their effect on delicate and elaborate ornamentation; such decorations as paneling, carving, painting, and gilding may be readily enough obtained where a clever, industrious, efficient pair of hands can be hired for a few spoonfuls of rice per diem, but not so easily in a country where everyone is as good as his neighbor "and better," and where ordinary mechanics ask and get two or three dollars for a day's work. The irregular Italian, and the later modifications of the Gothic, are the most useful types to analyze; but the flat-terraced roofs of the first have to be avoided on account of the snow, and the latter has to be adapted to the use of verandas before it can be acceptable. Nor is this all: there is in this country a perpetual necessity for compactness of plan, however large the house may be, because, as it is invariably difficult to get efficient servants, it is desirable to save labor in every possible way. In this particular neither the Italian nor the Gothic examples help us materially; they delight too much in halls and passages, long corridors and wide vestibules, galleries, and staircases. This sort of rambling arrangement does not answer here—the difficulties of heating and service render a closer attention to concentration desirable—nevertheless, a sufficient privacy, and a freedom from any appearance of meanness, is the right of every house, however small its scale. The English country houses and cottages have undoubtedly claims to our best consideration; but it is from an examination, by means of illustrations, of what is going on at home, called forth by the actual needs of people, more than from a study of foreign examples, that the general taste for architectural comfort and beauty in country houses is likely to improve. Any genuine step in advance will be responded to at once by the sympathetic perceptive faculties of individuals who may notice it, and the result, so far as it bears on their needs, will remain daguerreotyped in the memory. Whatever, on the other hand, has no reference to local habits and experience will be passed over without receiving much consideration. Every active-minded man is in a position to understand and criticize such examples, and though they may have little of the pretension or extent that specimens of villa architecture in other differently constituted countries would afford, they will have the practical advantage of offering definite starting points for farther improvement at home.

This would hardly hold good if there was very little doing; but such is not the case. There has been latterly an immense number of buildings of this nature going up in all parts of the United States; numberless villages have sprung into existence, and much thought has been given to the subject. A very transient visit into any part of the country shows, however, that most of the villas and cottages are erected without regard to artistic propriety, and at considerable loss to their owners from the useless outlay incurred by adopting ill-considered plans, and the subject, as well as the majority of the houses, would be improved by a little more ventilation. Square boxes, small and large, are springing up in every direction, constructed without any attempt at proportion, or the slightest apparent desire to make them agreeable objects in the landscape. These tell their tale simply and unceremoniously: they are the natural result of the migratory, independent spirit pervading the industrious classes in America, and offer interesting evidences of the genuine prosperity of the country, for they show not only that the landlord and tenant system is disliked, but that almost every storekeeper and mechanic can contrive, even when quite young, to buy his own lot and live in his own house. On the other hand, however, they demonstrate that the capacity for enjoyment and the appreciation of what is really desirable in life, that should naturally accompany this active and successful industry, are wanting. Each of these bare, bald, white cubes tells its monotonous story of a youth passed with little or no cultivation of the higher natural perceptions, and of a system of education in which the study of the beautiful in its most simple elements is neglected and apparently despised. The lack of taste perceptible all over the country in small buildings is a decided bar to healthy social enjoyments; it is a weakness that affects the whole bone and muscle of the body politic; and it is a needless inconsistency, for a full exercise of freedom of speech and action should naturally result in a full, free exercise of the innocent enjoyment that unfettered industry renders possible, and a refined propriety and simple, inexpensive grace ought habitually to be the distinctive marks of every habitation in which a free American dwells.

Unfortunately, however, this is not the case. Even the village school itself, in which the earliest and most active germs of progressive thought are commenced, is almost universally a naked, shabby structure, without a tree or a shrub near it, and is remarkable chiefly for an air of coarse neglect that pervades its whole aspect. The improvement of the village schoolhouse is probably the most powerful and available lever that can be applied toward effecting a change for the better in the appearance of rural buildings generally: all see it, all are interested in it, and all are more or less influenced by its conduct and appearance. It is placed under the control of the leading men in each place, and it might easily be made the most cheerful and soul-satisfying building in the neighborhood, instead of, as at present, a God-forsaken, forlorn-looking affair, that is calculated to chill the heart and insult the eye of every thoughtful beholder. The cost would be utterly incommensurate with the advantage to be obtained. An extra hundred or hundred and fifty dollars at first starting would do much. The roof might then have a good projection, and be neatly finished. Some sort of simple porch might be added; the chimney might be slightly ornamented, and the rest would then depend on proportion, color, and surrounding the building from time to time with shrubs, creeping vines, and young trees. These, in afteryears, would offer a welcome shade, and give an air of domestic comfort and liberal vitality to the whole effect. A similar result, through precisely similar means, would probably, in course of time, be arrived at in the small cottages in its vicinity, and, as success would be cheap and invariable, the example would have a fair chance of spreading. [pp. 30–37]

One especial disadvantage that rural art labors under in America is that the plans of country towns and villages are so formal and unpicturesque. They generally consist of square blocks of houses, each facing the other with conventional regularity; and this arrangement is so discordant with the varied outlines characterizing American scenery, that Dame Nature refuses, at the outset, to have anything to do with them, and they never seem afterward to get any better acquainted with her. Except, perhaps, in a very large city, there is no advantage gained by this intense monotony of arrangement, and it is much to be regretted that in the many new villages that are being erected the same dull, uninteresting method is still predominant.

The great charm in the forms of natural landscape lies in its well-balanced irregularity. This is also the secret of success in every picturesque village, and in every picturesque garden, country house, or cottage. Human nature, when allowed a free, healthy scope, loves heartily this well-balanced irregularity, and longs for it in life, in character, and in almost everything. It is the possession of this same quality, even when the balance is incompletely kept, that makes the stirring, unconventional, free-spirited man so much more interesting and agreeable than the cold, correct, and somewhat unsympathetic gentleman who never does any harm to anyone, and whose equanimity is never disturbed. We want far less formality and restraint in the plans of our new villages. The roads should wind in graceful, easy curves, and be laid out in accordance with the formation of the ground and the natural features of interest. A single existing tree ought often to be the all-sufficient reason for slightly diverting the line of a road, so as to take advantage of its shade, instead of cutting it down and grubbing up its roots. In a case that recently occurred near a country town at some distance from New York, a road was run through a very beautiful estate, one agreeable feature of which was a pretty though small pond that, even in the dryest seasons, was always full of water, and would have formed an agreeable adjunct to a country seat. A single straight pencil line on the plan doubtless marked out the direction of the road; and as this line happened to go straight through the pond, straight through the pond was the road accordingly carried, the owner of the estate personally superintending the operation, and thus spoiling his sheet of water, diminishing the value of his lands, and increasing expense by the cost of filling in, without any advantage whatever: for a winding road so laid out as to skirt the pond would have been far more attractive and agreeable than the harsh, straight line that is now scored like a railway track clear through the undulating surface of the property; and such barbarisms are of constant occurrence. Points of this nature deserve the utmost attention, instead of the reckless disregard they generally meet with. When once a road is laid out, its fate is settled, and no alteration is likely to be made: it is, therefore, the more desirable that its direction should be well studied in the first instance.

[pp. 39–40]

9

James Jackson Jarves, ART-HINTS. / ARCHITEC-
TURE, SCULPTURE, / AND / PAINTING (New
York, 1855), pp. 11–14; THE / ART-IDEA: /
SCULPTURE, PAINTING AND ARCHITECTURE IN
AMERICA (New York, 1864), pp. 286–314.

James Jackson Jarves (1818–1888) was an American
author and art collector who traveled widely not only in
Europe but also in South America and in the Pacific. He wrote
as an "amateur" in the arts (and as a sort of "amateur"
cultural anthropologist), though it should be noted that his
word "amateur" reflects the fact that the history and criticism
of art was not regarded as a profession in nineteenth-century
America. His point of view toward the arts and toward what
he called the "principles" of the countries in which he
traveled and lived is characterized by his phrase "as seen
through American spectacles," spectacles that had a decidedly
Emersonian focus. "Art in America" he regarded with qualified optimism: "Freedom gives Art birth; but virgin soils
also produce choking tares. Cultivation is requisite to weed
them out." It was Jarves's announced intention to write "in
a popular form" in the attempt to accomplish that requisite
cultivation of his countrymen.

From Chapter I, "Introductory," in ART-HINTS (1855)

America—I mean the United States—is but just girding
her loins for the race set before her. While men have to
contend with stern nature, winning civilization step by step

from the wilderness, they have no leisure for aught but the necessary. The useful is the next step. Then come the requirements of ease and luxury, and their attendant train of degenerating influences. In the United States we have arrived at that period of our national career; or rather, while on our frontiers, the strife of man with nature is in constant progress, on our seaboard we have enslaved her to the administration of our sensual comforts to a degree that no other nation has ever rivaled on so gigantic a scale. History tells us there is danger in this. Upholstery, dainty furniture, mechanics racked to construct in quantities those things that tend to glitter or mislead, machinery multiplied for the fabrication of all objects, not only of use but of ornament, art degraded to manufacture, all bespeak a people with their eyes yet unopened to a sense of their full capacity for greatness and refinement. There is no halting place in a nation's career. She advances or recedes. If she mistake the road, others advance on the right track and secure the prize. There is more hope for America in her future than for any other nation. In proportion to her hope is also her danger, for the principle which bids her soar is equally active to bring her down. This principle is freedom of mind. Elsewhere the governments make their subjects; in America, alone, individuals make their governments; as is the individual so is the government. The importance, then, of rightly directing not only the principles but the taste—in its full significance, to be hereafter defined—is self-evident. The love and fear of God is indeed the keystone to the political arch. In proportion as religion demonstrates these principles in their acceptance to man, in that proportion are they wise for this life and safe for another. But strip religion of its element of beauty, crush the taste and refinement of a nation in the anaconda grasp of bigotry, and you shut out heaven from earth, and turn earth itself into a wilderness of unprofitable duties. Heroic virtues and stern self-denial are for times of trial, when the soul's energies must be concentrated by the struggles of existence into mighty efforts. But with the passing of the storm comes the sunshine. Hearts are to soften and expand under its genial warmth. Love is to elevate and taste to refine them. The energies which have raised America to the position of an enigma for all nations must still find employment. License, the fruit of misdirected passion, and effeminacy, the canker of luxury, are equally stumbling blocks in her progress. She has strength and wealth, freedom and mental activity. The right direction to be given to each is the problem to settle. Art looks to America with open arms. How is it to be carried there? Not by misses who run over Europe and bring back a cabinload of new bonnets, with dresses and trinkets to match; neither by women whose aim is display and ruling principle vanity; nor by young gentlemen whose attainments are limited to the run of "cafés" and gambling saloons. We have too many of them, and too many of such families as that of Santa Maria della Salute, whose sole reminiscences of European travel are the number and not the quality of sights. We need art students, men of sincerity and labor, who will not hesitate to go on their backs and knees, if need be in the dust, to read the soul-language of the mightiest minds in Europe.

Europe is a storehouse of art, but its value and lessons are lost in a great measure upon the nations that gave it birth. Still those silent voices speak. Out of old churches, moldering tombs, time-honored galleries, there go forth eternal principles of truth, if rightly studied able to guide the taste and warm the heart of young America, and urge her on in the race of renown. I do not advocate blind copying of mind or the reception of laws, whether of taste or morality, without fully proving their spirit; but I do advocate, and would press home to the heart of every American who goes abroad, the necessity, if he would do his duty to his own country, of reading and interpreting to his countrymen, so far as in him lies, these sacred writings on the wall. Talent is lent by God. We are to return it with usury. I write not for those light minds who find pleasure only in frivolity, and who travel simply for excitement; their case is hopeless. I write for my young friend of the Venetian church. With earnest souls like his lies the artistic hope of America.

[pp. 11–14]

From THE ART-IDEA *(1864)*

CHAPTER XVII / REVIEW OF AMERICAN ARCHITECTURE, PAST
AND PRESENT—THE PROSPECT BEFORE IT—SUMMARY OF
FUNDAMENTAL PRINCIPLES

Our synopsis of the art-idea would be incomplete without
referring to the condition of architecture in America. Strictly
speaking, we have no architecture. If, as has happened to
the Egyptians, Ninevites, Etruscans, Pelasgians, Aztecs, and
Central American races, our buildings alone should be left,
by some cataclysm of nations, to tell of our existence, what
would they directly express of us? Absolutely nothing! Each
civilized race, ancient or modern, has incarnated its own
aesthetic life and character in definite forms of architecture,
which show with great clearness their indigenous ideas and
general conditions. A similar result will doubtless in time
occur here. Meanwhile we must look at facts as they now
exist. And the one intense, barren fact which stares us fixedly
in the face is that, were we annihilated tomorrow, nothing
could be learned of us, as a distinctive race, from our architecture. It is simply substantial building, with ornamentation,
orders, styles, or forms, borrowed or stolen from European
races, an incongruous medley as a whole, developing no
system or harmonious principle of adaptation, but chaotic,
incomplete, and arbitrary, declaring plagiarism and super-
ficiality, and proving beyond all question the absolute poverty
of our imaginative faculties, and general absence of right
feeling and correct taste. Whether we like it or not, this is
the undeniable fact of 1864. And not merely this: an explorer
of our ruins would often be at a loss to guess the uses or
purposes of many of our public edifices. He could detect
bastard Grecian temples in scores, but would never dream
they were built for banks, colleges, or customhouses. How
could he account for ignoble and impoverished Gothic chapels,
converted into libraries, of which there is so bad an example
at Cambridge, Massachusetts, or indeed for any of the architectural anomalies which disfigure our soil and impeach our
common sense, intensified as they frequently are by a total

disregard of that fundamental law of art which demands the harmonious relation of things, condemning the use of stern granite or adamantine rock in styles where only beautiful marbles can be employed with aesthetic propriety, or of cold stones in lieu of brick, or the warmer and yet more plastic materials belonging of right to the variety and freedom of Gothic forms? If the mechanical features of our civilization were left to tell the national story, our ocean clippers, river steamers, and industrial machines would show a different aspect. They bespeak an enterprise, invention, and development of the practical arts that proclaim the Americans to be a remarkable people. If, therefore, success attend them in whatever they give their hearts and hands to, it is but reasonable to infer that cultivation need but be stimulated in the direction of architecture to produce results commensurate with the advance in mechanical and industrial arts. If one doubt this, let him investigate the progress in shipbuilding from the point of view of beauty alone, and he will discover a success as complete in its way as was that of the builders of Gothic cathedrals and Grecian temples. And why? Simply, that American merchants took pride in naval architecture. Their hearts were in their work; their purses opened without stint; and they built the fastest and handsomest ships.

To excel in architecture we must warm up the blood to the work. The owner, officer, and sailor of a gallant ship love her with sympathy as of a human affinity. A ship is not *it,* but *she* and *her,* one of the family; the marvel of strength and beauty; a thing of life, to be tenderly and lovingly cared for and proudly spoken of. All the romance of the trader's heart —in the West, the steamboat holds a corresponding position in the taste and affections of the public—goes out bountifully toward the symmetrical, stately, graceful object of his adventurous skill and toil. Ocean clippers and river steamers are fast making way for locomotive and propeller, about which human affections scarce can cluster, and which art has yet to learn how to dignify and adorn. But the vital principle, *love of the work,* still lives, that gave to the sailing vessel new grace and beauty, combining them with the highest qualities of utility and strength into a happy unity of form. As soon as an equal love is turned toward architecture, we may expect as rapid a development of beauty of material form on land as on the ocean.

Our forefathers built simply for protection and adaptation. Their style of dwelling houses was suited to the climate, materials at hand, and social exigencies. Hence it was true and natural. They could not deal in artifice or plagiarism, because they had no tricks of beauty to display and nothing to copy. Over their simple truth of expression time has thrown the veil of rustic enchantment, so that the farmhouses still standing of the period of the Indian wars are a much more pleasurable feature of the landscape than their pretentious villa-successors of the nineteenth century.

The public buildings of our colonial period are interesting solely from association. Anything of architectural pretense, more destitute of beauty, it would be difficult to originate; and yet, as meager a legacy as they are of the native styles of ancestral England and Holland at that date, they avoid the worst faults of ornamentation and plagiarism of later work. Any of them might have been sent over the seas to order, like a dress coat, and placed wherever needed, without other thought than to get a substantial building for as little money as possible. Yet there is about them, as well as the aristocratic mansions of colonial times, a certain quiet dignity of constructural expression which bespeaks conscious rank and gentlemanly breeding. It is true, they have misplaced pilasters, pillars, and other incongruous thefts of classical architecture, in mathematical rank-and-file order upon wall surfaces, with which they have nothing in common in feature or spirit, but, notwithstanding the pettinesses of the pettiest of the imitators of Wren or Jones, they are not overborne and crushed by them, but wear them with as self-possessed an air as their owners did foreign orders and titles, rejoicing in possessing conventional distinctions of rank not had by their neighbors.

Fergusson* says, "There was not a building erected in the United States before A.D. 1814, worthy of being mentioned as an example of architectural art." This sweeping assertion may disturb the serenity of those who look upon the City Hall of New York, the State House at Boston,† and buildings of their time and class as very wonderful. We agree entirely with the judgment of Fergusson from his standpoint of

* James Fergusson (1808–1886), Scottish architectural critic and historian.
† The City Hall of New York (1811), designed by Joseph-François Mangin (active 1794–1818) and John McComb, Jr. (1763–1853); the State House at Boston (1795–1798), designed by Charles Bulfinch (1763–1844).

criticism. But there are details and features in many of the earlier buildings that are pleasurable and in good taste, while the edifices, as a whole, are not displeasing. The Boston State House is a symmetrical, well-proportioned building, simple and quiet in its application of classical details, with an overgrown lantern on a diminutive dome, but, as an entirety, effective and imposing. Its good taste is more in its negative than positive qualities, and happy adaptation of foreign styles to our wants, which at this early period almost savors of a germ of new thought. The New York City Hall is a meager, Renaissance building, with nothing new in expression or adaptation, and would find itself at home almost anywhere in Europe, without attracting notice of any kind.

Fergusson, who is an excellent guide in the forms of universal architecture, further states as a reason for our deficiency of original thought, that "an American has a great deal too much to do, and is always in too great a hurry to do it, ever to submit to the long, patient study and discipline requisite to master any style of architecture perfectly. Still less is he likely to submit to that amount of self-negation which is indispensable if a man would attempt to be original." This is too true for any one to gainsay it; neither would it lessen its force, to retort on the weak points of his countrymen. But perhaps he overstrains criticism in stating that "the perfection of art in an American's eyes would be the invention of a self-acting machine which should produce plans of cities, and designs for Gothic churches and classic monumental buildings, at so much per foot super, and so save all further thought or trouble." Resentment at this caricature is checked when we remember that our countrymen have actually patented machines for producing sculpture, whether from life or copy; and that almost every new town *founded*— once they were allowed to grow—is on a rectangular gridiron plan, utterly devoid of picturesque beauty or aesthetic design, as monotonous and unrefreshing as a table of logarithms. Such towns have no organic structure. They are all extremities, as if the human being was made up only of arms and legs, and his sole function to get about at right angles. The saving feature of Boston is that it has a heart, head, and lungs, as well as extremities. We refer to our towns in this connection, because the absence of taste and inventive thought in laying them out is at the root of corresponding weaknesses in architecture. "It is in vain to urge," says the same author, "the prosiac ugliness of such a system of laying out towns, or the vices of the way our architects *edit* buildings, after the free manner of using the scissors in making up a newspaper, when there is no feeling to perceive the deformity of the one, or knowledge to comprehend the absurdities of the other." It will be a healthful symptom of progress when we are willing to confess our deficiencies and seek remedies, instead of endeavoring to disguise them by lauding to the skies buildings styled architectural by those who erect them, but which do not possess the first principles of correct taste or beautiful design. Could the public criticize these edifices with the same warm feeling and appreciative knowledge that is applied to naval architecture, we should soon see a different state of things, the sooner because, having no examples of high art in architecture on our soil, we could more rapidly develop a style of our own.

When our people were seized with a mania of fine buildings, one generation ago, their taste turned to classical models. Although the men of Athens to whom Paul spoke might not have viewed the buildings we call Grecian with the same admiration which was bestowed on them here, put as they are to uses foreign to their spirit, and debased by utilitarian details and changes which destroy their true character, yet our builders did succeed in erecting tolerable copies of the Parthenon, and temples of the Doric, Ionic, and Corinthian orders, converted into nineteenth-century banks, customhouses, colleges, and churches. The influence of these examples spread like wildfire over the country. Cottages were hid behind wooden porticoes, while lean or bisected columns, lank pilasters, triangular masses of framework dubbed pediments, rioted everywhere, upheld by a fervor of admiration because of their origin, which now to look back upon borders on the absurd. It was indeed an invasion of Hellenic forms, but distorted into positive ugliness by ignorance of their meaning and want of taste in their application. We do not believe that Grecian architecture, born of a widely different race, country, and religion, can be adapted to America. A literal copying of it only makes it appear still more misplaced; especially, torn as it is from high places to be crowded into narrow streets, overtopped by lofty houses, and confronted with buildings of a wholly opposite character. Indeed, the attempt to reconcile it to our purposes was so manifestly preposterous that it was speedily given up.

Then we had a Gothic flurry, which ended still more absurdly, owing to entire ignorance of the forms and character of Gothic architecture. The Girard College and old United States Bank, at Philadelphia, and the United States Sub-Treasury, Wall Street, New York,* could indeed instruct the public eye as to the external anatomy of Grecian temple architecture, but the buildings that were erected as Gothic out-Heroded Herod in their defiance of its instinctive spirit. Anything pointed, having a parapet or towers with obelisk-like blocks perched about them, was palmed off as Gothic. The churches of Boston built a score or more years ago, and the Masonic Temple, are absurd caricatures and wretched parodies of their father style. Peaks and points even invaded our domestic architecture with a wanton enthusiasm, like that which just before multiplied columns and pilasters everywhere. It is only necessary to state the fact, for individuals to select examples of either architectural folly by thousands in every state. We no sooner acquired a dim idea that ornament was needed, than builders turned to their books, and made an indiscriminate raid on whatever was given as Gothic or Grecian, perverted temple and church to false uses, wrenched old forms from their true purposes and positions, and stuck our houses all over with a jumble of ill-applied details, degraded to one low standard of masons' or carpenters' work. We do not disparage the mechanical arts. They are as honorable as they are useful. Whenever our mechanics confine themselves to those utilitarian arts the knowledge of which is their professional study, they make their work as perfect of its kind as that of any other people. But when they seek to superadd beauty, a new principle comes into play, which requires for its correct expression not only a knowledge of aesthetic laws, but a profound conviction of their value. A boatbuilder may make a respectable boat, but he is

* Girard College was designed (circa 1833–1847) by Thomas Ustick Walter (1804–1887); it is difficult to believe that Jarves means the first Bank of the United States, a three-story house similar to the Salem and Boston mansions of the 1790's, and it is more probable that Jarves has in mind Benjamin Latrobe's Bank of Pennsylvania (see illustration 7); the United States Sub-Treasury was designed circa 1822 by Martin Thompson who later (1826) became a partner of Ithiel Town's (see pp. 298 ff.). The façade of Thompson's building was reconstructed as the south façade of the American Wing of the Metropolitan Museum of Art.

not the man our merchants would entrust to model a sovereign of the seas. So a master mechanic may plan a building every way adapted to common uses, but be incompetent to erect temples and cathedrals, or even a bank or railway station.

Architecture naturally grows out of the wants and ideas of a people, and its ornamentation should be in harmony with them. Our Grecian and Gothic manias were nothing of this kind. Their forms were simply old fashions, of foreign origin, made ridiculous by ignorant application, just as a savage with new-found trousers is as likely to put his arms through the legs as to wear them properly. We laugh at the mistake of the savage, but tens of thousands of buildings in America betray an ignorance of the elementary principles of architecture quite as great as that of the wild Indian of the uses of a white man's garment. In this relation stands the placing steeples astride of porticoes, or thrusting spires and domes apparently through roofs, and sticking pinnacles and pillars anywhere and everywhere, without regard to their true meaning and uses; the breaking up and confusing Grecian horizontal lines with Gothic angular and pointed, in an attempt to unite two antagonistic styles which can no more mingle than oil and water; and, the climax of solecism, trying to put the new wine of American life into the old bottles of departed civilization. Copying does not necessarily imply falsity. Imitators occasionally gave us clever examples of their originals, like the Doric portico of the Tremont House, Boston, and the circular colonnade of the Exchange, of Philadelphia;* but, in general, the whole system of imitation is simply a subterfuge to avoid thought and study. Although it may be carried out at times with good taste, it is essentially extraneous art, like a foreign literature, the delight of a learned few, but having no root in the ideas and affections of the people. The classical and Gothic phases of building of the past generation had no germinating force, because they were not the vernacular speech, but only dead tongues and obsolete characters galvanized into a spasmodic life by transitory fashion. Since then, though there have been no more repetitions of Grecian architecture on a large scale, we have had some better imitations of mediaeval Gothic, especially for ecclesiastical pur-

* Tremont House (1828–1829), a hotel designed by the Boston architect Isaiah Rogers (1800–1869); the Exchange (1832–1834) was designed by William Strickland (1788–1854).

poses, and with a truer expression of its intention. New York City furnishes conspicuous examples of copies of several of its styles, as well as of early Italian, a mode which has been followed elsewhere, both for civic and commercial purposes, not to enumerate the attempts to adapt it to domestic architecture.

The question of its adaptability to every need of modern life is not one easily decided. But the underlying spirit of the Gothic, namely, the right of free growth as of nature herself, borrowing from her the models or forms into which it incarnates its fundamental ideas, the same as vegetation, although of one great family in relation to the planet, yet adapts itself, by an infinitude of beautiful shapes, to every variety of soil—this spirit, we think, coexisting with nature herself, is capable of responding to every architectural desire. If this be a correct view of the Gothic idea, the medievalists, so far from having exhausted its scope and variety of application, have left us only on the threshold of its power. Grecian architecture was a perfect, organic, disciplined whole, limited in intent, and condensed into a defined aesthetic code, outside of which it could not range without detriment to its rule of being. Gothic, on the contrary, has no settled, absolute boundaries. Its essence is freedom of choice, to the intent to attain diversity of feature. Hence it is both flexible and infinite in character, affording working room for every intellectual and spiritual faculty. The sole limit of its being is the capacity of invention and adaptation of the workman. We perceive that he was never conventional. He might be rude, grotesque, wild, or wonderful, but the free play given individual fancy saved the Gothic from sameness and repetition. Genuine Gothic buildings of every class possess as marked individuality of expression as the human countenance, because in each the human soul, animated to excel, and vary what had been already done, is permitted free expansion of character. Its novel and beautiful doings are a perpetual surprise and delight, overflowing with exhaustless poetry and spiritual joy. In fine, believing Gothic architecture to represent and be founded upon the fundamental ideas of natural and spiritual freedom which are born of Christianity, we can limit its adaptation to human wants only by the power of the gospel to make men free and wise, and its variety and quality of expression only by the variety and quality of Christian life. Therefore, in whatever nation the promise of these is the highest, there may we look for the highest types of this architecture.

But the present question is confined to our varied, mongrel, generally mean, and rarely good imitations or copies of its past features. The fact that we are sufficiently advanced in our appreciation to borrow them for church edifices augurs well for its future career among an inventive people, and it does noble service to the principle of worship, by rescuing it from styles which are permeated by sensual, sensuous, or sordid influences. The interiors of too many fashionable churches are planned to suit the luxurious requirements of modern disciples of Jesus, with every facility for corporeal ease and none for spiritual watchfulness; while not a few are no better than a hybrid union of Mammon and Sectarianism, preaching and singing above, below, magazines of merchandise or a "depot" of ice cream, of which we have had a notable instance in one of the most conspicuous meeting houses in Boston. A plagiary which redeems sacred buildings from such incongruous uses is a cause of thankfulness, for it shows that we have got a step beyond the notion that, because a building or a portion of it is beautiful, it is desirable to repeat it without regarding the original intent, thus degrading architecture from a creative to an imitative process, and putting its forms upon a level with the copies of old masters which are imported by thousands as furniture decoration for our walls. The buildings we fix in our streets are like so many Old-World cousins come over on a visit, not having had time as yet to get other naturalization than Yankee sharpness and awkwardness of outline. We are glad to see them, though they bluntly tell us that we have many masterbuilders but no Giottos. It is encouraging, however, to begin to have a taste for what Giotto loved, though unable to create art in his spirit. In his day men *created* art. That is to say, they invented, designed, and composed with reference to home thoughts and needs. True architecture is not what so many fancy, simply ornamental building, but, as Fergusson emphatically observes, the accumulated creative and constructive powers of several minds harmoniously working out a great central idea. Everything is designed from a penetrative insight into its latent meaning, with reference to a certain position and use. The best men of each craft that enters into its constructive expression, painters, sculptors, carvers, molders, stainers of glass, mo-

saicists, masons, carpenters, the very hodmen, all labor in
unity of feeling for the one great object, which becomes to
them the incarnated ambition of their lives, and into which
enters a variety of language, fact, and feeling, having a word
to all men, and commensurate with the harmonious variety
of human capacity when stimulated to its fullest power. Not
before we appreciate the possibilities of architecture in a
grand combination of the intellectual and spiritual faculties,
aroused to action by the deepest emotions, can we expect to
create work to rival that of olden time. That was the product
of many brains. A medieval cathedral was a miniature commonwealth. Embracing in its erection and purposes an entire
community, the very names of the designers finally become
lost in the edifice. They did not think of a monument to themselves, but of a monument worthy of their faith and lineage.
Gradually the system changed. Architecture dwindled to the
business of a class. What had been the care and joy of a
people was delegated to a professional one. A great structure
no longer *grew,* but was made by contract. The old men
thought only how they should construct the best possible
building for the intended purpose. The new man, now architect by distinction, designed the whole, and he alone, not the
buildings, grew famous. The public copyrighted his work for
him. Instead of the ever-increasing variety of Gothic forms,
there was a monotony of one man's talents. In England, Inigo
Jones and Wren for centuries held almost supreme sway. In
Italy, Alberti, Brunelleschi, Michelangelo, Palladio, Sanso-
vino, and their scholars dominated the public taste. Indeed,
Italy, after the Gothic freedom of hand and thought died out,
in the persons of her architects virtually made a conquest of
Europe, not absolute, but enough to show the force of mere
fame, and the injury to originality by the supremacy of a
system which concentrated into the hands of a single man
what had been sufficient for ages before to employ the entire
energies of many. The fatal effect upon architecture was not
immediately perceived, for the men of genius, having lofty
conceptions and noble aims, invented new combinations suited
to the new era of European life. But their followers either
were incapable of this, or else they were seduced to display
their learned adroitness or tempted by sordid views. Their
work speedily degenerated into mechanical conventionalism,
based upon the ideas and inventions of their predecessors. It

could not be otherwise; for to no one person is given the
power of revolution, any more in art than in government.
External change must be predicated on the growth of fundamental ideas and the cooperative magnetism of multitudes.
Architecture delegated to a professional priesthood had lost
its power of growth. It had but one step lower to fall. Having
ceased to be practiced to develop beauty, it passed into the
keeping of tasteless, superficial professors, who, having enslaved art to vulgar sentiments, in turn easily became the
slaves of ignorant patrons, in whose minds utilitarian or ego-
tistical considerations reigned paramount. The old men would
have scorned such bondage. If they had not, their public,
appreciating the dignity of architecture, although ignorant
of so much that the nineteenth century considers school
education, would have scorned them.

The largest and most expensive of our public buildings are
at Washington. If the nation possess no architecture of its own
at its Capital, it is not owing to any stint of pecuniary stimulus, but to the causes already mentioned. The Smithsonian
Institution* is an example of a solitary effort, on an extended
scale, to introduce into the chief city of the Union a species
of modernized Norman style suited to scientific uses. It represents an abbey church of the eleventh century in plan, but
gives nothing new or beautiful by way of modern adaptation,
and so must be classed among the blundering imitations of
medievalistic architecture which have so numerously over-
spread the land with corruptions, very often in wood, of the
several styles of Gothic known as Tudor, Elizabethan, Flam-
boyant, Perpendicular, Castellated, and are now, for variety's
sake, invading the Lombard, Tuscan, Romanesque, Pisan, and
German. Of the other public buildings it is not necessary to
speak, because they are even more unfortunate debasements
of Old-World prototypes. The classical feeling rules at Washington. It is better suited to its chessboard outlines than the
Gothic. Indeed, a true palatial style, such as its eminent
Italian originators composed out of the Roman and Grecian
architecture, would suit well with the purposes of the national
Capitol. Leon Battista Alberti, Palladio, or Sir Christopher
Wren would have rejoiced in the opportunity which Washington affords for a display of the finest qualities of the Renaissance. Either one could have created a city to be proud of.

* Designed (1846–1855) by James Renwick (1818–1895).

But the only building, thus far, which answers in a respectable degree to the lofty and elegant spirit of that composite style, is the Capitol.* Before its recent enlargement it was in many features beautiful; but its simplicity of external detail and general symmetry have been marred by the disproportionate height of the florid cast-iron dome, and the crushing effect it has, placed upon the roof of an edifice complete and beautiful without it, and whose slender, detached columns, whether of the portico or peristyle, seem illy calculated to sustain the immense weight that towers above. A tall dome is of itself a delightful feature, full of majesty and dignity, and has been used by men of the caliber of Brunelleschi, Michelangelo, Wren, and Mansard, with powerul effect, as may be seen in the Duomo of Florence, St. Peter's at Rome, St. Paul's at London, and the Hôtel des Invalides at Paris. But even with these examples, and borrowing their architecture entirely from Europe, the projectors of the Capitol have failed in harmoniously uniting the two great parts of the edifice.

The Washington Monument,† apart from the extraordinary portico of pillars contemplated in the original design, is a lofty idea, borrowed in motive from the Greek phallus, and identified with Egypt's history under the form of her obelisks. As old as the earliest dawn of civilization, the symbolism of this form of a monument is not inappropriately applied to the Father of his Country; and as his moral grandeur overtops that of every other soldier and statesman, it is fitting that his monument should pierce the skies. Equally significant of uncompromising Puritanism is the stern nakedness of the Bunker Hill shaft. But in neither of them is there anything of a monumental character born of American invention.

Another style of foreign origin is making progress in America, known as the French Renaissance, of which the new City Hall, Boston,‡ is an example. Destitute of the ornate richness of its prototype, it gives no adequate conception of it except in making conspicuous its specific defects, and is stilted and forced compared with the best Italian Renaissance style. Cut up and overladen with alternate courses of tall and

---

* Designed by William Thornton (1759–1828) and others, including Charles Bulfinch and Benjamin Henry Latrobe. The addition Jarves condemns was designed (1851–1865) by Thomas Ustick Walter.

† Designed (1815) by Robert Mills (see pp. 80 ff.).

‡ Built by G. J. F. Bryant (1816–1899) and Arthur D. Gilman (1821–1882) in 1862–1865.

stunted pilasters having nothing to do, its ornamentation a meager theft of classical orders, or a meaningless exhibition of horizontal or perpendicular lines and the simplest geometrical forms, robbing the building of simplicity without giving it dignity, there is not a single element of original thought in it. Architects who design buildings of this character are mere parasites of art, obstructing natural and tasteful growth, and impeding the right men from being felt and heard. A city given over to their hands, so far as indigenous development of art is concerned, becomes a mean sham. If we do not speedily outgrow the present system of erecting public edifices, they will be so many monuments of our moral and intellectual dullness, instead of, as they might be, the incarnation of vivifying thoughts and new shapes of beauty. It is to be conceded that the City Hall is imposing from its height, and attractive from the bright solidity of its material, though the use of granite for the fine and free carving required in the Corinthian order is a waste of money and hard labor not to be commended. But the building cannot be too strongly condemned on account of the entire want of keeping of the conspicuous rear portion with its front and sides. The least that the architect ought to have done was to make that conform to the remainder of the edifice. Instead, it would appear as if, tired of his work by the time he arrived at the farther angles, he gave it to his youngest office boy to finish, who, at a loss for what to put in, by a happy thought turned to one of his early copybooks in writing for aid. Opening to the page which precedes the pothook period, he espies a multitude of upright lines. *"Eureka!"* He marks an equal number, divided by window spaces, all over the great wall surface, and at last we have an original American style of architecture. Such work is an insult alike to those who pay for it and those who have to look at it.

But meager imitation does not wholly bear sway. There is, besides, a restless, inquiring, experimentive spirit, approaching the inventive, in our building. At present it is chaotic and capricious, with an imperfect comprehension of beauty. Still, it is an active instinct seeking something new. Evidently the architects are called upon to vary their old hole-in-the-wall styles, a house being a brick box pierced with oblong apertures, or else their patrons are taking the matter in hand, and with a crude, experimental zeal are striking out new shapes and combinations. Individuality, or the expression of personal taste in architecture, is a spirit to be encouraged; for it is rooted in the freedom of choice which first begat rude Gothic forms, and subsequently developed them into ripe beauty and infinite variety. We could name many buildings for private purposes which manifest this spirit of new life, in some cases almost arriving at the grotesque, and frequently at that climax of bad taste known in Europe as Rococo, but which are refreshing to view because of their departure from old conventionalisms and servile copying. The Boston Organ in its architectural features is a striking example of Rococo. The organ, being essentially a Christian instrument of music, requires a case in harmony with its spirit and purpose, or, if put into any other, the details should be kept strictly in unity with its animating spirit. Instead of this, we have an incongruous, grotesque whole, made up of details partly taken from the Christian art-idea and partly from the pagan, gigantic caryatids and classical masks intermixed with puny cupid-angels, a feeble St. Cecilia, and inane and commonplace ornamentations; fine workmanship throughout substituted for fine art; and the entire mass made the more emphatic in its offensiveness by its want of adaptation to the size and aesthetic character of the hall over which it domineers so unpleasantly.

Though individual taste has not yet accomplished anything worthy of perpetuation or to be an example to other peoples, still recent enterprise is eminently suggestive and hopeful. This new movement springs from a rising passion for something novel and beautiful in the dwellings and places of business of our merchants. They clamor for carving and color, for something that expresses their taste or want of it. Decoration is not wholly left to the architects. People's hearts being with their treasures, it is as natural that they should strive to embody them in appropriate forms as that the medievalist, stimulated by his hopes of heaven and fears of hell, should put his treasure into cathedrals and monasteries. The estimation in which our merchants hold their stores and houses, as compared with their churches and civic edifices, is fairly shown in the relative sums expended on them. Many private buildings cost far more than public. In no respect is the contrast between the spirit of the medievalist and the modernist more striking than in their respective expenditures on their sacred and civic architecture. The one gloried in whatever adorned his city or exalted his religion in the eyes of the world; the other reserves his extravagance for private luxury and the exaltation of the individual in the estimation of the community. Not a few dwelling houses are built on so extravagant a scale, compared with the needs of the proprietor, as to come to be called, in popular talk, such a one's "folly." No public building has ever been made obnoxious to a similar term on account of lavishly exceeding its uses and appropriate ornamentation, though millions of dollars have been profitlessly buried in them by the machinations or peculations of unclean hands.

Without investigating the causes of the differences in the above respects between the merchant of the fourteenth century and his brother of the nineteenth, or enlarging upon their social consequences, we feel justified in stating that our citizens have entered upon a phase of feeling which prompts them to love display in their marts of business and their homes; to feel after beauty, as the untutored mind feels after God, if haply it might find him. We hail this as a fruitful promise of final development of fresh architectural forms, which shall make our century, before its completion, a fit companion in aesthetic progress to any one that has preceded it. True, the motive now is strictly personal, and, therefore, not the highest. But give man liberty, and the good in him is ever striving to assert itself. Already we find solid and handsome blocks of stores, in more or less good taste, appropriate to their purpose, effective as street architecture, and novel in many of their features. This improvement is greatly owing to the infusion of his own individuality, and the greater latitude the merchant gives his architect in designing an edifice which is to distinguish his business than committees do in plans of a public character. So, too, with dwelling houses. Doubtless we have as bad, perhaps the worst, specimens of expensive domestic architecture of any country. Certainly, nothing more mixed, vulgar, overdone with inappropriate ornament, mechanical, presumptuous, and mannered, can be found elsewhere. At the same time, no other country affords more hopeful indications of varied styles for domestic purposes, combining the modern constructive and utilitarian requirements with the privacy, refinement, and luxury that appertain to the Anglo-Saxon ideas of home. Boston, which is so poor in public buildings, is the most advanced in private architecture, both for domestic and commercial uses. If more regard were paid to specific fitness and beauty in details and a better disposition and harmony of masses, Boston might become an elegant as well as picturesque city; all the sooner, too, if her citizens would admit into public edifices, with a view to their own honor and dignity, lavish adornment, and freedom of inventive design similar to that they bestow upon private buildings. In Hammatt Billings* they possess an architect capable of fine work. The Methodist Church, on Tremont Avenue, a Gothic group, the Bedford Street Church, and the adjoining building for the Mechanics' Association, the finest public architecture Boston has, are but meager examples of what his taste could do if scope were given. One turns instinctively to the Roman Catholics for ecclesiastical architecture commensurate to the aesthetic nature of their ritual. But the Church of the Immaculate Conception is an agglomeration of the worst faults of the most debased types of architecture. Externally, it presents a sort of jumble of the fashions in which we build factories and jails, with much vicious and misplaced ornamentation, or what is meant as such, but, as applied, resulting in absolute ugliness. Internally, it has the air of a bank and café in its staring, hard, common look; no religious repose, abundance of sham decoration, and not one gleam of real spiritual significance. It is inconceivable how a sect with so much feeling in general for religious art, and so liberal in their contributions, should have erected a building for a sacred purpose, which violates so preposterously the aesthetic spirit and aim of their faith. Stranger still is it that a Puritan sect, "Orthodox up to the hub," as we were told by one of its members, should have built the Shawmut Church, on Tremont Avenue. The style is early Lombard, somewhat meagerly carried out, with slight modifications for special purposes. But its distinctive features are essentially anti-Puritan and of Roman Catholic origin. These are the detached, massive, lofty clock tower, or campanile, which makes so conspicuous an object in the air line of the city; the superabundance of stained glass, causing the interior to sparkle with brilliant colors, and rendering it fervid with spiritual symbolism; its low-toned frescoed walls and

---

* Hammatt Billings (1818–1874), an American architect, illustrator, and water-colorist, who began his career as an architect in Boston and later moved to New York where his role as illustrator took precedence in his career.

grandly treated roof, its harmonious adaptation of aesthetic taste and design to the requirements of Protestant worship, and chiefly the numerous carved crosses on the outer walls, and *credat Judaeus*, surmounting the very church, astounding innovations, but surpassed by that climax of religious horror to Calvinists, placed over and above the pulpit, the crucified Saviour in stained glass, answering to the crucifix of the Romanists. The persecuting Saul of art among the prophets! Puritanism arraying itself after the fashion of the scarlet lady of the seven-hilled Babylon! Is not this a change of sentiment worthy of historical note? The gentleman who assured us that the church was orthodox up to the hub also added that at first he did not like these innovations on their old system of white-wash and absence of all beauty, but had come to like them. He will find, later, that what he now likes will become indispensable, for it is the unlocking of a divine faculty which has been long closed in his sect through misapprehension of its true nature. And the example of the Shawmut Church is a striking and unlooked-for illustration of the rapid growth, in this instance revolutionary in its abrupt force, of aesthetic taste in America, confirming in a welcome manner our theory of its eventual destiny.

We do not purpose, however, to criticize in detail, but to point out the general grounds of our faith in the aesthetic future of our architecture. Its foundation is the variety of taste and freedom of inventive experiment shown by private enterprise. If a knowledge of the fundamental principles of architecture equaling the zeal displayed in building could be spread among all classes, a better order of things would soon appear. To this end, we condense from the best authorities a number of axioms or truths, which, once comprehended by the public, will go a great way to counteract bad work.

Pugin* tells us, "The two great rules for design are: First, that there should be no features about a building which are not necessary for convenience, construction, and propriety; Secondly, that all ornament should consist of enrichment of the essential construction of the building"; and adds that the neglect of these two rules is the cause of all the bad architecture of the present time.

---

* Augustus Northmore Welby Pugin (1812–1852), an English architect and designer, instrumental in the revival of Gothic architecture in nineteenth-century England.

Another English authority who treats architecture comprehensively, J. B. Atkinson,* sums up its living principles somewhat as follows:

Construction (or use) is the ground or root out of which decoration (delight) should germinate. It is the bone, marrow, muscle, and nerve of architecture as a decorative art. Architecture is capable of any variety and expression, based on the above principle.

Construction must be decorated; not decoration *constructed*.

Decoration must accord with conditions of situation, fitness, and use.

Each genuine style of architecture demands a corresponding type of ornamentation. Specific types grow out of cognate forms in the outer world, so that decorative art becomes intimately or remotely the offspring of nature.

Decoration is not only the reproduction of external form, but also the representative of inward ideas, the symbol of thought and fancy, and the earnest expression of faith. Consequently, decoration has a distinctive character and is subject to classification, as naturalistic, idealistic, symbolistic, geometric, and descriptive or illustrative.

Naturalistic decoration should accord with natural forms and conform to the principles of organic growth. The flower or leaf should represent its natural qualities or organic structure; so, too, of birds, animals, and so on; of which the public can see some fine examples of carving by workmen after nature in Central Park, New York, a beginning in the right direction, and there to be contrasted with conventional or the architects' work, from similar subjects.

Idealistic ornament is usually natural forms subjected to the control of some governing *idea*. It may be conventional or creative; the one extreme tending to mannerism, the other to extravagance.

Allied in certain points to idealistic is symbolic ornament, or the outward manifestation by form of an inward thought or abstract truth.

Geometric ornament consists only of the symmetric distribution of space and a balanced composition of lines, pointing to a central unity and radiating into erratic variety. The

* *Fine Arts Quarterly Review*, London, No. 2 [Jarves's note].

Saracens, whose religion forbade images, were the masters of this style.

Architecture admits also of descriptive, historical, and pictorial painting on wall spaces; also of color, to enhance the effect of light and shade, produce relief, and add emphasis to articulate form, and for purpose of aesthetic delight generally.

The final purpose of decoration being beauty to promote pleasurable delight, it is of paramount importance that every design or detail should conform to aesthetic laws.

Every style must be judged from its peculiar standpoint of principle and aim.

In fine, architecture is, we emphatically repeat, the materialistic expression of the life, manners, needs, and ideas of a people. It reflects them; expands and develops as they themselves do. Endowed with life of its own, it is GROWTH; man's objective creation as distinguished from nature's.

[pp. 286–314]

10

Samuel Sloan, SLOAN'S / HOMESTEAD ARCHITEC-
 TURE, / CONTAINING / FORTY DESIGNS FOR
 VILLAS, COTTAGES, AND FARM HOUSES, /
 WITH ESSAYS ON / STYLE, CONSTRUCTION,
 LANDSCAPE GARDENING, FURNITURE, ETC.
 ETC. (Philadelphia, 1861), pp. 25–30.

Samuel Sloan (1815–1884) was a Philadelphia architect, remarkable for the number and variety of commissions
he undertook, and equally remarkable for the number and
variety of styles in which he worked—from the most animated and elaborate Oriental villas through the whole pictorial spectrum to what he described as "the staid repose" of
Renaissance and classical public buildings. In 1868 Sloan
founded and published the first architectural magazine in this
country, the *Architectural Review and Builders' Journal*. His
basic assumption was that "the requirements of living had
become more complicated with the growth of refinement"
(by which he meant *moral* refinement); and he was an ardent
advocate, as well as practitioner, of the ornate eclectic styles
that were regarded as "elegant architecture" and therefore as
consonant with the "moral refinement" of his period.

Remarks on Style

When we speak of a building being in the Grecian, Italian,
Gothic, or any of the numerous well-known *sub*-styles, we
mean that the spirit rather than the sum total of the peculiarities of that style has been seized upon and infused into it.

No design in this work can be pointed out as a facsimile of any ancient or foreign specimen of architecture; but ancient forms and details have too long appealed to the tastes or prejudices of mankind for the architect to dream of their abandonment. They have been consecrated to architecture by long-continued use and the admiration of bygone ages; and, so far as their existence depends on intrinsic beauty of form and the laws of proportion, they are bound to be immortal. The orator or poet would not be more culpable for laying aside the teachings of the past than would the architect for neglecting the precedents set before him in the works of the ancient masters. Each might substitute a chimera of his own, and the failure of all would be alike pitiable. Instead of eloquence and poetry, the listening audience would be fed on the rudiments of an unintelligible language; and instead of a pleasing combination of forms resulting in the most happy effects, unmeaning piles of brick and stone at every step would greet our vision.

By the adoption of some one of the known modes or styles of building, the structure is invested with an interest that it would not otherwise possess. The popular mind is easily reached through a medium combining beauty of aspect with antiquity of origin; it is affected by an appreciation of the present interwoven with a veneration for the past. Hence the architect who studies the ancients, to imbibe the spirit of their performances rather than to follow them servilely through beauty and deformity, is certain to be most successful in the production of good designs for the present day.

The Gothic or pointed style, and the Grecian or horizontal style, are the types of the two great elements of architectural design. All the divisions and subdivisions that figure so largely on the page of the historian and tourist are merely so many petrified phases of national practice at a given time, handed down to us under the name of the nation or people under whose auspices they assumed their distinguishing peculiarities. It is, however, foreign to our present purpose to trace any of these to their fountainhead, and show how, step by step, they reached their highest perfection, or how, in the hands of skillful masters, they were combined with each other to astonish and delight the art world: it is enough to remark that the American architect has a living source of satisfaction in the thought that it is possible for him to aid in setting a national stamp on the architecture of his country. That this is possible, a convincing proof is furnished to our hand in "beautiful Venice, the bride of the sea." Look for a moment at the church of St. Mark. Roman, the legitimate descendant of Grecian art, but not less national, had reached its climax, and the fountain of Gothic beauty seemed exhausted, when lo! we see a structure arise bearing the impress of Roman and Gothic art harmoniously blended, and yet developing a character so clearly and decidedly its own that none have ventured to gainsay or question its nationality.

Grecian architecture and its lineal successors, Roman and Italian, are imbued with a spirit of repose and quietness that contrast powerfully with the lively character of the Gothic mode. The origin of this apparent antagonism is attributable to the prevalence of horizontal lines in the former and of vertical in the latter. That these can be reconciled to each other with happy effect is verified in the example alluded to, as well as in the famous Milan Cathedral and many contemporary buildings. But the accomplishment of such a feat is the highest evidence of artistic skill that an architect can stamp on the face of his performance: few dare it, and of the few, not a moiety can be said to be successful.

Domestic architecture in ancient nations seems to have been neglected, or at least to have occupied but an inferior position. While temple after temple was reared to their gods, and tomb and triumphal arch to their heroes and kings, the Grecian and Roman people lived in hovels. The same may be said of the people of Britain and the Continent during the palmy days of Gothic art. As the equality of mankind approaches nearer to being acknowledged as a fixed element in human society, we see a change taking place, and for centuries back the masses have been gaining ground on the aristocracy. And when the dwelling of the private citizen finally became a subject for the display of the taste and genius of the architect, he naturally enough looked to the most magnificent specimens of ancient or contemporary public architecture for his guide in the selection of forms and details; and as a consequence we see domestic buildings, even down to modern times, wearing the exact dress of the heathen temple, or the livery of the medieval church or castle. By degrees, however, domestic architecture is improving, and that improvement is accelerated by copying nothing ancient or foreign further than its application is in strict consonance with the requirements of domestic life. In public buildings, we may, if we choose, with some degree of propriety and prospect of success, copy the Grecian or Roman temple or the Gothic cathedral; but for the citizen's home, the introduction of details derived from those sources presupposes their entire subordination to the domestic character of the building of which they are to form a part. What we mean to say is that architectural *style* should never seem to rule out the expression of the END IN VIEW. This may be more fully explained by the following incident: In passing by a fine residence, the location of which we need not name, a friend inquired whether it was a church, college, or courthouse; which we were not able to answer until we approached close enough to determine by the drapery in the windows that it was a dwelling house. It was a classic building and a fine specimen of architecture; but was it domestic architecture? Someone has very well said that the ancient practice should be treated as a *servant*, not as a master. Without doubt the gentlemanly proprietor of the classic house above spoken of would have scorned to receive from the painter's hand the picture of Apollo as his own portrait, and yet he has permitted his architect to disguise, under the semblance of a heathen temple, the real character of his place of residence, although one is not more at variance with the true spirit of living art than the other.

Without condemning what has been done, and with great hopes for the future of rural building, we pass sentence on servile imitation as being unworthy of the genius and spirit of the American people. There is an element of originality in American enterprise that seems to have slumbered in nothing more than in the pursuit of architecture as a fine art, and once fully awakened to the importance of its cultivation, it is destined to set its mark high in the record of nations. But this can be done only by the application of the best talent the country can afford, irrespective of the profits likely to accrue to the leaders of the profession. So long as the uneducated builder is permitted to take the lead in designing and constructing our edifices, to the exclusion of the true architect, so long must we fall short of the high standard within our reach.

Admiration of ancient forms and details leads the uncultivated judgment to apply them without regard to order or congruity, and the result is always offensive to the refined perception of the true artist. The constituent elements of style are proportion, beauty of form, harmony of arrangement, and unity of effect; without these, no style can exist, nor can a building be said to be an architectural composition in which any of these elements are neglected.

But first of all, in domestic structures let attention be paid to unity; that is, the production of a WHOLE, and the expression of the END IN VIEW, the latter being manifested by chimney tops, verandas, entranceways, windows, and so on, the absence or concealment of any of these features being destructive to the domestic character of the building. Then let the proportion of parts be considered, for without this no real satisfaction will be derived from the inspection of a building of any kind. Whatever details are introduced of an ornamental character should be the best, chosen with regard to gracefulness of form, never so elaborate as to produce a striking contrast with larger masses of plain surface, but culminating in extreme points or exhibited lines of construction, as in nature the flowers grow not on the stalk but on the branches.

Harmony expresses the radical idea conveyed by the term as employed in musical composition, and its importance cannot better be illustrated than by the momentary violation of its principles in the choir or orchestra. Mr. Loudon* says the term is "transferred from music to architecture, and implies such a composition of lines and forms as will produce a powerful, a varied, and an agreeable whole. Where great contrasts exist among the parts, and yet all of them are in accord, the effect is harmony," and "harmony therefore supposes unity, contrast, variety, order, proportion, and various other subordinate beauties. Notwithstanding this, however, harmony in architecture as in music may exist independently of ornament or of any distinctive character."

[pp. 25–30]

* John Claudius Loudon (1783–1843), a Scottish botanist and landscape architect, founder and editor of several magazines, including the influential *Architectural Magazine*.

11

Catherine E. Beecher and Harriet Beecher Stowe,
THE / AMERICAN WOMAN'S HOME: / OR, /
PRINCIPLES OF DOMESTIC SCIENCE; / BEING /
A GUIDE TO THE FORMATION AND MAINTE-
NANCE OF ECONOMICAL / HEALTHFUL, BEAU-
TIFUL, AND CHRISTIAN HOMES (New York,
1869), pp. i–xii, *passim*, pp. 23–42.

Catherine Esther Beecher (1800–1878) was described
in obituaries as a brilliant, rather eccentric woman. She was
a dedicated philanthropist and indefatigable in her efforts—
writing and organizing schools and societies—to advance the
education of women; her insistence was that women should
be educated "for their peculiar duties . . . domestic employment" just as men are educated for their worldly employments.

Her sister, Harriet Beecher Stowe (1811–1896), was no
less brilliant or eccentric. Her twentieth-century reputation
is based on *Uncle Tom's Cabin* (1851–1852), one of her two
didactic antislavery novels. Among her contemporaries she
was reputed not only for her polemics about slavery and
woman's moral supremacy (*Lady Byron Vindicated*, 1869)
but also as the author of a series of rambling and comforting
novels about quiet New England life.

The excerpts from the Table of Contents included below
reflect the complexity of what an architecture, both practical
and expressive of the *"soul,"* could mean in the context of
nineteenth-century domestic reform idealism.

From "Table of Contents"

INTRODUCTION

I / THE CHRISTIAN FAMILY

II / A CHRISTIAN HOUSE

etc.—Laundry—General woodwork—Conservatories—Average estimate of cost.—Pages 23–42.

III / A HEALTHFUL HOME

Household murder—Poisoning and starvation the inevitable result of bad air in public halls and private homes—Good air as needful as good food—Structure and operations of the lungs and their capillaries and air cells—How people in a confined room will deprive the air of oxygen and overload it with refuse carbonic acid—Starvation of the living body deprived of oxygen—The skin and its twenty-eight miles of perspiratory tubes—Reciprocal action of plants and animals—Historical examples of foul-air poisoning—Outward effects of habitual breathing of bad air—Quotations from scientific authorities.—Pages 43–58.

IV / SCIENTIFIC DOMESTIC VENTILATION

V / STOVES, FURNACES, AND CHIMNEYS

VI / HOME DECORATION

Significance of beauty in making home attractive and useful in education—Exemplification of economical and tasteful furniture—The carpet, lounge, lambrequins, curtains, ottomans, easy chair, center-table—Money left for pictures—Chromos—Pretty frames—Engravings—Statuettes—Educatory influence of works of art—Natural adornments—Materials in the woods and fields—Parlor gardens—Hanging baskets—Fern shields—Ivy, its beauty and tractableness—Window, with flowers, vines, and pretty plants—Rustic stand for flowers—Ward's case—How to make it economically—Bowls and vases of rustic work for growing plants—Ferns, how and when to gather them—General remarks.—Pages 84–103.

VII / THE CARE OF HEALTH

VIII / DOMESTIC EXERCISE

IX / HEALTHFUL FOOD

X / HEALTHFUL DRINKS

XI / CLEANLINESS

XII / CLOTHING

XIII / GOOD COOKING

XIV / EARLY RISING
A virtue peculiarly American and democratic.

XV / DOMESTIC MANNERS

Good manners the expression of benevolence in personal intercourse.

XVI / GOOD TEMPER IN THE HOUSEKEEPER

XVII / HABITS OF SYSTEM AND ORDER

XVIII / GIVING IN CHARITY

XIX / ECONOMY OF TIME AND EXPENSES

XX / HEALTH OF MIND

XXI / THE CARE OF INFANTS

XXII / THE MANAGEMENT OF YOUNG CHILDREN

XXIII / DOMESTIC AMUSEMENTS AND SOCIAL
   DUTIES

XXIV / CARE OF THE AGED

XXV / THE CARE OF SERVANTS

XXVI / CARE OF THE SICK

XXVII / ACCIDENTS AND ANTIDOTES

XXVIII / SEWING, CUTTING, AND MENDING

XXIX / FIRES AND LIGHTS

XXX / THE CARE OF ROOMS

XXXI / THE CARE OF YARDS AND GARDENS

XXXII / THE PROPAGATION OF PLANTS

XXXIII / THE CULTIVATION OF FRUIT

XXXIV / THE CARE OF DOMESTIC ANIMALS

XXXV / EARTH CLOSETS

XXXVI / WARMING AND VENTILATION

XXXVII / CARE OF THE HOMELESS, THE HELPLESS, AND THE VICIOUS

XXXVIII / THE CHRISTIAN NEIGHBORHOOD

Spirit of Christian Missions—Present organizations under church direction too mechanical—Christian family influence the true instrument of Gospel propagation—Practical suggestions for gathering a Christian family in neglected neighborhoods—Plan of church, schoolhouse, and family dwelling in one building—Mode of use for various purposes—Nucleus and gathering of a family—Christian work for Christian women—Children—Orphans—Servants—Neglected ones—Household training—Roman Catholic Nuns—The South—The West—The neglected interior of older states—Power of such examples—Rapid spread of their influence—Anticipation of the glorious consummation to be hoped for—Prophecy in the Scriptures—Cowper's noble vision of the millennial glory. —Pages 453–461.

[pp. i–xii, *passim*]

II / *A Christian House**

In the Divine Word it is written, "The wise woman buildeth her house." To be "wise" is "to choose the best means for accomplishing the best end." It has been shown that the best end for a woman to seek is the training of God's children for their eternal home, by guiding them to intelligence, virtue, and true happiness. When, therefore, the wise woman seeks a home in which to exercise this ministry, she will aim to secure

* The sketch at the head of this chapter represents a small Gothic cottage, similar to but somewhat simpler than the cottage shown in illustration 11.

a house so planned that it will provide in the best manner for health, industry, and economy, those cardinal requisites of domestic enjoyment and success. To aid in this is the object of the following drawings and descriptions, which will illustrate a style of living more conformed to the great design for which the family is instituted than that which ordinarily prevails among those classes which take the lead in forming the customs of society. The aim will be to exhibit modes of economizing labor, time, and expenses, so as to secure health, thrift, and domestic happiness to persons of limited means, in a measure rarely attained even by those who possess wealth.

At the head of this chapter is a sketch of what may be properly called a Christian house; that is, a house contrived for the express purpose of enabling every member of a family to labor with the hands for the common good, and by modes at once healthful, economical, and tasteful.

Of course, much of the instruction conveyed in the following pages is chiefly applicable to the wants and habits of those living either in the country or in such suburban vicinities as give space of ground for healthful outdoor occupation in the family service, although the general principles of housebuilding and housekeeping are of necessity universal in their application—as true in the busy confines of the city as in the freer and purer quietude of the country. So far as circumstances can be made to yield the opportunity, it will be assumed that the family state demands some outdoor labor for all. The cultivation of flowers to ornament the table and house, of fruits and vegetables for food, of silk and cotton for clothing, and the care of horse, cow, and dairy, can be so divided that each and all of the family, some part of the day, can take exercise in the pure air, under the magnetic and healthful rays of the sun. Every head of a family should seek a soil and climate which will afford such opportunities. Railroads, enabling men toiling in cities to rear families in the country, are on this account a special blessing. So, also, is the opening of the South to free labor, where, in the pure and mild climate of the uplands, open-air labor can proceed most of the year, and women and children labor out of doors as well as within.

In the following drawings are presented modes of economizing time, labor, and expense by the close packing of conveniences. By such methods, small and economical houses can be made to secure most of the comforts and many of the refinements of large and expensive ones. The cottage at the head of this chapter is projected on a plan which can be adapted to a warm or cold climate with little change. By adding another story, it would serve a large family.

Fig. 1 shows the ground-plan of the first floor. On the inside it is forty-three feet long and twenty-five wide, excluding conservatories and front and back projections. Its inside height from floor to ceiling is ten feet. The piazzas each side of the front projection have sliding windows to the floor, and can, by glazed sashes, be made greenhouses in winter. In a warm climate, piazzas can be made at the back side also.

In the description and arrangement, the leading aim is to show how time, labor, and expense are saved, not only in the building but in furniture and its arrangement. With this aim, the ground floor and its furniture will first be shown, then the second story and its furniture, and then the basement and its conveniences. The conservatories are appendages not necessary to housekeeping, but useful in many ways pointed out more at large in other chapters.

The entry has arched recesses behind the front doors, furnished with hooks for overclothes in both—a box for overshoes in one, and a stand for umbrellas in the other. The roof of the recess is for statuettes, busts, or flowers. The stairs turn twice with broad steps, making a recess at the lower landing, where a table is set with a vase of flowers. On one side of the recess is a closet, arched to correspond with the arch over the stairs. A bracket over the first broad stair, with flowers or statuettes, is visible from the entrance, and pictures can be hung . . .

The large room . . . can be made to serve the purpose of several rooms by means of a *movable screen*. By shifting this rolling screen from one part of the room to another, two apartments are always available, of any desired size within the limits of the large room. One side of the screen fronts what may be used as the parlor or sitting room; the other side is arranged for bedroom conveniences. . . . the front side [is] covered first with strong canvas, stretched and nailed on. Over this is pasted panel paper, and the upper part is made to resemble an ornamental cornice by fresco paper. Pictures can be hung in the panels, or be pasted on and varnished with white varnish. To prevent the absorption of the varnish, a wash of gum isinglass (fish glue) must be applied twice.

. . . the back or inside of the movable screen [is] toward

the part of the room used as the bedroom. On one side, and at the top and bottom, it has shelves with *shelf boxes*, which are cheaper and better than drawers, and much preferred by those using them. Handles are cut in the front and back side. . . . Half an inch space must be between the box and the shelf over it, and as much each side, so that it can be taken out and put in easily. The central part of the screen's interior is a wardrobe.

This screen must be so high as nearly to reach the ceiling, in order to prevent it from overturning. It is to fill the width of the room, except two feet on each side. A projecting cleat or strip, reaching nearly to the top of the screen, three inches wide, is to be screwed to the front sides, on which light frame doors are to be hung, covered with canvas and panel paper like the front of the screen. The inside of these doors is furnished with hooks for clothing, for which the projection makes room. The whole screen is to be eighteen inches deep at the top and two feet deep at the base, giving a solid foundation. It is moved on four wooden rollers, one foot long and four inches in diameter. The pivots of the rollers and the parts where there is friction must be rubbed with hard soap, and then a child can move the whole easily.

A curtain is to be hung across the whole interior of the screen by rings, on a strong wire. The curtain should be in three parts, with lead or large nails in the hems to keep it in place. The woodwork must be put together with screws, as the screen is too large to pass through a door.

At the end of the room, behind the screen, are two couches, to be run one under the other. The upper one is made with four posts, each three feet high and three inches square, set on casters two inches high. The frame is to be fourteen inches from the floor, seven feet long, two feet four inches wide, and three inches in thickness. At the head, and at the foot, is to be screwed a notched two-inch board, three inches wide. The mortises are to be one inch wide and deep, and one inch apart, to receive slats made of ash, oak, or spruce, one inch square, placed lengthwise of the couch. The slats being small, and so near together, and running lengthwise, make a better spring frame than wire coils. If they warp, they can be turned. They must not be fastened at the ends, except by insertion in the notches. Across the posts, and of equal height with them, are to be screwed head and foot boards.

The under couch is like the upper, except these dimensions:

posts, nine inches high, including casters; frame, six feet two inches long, two feet four inches wide. The frame should be as near the floor as possible, resting on the casters.

The most healthful and comfortable mattress is made by a case, open in the center and fastened together with buttons, to be filled with oat straw, which is softer than wheat or rye. This can be adjusted to the figure, and often renewed.

Fig. 10 represents the upper couch when covered, with the under couch put beneath it. The coverlid should match the curtain of the screen; and the pillows, by day, should have a case of the same.

Fig. 11 is an ottoman, made as a box, with a lid on hinges. A cushion is fastened to this lid by strings at each corner, passing through holes in the box lid and tied inside. The cushion to be cut square, with side pieces; stuffed with hair, and stitched through like a mattress. Side handles are made by cords fastened inside with knots. The box must be two inches larger at the bottom than at the top, and the lid and cushion the same size as the bottom, to give it a tasteful shape. This ottoman is set on casters, and is a great convenience for holding articles, while serving also as a seat.

The expense of the screen, where lumber averages $4 a hundred, and carpenter labor $3 a day, would be about $30, and the two couches about $6. The material for covering might be cheap and yet pretty. A woman with these directions, and a son or husband who would use plane and saw, could thus secure much additional room, and also what amounts to two bureaus, two large trunks, one large wardrobe, and a washstand, for less than $20—the mere cost of materials. The screen and couches can be so arranged as to have one room serve first as a large and airy sleeping room; then, in the morning, it may be used as sitting room one side of the screen, and breakfast room the other; and lastly, through the day it can be made a large parlor on the front side, and a sewing or retiring room the other side. The needless spaces usually devoted to kitchen, entries, halls, back stairs, pantries, storerooms, and closets, by this method would be used in adding to the size of the large room, so variously used by day and by night.

Fig. 12 is an enlarged plan of the kitchen and stove room. The chimney and stove room are contrived to ventilate the whole house by a mode exhibited in another chapter.

Between the two rooms glazed sliding doors, passing each

other, serve to shut out heat and smells from the kitchen. The sides of the stove room must be lined with shelves; those on the side by the cellar stairs, to be one foot wide, and eighteen inches apart; on the other side, shelves may be narrower, eight inches wide and nine inches apart. Boxes with lids, to receive stove utensils, must be placed near the stove.

On these shelves, and in the closet and boxes, can be placed every material used for cooking, all the table and cooking utensils, and all the articles used in housework, and yet much spare room will be left. The cook's galley in a steamship has every article and utensil used in cooking for two hundred persons, in a space not larger than this stove room, and so arranged that with one or two steps the cook can reach all he uses.

In contrast to this, in most large houses, the table furniture, the cooking materials and utensils, the sink, and the eating room are at such distances apart, that half the time and strength is employed in walking back and forth to collect and return the articles used.

Fig. 13 is an enlarged plan of the sink and cooking-form. Two windows make a better circulation of air in warm weather, by having one open at top and the other at the bottom, while the light is better adjusted for working, in case of weak eyes.

The flour barrel just fills the closet, which has a door for admission, and a lid to raise when used. Beside it is the form for cooking, with a molding board laid on it; one side used for preparing vegetables and meat, and the other for molding bread. The sink has two pumps, for well and for rain water—one having a forcing power to throw water into the reservoir in the garret, which supplies the water closet and bathroom. On the other side of the sink is the dish drainer, with a ledge on the edge next the sink, to hold the dishes, and grooves cut to let the water drain into the sink. It has hinges, so that it can either rest on the cook form or be turned over and cover the sink. Under the sink are shelf boxes placed on two shelves run into grooves, with other grooves above and below, so that one may move the shelves and increase or diminish the spaces between. The shelf boxes can be used for scouring materials, dishtowels, and dishcloths; also to hold bowls for bits of butter, fats, etc. Under these two shelves is room for two pails, and a jar for soap grease.

Under the cook form are shelves and shelf boxes for unbolted wheat, cornmeal, rye, and so on. Beneath these, for white and brown sugar, are wooden can-pails, which are the best articles in which to keep these constant necessities. Beside them is the tin molasses can with a tight, moveable cover, and a cork in the spout. This is much better than a jug for molasses, and also for vinegar and oil, being easier to clean and to handle. Other articles and implements for cooking can be arranged on or under the shelves at the side and front. A small cooking tray, holding pepper, salt, dredging box, knife and spoon, should stand close at hand by the stove.

The articles used for setting tables are to be placed on the shelves at the front and side of the sink. Two tumbler trays, made of pasteboard, covered with varnished fancy papers and divided by wires, save many steps in setting and clearing table. Similar trays for knives and forks and spoons serve the same purpose.

The sink should be three feet long and three inches deep, its width matching the cook form.

Fig. 17 is the second, or attic, story. The main objection to attic rooms is their warmth in summer, owing to the heated roof. This is prevented by so enlarging the closets each side that their walls meet the ceiling under the garret floor, thus excluding all the roof. In the bedchambers, corner dressing tables, as Fig. 18, instead of projecting bureaus, save much space for use, and give a handsome form and finish to the room. In the bathroom must be the opening to the garret, and a stepladder to reach it. A reservoir in the garret, supplied by a forcing pump in the cellar or at the sink, must be well supported by timbers, and the plumbing must be well done, or much annoyance will ensue.

The large chambers are to be lighted by large windows or glazed sliding doors, opening upon the balcony. A roof can be put over the balcony and its sides enclosed by windows, and the chamber extend into it, and be thus much enlarged.

The water closets must have the latest improvements for safe discharge, and there will be no trouble. They cost no more than an outdoor building, and save from the most disagreeable house labor.

A great improvement, called *earth closets*, will probably take the place of water closets to some extent; though at present the water is the more convenient. A description of the earth closet will be given in another chapter relating to tenement houses for the poor in large cities.

The method of ventilating all the chambers, and also the cellar, will be described in another chapter.

Fig. 19 represents a shoebag that can be fastened to the side of a closet or closet door.

Fig. 20 represents a piecebag, and is a very great labor and space-saving invention. It is made of calico, and fastened to the side of a closet or a door, to hold all the bundles that are usually stowed in trunks and drawers. India rubber or elastic tape drawn into hems to hold the contents of the bag is better than tape strings. Each bag should be labeled with the name of its contents, written with indelible ink on white tape sewed onto the bag. Such systematic arrangement saves much time and annoyance. Drawers or trunks to hold these articles cannot be kept so easily in good order, and moreover, occupy spaces saved by this contrivance.

Fig. 21 is the basement. It has the floor and sides plastered, and is lighted with glazed doors. A form is raised close by the cellar stairs, for baskets, pails, and tubs. Here, also, the refrigerator can be placed, or, what is better, an ice closet can be made, as designated in the illustration. The floor of the basement must be an inclined plane toward a drain, and be plastered with water-lime. The washtubs have plugs in the bottom to let off water, and cocks and pipes over them bringing cold water from the reservoir in the garret and hot water from the laundry stove. This saves much heavy labor of emptying tubs and carrying water.

The laundry closet has a stove for heating irons, and also a kettle on top for heating water. Slides or clothes frames are made to draw out to receive wet clothes, and then run into the closet to dry. This saves health as well as time and money, and the clothes are as white as when dried outdoors.

The woodwork of the house, for doors, windows, and so on, should be oiled chestnut, butternut, whitewood, and pine. This is cheaper, handsomer, and more easy to keep clean than painted wood.

In Fig. 1 [the ground floor] are planned two conservatories, and few understand their value in the training of the young. They provide soil, in which children, through the winter months, can be starting seeds and plants for their gardens and raising valuable, tender plants. Every child should cultivate flowers and fruits to sell and to give away, and thus be taught to learn the value of money and to practice both economy and benevolence.

According to the calculation of a house carpenter, in a place where the *average* price of lumber is $4 a hundred, and carpenter work $3 a day, such a house can be built for $1,600. For those practicing the closest economy, two small families could occupy it, by dividing the kitchen, and yet have room enough. Or one large room and the chamber over it can be left till increase of family and means require enlargement.

A strong horse and carryall, with a cow, garden, vineyard, and orchard, on a few acres, would secure all the substantial comforts found in great establishments, without the trouble of ill-qualified servants.

And if the parents and children were united in the daily labors of the house, garden, and fruit culture, such thrift, health, and happiness would be secured as is but rarely found among the rich.

Let us suppose a colony of cultivated and Christian people, having abundant wealth, who now are living as the wealthy usually do, emigrating to some of the beautiful southern uplands, where are rocks, hills, valleys, and mountains as picturesque as those of New England, where the thermometer but rarely reaches 90° in summer, and in winter as rarely sinks below freezing point, so that outdoor labor goes on all the year, where the fertile soil is easily worked, where rich tropical fruits and flowers abound, where cotton and silk can be raised by children around their home, where the produce of vineyards and orchards finds steady markets by railroads ready made; suppose such a colony, with a central church and schoolroom, library, hall for sports, and a common laundry (taking the most trying part of domestic labor from each house)—suppose each family to train the children to labor with the hands as a healthful and honorable duty; suppose all this, which is perfectly practicable, would not the enjoyment of this life be increased, and also abundant treasures be laid up in heaven, by using the wealth thus economized in diffusing similar enjoyments and culture among the poor, ignorant, and neglected ones in desolated sections where many now are perishing for want of such Christian example and influences?

[pp. 23–42]

Part III: The New Technology (1820-1880)

1. Introduction

The Yankee ingenuity that is so deeply ingrained a part of our mythology about the American past came into its own with a flourish in the opening decades of the nineteenth century. Our mythology presents the image of an ingenuity that was not intellectual and theoretical but native wit and rule of thumb; and, like most mythological images, this one is both true and untrue. The new technologies of construction did develop in part by rule-of-thumb ingenuity, but they also involved both scientific thought and formal engineering techniques. In effect, the new technologies in nineteenth-century America were the result of a tangled interchange among science, engineering, and what John A. Kouwenhoven has called "the vernacular tradition" (*Made in America*, New York, 1948).

Nineteenth-century technology was in part the heir-apparent of eighteenth-century rational technology. The eighteenth-century point of view is effectively characterized by Count Rumford's remark that what he strove for was "the application of science to the common purposes of life." Count Rumford of Bavaria (1753–1814) was born Yankee: Benjamin Thompson of Woburn, Massachusetts. He combined in himself a political opportunism, a native ingenuity, and a scientific curiosity reminiscent of some aspects of Benjamin Franklin's personality. Rumford's approach, by his own assertion, was to reason from general theory toward practical application; in the 1790's he recorded what seemed to be his progress from a general interest in the phenomena of heat to a mathematical analysis

of the fireplace and the way it functioned, and from analysis
to recommendations and specifications. What he established
as general theory was that the fireplace was a source not of
direct heat from the flame or of indirect heat from hot air,
since that went up the chimney, but of radiant heat from the
brick sides and back. He established a system of ideal proportions for the chimney that were in effect the invention of
the smoke chamber and of the smokeless fireplace. He determined ideal angles for the relations front to side and side to
back, and he recommended that the fire be built directly on
a bed of ashes that was high in the front and sloped downward toward the back. What he seemed to have achieved was
a "classic" rational sequence, an investigation that ran the
gamut from thermodynamic theory through the mathematical
analysis of phenomena to practical recommendations and
advice. But in his *Treatise* it becomes apparent that the
"classic" sequence holds because Rumford made it hold. The
Treatise is a set piece, a rhetorical demonstration of reason
in action, rather than an accurate description of the life
history of Rumford's practical ideas. This emphasis on
rhetorical presentation was dictated by the eighteenth-century
rational dogma that maintained that the universe was organized as a hierarchical pyramid, from universal law at the apex
to specific phenomena at the base. The "classic" sequence,
even though it was rhetorical rather than analytic, has lingered
into our own time as "common sense" about technological
innovation, and this common sense confuses our attitudes
toward the history of technological development: we tend to
expect that the innovations of the past have developed from
the inventor's grasp of general law toward specific application—whereas in actuality (and beneath the rhetoric even in
Rumford's case) innovation involves a continuing dialogue
between mind and hand, between theory and native wit, between innovative thought and practical implementation; and
it was this dialogue that was the vital force in Yankee
ingenuity.

Rumford's recommendations for the fireplace were so
demonstrably effective that within a few years after the
publication of his *Treatise* New England brickyards were
offering for sale bricks precast with the angles that Rumford
had determined for the relation of side to back in the fireplace. This immediate readiness to make innovations prac-

tically available is one key to the dialogue of the Yankee approach. In effect, Rumford's brick was prepared for the use of the skilled amateur rather than of the skilled professional, and this in turn suggests that there was a wide dissemination of a variety of skills rather than a concentration of specialized skills. Highly trained craftsmen were in short supply in early nineteenth-century America, and basic to an understanding of the technological revolution is a recognition of what the labor force was: literate and resourceful, generally skilled in making shift, but not professional in the craft sense. Eli Whitney, who is understandably famous for his invention of the cotton gin, should be even more famous for his grasp of the technological potential of interchangeable parts. It was Whitney's grasp of this potential that made a semiskilled labor force capable of large-scale production. In 1798 Whitney contracted with the Federal government to manufacture 10,000 rifles in two years; this unprecedented contract was based not on the highly skilled art of the professional gunsmith but on machine-made interchangeable parts that could be fitted and assembled by the generally skilled amateur. Whitney conceptualized this as the substitution of "correct and effective operations of machinery" for the skills of the craftsman; what Whitney and his like-minded contemporaries achieved was an extraordinary release of productive energy.

The intelligent technological use of rudimentary skills is one of the dominant themes of nineteenth-century structural technology. Ithiel Town's truss is a case in point. When Town solicited a letter recommending his truss from Whitney, Whitney responded by emphasizing, among other things, "the great facility in taking out any piece of timber and replacing it with another"; that is, the truss was composed of interchangeable parts, easy to duplicate and relatively simple to assemble and disassemble. The truss also implied a sort of prefabrication: its parts could be manufactured in a mill under skilled supervision for subsequent assembly at the bridge site. Much the same sort of thematic pattern emerges in Bogardus's development of the cast-iron building in the 1850's. He conceived of cast-iron structures in terms of factory-molded, prefabricated interchangeable parts that, in his characteristic overstatement, "may be adjusted and secured by the most ignorant workman"; semiskilled labor could achieve the results of skilled construction. Much the same can be said for Etzler's visionary mechanics and for Fowler's rationalization of the gravel wall (poured concrete); Fowler and Etzler, who were not practical men, thought in terms of prefabricated, interchangeable structural modules that could be assembled by semiskilled labor. And the same is true of the balloon frame in the 1830's: once the development of sawmilling techniques had made possible large-scale production of standard lumber sizes and once nail-making machines had been developed,* the prefabricated modular units basic to balloon framing (the nail and the two by four) were available. The skills involved in fitting and assembling the balloon frame and the diagonal sheathing that made it rigid were rudimentary and mathematical, dependent on literacy, in contrast to the hand skills (carving pegs, mortising and tenoning, and so on) involved in heavy timber ("drop girt") framing.

It was patently impossible for early nineteenth-century America to build as much and as rapidly as the need seemed to require and also to take time to train specialists in the traditional European structural crafts. The sheer quantity of construction stands as a monument to the resolution of the problem, a resolution symbolized by the common emphasis that Town's truss, the balloon frame, and Bogardus's system of cast-iron construction put on the economical use of semiskilled or, more accurately, of literate and generally skilled but unspecialized labor. To argue that this emphasis was the application of a rational principle would be to dignify as a formal concept something that was "in the air" as a general "bent of the mind." Not only did the professionals, Town and Bogardus and Bell, grasp aspects of this principle but also Etzler and Fowler, the nonprofessionals, appear to have grasped it. It would be equally inaccurate to argue that this radical departure in the use of labor was the simple result of economic demand; the stimulus seems to have been an intermesh of economic demand, the rapid development of machine tools, a flexible and literate labor force capable of following skilled direction, and the emergence of a new, innovative approach toward engineering know-how and its implementa-

* A skilled modern blacksmith can make 200 nails a day (*New York Times*, May 31, 1965). A modern carpenter on a "nailing day" can drive from 4,800 to 7,200 machine-made nails.

tion. The professionally trained architect was at times hampered in this new environment; the career of Benjamin Henry Latrobe offers a case in point. His training in England made him capable of the design of domed and arched masonry buildings, but masonry involves skilled artisans, and Latrobe was repeatedly hampered by the shortage of skilled masons in this country. The traditional skills of the trained architect depended on the traditional skills of the mason with years of painstaking apprenticeship behind him. The new technology, as symbolized by Town's truss, in effect altered this relationship: the skills of the designer could compensate for the workman's lack of craft skills and could at the same time capitalize on the workman's rudimentary skills, on his literacy and on his ability to "talk back."

That this technological "breakthrough" was "a bent of the mind" rather than a result of specialized training is reflected in Bogardus's career as an inventor. Bogardus was trained as an apprentice watchmaker and engraver. His first patented inventions were in the field of his expertise, but once his career had been launched he turned his hand to fields as various as textile machinery, architectural engineering (cast iron), rubber-molding machinery, dry gas metering, sugar milling, and so on. The experience of his first inventions seems, in retrospect, to have given him a habit of inventiveness that was not so much an increase of skill in one field as it was the development of general skills in many. This habit of inventiveness also did not put as much emphasis on originality as we tend to associate with invention; the real emphasis was on adaptation and implementation. Bogardus's invention of a cast-iron structural system was not an original idea so much as it was the imaginative adaptation and implementation of prior art; nor was it singular as an invention: Bogardus's system in the 1850's, like Town's truss in the 1820's and 1830's, was only one of many more or less equally innovative, competing systems.

Another hallmark of the new technology was a renewed interest in materials and a fresh look at what they could do. Town's truss reflects, in its handling of wood and its implications for metal, a major breakthrough. Traditionally wood had been used post-and-lintel fashion for bridging; it had also been used to fabricate structural imitations of the stone arch. It is interesting that the first cast-iron bridge (at Sunderland in England, 1793–1796) was designed as an abstraction of a stone arch. Town's truss (as any truss) is a framework of ties and struts arrayed so that the whole pattern acts as a beam. The truss beam exploited wood (or metal) for its strength under tension strain where traditional modes had treated wood and metal in imitation of stone, and therefore in imitation of the strength of stone under compressive strain. This new attitude toward materials and their use is also apparent in the balloon frame. The balloon frame was named in derision and was regarded by traditional architects as "no frame at all." The balloon frame depends for its strength not on the strength of a single member but on the whole pattern of vertical studding, diagonal sheathing, and horizontal siding; the strength of the whole is greater than the strength of the individual parts. In heavy timber framing, the reverse is the case. Both Town's truss and the balloon frame emphasize design pattern, and both imply a conservation of materials. They also require a working knowledge of mathematics and geometry on the part of the laborer, as is apparent in Bell's handbook. This fresh look at materials and their uses is perhaps more impressive in relation to traditional materials such as wood than it was with cast iron in the 1850's or structural steel in the 1870's, since iron and steel, once they were available in quantity, were "new materials" demanding an original investigation of their potentials and uses.

The history of Town's truss, the balloon frame, and Bogardus's system of construction calls into question our conventional expectation that necessity must have mothered these inventions. Each of them seems in retrospect to have been invented before the crisis of need rather than after it. The need for level-bedded bridges was not as pressing in 1820 when Town patented his truss as it was to be in the 1830's and 1840's when the railroad was revolutionizing transportation. The balloon frame was developed in Chicago as early as 1833, when the population of the city was only 550—before and not after the population explosion in the Chicago area put such a premium on quick and inexpensive methods of construction. Similarly, Bogardus's innovations in the 1850's occurred before the inflation of urban real-estate values (in the 1860's and 1870's) had dictated the skyscraper; and Otis's fail-safe elevator, which was to make the skyscraper habitable, had also been developed in the 1850's. This rela-

tion of invention to need also suggests that inventions are
not singular, isolated innovations but integral parts of a
complex web—as Buckminster Fuller metaphorized it: "The
automobile is only one-half of the invention; the concrete
highway is the other half." In the nineteenth century new
structural systems were only a small part of the rapidly
growing invention complex; and while it is convenient to
study the structural engineering aspects of architecture in
isolation, we can mislead ourselves into imagining that all
the nineteenth-century architect needed to fulfill the dream
of a "new architecture" was a knowledge of specific materials
and specific structural systems, when what he actually needed
was a comprehensive vision of the whole technological revolution, embracing everything from new steel processes and
new machine tools to the new farm machinery, the slaughterhouse techniques, and the railroad transportation that could
supply the new urban concentrations.

It is small wonder that the radical transformation of the
space-time environment between 1820 and 1870 resulted in
a deepening three-way split between what the hand could do,
what the eye could see and synthesize, and what the mind
could ask for and yet control. One reflection of this deepening split was the growth in the 1850's and 1860's of a
three-cornered opposition among art, technology, and economics in architecture (see Part III, Chapter 6). Art was
increasingly assumed to be the province of the architect,
technology of the engineer, and economics of the client or
patron. As the Scottish architectural historian and critic James
Fergusson, put it, "Where the engineer leaves off the art of
the architect begins." This assertion implies that the art
of architecture consists of decorating the engineered structure. Fergusson's assertion was poeticized by Ruskin into the
strange dogma, "True architecture does not admit iron as a
constructive material." And this dogma in turn gradually
fused with the growing aesthetic reaction against the urban-
industrial uglification of the landscape—a reaction that for
William Morris stemmed from his vision of the English
Midlands, "six counties overhung with smoke." The reaction,
with its suspicion of technology, was further hardened by what
must have seemed the bewildering pace of technological innovation and exploitation. For example, as late as the 1870's,
professional architects were still contemptuous of, and in part

ignorant of, the design-materials-labor potential of the balloon frame. Conversely, the engineer-technologist grew contemptuous of the architect, and tended to regard him as a mere dilettante and decorator. But as opposed as the two personalities sound, they were still being combined in one man, for example in George B. Post (1837–1913) whose Manufacturers Building at the World's Columbian Exposition in Chicago combined a brilliantly engineered roof truss spanning 385 feet with an impenetrable disguise of exuberant neo-Renaissance classicism.

Nor was this opposition simply architect versus engineer; the client-patron-public has to be included in the tangle. The present attempt by architectural historians to pinpoint "the first skyscraper" sheds interesting light on the role of client-patron-public. The skyscraper, by definition, should be a steel cage with curtain walls; why, then, did engineer-architects of the first skyscrapers, men like William Le Baron Jenney (1832–1907), disguise their buildings to look as though they were stone-bearing structures? The answer to this question is usually couched in terms of praise for the engineer who designed the structure and blame for the architect who designed the disguise, but this answer omits consideration of what the public eye in the 1880's would have read and accepted as a safe and useful building. The public eye had been trained to see in terms of stone-bearing construction— heavy at the bottom, progressively lighter toward the top. The cast-iron cage of the 1850's and the steel cage of the 1880's would have read as top-heavy buildings, lacking the familiar pyramidal base. The response to this public opposition was: on Bogardus's part, argument and overstatement in advertising pamphlets; on the part of Jenney and others, a "fool-the-eye" compromise—until the public eye had been retrained by experience of steel cage and suspension bridges, of factories, grain elevators, and other industrial buildings to read and accept the steel cage as structurally sound.

The selections in Part III are presented only as indicators of a climate of mind, as brief glimpses of the extraordinary technological revolution that was altering both the needs for architecture and the methods and materials of architectural construction. The selections also suggest a spectrum, from

Town, who was both architect and engineer, to Bogardus, who was inventor-engineer, to the quasi-anonymous carpenters who evolved the balloon frame. Etzler and Fowler are included as reformers whose imaginations were building in the modes that were being developed by the practical innovators.

Ithiel Town, A / DESCRIPTION OF / ITHIEL TOWN'S / IMPROVEMENT IN THE CONSTRUCTION / OF / WOOD AND IRON BRIDGES: / INTENDED AS A / GENERAL SYSTEM OF BRIDGE-BUILDING / FOR RIVERS, CREEKS, AND HARBORS OF WHATEVER KIND OF BOTTOMS, / AND FOR ANY PRACTICABLE WIDTH OF SPAN OR OPENING, / IN EVERY PART OF THE COUNTRY (New Haven, 1821).

Ithiel Town (1784–1844) was not only an inventive engineer but also a skilled and sensitive architect in the current revival styles, Greek (see illustration 13), Gothic, and Tuscan Villa. He was a bibliophile with a library of 11,000 books and thousands of engravings; he was an indefatigable student of art history and a liberal influence in the evolution of American culture in the second quarter of the nineteenth century. The lattice truss described in this pamphlet was patented January 28, 1820. The royalties from the truss made Town a rich man; and he continued to study and improve the engineering of truss and bridge designs throughout his career. After 1829, as senior partner with the draughtsman and "architectural composer" Alexander Jackson Davis (1803–1892), Town turned his attention increasingly to architectural design. The firm of Town and Davis advertised itself, not entirely accurately, as the first professional architectural firm in America, but in revival architecture the firm had considerable influence on the American architectural scene, setting and maintaining relatively high standards in both its buildings and its copybooks.

13. Ithiel Town and Alexander Jackson Davis; David Hoadley, builder, Russell House (1828–1830), now the Honors College at Wesleyan University, Middletown, Connecticut.

A Description

To establish a general mode of constructing wooden and iron bridges, and which mode of construction shall, at the same time, be the most simple, permanent, and economical, both in erecting and repairing, has been, for a long time, a desideratum of great importance to a country so extensive, and interspersed with so many wild and majestic rivers as ours is. It has been too much the custom for architects and builders to pile together materials, each according to his own ideas of the scientific principles and practice of bridge-building, and the result has been, 1. That nearly as many modes of construction have been adopted as there have been bridges built. 2. That many have answered no purpose at all, and others but very poorly and for a short time, while most of the best ones have cost a sum which deters and puts it out of the power of probably five-sixths of those interested in ferries, to substitute bridges, which would obviate the many dangers and delays incident to them.

That architects and builders adhere to their own ideas in the construction not only of bridges, but of buildings, is almost universally true; they are obstinately opposed to the adoption of any other mode than their own; consequently it is as true, and it is seen to be so, throughout the country (and it is much to be regretted), that in very few instances, either in erecting bridges or buildings, there is any model either uniform, or, in general, very good. But in bridges and public buildings, it would seem, something better might be expected, if men scientifically and practically acquainted with such subjects would step forward, in a disinterested manner, and determine between principles which are philosophical and those which are not, and between modes of execution which are founded in practice and experience and those which are founded in ignorance and inexperience; and in matters of taste, if they would determine in favor of classic and well-established taste, and that which is the offspring of unimproved minds and whimsical fancies, which are ever upon the rack to establish new things, the creation of their own imaginations; and which are therefore sure to be wrong for this good reason, that their authors are so.

14. Model of Ithiel Town's Lattice Truss.

Perhaps the following proposition comprises what is the most important to be determined with regard to a general system of bridgebuilding, viz.:

By what construction or arrangement will the least quantity of materials, and cost of labor, erect a bridge of any practicable span or opening between piers or abutments, to be the strongest and most permanent, and to admit of the easiest repair?

In giving the best answer to this proposition which I am capable of after a number of years' attention to the theory and practice of this subject, I shall refer to the plates accompanying this article. The mode of construction is so simple and plain to inspection as to require little explanation of them.

Figure 1 is an elevation of one of the trusses of a bridge; one, two, or three of those trusses placed vertically upon piers are to be considered as the support of the bridge, and are to be of a height at least sufficient to admit a wagon to pass under the upper beams, which lie horizontally upon the top stringpiece of the side trusses; and on these same side stringpieces rest the feet of rafters, which form a roof to shingle upon. In this case, a middle truss is used, which will always be necessary in bridges of considerable width; the height of it will be as much greater than the side ones as the height or pitch of the roof. The height of the trusses must be equal to the whole height of the bridge required, and is to be an exact continuation of the work represented in Fig. 1.

The height of the trusses is to be proportioned to the width of the openings between the piers or abutments, and may be about one-tenth of the openings, when the piers are fifteen feet or more apart—a less span requiring about the same height, for the reasons before stated.

The diagonal bearing of these trusses is composed of sawed plank ten or eleven inches wide, and from three to three and a half inches thick; it may be sawed from any timber that will last well, when kept dry. White pine and spruce are probably the best kinds of timber for the purpose, on account of their lightness and their not being so subject to spring or warp as white oak.

The nearer those braces are placed to each other, the more strength will the truss have, and in no case are they

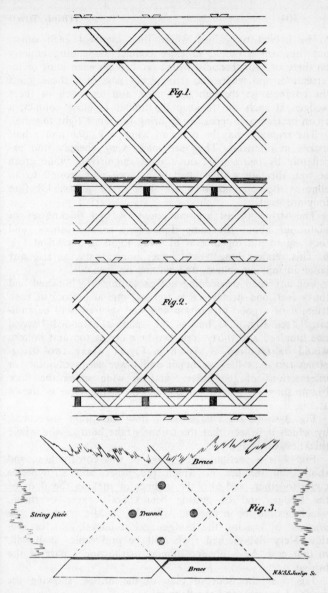

Fig. 1.

Fig. 2.

Brace

String piece   Trunnel   **Fig. 3.**

Brace

N.&S.S.Jocelyn Sc.

15. Ithiel Town, Structural Diagrams, Lattice Truss.

to be halved or gained where they intersect each other; but they are to stand in close contact, depending entirely on three or four trunnels, which go through each joint or intersection, and where the stringpieces pass over these joints the trunnels go through them also, and are each of them wedged at each end to keep the timber in close contact; a chain or clamp is necessary to bring the work tight together.

The trunnels may be made of white oak, one and a half inches in diameter. They are made very cheaply and excellently by being rived out square and driven, while green or wet, through a tube fitted to a block and ground to an edge at the top end; they are then to be seasoned before they are used.

The string pieces are composed of two thicknesses of plank, of about the same dimensions as the braces, and they are so put together as to break joints as shown at Fig. 6. This renders long hewn timber unnecessary, as also any labor in making splices, and putting on ironwork.

For any span or opening not exceeding one hundred and thirty feet, one stringpiece at top and one at bottom of each truss, if of a good proportion and well secured, will be sufficient (see Fig. 2.); but as the span is extended beyond one hundred and thirty feet, two or more at top and bottom would be required as shown in Fig. 1 where two stringpieces run over the two upper and lower series of joints or intersections of the braces, and in wide spans the floor beams may be placed on the second stringpiece as shown at Fig. 1.

Fig. 3 shows on a larger scale how each joint is secured, by which it is seen that the trunnels take hold of the whole thickness of each piece.

Fig. 4 is a section of a bridge of this construction, and shows the manner in which the brace and stringpieces come together, and also the manner of making the floor of the bridge, and of putting beams and braces overhead, which are to be connected with the middle truss for the purpose of bracing the bridge against lateral rack or motion. Very flat pitched roofs will be preferable, as it will, in that case, be a greater support to the upper part of the bridge.

Fig. 5 is the floor or plan of the bridge, showing the mode of bracing and the floor joist.

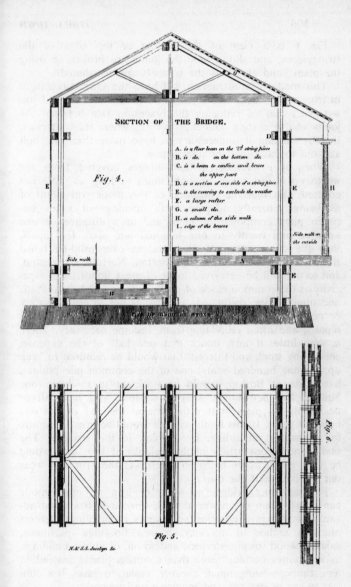

SECTION OF THE BRIDGE.

A. *is a floor beam on the* 2d *string piece*
B. *is do.   on the bottom do.*
C. *is a beam to confine and brace the upper part*
D. *is a section of one side of a string piece*
E. *is the covering to exclude the weather*
F. *a large rafter*
G. *a small do.*
H. *a column of the side walk*
I. *edge of the braces*

Fig. 4.

Side walk

Side walk on the outside

Fig. 5.

Fig. 6.

N. & S. S. Jocelyn Sc.

16. Ithiel Town, Structural Diagrams, Lattice Truss.

Fig. 6 is a view of the bottom or top edge of the stringpieces, and shows how the joints are broken in using the plank, and also how the trunnels are distributed.

This mode of construction will have the same advantages in iron as in wood, and some in cast iron which wood has not, viz., that of reducing the braces in size between the joints and of casting flaunches to them where they intersect, thereby making it unnecessary to have more than one bolt and nut to each joint or intersection.

When it is considered that bridges covered from the weather will last seven or eight times as long as those not covered, and that the cheapness of this mode will admit of its being generally adopted, with openings or spans between piers composed of piles, and at a distance of one hundred and twenty to one hundred and sixty feet apart, then the construction of long bridges over mud-bottomed rivers, like those at Washington, Boston, Norfolk, Charleston, and so on, will be perceived to be of great importance, especially as the common mode of piling is so exposed to freshets, uncommon tides, driftwood, and ice, as not to ensure safety or economy in covering them, and consequently continual repairs, and often rebuilding them, become necessary. There is very little, if any, doubt that one half of the expense, computing stock and interest, that would be required to keep up, for one hundred years, one of the common pile bridges, like those at Boston, would be sufficient to maintain one built in this new mode, keep it covered, and have all or nearly all the piers built with stone at the end of the one hundred years. If this be the case, it would be great economy to commence rebuilding, by degrees, in this manner. The saving in the one article of floor planks, if kept dry, would be very great, as by being so much wet they rot and wear out in about half the time.

For aqueduct bridges of wood or iron no other mode can be as cheap or answer as well; this mode has equal advantages also in supporting wide roofs of buildings, centers of wide arches in masonry, trussed floorings, partitions, sides of wood towers, steeples, and so on, of public buildings, as it requires nothing more than common planks instead of long timber—being much cheaper, easier to raise, less subject to wet or dry rot, and requiring no ironwork.

Some of the advantages of constructing bridges according to this mode are the following:

1. There is no pressure against abutments or piers, as arched bridges have, and consequently perpendicular supports only are necessary; this saving in wide arches is very great, sometimes equal to a third part of the whole expense of the bridge.

2. The shrinking of timber has little or no effect, as the strain upon each plank of the trusses, both of the braces and stringpieces, is an end-grain strain or lengthwise of the wood.

3. Suitable timber can be easily procured and sawed at common mills, as it requires no large or long timber—defects in timber may be discovered, and wet and dry rot prevented much more easily than could be in large timber.

4. There is no ironwork required, which at best is not safe, especially in frosty weather.

5. It has less motion than is common in bridges, and which is so injurious and frequently fatal to bridges—and being in a horizontal line, is much less operated upon by winds.

6. A level roadway is among the most important advantages of this mode of construction.

7. The side trusses serve as a frame to cover upon, and thereby save, any extra weight of timber, except the covering itself—and the importance and economy of covering bridges from the weather is too well understood to need recommendation after the experience which this country has already had.

8. Draws for shipping to pass through may with perfect safety be introduced in any part of the bridge, without weakening it as in arched bridges, where the strength and safety of the arches depend so much on their pressure against each other and abutments, that a draw, by destroying the connection, weakens the whole superstructure.

9. The great number of nearly equal parts or joints into which the strain, occasioned by a great weight upon the bridge, is divided is a very important advantage over any other mode, as by dividing the strain or stress into so many parts, that what falls upon any one part or joint is easily

sustained by it without either the mode of securing the joints, or the strength of the material being insufficient.

10. The expense of the superstructure of a bridge would not be more than from one-half to two-thirds of other modes of constructing one over the same span or opening; this is a very important consideration, especially in the southern and western states, where there are many wide rivers, and a very scattered population to defray the expenses of bridges.

11. This mode of securing the braces by so many trunnels gives them much more strength when they are in tension strain than could be had in the common mode of securing them by means of tenons and mortises, for tenons, being short and not very thick, compared with this mode, nor having so much hold of the pins or trunnels as in this case, will, of course, have much less power to sustain a tension or pulling strain, and it is obvious that this strain is in many cases equal to, and in others greater than, the thrust or pushing strain. It is also very obvious that this pushing or thrust strain in the mode of tenons and mortises receives very little additional strength from the shoulders of the tenons, as the shrinkage of the timber into which the tenon goes is generally so much as to let the work settle so far as to give a motion or vibration, which, in time, renders them weak and insufficient.

12. Should any kind of arched bridge, for any reason, be preferred, however it may be arched either at top or bottom, or both, still this same mode of combining the materials will have all the advantages as to cheapness and strength, over the common ones of framing, as in case of the horizontal or straight ones before described. In cases where abutments are already built, it may sometimes be preferred.

Sidewalks may with equal ease be constructed, either on the outside or inside of the main body of the bridge, which particular, as also the great strength of the mode, and so on, may be better seen by examination of the models which are (or soon will be) placed in most of the principal cities of the United States, and no merit is either desired or claimed in this new mode of construction by the patentee, which the mode itself does not command, even on the most strict philosophical investigation as to its mathematical principles, the easy, practicable, and advantageous application of materials, the advantages it possesses in mechanical execution, and its simplicity, strength, economy, and durability, as a general and uniform mode of bridgebuilding.

Science and practice will, in a short time, decide on this question so important to this extensive country.

I shall conclude this article by a few ideas taken from the celebrated Robert Fulton's treatise on canal navigation, page 117, and subsequent pages.

In England, the attention of engineers has of late years been much engaged on bridges of iron. These bridges, as experience produces courage, are progressively enlarging their dimensions, nor should I be surprised if genius should, in time, produce the mechanic rainbow of one thousand feet over wide and rapid rivers. In crossing the rivers in such countries as Russia and America, an extensive arch seems to be a consideration of the first importance, as the rivers or even rivulets, in time of rain, suddenly swell to a great height, and in the spring, on breaking up of the ice, the immense quantity which is borne down with a rapid stream would, if interrupted by small arches and piers, collect to such a weight as ultimately to bear away the whole. It is therefore necessary that, in such situations, an arch should be extended as far as possible, and so high as to suffer everything to pass through, or the inhabitants must, without some other expedient, submit their passage to the casualties of the weather.

The important objection to bridges of wood is their rapid decay, and this objection is certainly well founded when particular situations are alluded to where timber is scarce and consequently expensive. But in such countries as America, where wood is abundant, I conceive it will be a fair criterion to judge of their application by calculating on the expense of a bridge of stone, and one of wood, and then compare the interest of the principal saved in adopting the wood bridge, with the expense of its annual repairs.

I have before exhibited the necessity of constructing bridges in America of an extensive span or arch, in order to suffer the ice and collected waters to pass without interruption: and for this purpose it must be observed that a wood arch may be formed of a much greater length or span than it is possible to erect one of stone; hence wooden bridges are applicable to many situations where accumulated waters, bearing down trees and fields of ice, would tear a bridge of stone from its foundation.

It therefore becomes of importance to render bridges of wood as permanent as the nature of the material will admit.

Hitherto, in bridges not covered from the weather, the immense quantity of mortises and tenons, which, however well done, will admit air and wet, and consequently tend to expedite the decay of the weak parts, has been a material error in constructing bridges of wood.

But to render wood bridges of much more importance than they have hitherto been considered, first from their extensive span; secondly from their durability; two things must be considered, first that the wood works should stand clear of the stream in every part, by which it never would have any other weight to sustain than that of the usual carriages; secondly, that it will be so combined as to exclude as much as possible the air and rain.

When the true principle of building bridges of wood is discovered, their progressive extension is as reasonable as the increased dimensions of shipping; which, in early ages, was deemed a great work if they amounted to one hundred tons' burden; but time and experience have extended the art of shipbuilding to two thousand tons, and in the combination and arrangement of the various and complicated parts, there certainly is more genius and labor required than in erecting a bridge of five-hundred- or one-thousand-feet span: but the great demand for shipping has rendered their formation familiar, and their increased bulk has gradually grown upon our senses. But had a man, in the infancy of naval architecture, hinted at a vessel of two thousand tons, I am inclined to think his contemporary artists would have branded him as a madman.

NOTE

Those who wish to purchase rights, and to obtain particular directions for building bridges according to this improvement (the description of which is annexed), will please to write to me at the City of Washington in the District of Columbia, where myself or an agent will at all times attend promptly to the business.

ITHIEL TOWN

3

J. A. Etzler, THE PARADISE / WITHIN THE REACH OF ALL MEN / WITHOUT LABOR, / BY POWERS OF NATURE AND MACHINERY, / AN ADDRESS / TO ALL INTELLIGENT MEN (London, 1836), pp. 62–65.

John Adolphus Etzler was a Pennsylvanian whose *Paradise* was first published in Pittsburgh (1833) but eventually was more popular in England than in America. He was so little known in his own time that he was identified in one magazine as "that Englishman." Etzler and many of his contemporaries conceived visionary and at times weird utopian schemes for the perfection of man and his society. Classical utopias such as Sir Thomas More's present "ideal states" as a means of dramatizing the inadequacies of contemporary states, but in Etzler's *Paradise* the dream of moral and intellectual improvement is interwoven with visionary mechanical ideas. As Thoreau remarked in his review of Etzler's book: "It appears there is a transcendentalism in mechanics as well as in ethics." In effect, the mechanical ideas with their suggestion of feasibility assert the possibility of actual utopian achievement. The brief section of Etzler's book quoted here is yet another reflection of an idea which was "in the air" in the second quarter of the nineteenth century, the idea of prefabrication and modular construction.

Architecture

Earth may be baked into bricks, or even to vitrified stone, by heat. Stones may be cemented together so as to break to pieces before their cement yields; a proof that cement is then harder and more cohesive than the stones themselves. Sand and stones ground to dust may be turned into glass or vitrified substance of the greatest hardness and cohesion, by great heat. Hence we may bake large masses of any size and form into stone and vitrified substance of the greatest duration, even for thousands of years, out of clayey earth or of stones ground to dust, by the application of burning mirrors. This is to be done in the open air without other preparation than gathering the substance, grinding and mixing it with water and cement, molding or casting it into adapted molds, and bringing the focus of the burning mirrors of proper size upon the same.

Wood, cut and ground to dust, and then cemented by a liquor, may be also molded into any shape and dried, so as to become a solid, consistent wooden substance that may be dyed with various colors, and polished.

Thus we may mold and bake any form of any size, entire walls, floors, ceilings, roofs, doors, channels for canals, ditches, aqueducts, bridges, pavement of walks and roads, chimneys, hollow cylinders for machineries and mines and wells, plates for any purpose, vessels for holding dry and liquid materials, pillars, columns, balustrades, statues, postments, and other ornaments, figures of any description, reliefs, sculptural works, pipes, furnitures for household, kitchen utensils, pieces of machineries, and numberless other things, of all shapes, sizes, colors, fashions, and fancy; in short, any thing of hard material. When once the mold is made, it may serve forever for thousands of thousands of other pieces, no matter how artificially it be shaped, without ever requiring any further labor of man. The substance may be polished or glazed, and then serve for burning mirrors.

Foundries of any description are to be heated by burning mirrors, and require no labor, except the making of the first molds, and the superintendence for gathering the metal and taking the finished articles away.

Flexible Stuff

There is one yet great desideratum; this is the making of flexible or pliable stuffs, and finishing all the articles out of them for use, such as for garments, couches, and all other commodities and ornaments, without labor. If this can be effected without labor, then the problem of superseding all human labors is resolved completely.

This can be done, without spinning, weaving, sewing, tanning, and so on, by a simple proceeding. There are cohesive substances in superabundance in nature, in the vegetation and animal kingdom, which need but be extracted; they are of various qualities: some resist water, some heat, some both, some are elastic, some soft, some hard. They all may be hardened or dissolved into fluids, just as required. They are made use of already for various purposes. In dissolving them into adapted fluids, and mixing the same with fibers of vegetables of convenient fineness or other flexible stuffs fitly prepared, they will glutinate them together. By a proper contrivance sheets of any size and form may be formed, in a similar manner as it is done with manufacturing paper. This stuff may be made as fine, and as thin or as thick as it may be desired. It may be made of any degree or stiffness or softness, which is depending from the mixture of stuffs, and from the manner of preparation and finishing. It may be calendered and polished for the sake of ornament, or for mirrors. It may be made of any color, or pattern, without any additional trouble, except admixture of dying stuff. It may then be used for any purpose, instead of any woven stuff, of leather, paper, fur, and so on. It may be cast not only in sheets of any size or form but also into any shape whatever; thus ready-made clothes of any fashion, vessels for holding dry or liquid materials, of any shape or size, any other article of commodity may be at once cast or molded into the appropriated form or mold.

So there will be no sewing or any kind of finishing by hands. There is no object of pliable stuff to be thought of which could not be made completely in this way, so as to supersede all articles of that kind actually in use.

[pp. 62–65]

4

O. S. Fowler, A / HOME FOR ALL / OR / THE
GRAVEL WALL / AND / OCTAGON MODE OF
BUILDING / NEW, CHEAP, CONVENIENT, SUPE-
RIOR / AND / ADAPTED TO RICH AND POOR. /
SHOWING THE SUPERIORITY OF THIS GRAVEL
CONCRETE OVER BRICK, STONE, AND FRAME
HOUSES; MANNER / OF MAKING AND DEPOSIT-
ING IT; ITS COST; OUTSIDE FINISH; CLAY
HOUSES; DEFECTS IN SMALL, LOW, / LONG-
WINGED, AND COTTAGE HOUSES; THE GREATER
CAPACITY, BEAUTY, COMPACTNESS, AND /
UTILITY OF OCTAGON HOUSES; DIFFERENT
PLANS; THE AUTHOR'S RESIDENCE; / GREEN
AND ICE HOUSES; FILTERS; GROUNDS; SHRUB-
BERY; FRUITS, AND / THEIR CULTURE; ROOF-
ING; SCHOOL-HOUSES AND CHURCHES; /
BARNS AND OUT-BUILDINGS; BOARD AND
PLANK WALLS; THE WORKING-MAN'S DWELL-
ING, ETC. ETC. (New York, 1853), pp. iii–iv,
12–20, 56–62, 67–70, 80–89.

Orson Squire Fowler (1809–1887) was noted as the
founder of practical phrenology in the United States and
also as an ardent reformer in both the abolition and temperance movements. The central emphasis of his entire career

is "improvement"—of memory, intellect, marriage, society, and humanity, and, in the case of the book quoted here, housing. Fowler's influence was widespread as a result of his writings, which were voluminous, and as a result of his indefatigable persistence as a lecturer. *A Home for All* is an attempt at a comprehensive rationalization of both design and construction, not unlike Fowler's phrenology, which was a similar attempt to rationalize and improve all aspects of human mental behavior. In passages not quoted here, Fowler discusses at length problems of circulation in housing; he generalizes the octagon form to include schools and churches; and in one passage he speculates on prefabricated and reusable forms for the concrete construction which he regards as a universal common denominator.

Preface

To cheapen and improve human homes, and especially to bring comfortable dwellings within the reach of the poorer classes, is the object of this volume—an object of the highest practical utility to man. It delineates a new mode of enclosing public edifices and private residences, far better, every way, and several hundred percent cheaper, than any other; and will enable the poor but ingenious man to erect a comfortable dwelling at a trifling cost, and almost without the aid or cost, as now, of mechanics. Except in a single particular, and this he has greatly improved, this mode is the invention of its author, and occurred thus. Till past forty, his profession engrossed too much of his time and means to allow him to procure a comfortable home; yet for ten years he has been making observations, in all his professional peregrinations, and cogitating by months, upon the best mode of building the home of his future years. These have at length brought him to results, now reduced to practice. Let no one suppose that he has forsaken, or even turned aside from, phrenology —that first and only occupation of his enthusiastic youth, and the idol of his matured and declining years. He has turned aside only to build him a good home, and in doing so, has made and learned improvements to adopt which will greatly increase *home comforts;* and this work is written to propagate them, rather than as a complete architectural production.

As its author is a phrenologist, not a builder, it may lack occasional details and specifications, yet will give everything peculiar to *this mode* of building. Specifications respecting doors, floors, windows, etc., common to this and other modes of building, can be learned from scientific works on this subject.

The octagon form and the gravel wall are its two distinct characteristics. The form, as applied to domestic residences, is wholly original with the author, and the latter greatly improved upon, and at the other principles and suggestions the author has arrived while planning and studying out his own house. The work is offered, not as beyond improvement, for "progress is a universal law," but to apply this law of progress to housebuilding. Why so little progress in architecture, when there is so much in all other matters? Why continue to build in the same square form of all past ages? Is no *radical* improvement of both the external form and internal arrangement of private residences, as well as *building material,* possible? Let this work answer.

[pp. iii–iv]

From Section I, "Principles, Facts, and Common-Sense Suggestions About House-Building"

THE PLEASURES OF BUILDING

Nor is man constituted merely to *require* houses, but also adapted to build them, by being endowed with a building faculty. Not merely does nature double and quadruple most of life's pleasures by means of houses; but she has made their erection absolutely certain, by rendering the very building itself most pleasurable. Behold how happy yon birds, in gathering materials, and building up day by day, a sweet little home for themselves and their prospective offspring; and say, ye who have ever built a residence for your own self and family, if its planning, its preparation, and its erection, from its very cornerstone, were not all pleasurable, so as literally to form an epoch in your history, and to overbalance even its expensiveness. And if it were conducted in the best manner, it might all be pleasurable. Building too hastily, or at great disadvantage, or unwisely is more or less irksome, as is the nonobedience of all nature's other laws; but to see this room finished today, and that tomorrow; this excellent fixture begun, and that added, is exultingly pleasurable. No labor of my life has given me more lively delight than the planning and building of my own house; and to all it can likewise be rendered almost intoxicating.

Not withstanding its expensiveness, men have a literal mania for building, which increases with civilization, and should continue till all are supplied with comfortable homes. Houses being so absolutely necessary, nature has made their erection absolutely certain, by rendering it thus pleasurable. This pleasure is consequent on its gratifying those two primitive faculties, inhabitiveness and constructiveness, along with several others; without the former of which he would never wish to build if he could; and without the latter, could not if he would. How perfect this home-erecting arrangement of nature! Then let it be cultivated by all.

These two faculties make men prefer to *build* their own houses, rather than to buy those equally good built by others. Hence, houses can always be bought cheaper than built. But, as birds, instead of living in some vacated nest, prefer to build a new one to their own liking, so men, unless too poor, should rather build than buy; for, otherwise they will wish this different, and that bettered, all their lives, and probably spend more in "alterations" than the extra cost of a new house. One may well be content to live in the old family mansion, consecrated by the joys and sorrows of his parents and ancestors, and by the sacred reminiscences of his childhood; but give me a relatively poor house of my own erection, in preference to one built by some stranger.

WHAT CONSTITUTES A PERFECT HOME

THAT which combines the most instrumentalities for comfort and enjoyment, especially domestic—the only rational end of any dwelling—only a few of the most important of which we will now name, leaving others to be developed as we proceed.

To ENCLOSE SPACE is the first and main object. This is effected by making walls, floors, roof, etc.

STRENGTH and TIGHTNESS are required; the former to resist winds, and the latter to exclude rains and colds, and include warmth. LIGHT is needed, and secured by windows, as is also WARMTH, which should be easily created, cheap, governable, and complete; for what comfort can be taken in an open barn of a house, the chilling blasts pouring in through a thousand insolent apertures, freezing one side while you roast the other, and exposing you to every sudden change of temperature.

COMPLETE VENTILATION, under control, is another; for every human being requires a copious and constant supply of this commodity, so indispensable not merely to human comfort but even existence.

A SUITE OF ROOMS is also requisite; one for cooking, another for family use, others for sleeping and other purposes, and all so arranged as perfectly to subserve their respective ends, and, of course, easily accessible from each to all, effected by doors, stairs, entry, etc. And these rooms should be conveniently located, as regards each other, and especially adapted to facilitate family ends, housework in particular. Practical housekeepers know that it takes twice the labor to do up a given amount of work in some houses as in others. To have each room and its appurtenances, and all the rooms, as regards each other, so placed and arranged as to have everything handy and convenient, and a place for every thing, is indeed a great desideratum. How much fretfulness and ill temper, as well as exhaustion and sickness, an unhandy house occasions. Nor does the evil end here. It often, generally, by perpetually irritating mothers, sours the tempers of their children, even *before birth*, thus rendering the whole family bad dispositioned *by nature*, whereas a convenient one would have rendered them constitutionally amiable and good.

Beauty is also desirable, as gratifying an important human faculty.

A GOOD BUILDING SPOT is also necessary, and one adapted to the proposed kind of house. The same money will often build a far better house on one site than on another. A superb building spot was one of the three motives which induced me to build where I did—the other two being good water and an excellent fruit locality.

As to what constitutes a good building spot, "many men have many minds." Some prefer valleys, streams, and lawns; others water scenery, elevations, and sightly prospects; but I confess partiality for the latter. Give me a beautiful landscape and an elevated site. This also guarantees a fresh, dry atmosphere, in place of valley fogs and miasmas, together with whatever summer breeze may be afoot. And what if it is exposed to winter's bleak winds? Are they not bracing and healthy? Yet a plan will soon be proposed which will enable you to defy them, yet enjoy summer's balmy breezes. At least, do not build in a mudhole. Yet good water, and handy, is most desirable, and springs exceed wells.

But, be your site where and what it may, let it and your house be *adapted to each other*. Some sites are admirably adapted to one kind of house, yet miserably unfitted to another, and the reverse. Choose your site with reference to your general plan, and then modify the latter till you effect a perfect correspondence of each to the other, and adapt both to your own wants and taste.

From Section II, "The Gravel-Wall Plan"

NATURE'S BUILDING MATERIAL

Nature has made ample provision for supplying every legitimate want of all her creatures. Behold in this her tender fondness, her maternal care. Hence, since a comfortable home is one of these natural wants, has she not made perfect provision for this home demand of all her creatures? Nor for rich merely; for, does not her provisionary care extend to her *needy* creatures quite as much as to her more favored children? Is nature so aristrocratic as to provide homes only for the rich? Does not her vast laboratory abound in some "coarse homespun," about as promotive of human comfort as her more expensive materials? Ye homeless poor, be assured your mother has not forgotten you. She has provided some cheap and comfortable building material, if you only knew what it is. And in various climes it is exactly fitted to each clime—in cold latitudes, one every way fitted to withstand and keep out cold; another in warm climes adapted thereto; in damp places, something adapted to them; and thus of all the other conditions of all climates, for nature's provisions are all *perfect*.

Before considering what this material is, let us see what it is *not*. Nature's building material is abundant everywhere, cheap, durable, and complete throughout. Of course, what is objectionable is not hers.

WOOD IS OBJECTIONABLE

Because the whole of the earth's surface is or will ultimately be required for raising food for man. All nature's economies point to the greatest possible number of human beings she can feed and clothe. For a time yet, or till she is well stocked with human beings, that surface is of little account, and can just as well be spared for raising timber for lumber as not. But let earth's population increase for five hundred years to come, as fast as it has for one hundred past—and it is sure to do far more than this—and her entire surface will be densely populated. But to raise wood enough to erect and repair all the human habitations then needed will require immense tracts of land, which otherwise could be appropriated to raising food, which would allow a far greater number of human beings to inhabit and enjoy earth and her luxuries if there were some other building material than if wood were mainly used. The strife will then be between tree and man, and will be short. The great consumption of food then will also render land so valuable for horticulture as to render wood too dear to be bought for building, even by princes. It is even now becoming enormously high in New York, namely, good pine $35 to $45 per 1,000 feet. Then what must it become in fifty years?

Wood decays, whereas economy requires that houses, once up, endure like time, and improve by age. This being obliged every few years to paint and repaint, to repair and re-repair, and even then to have your house perpetually rotting down upon you, is a defect too palpable to characterize a proper building material.

Wood houses burn down, often in half an hour; whereas a complete house must be incombustible. The ravages of fire in cities and towns are horrible, beyond almost any other horror to which man is subjected; and even a country fire,

if only a stable, is awful. No! nature's building material will
not render her occupants liable to be turned by thousands
in an hour out of comfortable rooms into houseless streets,
perhaps in a night of darkness and storm, of snow and blow,
terrible of itself when warded off by a comfortable house, but
awfully horrid when forced out of a comfortable house and
warm bed, perhaps sick, or aged, every article of comfort and
luxury, the accumulated toil of years, consumed in a moment,
perhaps a beloved child or companion scathed by flame and
suffocated by smoke, burned to a crisp. No, no! wood is not
nature's building material although a wood house is indeed
better than none, and will do for man when he can afford
nothing better.

BRICK

Ah, now we have it. Slow to decay, incombustible, requiring little of earth's surface for its production—yes, brick must
be the very thing, says one. Not so fast. It wastes by time, is
marred by frost, expensive, both in cost and laying—too much
so to be nature's staple building material—for nature cares
for her poorest sons and daughters, and will not put good
homes beyond their reach. Still, brick is by far preferable to
wood, and will do in many localities, especially where it
can be made *on the spot,* yet is too costly to transport far.
An anecdote. A proud English lord spent an immense sum
in erecting a magnificent manorial mansion, and invited
another noble lord to examine, and say what he thought of
it—proud to exhibit his riches and his taste. As his opinion
was solicited, the visitor replied: "Well done for a *mud*
house." The muddy adjective so stung the owner, that he
removed every brick, and rebuilt of stone. "Then," it is
replied, "you recommend *stone houses.*"

Not exactly. Very laborious to hew them into shape, very
cold in winter, and damp in wet weather, either expensive or
else unsightly—there must be something else better than this,
than brick, or wood—some *perfect* building material. What
is it?

THE LIME, GRAVEL, AND STONE WALLS

Simplicity and efficiency characterize every work of nature. Her building material will therefore be simple, durable, easily applied, everywhere abundant, easily rendered beautiful, comfortable, and every way complete. All this is true of the *gravel wall*. It is made wholly out of lime and stones, sand included, which is, of course, fine stone. And pray what is lime but stone? Made from stone, the burning, by expelling its carbonic acid gas, separates its particles, which, slaked and mixed with sand and stone, coats them, and adheres both to them and to itself, and, reabsorbing its carbonic acid gas, again returns to stone, becoming more and still more solid with age, till, in the lapse of years, it becomes real stone. By this provision of nature, we are enabled to mold mortar into whatever form we like, and it becomes veritable stone, and ultimately as hard as stone, growing harder and still harder from age to age, and century to century. Even frost and wet do not destroy its adhesive quality, after it is once fairly dry. The walls of my house stood one severe winter entirely unprotected even by a coat of mortar, *without a roof,* yet neither peeled nor cracked nor crumbled one iota. Does frost crumble or injure a brick wall? Yet what but lime forms its bond principle? Nothing? Then why should frost injure any wall having lime for its bond principle?

Reader, reflect a moment on the value of this lime principle. What would man do without it? How useful to be able to cast or spread mortar into any shape, and have it harden into stone. Without lime, of what use brick? How could we make inside walls, or hard finish them? Let us, while enjoying the luxuries secured by this law, thankfully acknowledge their source.

Obviously, this hardening property of lime adapts it admirably to building purposes. Mixed with sand, formed with brick or stone into any shape we please, it petrifies and remains forever. How simple! How effectual! How infinitely useful! Like air or water, its very commonness and necessity makes us forget its value.

And can not this hardening principle be applied to other things as well as to mortar? Especially, can it not be applied as effectually to *coarse* mortar as to fine? Aye, better! If it will bind fine sand particles together, why not coarse stones? Especially, coarse stones embedded in fine mortar? Lime sticks to anything hard, and sticks together any two or more hard substances coated with it and laid side by side, whether large or small. It fastens stones and brick together, as now usually laid up by the mason, then why not if thrown together promiscuously? Fact and philosophy both answer affirmatively.

In 1850, near Jaynesville, Wisconsin, I saw houses built wholly of lime, mixed with that coarse gravel and sand found in banks on the western prairies, and underlying all prairie soil. I visited Milton, to examine the house put up by Mr. Goodrich, the original discoverer of this mode of building, and found his walls as hard as stone itself, and harder than brick walls. I pounded them with the hammer, and examined them thoroughly, till fully satisfied as to their solidity and strength. Mr. Goodrich offered to allow me to strike with a sledge, as hard as I pleased, upon the inside of his parlor walls for six cents per blow, which he said would repair all damages. He said, in making this discovery, he reasoned thus: Has nature not provided some other building material on these prairies but wood, which is scarce? Can we find nothing in our midst? Let me see what we have. Lime abounds on them everywhere. So does coarse gravel. Will they not do? I will try. He first built an academy not larger than a schoolhouse. Partway up, a severe storm washed it, so that a portion fell. His neighbors wrote on it with chalk by night, "Goodrich's folly." But, after it was up, he wrote in answer, "Goodrich's wisdom." It stood; it hardened with age. He erected a blacksmith's shop, and finally a block of stores and dwellings; and his plan was copied extensively. And he deserves to be immortalized, for the superiority of this plan must certainly revolutionize building, and especially enable poor men to build their own homes.

All the credit I claim is that of appreciating its superiority, *applying* it on a large scale, and greatly improving the mode of *putting up* this kind of wall.

[pp. 12–20]

From Section III, "Defects in the Usual Shapes of Houses"

Since some shaped houses contain twice and even thrice as much room as others, compared with their amount of wall, and that much better adapted to household purposes, the best *form* for a house becomes a matter of prime importance —even a governing condition—and requires judicious investigation. How can I enclose the most *space*, so shaped that it can be partitioned off into rooms best adapted to my requisitions? should be your great inquiry. This brings up the defects of most houses.

HIGH AND LOW HOUSES

Low houses cost much more, compared with their room, than high ones. Foundation and roof cost the same for a one-, as for a four-story house, yet the latter contains *four times* as much room, or four houses in one; and all for less than double the expense—a saving of about one-half.

"But I want all my rooms on *one floor*, for I don't like this running up and down stairs—this living in the garret and cooking down cellar!" exclaims some weakly fidget, as horrified at the sight of stairs as a mad dog at that of water. Then build as you please, but for one, I dislike to sleep on the first floor, because more or less dampness will ascend, causing colds, fevers and premature death. Nor do I like to sleep directly under the roof, because so insufferably hot evenings as to induce one to throw off all the bedclothes on retiring, yet rapidly cooling toward morning, by dew or rain, so as to cause chills and colds, but decidedly prefer an *intermediate* story, so as to escape both these evils, and secure dryness, and as *even* a temperature as possible. To human health and happiness, sound sleep is second in importance only to air and food, so that good sleeping apartments are more important than even a good parlor; and these can not be had in a house less than two and a half or three stories. It is especially bad to sleep right over an unventilated *cellar*; for the poisonous gases generated by stale or decaying vegetables are both noxious and insidious.

Ventilation, too, is as important in a house as breath to human life and strength. Yet no one-story house can be well ventilated; much less if located low, whereas a high house naturally causes the air to draw *up* from bottom to top, because the atmosphere is lighter above than below, which naturally not only facilitates and increases all breezes, but even *creates* a draft when there is no breeze on the principle that a high chimney promotes draft. And the higher the house, the cooler and more complete this ventilation in summer, and the warmer in winter. Hot air naturally ascends, which cools the house in summer, and warms it in winter, whereas, in a low house, it escapes *out* of doors, instead of into upper rooms; which renders heating it much more expensive.

And are not the rooms even more accessible in a high than low house? Suppose you require the room of a three-story house 30 by 40, is it not easier to ascend 10 feet than go from 40 to 50 on a level, and to ascend 18 feet than walk 60 to 100?

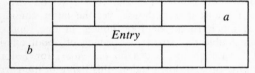

Fig. 1

Thus, how much more difficult is it to ascend two flights of stairs than to walk from *a* to *b*, which is over 100 feet on a scale of 16 feet to the inch. And then see how much more room is consumed by the entry than if you had merely a stairway. To accommodate a large family takes a good many rooms, which, if all on one story, would require an immense roof and foundation, and must be every way awkward and inconvenient, besides looking so low. And why is not a bedroom as handy on the second story as first? Is going upstairs twice a day—once, to prepare the bed, and again to occupy it—or even more, so *very* irksome? Even to cook a story below where you eat is not so bad, if a dumbwaiter is provided to transport food and dishes back and forth. Yet a light, airy basement is no inferior eating place. Both to look well proportioned and to be convenient, houses require to be about two-thirds as high as wide. Small houses should be at least a story and a half, and large ones two or three stories, according to size.

LARGE AND SMALL HOUSES

A small house, compared with its room, costs much more than a large one, and is much less comfortable, because, first, it requires more wall to enclose it, as compared with its number of square feet. Thus, a mile below St. Charles, Illinois, is a one-story stone house, ten feet square, and its walls one foot thick. Of course, it is 8 feet square inside, and contains 64 square feet to 40 feet of outside wall, or about one and a third feet of wall to every square foot of room. Now, a house 20 feet square inside gives 400 square feet of room to 80 feet of wall, or 5 feet of room to 1 foot of wall, which is more than 350 percent more inside room, compared with its outside wall, than the 10-feet house. But a 40-feet house gives 1,600 square feet to 160 feet of wall, or 10 feet of inside room to every foot of outside wall. Observe, reader, some *nine times* more room in the large house, compared with its outside wall, than in the small one! Verily, are not these small houses more expensive, compared with what room they yield, than one would suppose? One 80 feet square, gives 6,400 square feet for 320 feet of wall, or 20 feet of inside room to one foot of wall, which is fifteen times more room in the large than small house, compared with its wall. It would, then, take *one hundred* of these 10-feet houses to give as much room as is given in one 80-feet house. To present this in a tabular form, omitting thickness of walls:

Sized House.	Outside Wall.		Square Feet.	
10 feet takes	40 feet,	gives	100 inside room
20 ″	80 ″	″	400 ″
40 ″	160 ″	″	1,600 ″
80 ″	320 ″	″	6,400 ″

Now reduce these by division to their lowest denominations equally by cutting off their ciphers, and we have the following proportions:

1	2	4	8	sized house.
1	2	4	16	outside wall.
1	4	16	64	inside room.

Observe the *law* here involved. While the increase of wall is 1. 2. 4. 8, that of capacity is *four times* greater, or 1. 4. 16. 64. By increasing the wall only from 1 to 8, you increase the *room* from 1 to 64. That is, the wall of the 10-feet square house is *sixty-four times* more expensive, for its room, than one of 80 feet; or deducting thickness of wall from all, above *ninety* times. In other words, ninety dollars go no farther in making the outside walls of a 10-feet square house, than one dollar goes in making one 80 feet square. Of course, this does not reckon the partitioning of the large house, yet inside partitions are far less expensive than outside walls.

But see with what force this law applies to large and small *rooms*. A bedroom 7 by 9 takes 32 feet of wall, yet gives only 63 feet of room; and if only 7-feet ceilings, 441 cubic feet of air; whereas, one 20 feet square takes 80 feet of wall, and gives 400 square feet of room, or over *six times* more room in proportion to its wall, or six rooms in one; and if 13 feet high, gives 5,200 cubic feet of breathing timber, or almost twelve to one. Now, what will be the additional cost of this large room over the small one. It costs no more for doors and windows, for one of each will serve the large just as well as the small one; and only two and a half times more studding, lathing, baseboards, and plastering, and not two and a half times as much labor; for it takes no more time to *lay out,* or mark off, the large than the small room, or to strike 20-feet lines than 7 or 9, no more trouble to erect the *scaffoldings* for placing them, or for lathing or plastering, and not much more time, when once at it, to stud or lath or plaster. Of course, you have six times as much floor and ceiling, yet it takes much less labor in proportion, and wastes much less stuff to lay a large floor than a small one.

As to the height, pray how much more does it cost to make a high than low room? Studding comes never less than 12 and usually 13 feet. Hence, if your walls are only 7 or 8 feet high, you must cut off 5 or 6 feet of each stud, to be *wasted,* as to splice costs more than new. It costs no more to *place* a long stud than a short one; and hence a high room costs no more for doors, windows, floors, studdings, or baseboards than a low one, and only more for lath, plastering, and mortar. Then, pray, how much for that? A room 7 by 9 is 11 yards round. Now since, as just seen, it costs no more for studs or placing them, or for doors, windows, floors, ceiling (by which is meant *overhead* ceiling), or baseboards, the only additional expense of a room 13 feet high over one 7, is the *lath and plastering*. Lath, at $1.75 per thousand, costs 2½ cents per square yard, and putting on and plastering about 5, 6, or 7 more, say outside at 10 cents in all. Now a room 7 by 9, 13 feet high, has 22 yards more of plastering on its sides than one 7 feet high, and therefore at 10 cents per square yard, costs only $2.20 more. A room 20 feet square and 13 feet high has about 54 square yards more of lathing and plastering than one 7 feet, and of course costs, at 10 cents per yard, $5.40, the interest on which for one year is only 38 cents, or only about *one mill* per night, yet contains *almost twelve times* as much of life's great staple, *air*. The studding of the large room, at $10.00 per 1,000 feet, will cost about $8.00, and for the small one about $3.25, difference, $4.75; baseboards for large room, $1.50, small room, 65 cents, difference, 85 cents; putting up studding, baseboards, etc., say difference $1.00; lathing and plastering large room, $5.40, small room, 32 cents, difference, $5.08. The difference of cost in the floor is about proportionate to the size of room, except that one can lay a large floor much faster and at less waste of stuff than a small one. The large floor may possibly cost the most by $10.00. The doors and windows will be about the same, only a little larger—the same number of pieces, only longer, for frames, casings, etc., and worth about the same. The difference would not probably exceed a dollar or two, at most. A room 20 by 20, and 13 feet high, might possibly cost more than one 7 by 9, and 7 feet high, from $30.00 to $35.00, which, at 7 percent interest, is only about one-half of a penny per night; yet the small one contains only 441 feet of air, while the large one contains 5,200! or almost *twelve-times* as much, and all for only half a penny per night rent, or one-fourth the price of a cigar! Now for which, reader, prefer you to lay out your earnings, for one-fourth of a cigar per day, and 440 feet of breathing timber at night, or for 5,200 feet of this precious life-giving element without the cigar? How can you spend a penny per day so as to obtain any thing like as much real good, and even sumptuous *luxury*, as for this large sleeping room. In your small room you are obliged either to breathe your air over and over again for the twentieth time every night, or sleep with the wind blowing directly on you. And if two occupy the same bed, how doubly bad in the small, and good in the large one. Contrast your feelings in the morning. Waking up in the small room, you feel dull, stupid, gloomy, oppressed, yawny, lax, and all unstrung in body and mind, because almost stifled for want of breath; in the large one, fresh, lively, strong, bright, happy, and healthy. And how much more can you enjoy and accomplish during the day! Especially during a lifetime! In the spent air of your small room you discharge the poisonous carbonic acid gas, generated by the life process, but slowly, or, rather, *re-inhale*, about as fast as you discharge it, and this will soon leave your system loaded down with disease, and cause a fit of sickness, which will cost more for doctor's bills and loss of time than several such rooms. If poor, this is the very reason why you should sleep in large rooms, lest you get sick, especially since it need cost only half a penny per night. The poorer you are, the better you can afford to pay this large-room life and health insurance of some two dollars per year.

The same general principles apply to large and small sitting rooms, and particularly to warming them. A small room heats up quickly and cools off rapidly, and this perpetual *change* of temperature is as detrimental as uncomfortable. Who has not noticed, on first entering a small room containing several persons, how terribly repulsive and suffocating its atmosphere, rendered so by so many breaths in so small a room. To retain a comfortable, even temperature in a small room *is not possible*. To occupy them is wicked, because destructive of health and life, and therefore *suicidal*. And how much more so in sickness?

Another advantage of a large over a small house is that outside wall costs far more in proportion than inside, and still another, that having less surface, it receives and evacuates less heat and receives less cold. Thus, as a house 15 by 25 has only about four square feet per one of surface, whereas one 40 feet square has 10. Of course, the former in a very hot day becomes twice and a half times as hot, and in very cold weather evacuates fire heat, and receives out-of-door cold, twice and a half times faster than the large one. In a large house the sun shines on only a small part of any one room at a time, the other walls of the room being screened from the sun's rays by adjoining rooms. A like principle applies to cold, and to one- and five-story houses.

[pp. 56–62]

LONG AND NARROW HOUSES

Besides being out of all proportion, [these] are very inconvenient, obliging you to perform quite a journey in going from one extreme to another. *Compactness* of room is most desirable, because it facilitates the grouping of rooms around or contiguous to one another, thereby rendering the passage from room to room both short and easy, which, in a long and narrow house, is absolutely impossible.

It also takes more *wall* to enclose the same number of square feet in a long and narrow than square or round shape. To illustrate by diagrams.

Suppose Fig. 2 is four inches long by a quarter of an inch wide, it will contain one square inch.

THE LONG AND NARROW FORM

Fig. 2

Fig. 3 is two inches long by half an inch wide, and contains one square inch.

THE LONG AND NARROW FORM

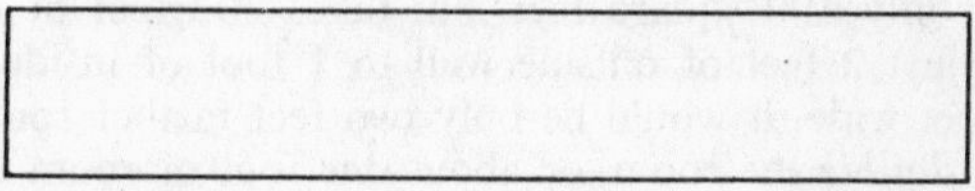

Fig. 3

Fig. 4 is one inch square, and contains one square inch.

THE SQUARE FORM

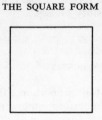

Fig. 4

THE CIRCULAR FORM

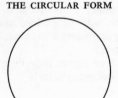

Fig. 5

Now let Fig. 2 represent a box four feet long and a quarter of a foot wide: it contains only one square foot; yet its *outside wall* is *eight* and a half feet. Let Fig. 3 represent one two feet long and half a foot wide; it also contains one square foot, yet it is only *five* feet in circumference; while a box one foot square contains just as much room, yet is only *four* feet round—less by one half than Fig. 2, yet of the same capacity.

Surprised at this result, you, perhaps, inquire how is this possible? Observe: A house 100 feet long and 1 foot wide contains only 100 square feet, but takes 202 feet of outside wall, or just 2 feet of outside wall to 1 foot of inside room. If two feet wide, it would be only two feet farther round, yet contains *double* the room, or about one foot of room to each foot of wall. If 5 feet wide, it is 210 feet round, yet contains 500 square feet, or some two and a half feet of room to one of wall, whereas the first was less than half a foot—an *increase* of *five hundred* percent. Carry up the supposition to 100 feet wide—it gives 10,000 square feet to 400 feet of wall, or over 22 feet of room to one of wall, instead of half a foot, as in the one-foot wide house, which is *forty-five times* more room in proportion to wall. Please ponder over and reread this point till you have mastered it, and till you both see that it *is* so, and *why*.

This same law, which governs all measurements, renders the circumference of the circle, in proportion to its capacity, less than that of any other figure; and, of course, the nearer any figure approaches to the spherical, the greater will be its capacity, compared with its surface.

Since, then, the circle gains even on the square, of course a square house holds more, for its wall, than a long and narrow one, and a round one than a square one. Consequently, long and narrow houses cost more for wall, foundations, and so on, than square ones, compared with their room.

To enclose a house 100 by 10, you have to build 220 feet of wall, yet have only 1,000 square feet. One 30 by 80 takes the same 220 feet of wall, yet gives 2,400 square feet, or almost *twice and a half* as much room for the same wall. Put this wall into a square form, we have a house 55 feet square and 3,025 square feet, yet only the same 220 feet of wall. That is, the latter contains as much room as *both the former,* lacking only 72 square feet, yet has not one inch more wall.

This result, stated in a former edition, was stoutly denied by a neighboring mechanic, because he could not see HOW it should be. I inquired, "Erect a building 50 by 10, how many feet of wall does it take?" He replied, "120." "Now, how many square feet does it contain?" "Ten times fifty, or 500," he answered. "And how many feet of wall does it require to enclose one 30 feet square?" "Four times 30 are 120, the same as the other," he rejoined. "And how many square feet does it contain?" "Thirty times thirty of course, or 900." "Lacking only 100 square feet of being double," I replied. "Then build both walls *close together*—you have 100 feet of wall, and *no* space enclosed." "I see it *is* so, but can't see *why*," said he.

The reader is requested to master fully, and to remember, the *principle* here demonstrated, as we shall have frequent occasion to refer to it hereafter. Indeed, the knowledge of this law led to those architectural studies and improvements which this work was written to expound.

[pp. 67–70]

Another loss, not yet estimated, but consequent on the winged, cottage, and cross structure, is in their *corners*. Reference is now had not to the loss of time and materials consequent on constructing a wall of a given length all full of corners, compared with making a straight one of the same length—that is, the saving occasioned by building a square house with only four right-angles, compared with the loss of materials and labor consequent on making *twelve* corners, as in the cottage, cross, and winged styles—itself a very great loss—and all without gaining anything but a loss; but I refer to the loss *inside* the rooms—not to the loss of time and material of making twelve *inside* as well as outside corners, but to the *room* lost in the corners themselves. The corners of rooms are of little use anyway, because dark, far from the fire, disparaging to furniture, and rarely occupied. This is true of all corners, and of course the loss is *three times* as great in the cottage, cross, and winged styles as in the square one, because they contain four times as many corners, and these nearer together. And this loss appertains to both stories. Let the following diagram (Fig. 11) illustrate the principle here involved.

LOSS OCCASIONED BY CORNERS

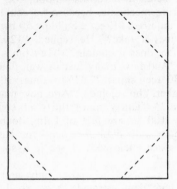

Fig. 11

A house with these corners left out, as in those dotted lines, would contain just about as much *available* or useful room as with them. Now suppose, instead of losing four corners in each story, you lose *twelve*, this loss amounts to considerable, in *addition* to all those other losses already pointed out. Away, then, with all three of these fancy styles. Those who fancy or adopt them must be either weak or thoughtless— weak if they cannot perceive their inferiority in every respect, and thoughtless if they can, but do not.

To sum up these results. Low houses are far more expensive, less comfortable, and every way inferior to high ones. Large houses are much cheaper, relatively, than small ones. The winged, cottage, and all irregular forms of houses cost far more than the square, yet are far inferior to it, besides making far less show in proportion to cost.

From Section IV, "Superiority of the Octagon Form"

IT CONTAINS ONE-FIFTH MORE ROOM FOR ITS WALL

But is the square form the best of all? Is the right angle the best angle? Can not some *radical* improvement be made, both in the outside form and the internal arrangement of our houses? Nature's forms are mostly *spherical*. She makes ten thousand curvilineal to one square figure. Then why not apply her forms to houses? Fruits, eggs, tubers, nuts, grains, seeds, trees, and so on, are made spherical, in order to enclose the most material in the least compass. Since, as already shown, a circle encloses more space for its surface than any other form, of course the nearer spherical our houses, the more inside room for the outside wall, besides being more comfortable. See figures 2, 3, 4, 5. Of course the octagon, by approximating to the circle, encloses more space for its wall than the square, besides being more compact and available. Why not employ some other mathematical figures as well as the square? These reasonings developed the architectural *principle* claimed as a real improvement, and to expound which this work was written. Hitherto men have employed the right angle, because it costs so much to frame other angles; yet our gravel-wall plan obviates this difficulty, it being as easy to corner at an octagon as rectangle. And since the *principle* here involved is the grand basis of that architectural superstructure attempted to be reared in this volume, the author may do well to elucidate it fully, and the reader to comprehend it perfectly. To compare the square with the octagon, see Figs. 12, 13.

Fig. 12 is four inches square. Let it represent a house thirty-two feet square, one inch representing eight feet. It is 128 feet in circumference, and encloses 1,024 square feet.

THE SQUARE FORM

Fig. 12

THE OCTAGON FORM

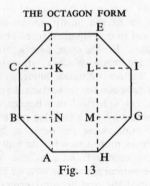

Fig. 13

Fig. 13 is an *octagon*, with sixteen-feet sides, on the same scale, and having of course the same circumference, namely, 128 feet. But it contains 1,218 square feet, as seen by the following demonstration:

	Square feet
A, D, E, H, is 16 by 39, and contains	624
B, C, K, N, is 11 by 16, and contains	176
I, G, M, L, is also 11 by 16, and contains	176
The four half-squares, A N B, C D K, E I L, and	
G H M, make two squares, each 11 feet	242
Total number of square feet in the octagon	1,218

But the square of the same circumference contains only 1,024 square feet. So that the octagon exceeds the square by 194 square feet—a gain of *one-fifth.*

To show this difference by reducing their respective numbers of square feet to fractions, dropping eighteen square feet from the octagon, and twenty-four from the square, the sum stands:

$$\frac{12}{10} \div 2 = \frac{6}{5} = one\text{-}fifth \ \text{gain}$$

in favor of the octagon. That is, an octagon of a given circumference contains more than a square of the same circumference by 100 square feet in every 500 square feet. Now, since a given length of octagon wall will enclose one-fifth more space than the same length of wall in a square shape, of course you can have the same-sized wall for one-fifth less money, or the wall of a house one-fifth larger for the same sum; for this gain is just as great in the foundation, siding, plastering, painting, whitewashing, and so on, as in the wall proper. It appertains alike to materials, labor, and *everything about the wall.* The doors and windows might be considered an exception, yet they are not. Given-sized windows will light a room more than those a fifth larger in the octagon than in the square—first, because the latter has deep, dark *corners,* which will be dark in a cloudy day however large your windows, which is not the case with the octagon; and also because the octagon form makes the same gain in the *depth* of the rooms that it does in the length of the walls, that is, the room is more *compact.*

To put together two important results at which we have thus arrived. We have seen that a square house of a given circumference contains more than an oblong one of the same circumference, and an octagon more than a square. Let us compare them. Take a house 24 feet front by 40 deep. Its circumference is, of course, 128 feet, the same as a 16-feet octagon, and a 32-feet square. But it contains only 960 square feet. The difference between it and the octagon is one-third, as reducing the square feet of both to fractions will show. Thus:

$$\frac{1218}{960} \div 8 = \frac{152}{120} \div 8 = \frac{19}{15} \div 5 = \frac{4}{3} \div 3 = \frac{1\frac{1}{3}}{1} \div 1 = \frac{1}{3}$$

equal to *one-third* more room in the octagon than in the 24-by-40-feet house, though the circumferences of both are exactly the same.

The *form* of our houses, then, is not so trifling a matter after all. The practical difference between building the outside of a house for $3,000, or just as large and good a one for $2,000, or in that proportion, is considerable, especially to those laborers who earn their money by bone and muscle.

But the difference between the octagon and the winged is still greater. Suppose the upright of a winged house to be 20 by 15 feet, and the wings 10 by 15 feet each. Its circumference will then be one hundred and thirty-two feet more than the circumference of the sixteen-feet octagon. The winged house will contain only $20 \times 15 + 15 \times 10 + 15 \times 10 = 600$, which compares with the octagon as follows:

$$\frac{1218}{600} \div 8 = \frac{152}{75} \div 6 = \frac{25}{12} \div 2 = \frac{12}{6} \div 6 = \frac{2}{1}$$

or not *one half*, though having more outside wall.

But suppose the upright to be two stories, while the wings are only one, which is usually the case, while the octagon is two stories, which it should be to look well, the winged will contain only 900 square feet, while the octagon will contain 2,436. Thus:

$$\frac{2436}{900} \div 12 = \frac{203}{75} \div 7 = \frac{29}{11} \div 11 = \frac{2\frac{1}{2}}{1}$$

two and a half times more room in the octagon than in the winged shape, though the latter is two feet more in circumference. Now the difference between building a winged house wall for $2,500, or just as large an octagonal one for $1,000, is something worth considering. Yet even all this saving, great as it is, is but a small part of the advantages of the style of building which this book was written to propound over others now in use, which we shall see as we proceed.

One other advantage of the octagonal style over the square, and especially over the cottage and winged styles, deserves to be reckoned in this comparison, namely, their *corners*. We have already seen, in Fig. 11, that the corners of a square room are of little account, because dark, useless for furniture, and rarely occupied for any purpose. In fact, an octagon, drawn *within* the square, furnishes about as much *available* room as the square, yet contains only eighty feet to the square's ninety-eight:

$$\frac{98}{80} \div 2 = \frac{49}{40} \div 10 = \frac{5}{4} \div 4 = \frac{1\frac{1}{4}}{1}$$

a loss of *twenty-five percent* in the amount of wall in the square over and above the same amount of *available* room in the octagon. But suppose, as in the winged and cottage styles, there are twelve right angles, instead of four, the loss is in the same proportion:

$$\frac{98}{54} \div 6 = \frac{16}{9} = \text{almost 40 per cent.}$$

Fig. 11 also enables us to show—what has doubtless puzzled some readers—*why* this gain by the octagon over the square. It consists in the fact that it requires more wall to enclose the corners, in proportion to the number of square feet which they contain, than the house as a whole. Thus, those eight lines which form the four right angles of the four half squares in the corners of the square, which are omitted by the dotted lines of the octagon, are seven feet per side, making together fifty-six feet. Yet they enclose only two seven-feet squares, or ninety-eight square feet, or four feet of wall to seven square feet enclosed. That is, a foot of corner wall encloses less than two square feet, whereas the octagon has only 80 feet of wall to its 478 square feet, which is:

$$\frac{478}{80} \div 10 = \frac{48}{8} \div 8 = \frac{6}{1}$$

or six square feet for every foot of wall; whereas the four
corners omitted by the dotted lines contain only two square
feet for every foot of wall. That is, the octagon encloses six
square feet to every foot of wall, while the triangles, or
corners of square rooms, enclose only two square feet to every
foot of wall—a difference of three to one, which is lost in the
corners of the square over the octagon as a whole.

The gain in twelve, sixteen, and twenty-sided figures over
even the octagon, is greater, and still greater in proportion as
the figure approaches the circle. Yet so many corners cost
more extra than they save.

THE COMPARATIVE BEAUTY OF THE DORIC, SQUARE, AND OCTAGON FORMS

The *beauty* of a house is scarcely less important than its
room. True, a homely but *convenient* house is better than a
beautiful but incommodious one, yet beauty and utility, so
far from being incompatible with each other, are as closely
united in art as in nature; that is, are *inseparable*. It is hardly
possible to have a truly handsome house without its being
capable of being made as handy inside as it is beautiful outside; nor can a homely-looking house well be made convenient. I repeat, beauty and utility are as closely united in architecture as they are throughout all Nature. If, therefore, the
square or winged form of house is the best, it will *look* best,
and if it is the most beautiful, it can be made the most
comfortable.

Form embodies an important element of beauty. Yet some
forms are constitutionally more beautiful than others. Of
these the spherical is more beautiful than the angular, and the
smooth and undulating than the rough and projecting. *Why*
is it that a poor animal, or a lean person, is more homely than
the same animal or person when fleshy? Because the latter are
less angular and more spherical than the former. Why do we
behold flat, smooth stones with more pleasure than those
which are rough and irregular, but because there are less
angles in the former than the latter? Why is the shape of

apples, peaches, etc., more beautiful than of chestnut burs? This principle answers, excepting what beauty is imparted by color. And the more acute the angle, the less beautiful; but the more the angle approaches the circle, the more beautiful. Hence a square house is more beautiful than a triangular one, and an octagon or duodecagon than either. Of course, then, the far greater number of right angles in the winged and cross styles than in the octagonal, and the high peaks of the roofs of the doric, prove them to be less handsome than a square house, and doubly less than the octagon. For one, I cannot consider cottages or wings handsome. They always strike me as unsightly and well-nigh deformed. And the basis of this sentence is an immutable law of Nature. Look at a dome, and then at a cottage roof, full of sharp peaks, sticking out in various directions, and say if the undulating regularity of the former does not strike the eye far more agreeably than the sharp projections of the latter. This is not one of those fancy matters which allow of diversity of opinion, but is a fixed ordinance of Nature, and passes no enviable sentence on the tastes of those who claim to possess as great a preponderance of good taste as of property, besides their other prerogatives. And facts sustain this theory, as all will say who compare figures 2, 3, 4, 5, 6, 7, 9, 10, and 13 with each other.

Since, then, the octagon form is more beautiful as well as capacious, and more consonant with the predominant or governing form of Nature—the spherical—it deserves consideration.

"But," some will ask, "how happens it that our author is so very much smarter than all the world besides? Why has not this plan, if really so superior, been seen and put in practice long ago, especially since men are racking their inventions in search of building improvements?" Because of the greater ease of *framing* the right angle than any other; and unless this difficulty can be overcome, it will be cheaper, after all, to build on the square than on the octagonal plan. This difficulty is wholly obviated by our gravel-wall plan, which enables us with little extra expense, and a great increase of strength, to secure our octagon form.

But can this octagonal form be *partitioned off into rooms* as advantageously as the square? *Far more so*. Let us see.

[pp. 80–89]

5

William E. Bell, CARPENTRY MADE EASY; / OR, / THE SCIENCE AND ART OF FRAMING, / ON A NEW AND IMPROVED SYSTEM. / WITH SPECIFIC INSTRUCTIONS FOR / BUILDING BALLOON FRAMES, BARN FRAMES, MILL FRAMES, WARE- / HOUSES, CHURCH SPIRES, ETC. / COMPRISING ALSO / A SYSTEM OF BRIDGE BUILDING; / WITH / BILLS, ESTIMATES OF COST, AND VALUABLE TABLES (Philadelphia, 1858), pp. 3, 7–13.

William E. Bell (1815–circa 1890) described himself as "architect and practical builder." He was born in Virginia, moved to Seneca County, Ohio, in 1832 where he worked as apprentice carpenter and joiner in the summers and taught school in the winters. His employer remarked that he was, after three years, "as good a mechanic as ever went out of the shop." But when he went into a larger shop in Michigan City, Indiana, in 1835, Bell reported that he was surprised to learn how little he knew about his trade. This remark (made in an interview in the 1880's) suggests that Bell was exposed to new techniques in Michigan City; whether these techniques included balloon framing it is impossible to say, but the balloon frame had been used as early as 1833 by Augustine Deodat Taylor in the construction of St. Mary's Catholic Church in Chicago. Bell lived in Tiskilwa, Bureau County, Illinois, from 1836 to 1846; from 1846 until his death, in Ottawa, La Salle County, Illinois. He built not only houses, churches, and so on, but also railroad bridges and shops. By

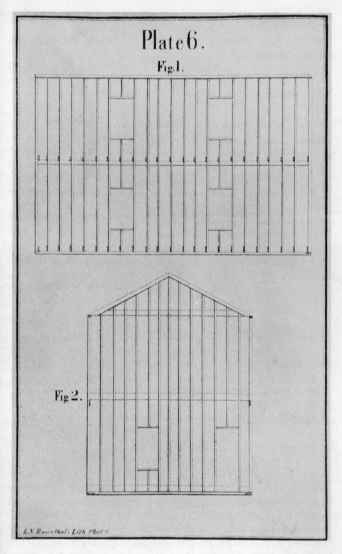

17. William E. Bell, Diagram for a Balloon Frame, from *Carpentry Made Easy* (1858).

1886 he had earned a reputation as "one of the best mechanics in the state."

Preface

The author takes great pleasure in acknowledging the
eminent services rendered him in the literary and scientific
portions of this work, by E. N. Jencks, A.M., Professor of
Mathematics and Natural Sciences; and the public cannot fail
to appreciate the value of his labors in these departments.

The inception of the work, its original designs, and the
entire system are mine. Whatever is found in it purely literary
and scientific, I cheerfully attribute to his assistance. And
believing that the work will supply a pressing want, and will
be useful both to those who are devoted to the mechanic arts
and to amateurs who have felt the necessity of a faithful
guide in house-building and other structures, especially in
new settlements, I can confidently commend it to them as
supplying this deficiency.

WILLIAM E. BELL

Ottawa, Ill., 1858

[p. 3]

Introductory Chapter

SUMMARY VIEW

THE SCIENCE AND THE ART OF FRAMING

No apology is offered for introducing to the public a work
on the science and art of framing. By the *science of framing*
is meant the *certain knowledge* of it, founded on mathematical
principles, and for which the master of it can assign intelligent reasons, which he knows to be correct; while the *art of
framing* is the system of rules serving to facilitate the *practice*
of it, but the *reasons* for which the workman may or may not
understand. That carpentry has its rules of science as well as
its rules of art, no intelligent mechanic can doubt. The rules
of the art are taught by the master workman at the bench;

or, more commonly, insensibly acquired by habit and imitation. But by whom have the rules of the *science* been laid down and where have its principles been intelligibly demonstrated?

SOMETHING NEW

It is believed that this is the very first attempt ever made to bring the science of carpentry, properly so called, within the scope of practical mechanics.

DEFICIENCIES OF FORMER WORKS ON CARPENTRY

Whatever has formerly been published on this subject, that can, with any degree of propriety, be classed under the head of science, has been only available by professional architects and designers, being written in technical language and mathematical signs, accompanied by no adequate definitions or explanations; and are as perfectly unintelligible to workingmen of ordinary education as Chinese or Choctaw. On the other hand, the numerous works upon the art of carpentry, designed and published for the use of workingmen, are sadly deficient in details and practical rules. They seem to take it for granted that the student is already familiar with his business; they furnish him with drafts and plans to work from; they tell him authoritatively that such or such an angle is the proper bevel for such a part of the frame; but they neither tell him *why* it is so, nor inform him *how* to begin and go on systematically with framing and erecting a building. These works are, in fine, chiefly valuable for their plates; and even these it is not always possible to work from with confidence and accuracy, because no man can work with confidence and accuracy in the dark: and he certainly is in the dark who does not understand the reasons on which his rules are founded.

THE AUTHOR'S EXPERIENCE

These facts and reflections have been impressing themselves upon the mind of the author of this work for twenty years past, while he has been serving the public as a practical carpenter. During much of this time it has been his fortune to have large jobs on hand, employing many journeymen mechanics, who claimed to understand their trade, and demanded full wages. But it has been one of the most serious and oppressive of his cares that these journeymen knew so little of their business.

FEW GOOD CARPENTERS

They had, by habit, acquired the use of tools, and could perform a job of work after it had been laid out for them; but not more than one man in ten could himself lay out a frame readily and correctly.

WHY APPRENTICES DO NOT LEARN

Now, it is not commonly because apprentices are unwilling to learn, or incapable of learning, that this is so, but it is because they have not the adequate instruction to enable them to become master workmen. Their masters are very naturally desirous to appropriate their services to their own best advantage; and that is often apparently gained by keeping the apprentice constantly at one branch of his business, in which he soon becomes a good hand, and is taught but little else; and when his time is his own, and he comes to set up business for himself, then he is made to feel his deficiencies. Should he have assistants and apprentices in his turn, he would be unable to give them proper instruction, even were he well disposed to do so—for he can teach them nothing more than what he knows himself.

In this condition, the young mechanic applies to books to assist him to conquer the mysteries of his art; but he has not been able hitherto to find a work adapted to his wants. He anxiously turns the pages of ponderous quarto and folio volumes; he is convinced of the prodigious learning of the authors, but he is not instructed by them. On the one hand, their practical directions and rules are too meager; and, on the other hand, their mathematical reasoning is too technical to yield our young workingman any real benefit or satisfaction. May not these faults be remedied? Is it not possible for instruction to be given which shall be at once simple and practical in detail, and comprehensible and demonstrative in mathematical reasoning?

DESIGN OF THIS WORK

An attempt has been made, in this little work, to answer these questions affirmatively; and thus to supply a positive want, and to occupy a new field in the literature of architecture. Its design is to give plain and practical rules for attaining a rapid proficiency in the art of carpentry; and also to prove the correctness of these rules by mathematical science.

IMPORTANCE OF GEOMETRY TO CARPENTERS

No certain and satisfactory knowledge of framing can be gained without a previous acquaintance with the primary elements of arithmetic and geometry. It is presumed that a sufficient knowledge of arithmetic is possessed by most mechanics in this country; but geometry is not so commonly understood. It is not taught in our district schools, and is looked upon as beyond the capacity of common minds. But this is a mistake. To mechanical minds, at least, the elements of plane geometry are so easily taught that they seem to them to be almost self-evident at the first careful perusal; and mechanics have deprived themselves of much pleasure, as well as profit, in not having made themselves masters of this science.

GEOMETRY IN THIS WORK

Part I is therefore devoted to so much of the science of geometry as is essential to the complete demonstration and thorough understanding of the science and art of carpentry; and it is recommended to all mechanics into whose hands this volume may fall, to give their days and nights to a careful study of this part of the work. It is true that our rules and instructions in carpentry are so plain and minute that they are available to those who do not care to study geometry at all; but the principles on which those rules are founded, and consequently the *reasons why the rules are as they are,* cannot, from their very nature, be made plain and intelligible to any one except by a course of geometrical reasoning.

NEW RULES OF CARPENTRY

Part II comprises the main body of the work, and is devoted particularly to the framing of buildings. The rules for obtaining the bevels of rafters, joists, braces, and so on, as explained in this part of the work, it is believed, have never been published before. That such bevels could be so found has been known, for several years past, among master builders; and, to a limited extent, has by that means been made public; but this feature of the work will, no doubt, be new and useful to some mechanics who have followed the business for years, and will be especially useful to apprentices and young journeymen who have not yet completed their mechanical education.

THEY ARE PROVED AND EXPLAINED

These rules have been here demonstrated by a new and rigid course of geometrical reasoning; so that their correctness is placed beyond doubt. The demonstrations are often given in footnotes and in smaller print, so as not to interrupt the descriptive portion of the work, nor appall those who are not mechanically learned, by an imposing display of scientific signs and technical terms. In fact, it has been made a leading object, in the preparation of this work, to convey correct mechanical and scientific principles in simple language, stripped as much as possible of all technicalities, and adapted to the comprehension of plain workingmen.

BRIDGEBUILDING

Part III comprises a brief practical treatise on the framing and construction of bridges, with bills of timber and iron given in detail, by the use of which intelligent carpenters can construct almost any kind of a bridge. This part of the work does not, however, make any special claims to new discoveries, or to much originality; nor is it intended to supersede the use of those works specially devoted to bridge-building; but it is believed it will be found more practically convenient and simple than some others of more imposing bulk and of higher price.

VALUABLE TABLES

Part IV contains a valuable collection of tables, showing the lengths of rafters, hip rafters, braces, and so on, and also the weights of iron, the strength of timber, and so on, which will be found of the greatest convenience, not only to common mechanics but to professional designers, architects, and bridgebuilders. Some of these tables have been compiled from reliable sources; but the most important of them have been calculated and constructed, at a considerable amount of expense and labor, expressly for this work.

PLATES AND ILLUSTRATIONS

Nor has any expense been spared in the preparation of the plates and illustrations, which are *"got up"* in the highest style of the art; and it is hoped, and confidently expected, that the work, as a whole, will prove to be satisfactory and remunerative equally to the public and to their

Humble and obedient servant,

THE AUTHOR

[pp. 7–13]

6

James Bogardus, "Construction of the Frame, Roof, and Floor of Iron Buildings," UNITED STATES PATENT OFFICE (1850); CAST-IRON / BUILDINGS: / THEIR / CONSTRUCTION AND ADVANTAGES, "by James Bogardus," authored by John W. Thompson (New York, 1858), pp. 1–16.

James Bogardus (1800–1874) was a versatile and productive inventor and manufacturer. Trained as a watchmaker and engraver, he invented not only clocks, among them a three-wheeled, eight-day chronometer, and various engraving machines and processes, but also improvements in textile machinery, machines for pressing glass and for cutting and working India rubber; he invented the first dry-gas meter and the eccentric mill, in which both stones turn in the same direction but at different speeds. Bogardus's contributions to cast-iron construction can easily be overrated if they are overgeneralized. There was considerable prior art, in the cast-iron store front in this country and in structural uses of cast iron, particularly in England. Many of Bogardus's contemporaries were competing for primacy in the field; and Bogardus was also concerned with other new inventions and with the manufacture of a variety of his established inventions. Bogardus's inventiveness in cast-iron construction departed in two ways from the prior art and the art of his contemporaries: (1) In detailing he developed systems of interchangeable parts for joining the cast-iron modules of a structure (see Patent 7337, pages 352 ff.); (2) in imaginative terms he saw the potential of a universal system of construction in the combination of the cast-iron skeleton with nonbearing curtain walls (see illus-

18. James Bogardus, Shot Tower (1855), McCullough Shot and Lead Company, New York City. Photograph taken during demolition in 1908.

tration 18). This 175-foot shot tower with its cast-iron skeleton and curtain walls of brick was erected in two months in 1855, and was, in one stroke, the prophecy of the sky-scraper.

United States Patent Office

JAMES BOGARDUS, OF NEW YORK, N.Y. / CONSTRUCTION OF THE
   FRAME, ROOF, AND FLOOR OF IRON BUILDINGS / SPECIFICA-
   TION OF LETTERS PATENT NO. 7,337, DATED MAY 7, 1850

To all whom it may concern:

Be it known that I, JAMES BOGARDUS, of the city, county, and State of New York, have invented certain new and useful Improvements in the Method of Constructing Iron Houses, and that the following is a full, clear, and exact description of my invention of the principle or character which distinguishes it from all other things before known and of the method of making, constructing, and using the same, reference being had to the accompanying drawings, making part of this specification, in which—

Figure 1 is a front elevation of the frame of a house on my improved plan, Fig. 2, part of a top view with the roof removed, Figs. 3 and 4, horizontal sections taken at the lines A, *a*, and B, *b*, of Fig. 1, Fig. 5 a vertical section, Fig. 6, a like section with the roof and floors, Figs. 7, and 8, plan and bottom views of the roof and floors, and Figs. 9 and 10, elevation and cross section on a smaller scale of a separation wall or partition.

The same letters indicate like parts in all the figures.

The first part of my invention consists in making the horizontal beams, which form the horizontal parts of the framework, in sections cast with flanches through which longitudinal bolts pass to secure and draw together the sections at their junctions, their upper and undersurfaces being horizontal and parallel flanches, when this is combined with vertical columns, pilasters or posts, also cast with horizontal flanches at top and bottom provided with bolt holes corresponding with bolt holes in the horizontal flanches of the beams, the top end of one column, pilaster, or post and the bottom end of another being bolted to the lower and upper

19. James Bogardus, Diagram for Patent 7337 (1850).

horizontal flanges of two beams to bind together same, in addition to the bolts which draw together the beams.

The second part of my invention, which relates to the method of making the floors, consists in making such floors of narrow plates or sheets of metal with tongues and grooves made on the edges by riveting to the under surface of the plates or sheets a strip of sheet iron to form the tongue, and one or two strips to form the groove, the said strips acting at the same time as ribs to give stiffness to the plates or sheets which constitute the floor, all the said plates being arranged, when put together, to break joints, by which means I am enabled to make a floor which, for rooms of ordinary size, needs no intermediate supports.

The third part of my invention, which relates to the method of covering the roof by means of a series of plates, consists in making one edge of each plate with a groove, in the same manner as in the floor plates, to receive the opposite edge of the next plate, and thus make one plate lap over the other and bind the two together, that they may not be separated to permit the passage of water, these plates being also provided with cleats or small plates riveted on one end of each plate and made to overlap the end of the next and projecting beyond the lower edge of the large plate to lap over a corresponding and like plate or cleat on the next plate and thus lap all the joints of the roof.

In the accompanying drawings (*a*) represents a horizontal square framework which girds the house, that is, which passes entirely around. One such framework constitutes the base of each story. The beams (*a*), constituting these frames, are cast in sections, hollow, with the inner face open, the top and bottom being horizontal flanges (*b, b,*) from the outer face. The ends of each section are formed with flanches (*c, c,*) projecting inward, so that by means of screw bolts (*d, d,*) passing through such flanches the sections are united and drawn together to make close joints. Before putting together the different sections their ends should be faced perfectly true and at right angles with the top and bottom surfaces, which last-named surfaces should be made as nearly parallel as possible. One of these frames, made and put together as above described, is placed on the foundation (*c'*) and on it are erected a series of semi-columns (*f*) cast with flanches so as to present externally the appearance of columns or pilasters, but hollow inside to make them light, while the curves of their cross sections gives them stiffness. At each end they are cast with flanches (g, g,) the lower one at the base to rest on the base frame, and the other at the cap to receive the next frame (a) which forms the base of the next story or floor. These semi-columns are placed over and under the junctions of the sections of the beams (a, a,) and are secured thereto by screw bolts (h, h,) passing through the flanches (b, b,), so that every column at each end is secured to two sections, and, therefore, the sections of the beams (a) are held together not only by the screw-bolts (d, d), that pass through the end flanches (c, c) but by the columns also, by reason of the attachment of each column to the adjacent ends of two sections. In this way one story may be erected on another, and, when thus put together, each side of the house or structure constitutes a frame, and when the four sides are united all these frames brace each other, and make a strong and light structure, which, in the casting of the parts, may be made as plain or as highly ornamental as may be desired, and according to any order of architecture.

When the extent of the building requires it I introduce a cross-beam (j) cast with a central vertical rib with a top and bottom flanch on each side like the flanches (b, b,) of the beams (a) and with end flanches (k) through which bolts pass to secure it to the beams (a).

The spaces between the flanches (b, b) of the beams (a) and (j) form recesses to receive the ends of floor beams (l) which rest on the lower one of these flanches, so that the upper and lower surfaces can be made either flush with the top and bottom surfaces of the beams, or so much within those surfaces as to make the floor and ceiling flush therewith.

The floor beams (l) I make with the top (m) level, that is, in a straight line or nearly so and the underpart in arch form, and cast them onto wrought iron tension rods (n) to make them light and stiff. The ends which constitute the abutments are formed to fit in the space between the flanches (b, b,) of the beams.

The floor (o) is formed of narrow and thin plates (p) of sheet rolled iron with their edges parallel. To their under-surfaces and near one edge I secure by rivets a narrow strip of metal (q) and under this another strip (r) one edge of which is on the same vertical plane with the edge of the plate, thus forming a groove. On the other edge of these plates is secured in like manner a strip (s) which projects sufficiently beyond the edge of the plate to form a tongue. In this way every plate has a tongue formed on one edge and a groove on the other, so that in laying the floor, the tongue of one plate fits into the groove of another, the upper surfaces of all being flush. The strips of iron, riveted as above set forth to the plates form the tongues and grooves, and add stiffness to the floor. The plates in laying the floor are put together breaking joints, that is, the ends of two in the same line are placed midway between the ends of the one alongside. By these two means a floor for a room of ordinary size can be made of sufficient strength and stiffness, by resting at the edges on the beams only and without intermediate supports; but when the room is of a very large size, one or more floor beams (l) may be introduced.

The spaces between the columns, pilasters or posts are filled up by plates of cast or sheet iron (t). If the outer surface be required to be smooth, the plates are formed on their edges with tongues and grooves as in the manner of making the floors above described; but if it be desired to make the outer surface in imitation of weather-boarding, then a groove is to be formed on one edge of each plate, the other edge of the plates answering the purpose of a tongue to fit in the grooves, so that the plates, when put together, will overlap one another. The plates prepared after either of the above modes and cut of the required lengths are inserted one by one in the upper end of grooves formed in the columns, pilasters, or posts, and let down and fitted into each other, the flanches forming the grooves for the reception of the plates being cut out at the top the breadth of one plate to admit of their insertion, the last of the series of plates being secured in place by pins driven into holes made for that purpose in the columns, pilasters, or posts.

When windows or doors are to be put into the panels or spaces between the pilasters etc., the said pilasters are either cast with the requisite recesses or rabbets to receive the windows or doors, or otherwise adapted to receive the window or door frames. For windows I usually insert a cast-iron panel (u) cast with or without ornaments, the upper edge of such panels being properly formed to constitute the window or sill.

The cornice (v) is cast in sections like the beams (a) with

flanches on their ends projecting inward that they may be drawn and secured together by screw bolts in the same manner as the beams (*a*). After the sections have been united, they are then secured to the upper ends of the columns, pilasters or posts in the same manner as the beams (*a*). In this way, the cornice is made to constitute the upper frame of the structure.

The framing for the roof is formed as shown at (*w*) in the drawings, and rests on the part (*x*) of the cornice and within the ornamental part thereof, which is to be pierced at the proper places for the reception of spouts to carry off water. The covering for the roof is made of a series of plates formed with a groove on the lower edge in the manner of making the plates for the floors, the upper edge of one plate being fitted into the groove at the lower edge of the next plate above, so that the plates overlap each other from the top to the bottom, thus effectually preventing leaks. The plates should be of sufficient length to extend from the middle of one rafter (*w*) to the next. For the purpose of covering the end joints and preventing leaks, to one end of each plate is secured a cap-plate (*y*) which extends or laps over the end of the next plate, and also over a like cap-plate (*y'*) below it. In this way all the joints are completely covered and the plates are effectually prevented from sagging or bending to make a leak. At the angles of the roof the plates are bent to the required form that there may be no seam at the angles.

The pilasters are represented as being hollow semi-columns with projecting wings or flanches to give breadth of support at the ends where they join the horizontal beams. This is the form which is best adapted to the purpose as it unites strength and beauty with lightness; but so long as the flanches are retained this form may be varied at pleasure. Where it is to form a division between two houses I prefer to make the pilasters flat with projecting flanches at top and bottom as represented at Figs. 9 and 10. When thus constructed, I fill up the space between the pilasters or posts and the horizontal beams with masonry or with metal panels, as above described.

I have above stated that the floors, roof, and paneling between the columns, pilasters, or posts are made of sheet iron, but I do not wish to confine myself to the use of rolled sheet iron, as thin plates of cast iron, with strips riveted to their undersurface to form the tongues and the grooves and to give stiffness, will answer a good purpose, although I prefer rolled sheet or plate iron, such as thin boiler iron.

What I claim as my invention and desire to secure by Letters Patent is—

1. The method, substantially as herein described, of making the framework of iron houses of more than one story by means of beams cast in sections with end flanches which receive bolts for uniting and drawing them together and with top and bottom parallel flanches, when this is combined with columns, pilasters, or posts cast with horizontal flanches at top and bottom, the top flanch of one column, and the bottom flanch of another being secured by bolts to the horizontal flanges of two beams one column above and the other below the point at which the beams are joined for the purpose and in the manner substantially as described.

2. I also claim the method, substantially as herein described, of making the floors by means of thin plates of metal formed with a groove on one edge and tongue on the other by riveting narrow strips of metal to their undersurface and near the edges, the plates so formed being put together breaking joints, substantially in the manner and for the purpose specified.

3. I also claim the method, substantially as described, of covering the roofs of houses by means of series of thin metal plates, formed each with a groove on one edge, by riveting narrow plates or strips to the undersurface thereof, that the edge of one plate may fit into the groove on the lower edge of the next above and so on throughout the series, substantially as described, when these plates are also provided with the lapping pieces or plates riveted or otherwise secured to the upper surface of one end of each plate in each series to lap over the end of the contiguous plates of the next series, the said lapping pieces of each series being also made to lap one over the other, substantially as and for the purpose specified.

                                                      JAMES BOGARDUS

Witnesses:
    JOHN LONDON
    C. BROWNE

Cast-Iron Buildings (1858)

So much that is erroneous has been said and written concerning iron architecture, and so little that is authentic, that but few are yet properly acquainted with either its merits or its history. To furnish correct information on this important subject is the object of this pamphlet.

The first complete cast-iron edifice ever erected in America, or in the world, was that of the inventor James Bogardus—being his manufactory on the corner of Center and Duane streets, New York. Its foundation was laid in May, 1848: but a model of it had been freely exhibited to visitors at his factory, since the summer of 1847. Previous to this period, the opinion of most men of scientific reputation was unfavorable to the use of cast iron for this purpose; and, amongst all classes, there was a very strong and general prejudice against it. Some accidents had happened from the breaking of cast-iron beams in England, and their cause was ignorantly attributed to the material employed; whereas, the fault lay in the want of proper knowledge and skill in constructing them. These accidents, however, helped to swell the popular prejudice against cast iron as a material for buildings, and they were frequently quoted in opposition to the inventor; until, by the erection of the building already mentioned, he demonstrated their untrustworthy character. Since that period, he has erected many structures of the same description, not only in New York, but also in many other cities; and persons capable of passing judgment on their merits, have, after a careful investigation, been profoundly convinced of their superiority—that they alone embrace the true principles of safety, durability, and economy. And the inventor himself firmly believes that, were the public fully aware of its great advantages, cast iron would be employed, for superior buildings, in every case, in preference to granite, marble, freestone, or brick.

It was whilst in Italy, contemplating there the rich architectural designs of antiquity, that Mr. Bogardus first conceived the idea of emulating them in modern times, by the aid of cast iron. This was in the year 1840; and, during his subsequent travels in Europe, he held it constantly in view;

20. James Bogardus, Cast-Iron Building (1848), Washington and Murray Streets, New York City.

and cherished it the more carefully, as he became convinced, by inquiry and personal observation, not only that the idea was original with himself, but that he might thereby become the means of greatly adding to our national wealth, and of establishing a new, a valuable, and a permanent branch of industry.

It is impossible for the reader to realize to their full extent the difficulties which Mr. Bogardus had to encounter in the erection of his first building. Whilst burdened with the care of his factory, and with limited means at his command, he had not only to superintend every detail of its construction, but to hear and answer daily the same predictions of failure. One would not live in it, if he had it as a gift, for fear lest it would crush itself by its own weight; another would not, for fear of lightning; a third was sure that it was not perpendicular, and that sooner or later it would topple to the ground; and a fourth foretold that if a fire should happen, it would melt the columns, and the whole would fall with one tremendous crash. Others declared, as the universal voice of science, that, in consequence of the expansion and contraction of the metal, it contained within itself the elements of early and rapid decay; and some even asserted that the experiment had already been made in England; that its disastrous failure there had been attended with a great public calamity; and that, in consequence thereof, an act of Parliament was actually then in force, forbidding the erection of cast-iron buildings. But these and other objections, Mr. B. had already thoroughly considered, and found them either to be groundless altogether, or to involve only such difficulties as might be obviated by mechanical means. Meantime, the work on the building, which had hitherto been steadily progressing, though but slowly, wholly ceased for a time. This was, to many, a convincing proof that something was wrong; and the poor unfinished skeleton they christened Bogardus's Folly—not knowing that, in the interval, he had commenced and finished the fronts of several other stores.

It may be also added that complaints were made to the city authorities against it, and that some of the tenants of neighboring buildings actually left their houses through fear of danger: this created some delay, until informed by the chief engineer of the fire department that the committee had made a favorable report.

This first cast-iron building, Mr. Bogardus's present factory, is of five stories, and was designed to be a model of its kind. Since its erection, it has not been difficult to convince anyone who will take the trouble to examine it, that SUCH BUILDINGS COMBINE UNEQUALED ADVANTAGES OF ORNAMENT, STRENGTH, DURABILITY, AND ECONOMY; WHILST THEY ARE, AT THE SAME TIME, ABSOLUTELY SECURE AGAINST DANGER FROM FIRE, LIGHTNING, AND AN IMPERFECT FOUNDATION.

Whatever be the advantages of cast iron as a building material, they would be all unavailable were they not accompanied with stability of structure. But, simple as this problem now appears to be, had it not been hitherto esteemed impracticable, it would not have been left for Mr. Bogardus to solve it. As it is on this point, mainly, that his merit as its inventor depends, a short description is subjoined; and the reader should remember that the simpler the invention, it is the more meritorious.

The cast-iron frame of the building rests upon sills which are cast in sections of any required length. These sills, by the aid of the planing machine, are made of equal thickness, so as not to admit of any variation throughout the whole: they are laid upon a stone foundation, and are fastened together with bolts. On the joint of the sills stand the columns or pilasters, all exactly equal in height, and having both their ends faced in a turning lathe so as to make them perfectly plane and parallel; and each column is firmly bolted to the ends of the two adjacent sills on which it rests. These columns support another series of sills, fascias, or cornices, in sections, of the same length as the former, but of greater height, according to the design of the architect: they are separately made of equal dimensions by the planing machine, and are bolted to the columns, and to each other, in the same manner as before. On these again stands another row of columns, and on these columns rests another series of fascias or cornices; and so on, continually, for any required number of stories: the ends of the columns and fascias having been, of course, all previously drilled so as to receive the bolts. The arches are bolted together in the same simple and effectual manner; and the spaces between the columns are filled up with windows, doors, and panels, which may be ornamented to suit any taste.

It may be here remarked that, in certain cases, the first layer of sills may be dispensed with altogether; and also that, immediately before uniting the pieces, it is the practice of Mr. Bogardus to apply a coating of paint to those parts which are designed to be in contact with others; thus rendering the joints absolutely air-tight.

From this description it will be seen, that each end of every column acts as a strap to the adjacent joint of the cornice, and that the separate parts are all united so firmly as to form one stable whole, equivalent in strength to a single piece of cast iron. Hence, such a structure must be far more firm and solid than one composed of numerous parts, united only by a feeble bond of mortar. On this account it may be raised to a height vastly greater than by any other known means, without impairing its stability in the least; and, were all the columns of any story removed or destroyed by violence, except the four corner ones, or others equivalent in position, the building would still remain firm as an arch; and the greater its height, the firmer it would be.

It is also plain that such a building may be erected with extraordinary facility, and at all seasons of the year. No plumb is needed; no square, no level. As fast as the pieces can be handled, they may be adjusted and secured by the most ignorant workman: the building cannot fail to be perpendicular and firm. Wedges, mortises, and chairs are all ignored: they are the subsequent inventions of interested individuals, in order to evade the patent; and to render less dangerous, or less apparent, their imperfect and unstable joints. Strength is secured in the simplest and surest way, and at the least possible expense.

It also follows that, a building once erected, it may be taken to pieces with the same facility and dispatch, without injuring or destroying any of its parts, and then re-erected elsewhere with the same perfection as at first. The size and form of the pieces greatly favor their portability, which has enabled Mr. Bogardus to construct them in New York, and export them to distant cities. This quality is of the greatest importance; for it renders every cast-iron building not only a present, but a permanent addition to our national wealth. Who could estimate the annual saving to the city of New York alone, were all its buildings of this character? The progress of improvement would no longer be accompanied with the work of demolition; instead of destruction, there would be a removal only—a simple change of location. And to make the calculation properly, we should know not only the present worth of the buildings destroyed, but what was their original cost.

These superior qualities of cast-iron buildings depend mainly upon their mode of structure, without which the rest would be of little avail. We now proceed to consider those superadded advantages which arise more directly from the character of the material employed.

Cast iron does not indeed possess the character of wrought iron for resisting tensile strain, but it is far superior to it in resisting a crushing force; and it is vastly superor to granite, marble, freestone, or brick in resisting any kind of force or strain. It may, however, for building purposes, be considered crushing-proof. According to the tables of our best authorities, which have been often verified, a cubic inch of cast iron can sustain a weight of eighty tons. Now, since a cubic foot weighs four hundred and fifty-five pounds, it follows, by an easy computation, that a column of cast iron must be ten miles in height, before it will crush itself by its own weight. It will be readily seen that the joint invented by Mr. Bogardus effectually secures the whole of this important quality: and that thereby he would be enabled to erect a tower or building many times the height of any other edifice in the world, which would be perfectly safe to visitors, in the face of storm or tempest, though they filled it throughout every story, to its utmost capacity.

The great strength of cast iron enables us also to enlarge the interior of a house, by lessening the thickness of its walls: a very important item in this city, where ground is of great value.

Cast iron also possesses the quality of great durability. Unlike wrought iron and steel, it is not subject to rapid oxidation and decay by exposure to the atmosphere. And whatever tendency it may have of slowly imbibing oxygen in a moist atmosphere can easily be prevented by a proper coating of paint; and thus, at a very small expense, it may be made to endure a thousand years, unaffected by the winds or the weather. On account of this quality, cast-iron houses do not tax their owners with the cost and the trouble of repairs which are incident to other buildings, in consequence of their perishable character.

Another recommendation of cast iron is "its happy adaptability to ornament and decoration." Were only a single ornament required, it might perhaps be executed as cheaply in marble or freestone: but where a multiplicity of the same is needed, they can be cast in iron at an expense not to be named in comparison, even with that of wood; and with this advantage, that they will retain their original fullness and sharpness of outline long after those in stone have decayed and disappeared. Fluted columns and Corinthian capitals, the most elaborate carvings, and the richest designs, which the architect may have dreamed of, but did not dare represent in his plans, may thus be reproduced for little more than the cost of ordinary castings. Ornamental architecture thus becomes practicable, even with our limited means; and its general introduction would greatly tend to elevate the public taste for the beautiful, and to purify and gratify one of the finest qualities of the human mind.

Indeed, so apparent have become the advantages and economy of cast iron for ornamental purposes that there is danger lest the public overlook the character of the structure of a building, in the contemplation of its architectual beauty; and that, deceived thereby, and by the name of the material employed, they imagine themselves to be admiring a building which has all the superior qualities already described: whereas, being without stability in the combination of its parts, it is in reality more insecure than our ordinary buildings.

Some have asserted, and it is still by many believed, that, as iron is so good a conductor of heat, it would expand and contract so much by the changes of temperature as to dislocate its joints in a short time, and render the building unsafe. It has been already mentioned that the assumed impossibility of forming a safe and economical joint for massive structures of cast iron was the probable cause why such buildings had not been earlier introduced. It may now be added that the supposed necessity of making some provision for the expansion and contraction of the mental was the probable reason why greater efforts were not made to overcome this difficulty. Indeed, such has been the prevalence of this belief that even lately a writer in the *Daily American Organ*, published at Washington, has said:

Nothing prevents the speedy and general adoption of iron for building purposes, but the practical difficulty in applying it to the substantial portion of architecture, resulting from some of its elementary properties: these are its expansive and contractable action under the influences of heat and cold, and its extraordinary conducting powers.

And in support of his statement respecting the destructive effects of metallic action, he makes the following quotation from another writer:

The first difficulty arising from this source is the comparatively slight but constantly disorganizing force exerted upon structures of iron or other metals, by expansion from solar heat and contraction by severe cold—a difficulty great in Europe, but much more formidable in this country, where we have such extraordinary extremes of temperature. A distinguished scientific gentleman, speaking of this subject, refers to the monument Colonne de la Place Vendôme, erected in honor of Napoleon the 1st, and covered with bronze made from captured cannon. "In this monument," he says, "there was experienced much trouble from contraction and expansion. The bronze plates, firmly united by rivets, acted as one stupendous sheet, and buckled under the sun's rays in a most extraordinary manner, acting as a real great pyrometer."

If these statements are intended to apply to cast-iron buildings—as they are doubtless meant to do—they are nothing more than the reiteration of all previous writers on the subject, and arise from sheer ignorance: they have been the great bugbear to inventors in this department of art; for, although more or less true in reference to copper, bronze, and certain other metals, they are utterly unfounded when applied to cast iron. We do not say that cast iron is without expansibility: we simply assert that the temperature of our climate, throughout its utmost range, from the greatest cold to the greatest heat, exerts upon it no appreciable effect.

A complete proof of this assertion may be had by examining any of the numerous cast-iron structures erected by Mr. Bogardus. His factory building has now, for a number of years, been exposed to every change of atmospheric temperature without, and to the heat of steam boilers and the operations of a steam engine and heavy machinery within—and, it should be observed, his engine of twenty-five horse power is placed on the second story, purposely to show the great stability of the building—and yet, so perfect are all its joints, that the blade of a lancet cannot be thrust into one of them; nor can there be discovered, by continual and close observation, where its walls adjoin the neighboring houses, the displacement of a single grain of dust.

The writer of the quotation in the *American Organ* continues thus:

Although ingenious and complicated devices may have partially overcome the effects of expansion arising from this source, they have been wholly inadequate to overcome the much greater expansion from artificial heat in contiguous conflagrations. Iron buildings, as usually constructed, although expressly designed to resist conflagrations in compact cities, have been wholly ineffectual for this purpose. It was found in the great fires at San Francisco that the iron columns and framework of buildings were expanded, and thus warped and thrown out of line, by the heat of fires across the streets, and that the buildings were ruined even before contact of the flames.

From these remarks it may be inferred that their author either did not know that there was such a thing as cast-iron buildings in existence, or that there was any difference between them and those made of wrought iron. The houses of San Francisco, which are described as shriveling like paper before they came in contact with the flames, were built of sheet iron, either plain or corrugated; nailed, in most cases, to wooden posts: or, like the better class of English iron houses, riveted to cast-iron columns, and thence ignorantly described as cast-iron buildings.

Cast-iron houses are perfectly fireproof. Were such a building as Mr. Bogardus's factory filled with the most combustible goods, such as cotton or resin, and its entire interior to burn until the whole was consumed, the building itself would remain firm and unimpaired. Some have said that the columns might melt, and thus precipitate the whole; but this is simply an absurdity, said without reflection: for, it is well known, not only a high and intense heat, but the use of a blast, is required to reduce iron to a molten state; and never yet, in any conflagration, has it been found melted, except in pieces of minute dimensions, and in such situation that the current of the flames created around them an artificial blast. Others compare iron houses to stoves, and tell us that if certain parts be made red hot, and cold water then thrown upon them, it will warp and crack the metal: but this only shows a mechanical defect in their construction; for it is quite possible so to construct a stove that it would stand such a test without damage, though it were repeated many times a day, for years. And that the several parts of Mr. Bogardus's buildings are carefully modeled so as to run no risk of this disaster, he has ascertained by direct experiment for this purpose.

This experiment has been repeatedly verified since in the following way. It has sometimes happened that his columns would be found warped when they came from the foundry. To remedy this defect, he made the column red hot; and whilst in this condition, by means of powerful screws, forced the parts not only to the position required, but in some cases as much as six inches beyond it: yet, after cooling, he has invariably found them to be warped exactly as at first. It may be here added that, in his later experiments, he endeavored to secure the set of the column by dashing cold water upon it when red hot, but equally without success.

It is desirable, in most cases, that the floorings and partitions should be also fireproof; so that, should a fire occur, it may be confined to the room in which it originated. This may be accomplished by various devices, extensively practiced in Europe, but too much neglected in our country. Mr. Bogardus has also devised for this purpose, and secured by letters patent, a plan of iron flooring, to be supported by iron beams, in combination with his own new sectional truss girders, which may be seen in use in the buildings of Messrs. Harper & Brothers, the well known publishers. These girders, which may be made highly ornamental, can sustain a heavier load than any others of the same weight yet known, and are therefore more economical. He is also prepared to furnish other modifications, varied as ornament or extent of flooring may require.

Cast-iron buildings are also perfectly safe during thunderstorms; no accident from the electric fluid can happen to any person within them. The metal being a good conductor, and presenting so great a mass to the overcharged clouds, conveys all the electricity silently to the earth, and thus obviates all danger from disruptive discharges. An iron building, for this reason, requires no lightning rods, because it is a huge conductor itself. This is a feature deserving consideration; for many ordinary buildings with rods attached to them have been struck with lightning, whereby a number of persons have lost their lives; accidents which can never occur in cast-iron buildings. In them the intensity current is instantly diffused throughout the entire mass, and thus changed into a current of quantity; so that, in any one part, the electricity must be very feeble and therefore not dangerous to life.

Every style of architecture and every design the artist can conceive, however plain or however complicated, can be executed exactly in cast iron; and, in consequence of its having greater strength than any other known building material, it furnishes us with new ideas of the proportional fitness of parts, and thus opens a wide field for new orders of architecture. Hitherto its use has been confined to factories, stores, lighthouses, and bell towers; but we hope the day is not distant when we shall see it in our city halls, our state houses, our churches, and their spires. And Mr. Bogardus himself firmly believes that had his necessities required him to construct a dwelling house rather than a factory, it would now be as popular for this purpose as it is for stores. They would have, moreover, this advantage: being free from damp, they are ready for occupation as soon as finished; and since they cannot absorb it afterward, they are not liable to mildew, and therefore more healthful.

When Mr. Bogardus commenced this business, the use of cast iron for building purposes was, in this city, only to be seen in the occasional substitution of a water pipe, or a rude solid pillar, for the ordinary stone posts of the first story. It needs not be told here how extensively it is now used. There is scarce a street in our city, and scarce a city in our country, in which are not to be seen either copies or imitations of his beautiful and costly patterns. His mode of forming capitals, a valuable invention which he did not patent, is now in universal use: and, not content with the gift of this great addition to their business in the construction of columns for the first story, some have already attempted to evade his patent for house building. As a substitute for his safe and simple joint, wedges, mortises, chairs, and other complicated devices have actually been patented; and in order to secure their columns, some have fastened them with tie bars to the wooden girders! Of these contrivances, which are, all of them, mere subterfuges for the evasion of his rights, some are absolutely dangerous; and of the remainder, the best are not only inferior in stability—being liable to dislocation by the displacement of the wedges—

but so much more expensive that the value of the extra iron necessary for their construction, without any regard to the work spent upon it, would alone be sufficient to pay for the cost of erecting a superior building. Far from attempting or desiring to monopolize the business—for the demand promises to be sufficient to support very many large establishments—he is ready to grant the privilege to build for a fair remuneration, so small as to leave no inducement to infringe his rights as the inventor.

It may be here added that the validity of the patent of Mr. Bogardus has been contested by the City of New York, and already decided in his favor.

Mr. Bogardus is prepared to carry out designs in cast iron for public and private buildings of every description, lighthouses, towers, and so on, and refers to the following gentlemen for whom he has already erected buildings:

Messrs. Tatham & Brothers, Dr. J. Milhau, Messrs. Blune & Syms, Messrs. Harper & Brothers, The McCullough Shot & Lead Co., Messrs. Spofford & Tileston, Robert J. Dillion, Esq., Mr. Douglas Robinson, The Emigrants' Industrial Savings Bank, Messrs. Christal & Donohue, Messrs. F. Hopkins & Brothers, Messrs. H. Sperry & Co., Messrs. McKesson & Robbins, Mr. John H. Sherwood, Mr. George Bruce, Wm. H. Munn, Esq., Charles O'Connor, Esq., New York; Mr. S. H. Ransom, Albany; Mr. Isaac H. Burch, Mr. Peter Page, Messrs. A. G. Burley & Co., Mr. Tuttle, Chicago; Mr. Wm. M. Swain, Philadelphia; Mr. A. S. Abel (Sun Building), Mr. E. Larrabee, Mr. M. S. Schoonmaker (of Adams & Co.'s Express Co.), Baltimore; F. Coyle, Esq., M. Shanks, Esq., Messrs. Adams & Co. (Express Office), Washington, D.C.; Mr. Daniel Mineu, Charleston Hotel, Charleston, S.C.; Mr. John Parrott, San Francisco, California; La Sociedad de Aiwauenes de Marimielena, The Santa Catalina Warehouse Company, Havana, and so on.

7

THE AMERICAN ARCHITECT AND BUILDING NEWS, selections from editorials and letters, Vol. V, No. 174, through Vol. VI, No. 199, Boston, April 26, 1879–October 18, 1879.

This three-cornered exchange was initiated by the editors of *The American Architect and Building News*. Their argument was answered by E. A., Edward Atkinson (1827–1905), an American economist and amateur inventor who was president of the Boston Manufacturers Mutual Fire Insurance Company. C., the architect who enters the discussion in Vol. V, No. 178, has been tentatively identified by Professor William H. Pierson of Williams College as the Boston architect Charles Cummings (1833–1905). Cummings combined in his career an emphasis on thorough engineering with a careful and somewhat dry archaeological preference for Florentine and Gothic prototypes. At the outset the discussion reflects three conflicting interests: economic considerations (clients and underwriters), utilitarian concerns (engineers), and "picturesqueness or even grace" (architects). This triangular conflict provides a clear image of the complexities involved in any attempt to resolve the various oppositions among architects, engineers, builders, and clients. As the discussion continued, it focused increasingly on an examination of technological details of slow-burning construction, wood-framed construction that would burn slowly and at a rate that could be calculated to the advantage of fire-fighters and salvage crews. Slow-burning construction stood in contrast not only to the tinderbox construction against which Atkinson inveighed, but also to cast-iron construction, since cast iron, in spite of Bogardus's protests, was subject to sudden and disastrous collapse in the event of fire.

In retrospect, the resolution of the controversy seems simple: sheathed structural steel; and that resolution was to come in the two decades after the 1870's in the work of William Le Baron Jenney and the Chicago school.

Vol. V, No. 174, p. 129; April 26, 1879

It would be difficult to find surroundings more deadening to the sensibilities, more uncongenial to art, than are to be found in any New England factory town, with its regular hours, its ceaseless clatter and confusion of sounds, its population with minds all intent on one thing, and its monotony of unsightly buildings; for somehow or other picturesqueness, or even grace, and utility are thought to be quite incompatible when it is a question of building a cotton or a woollen mill. To the architect more than to anyone else such a building is an eyesore; to him it represents the minimum of result and almost the maximum of wasted opportunity. Knowing it for the work of the builder and the engineer, he knows too that its unsightliness is not essential to its strength or to its serviceableness. He can recall scores of engineering structures which are at once pleasing to the eye and useful, and he wonders how it happens that all owners of mills are affected by the same unappreciativeness of architectural effect. If he inquire diligently, he will find that the responsibility rests not wholly with the owners, but in a great measure with the underwriters who insure them against fire loss. They have formulated the conditions which a mill must fulfill before they will accept a risk on it, and having found them to be such as master builders and engineers can fulfill to their satisfaction, they have discouraged, intentionally or unintentionally, the employment of architects. They even go so far as to themselves provide plans and specifications. This hostility to architects, which is a fact to be regretted rather than complained of, is not, to be sure, felt by all insurance companies; for there are wildcat companies, in the scheme of whose operations the aleatory element is given prime consideration, so that an architect's mistake is as often a matter of profit as of loss. In the East, at least, the responsibility for much of this bald work rests with a combination of seventeen mutual fire insurance companies, which make a specialty of insuring mills. Without reflecting on the propriety and wisdom of the regulations which these companies have established, we can express the wish that they may find it possible hereafter to take a more liberal view of the architectural needs of mill buildings.

—THE EDITORS

*Vol. V, No. 176, pp. 151–152;
May 10, 1879*

THE ARCHITECTURE OF MILL BUILDINGS

BOSTON, MASS.

TO THE EDITOR OF *The American Architect:*

Dear Sir,—I have the honor to acknowledge the receipt of No. 174 of your paper, in which it is alleged that the modern cotton or woollen factory represents to the professional architect "the minimum of result and almost the maximum of wasted opportunity." "Knowing it for the work of the builder and the engineer, he knows too that its unsightliness is not essential to its strength or to its serviceableness." Granted in part. There can be no good architecture unless art and utility are combined in a consistent way.

The dreariness of the factory town and the want of appreciation of architectural effect is further imputed to the underwriters, and to them is also imputed "hostility to architects."

In reply to this last very serious charge I beg leave to say that it has but little foundation in fact. The factory underwriters are the factory owners insuring each other under a mutual system, and working through officers whose business it is to study the right methods of construction of the factory and auxiliary buildings, and to advise the owners what rules of construction they must follow in order to reduce the risk of loss by fire to a minimum.

The factory owners constitute a class who have given much employment to architects in the construction of dwellings, warehouses, and churches, and it has always been a matter of great surprise to the writer, especially after the great fire, that they have not required their architects and builders to adopt the same methods of construction and modes of preventing loss by fire that have compassed the safety of their factories. This will not be accomplished until professional architects cease to class the engineer and the builder as having a function in the construction of buildings separate and distinct from their own.

These officers of insurance companies, of whom the writer is one, have no hostility to true architects whatever, but as underwriters they are compelled to take the position of hostility to the work of very many of the professional architects, for the following reasons: In several cases in which the writer has had knowledge of their work, in the construction of factories, workshops, or other buildings intended for industrial purposes, they have constructed buildings that were either unsafe to insure, not strong enough for the work to be done in them, or unfit in some important way for their proposed use; or else, the plans presented and sometimes adopted have involved an expense for mere architectural effect entirely inconsistent with the necessary conditions of the work to be done in the buildings. The writer could designate cases in which factory owners have incurred very heavy expenditures in altering the work done under the direction of the professional architect, in order to secure safety and fitness in the buildings constructed.

Furthermore the mutual underwriter distrusts the work of many of the professional architects because in most of the city buildings lately constructed under their control or supervision the method of construction is such as to *assure the maximum of risk from the minimum of fire.*

Much attention has been given in these late years, by professional architects, to the building of churches. They have but to ask any underwriter and they will learn that with scarcely an exception churches are considered very bad risks, and for the best of reasons, since what are called brick and stone churches are very apt to burn. Next to churches the chief attention of architects appears to have been given to warehouses and shops. With few exceptions the new structures in the burned district of Boston could not be admitted to the mutual system of factory insurance if placed separately near the factories and under the protection of their fire apparatus, because many of the worst faults of the old buildings that were burned have been repeated in the new.

In very many of them also the use of the interior has been subordinated to the architectural effect of the exterior; hence they are not only unsafe but in some measure unfit for their purpose.

Hotels are among the worst risks taken by underwriters, yet in some of the apartment buildings now being constructed some of the worst faults and gravest causes of danger are being repeated.

Schoolhouses can be constructed in such manner that no fire could exist in one under such conditions as to cause the danger of a panic among the children, such as was lately prevented in New York by the courage of the female principal. There is one private schoolhouse that would meet this condition in Boston, but the last public schoolhouse built could not be insured in a well-managed mutual factory insurance company, and the faults which make it unsafe have made its construction more expensive than a safe construction would have been. I think you will admit that if there is any ground whatever for the following allegation, which I do not hesitate to make—that it is a more hazardous business to insure stone churches, city warehouses, and brick or stone hotels than it is to insure factories used for the extra-hazardous purposes of manufacturing cotton and wool—it is time to question the capacity of those who under the name of architects have constructed these buildings.

In your comments upon the record of the fires in factories you cite in evidence of the alleged hostility of the factory underwriters to the architects that they (the underwriters) "even go so far as to provide plans and specifications" for factories. I send you herewith one of these plans, but before you copy it would it not be well to ask from your contributors sketches and specifications for a factory building say 350 feet long, 72 feet wide, and four stories high? The elevation should be accompanied by a sectional plan showing the mode of construction of the floors and roof, and the specifications should give the detail of all the material to be used. You may then have the opportunity to compare our plan with any that may be submitted, and we may then ask the question, Which is the true architect, he who subordinates architectural effect to the conditions of safety and fitness for intended use, or he who sacrifices either or both of the latter to the former?

In the number of your paper which you have sent me I find

eight pages of letterpress and four pages of illustrations; aside
from the paragraphs to which this communication is a reply
there is not a single sentence treating any question of the right
construction of a building. In connection with the picture of
a church, there is nothing to show whether it was really built
of stone, or whether it is a stone sham screening a combustible
timber church inside, or whether it is provided with such an
arrangement for the furnaces as to make it safer to insure
it to burn than to insure it not to burn; of which description
of church I can point out to you several examples within
the limits of an afternoon's walk from your office.

Will you kindly send me a number of your paper containing a study or design for a factory or workshop, in order that
I may compare the method of construction of the professional
architect with the requirements of the underwriter.

Very truly yours,

E. A.

The editors of *The American Architect* replied by apologizing for the word "hostility" in their initial comment, and
then they continued in part:

. . . Architects who have built mills have had their minds occupied
with ideas of their own, and, not being familiar with these
practical conditions, have too often neglected to study and provide
for them. The owners have found that engineers, by the nature of
their occupation, were more prone to concentrate their attention
upon these conditions, or have turned to builders as men whom
they could more directly order in the carrying out of their work,
and who asked no fee for architectural services. . . .

It is desirable that mills and factories should be made architecturally as presentable as possible, for they and like buildings
give the whole character to the aspect of many of our towns, and
of the outskirts of most large cities. Three or four centuries ago
they could certainly have been made picturesque and interesting,
and perhaps we may yet make them so, more or less; at present
they are unspeakably dreary and repellent, and their fault is not
merely that they are ugly in themselves, but that they spoil whole
towns which might else be attractive.

Vol. V, No. 178, p. 167; May 24, 1879

WHY BUILDINGS ARE NOT MADE FIREPROOF

BOSTON, May 12, 1879

To THE EDITOR OF *The American Architect:*

Dear Sir,—I suppose that most of your professional subscribers have, like me, read E. A.'s letter, published in your last issue, with great interest, and also with no small pleasure, although we may think that his remarks about architects and their work convey an impression, the injustice of which we feel the more keenly, because the writer's intention so evidently is to show them fairness and courtesy. E. A. says he is surprised that the owners of dwellings, churches, warehouses, and so on, after the lesson of the great fire, have not required their architects to adopt the same methods of construction and modes of preventing loss by fire that are so successful in factories. So are we, and our surprise is as much greater than E. A.'s as our knowledge of the simplicity of the means by which comparative security can be attained is, with all due respect to him, greater than that of a nonprofessional is likely to be.

But E. A. goes on to speak of the combustible character of stores, hotels, churches, and so on, as usually built, and concludes with the following defective piece of logic, that "if it is more hazardous to insure stone churches or brick hotels than cotton factories, it is time to question the capacity of the architects who constructed them." To make this reasonable, the premise must be supplied that the architects controlled the mode of construction. In how many cases is this true? Does E. A. suppose that any decent architect does not know how to build a building with any required degree of fireproof quality, if he is instructed, or rather permitted, to do so? Or did he ever see an architect who, in discussing a project for a new structure, did not timidly suggest modes of obtaining greater security against fire than was possible with the ordinary construction? I know of no habit more invariable with any class of people than is that among architects of trying to suggest such improvements on the ordinary fashions, unless it be the corresponding habit among their clients, or patrons, of summarily crushing such aspirations. And we, perhaps, have had occasion to think even more deeply on the subject than E. A., and have seen that the owners are, from their point of view, right. Let us present to E. A. an example. Suppose he has in mind to build a hotel, to cost a hundred thousand dollars if built in the ordinary manner, which, it must be remembered, is also the cheapest manner. His architect, who keeps all these figures at his fingers' ends in the vain hope that some time they may be of use to him, tells him that at the present price of iron he can make it practically fireproof for about 18 to 20 per cent increase in the cost. E. A. thinks other people are foolish not to make the additional outlay: how would he figure in his own case? "If I build it fireproof," he would think, "I shall need no insurance. With the ordinary construction the premium will be about one per cent for five years, or $200 per year. To make it fireproof will cost say $20,000 more. Interest on $20,000 at six per cent is $1,200. I was then," he would remark to himself, with considerable asperity, "about to sacrifice a thousand dollars a year to a mere sentiment, or in order to gratify the whims of this architect." The agent tells him that he could not get any more rent on account of the fireproof qualities of his building, and the welfare of humanity in general and the initiation of better modes of construction are left for the next man to take care of.

Every architect knows that this is true; have not underwriters yet found it out? People will not build securely, simply because it is not for their interest to do so. Now and then parties who carry valuable stocks of merchandise can figure out a profit in building a fireproof structure to contain them; or where, as in the case of the manufacturers' mutual insurance companies, the influence and interest of a great number are combined to impose precautions upon a single member, a certain amount of security is enforced; but except under such circumstances, all architects will unite in saying that it is next to impossible to induce owners to expend money in extra protection against fire.

The writer, in a youthful enthusiasm for good construction, finding that at least half of the fires in frame houses could be prevented by building the chimney walls eight inches thick instead of four, began by drawing all his chimneys in this way, hoping that someone, seeing it done, might approve his intention, or might overlook it, and thus without his consent be saved from burning alive. It was of no use; the plans would be submitted to a builder, and brought back with the invariable question, "Why do you make these chimneys so thick?" "Oh, that is for protection against fire." "How much will it cost more than the common way?" "About a hundred dollars." "Is it often done so?" "Well, no; but if it were, scores of children who have been burned in their beds would now be—" "Never mind about that, the ordinary way is good enough for me; please have the plans changed." After repeated experiences of this kind, he contented himself with suggesting the extra thickness of the flue walls as extremely desirable, but to this day he has never found an owner who would consent to have it done, unless he were compelled by law.

Most of us, after we have had a few of our clients leave us because "they didn't want the architect's ideas crammed down their throats," get shy of preaching unpopular doctrines, and content ourselves with looking after our four-inch walls as well as we can. It is all we are allowed to do, and I claim that we do it well. Most persons know that a house designed and superintended by a competent architect is far less likely to burn than the ordinary carpenter's construction. They are both restricted to the same materials and modes of building, but to the superior care and knowledge of the architect is due the increased security that he attains.

It is strange that anyone should lay at the door of architects the reckless fashions of building. Where alone is there any attempt to impose some conditions of safety? In the large cities, by the help of building laws, all of which have been proposed, drawn up, urged to enactment against bitter opposition, and carried to enforcement, by the efforts of architects. What more can they do? If anything further in that direction is to be accomplished, they must have the assistance of some other influential class. Why should not the underwriters themselves help them, instead of abusing them?

E. A. comments upon the failure of architects to design factories which were suitable in all respects for their purposes. There is nothing surprising in that. Judging from the results, the architects employed to design factories are seldom of the first class, and the best would need much help from the mill engineers in their first attempt at such constructions, but it does not follow that with the aid either of their own or other's experience they would not be able to be of much use to the owners of the mills. Nor must it be forgotten that a building cannot be made beautiful without some sacrifice of money or convenience. A mill may be perfectly convenient and perfectly beautiful, but cannot at the same time be perfectly economical. A poor architect may be unsuccessful with ample means, just as a second-rate tailor can use a bale of cloth without making a well-fitting coat; but the best tailor cannot make a coat elegant which reaches only two inches under the arms, nor can any architect make a rectangular box with a flat roof picturesque, whatever directors may think.

C.

Vol. V, No. 180, pp. 182–183 (passim); *June 7, 1879*

SLOW-BURNING CONSTRUCTION

BROOKLINE, May 26, 1879
To the Editor of *The American Architect*:

Dear Sir,—I am under great obligation to your correspondent C. for the kind manner in which he has replied to my last communication, and I greatly regret if I have appeared to do an injustice to the members of a profession among whom I count many of my best friends. We agree in the main in regard to the unsafe character of many of the city structures, but I cannot admit as yet that the "knowledge of the simplicity of the means by which comparative security can be attained" is attained more surely by the professional architect than by the nonprofessional underwriter. I say this with all respect to C., because the very title with which he heads his rejoinder proves that he has missed the point of my first letter. I have not raised the question "why buildings are not made fireproof," because I am well aware that the cost would be too great for common uses, and that either the architect, builder, or mill engineer who proposed such a construction for ordinary buildings would fail to get much employment.

Our mills are not fireproof, but if kept clean and in good order they are *slow-burning*. The contents may burn with great rapidity, but the structures themselves are built with a view to slow combustion.

The underwriters claim that the same quantity of material commonly used in the construction of a city warehouse, schoolhouse, or church, and usually put together in such manner as to make a very combustible structure, can be so combined as to make a very incombustible one, at the same time not more expensive, and in many cases more fit for use, than the ones now built.

The dwelling house constitutes a more difficult problem because of the numerous partitions, but even here we think a truly skillful architect could get some useful hints from the factory methods.

The city structures to which we take exception are many of them those in which money has not been spared, and where owners, architects, and builders appear to have desired to compass safety; yet in such buildings we find faults which our experience has taught us to be grave causes of danger. It would not be fit for me to designate the exact buildings, lest I should do harm to some individual; but I have now in mind one in which the intention has been to secure complete safety, as nearly as possible, short of an absolutely fireproof construction, yet its flat roof and the inside finish of its upper story are so combined as to make it dangerous. It could not be insured by the mutual underwriters, even if alongside a factory fire pump, without a considerable altera- tion, or a heavy expense for sprinklers in the hollow spaces between its flat roof and its false ceiling; in which concealed and inaccessible space enough wood has been uselessly placed to assure a very great damage and probably complete destruc- tion of its upper stories if fire ever gets there. Rats may set it on fire at any time if oily rags, such as are often used in cleaning furniture or woodwork, should happen to come within their reach. We have several proved cases where rats have caused spontaneous combustion by building their nests of oily waste in such hollow roof-spaces as I have described.

In other buildings, not far from your office, faults of the most serious kind can be pointed out that would have been remedied at even less cost than has been incurred; in other cases, a little of the money spent in excessive exterior decoration, if expended in the interior, would have made the buildings far safer and better for use.

I am well aware of the difficulty which architects often meet when suggesting changes in method, but it is not always so, and I cannot but think that the great attention that has been given to architectural effect and to decorative art has been, in part at least, misapplied, and that it is because of this tendency to develop unduly the fine-art side of the profession that the architect has been so little consulted by those who must of necessity be controlled by the uses to which the building must be put.

During the last ten days the writer has visited one new factory, not yet occupied, for which a professional architect was employed to prepare the plans. It is safely built, but it is greatly injured for use because the arrangement of its windows and the construction of its roof have been subordinated to the architectural effect. It has an unusually good effect, but its owner will pay a heavy annual tax for its enjoyment. . . .

In reply to the proposition made by C. as to the writer's probable course were he called upon to build a hotel, he begs to say that he probably would not attempt an absolutely fireproof construction, but that he would endeavor to apply the principles of slow combustion, and would also endeavor to build in such a way that the rats in their passage from the cellar to the attic in the concealed flues in the woodwork should not awake him up by stirring the shavings and rubbish over which they traveled, an occurrence which has not been infrequent in some hotels that might be named, and one which probably accounts for the fact that hotels stand at the head of the list in the enumeration of fires.

E. A.

Vol. V, No. 182, pp. 199–200 (passim);
June 21, 1879

This letter turns the controversy from a discussion of principles toward a discussion of technological details.

SLOW-BURNING CONSTRUCTION

To the Editor of *The American Architect*:

Dear Sir,—If you can spare a little more space for discussion of the subject of slow-burning construction, I would like to make a few comments on E. A.'s last letter, and hope that my reply may be half as interesting and instructive as his communication.

Before proceeding to practical matters, I wish to defend the profession from being considered responsible for schoolhouse construction. How much the real architects have to do with such buildings may be inferred from a little story, to which I imagine there are many parallels. A member of the Institute once submitted designs in competition for a schoolhouse in a certain city. He was afterward told that his design was adopted, but for a long time heard nothing further. Being a gentleman, and unwilling to importune the committee, he waited until one day, passing the spot, he saw his schoolhouse half built. He applied to the committee for an explanation, and was told that he was too expensive an architect for them, and they had found one who agreed to take his sketches and make the working drawings and specifications for forty dollars, and they had given him the job. I venture to say that it is the forty-dollar architects who have done the larger part of the schoolhouse construction, and between them and the committees who employ them, the public gets all the safety and convenience that it need expect.

However, I am far from claiming that architects do all that they might in promoting good construction. Long habit, the opposition of builders, and the indifference of owners have induced careless ways which are much to be regretted; but I think that few of the respectable ones are unfamiliar with most of the precautions which E. A. mentions. At the same time there are many details about which they would be glad to learn from one who certainly shows himself well qualified to inform them. In the hope that he will be disposed to give us the benefit of his experience, I will make a few inquiries, rather than criticisms, about the mode of factory construction which he describes, with reference to its application to more finished buildings. . . .

Part IV: Coordination of Theory and Practice (1880–1910)

1. Introduction

The post–Civil War period in this country seems to have been on the one hand a period of excitement and elation about the pace and scale of expansion and on the other hand a period of anxiety and at times not a little depression about disorientation and displacement. The stock image of the expansion of the period is the accelerated settlement of the West, the rapid elimination of the frontier—a stock image that supports the insistent American dream of this country as essentially agrarian, or grass at its roots. Perhaps more important was what seemed the thunderclap explosion of the Industrial Revolution—a revolution that had not been so much delayed as it had been leisurely in the pre-Civil War period. The Civil War itself, with its extraordinary concentrations of men and materials, had reflected the potentials of an industrialized society, and in the period from 1865 to 1914 those potentials were realized at an accelerated pace (and with a waste of resources) that still staggers the imagination. Not only did industrialization transform the physical landscape; the new wealth it created transformed attitudes toward life, and geometrically increased the capacity to manipulate both the physical and human environments. The rapid growth of population (from 31 million in 1860 to 76 million in 1900) was dramatized in the rapid growth of urban concentrations (New York City, from 800,000 in 1860 to 3½ million in 1900; Chicago, from 109,000 in 1860 to 1,700,000 in 1900); and the new urban concentrations were a radical alteration of the human landscape. The dream of America as simple, moral, and agrarian, lively as the dream still was (and perhaps is), came into sharp conflict with the realities of the new cliff dwellings and of "the Cross of Gold."

If "expansion" was one of the dominant metaphors of the period, the other and corollary metaphor was "conquest"—the conquest of the West, of the frontier wilderness (of the buffalo), and ultimately, the conquest of nature and of time and space by the new combination of science, technology, and industry. The metaphor of conquest, supported directly by the evidence of the transformed physical environment, was reinforced by the popularization of Darwinian ideas, notably "survival of the fittest," generalized to incorporate metaphors of conquest in social, economic, and political behavior.

The impact of this accelerated growth and flux on architecture was an intensification of a variety of pressures. The expansion created an obvious increase in the demand for housing and for all kinds of enclosures of space; the expansion altered functions that had to be housed, the uses to which structures were to be put; the expansion increased urban real-estate values and dictated a new architectural economy; and the technological revolution made available new and different structural materials and systems. All this could have been romanticized as the excitement and challenge of expanding horizons had it not been for an equal and opposite popular and professional reaction in favor of architectural conformity—what William Henry Furness remarked as the reaction against the "odd," against the "new . . . If we have never seen it before, either in buildings, or in prints and photographs . . ."—as though architecture was to be required to remain fixed and dependable in the midst of expansion and flux.

Contemporaneous with the pressures of expansion and the counterpressures for conformity to the architectural past was a renewed demand for a "new architecture." Where that demand in the 1830's and 1840's had been idealistic and nationalistic, in the 1870's and 1880's it lost the tinge of nationalism and reflected instead an interest in the new technologies and in changing architectural needs. Apparently this demand for the "new" had become so lively in the 1880's that Mrs. Van Rensselaer felt called upon in 1888 (two years after Richardson's death) to defend him as at least "sufficiently new" to merit his reputation. Her defense implies that Richardson's use of the traditional technology of stonemasonry and his revival of Romanesque forms were already under attack by the *avant-garde*.

The odyssey of the phrase "form follows function," as its meanings shift and change, reflects the impact of changing technologies and needs. When Greenough used an approximation of the phrase in his 1851 letter to Emerson (see page 123), he was writing from Washington, D.C., where his specific concern was with the architecture of government buildings and with his reaction against "foreign and hostile systems" in their design. Emerson's response was generalized; Thoreau's response (see page 173) transposed Greenough's concern with public buildings into a concern with domestic housing. By implication, "architecture" in the 1850's meant government buildings, churches, and homes. Within fifty years "architecture" had evolved to include, from Sullivan's point of view, bridgebuilding technology, the office building, the apartment building, the warehouse, and the factory. In this transformed context the slogan "form follows function" shifted its meanings: function was not, for example, the expression of national identity in a government building or of domestic order and felicity in the forms of a private home; function related to urban economy and the elaborate office machinery that coordinates that economy and makes it possible. The same ideal of a direct relation between form and function is given a more explicit treatment in 1881 by Leopold Eidlitz, who stressed the relation between architectural forms and the function of the structural materials and systems that make them possible.

In addition to the different meanings that derived from changing needs and technology, "form follows function" was also modified by shifting emphases in modes of thought. Greenough conceived of form and function essentially in a context of biological metaphor, the fitness of an animal's form and structure to its environment and its functions within that environment. Eidlitz contextualized form and function in a metaphor much more closely linked with the concerns of the practicing architect. Sullivan's preoccupation with "power" and Wright's with "plasticity" also variously condition the meanings of form and of function and the nature of their interrelation.

The slogan and its implications were, in effect, a literary ideal in the 1850's; and it was not the emergence of the ideal itself or a change in its meaning that made the new architecture, but a displacement of literary preoccupations and a shift to an emphasis and a vision that were essentially architectonic. This shift is reflected in the concentrated focus of Eidlitz's attempt to deal in solidly architectural terms with "the nature and function . . . of architecture"; and it is reflected in the forthrightness of Richardson's architecture. Richardson worked within the limits of traditional materials and techniques and within the limits of revived architectural forms; but his Romanesque forms are a new architecture because Richardson did not treat them as applied or literary decoration. Richardson designed in terms of the strength and weight of structural elements in interrelation with the strength and weight of a building's masses and spaces. He combined a renewed interest in the stuff of his materials with the attempt at direct, rather than theoretical, architectural conception. His attitude toward the past was not that of the literary or archaeological imitator of achieved forms; as Richardson put it, his interest was in "how those old fellows had done"—how, not what—an interest in method as against an interest in end product. If iron was to have its "honest credit," as William Henry Furness wished, iron would have to be treated with an attitude analogous to Richardson's attitude toward brick and stone.

Sullivan and John Wellborn Root both reflect the emergence of this new attitude toward materials, compounded with a new ability to think directly in terms of engineering. Sullivan's surprised realization as a child that he was "actually thinking in terms of mathematics," and his later realization that he was actually thinking in terms of engineering, put engineering in a new role. Engineering is no longer conceived as what is done to hold the building up after the building's forms have been determined; engineering is throughout an integral aspect of the process of design.

The period 1880–1910 is impressive to the mid-twentieth-century critic as a time of revolution in architecture, a period dominated in three quick generations by the work of Richardson, Sullivan, and Wright. Legitimate as it is, the emphasis on these three masters can distract us from the fact that they were surrounded by architects who were perhaps lesser artists but who were their peers. Eidlitz is not remembered for his architecture, but his book is as clear and positive a statement of the new architectural principles as his generation or the next was to produce. Without Sullivan, the Chicago of the 1880's and early 1890's would still be regarded as having realized a major architectural revolution. Conversely, if we overdramatize the "isolation" of the three masters, we are in danger of regarding them (as Sullivan and Wright sometimes regarded themselves) as lonely giants, single-handedly holding out against overwhelming hordes of Philistines. The chronic concern with the necessity for aesthetic education of the American public from the 1830's on clearly indicates that the Philistines were there in force, and by the 1890's the new wealth had made them formidable opponents; but there were also *Davidsbundler*. Sullivan and Wright had protagonists and admirers; and in part the image of them as lonely and embattled men derives from a tendency characteristic of biography, the tendency to confuse their personal lives with their public careers as architects. The Philistine power's ultimate victory as Sullivan and Wright saw it certainly did take place, but not in the same terms or at the same odds as their autobiographical dramatizations tend to portray.

One more question remains to tease and unsettle the contemporary critic: We conceive of this period as the dawn of modern architecture, as a period that achieved a synthesis of theory and practice, of art and technology. But for all the apparent accord that evolved in the period, there is a subtle and nagging divergence, implied by Sullivan's preoccupation with large-scale architectural forms in the new industrial-urban economy and Wright's preoccupation (1890–1910) with forms essentially domestic in scale and rural-agrarian in their overtones. This divergence can be minimized by the argument that the differing contexts implied the differing architectural solutions, yet the divergence remains as a deep-rooted discord in twentieth-century architecture: the opposition between the urban realities of the American landscape and the insistent agrarianism of our unstated preferences.

2

William Henry Furness, "Closing Address," PRO-
CEEDINGS OF THE FOURTH ANNUAL CON-
VENTION OF THE AMERICAN INSTITUTE OF
ARCHITECTS, November 8, 9, 1870 (New
York, 1871), pp. 247–254.

W. H. Furness (1802–1896) was a Unitarian clergy-
man, born in Boston, educated at Harvard, and minister of the
First Unitarian Church of Philadelphia from 1825 to 1875.
He was a close and lifelong friend of Emerson's, and he
stands, through the person of his son Frank, as a tenuous
link between the Emerson-Greenough-Thoreau complex and
the early years of Louis Sullivan's career. Sullivan, after his
year (1872–1873) in the "cemetery of orders and styles" at
Massachusetts Institute of Technology, spent a few months
as draftsman in the architectural offices of Furness and
Hewitt. Sullivan was attracted and excited by Furness's work:
"something fresh and fair . . . a human note, as though
someone were talking." (See *The Autobiography of an Idea,*
pages 190–196.) Frank Furness (1839–1912) was W. H.
Furness's son; another son, the portrait-painter W. H. Furness, Jr., was referred by Emerson to Greenough at W. H.
Furness's request in 1852. It is interesting that one of
Greenough's favorite themes (in their workshops "the old
artists taught each other") crops up in Sullivan's account
of Furness's office: "The atmosphere was the free and easy
one of a true workshop savoring of the guild where craftsmanship was paramount and personal." The tenuous line of
argument thus runs: as Emerson (and Greenough) had taught
the father, so the father taught the son, and the son taught
Louis Sullivan.

The Chairman introduced Dr. Furness, who addressed the Convention as follows:

Sydney Smith tells us that Mr. Fox used very often to say, "I wonder what Lord B. will think of this." As it happened that Lord B. was not a very bright gentleman, the curiosity of Mr. Fox's friends was naturally excited to know why he attached such importance to the opinion of so commonplace a person. "His opinion," said Mr. Fox, "is of much more importance than you are aware of. He is an exact representative of all commonplace English prejudices, and what Lord B. thinks of any measure, the great majority of English people will think of it." And Sydney Smith goes on to say that it would be a good thing if every cabinet of philosophers had a Lord B. among them. He expresses his astonishment at the neglect of the British Ministry of his day in not providing themselves with a *foolometer,* that is, with the acquaintance and society of some Lord B., or regular British fool, as a test of public opinion. He states that he himself had a very valuable instrument of the kind, which he had used for many years, and that no one, at all accustomed to handle philosophical instruments, could have failed to predict by it the storm which was then brewing in the public mind, caused by a certain bill that had just been passed by Parliament.

GENTLEMEN OF THE INSTITUTE: While I am very much obliged to you for the honor you have done me in the invitation, with which I am now complying, to address you, without meaning to indulge in any strain of self-disparagement I must needs admit your wisdom in providing that an address shall be delivered at your session by a nonmember, by one of the outside multitude, by one of us who are, *quoad Architecturam,* to speak plainly, fools to you, and any one of us a foolometer of all the rest. I take it for granted that, thorough fanatics in your art, you look upon architecture as the final cause of human existence, at all events as the one thing which you were born and which you have come into the world expressly for. Certain it is that no man ever achieves anything great, anything beyond keeping body and soul together for a few years, unless he is possessed of a certain divine fanaticism for his art or pursuit, whatever it may be. I take it for granted, therefore, I say, that the zeal of the house, the ideal house, hath eaten you up, and that, consequently, you cannot have any respect, even if you ought, which is more than doubtful, for the architectural wisdom of outside critics, who, as is so often the case, torment you by dogmatizing about your art to you who are giving your best powers, your whole lives, to it.

I think I understand the case, gentlemen. You have not invited me, and you do not expect me, to instruct you in architecture. If I were able to do that, I should be ineligible to the office with which you have honored me, and which I am now discharging. Could I teach you in your art, I should be, not a nonmember, but your fellow member, in high standing, and, by good rights, your President. Most emphatically am I a nonmember of your Institute. I know nothing of architecture. I never could have made even so much of an architect as, I am told, any man may become, for all practical, that is, money-making purposes, by simply subsisting on other men's brains, ancient and modern. Yankee as I am, I never could even whittle with any satisfaction, suffering much "from the obscure trouble of a baffled instinct." No, sirs, I know nothing of your art, but I respect it so much that I have not insulted it by undertaking to cram for this occasion in the few days since your invitation came to me. I cannot breathe a syllable that will lead anyone to mistake me for a fellow member of yours. I am your very humble and devoted nonmember, representing for the moment the large and respectable nonportion of your honorable body.

You will pardon me if I have transgressed in spending so many words upon myself. The position is so novel to me that I should not be an American if I were not anxious to define it.

It is very natural that you should wish to hear a word from us outside, to obtain occasionally, in one way or another, some popular and public recognition of your high calling. You are obviously, in a special manner, dependent upon us. You could not exist but for your nonmembers. You cannot employ yourselves. You must have employers. You cannot go on building ever so many blocks of dwelling houses, and palaces and churches, for your own amusement and at your own expense, relying upon chance purchasers, just as a painter multiplies his pictures. If there is any considerable number of you that can do as much as build a moderately sized house, each for himself, letting alone architectural decorations, all that can be said is that you must be much more successful than your brother artists in other departments. Your ideas cost somewhat, if they are to be realized. Capital is your indispensable helper. And you must do all that you can to secure its help. To this end, a taste for art is to be awakened and cultivated in the community at large. There is hardly anything more wonderful in these days and in this country than the rapidity with which wealth is created. The means of erecting the costliest structures, public and private, are amassed in ever-increasing abundance. And only the love of art, animating the public generally, is wanting to give artists of every description as much as they can do, were there ten times the number. You cannot help being concerned, therefore, in winning attention, in all ways possible, to your particular art.

And all the more concerned, because it is your misfortune, or your trial, to live in a country so young in everything, especially the high arts, that architecture is hardly yet appreciated as an art, or its professors and students esteemed as anything more than builders and working mechanics. Builders and mechanics are, by the way, honorable after their kind, and not the less honorable, but the more so, when they are loyal to their position, and make no pretense of being what they are not. Indeed, some architects themselves seem to have no higher idea of their art than what the word architect literally signifies: *chief of the builders or works*. If this is really all that it imports, then, as it has well been suggested, "The *fine* art—the art which divided with painting the affections of Giotto, Michelangelo, Da Vinci, and Raffaello, and produced the Greek temple, the Gothic abbey, and the Venetian palace—may as well look about for some other name."

The consequence of this confounding of artists with mere mechanics is that your art is not only defrauded of its dignity, it is without its rightful authority; and you have incessantly to submit to the humiliation of discussing as questions of taste what are no questions of taste at all, but matters of knowledge, of fact, with persons who, so far from having studied them, have never given a thought to them before— with persons who, if they knew what makes for their salvation (architecturally speaking) would sit silently at your feet, and listen and learn. I sympathize with you, gentlemen, as every humane man must, when, knowing the reason and principle of your work, you have to hear it questioned and caviled at by those who, sound as their judgment may be in the stock market, or as to the quality of this or that article of commerce, know nothing of architecture—a trial as great as it would be to a mathematician to hear his axioms disputed, or the sum of two and two, for instance, questioned.

Mr. Ruskin is not altogether to my liking. He is too intolerant, speaks too much *ex cathedra* for one who is not exactly an artist himself, but an amateur. Yet one cannot help bowing to him, when after elaborately setting forth the merits of Turner's works, he says that he trusts he has convinced the public that they have no right whatever to criticize Turner, that they have nothing to do but to look at his works and be edified. Whether or not Turner were the great man Mr. Ruskin holds him to be, there have been artists—painters, sculptors, and architects—who had this high authority, and before whose works criticism is dumb. Not to mention edifices nearer home, we are told of a structure even in the far-off barbarian East—is it the tomb of Nourmahal?*—of such overpowering beauty that an English traveler, upon entering it, burst into tears.

What art has a better right than architecture to be called a fine art, the art which has been pronounced, in one sense, "the most perfect of the arts, because the laws of proportion and of beauty are in no other art so strictly and so accurately defined," "the only art," it has been said, "which, in its effects, approached nature," and the impression of the grander works of which "is less akin to admiration of the talent of an artist, than to the awe and veneration which the traveler feels when he first enters the defiles of the Alps." This blood relationship of architecture to nature—how beautifully is it affirmed in one of the finest brief poetic utterances that we have had since Milton:

> Know'st thou what wove yon woodbird's nest
> Of leaves, and feathers from her breast?

* Nourmahal is one version of the name of the favorite wife of the Mogul emperor, Shah Jahan. She is better known by the name Mumtaz Mahal. It was for her that the Shah built the incomparable Taj Mahal (1632–1645) as a mausoleum.

Or how the fish outbuilds her shell
Painting with morn each annual cell?
Or how the sacred pine-tree adds
To her old leaves new myriads?
Such and so grew those holy piles,
While love and terror laid the tiles.
Earth proudly wears the Parthenon,
As the best gem upon her zone;
And Morning opes with haste her lids
To gaze upon the Pyramids;
O'er England's abbeys bends the sky
As on its friends, with kindred eye;
For out of Thought's interior sphere
These wonders rose to upper air
And Nature gladly gave them place,
Adopted them into her race,
And granted them an equal date
With Andes and with Ararat.*

Architecture has its ideals, magnificent for their beauty and grandeur, as we know from what has been realized, from the temples of the ancient world and the cathedrals of Christendom. And they who devote their lives to the study of these ideals are bound to exercise an authority in matters of taste which only the most arrant flippancy can presume to question.

You remember the anecdote told of Turner, how when he was once painting, with a brother artist looking over his shoulder seeing him work, he dashed a brushful of red into the water which he was painting, and when the looker-on exclaimed, "Mr. Turner! I never saw that effect in nature!" he dropped his hand from the canvas, and turned and looked at his critic and said: "Don't you wish you could?" A great deal of the criticism passed, upon your art especially, proves nothing but the blindness of your critics. We, the people, are to be taught that, although this is a free country, and every man is at liberty to speak his mind, this liberty is conditioned upon his possessing a mind to speak. It is egregious self-flattery in a man to imagine that he has so much as a fragment of a mind upon matters of which he knows nothing. And when, in this case, he undertakes to express an opinion, his talk is no better than inarticulate babble, and he should be abated as a nuisance—coughed down.

* Ralph Waldo Emerson, "The Problem," lines 25–44 (1839/1840).

I verily believe, gentlemen, that the idea of the excellence of any given edifice depends with most of us nonmembers upon whether it is old or new. If we have never seen it before, either in buildings or in prints and photographs, we pronounce it odd; and when we call a thing odd, we find it difficult to see how it can be called beautiful. With all our freedom, we do not tolerate oddness. We insist, in this country, upon everything's being cut to one pattern. Only think what a long day of it, one particular style of building (the Quaker style—marble steps and wooden shutters) has had here in Philadelphia. What man is there of us, of any social standing, whose mind does not misgive him, when he crosses the street anywhere but at the regular crossing, that he must stop on the curbstone and explain himself—define his position? It is an adventurous thing in this land to set before us anything of which we cannot at once tell what to think. We resent it as a personal insult and take satisfaction—the law of taste—into our own hands, and condemn it. It is a great gratification of one's pride, an evidence of good judgment, of which we do not like to be defrauded: to decide upon a thing offhand, to be able instantly to say, it is good or it is bad.

In one of the fine arts, music, I think we are all learning a becoming modesty, learning what is meant by suspending one's judgment. We are finding out that we must hear a musical composition over and over again before we can decide upon its merits. I do not see why we should not exercise the same restraint in regard to architectural compositions and learn to look more than once before we express an opinion. I appeal to you, who are learned in the art, have you not seen buildings which you thought at the first very much out of the way, and which you have subsequently come to consider very fine? If such be ever the case with you, how much more likely is it to be frequently the case with us of the laity, if we only have patience enough to look and study and magnanimity enough to confess a change of mind?

Without meaning to insinuate any commendation whatever of your noncommittal men in politics—a race, I trust, which has nearly disappeared—they were very much in the way at one time—before the war—I do hold it a great part of wisdom to be always on our guard against a hasty expression of opinion, in matters of art, as in everything else. The instant the decisive word has passed our lips, up leaps our pride to make good the position to which we have committed ourselves; and, if we are wrong, there is no telling the extent to which the finest understanding may become perverted in the fruitless endeavor to make the false true. But the wisdom of this prudence how few show! Only those, I fear, slow-minded people, who would be as hasty as the rest of us if they could.

In fine, we express opinions upon all subjects offhand with the greatest confidence, when, in fact, we know so little of the things whereof we affirm, that, as I say, we have no right to have any opinion about them at all, when our taste is wholly uneducated, and what we are pleased to call our taste is the mere whim of our fancy or our mood, mere use and wont and hearsay, not referable to any principle whatever.

Such is the state of things, gentlemen. Such is the competency of the generality of us to appreciate your great art.

And what makes the matter worse, confounded as architects are with simple builders and mechanics, with those who avowedly work for pay, to earn their living, an honest living indeed, but still to earn a living, there is but little or no faith that you are striving ever to realize ideas, high and beautiful, to make the structures you create speak to us.

Far be it from me to utter a syllable in derogation of the dignity of the humblest mechanical labor. There is no workman, whether toiling in a shop or a brickyard—there is not a hodcarrier, over whom an ideal perfection of work does not hover, and which he may not aim to render a reality. And there is no mere official position, however high, no throne, no presidential chair, even of these United States, that can command the respect which this aim, faithfully pursued, inspires. Honor now and always to the man who, working in the lowest spheres of human labor, is so possessed with a passionate desire to do his work well, rendering it perfect after its kind, that he would rather starve than produce for his employer anything less than his best! I would rather a thousand times over be such a man than the most accomplished man breathing, architect or what not, who has no object in life but his miserable little self.

As the world goes, however, and defective as is the general culture of those engaged in mechanical and manual labor, it would savor strongly of romance to imagine that any higher purpose animates the generality of the working classes so-called than to sell their time and skill in as honest a way as they can, for as much money as they can. And in this, have they not the warrant of universal example? What is all the world agog for, but to make money? I am not going to denounce it, as you may suspect from my profession. I only refer to the fact. I am free to confess that, if this stimulus were suddenly to lose its effect, I don't know what would become of us all. Everything would be at a standstill. You architects would have precious few houses to build. And the clergy, the country clergy especially! Heaven take pity on them—it is but little of this world's wealth that they get anyhow. It would be sad indeed if, under the good Providence that makes even so mischievous a thing as the wrath of man to praise it, some good did not come from the ruling passion for moneymaking. But its evils are manifold and glaring. And the one of them which it specially concerns us to note now is that, as architects are confounded with the money-seeking working classes, and are supposed to be all one with builders, contractors, and mechanics, having and making common cause with these, bent upon wringing out of their jobs as much money as they can, it is not clearly understood that your true architect is, in the highest sense of the word, an artist, having always an infinitely dearer purpose than moneymaking. He has priceless visions of truth and grace, which he is living and dying to express in wood and iron and stone, and he would as soon think of falsifying a revelation from Heaven as of sacrificing them for the sake of money. Were he recognized in this, his true character, as a real, out-and-out worshipper of art, seeking in his way to speak the truth with power to the highest or deepest within us, the recognition could not fail to be reverential, and, instead of being flippantly caviled at, he would be listened to as an oracle. But as it is, he is not so recognized. He is not so listened to.

And then again, gentlemen, it is the peculiarity of your art that you must execute your work out of doors. Other artists, sculptors and painters, work in the stillness and seclusion of their ateliers and studios, and no eye sees what they are doing, but at their pleasure. It is true you can devise and work out your plans in like privacy. But when it comes to the execution, you must go out under the open sky, into the thick of the crowded city, and, in the loud language of brick and stone, utter your high aspirations—say your prayers like the Pharisees of old, though not in their spirit, at the corners of the streets and in the marketplaces, with all the world looking on at every stone that is laid. I wonder whether we should have had so many great paintings if the old masters had been compelled to set up their easels on the sidewalks, and to work with thousands of curious eyes looking on, and to hear all sorts of thoughtless and ignorant criticism.

I call this the peculiarity of your art: its essential and inevitable publicity. It has its trials, and you would, doubtless, be glad oftentimes if, by some magic, you could render your work invisible while it is going on, and until it is finished; at least so long as a just appreciation of your art on our part is so rare. But I cannot say it is a very great disadvantage.

It suggests that you must make up your minds once for all, and consider it an indispensable condition of an architect's existence, that he is to be criticized and wondered at and laughed at, at every stage of his work. As you put your work right before our eyes, and you have to do that, unless we shut our eyes and run the risk of putting them out altogether by tumbling over your materials, we must see your work. And seeing it, it is not in human nature, at least in its present state of architectural ignorance, that we should not think and talk about it, unwisely of course. So you see what a very discipline of personal religion the publicity of your art is; putting you under the blessed necessity of learning and practicing a large and unfailing charity for your ignorant fellow creatures, tending to make pattern Christians of you.

And furthermore—pardon me, if I seem to be preaching to you—I do not mean it—the publicity of your art admonishes you that you are engaged perforce in the great work of public instruction. You are, by the ordination of Heaven, street preachers, and whether you hold forth sound doctrine or false, we must listen to you. We cannot forbear. People may go to sleep inside the churches that you build, and hear nothing, unless indeed you make the interiors so much more eloquent than the preachers that the people must needs keep awake and receive edification through their eyes, but your sermons are written outside as well as in; there is no evading them. You can fill and enlarge and elevate our minds, breathing into us with the light a new sense of truth and beauty. You may minister to the general cheerfulness by gratifying our eyes with lines of beauty and fair proportions, or you can put us out of temper by the reverse, and without our knowing how it is done, which only makes us worse. I find for myself a cheering effect in all architectural ornamentation, whether it be good or bad. Be it ever so bad, it hints of plenty. It is an assurance that people have more than they absolutely need. And this it is, by the way, that renders traveling in New England so delightful. The dwellings, surrounded by gardens, show such attempts at architectural ornament as imply that their owners had more money than they knew what to do with. And the impression is that it must be *millionaires* who live in those fine houses, the probability being that they are occupied by clerks and industrious mechanics. In this state of Pennsylvania, you must look at the broad fields under cultivation, and the opulent barns of our farmers, if you would be assured of their wealth, and not at their habitations which are, or were a few years ago, no better than log houses and shanties. I understand they are better now. Certain it is that the suburbs of this city once so homely have begun to blossom as the rose, and the beauty is stealing abroad and promising to make the whole state our city park. Our multitudinous places of worship, covered though they be with the commonest of church decorations, pinnacles and mortgages, make it interesting to go through the streets, or rather round the streetcorners, where, for the most part, they are, very properly placed to be seen of men. I confess to you, I have been much pleased with myself, when I have learned that the style of a building was designed to express the very feeling which it had already awakened in me. But I shall not venture in this presence to specify my small architectural experiences. By so doing, I should only be giving you what you do not need, additional evidence that it is a nonmember of the Institute who is addressing you. But I am growing garrulous. Venerators as you are of antiquity, you will pardon the infirmities of age.

I have spoken of your art as if its sole or chief office were to inspire cheerful thoughts and contribute to the general good humor; and of this I have spoken because it is a thing which we can all understand, and of which I have honest experience myself. Were this all that you are doing, it would be worth all your labor, all your enthusiasm. In a silent, quiet way, like the liberal light of heaven, the influence of your works steals insensibly into the minds of men, adding an amount that cannot be computed to the sum of human happiness. It is a great service rendered to put and keep men, anxious men of business, in good spirits; and without their knowing whence the cheering influence comes. Who does not know how powerfully localities minister to deepen the sacred love of home and of country, how the exile in a foreign land feeds upon memories of old familiar places, and of buildings, any stone of which he would give his eyes to behold once more, and what strong and endearing associations are wreathing themselves for young and old, all round and all over your architectural devices? How beautiful, and what an exquisite piece of English, is Charles Lamb's lament over the disappearance of the artificial fountains of London! Although you may have the passage by heart, you will not weary of hearing it. "Most of the fountains," he says, "are dried up or bricked over. Yet where one is left, as in the little green nook behind the South Sea House, what a freshness it gives to the dreary pile! Four little winged marble boys used to play their virgin fancies, spouting out ever-fresh streams from their innocent-wanton lips, in the square of Lincoln's Inn, when I was no bigger than they were figured. They are gone, and the spring choked up. The fashion, they tell me, is gone by, and these things are esteemed childish. Why not then gratify children, by letting them stand? Lawyers, I suppose, were children once. They are awakening images to them at least. Why must everything smack of man and mannish? Is the world all grown up? Is childhood dead? Or is there not in the bosom of the wisest and best, some of the child's heart left, to respond to its earliest enchantments? The figures were grotesque. Are the stiff-wigged living figures, that still flitter and chatter about that area, less Gothic in appearance? Or is the splutter of their hot rhetoric one-half so refreshing and innocent as the little cool, playful streams those exploded cherubs uttered?"

But I am far from implying that your art has not far higher offices than those at which I have hinted. Does it not in all times and countries repay in kind the debt of inspiration which it owes to the religious sentiment? Does it not awaken emotions none the less deep because they are indefinable? Can the most skeptical or the most frivolous be insensible to the solemnity, the sanctity, the mysterious awe breathing from the structures which your art has reared?

I do not know whether in any department, whether even in literature, with Shakespeare at its head, there has been a more imposing display of human genius than in architecture. Every creative age in art is naturally followed by an imitative age. So strikingly is this the case in architecture that it is affirmed that "There is now no such thing as a really original design, while some centuries ago there was no design that was not original." Even, then, if the monuments of the creative periods of your art were no longer extant, we might safely infer the greatness of those periods from the fact that they have been followed by ages of imitation.

You have every reason, gentlemen, to assert the dignity of your calling, to exalt your office. Having faith in that, penetrated with a self-forgetting devotion to the high purposes of your profession, you will be open to receive the inspirations of that creative spirit which those who have gone before you have not exhausted, nor could they, and which comes and goes mysteriously, like the wind, blowing where it listeth, we know not whence nor whither. Receiving of that spirit, you will cease to repeat. You will create. "Amidst the ruins of Rome," I use the words of another, "the great Italian architects formed their tastes. They studied the relics of ancient grandeur with all the diligence of enthusiasm. But when they were employed by the piety or magnificence of the age, they never restored the examples by which they were surrounded, and which were the objects of their habitual study. The architects did not linger in contemplation of their predecessors; former generations had advanced, and they proceeded."

Inspired by the ideal of your art, you will be lifted high above all mutual jealousies, for you will perceive that the success of one is a new inspiration for all. Every actualization of truth and beauty will animate your faith in them, and bring you all into closer fellowship. It is only mercenary aims that engender feuds. Charles Reade tells us in one of his books that the old masters in art loved one another. And should this seem incredible, he reminds us that Christians loved one another once.

What has been shall be again. What achievements are

there of the past in architecture, or in any of the arts, which the future will not surpass, since science by its amazing activity and its splendid achievements is arraying man in the regalia of his empire over the inexhaustible resources of the physical world?

Some fifty years ago, the reason given for the general lack of taste in architecture was the absence of monuments of approved design among us, such as the great Italian architects studied, and the impossibility of giving to the public at large any idea of the celebrated structures of the ancient world. People might know and did know something about painting and sculpture, because they had copies and engravings of the masterpieces of those arts. But no engraving, it was said, could give any idea of the grandeur of those ancient monuments, and even if it could, it was costly and limited to a few.

But photographs and stereoscopic views—have they not changed all this? Have they not opened a new era? Brought acquainted by these magical instruments of science with the great ruins of Egypt, for example, have we not the same sense of sublimity that fills the mind of one standing before the originals, only so much less vividly, as seeing the originals at a little distance through a good spyglass differs from seeing them close to? Indeed, the impression made upon my mind by these works of the sun is such that I have often thought how much trouble and expense my invalid clerical brothers, who go abroad to be cured by sight-seeing, would be saved if their physicians would only put them upon a course at home of stereoscopic views, Egyptian, Swiss, or Italian. But whether these miracles have any medical virtue or not, they are certainly efficacious in producing a healthier, healthier because more enlightened, state of the general mind in matters of art, and of architecture especially. They are teaching us and so helping you.

Finally, gentlemen, who can doubt—you surely do not—that in this country, so richly blest of Heaven, with these gloriously free institutions, offering opportunity, invitation, incitement to every human faculty to spring forth and help to enrich human life, the weary age of imitation will come to an end, and that a brilliant age of creation will succeed for your noble art? "Every work of genius is an impossibility until it appears." But when it does appear, it comes with such spontaneous ease and grace that we lift up hands and eyes in wonder that it had never been thought of before.

That you are hopeful of a better day, the existence of this Institute is no uncertain sign. As it is a result, so will it prove an active cause, of progress. Some years ago, a distinguished member of your body, in talking of his art, remarked that we are building now of iron, and we require new styles of building fitted to this material, so that iron shall have its honest credit and publish its massive strength, looking like what it is, and not like wood or stone. Shall this homely, stolid substance have its rights, and will not universal liberty, now no longer a dream, but a fact, a component of the heart's blood of forty millions of people, no longer a dead letter, but a spirit, a vital principle, will it not demand —will it not create—new orders of architecture? Answer us, gentlemen, please, in your works.

3

Leopold Eidlitz, THE NATURE AND FUNCTION OF
ART / MORE ESPECIALLY OF / ARCHITECTURE
(London, 1881), pp. xx–xxi, 33–36, 42–43,
57–58, 251–253, 261–264, 269–291, 481–
489.

Leopold Eidlitz (1823–1908) was born in Prague and
educated at the Polytechnic in Vienna; he emigrated to New
York in 1843, and entered the office of Richard Upjohn, whose
specialty was an extraordinarily sensitive and painstakingly
archaeological Gothic revival (see illustration 10). At the
beginning of his career Eidlitz was capable of the assertion:
"Gothic is adequate to every expression." By midcareer experience and reassessment had led him to a devastating
conclusion: "American architecture is the art of covering
one thing with another thing to imitate a third thing which,
if genuine, would not be desirable." Eidlitz's most famous
designs were the result of his cooperation with Henry Hobson
Richardson and Frederick Law Olmsteed in the revision and
completion of the New York State Capitol in Albany. In
retrospect he seems far more perceptive and important as
critic and theoretician than he does as practicing architect,
though it should be noted that the book excerpted here
seems to have had but little impact on Eidlitz's contemporaries.

From "Introduction"

To devise remedies which shall arrest the decay of art,
and especially of architecture, to arrive at a clear under-

standing of its nature and function, and to mature a system
which shall direct its practice in the right channel, it becomes necessary, first, to review the peculiarities of its
present condition, the views held by the public, and more
especially by those who are recognized as of authority on
such matters; to examine the relation of the professional
architect to his client, to the public at large, and more especially to the church, which has ever been the greatest
patron of architecture; and, finally, to consider the existing
theory of art in general, and its influence upon architecture.
The philosophy of art has heretofore mainly discussed the
nature of beauty, and of the pleasurable emotions caused by
it, with sole reference to the relation of these two phenomena,
and without taking cognizance of the intellectual function
and meaning of art. That art deals with ideas is universally
admitted; but it seems desirable to know exactly how the idea
is finally expressed in matter: that is, how it assumes a
physical form. The exact definition of this process may lead
to a better understanding of the nature of beauty, and hence,
also, to the nature and function of art.

The boundary between the industrial arts and the fine
arts, the properties possessed in common by works of fine
art and those of nature, and the exact meaning of the ideal,
of imitation, of the ugly, the ludicrious, and the sublime,
depend upon a clear understanding of the materialized idea,
as we find it in art.

Architecture demands special consideration to show the
application to it of the law of the ideal and imitation as
governing art in general; and, further, to elicit the exact
conditions of proportion, and the use of carved ornament and
color decoration.

If architecture is to be a living and creative art, the study
of styles must be directed to the art principles manifested
in the relation of their forms to contemporary ideas and
knowledge of construction, to the end that new forms, based
upon modern ideas and the present development of construction, may supersede the forms of the past.

[pp. xx–xxi]

From Chapter II, "The Aim of Architecture," in Part I, "Present Condition of Architecture"

Science, common sense, and taste supply the world with knowledge. Let us see how art, and more especially architecture, are thriving with the help of this knowledge. In order to form a correct view of the condition of architecture, it will be well to examine its great aim at the present day, to create a new style.

The present condition of architecture may be inferred from the question constantly asked, "Will the civilized world, England, America, France, or any other civilized country, ever have a new style of architecture?" There is no indication that this question was ever asked by the Egyptians, Greeks, and Romans, or by the nations of Europe during the Middle Ages; nor are the Chinese, Japanese, and Persians interested in it at the present day; it is eminently the concern of the so-called civilized world and of the nineteenth century.

If architecture as an art were complete, or if it ever had been perfect at any one time, that is to say, if all the demands now made upon it could be fully supplied by past experience, or if we could find in any one period of its history an answer to every current aesthetic question, there would be no need of progress in architecture; new styles would arise from time to time as society changed its needs and nature, and as human ingenuity multiplied its material; we should then see springing up around us buildings of a character entirely new in expression, representing the many new ideas and wants of civilized society made possible by modern science, and called forth by political, social, and religious changes, and by a vast increase in the best building material. We should be overwhelmed with new architectural forms and combinations, and have not only a new style of architecture, but a constantly growing and changing style. Indeed the *various* styles of the present century would be spoken of with confidence and approval. The present activity in building has no parallel in the history of the world. The complexity of modern society demands more various build-

ings than are furnished by any past period of architecture,
or by all past periods put together, and the conditions which
govern erections vary constantly from those which preceded
them. What state of things ever seemed more forcibly to
compel a new style in architecture than that in which we
live?

And yet, though monuments are built of new materials,
in new places, to answer new and heretofore unknown purposes, they merely repeat, when they do not caricature, past
architecture, and we call in vain for a new style. A new
style, it is evident, will not come simply because it is called
for, or hoped for. Architects think of it and dream of it;
attempt it and fail; and finally, in despair, change their
designs from one style to another, vaguely hoping to stumble
upon one that contains all the elements they need, in the
combination in which they need them.

As we know of no such struggles in the past, we come
to the conclusion that architecture is dead, and that we can
do no more than to dig up its varied forms from the past
and apply them to the need of the present. The question then
becomes, What forms are we to take, Egyptian, or Greek,
or Roman, or medieval? The current answer to this question
is, Take them all, familiarize yourself with them all; but when
you reproduce them, be careful to keep them separate, and
to use only such as were originally used together, lest by
mixing forms of different periods you produce discord.

And thus the student reads the history of architecture,
and if he is very clever and industrious he dives deep into
archaeology. Give him a section of a label molding, or of an
abacus, and he will reconstruct the building for you from
which it is taken. His mind is a museum of architectural
history, and architecture becomes to him a knowledge of
forms, connected with dates and places, but not quite clearly
with the ideas which have given them existence. He finds
that these forms harmonize best in the relation in which
they are placed by their authors; and in order to preserve the
harmony and unity of works of architectural art as they
appear in the past, he copies them in the exact relation in
which he finds them. Hence mere division into styles no
longer affords a well-arranged index of art. It becomes necessary to divide and subdivide styles, until there are as many
types almost as there are individual monuments, and when

the problem of designing a new structure is met face to face, and it is found that its requirements do not agree with those of any monument erected at least five hundred years ago, the architect becomes indignant at modern wants, and declares them to be outside the pale of architectural art.

[pp. 33–36]

It would be unjust to the profession not to remember some good results of this lamentable condition of things, viz., the archaeological work in the excavations of antique, and the active and successful restoration and completion of medieval monuments.

Nevertheless architecture today is practically nothing more than a collection of assorted forms, the elements of which are but little considered, and the origin of which is hardly known. When architects speak of progress in architecture, they mean possible new forms which must be *invented* with great labor of the imagination. When old forms are applied, it is done without reference to construction and material. A cornice is supposed to be a sort of architectural decoration, and not a stone covering a wall, hence wooden and zinc cornices, cast-iron capitals, gargoyles in places where no water runs, and buttresses where there is no lateral pressure, arches of lath and plaster where there is no abutment, columns which support nothing; balustrades in places where no one can possibly walk, and battlements upon peaceful libraries and schoolhouses. It is true that a very respectable number of modern architects are never guilty of these gross errors, but how many are there who are willing to forego a tower simply because it is not needed either physically or aesthetically, or a flying buttress, if by an ingenious argument it may be justified?

Architectural forms, like musical compositions, contain but few elements, but these are capable of a great number of combinations. Nor is it necessary that these combinations should be laboriously sought for; they arise naturally out of the conditions of the structure, out of the idea which has given rise to it, and out of the material used in its construction. They are of value only in expressing all these conditions, and of no art value whatever if brought about in any other away.

The modern architect, for reasons which will hereafter

be discussed, but rarely refers an architectural composition to the idea which has given rise to it. He often ignores or neglects the construction and the possibilities of the material employed, as technical matters beneath his notice, but imagines that after a structure has been technically designed, so far as it is necessary to answer its practical purposes, either by some engineer or by himself, *then* the labor of the architect begins by enclosing the structure on the outside and lining it on the inside with a skin of architectural forms gathered from his general fund, in accordance with the dictates of his *taste*.

[pp. 42–43]

From Chapter IV, "Architecture," in Part I, "Present Condition of Architecture"

It would be a waste of time here to enumerate the popular errors as to the nature and function of architecture, or to enlarge upon those of professional architects and writers on this subject. It is enough to show that leading architectural minds who are habitually quoted as authorities on the philosophy of the art look upon an architectural monument, not as the logical expression of an idea, but as an accidental makeshift to supply certain physical needs, which, subsequent to its creation is to be in some way adorned. This adornment again is not considered as an integral element of the structure, but as a thing which shall somehow please the public, either by furnishing artificial shadows to cover inherent nakedness, or by introducing extraneous artwork, which by its nature shall, independently of the structure, produce art effects which the structure itself is not capable of doing, or in the doing of which it can take no other part than that of the frame of a painting.

To sum it all up, it appears to be the accepted opinion that the sole function of architecture as an art is to make monuments pleasant to behold; that this may be done in any way which to the author of the monument may promise good results; that it is useless to seek for a clue to all this in the organism of the monument itself, or in the nature of the idea which has called it into existence, or to seek to establish an organic relation between the ornament and the structure. The forms of past architecture are valued in the degree in which they please individual authors; their function and meaning are unknown, and where known they are disregarded. New forms are looked forward to which shall be the off-spring of the mind or of the imagination. Their conditions also are not that of an expression of certain mechanical work performed which connects the material with the ideal, with a system, a principle, or a law, but they result simply from the dictum of the author's taste. What must become of the value of this taste when all thought bearing upon the subject is rejected as extraneous may be readily imagined, and its results may be observed in the work of the last four centuries. That such a looseness in the definition of the nature of architecture must lead to false conceptions of its characteristics and to other illogical reasoning must be apparent, but will be more circumstantially illustrated in the next chapter.

[pp. 57–58]

From Chapter XVIII, "Monuments," in Part III, "Nature of Architecture"

In creating a monument, the problem is mainly to give expression to the acts performed within its walls, which is done by giving to the structure a form which will correspond with the groups performing these acts, and to its parts such masses, modeling, carved and color decoration as will express precisely the degree of stability, dignity, and elegance which corresponds with the import of the acts to be expressed. The form of a monument is determined, therefore, by the human groups which are accommodated in its interior, and must contain as many single cells as there are prominent groups. The expression of strength and elegance must relate to the mechanical functions performed by structural parts, and is, therefore, referable to mechanical laws. It is the purpose of every architectural monument, also, to supply such physical needs as shelter and comfort to the persons who occupy it; and we may, therefore, sum up the conditions which surround the creation of a monument, as the idea which called it into being, the acts which illustrate this idea, the emotions which are produced by these acts in the human groups which occupy the structure, the degree of strength and elegance which corresponds with these emotions and with the nature of the materials which serve for the erection of the monument, and the knowledge possessed by the author of the monument of both the mechanical and aesthetic relations of the matter which serves to form the organism of his structure. All these conditions appertaining to the development of monumental forms may be likened to the environments of natural organisms, with this difference, that the art force in natural organisms is absolutely adequate, while in an artwork, created by human effort, the degree of creative force varies with the ability and learning of the artist. But it must be clear that man cannot invent artistic forms, but that he may permit himself to be led into the development of forms in precisely the same way as nature develops her forms. In nature environment compels functions, and the organism fully responds to these functions; hence it is possessed of perfect expression. In an architectural monument the functions of the structure are first determined, and next to these the methods of expression, all of which is in imitation of nature by referring development at every stage to nature's own laws pertaining to such organism, namely, the laws of statics. Hence these laws, together with the nature of the fundamental idea which is the origin of the monument, the material of which it is built, its situation with reference to the sun, the climate of the country in which it is built, constitute environments of physical development, which must be understood and responded to by the architect.

The development of monuments in the past, however, does not show even an approximation to a prompt and full appreciation of the conditions controlling the creation of monuments by those who built them. Antique and medieval monuments reached perfect development at a time when the ideas which called them into being had long culminated and begun to decay, if that term can be used in relation to an idea—undergoing a change in its nature, or yielding its place to another idea related to it indeed, but so materially modified as not to be readily recognized as the same.

The monuments erected under Pericles, those of the Roman Empire, and the cathedrals of the twelfth and thirteenth centuries are all illustrations in point. The decay of Catholicism, and of the polytheism of Greece and Rome, occurred simultaneously with the perfection of the monuments illustrative of these religious ideas.

[pp. 251–253]

The confessional, the mass, the saints, and all the methods of Catholic worship pertaining to these, are examples of material expressions of ideas as created in the past. They must continue to command our respect, and will continue to live in Christian poetry. We have discarded them. We should now prove to the world that we are capable of replacing them with other and better expressions of religious ideas. If the present class of recurring religious, social, and political questions should condense and crystallize into tangible ideas worthy of the intellectual condition of the age, and society should, upon sober reflection, discard the aberration of the so-called fashions, and apply itself to clothing its thought in dignified and speaking art forms, then architecture will be able to respond to the demand made upon her. The architectural mind, which is now filled with multitudes of created forms, may well doubt whether new forms are a possibility; but as long as ideas are developed, fitting art forms to express them will be the logical result, provided architecture remains a living art.

A moment's reflection will show that architecture, in spite of the goodly age of this globe, is still in its infancy. We have seen in a former chapter that it deals with single cells, groups, and piles. In truth, the art has not yet fully risen above the single cell. In medieval architecture we certainly find groups of cells and exceptionally rambling piles; but the former are not fully developed, and the latter are mere accident, not premeditated—hence not artwork in that sense. In early human monuments, as the Pyramids, it was required that they should be enduring, and the expression of their import was sought solely in magnitude. It is but natural that the symbol to express greatness which first presented itself to the mind of man should be physical magnitude. Modern architects are still somewhat possessed by an art superstition of this kind. Magnitude is cited as one of the elements of beauty, and this question is seriously debated somewhat in this wise: The larger a monument, the more impressive, the more beautiful it is. Is there any limit, then, to this largeness?

For if magnitude constitutes beauty, unlimited magnitude must be the correlative cause of unlimited beauty; and this leads to serious practical difficulties. The answer made to it is not as logical as the question. It is held that the magnitude of a monument should not exceed what you can overlook from one point of sight. This can be true only when the monument is the result of an isolated idea, or of a single act illustrating an idea. If, on the other hand, there are a series of acts to be represented, it would be well for the clearer representation of the idea in matter that we should observe the various acts in succession. Moreover, these various acts and emotions are not of equal importance. Hence different magnitudes must come into play, and the rule, "the larger the better," must yield to some sort of system whereby magnitude is determined, not perhaps in feet and inches, nor in diameters of columns, nor in magical numbers, but by a rule of relation which shall apply in all cases.

The eagerness to build high towers in connection with medieval cathedrals is a remnant of this crude art system; and the method of placing these towers in immediate connection with the nave, or, what is worse, over the transepts, serves as a striking proof that the single cell was ever present to the mind of medieval architects. The force which is inherent in the tower is belittled by the proximity of the church, and the idea of power to be imparted to the church is frustrated by the proximity of the tower; or, in other words, as cathedrals are arranged, the tower belittles the church, and the church belittles the tower. The cathedral without the tower is a melody which relates dignified ideas in a masterly manner; the tower is the base note, well calculated to strengthen the score. A visible separation, however, of the two is needed fully to attain the desired effect.

Another strong indication of the prevalence of the single-cell system is the crystallization of the cathedral masses around a central line. This is what is usually known under the name of symmetry. It is a fundamental law of both art and nature, but does not extend beyond the limits of organisms of a single function. In nature the moment there is a change of function there is also a change of crystallization in magnitude, form, and direction. Art, to be in imitation of nature, must utilize this very important fact by accepting it as a law, and will thus gain in the expression of the idea.

The composition of architectural groups is a problem reserved for the future, and must be perfected before the relation of architectural piles can be successfully considered. This opens to us a vista of activity, which, when fairly reached, will generate works compared to which the cathedrals of the Middle Ages and Greek and Roman temples are the alphabet of art. There are but few notes in the octave, but few colors (pure colors) in nature; but the development of music and color decoration depends more upon combination than upon the number of original elements. Architecture must seek its ultimate development, and will find it, too, in the same way.

[pp. 261–264]

Chapter XIX, "Form and Construction," in Part III, "Nature of Architecture"

Architectural construction teaches the application of well-known mathematical reasoning to questions arising in statical mechanics. It deals primarily with the laws which determine the just proportions of matter under a given relation, and with the use of certain given materials; and, secondly, it investigates possible forms or possible relations of material, as also the application of mechanical laws to all available materials for all possible purposes. In this manner methods of construction are mutiplied, and new materials are brought into use. Methods of construction are geometrical demonstrations in matter of mechanical ideas, and are for that reason not works of fine art. Fine art means representation and not demonstration. The author of a demonstration of an idea is, therefore, not an artist—but inasmuch as the work produced by him is to the uninformed mind often a satisfactory representation of an idea, without becoming absolutely a demonstration (which can be the case only when the construction is mathematically understood), the effect upon the subject is very much akin to that of a work of fine art in this, that it produces surprise, or, as it is commonly called, a pleasurable emotion.

Surprise is enhanced in the degree in which the construction excels as a scientific achievement, and also in the degree in which the essence of the argument involved is sufficiently revealed to betray, not the scheme itself, but its fitness for the purpose.

Methods of construction also appeal to the imagination, and compel admiration for boldness of conception, daring, and enterprise. Hence it follows that superior or inferior methods are applied to monumental structures in the degree in which these monuments rank in the scale of ideas represented by them.

It needs no special argument to show that form is the result of construction, and that construction determines the elements of form. Form and construction are indeed so intimately related that they may be advantageously connected in the same chapter, that we may, as it were, step from one to the other, and gain thereby in the understanding of both.

It is rarely the case that one and the same structure represents more than one idea; but inasmuch as fine art deals with acts and emotions (phases of an idea), we can point to but few modern monuments which do not involve the consideration of a number of acts and emotions; and it needs to be considered what elements of form and construction may be used to serve the architect in expressing them. To illustrate: the Greek temple contemplates the idea *religion*, also a *habitation* for its services, a receptacle of the god, accessible only to a priest, whose act, whatever it may be, forms no element in the structure, as this act is not observed by anyone. No congregation is admitted inside the temple. So far as the people are concerned this temple is the habitation of a statue without function or motion; and it follows that this purpose may be represented by a single cell which needs expression only on the outside. A Christian church, on the other hand, admits into its interior the whole congregation, and accommodates various groups as they range themselves for prayer, private and congregational, music, confession, baptism, the communion, processions, and sermons. The service and government of the church also demand vestry rooms, a chapter house, corridors, and cloisters; and thus a church structure may be termed a group of cells. In this case, as in many others, cells need not be separated from each other by walls, but may be indicated by colonnades, screens, or archways, for the reason that the separation does not arise from a physical necessity but from an aesthetic necessity which demands a representation of the separate acts which illustrate the idea in the organism of the group; and also for the purpose of distinguishing special acts by giving greater height to the cells devoted to them, and a more refined treatment in modeling and decoration.

It frequently occurs that the architect is called upon to join two or more groups, as is the case, for instance, in parliamentary structures. Such a combination of groups becomes a pile, wherein the groups are separated sufficiently to prevent practical inconvenience, and mainly to give an expression to the whole, which will tell the story of the functions of each group, and hence of the whole pile.

A series of single cells, coordinate in their import and use, may be treated as divisions of one great single cell, as, for instance, the rooms of a hospital, prison cells, warehouse divisions, clerks' rooms attached to one and the same department, committee rooms, and so on. If in such a hive it becomes necessary to distinguish one or more special cells, it may be done by simply accentuating and grouping their openings as well as by distinguishing them from others in magnitude, special modeling, and decoration. This may be done, say, in a warehouse where the proprietor's office occupies an appreciable part of the building; or in the case of a physician's room in a hospital, and so on. But in structures of a monumental character it should be the care of the architect to see that the representation of no separate purpose of the structure be omitted, for all features of it, if justly treated, contribute to its expression.

It is the function of the architect, in the first place, to master the idea to be expressed, to understand the various methods used to illustrate it by acts, and to appreciate the import of the resulting emotions, that he may be able to designate the various human groups which form the basis of his design.

It is often the case that the proprietors of buildings, or managers of building enterprises, commissioners, committees, or other persons do not understand the relation between the idea and the structure, or the meaning of the structure as a work of fine art. In that case the architect must supply the defect and point out these relationships; he must, if need be, awaken a sufficient interest to supplant the prevailing prejudice that a structure is merely intended as a convenient shelter for its occupants.

The next step is to determine the magnitude and form of the single cells and their relative positions, the modeling, as it were, of the group. This process is impossible either as a problem for the imagination, or as a fact to be reduced to drawing, without a thorough knowledge of methods of construction and of the principles which govern these methods. We cannot think of spaces merely; we must think of them as surrounded by matter. This matter is called into use, and its mass is determined by laws of mechanical construction. Now, it is not true that a structure (a monumental structure) is, first of all, a shelter, a place for human convenience, and afterward an object of fine art—that the domain of architecture begins when the engineer and builder have done their work of planning. It will be too late then. Architectural art must, as we have seen, initiate the work and take hold of it at the very beginning.

Why is it, then, that a different view of the functions of construction and architectural art is entertained by a large majority of modern architects? An examination of this may help us to a better understanding of the true relations of construction to architecture as a fine art. Many architects believe that every structure is a single cell, the outer form of which has no special relation to its interior. Architects love to modify this single cell in its outline, especially if it be of a respectable magnitude; but these very modifications amount only to arbitrary projections which are not the result of a relation of parts. In addition to this they view a structure as consisting of three parts—an exterior and an interior (which need artistic consideration), and the construction proper, which is placed between the two, and which needs no artistic treatment. This construction is to be overlaid on both sides with forms which please the fancy of their author. These forms do not involve mechanical ideas, inasmuch as they may be affixed to, or supported by, the real construction. Can this be architecture? No. If construction were the vulgar thing it is said to be, the work of the mere builder or engineer; if this construction were not an integral part or motive in the aesthetic development of a monument, and if it were not possible so to modify this vulgar thing as to make it an artwork, why then, surely, it would be well to conceal it from sight with something that is recognized as a work of fine art, say with hangings, screens, and paintings, with anything that is capable of expressing an idea in matter, and which is not itself a mechanical construction. But what is really done is this: the real construction is covered with a false construction which is not applicable here, or with an impossible construction not borrowed from anything real, but purely the result of architectural aberration, a thing which, if really built of stone or wood or any material capable of doing mechanical work, would fall to pieces by reason of its own weight, but which the ingenious artist persuades to stay in its place by making it of plaster, zinc, cast iron, or something else in imitation of stone, or wood, and sustaining it by means of nails and bolts.

Now, why do architects do this? Obviously because they prefer this sham construction to the real construction; they like its form better. Then the question arises, Why not use the construction they prefer, and discard the one really employed? The reason why this is not done is that they have lost the art of architecture, the art of building. The forms they affect are not regarded by them as constructions at all, but as an aggregation of pretty things derived from interesting antique and medieval monuments, where they have a charming effect.

The Greeks covered the walls of their temples at the top with a liberal stone which reached over far beyond the outside of these walls, and protected them from the weather. The modeling of these cornices from the beginning of the architrave to the corona shows a movement everywhere constructively exquisite and expressive of the function of protection which this member afforded to the walls beneath. Let us see how Mr. Fergusson,* an ardent admirer of antique work, contemplates these moldings. He tells us that "the first and most obvious of these (carved ornaments) are mere moldings, known to architects as scotias, cavettos, ogees, toruses, rolls, etc.—curves which, used in various proportions either horizontally or vertically, produce, when artistically combined, the most pleasing effect."

To him evidently these moldings are not a modification of matter in order to express parts of a structure, or to em-

* James Fergusson (1808–1886) was a Scottish writer on archaeology and architecture; his comprehensive *History of Architecture in All Countries from the Earliest Times to the Present Day* (1867–1876) was the bible of late nineteenth-century eclecticism.

phasize their function, but they are things of no meaning which may be artistically arranged, and thus produce a pleasing effect. What a pity that Mr. Fergusson gives no definition of this "effect," nor explains in some comprehensive manner how these ogees and toruses may be artistically combined!

The first and foremost element of art expression in architecture is to be attained in the form of its masses. This form is not accepted as the result of mechanical relations, but of certain laws of proportion otherwise determined. Stability, massiveness, strength, elegance, and repose—all of them qualities which in a greater or less degree must exist in every monument—are clearly expressions of a statical condition of matter of which the mechanical relation is a constant function; and yet proportion in architecture is supposed not to refer to those laws, nor, in fact, to any real law whatever.

If structural masses could be piled up without reference to the mechanical laws of construction, and yet without risk of danger to the stability of the monument, a relation of masses which gives the expression of stability would still remain a desideratum. Architecture as a fine art deals most prominently with this very expression. Should we then seek it in the laws of mechanics or in the magical numbers of so-called proportions? What man has invented a system of proportion in masses that perform mechanical functions more just or better adapted to the purpose than that which is dictated by a law of nature? Where are we to find him? Has he written a book on the subject? Mr. Fergusson gives us some hints. Let us see if we can understand them and make use of them in following this path of art without the guidance of nature. He says:

Construction has been shown to be the chief aim and object of the engineer; with him it is all in all, and to construct scientifically, and at the same time economically, is the beginning and end of his endeavors. It is far otherwise with the architect. Construction ought to be his handmaid, useful to assist him in carrying out his design, but never his mistress, controlling him in that which he would otherwise think expedient. An architect ought always to allow himself such a margin of strength that he may disregard and play with his construction; and in nine cases out of ten the money spent in obtaining this solidity will be more effective architecturally than twice the amount expended on ornament, however elegant and appropriate that may be.

The advice here offered to the architect, "that construction ought to be his handmaid," "useful to assist him in carrying out his design," clearly explains it to be the author's opinion that a contemplated design has existence outside and independent of construction; that this design represents a monument possessed of the qualities of massiveness, strength, elegance, and repose, which qualities are not derived from any law that determines these mechanical conditions, but from some other source. The nature of this source is explained in the following sentence: "That the architect should do what 'seems to him expedient,' " and not what the poor vulgar engineer finds to be scientifically just. Can it be expedient at any time to change that which is dictated by a law of nature? But then we are to make our masses much larger than they would be if we were governed solely by the dictates of sound mechanical construction? This is wise, no doubt. A monument cannot well be made too strong, nor very often too massive. But we are not to permit posterity to be benefited by this massiveness; we are to "play" with it, to reduce it here, and increase it there, in "disregard" of the laws of construction, to gain what? This Mr. Fergusson omits to tell us; but it cannot be doubted that he intends in some way to improve the relation of these masses. Can this be done? This is a very serious question, and no one has, as yet, answered it; for in no phase of architectural art which is now universally recognized as true art has this been attempted; quite the contrary. In all good architectural work we find a strict adherence to mechanical laws, which is the more surprising, because we understand the theory of these laws so much more clearly than did the architects who produced those works. We may be sure that they did not play with this matter, whatever they did. We must give them credit for a zealous regard for construction, and for untiring efforts to make construction the prime element of art. They may not have always expressed ideas which we admire, or are willing to adopt; but the ideas which they believe in they expressed faithfully and well. Construction, the most perfect and the boldest, the most refined methods of dealing with matter, were the principal element of their artwork. And when we go back to the temples of Egypt, to Karnak, where one half of the area of an architectural monument is devoted to walls and columns, we still find no disregard of construction, no attempt to play with masses for fantastic and imaginary purposes, for lights, shadows, sentiment, and effects, which are so much talked about in our day, but which have, as yet, yielded no results worthy of being embalmed in *too much* of nature's stone, nor in *too much* of human labor.

In pursuing further Mr. Fergusson's remarks on the subjuct of construction, we learn that

the Egyptians and the Greeks were so convinced of this principle [of allowing a margin of strength to be played with] that they never used other constructive expedients than the perpendicular wall or prop, supporting a horizontal beam; and half the satisfactory effect of their buildings arises from their adhering to this simple though expensive mode of construction. They were perfectly acquainted with the use of the arch and its properties; but they knew that its employment would introduce complexity and confusion into their designs, and therefore they wisely rejected it. Even to the present day the Hindus refuse to use the arch, though it has long been employed in their country by the Mohammedans. As they quaintly express it, "The arch never sleeps"; and it is true that by its thrust and pressure it is always tending to tear a building to pieces in spite of all counterpoises. Whenever the smallest damage is done, it hastens the ruin of a building, which, if more simply constructed, might last for ages.

If the system of piers and lintels is pronounced a superior construction to that of the arch, on the ground of its superior stability, that system must for the same reason yield the palm to the solid pyramid; and progress in architecture can be attained only by retrogression.

At the bottom of all this we may see a misconception of the laws of construction. All matter is subject to gravitation, and every organism in consequence deteriorates with time. Whether this time shall be short or long depends not upon the magnitude of the masses employed so much as upon their relation. It depends upon this: whether the relation is in accordance with the principles involved in the construction adopted or not.

To say that the Egyptians and Greeks knew the arch system of vaulting as we find it in medieval cathedrals, or as the arching of spaces may be done in the light of modern mechanics, is probably not what the author of the *History of Architecture in All Countries* intended to convey. He probably refers merely to the arch over an opening in the field of a wall. That the arch never sleeps means only that all matter is possessed of the property of gravitation, the law of which is not as universally understood in the case of the resultant lateral pressure of the arch and its order of equilibrium as the more simple law of the pressure of the lintel. We cannot advance the process of expressing an idea in a monument, either by resorting exclusively to primitive methods of construction or by ignoring its laws in trifling with structural masses to suit our fancy. All known constructions, from the simplest to the most refined or complicated, should be brought into requisition by the architect as a means to express corresponding ideas, simple or complicated, materialistic or refined. It is perfectly consistent with the stability of a monument to employ a system of vaulting, provided its lines and abutments are mechanically considered and arranged. Such a structure can be made fully as stable as a mere pile of stones in a pyramid.

When a group of cells is projected in a ground plan, and the altitude of the cells determined with due regard to their individual importance, the various roofs outlined, and the openings for light are arranged, as to size and position, with reference to practically lighting and aesthetically illuminating the interior; if the structure is composed in accordance with mechanical principle, and a perspective view of such a composition painted on canvas in black against a light background, it will fairly represent the masses in the rough, and will effectually express the nature of the structure, and the accruing forms will be aesthetically correct. Such a picture is, as far as a drawing on a reduced scale can be made to be, a representation of the phonetic expression of the contemplated monument. No additional expression can be attained by modeling, by carved and color decoration, or the introduction of statuary. All these serve only to accentuate or to heighten the expression inherent in the structural masses, but not to add to it. If this picture seems still lacking in expression the artist must look for the probable defects, first, in a misapprehension of the idea; second, of the acts illustrating the idea; and, third, of the groups prompted by the emotions arising from the acts; fourth, in the absence of a just arrangement of the cells in relation to each other; and, finally, in bad or feeble construction. The latter may be bad because, first, the author of the design does not understand the principles involved; or, second, he may understand those principles, and fail to apply them; or, third, he may not be familiar with known methods of construction, or capable of devising methods to suit the case; or, fourth, because the order of elegance of constructive methods does not correspond with the importance of the individual cells.

It would be of no use to retouch an unsuccessful group of this kind without due reasoning, merely in accordance with personal feeling, or in accordance with forms which at some time have made a favorable impression upon us; nor to pile on additional features that have no foundation in fact; nor to strike out those that have this foundation in fact; nor to make the whole larger or smaller. It will not help us to add favorable surroundings which do not exist; nor to fret and fume over it and wipe it all out, in order to substitute something else which foggily exists in our brain; nor to rush to a collection of books and photographs to look for better things, unless it be for the purpose of examining them critically in their individual relation, and to find by that means where, in our composition, we have failed either to do that which is true and just, or to achieve an expression as truthful and brilliant as may seem desirable under the circumstances.

If you find that your dining hall bears no proper relation to your library, and upon examination you are convinced that it is not your fault, but that your client either studies or eats too much, let it be so. The structure must express the *morale* of your client, not yours.

But above all things do not search for special effects. Do not expand a plain country house into a palace, nor squeeze it into a cottage, nor into any known or given shape, because you admire that shape more than others. Do not add battlements when there is no opportunity to walk behind them, because you think this a fine medieval feature. Do not build a buttress because you think you would like to have a mass in this place and a shadow next to it. Do not sketch balconies where the orientation of the structure or the surrounding landscape does not warrant such a feature; nor bay windows, nor porticoes, nor any other appendage of this nature, unless they are needed, not merely physically but aesthetically; that is, unless the going out upon such balconies, or the entering into bay windows affords a mental entertainment which cannot otherwise be reached, or at least so fully enjoyed.

But if, after close scrutiny and correction for good aesthetic reasons, the groups or the pile fail to please you, what then? Consider that this may be owing to the fact that you are not familiar with the forms which result from your idea and its phases. The forms you know and love represent other ideas than those you are endeavoring to treat; and you may be sure if you have otherwise committed no error of judgment, you are on the road to a good architectural result. Proceed with your work, model the parts, decorate them in accordance with their functions, and before long the thing will speak to you in a new language expressing new thoughts; it will speak to you intelligibly, and with surprising force, and you will admit that this is by far the best arrangement of forms, *better* than you could have imagined them in your most enthusiastic moods.

The question may now be asked, Which of the many scientific constructions is the architect to select for use in his monuments? All of them. None must be rejected; none can be rejected; our *repertoire* is small enough as it is. But the Egyptians and the Greeks did not make use of the arch, and the Normans did not use the pointed arch. The Egyptians, the Greeks, and the Normans did perfectly right in not doing what they did not know of. You can have no such motive. You know the arch in all the forms in which it has been used, and in forms in which it has not been used, as yet, to any extent; you know a catenary arch, an arch which is purely a curve of pressures; use it, use them all, not indiscriminately, not unwisely, but, as they are all at your command, use each of them whenever it is the best thing to be used.

What is sad to see is a flat ceiling divided into impossible panels, supported by impossible girders which are not the result of any construction whatever—a ceiling which, if it were attempted to be built in stone or wood, would drop down by its own weight, but which is worked in plaster upon a framework of wood, and tied to the floor beams above.

Look at the constructions that have resulted from the modern invention of the rolled iron beam. All of these are mere attempts to cover this unfortunate beam (one of the cleverest expedients of the age), and none to make the beam itself presentable, to arrange the arches between the beams in a logical manner that they may be sightly, and an aesthetical element.

Look at the treatment of cast-iron columns and other structural parts made possible by modern use of metals. They are more or less imitations of stone and wood constructions; but few of them devised by architects are modelings which can possibly result from the nature of the metal, yet the engineer has developed pure metallic forms unknown before, simply because he derives his wisdom from the laws of mechanics. But how can we preserve purity of style in architecture if we are to use and to exhibit constructions which find no place in the style we are working in. This subject of style we must reserve for a separate chapter, of which it is well worthy. But we may ask here, Did the architects of the Norman or Gothic school neglect constructive elements because they interfered with the style of the day or of their past? If this had been so, we should be still engaged in building pyramids. The elements of the architectural results of any time are construction (in its methods and perfection), materials, fundamental ideas, mechanical and artistic skill in their development. Of all these the progress of construction has exercised the most potent influence upon past development of architecture. This is true of the state of architecture in Europe up to the fourteenth century, but not since.

A post, column, or strut of stone or wood, meaning a part of a structure which is subject to a negative strain (compression), is strongest (the transverse area being the same) if it is circular in ground plan. Although this fact is not generally known to laymen, or thought of much by architects, it happens that when we see a post or pier which has a circular or octagon ground plan, it seems to us stronger than a square pier containing the same area and length.*

From this there is but a short step to the impression that round piers or columns look strong. Hence it is that the jamb of an opening seems more rigid if we chamfer its corners. This is actually done, not only in the case of door and window jambs and posts, but also at the intrados of arches and ribs,

---

* The experiment is easily tried by comparing a square and round post of equal length and area; the diameter of the square post will be proportional to the diameter of the round post as 1.7 is to 2.—Eidlitz's note.

in fact, in all parts of structure which are subject to compression. More frequently the reduction is accomplished by modeling the corners in a manner which still more heightens this effect by imparting to it an expression of strength and elegance as well as of rigidity. The transition of piers to their bases and capitals, the underside of projecting corbels, sill courses, and cornices are all treated in a similar manner. The Greeks were familiar with this process, and practiced it in modeling their columns and cornices, but did not extend it to the jambs of their doorways.

The purpose of modeling masses in architectural work is to make the functions performed more apparent, and to heighten the expression of rigidity in the direction in which the forces are acting; also, in some cases, to multiply the apparent surface of the matter treated. When surfaces are molded, light and shade are the natural result; but light and shade are not the object of the process, they are merely an incident.

When two or three modeled groups of a structure succeed each other perpendicularly, the organization of the lower part must be more simple than the one immediately above it, and there should be a relation of mass between the parts whereby they continue each other. The lower pier, may, however, be a simple shaft, unless the organism immediately above it is so highly organized as to produce a contrast which would make the inferior organism rude, or the superior one weak or meager. This process of subdividing masses by modeling was undoubtedly carried to excess in late medieval work. This is evidently owing to an erroneous tendency to attentuate matter for the purpose of giving a sublime spiritual expression to the work, which well accords with the ideas of Christianity of the times, as well as to express function minutely. The times have changed, and with the times our ideas have changed; we do not now look upon matter as the despicable thing it was then held to be. This is no reason, however, why we should reject the scheme of Gothic architecture, as it is vulgarly termed, or Christian architecture, as Kugler properly calls it. The architecture of the medieval cathedrals, considered as a system, especially when we contemplate it in its principles rather than in its completed forms, may, without fear, be accepted as the most perfect development of architectural art known to us, and may well serve as a proper starting point for future efforts—always provided that we confine ourselves to the principles manifested in it, and not to its forms; and that we apply these principles to create such forms as will express our own ideas, and not those of the Middle Ages.

The analysis of the human body is the work of the anatomist, but to depict human emotions in stone or on canvas is the work of the artist. He deals with the material motions of the human figure, and must, therefore, understand its anatomy. More than this, the human frame is created to the artist's hands, and we may presume that nature has adopted the most brilliant construction which could be devised to combine expression with function. It is the problem of the architect to depict the emotions of the structure he deals with; to depict, as it were, the soul of that structure. But the emotions of this soul, like the emotions of any soul, can be depicted only by representing modifications of the body under the influence of emotions; and for that purpose the architect must understand the anatomy of his structure, which amounts to an analytical knowledge of its construction. More than this, the architect's structure, unlike the painter's or the sculptor's, is, in the first place, necessarily a human creation; not a natural organism which contains within itself a perfect system of mechanical construction, not only the best to perform the functions assigned to it, but also the best to give expression to those functions, to the end that man may, if not understand, at least know them without a scientific analysis. Thus the architect must create his structure (while the sculptor and painter only re-create) upon principles supplied him by nature, which are the principles of mechanics. It is necessary, moreover, that his construction should perform not only certain physical functions, but also others superadded to these, which may be termed ideal functions, and which pertain solely to the ideas which have called together the persons occupying the structure; and, finally, this construction must be capable of an expression which conveys the idea of the motive for the existence of the monument.

This knowledge of mechanical construction should be also sufficiently positive to furnish the architect, at every stage of the composition, with a clear view of the mechanical relation of the parts of the structure as he develops them, that he may at all times in the production of an organism, and afterward, in the external modeling of its parts, justly express its functions.

Carved ornament and color decoration have no other purpose than to heighten the expression of mechanical resistance to load and pressure in architectural organisms. They do this (as will be hereafter more minutely shown) by their density, magnitude, projection, form, and the direction in which they are placed, which direction must coincide with the direction of resistance to load and pressure. They do it also by the peculiar treatment known as conventionalizing ornament, by which natural forms of animals and vegetables are so modified as to conform to the nature of the material in which they are wrought, and to the mechanical work which they perform.

The motives which influence modern architects in composing a design, and the quality of mind which enables them to compose, may be summed up as personal notions of the proper character of the structure, and of the effect which it may produce upon themselves and others; all of which is matter of *taste*. This taste some admit to need cultivation, and this cultivation is exclusively sought in the contemplation of the architectural work of the past, which is not applicable to the needs of the present, and which tends to fill the imagination of the zealous student with pictures which it would be better he should not know, if he is not to analyze them intelligently; for the greatest and first lesson which they teach is how not to do it.

The motive which governs the modern architect in composing a monument may be stated as a desire to please the public, or, as he says, produce a favorable effect. The education of the architect consists in looking at architectural forms which have produced favorable effects upon others. Such a course of education cannot certainly be productive of new forms or of a proper use of old forms. In truth a proper art use of old forms under new conditions is a practical impossibility. To illustrate: a painter who depicts the warrior paints him in medieval armor; he thinks a knight in armor exceedingly picturesque. The word "picturesque" with him embodies all that is good and proper in the way of dress, accoutrement, and physical development responding to a system of attack and defense carried on with certain given weapons and with an armor devised to resist these weapons. If you visit the studio of this artist you will find there swords, foils, breastplates, helmets, spears, and chain armor—in fine, every contrivance of offense and defense known in the Middle Ages. The artist has lived among these objects so long that he is able to draw them on paper or paint them on canvas in every conceivable combination consistent with their use. What is more, he has acquired a love for these forms, and he deems them eminently beautiful. Now let us imagine that a patron of this painter demands a picture of a warrior which shall not be a medieval knight, nor a Roman, or Greek, or modern soldier, but purely an ideal invention. Could the artist invent the figure of a warrior by merely trying to sketch and paint one? Certainly not. He could produce nothing but Greek, Roman, medieval, and modern warriors, or imperfect and incongruous combinations of all of these. Is the thing impossible? No, it is not impossible; but the process demands a species of skill not possessed by the artist. In the first place, a series of weapons would have to be devised upon principles heretofore not applied, and then an armor to resist these weapons. All this may be theoretically done by some person versed in possible methods of war, revised and corrected by an able military engineer, practically executed by a skillful armorer, and then the painter could paint a picture of an ideal warrior which would rank in beauty with pictures of the warriors of the past. If architecture is to be equally successful, the architect must combine with his art other technical skill corresponding to that of the general, the military engineer, and the armorer, and which in his case amounts simply to a thorough knowledge of the theory and practice of mechanical construction.

Relations of matter cannot be clearly understood nor successfully reasoned upon unless they are numerically considered. To say that the earth moves around the sun, conveys an idea; but it is a very confused idea, which cannot be made positive until we know that it completes a revolution around the sun in one year, and that the mean radius of its orbit is ninety-two millions of miles long. Now, when we say that this latter statement gives us a positive idea of the motion of the earth in its orbit, it is not meant to be an assertion that we can form in our minds a picture of that orbit or of the velocity of the motion of the earth; but that we can proceed to reason from these data with certainty, and arrive at the final conclusion that the earth moves in its orbit around the sun during a second of time over a space nearly 18.5 miles in length. It is true that a velocity of 18.5 miles per second is as much an enigma to the human mind as ninety-two millions of miles measured out in space; but with the help of the figures presented to us we can proceed to reason from one step to another without fear of error; in fact, with the certainty that every conclusion arrived at will be numerically correct.

Now, architecture is the art of representing ideas by masses of matter. We can gauge these masses, we can mathematically determine their dimensions under certain conditions of work to be performed by them, and also under certain conditions of apparent energy in resisting a given load.

Shall we abandon this opportunity to reason numerically? If we do so, we relinquish the only method of reasoning which never fails, and we must drift into a shoreless sea of architectural aberration.

[pp. 269–291]

*From Chapter XXVII, "Cultivation of Architecture," in Part III, "Nature of Architecture"**

This is not the place to enter into the detail of instruction, but it is desirable to make it perfectly clear that the architect, to compose well, must compose a monument which he may jot down as he proceeds in the form of a drawing, and he must not compose a drawing, which, when executed, may be a monument.

Only those who are capable of analyzing the relation of the various external elevations of modern monuments to each other, and to their internal sections, and who perceive the existing discords, can realize the pernicious influence of the modern system of doing architecture purely through drawings.

How shall I build this thing? should be the constant question of the architect while composing, instead of What form

---

* This section of Chapter XXVII Eidlitz describes in his table of contents, p. xv, as "relation of form to function."

shall I give to it? If the former question is responded to in our composition; if this question is intelligently answered at every step of progress, forms will grow out of it; but if we design monuments in response to the latter question, the monument is never contemplated seriously, scientifically, or artistically as a whole, but as an aggregation of disjointed parts; hence the other question, How can I join this and that together with architectural propriety? is the question which most frequently occurs in modern architectural composition. The moment the architect finds it necessary to ask or answer this fatal question, he may be sure that he is pursuing the wrong course. He has started his work with completed forms, and is not developing them.

All parts of structure perform mechanical functions; hence their form must be primarily determined by mechanical laws. The modern architect ignores this fundamental law. He believes that there is a relation of a mechanical nature between superincumbent mass and the area of the supporting pier, between the lateral thrust of an arch and the resistance of its abutment, but he deems it an intrusion to remind him that no part of structure can be determined in its mass or outline without due mathematical consideration.

It is not intended in these pages to enter upon a detailed analysis of this principle and its practical application. The subject is too large to do justice to it in the short space which can be devoted to it here; but to make the principle more clear, by an illustration, we may mention one special structural feature, namely, the capital, which is almost invariably misunderstood in modern practice. By many it is imagined that its height, for instance, depends mainly upon the diameter of the column which it crowns. This is the Renaissance error, and is derived from the rule now taught, that the height of a capital may be expressed in diameters of the column, or that it must bear a certain fixed relation to the thickness of the column. Others, again, design the capital to correspond with the length of the column which supports it. Exaggerated capitals of this kind are to be frequently found upon the thin and long wall shafts of modern Gothic structures. Many others, again, refer the size and shape of the capital to the general form and dimensions of length and diameter of the whole organized pier of which it forms a part. Very few, indeed, seem to understand its function and true mechanical value. The capital is the cornice or crowning stone of a shaft or pier, and connects this shaft with its load, which is always of larger area than the shaft at the point of connection. This difference of area itself depends upon mechanical considerations, which, for this present purpose, may be omitted, but it alone determines the projection of the capital. Now, the height of the capital is the resultant, first, of the needed projection; second, of the position in relation to the eye; third, of the shape of its own bell, whether it be concave or convex; fourth, of the nature, strength (capability to resist pressure), of the material it is made of; and finally, of the degree of strength and elegance pertaining to the monument in question. It is not intended to convey the idea that all these elements which constitute the proportions of the capital must, or always can be, mathematically demonstrated; but it must be clear that, inasmuch as they form the mechanical elements of its mass, they must be mechanically considered, and at least approximately realized, to enable the architect to attain to the best and most expressive form possible.

It is a well known fact that in the construction of roofs, bridges, and trusses, made possible by the invention of modern rolled iron, the calculation of the strains of a projected construction, and the determination of the sectional area of the various parts which resist these strains, are the least part of the engineer's labor in designing these roofs, bridges, and trusses. The greatest part of the work is, of necessity, bestowed upon the connections where strains are concentrated upon bolts or divided upon rivets, and where the material is constantly weakened by perforations, and must be constantly strengthened again by additional plates or special castings. Now when we look upon a structure of this kind, one that is well and conscientiously designed, these connections, or knots, as they are called, address us very forcibly, and convey a convincing expression of their strength and adequacy to do the mechanical work they perform. In them, nothing is attempted beyond this adequacy of strength; but inasmuch as, by reason of economy and mechanical convenience, this cannot be attained by the mere weight of abundant material, but only by the most scientific application of the material at the disposal of the engineer, the result of these constructions is a species of art form, which speaks

forcibly of mechanical work done, and is hence possessed
of beauty. We perceive in these works of the engineer the
true spirit of art force and the resultant pleasurable emotion. Some of these iron structural parts have been successfully treated by the architect with color decoration and
ornament wrought in metal, and thus been elevated into
works of fine art. It is for their primary development of form,
however, that they should be recommended to the student
of architecture as a potent schooling in the mechanical consideration of the material function of structural parts.

An architect may design a very clever capital, bracket, or
cornice, and so on, by groping for it, and elaborating and developing it out of his inner consciousness. But it must be remembered that to do a work of fine art is to do it with
premeditation, that the artist must know what he is driving
at, and must possess the technical skill to approach it and
bring it to completion by direct methods. This technical skill
is acquired by long-continued practice. While the knowledge
of what is to be done is of a scientific nature, it is positive,
logical, and analytical in its character, and must be diligently
studied and mastered by the architect if he is to do his work
with premeditation, for only then is it a work of art.

As soon as the student has mastered his mathematical
studies, and become an expert draftsman, and has been
taught the principles of architectural modeling and decoration, and the use of color in application to structural forms,
he should be initiated into architectural composition by
problems involving, at first, merely parts of structures, as,
for instance, a pier supporting a given wall imposed upon an
arch or lintel; the cubic contents of the wall being known
and the height of pier given, the transverse area of the pier
may be readily determined. Now the pupil should be made
to model this pier, arch, and wall for a series of structures
of different degrees of strength and elegance, from a servant's
hall up to a church aisle. He should elaborate some of these
drawings with carved ornament and color decoration. He
should be made to prepare two or three examples of each
kind varying in richness, and should in this process be
corrected as to the proper relation of modeling to be adopted
in each part. From this simple example the pupil should be
gradually permitted to advance toward more extensive combinations, and finally to whole structures of a simple kind,

and so on to the end of the chapter. There should not be one word spoken of style; in fact, the study of art history may be safely postponed to the last year of instruction; or, if the pupil has dabbled in art history before it is good for him to do so, he should be promptly impressed that what he finds there is not to be a criterion of what he is to do, but simply a statement of what others have done under circumstances which will not occur again.

The character of his work must refer solely to construction, and the construction to the idea which is to be expressed and to the material which is at his command for that purpose. He should learn in this practice the difference of treatment which is due to the material used; that wood needs different modeling from stone, and stone different modeling from metal; and he should learn also the methods of conventionalizing decorative ornament, which depend upon material and function. A dozen pupils of fair abilities and general education, well grounded in mechanics and drawing, guided by a teacher who is not a professed militant in the battles of style, will, if trained in this manner, produce an era in architecture, always provided that they are permitted to do work and not to spend their time in preparing drawings for the approval of persons who have enjoyed no architectural education whatever.

A child could not well be taught the English language if we insisted on beginning with the dialect of Chaucer, and so going on to the English of today. Astronomy is read at universities as developed at this time, not as it was at the time of Hipparchus. Of what use would it be to teach geography upon a map of the Roman Empire, or science according to the theories of Swedenborg? There is no doubt a historical value in all such teaching, but the student cannot well commence the study of the theory and practice of a living art by a perusal of an art that is dead. The radical error is to be found in the opinion of those who teach. They do not believe that Greek architecture is dead; they would have us think that it still lives, and try to think so themselves; but it *is* dead, and so are Roman, Byzantine, and Gothic architecture just as surely dead as the language of Chaucer and the astronomy of Hipparchus. These styles are all metals which have undergone various combinations with oxygen, one and all oxides of architecture; you may, if you please, apply to them the poles of your analytical battery, and extract grains of pure iron from this historic rust; but if you wish to have your horses shod today, *now,* because you need them, let the smith take metal from his own store and let him forge it into shoes that are serviceable *now,* at once, lest, if he wait for the operations of your battery, the horses die before you procure iron enough out of the shield of Piramus or the spear of Achilles.

Greek poetry and sculpture stand foremost in the ranks of art, both in their intrinsic and relative value; they have never been surpassed. Greek science and architecture, considered as the outcome of an early civilization, form an epoch in the cosmic history of human culture and art, which, in brilliancy of attainment, also has no parallel in subsequent relative progress; but both science and architecture have grown since the days of Pericles. The science of the nineteenth, and the architecture of the thirteenth, century manifest a conscious manly mastery of the multitude of questions which have arisen in science and art since Greece dazzled the world with her childlike dallying with their rudiments. Her genius will ever command our admiration, but we cannot afford to deny our manhood by neglecting the earnest work of our time in the continuous worship of a divine example.

Young men between the ages of twenty and twenty-five, who should be engaged upon something which will make them useful members of society, are made to bend over the drawing board for six hours daily, drawing an acanthus leaf and a volute, as the sum and substance of carved decoration. They are told that the Corinthian capital is the greatest triumph of architectural art. There is no truth in all this. The acanthus leaf was never treated in Greek architecture so as to express capacity to carry a load; there are too many leaves in the Corinthian capital; they are weak, drooping— not strong at all—and so are its volutes. What is the use of nursing enthusiasm for the poor Corinthian capital? Let us respect it as a work of art in the place where we find it, and for the time in which it was made; but to say that it is the sum and substance, the ultimatum of human art, that there is nothing more to be done by young men who are possessed of souls but to draw that thing over and over again, that they may become architects and draw this same thing again during their natural lives, and go into ecstasies over it, and call it art, and try and make others believe that nothing else can be produced which is equally good, is a sin, for it is a falsehood, and a gross one. Nor is the pursuit of this sort of architecture art in any sense. Suppose that it were true that the architecture of Athens is perfect, that it answers all purposes for all time to come; that the proportions of its structural parts are settled beyond doubt or possible change; that its decoration and carved ornament are things finished and completed, then what is the use of academies of architecture? There are many clever mechanicians of our day, who will construct a machine which will produce endless designs of this kind for all time to come. This perfection and infallibility of antique architecture has remained undisputed long enough; it has done all the harm that can be reasonably conceded to any one human prejudice or error. It has been treated by its very opponents with great courtesy and forbearance. There is gathered around it a halo of poetry, of physical human vigor, of human virtue, courage, and patriotism, of human rights and philosophy, which must deter all thinking men from disturbing its intellectual and moral radiance. But it cannot be necessary that it should be dragged from its proper place to do duty and perform a function to which it is ill calculated to respond. As sincere and earnest partisans of its historical glory, we should desire that it remain forever in its historical shrine.

The dilettantism of modern architecture must be rooted out before the art can revive and exercise a wholesome influence upon society. It must be understood by all, and more especially by those who desire to become architects, as the first and most important lesson of their education, that the road to architecture is long, tortuous, and thorny, and not a well-paved highway upon which man may amble into fame; that the days of false taste are numbered, and that the time is not far distant when *style* will follow in the same direction, and nothing be left but to pursue architecture pure and simple.

[pp. 481–489]

4

Mariana Griswold Van Rensselaer, HENRY HOBSON RICHARDSON AND HIS WORKS (Boston and New York, 1888), pp. 36, 58, 64, 111–119, 132–138.

(Mrs.) Mariana Griswold Van Rensselaer (1851–1934) combined in one career the interests of a research historian (*History of the City of New York in the Seventeenth Century*, 1909) with the interests of a sensitive and appreciative critic of the arts. Her research scholarship as a historian was thorough, though not particularly original; and her historical writings are distinguished by the breadth and tolerance of a cultivated combination of research materials. Similarly, her art criticism is not so abrupt and polemic as that of many of her contemporaries; on the contrary, it is balanced and considerate; this is not to say that she was unsure of her evaluations, but that she delivered her evaluations with a cultured poise that was contemplative rather than activistic.

She is included here to speak for Richardson (1838–1886) because she knew him well and, as was her style, asserts him rather than her own views; characteristic of the transparency of her style is the remark: ". . . I once heard Richardson say: 'The things I want most to design are a grain-elevator and the interior of a great river-steamboat'" (page 22). Had she been willing to intrude her own attitudes, she might have remarked instead: "Richardson wanted to combine in one career the extremes of utilitarian simplicity and of decorative exuberance." She was willing, however, to generalize Richardson's approach: "Richardson was no philosopher and very little of a theorist in any direction" (page 39). Louis Sullivan, who did not know Richardson as a person but only as an architect, recognized the nature

21. Henry Hobson Richardson, Allegheny County Buildings (1884–1886), Pittsburgh, Pennsylvania. Drawing from M. G. Van Rensselaer, *Henry Hobson Richardson* (1888).

of Richardson's approach in similar terms: "a copious, direct, large, and simple mind." Mrs. Van Rensselaer and Sullivan, from their different points of view, assert that Richardson did not arrive at his architectural forms through a conscious or literary program, but "directly"; and this may very well be a key to the difference between the rugged harmony of Richardson's forms and the self-conscious, more "literary" productions of his architectural contemporaries.

Mrs. Van Rensselaer argues that Richardson ". . . first 'got' his building as a whole and then got its features, working so that each feature should have its due relative importance and no more, and that all should act together to the enhancement of the main architectural impression" (page 53).

When Mrs. Van Rensselaer faces the problem of evaluating Richardson's work in the context of the critical assumptions of her more activistic contemporaries, the balance of her approach becomes quite clear:

In truth, the more we consider the conditions amid which he began and the preparations he had had,* the more vigor and individuality and power Richardson's early works seem to reveal. And if they do not reveal quite so much of either quality as we might expect, or show so much clearness in aim and consistency in effort, is it not rather because our instinctive demands are exaggerated than because his development was inconsequent? The results of his life as a whole show that he was a man of phenomenal power. But would he not have been a man of miraculous power had he come twenty years ago fresh from the schools of Paris with a ready-made anti-Parisian creed and at once began to build successful "original" structures, very various in purpose but consistent in themselves and among themselves to the precepts of that creed?

[p. 58]

I think it is hardly necessary to explain that it has never been part of an architect's duty to try to be original in the absolute meaning of the term, or that in these late days of art he could be so even if he tried his best. A process of intelligent adaptation is that which he must employ, and he has a clear title to be called original whenever he perfectly fits old features to new needs and

---

* A reference to Richardson's training at the École des Beaux Arts in Paris, a school characterized by what Louis Sullivan called "a fatal residuum of artificiality," in its preoccupation with a florid and eclectic neoclassicism.

schemes, or so remolds an old conception that a new conception is the result—not an effective piece of patchwork but a fresh and vital entity.

[p. 64]

From Chapter VI, "Last Days—Personal Traits"

During his early years in Europe* Richardson had had neither the time nor the money to travel. He had then seen only northern work and comparatively little of that. As he was fond of saying, "he knew his Paris," but he really knew very little else except on paper. Now for the first time he was visiting the South† with which his artistic nature sympathized far more deeply than with the North. For the first time he was seeing how men of like disposition with himself had worked in various lands and times; and in the western developments of Romanesque art he was studying forms and features which, as revealed in books and photographs, had already been embraced as his materials for self-expression.

Naturally he looked at them with an interest which a layman cannot fathom and which an architect with different leanings would by no means share—with a love and an intelligence immeasurably heightened by past experience and the prevision of future need. Many problems that had suggested themselves to him as new had, he now perceived, been long ago worked out by others. He often spoke of the singular delight it was to see "how those old fellows had done" the things he had been trying to do himself; and many qualities in their work impressed him far more forcibly than they had in pictures—qualities of simplicity and repose in general treatment as well as of exquisite refinement in detail.

This actual contact with southwestern Romanesque architecture established still more firmly his belief that it was the best source of inspiration for the modern artist. What had

---

* Richardson was in residence in Paris from 1859 to 1865; he returned briefly to the United States in 1862.

† Richardson traveled in southern Europe in 1882, four years before his death in 1886.

been a strong instinctive feeling, a passionately held and vigorously practiced faith, now became an assured dogma for which he could give much clearer reasons; and the special lessons he had learned showed at once in his work—not only in his plans for the Albany cathedral but also in the structures which he actually built. If we add to these gains the immense recuperation of energy and access of delight in labor which sprang from his long unresting rest, the renewed confidence in his powers and opportunities which grew from a comparison of his career with that of the average European architect, and the general broadening and freshening of his mind which were wrought by the varied scenes he had visited and the interesting persons he had met—if we add these other gains it will not seem strange that this journey should have been a second turning-point in Richardson's artistic life. With Trinity Church he had begun to do his true work; now, and only now, he was ready to do his very best work. Now, when there were but four years of life in store for him.

[p. 36]

Chapter XVII, "Characteristics as an Artist"

An artist cannot be tested as we must test almost every other man—by the average success of his results. The artist has a right to be called as great as his very greatest work. Yet the more frequently he succeeds, the higher, of course, we esteem his power. If Richardson had built nothing good but the Pittsburgh Courthouse he would still be entitled to the name of a great architect; but it is only when we consider all his works together, as a chronological panorama, that we realize the strength of his endowment. We cannot help judging them by a stricter standard than we apply to the works of others, yet even so we are astonished to find how few of them fall below a level of great excellence.

The fact seems the more remarkable when we note the versatility they reveal. This quality has sometimes been denied to Richardson; but only by those to whom versatility means a constant change in the garments of thought, not a constant freshness in thought itself. After his art matured he adhered to a single style. But to deny his versatility for this reason is as unjust as it would be to deny a poet's because he had expressed ideas of wide diversity in a dramatic or a lyric or an epic form alone. When, moreover, we analyze the similarity in style which marks Richardson's maturer works, we find that it cannot be called uniformity. It reduces itself to terms of very broad significance. Neither in deciding upon general outlines and proportions, nor in choosing special features, nor in elaborating details, did he work after set schemes or narrow rules. A man who could immediately follow up so romantic a structure as Trinity Church with so sedate a one as Sever Hall, and who could design in the same year the picturesquely varied Chamber of Commerce and the grandly monotonous Field Building, cannot be accused of mannerism. The more we study Richardson's works the more we feel that something deeper than style constitutes their individuality—that we must look behind his round arches and square-sectioned openings, his stone mullions, his arcades and loggias, and his Byzantinesque decoration to find the fundamental qualities which really reveal him.

These qualities are: Strength in conception; clearness in expression; breadth in treatment; imagination; and a love for repose and massive dignity of aspect, and often for an effect which in the widest meaning of the word we may call "romantic." The first is the most fundamental and important quality, and upon it depends to a very large degree the presence of the others.

The chief thing which made Richardson's works alike among themselves and unlike the works of almost all his contemporaries was his power to conceive a building as a whole, and to preserve the integrity of his conception no matter how various might be the features or how profuse the decoration he employed. Each of his best buildings is an organism, an entity, a coherent vital whole. Reduce it by distance to a mere silhouette against the sky, or draw it down to a thumb-nail sketch, and it will still be the same, still be itself; yet the nearer we approach it the more its individuality will be emphasized. This is because its character depends upon no one feature, no one line, but upon the concord of all and the vigor of the impression which all together give. No feature is of dominant importance, but each is of the right relative importance from any given point of view, and all are vitally fused together—the building seems to have grown, developed,

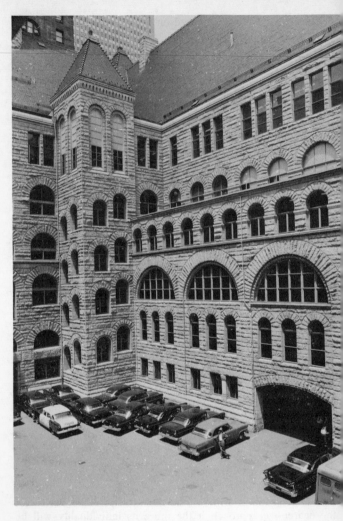

22. Henry Hobson Richardson, Allegheny County Buildings (1884–1886), Pittsburgh, Pennsylvania. Courthouse and courtyard.

expanded like a plant. We cannot dismember it in thought without hurting both what we leave and what we take away; and whether we study it up or down—from particulars to generals or from generals to particulars—there is no point where conception seems to end and mere treatment to begin. It would be as impossible, without injuring the conception, to change the surface character of the walls or the distribution of the ornament, as to alter the relative proportions of walls and roof or the size and position of the chief constructional features. When these facts are perceived together with the great difference in general aim which exists between Richardson's best buildings, his versatility is by implication confessed. It matters nothing that he drew from the same historic source most of the elements with which he built church and warehouse, civic palace and country cottage. In each case a radically different idea was needed and in each case it came to him.

In each case, too, it came as a strikingly appropriate idea. While conceiving and developing a structure as a whole, he worked from the inside out, not from the outside in. The nature of the service it should render was his first thought, its plan his next; and these rule his exterior in its major and its minor features. We do not find him taking schemes or features which were beautiful because appropriate in one building and trying to make them beautiful in another at the expense of fitness; and there is no favorite feature he does not sacrifice if fitness demands—not the last trace of decoration, not the visible roof which he loved to make so prominent, nor the round arch itself. Of course, he sometimes sinned against perfect appropriateness of expression, but his slips were few, and the longer he lived the rarer they became. Here lies the true greatness of Richardson's works—in the fact that they are true conceptions, clearly expressing an idea as appropriate as vigorous. The great value of the Quincy Library, for instance, or the Pittsburgh Courthouse, or—at the other end of the scale—of the Marion cottage, lies in the fact that it is a coherent vital entity and at the same time a speaking entity—unmistakably a library, a municipal palace, a gentleman's seaside home.

Another fundamental quality in Richardson's work is breadth of treatment. It is this which gives his results their air of "bigness"—not the actual size, which in many of them

chances to be great. Artistically speaking, his smallest structures are as big as his largest, and they are so because they
are as largely treated. Whatever his faults he never worked
in a small, hesitating, feeble way. Clearness in aim and
strength in rendering were the gods of his idolatry in art.
If combined with refinement, so much the better; if not, they
were still to be preferred to refinement without them. We are
sure that he excused the faults of a Rubens on canvas, of a
Michelangelo in architecture, but never those of a painter
who had microscopically elaborated a weak conception, of
an architect who had delicately adorned a fabric that was not
in the true sense a building. In his own work he was over-
exuberant at times, but, so to say, with a broad brush and a
vigorous touch, and with that truly architectural instinct which
makes ornament accentuate the meaning of constructional
lines. Of course, it was the strength of his basic conception
which encouraged him to be thus broad and definite in treatment. There was no temptation to fritter away his effect when
he felt that his fundamental idea would impress the imagination and charm the eye. There was every reason why he
should present this idea as frankly as possible, either in bold
simplicity or with lavish decoration which emphasized leading lines and important features. I have said that the greatness of his work rests first of all upon the strength and the
appropriateness of his conceptions; but perhaps the breadth
of treatment through which they were expressed is as important a quality. Certainly it is as rare a quality in modern
art.

The strong imaginative power which Richardson's works
reveal should perhaps not be called a separate characteristic,
being implied in the existence of those just named. Yet we
realize it most fully when we understand not only how strong
and vital his conceptions are and how unlike each other, but
how unlike they most often are to the conceptions of any
earlier day or of modern men in any other land. He took
the elements of the language with which he voiced his
thoughts from other thinkers, but his thoughts were his own.
Whenever fitness demanded—and with our novel needs this
was very often the case—he took counsel of his own imagination, began at the bottom of the problem, and produced a
result which differed essentially from all others. Yet he was

too true an artist to prize novelties as such, and he had too strong a faith in the individuality of his talent to fear that if he were not "original" he would not seem himself. He never needlessly sought for a new conception. It could never have occurred to him to wish merely to do something unlike what his predecessors had done or what he himself had already done. When a problem presented itself which was similar to some preceding problem, he frankly readapted the same idea which had already served. His versatility developed in the only way that it could have developed hand-in-hand with excellence—through the effort to fulfill the given task in the best possible manner, to find clear and full expression for the appropriate idea.

When such qualities as these are found conspicuous and persistent in an artist's work, his choice of style seems a matter of secondary importance. His thoughts have made his work great and individual, not the language in which he has expressed them. Yet Richardson's choice of language was by no means fortuitous or without deep and interesting significance. It is true that working in some other style he might as clearly have shown us the value of definiteness in conception and breadth in treatment, of harmonious effects of color and strong effects of light and shade; the beauty of a roof, the meaning of a wall; the nature of good surface treatment and of decoration which explains construction. But his chosen style was essentially favorable to the teaching of such lessons, as well as to the display of that romantic kind of beauty for which he had so strong a liking. And better than any other style it could meet his fundamental love for massiveness and repose.*

---

* By repose is not here implied quietness in the sense of simplicity of surface and a moderate number of features, but structural repose—repose of line and mass, repose in the form of features; and it is not too much to say that Richardson could best secure this quality by developing the suggestions of Romanesque art. Greek art, making all its lines straight and its horizontal accentuations preponderant, does not express repose so much as great strength gracefully bearing a downward-pressing load. We realize the fact when we study Egyptian art, which is similar in essence to Greek, minus the grace. Gothic art, accenting vertical lines, actually expresses motion—an upward lifting as of a growing tree; so much so that when, as in its Venetian forms, it strives to be more restful, we feel that it is not really itself, that it is trying to achieve a result which could have been more perfectly secured with round arches. Roman art, when it passed from the engineer's into the artist's hand, was not a simple concrete scheme, but a splendid bastard mingling of two alien schemes. Only when it was again stripped of its Greek overlay did it clearly reveal its intrinsic qualities. It is in Romanesque art only, and in

When he recognized the serviceableness of its forms he
instinctively preferred to study them in their southern developments. His temperament was essentially a southern one—
loving breadth and light and color, variety and luxuriance,
not cold grandeur, solemnity, and mystery. Refinement was
not one of his most fundamental qualities as an artist. Yet
his steady development toward a refined simplicity could not
have had its starting point in a paraphrase of Norman work.
It could only have begun with such a paraphrase of southern
Romanesque as we see in the Woburn Library.

In matters of treatment Richardson's attitude toward the
precedents of ancient art was the same as in matters of conception. He studied them with love and care but in no slavish,
idolatrous mood, and from a practical or purely aesthetic,
not from an antiquarian, standpoint. He viewed them as the
work of men of like nature with himself, not of demigods
inspired to a quality of performance which modern men
need not try to improve upon. They were helps for him, not
fetishes; starting points, not patterns. What he wanted was
their aid in building a good structure, not their prescrip-
tions how to build a "scholarly" one. He looked upon them
as a dictionary, not as a grammar, and still less as a collection of attractive features which might be stowed away in the
mind like quotations isolated from their context. None of
his pupils ever heard him say, "This is a charming thing—
someday we must manage to use it." The context, he knew,
was what made the worth of an architectural phrase. Only
when a man is sure of the general meaning he wants to express, the general effect he wants to produce, can he turn to
his predecessors for assistance.

In minor as in major matters Richardson invented when
he was obliged to and borrowed when he could. He took the
Romanesque art of the south of France as his chief but
not his only quarry. He was ready to draw from other sources
any special features which a special need required—later
medieval fashions furnished him with much material at the

---

those early Renaissance modes which were directly based upon it, that we
find that balance between vertical and horizontal accentuations which means
perfect repose. The semicircle demands neither that ascending lines nor that
retreating lines shall preponderate; and in itself it is neither passive like the
lintel nor soaring like the pointed arch. It seems to have grown to its due
bearing power and thus to remain, vital yet restful, making no effort either
to resist downward pressure or to press upward itself.—Mrs. Van Rensselaer's
note.

outset of his life, and toward its end he was more and more attracted by Byzantine forms and decorations. Whatever he took he remodeled as freely as he saw fit, and there was no more effort to conceal his alterings than his borrowings. What he wished was simply that to an intelligent eye his work should look right in the outcome; and if it did, then he knew it was right, though to a dull eye it might seem a copy or though to an antiquarian eye all the precedents of all the ages might seem to protest against it. Sometimes, of course, he was not entirely successful in his adaptations. But often he was, as in that tower of Trinity, the genesis of which has been described at length because it so clearly typifies his constant way of working.* No one could mistake this tower for an ancient one, wherever it might chance to stand. Yet the impression it produces is similar to that which good ancient works produce—an impression as of a vital, homogeneous entity. And, it cannot be too often said, this is the impression made by all of Richardson's best structures. Therefore, the more eclecticism appears when they are analyzed, the more cheering is their evidence with regard to the future of our art. In nothing did Richardson do us better service than in proving that the modern artist need not be cowed into a purist, straightened into an archaeologist, cramped and confined within the limits of a single narrow stretch of bygone years—or, on the other hand, thrown wholly on his own inventive powers—if he would do work to satisfy and delight us as the men of early years satisfied and delighted themselves. The tendencies of American art have been chiefly toward a reckless inventiveness. Those of foreign art are too strongly toward mere scholasticism. But Richardson, keeping to a middle path, worked as those whom we call the demigods had worked. Eclecticism is more patent in his results than in theirs, for the store of precedents which lay open to him was vastly wider than that upon which any of them could draw. But in spirit his process was the same as theirs. Many other modern artists have shared this spirit theoretically but very few have had the power to express it in work which can be compared with his for excellence. Few, indeed, have had the boldness to attempt the task as

---

* The forms of the tower of Richardson's Trinity Church in Boston (1873–1877) were based on the forms of the Spanish Romanesque Cathedral of Salamanca.

frankly. It is hard to say which fact proves Richardson's independence of mind and self-trust more—the fact that he dared so visibly to borrow the general scheme of so famous a piece of work as the Salamanca tower, or the fact that having borrowed it he dared to remold it with so radical a hand. One success of this kind is a better lesson for after-comers than a hundred correct and scholarly plagiarisms. Nor need we ask the antiquary whether or not it is a success. Perhaps he might say that the builders of Salamanca would not have approved of the tower of Trinity. But very likely the builders of the Parthenon or even of the Pantheon would not have approved of Salamanca. The world has had too much—infinitely too much—of such appeals to the artistic conscience of the past. It is time to remember that the past itself never had any artistic conscience except that of the current age, and that we in our turn should make the present our judge—or that if we look outside the present it should be forward and not back. The true question to be asked with regard to work like Richardson's is whether it has those fundamental qualities of harmony, vitality, appropriateness, meaning, and beauty which will make it seem good in the eyes of men born seven hundred years from now. How it would have looked in the eyes of men born seven hundred years ago—incapable of understanding our conditions, of sympathizing with our tastes, of seeing the currents which have been all this time at work in science and in art—is indeed a matter of small concern.

Yet, as has been hinted, there is another danger besides that which lies in an overweening respect for the past. We Americans are more ready than the rest of the world to acknowledge that adaptation, not imitation, should be the artist's formula. But we do not realize all that is meant by our own words when we add that of course adaptation must be sensible and skillful. We do not realize that it needs not only more power but more knowledge and labor to adapt well than to copy well. Here again Richardson's example is infinitely instructive. He adapted well—so well that the process was a creative one in the truest sense of the word—because he had thoroughly studied the principles of his art, and because he practiced it with an exceptional degree of love and patience.

[pp. 111–116]

From Chapter XVIII, "Characteristics as an Artist"

With regard to the benefit which Richardson received from his long early training, I cannot do better than quote the words of a brother architect:*

Richardson stands as a beacon light before the community, not only as a producer of distinguished architecture, but as a warning to impatient aspirants and their guardians against loose fancies on the subject of the education of the architect. He was no exemplar of the popular notion that all that creative genius has to do is to stretch forth its hand, however untrained, to accomplish everything that its heaven-born instinct impells it to. *Poeta nascitur, non fit*, it is true, but once born he cannot voice himself without mastering the symbols and signs of expression, and the more completely he masters them the more thoroughly and recognizably he will project himself. When once Richardson had passed through the chrysalis stage, he could not help designing in a grand way because he was a man of large caliber, of broad scope, and of lavish temperament. But he served a long apprenticeship, quite beyond the twelve or twenty-four months assigned by the average American parent as the unproductive pupillary stage of the gifted offspring. . . . The École course tends chiefly . . . to classic Renaissance expression, but that counted for little. The main thing is to get the discipline. The teacher's bias is nearly immaterial. Richardson's bent led him before long to handle the grammar of a certain architectural school closer than any other, though he almost always allowed himself entire freedom in the handling. But if by any chance his instincts or moods had led him to take hold of some other vehicle of expression than the one which soon became his choice, his training, we may be sure, would have stood him in equally good stead, and he would have equally mastered and equally illustrated it.

It is more difficult to explain the patient enthusiasm of Richardson's labor to those who never had the chance to follow—either at the time or afterward in drawings and descriptions—the genesis of one of his great structures. When a new problem appealed to him, some definite idea of a solu-

* A. J. Bloor, in *The Building Budget*, July, 1886.—Mrs. Van Rensselaer's note.

tion was very quickly born. But he was not quick to call it a good idea except in so far as it might seem rich in possibilities of improvement. Speaking of some fresh scheme he often said, "It is good, isn't it? But I mean to make it better. I don't see how just yet, but I shall find out." Meanwhile he seemed less to think about it than to wait for suggestions to present themselves. "I wait," he would say, "and go to bed on it, and carry it about with me while I am doing other things, and don't try to worry it out; and then after a while it comes." The artist as opposed to the manufacturer of art speaks in words like these; but it is only the well-trained artist who can be thus semipassive to good purpose, and who, when the inspiration has come, will realize that it is but the beginning of the matter. Richardson never forgot that only time and effort can turn a "good idea" into a good piece of work. It has been shown—though only in part—how he labored over Trinity Church, and how different its present aspect is from his first designs. So he always labored—not too proud to see when he had started wrong or too indolent to begin afresh, never satisfied with a thing which others found good if he could better it, never feeling himself beyond the necessity for a perpetual self-criticism broad in reach and minute in application, always open to fresh inspirations, always ready to take intelligent hints from his subordinates, always eager and ardent yet always trying to check impulse by reason. As his intelligence developed and his experience increased, his processes grew quicker and, naturally, left behind them less conspicuous traces than have been preserved in the case of Trinity. But they were always the same processes and always brought increase of excellence, as may be seen by comparing the competitive designs for the Pittsburgh Courthouse with the finished building.

About a fortnight before Richardson's death [writes Mr. Frederick Law Olmsted*], I was with him in Washington, and it is remarkable that he was led to speak in this last interview that I had with him of a point of professional economy of which he had been led to speak (by seeing a lot of rough tracings on a drawingboard) the first time he came to my house fifteen years before.

* Olmsted (1822–1903) was an American landscape architect who cooperated with Richardson and Leopold Eidlitz on the project to complete the New York State Capitol at Albany.

When I came into his room in Washington he was in a reclining chair, so exhausted after an attempt to take the air in a carriage that he had been for some time, as he explained, on the verge of losing consciousness. His eyes were bloodshot, his face red, his forehead studded with beads of sweat. He spoke feebly, hesitatingly, and with a scarcely intelligible husky utterance. While in this condition—I had been urging him and he had promised to go home the next day—a client came in. Something was said of the drawings of the structure Richardson was building for him, and then of the many successive drawings that had been made, revising the preliminary studies, the design always gaining as a turn of one detail led to the reconsideration of another, the gain being, as was intimated, steadily in the direction of simplification. Going on from this, Richardson repeated what he had first said to me at Staten Island. This was, in effect, that the most beguiling and dangerous of all an architect's appliances was the T-square, and the most valuable were tracing paper and India rubber. Nothing like tracing over tracing, a hundred times. There was no virtue in an architect more to be cultivated and cherished than a willing spirit to waste drawings. Never, never, till the thing was in stone beyond recovery, should the slightest indisposition be indulged to review, reconsider, and revise every particle of his work, to throw away his most enjoyed drawing the moment he felt it in him to better its design.

From something like this he went on discussing for the better part of an hour, growing to sit up erect, his voice becoming clear, his utterance emphatic, his eyes flashing, smiling, laughing like a boy, really hilarious, much as in some of our all-night debates years ago in Albany when he was yet a lithe, active, healthy fellow. I was afraid it would be too much for him, and, rising to go, said, "Eidlitz asked me to let him know how I found you: I shall have to tell him, never better in your life"; and he laughingly assented.

One phrase of Richardson's, repeated here, hints at something which it is important to make plain. An architect's revisings, he believed, should never end until his building is "in stone, beyond recovery"; and he exemplified this belief by altering much and often after construction had been actually begun. No one could have used preparatory pencil and paper more conscientiously, yet it was one of his firmest dogmas that they could not be implicitly trusted. If his scorn was great for the recklessness which says, No matter about the drawings—we can set things right as we build, it would have been just as great for the closet-spirit which

should say, No matter how the work is looking as it grows—
it was all right on paper. "The architect," he often explained,
"acts on his building, but his building reacts on him—helps
to build itself. His work is plastic work, and, like the
sculptor's, cannot be finished in a drawing. It cannot be fully
judged except in concrete shape and color, amid actual lights
and shadows and its own particular surroundings; and if
when it is begun it fails to look as it should, it is not only
the architect's privilege but his duty to alter it in any way
he can." Therefore he kept his judgment awake until his last
stone was set and his last touch of decoration had been given.
Therefore, too, he thought needful those long frequent
hurried journeys which must have done so much to sap his
strength. His representatives on the ground were capable and
conscientious. He knew that he could trust them to carry out
a design quite faithfully. But he could trust only his own
eye to see whether the design was carrying itself out well
or not, and so would leave the sickroom to find how some
far-off building looked which he had seen but a few weeks
before. As long as he possibly could he kept up his custom
of making monthly tours through all the distant towns where
he had work under way; and when journeys were at last
forbidden he sent one of his chief assistants to bring him
back verbal reports, and exacted daily detailed letters by
means of which he could follow the placing of every stone.

There are many architects, I believe, who hold a different
creed from the one which Richardson exemplified. They
point with pride to the exact correspondence between their
studies and their completed buildings, while Richardson delighted to explain the disparities in his. It would be idle to
try to lay down rules of right and wrong as decisive between
such opposite ways of thinking; yet the paramount success
of Richardson's results should at least be taken into account
by those whose own theories and methods are not yet
established.

[pp. 117–119]

Chapter XX, "Influence upon Profession and Public"

Richardson's influence upon the members of his profession extended far beyond the walls of his own office, and was both stimulating and ennobling. His success showed that good work might win wide popular appreciation, but that a class of work which had once seemed good enough would not seem so in the future; and the manner in which he had achieved success impressed the lesson that art is a serious matter and should be approached in a serious spirit. Upon the public, too, he exerted a very strong personal influence through contact with clients, friends, and even casual acquaintances. That self-assertion which to some eyes was a fault in his character seems in this connection his greatest merit. Nothing was more to be desired when he began his work than that American architects should have a better chance to show of what they were capable. No champion was more needed than one who should assert their right to do their own work in their own way—should proclaim and prove the fact that an artist knows more about art than the persons who employ him. Richardson's strength of will, directness of aim, genial manner, and beguiling tongue persuaded his clients to give him open opportunities and vigorous backing, to suppress their own crude ideas and wishes, and often to employ him on tasks of a sort for which an artist's help had seldom in the past been thought essential. The result has given us not only his own work but a better chance than we ever had before to get good work from others. In fighting his own battles he fought his comrades' battles, in widening his own path he smoothed and widened theirs, and in guiding and enlightening his clients he leavened the spirit of the whole American public. The unique position which he gained for himself has visibly raised the standing of the architectural profession throughout the whole country. There can be no American city into which some echo of Richardson's name and fame has not penetrated; and wherever they are even vaguely known the standing and the chances of his humblest brother artist are thereby improved.

No degree of personal force and charm, however, could by itself have been so powerful. The influence of Richardson's works upon the general public potently assisted the influence of his words. He was not the first American architect to build good and beautiful structures. But he was the first to build them in a way to attract the eye of every passer, and to win always respectful thought and almost always genuine, hearty admiration. Of all the services Richardson rendered us this is the most important. Of all his legacies the most valuable we possess is a newborn interest in the art of architecture, a growing belief that it may give us true pleasure and that we should therefore try to understand and foster it. The man was made for the place and hour. In other lands those who are capable of learning the value of art are taught by the precepts of long tradition and by the sight of ancient masterpieces. When Richardson began his work our love for art was growing strong but was still crude and ignorant. It was as vague in theory as in practice, and it was not half sure enough of its own value as a factor in national life. An influence like his was what we needed most—an influence which should give both an added impulse to our desires and an increased knowledge of how they might be gratified. Richardson himself knew this and rated his exceptional opportunity at its full worth. Not even his personal fame, dear though it was to him, so touched his imagination and fired his will as the consciousness that this fame was ennobling the attitude of the whole profession toward its work and of the whole public toward the profession.

The impress which Richardson thus made upon his generation has not been beneficial to architecture alone. He knew that architecture as the mother and center of all other arts and handicrafts should encourage them all for her own sake no less than for theirs. He was among the first American architects to preach and practice the fundamental precept that when walls and roof are standing a building is not finished, but still needs that its builder should concern himself with every detail of its decoration, perfecting it himself or calling upon other artists to perfect it in a way harmonious with his own results. No feature was too small, no object too simple to engage his thought. American glass stainers and decorative painters, architectural carvers in stone and wood, workers in iron and brass, cabinetmakers, carpenters, masons, potters—all today do work of a quality for which the last generation might have asked in vain. Those whom Richardson employed profited both intellectually and technically by the nature of the tasks he required and by the wise severity with which he criticized their performance. This was especially the case, of course, with those upon whom he most depended—his carvers and his masons; but a man could not even dig for Richardson without learning that there was a right way and a wrong way to dig.

Yet though he demanded much of the artisan, and firmly believed that he should be developed into something better than the name had implied in recent years, he was always eager to exchange his help for that of the higher artist. And when an artist's help had been secured, his policy of strict dictation gave place to one of brotherly cooperation. What he wanted was the best work other artists could supply for his particular purpose; and though he insisted that that purpose should be borne in mind, he remembered that what was true of himself was true of others: "No man can do good work who is perpetually cramped and thwarted." From the beginning to the end of his life he was always trying to bring the best sculptors, the best landscape gardeners, and the best painters of the country into his undertakings; and one of the chief facts which make Trinity Church a milestone to mark our progress in art is the fact that it was the first American church the interior decoration of which was entrusted as a whole to a painter of ability.*

Neither Richardson's own success nor his public usefulness could have been half so great but for his hearty optimism, synonym as it was for a thorough sympathy with his time and his surroundings. He was successful and influential because his nature was so intensely modern, so thoroughly American. His long familiarity with the triumphs of ancient art had simply inspired the belief that what had been done once could be done again and perhaps improved upon. And his long residence abroad had shown him that opportunities are both freest and richest here, and that latent talent, if not perfected skill, is at least as great. To his mind it argued

---

* John LaFarge (1835–1910), an American painter and muralist.

dullness of vision or weakness of will when an American architect wished he had been born in some other time or land.

There was little in surrounding circumstances or in the cast of Richardson's mind to lead him to talk of the conditions of artistic life in earlier ages. But he often discussed its present conditions in Europe, and always with expressions of thankfulness that his own lines had not been cast there. The priceless teaching of ancient monuments, he thought, could be absorbed by an American, while their distance from his actual place of labor gave him that greatest of all advantages—a free field, an open opportunity. What an architect can do in Europe is largely controlled by the neighborhood of historic works and by the traditions, faiths, and prejudices which antiquarian study has developed. What he can do in America depends only upon himself and upon the sympathy he can awaken in minds which if ignorant are unprejudiced, if untrained are intelligent, if unconscious of their wants are quick to recognize the value of anything which really appeals to them as a combination of good sense and beauty. In Europe a much more intelligent effort is made to secure the best architectural service than has been made in America. But when it is secured it is cramped in ways of which we know nothing—in France by the rule of certain official styles and formulas; in England by the sway of changing fashions, each as insistent for the time and as quickly abandoned, and often by the personal ideas of men high in political place; and everywhere by that archaeological spirit which demands first of all not that a building shall be sensible and beautiful but that it shall be scholarly, not that it shall represent an artist's own thought but that it shall show his acquaintance with the thought of some forerunner. The greatest difficulty with which our architects have had to contend is public indifference, the greatest with which foreign architects have to contend is public interference, and it is not difficult to see why Richardson thought the former much the smaller hindrance of the two. It seemed to him the one which personal force might more easily overcome in the end and meanwhile might more easily ignore.*

* The history of the Albany Capitol offers, indeed, an instance of public interference with architects' work. But professional voices then incited legislative action, and the case was in every way so exceptional that it does not affect the general contrast between American and European conditions.— Mrs. Van Rensselaer's note.

His last visit to Paris confirmed this attitude of mind. When he met the friends of his student days he found some of them at the very head of their profession—highly and securely placed, full of work, and rich in honor. But far from envying their position, he regretted that men of such ability should not have the same opportunities that were open to him. He deplored the fact that no one of them was able really to be himself—to discover what he would like best to do in art and then to do it. And when he came home it was with a renewed sense of intense delight in the freedom of his own path, the singleness of his dependence upon a public with fresh eyes and spontaneous instincts.

Such feelings may not be shared by men of different temperament from Richardson's—there is a degree of safety in tradition and prescription which strongly attracts all but the sturdiest spirits. But they were feelings which played a controlling part in his wonderful career. It is not talents or opportunities, he always maintained, which lack in the America of today, but merely the will to make good use of them, merely a truer recognition of what art really means and of what the artist's needs and obligations really are. It was the perception of the fact that these qualities are rapidly developing which made his confidence in the future of American art so great; and it was this confidence, this ever-forward, hopeful gaze, which made him so bold in doing his work and caused him to pursue with pupils, artists, and public alike, that policy of trust, encouragement, and inspiration which has borne such valuable fruit. His creed was the poet's:

I know that the past was great and the future will be great,

. . . .

And that where I am or you are this present day there is the
    center of all days, all races,
And there is the meaning to us of all that has ever come of races
    and days or ever shall come.*

Its value as a creed for the American artist may best be judged by its results in Richardson's buildings and in their influence upon the people.

It is difficult to explain why Richardson's work appealed so immediately and so strongly to the public. But the question

* Walt Whitman, "With Antecedents," lines 37, 40–41 (1881).

is of such importance that his biographer cannot escape from
the attempt to give at least a partial explanation.

The mere originality of any of his buildings can have had
little to do with the matter. Originality of one sort or another
has so long been the rule in American architecture that the
most striking novelty, if it is nothing more, can hardly excite
even a passing curiosity. The solid popular success of
Richardson's work—great at once and growing greater
year by year—has certainly been due in large degree to those
qualities which have already been described as setting it
conspicuously apart from modern architectural work in
general—to the clearness and vigor of the primary conceptions which it embodies, and to the consistency yet flexibility
in matters of treatment which it displays. The strength and
clearness of each of Richardson's conceptions attracted the
eyes of men whom mere scholarly arrangements of beautiful
features or elaborate schemes of decoration left unmoved—
putting before them a body which they could not help
noticing as a whole and which plainly showed what the aim
of the artist had been and what was the nature of his
aesthetic ideal. And then his steady yet pliant and sensible
adherence to the same ideal in the fulfillment of many
different aims impressed its character upon the observer's
mind, made him think not of each work by itself but of all
together, and thus caused him to realize the difference between an architectural creed and a mere succession of architectural recipes. It was Richardson who first proved to the
American public that the speech of a modern architect may
be something wholly different from a series of varying quotations or of ever-new inventions—that it may be a consistent
yet plastic language, one which inspires the artist yet is ductile
in his hands, one which borrows its terms from ancient
tongues yet has a thoroughly modern accent and can express
a fresh and powerful individuality. It was Richardson who
first proved this, and it is not strange, therefore, that he
should first have excited a genuine interest in the art he
practiced.

A part of the popularity of his works may in this way be
explained. But only a part—interest is not necessarily admiration, and they have excited an admiration which seems doubly
strong in contrast with the cool indifference that had greeted
the best works of his forerunners. This fact is best accounted
for, perhaps, by regarding him as the unconscious exponent

of an unconscious, latent, yet distinctly marked national taste in architecture. An artist so strong as he would in any case have impressed his generation deeply; but to have made the extraordinary mark he did seems to imply a peculiar concord in feeling between himself and his public.

Upon the question whether this concord was a fact turns the interesting question whether Richardson will be recognized by later generations as the founder and inspirer of a national architectural development. It does not involve the future of his fame as a great artist, or the vitality of his fostering influence upon our love for art in general and our understanding of architectural excellence. These in any case are well assured. And so, we cannot doubt, is the permanence in certain respects of his influence upon the actual character of American architecture. If the collective work of the American architects of today is compared with that of fifteen or twenty years ago, the effect of Richardson's example clearly appears—it would be hard to overstate the degree to which he should receive credit for the growth of this work in vigor, breadth, and simplicity, in coherence and clearness of expression. As far as such qualities as these are concerned his influence must endure. But they are not the only ones in which, at the moment, it is conspicuously embodied. His special schemes and features and types of decoration—his actual creed and style—have found so many adherents that they are fast setting a distinct impress upon the aspect of our towns. We have had many architectural fashions in America but nothing to compare with the vogue of that neo-Romanesque work which often seems to reproduce the true spirit of Richardson's art if at other times it seems merely to imitate or caricature it. And it is the permanence, the spread, the vital development, the eventual triumph in quality and in quantity of this special form of art which are involved in the question whether, in using it, Richardson merely expressed his personal taste or unconsciously expressed the taste of the American people too.

It is not important that we should discuss this question in advance, but it is imperative that we should recognize its exact form and bearing. It cannot be too often repeated that if the renewed Romanesque art which Richardson gave us does in truth continue to grow and flourish, it will not be because he taught us to like it but because when he produced it we liked it by native instinct. This cannot be too

23. Henry Hobson Richardson, Marshall Field Wholesale Store (1885–1887), Chicago, Illinois. From M. G. Van Rensselaer, *Henry Hobson Richardson* (1888).

often repeated, especially by the young architect for his own guidance. If he clearly understands it he will know that, however great his admiration for Richardson's success, the main thing he has to do is to seek within himself the direction which his own work should take. From the beginning to the end of his career Richardson frankly and emphatically expressed himself, and thus he did the very best that it was possible to do for the great talent which had been given him. It remains for the future to prove whether in expressing himself he really voiced a broad national instinct and thus was fortunate enough to do the best that could possibly be achieved for the art of his country. But no man can help this art or can assist Richardson's influence upon it by trying to work in Richardson's manner unless he feels as clearly as Richardson felt that it is the best manner.

To say this—to say that we should not blindly accept even Richardson as a guide in finding out the things which suit us best in art—is not to impugn his talent or his force. It needed immense talent and force to do what many cannot help believing that he did—clearly to reveal the fact that we had innate artistic tastes. To do more than this—to create tastes —is not within the compass of human power. A man may teach art in one way—by demonstrating its broad principles and by exciting a spirit which shall intelligently appreciate good results of every kind; and in this way Richardson was a very great teacher. But no man ever taught an art, in the sense of prescribing a special manner of practice, except to a people for whom he was the sympathetic spokesman. In fact, the highest praise we can give to an artist is to say that he was his public's spokesman. All narrowly individual merits pale before the great merit of being the one who says first what his fellow countrymen are eager to hear, and thus opens other mouths to give full expression to a national instinct. Not to be isolated but to be representative is to be a true leader, a true creator in art.

Richardson's right to this high title cannot now be decided. But the spirit in which he labored and the work which he produced have already done so much for us, and in the coming years will assuredly do so much more, that we may call him with confidence not only the greatest American artist but the greatest benefactor of American art who has yet been born.

[pp. 132–138]

5

Harriet Monroe, JOHN WELLBORN ROOT: ARCHI-
   TECT (Boston, 1896), pp. 94–109, 126–129,
   185–187, 190–192, 206–211. (Also quoted
   in this anthology, pp. 00–00).

   Harriet Monroe (1860–1936) was a poet and editor
whose present fame rests squarely on her achievement as
founder and editor of *Poetry: A Magazine of Verse* (1912–
1936). Under her leadership the magazine was of extraordinary
importance in its contribution to the environment and the
voices of the twentieth-century renaissance of poetry. Her biography of her brother-in-law, John Wellborn Root (1850–
1891), is on one level a tribute excited by Root's promising
career and his untimely death. On another level her book is a
sensitive and balanced presentation of Root's architectural
ideas and convictions. Root himself grew up in the "Chicago
School" of architecture and was, with Louis Sullivan, one of its
leading spirits. In the politics of architecture Root was, if anything, more influential than Sullivan; the measure of Root's influence is indicated by his appointment in 1890 as chairman of
the board of architects for the World's Columbian Exposition
in Chicago. While he is overshadowed by Sullivan in retrospect, Root's career is characteristic of the essential vitality
and creativity of the "minor" architects whose work provided
a solid and exciting context for the works of Sullivan and
Wright. Sullivan was not entirely complimentary about Root;
he regarded him as a man of "superficial nonsense" with
"the man of power" hidden beneath, but Sullivan "took joy
in him as a prospective and real stimulant in rivalry, as a mind
with which it would be well worth while to clash wits in the
promotion of an essentially common cause."

24. Burnham and Root, Monadnock Building (1889–1891), Chicago, Illinois.

From "His Ideas of Modern Architecture"

In another paper, read before the architectural class at the
Art Institute, and printed in the *Inland Architect* for June,
1890, he discusses, more specifically, "a great architectural
problem"—that of the design and construction of a large
modern office building. Its minute description of the system
of "Chicago construction" cannot be omitted, because this
system was partly his invention and his firm was among the
first to use and develop it. The paper begins by pointing out
the growing complexity of human habitations:

In the great monuments of early Egypt, of Greece, and even
of medieval Europe, as well as in such smaller buildings as have
survived to this day, very few and very simple ideas dominated
the whole structure as well as its art expression. . . . It was the
Renaissance, with its wonderfully vital and complex thought, which
first began to impress upon architecture the stamp of individual
whim or desire. . . . And with the enormous growth in wealth and
civilization since the Renaissance, especially since the beginning
of this century, the change has been beyond the wildest flight of
the imagination. The luxuries of kings are now necessities of life
to the day laborer; and following every modern necessity is a vast
nebulous train of luxuries, all in their turn to become fixed and
solid as necessities. These all demand accommodation and expression in modern architecture, and architecture must meet the
demand.

He points out that "sufficient time has not yet passed for
this expression to be fully wrought out," and continues:

Architecture is, like every other art, born of its age and environment. So the new type will be found by us, if we do find it,
through the frankest possible acceptance of every requirement of
modern life in all of its conditions, without regret for the past or
idle longing for a future and more fortunate day; this acceptance
being accompanied by the intelligent and sympathetic study of the
past in the spirit of aspiring emulation, not servile imitation. If
the new art is to come, I believe it will be a rational and steady
growth from practical conditions outward and upward toward a
more or less spiritual expression, and that no man has the right to
borrow from another age an architectural idea evolved from the

life of that age, unless it fits our life as normally and fully as it fitted the other. I say practical conditions, and this is fully meant— practical conditions without qualification or abridgment. Whenever in the past such a full acceptance occurred, and a building was erected in the effort frankly to express the conditions thus accepted, art has been willing and ready to consecrate the effort. But, on the contrary, whenever art has been evoked to abridge in architecture one of those normal conditions, she has been distant and cold. . . .

We live in an age beyond all others reasonable. The ethical and art status apparently reached by the Greeks and Venetians through processes almost intuitive, must be reached by us, if at all, through processes entirely rational. If the problem before us were the design of a temple to Jupiter, with its simple portico and cella, the whole attitude of the mind would be different from that which is demanded in the effort to design in homogeneous and expressive form a great and complex office building of twelve stories, constructed of steel and terra-cotta. Here the pure art expression can never be so high, perhaps, as in the simpler problem for reasons inherent in the problem; but if it is to be truly an art expression worth considering, it will be reached at the point where intellectual action, intensely concentrated upon vital conditions about and within us, passes into an unconscious spiritual clairvoyance. Here is the path which will lead us in the right direction, though we may not reach the end of it. . . .

The subject, then, of this paper is some of the processes by which a large office building in Chicago is evolved, from the time when the site is determined to the time of its occupancy. The subject is chosen because no class of buildings is more expressive of modern life in its complexity, its luxury, its intense vitality. The purely artistic side of the question will not be enlarged upon, because, as I have said, it is the practical and even commercial sides which at this moment need special attention, not so much for themselves, but as factors, and most important factors, in every aspect of a great problem; occupying a much greater and more significant relation to the ultimate art expression than has generally been conceded to them.

How much "percent" has always been considered foreign to art, and generally it is. Yet, curiously enough, it may sometimes guide art, if not positively foster it. Art has never grown vitally without some sort of check, whether in the limitation of the age, the narrow yet intense idea which was the inspiration of the epoch, the specialized occupations of the moment, or some other equally valid cause. And in this age the question, purely commercial, of "percent" often intrudes itself at a time when thoughtfulness is about to give way to mere lavishness, and asks of the mind the pertinent question "Why?" At the moment when an architect is entrusted with work to be executed by him "regardless of expense," let him beware that he lose not the thoughtful temperateness which should underlie even the most splendid effort. But when a certain income must be derived by revenue from the building designed, every question must be carefully weighed, investigated in every possible light, and the result is apt to be interesting, at least as expressive of thought; and if solved with truth and imagination, it will be interesting also from an art standpoint, as art in architecture is merely the expression in solid material that someone has thought for our comfort and delight.

Let us begin, then, at the moment when the questions involved in such a building arise and are propounded to the architect for solution.

Let us suppose that in the business center of this city a piece of ground has been purchased, lying upon the corner of two prominent streets, the dimensions of the ground being 150 feet north and south, 100 feet east and west, with a 16-foot alley on the south. It is surrounded by buildings averaging in height 9 stories, and the average width of the streets on which it fronts is 70 feet, being in one case 66 and in the other 80. Of course, the first radical question to suggest itself is that of light, and this will at once dictate certain general and preliminary conditions of the plan upon the ground. Experience has demonstrated that all spaces within the enclosure of four walls which are not well lighted by sunshine, or at least direct daylight, are in office buildings nonproductive. The elementary question, therefore, is how to arrange the building upon its lot so that every foot within it shall be perfectly lighted, and all spaces which would be dark thrown out.

Three floor plans are then presented and minutely discussed with reference to this problem of light, the decision resting upon the plan shown. The writer continues:

The next general question is the number of stories, and in Chicago, at present, the difficulty is not to determine how few, but how many. Nothing to a stranger seems more irrational than the present rage in Chicago for high buildings; but the reasons for it are obvious and the fact apparently fairly well established, so that we must accept it. Let us assume that twelve stories are determined upon.

The next step is to approximate the cost of the building; a question of keen interest, and one in which it would not be conceded generally that the architect puts his best foot forward. Here experience has shown that the cost may be obtained within a very small fraction by ascertaining the gross cubic contents of the building from the bottom of the foundations to the top of the roof, and inclusive, also, of all the space enclosed within walls in the shape of areas, and so on. Dependent upon the elaborateness of finish, the cost per cubic foot of such a building will vary from 25 to 40 cents, although in Eastern cities the latter figure is often greatly exceeded. Thus, a building of this sort, containing 2,500,000 cubic feet, will cost, according to its elaboration, from $625,000 to $1,000,000, the average being about $750,000.

The general plan being now determined, and the question of cost discussed, we proceed to other points relating more in detail to the arrangement of the building, and which still have especially to do with the question of revenue.

The writer then discusses nine such points, embracing height of stories, character of the main entrance, number and size of elevators, position of pipes and shafts, toilet room and barbershops, burglar-proof vaults, space in basement, plumbing and steam fixtures, and spacing of windows. He continues:

Think of the feelings of an Athenian architect of the time of Pericles, to whom the problem should have been presented to design a building of 14 stories, imposing the following conditions: All of the stories except two to be 10 feet 6 inches high, all windowsills to be exactly 2 feet from the floor, all lintels to be 6 inches from ceilings, and all windows to be in width not less than 4 and not more than 6 feet, and to be situated at distances apart of not more than 6 feet. If these conditions did not paralyze the architect, give him a few more: That all windows should have flat lintels, and that he must avoid as much as possible all projecting members on the façade, since these catch dirt and soot; and give him instructions to put on a few ten-story bay windows.

The next group of questions of vital importance relates to structure. The building must be fireproof. . . . The present fireproof structure is provided with metal columns and beams, all of which are enclosed in an envelope of hollow terra-cotta, which is fastened securely to the supporting metal. By this device heat is kept away from all metal work, and absolute safety is secured. Steel columns are coming rapidly into use instead of cast iron, for the reason that iron presents many unreliable features in the difficulty of obtaining perfect castings, and of ascertaining certainly whether the casting is perfect or not. The steel columns are made of rolled plates of steel which are bent into proper form and riveted together. Thus they may be inspected thoroughly, and they are absolutely trustworthy.

In the enormously tall buildings now erecting, scarcely any form of masonry is strong enough to use alone in the construction of the fronts; when, as noted above, windows must be placed at distances not much more than 12 feet apart, and should be at least 4 feet wide. This leaves a pile of not more than 8 feet at best, and this is often not strong enough to carry its load unless one makes it very thick, or strengthens it with metal. The first is costly, both in itself and because of the renting space it consumes. The second is entirely practicable and satisfactory. An iron or steel column is placed within the masonry pier, attached to it by anchors which do not interfere with any difference of expansion of the metal and masonry, and this column carries the loads of the various floors, the masonry being a mere protection against fire and weather. Another and still simpler method is to enclose the metal column in an envelope of hollow terra-cotta supported at each story on the column itself by brackets. In this case the column does all of the work, and any portion of the terra-cotta covering may be removed without injuring the structure.

Beneath all of these various supporting members foundations lie, which present some of the most interesting features of Chicago architecture or engineering. The greater portion of the center of the city is built upon a bed of clay, more or less soft, the firmest part of which lies at an average depth of 12½ feet from the grades of streets. . . . By tests made by the government, and also by individuals, this clay is found to be capable of carrying loads of not more than 3½ tons to each square foot. Practically this is greater than is safe, and the load generally assumed as conservative varies from 1½ to 2 tons, as greater loads per square foot create settlements so large as to be embarrassing. Into this clay, every building built upon it settles to a greater or less degree. In several cases this settlement is considerably over a foot.

The general theory of the foundation plan is exactly to proportion the area of each foundation pier to the amount resting upon it, keeping it free from every other foundation pier, so that the whole settlement will be equal, each pier being entirely independent. Thus a pier weighing, with the floors supported by it, 150 tons, should have footings of 100 square feet, and one of 75 tons, footings of 50 square feet. Several very nice variations must be made from this general law, but this is the rule.

How best to construct this floating raft is the vital question. Formerly it was made in the shape of a pyramid of stone laid in cement, but this is costly, filling up the basement with its bulk and adding often 20 percent to the gross weight of the whole pier. The present method is to lay down upon the level clay a thin bed of cement upon which are placed steel rails or beams, spaced at closer or wider intervals, according to the weights to be carried and the length of the beams. The rails are then filled between and covered by cement, thus excluding air and water; another set of beams is laid upon them, somewhat less in area, and so on, the whole forming a solid mass of cement webbed with a mesh or grill of steel, giving it very great transverse as well as crushing strength. Such a foundation is made, covering areas of 20 feet square or more, the total height of which is not over 3 feet 6 inches, thus leaving the basement unobstructed. Under the old system of construction a stone pyramid 12 or 14 feet high would have been necessary to do properly the same work, and this would have filled up not only the entire basement but some of the first story also.

I have said that whatever construction of foundations be employed, some settlement of the building takes place. This creates several very delicate and interesting problems. It frequently happens that a very heavy building is to be erected by the side of another already completed. The new building will, of course, settle, and in doing so will work injury to the old one, cracking its walls, destroying the level of its floors, and so on. Besides this, the old foundations are not large enough for the new and larger weights. To overcome this difficulty arrangements are made to underpin the old wall, and support it temporarily with heavy timbers extending far enough east and west to span the width of the proposed new foundations. While the wall is thus supported the new foundations are put in place, and that portion of the new wall begun which is needed to make, with the old, a composite wall strong enough for all of the work. The old wall, up to this time carried on timbers, is not reconstructed for some time, but instead of the timbers originally used jackscrews are substituted.

As the new construction proceeds, the new wall, with its foundations, slowly settles, and to hold the old wall and the building to which it belongs in place, the jackscrews supporting it are turned from time to time, becoming slightly lengthened, and thus keeping the former levels undisturbed. This it will probably be necessary to continue for a year or more, as the new building will continue to settle for that time. When all settlement has ceased, the jackscrews are removed one by one, and the space occupied by them filled with brick.

This is simple enough; but sometimes it happens that the old building adjacent to us is so occupied in the basement that we may not go into it without underpinning, and are thus prevented from using the above device. We cannot rebuild the foundations, yet we must not add to the load they carry. Here comes in one of the architect's best friends, the "cantilever."

Some distance from the old wall, columns are placed which are used as fulcrums of a lever. Farther away, on the long arm of the lever, another line of columns is placed, and against the old wall still another. Beneath these a foundation has been built, widest under the columns next the wall, and narrowest beneath the columns farthest from it. The columns next the old wall will

472   HARRIET MONROE

carry, on beams connecting them, whatever height of new wall we may require to be added to the old for the completion of our building. A very heavy girder runs beneath these three columns, and you will see by this diagram that if our calculations be correct, the column *A* will tend to settle most, the column *C* least, and the intermediate column *B* should settle exactly like all columns carrying simple and direct weights. Thus we carry our own new wall from within, and in no way disturb the neighboring building.

When the foundations are completely built, as I have indicated, large cast-iron shoes are put upon them to receive the base of the steel columns and distribute the loads carried by them over a larger area upon the footings. When the steel columns have been placed upon these shoes, and the structure has reached the first floor, the steel or iron beams are all bolted to the columns through wrought-iron brackets, and each beam is bolted to the next, forming a perfectly rigid skeleton of metal. To guard against all lateral movement from wind pressure or other causes, diagonal braces are carried along the tops of the beams between extreme points of the building, so as to tie the whole structure together like a truss. So strongly may this be done that a section of floor framing might almost be turned on edge and hold itself intact like a bridge truss. Thus, this great iron skeleton is slowly articulated from story to story, and during this process the flesh and skin begin to grow upon it.

It will not do to wait till the roof framing is done before covering the anatomy of the building with its fireclay, for here a nice point peculiar to our soil comes in. The plans of our foundations have been made necessarily for the completed building, and at each stage of the construction the same relationship, as nearly as possible, between the weights of each pier must be maintained as will ultimately exist in the completed building; otherwise one part will settle lower than another, and needless strain be imposed upon the building. If the soft clay kept its original condition after the completion of the building, the whole structure might resume its levels with completion, though, as just remarked, with considerable strain; but the clay is compressed by the loads placed upon it, and is drained of its water to some extent, thus becoming harder and capable of resisting greater pressure. Those weights which are placed upon it last do not settle so much as those placed upon it in the beginning. The whole construction of the building should, therefore, develop at the same time.

All that has been written relates to those portions of the building with which the public at large can have but little interest, but which are the inner and significant principle about which every external aspect must arrange itself. The truest and best forms which this external aspect is to present will be found by a reasonable appreciation of conditions of our civilization, of our social and business life and of our climatic conditions. Even a slight appreciation of these would seem to make it evident to every thoughtful man in Chicago that all conditions, climatic, atmospheric, commercial and social, demand for this external aspect the simplest and most straightforward expression. Bearing in mind that our building is a business building, we must fully realize what this means. Bearing also in mind—though this, like the other conditions, is not likely to escape us—that dust and soot are the main ingredients of our native air, we must realize what this means. Both point the same way. Every material used to enclose the structure we have seen raised must be, first, of the most enduring kind, and, second, it must be wrought into the simplest forms.

These buildings, standing in the midst of hurrying, busy thousands of men, may not appeal to them through the more subtle means of architectural expression, for such an appeal would be unheeded; and the appeal which is constantly made to unheeding eyes loses in time its power to attract. In them should be carried out the ideas of modern business life—simplicity, stability, breadth, dignity. To lavish upon them profusion of delicate ornament is worse than useless, for this would better be preserved for the place and hour of contemplation and repose. Rather should they by their mass and proportion convey in some large elemental sense an idea of the great, stable, conserving forces of modern civilization.

Enough has been said to suggest how radically new in type such edifices are, how essential is the difference between the modern and any of the preceding recognized architectural types.

One result of methods such as I have indicated will be the resolution of our architectural designs into their essential elements. So vital has the underlying structure of these buildings become, that it must dictate absolutely the general departure of external forms; and so imperative are all the commercial and constructive demands, that all architectural detail employed in expressing them must become modified by them. Under these conditions we are compelled to work definitely with definite aims, permeating ourselves with the full spirit of the age, that we may give its architecture true art forms.

To other and older types of architecture these new problems are related as the poetry of Darwin's evolution is to other poetry. They destroy, indeed, many of the most admirable and inspiring of architectural forms, but they create forms adapted to the expression of new ideas and new aspects of life. Here, vagaries of fashion and temporary fancies should have no influence; here the arbitrary dicta of self-constituted architectural prophets should have no voice. Every one of these problems should be rationally worked out alone, and each should express the character and aims of the people related to it. I do not believe it is possible to exaggerate the importance of the influence which may be exerted for good or evil by these distinctively modern buildings. Hedged about by many unavoidable conditions, they are either gross and self-asserting shams, untrue both in the material realization of their aims, and in their art function as expressions of the deeper spirit of the age; or they are sincere, noble, and enduring monuments to the broad and beneficent commerce of the age.

I am conscious of having preferred to quote from Root's essays passages which show his rebellion against the dry conventions of his art, and of having suppressed those which insist with equal emphasis upon a complete and thorough scholarship in its history and traditions. Such arguments as those I have omitted are more familiar, and may, perhaps, be left safely to the reader's intelligence. What I have wished chiefly to show here is the alert modernness of this man's sympathies, the broad foundation of humane reason from which his imagination took its flight.

[pp. 94–109].

From "His Work and Its Results"

It may be said, in general, that his quest of truth in an architectural expression of our modern civilization took, as its point of departure, the Romanesque churches and castles of southern France. Like Richardson, Root recognized in these a style arrested before completion, while still in the process of healthy development, and he found the spirit of it singularly suitable to the conditions before him. Though never limited to it, he based much of his work upon this early medieval system of design, adapting and molding it to his complex purposes with a fertility and energy of creative imagination which amazes those who try to follow the double-quick pace of his last ten years. Can this be the idle dreamer whom his father despaired of, this the lazy student who divined knowledge without digging for it?—this, one of the most prolific workers of his time!

Thus his more important work is based on Romantic, rather than classic motives. "Richardson introduced the Romanesque revival," wrote Mr. Henry Van Brunt in his able review of Root's work, and through the unexampled vigor of his personality, had already led it on to an interesting point of development when his career was interrupted by death; Root carried it still further toward the point of its establishment as the characteristic architectural expression of American civilization. The former conferred upon it power, the latter variety, and both, with their trained coadjutors in the profession, have already proved that the experiment is not merely a revival, barren of results, . . . but the introduction and probable acclimatization of a basis of design. . . . It seems to have been nearly proved that, in the hands of such a man as Root, upon this basis can be built an elastic system, capable of expressing any degree of strength or lightness, simplicity or complexity, force or refinement. It has also been proved, largely by his efforts, that the maintenance of the essential principles of the style does not depend upon the preservation of its peculiar original archaic character in structure or ornament, but that it can amalgamate elements from classic, Gothic, Saracenic, or even Indian sources without being diverted from its strong natural growth.

Root's allegiance to the style which he used with such freedom and boldness was by no means exclusive. Unlike Richardson, he did not confine himself to it, and he would have been the last to assert its superiority for all purposes. His work shows essays in many directions—in the style of Queen Anne, of medieval Holland, of the royal châteaus of France, of (freely adapted) colonial America, of Byzantine and Indian motives—some of these being among his admitted successes. The Flemish Gothic especially he delighted in; I think he would have confessed that he welcomed more than any other opportunity a subject which admitted of this motive. Its range was narrower than certain other styles, but he loved it. "We must beware," he wrote once,

of the servile imitation of those greatest and completest styles which mark the end of long periods of architectural development. To the use of these we have no right unless we shall have realized in our own mind the series of transitions by which the style was evolved, and for this reason it will be found often that a study of a transitional period is much more suggestive than a study of a complete style. Unity of design we must have, but unity must spring from within the structure, not without it. The great styles of architecture are of infinite value, but they are to be vitally imitated, not servilely copied. We must return continually to nature and nature's methods.

Up to the time of his death he had experimented little with the classic and its Renaissance outgrowths. Appreciating fully the beauty of Greek architecture, he felt, with Mr. Montgomery Schuyler,* that "this very perfection, which was only attainable when life was simple and the world was young, this necessary relation between the construction and the detail of Greek Doric, makes it forever impossible that Greek detail should be successfully 'adapted' to modern buildings." Yet perhaps "forever impossible" is too strong a phrase to express a mind so unprejudiced, so open to impression and conviction, as his. One cannot lay down limitations for the course his mind would have taken through the coming years. Many persons close in sympathy with him believe that he would not have continued to exclude the classic from his architectural repertory. One of these, a gentleman long in his office, says: "He didn't use the classic much, thought there wasn't much in it—for us. But how prettily he was playing with it before he died!—it was just beginning to tempt him a little. If he had lived, and people had begun to demand the classic from him, he would have given them better and fresher classic than they have had for centuries." I have heard him speak appreciatively of colonial architecture, of the skill of these isolated designers, who, in translating into wood a style created for marble, introduced modifications suitable to the expression of the lighter material.

[pp. 126–129]

From "Life and Thought"

We, living in the full light of the nineteenth century, freed from the thralldom of even our less fortunate brothers across the seas—we men of the Western Association of Architects can do what we please. For us no Jove thunders on high Olympus; for us no bloody despot wields autocratic power; for us no ignorant peoples grovel in the beaten paths of their own superstition. This is the age, and this the country of the great architectural go-as-you-please. I know of but one grave difficulty which besets us. This is the answering of the question, so constantly asked, "What is the style of that house?"

All of the old styles known in the books are obsolete or obsoles-

* See pp. 554 ff. in this anthology.

cent, and yet we still use their names. Why should we not frankly accept the actual condition of things and name our own styles? No one man may hope perfectly to do this; but I trust you will pardon a single, if only a feeble attempt, provided it be in the right direction.

Looking then back over the last twenty years of architectural development (for it is in the short space of twenty years that we have burst the last bonds of slaves), the first style to rise up and demand a name will be what we may call the Victorian Cathartic. This you will all readily recognize. You can see it in full flower in the London law courts. It came upon us all in the time of our virgin innocence when architecture seemed the vale of pure Arcadia, and Ruskin was its prophet. Seduced by the blandishments of this new Renaissance, we yielded ourselves easy victims to its sway, and since that fateful day what crimes against Beauty and Truth and Power and the rest of the seven lamps has it not led us to commit!

The Victorian Cathartic was too true to be good, and too good to be true. As long as its method of production remained secret (in the category of other patent medicines) it had a great and ready sale. But when some too trustful architectural chemist or some too inquisitive lay patient found out the formula, the sales ran down to nothing.

Then came the Tubercular Style, sometimes called by the facetious Queen Anne. This style is characterized by two sorts of eruptions, external and internal. It has for a long time held us in more or less complete control. Sometimes, when it looks as though we had got it out of our systems, it breaks out with new violence; and the troublesome thing about it is that no man can say where or in what fresh form it will manifest itself. Viewed externally, you will recognize this style by its varied and highly colored eruptive features. Generally the affected house is red as to the scalp, with a complexion of all colors, from cobalt blue to saffron yellow. Its eruptive tendencies manifest themselves in all sorts of things, from wens to carbuncles and ringworms.

In its interior manifestations the Tubercular Style often takes still stranger and more alarming forms. The house becomes, in its various functions, most strangely disarranged, and the various organs undergo the most extraordinary enlargements and contractions. I have seen Tubercular houses in which the heart and liver were so changed from their normal sizes that the hall was big enough for a castle, and the attending servant couldn't pass around the table when the family were at dinner. Yet it is singular that the history of medicine records the case of no man who ever died of a Queen Anne or Tubercular house.

Then there is the Cataleptic Style. This is supposed to have originated in New England in the last century. It can be recognized

by the careful suppression in its external aspect of all that would
indicate life. In general the house looks like a hard-featured Puritan at Meetin'—only more so. Viewed internally, it is so white and
bloodless as to be strongly suggestive of a prolonged cold-water
diet.

A style of work now in very common use and called the Romanesque might often be more properly called the Dropsical.
Here you note a general enlargement of all the members. The roof
especially becomes greatly distended and very heavy, and the
whole middle of the house is so swollen as to indicate plainly the
nature of the disease. In detail each member partakes of the generally enlarged type, and as a natural consequence of this enlargement, there is a tendency to obliterate all angles and corners,
creating instead rounded and protuberant surfaces.

Many other names applicable to styles of architecture now in
vogue will suggest themselves to all of us, and under each of the
general names I have suggested, many minor classifications might
be named. It is also true that where such wide freedom exists, the
difficulties of general classification are greatly augmented. All that
I can hope to do in a sketch like this is to convey a hint, which I
am confident you will be swift to act upon. A committee of architectural nomenclature might do much. I devoutly hope that by
conference between ourselves and the American Institute we may
in some way bring about the revision of this question. As it stands,
architectural nomenclature is a delusion and a snare.

                                                    [pp. 185–187]

There is no question [the article credits him with saying], that
a great school of art, enthroned on the traditions of the past and
dealing out oracles for the future, is, on the whole, a good thing.
It begets reverence for the correct, compels artists to be scholarly
and dignified in their work, and, so long as the school does not go
astray, certifies the production of works which will not be positively bad, even though they may not be emphatically good. Yet,
as Viollet le Duc acknowledged, a man born and reared in the
traditions of a great school of art is absolutely prevented from
looking at nature *de novo,* from taking a fresh point of view. His
eyes are inherited from countless generations, and their precon-
ceptions color what he sees. He is overburdened with learning,
and he cannot stand erect and walk freely. The modern French
artist is so involved with tradition that simplicity is lost to him.
He tries to paint madonnas, and gives us unsophisticated young
women with gold rings around their heads, as Bouguereau did in
his series on the life of the Virgin. He models a nude woman of
perfect figure, as Falguière did with his "Femme au Paon" in
this year's salon, and his compeers and critics pronounce it Greek,
when, after all, if we may believe the photographs, we have noth-

ing but a model with a fine form and inane smile posing in a self-conscious attitude in front of a peacock; also, in the handicrafts, one finds the French workman the most skillful in the world in his specialty, yet incapable of deviating a hair's breadth from the prescribed formulas. How beautiful, for example, are those cartouches, palm branches, and other devices which one finds carved in the stone of half the buildings in Paris! Yet each cartouche is exactly like all the others; the leaves of all the palm branches fall in exactly the same order, one crossing the others with the same tiresome, unalterable grace. An architect may draw careful designs of new cartouches for his building, yet when the façade is finished he will find the imperishable old ones reproduced in every line and curve. It is simply impossible to drag the French workman away from his traditions. The American workman, though untrained, is instinctively an artist. Alert, responsive, and intelligent, one can get anything out of him under proper teaching.

Now, in America, we are free of artistic traditions. Our freedom begets license, it is true. We do shocking things; we produce works of architecture, sculpture, and painting which are wholly, irremediably bad; we try crude experiments which result in disaster. Yet somewhere in this mass of ungoverned energies lies the principle of life. A new spirit of beauty is being developed and perfected, and even now its first achievements are beginning to delight us. This is not the old thing made over; it is new. It springs out of the past, but it is not tied to it; it studies the traditions, but it is not enslaved by them. It is doing original work, and it will do more.

Compare the best of our recent architecture—some of Richardson's designs, for example—with the most pretentious buildings recently erected in Europe. In the American works we find strength and fitness and a certain spontaneity and freshness, as of stately music or a song in green woods. They carry a message; they appeal to the heart. In the noblest sense they are works of art. Contrast with them the London law courts or the New Sorbonne. The English building is a barbarous mass of machine-made Gothic, absurdly inexpressive of its purposes, a travesty on the significance of true Gothic architecture, an affectation and an eyesore. As for the French structure, it is the same old French Renaissance which Louis XIV delighted in, and which has been worked over and over until its inspiration has died away.

[pp. 190–192]

In an essay entitled "A Utilitarian Theory of Beauty" he elaborates still further his ideas of the true relationship between art and science, as "parts of a co-related whole, complements of each other, standing to each other as the intellect to the affections, as the thought to the act." By utility he desires to express "the idea of use, of fitness—in a sense, of goodness itself; by beauty all those pleasure-giving qualities we define by words, from 'exquisite' to 'majestic.' Beauty is a utility, but not always an obvious utility." He considers it under three heads: "as a Utility of the Present, of the Past, and of the Future."

Under the first head he traces to fitness the beauty of natural forms—man, animals, plants, and the larger aspects of nature. He follows the development of the arts, and of each individual artist, through three periods:

First, the more or less symbolic type is manifest, in which nature is represented by partially arbitrary signs. . . . In the second period the race or artist studies more directly the methods of nature, and begins to copy her work with some degree of accuracy. But in this literal copy of nature much is reproduced which, being peculiar to the individual alone, detracts from the perfect expression of the type. The artist therefore systematically conventionalizes; that is, makes more prominent than in nature the essential character of the object copied. Art has now reached its climax. Hitherto nature has been studied, and into man's reproduction of natural objects have been infused nature's methods. Now sets in the third period and the process of decay; the artist begins to substitute his system for nature's; the eternal fitness of things gives way to vagaries and whims; fashion grasps at the novel, losing the underlying causes of novelty, and then come final imbecility and death. The period when art attains its fullest and most perfect expression comes when artists, by a careful analysis and synthesis of nature's methods, make nature's purposes clearer.

"Art attains its best expression," he insists, "only by following the natural law of utility or fitness. . . . It is a law of nature that she never makes in one material what she can make better in another. . . . This law of pure fitness is also a law of art, marking all the highest art the world has ever known." He traces the operation of this law in architecture, exemplifying with much detail "the only two completed and perfect styles of architecture, the Greek and the Gothic," and concluding that "in every art beauty is in direct proportion to fitness."

To maintain the truth of this proposition in the arts more remote from use, he considers Past Utility, looking to an earlier age, or (which is the same) to lower organisms, for the utility. . . . Man is an epitome of all previous life. . . . Each form of life through which the human family has developed has contributed its share to that vast fund of treasured experience known as man. And each race of men through which our ancestry might be traced have brought their lives as an offering to ours. . . . Our mental and physical structure is built up very much like the geological formations under our feet. First and nearest us are the shifting sand and the alluvial soil, so to speak, of our own conscious acquirement. These mark the individual, and with the individual partially disappear. Then we find these temporary characteristics fixed by transmission from father to son into family traits, which we may compare to the close and firm clay, resisting to some extent the action of the elements. Next, as generations go by, these family tendencies are solidified into the underlying sandstones of national life. In the fierce heat of internecine strife, national traits are fused into a more enduring form, constituting the granites which extend under vast sections of the earth's surface. But below these lie the primitive formations and the great seething mass of the Master Workman's furnace—the multitudinous life preceding us and surrounding us, out of which have come the fundamental elements of our own mental structure.

It is through this process that we have acquired the many intuitions which are in no sense conscious cognitions. We have simply learned lessons ceaselessly reiterated to our ancestors through countless ages. To them nature told truths face to face, and by a thousand forms of daily experience, while we simply inherit what they have so laboriously acquired. Among all things that we are affected by without knowing why, none move our emotional nature to such a degree as sound and color. Why music appeals so deeply to us we cannot, from our own history, ascertain; nor can we tell what events of our life or of our fathers' made abstract color a source to us of such endless pleasure. What direct utility there is to us in color we have but lately begun to ascertain; while as yet we can only speculate in the dark as to the immediate utility of music.

So he traces this utility back to "the vast underlying strata of preceding animal life," showing that the utility of color began in the interdependence of insect and plant life, of music in the love cries and war cries of animals, and increased through higher animal life by countless facts of daily experience.

From these lower lives we get our mental bias, so to speak; and what was to them a thing of common experience and of the highest personal utility has become to us a source of delight—a thing of beauty. These phenomena of sound and color have been passing down through the strata of the world's structure, until now they permeate the very foundation elements of all life. For this reason, because they have been and still are so useful, they have a profoundly recognized beauty. . . .

After considering in detail the historic development of these fundamental instincts into arts, he passes from the Utility of the Past to the Utility of the Future.

Art has at all times suffered from two things—lack of knowledge and lack of aim: Is there not in a utilitarian theory of beauty the possibility of both? In past times, as in the Italian Renaissance, art has had definite aims and lofty inspiration, but was hampered by lack of knowledge. At the present time our knowledge has increased, but we lack motive—inspiration. This fact is commonly attributed to the growth of a scientific spirit which opposes flights of the imagination. . . . Inspiration artists certainly do need; but if they have it not, they must blame themselves, not science. They endeavor to portray the beauty of nature while they refuse to learn from nature's methods in what that beauty consists. They sigh for inspiration, and scorn inspiration that science has placed at their very doors. Not such will be the artist of the future. He will gladly welcome every new fact of science as an aid to his work, and from the revelations made to him in the laboratory of nature he will gain fresh insight into the true principles of art. Is science dry and unimaginative? Does science crush the rising fancies of the poet or the painter? How grossly is he misled who thinks so!

Let him, so deceived, pass but one hour considering, from an art standpoint, such magnificent scientific theories as La Place's "Nebular Hypothesis" or Darwin's "Development of Species," and then ask if his poetic imagination need look further.

When artists thus faithfully study nature by the light of science, we shall no longer be in doubt as to the value of the arts. Portraying in forms of idealized beauty the natural principle of eternal fitness, each work of art becomes a lesson for better living. Based upon uses, art becomes useful. Artists will be then, as now, priests of the temple of natural beauty. But from that temple will then be lifted the veil of mystery, and men will see their goddess face to face—a deity surpassingly fair, because divinely good.

Thus in many lectures, as well as in talk less formal, he dwelt upon the sympathy between science and art, and urged upon artists that frank acceptance of the spirit of the age which has wrought such miracles for science. He did not despair over the preference of his time for the more exact forms of truth. He felt that art is vital only when it accepts and frankly expresses the spirit of its environment; and he marveled at the pessimism of certain scholarly lovers of the past who see no opportunity for art in the stress and thrill of the modern movement, who shut their hearts against the passion for beauty, for truth, for the happiness of others, which underlie its commercialism and skepticism. If the people of the great West had not yet been given an art which they could recognize, he knew that they were ready to welcome their own when it should come.

[pp. 206–211]

6

Louis H. Sullivan, from THE AUTOBIOGRAPHY OF
AN IDEA (New York, 1924), pp. 243–250,
257–259; from KINDERGARTEN CHATS (RE-
VISED 1918) AND OTHER WRITINGS (New
York, 1947), pp. 42–55.

Louis Henri Sullivan (1856–1924) is regarded (in both
his theory and his practice) as one of the major creative
influences in the "new American architecture" that emerged
in the 1880's and 1890's. Sullivan's formal architectural education began in an encounter with "the special course in
architecture" at The Massachusetts Institute of Technology
where "He felt the need and lack of a red-blooded explanation, of a valiant idea that should bring life to arouse his
cemetery of orders and styles. . . ." Quitting M. I. T., he was
apprenticed briefly in the Philadelphia offices of George
Hewitt and that "curious character" Frank Furness who
"made buildings out of his head." Displaced by the panic of
1873, Sullivan "discovered" Chicago (*"This is the Place for
me!"*) where he worked in the office of William Le Baron
Jenney, a brilliant engineer but, to Sullivan, "not an architect
except by courtesy of terms." By mid-1874 Sullivan was at
the École des Beaux Arts in Paris, "which, after all, was not
the reality he sought but an abstraction." And so, back to
Chicago and the beginnings of what was to be a brilliant,
though foreshortened, architectural career.

The verbal forms of Sullivan's *Autobiography of an Idea*
suggest that his architecture was the outgrowth of an evolved
critical and philosophical position, as, echoing Whitman,
Sullivan announces "There was a child went forth." But in
actuality the *Autobiography* was written as his career was

25. Louis Sullivan, Auditorium (1887–1889), Chicago, Illinois.

being frustrated into decline in the opening decades of the twentieth century; and this suggests that the critical and philosophical position was derived from the architectural practice, rationalizing and romanticizing it after the fact. The position Sullivan developed hinges on images of "power," "the super-power of Democratic Man," as Sullivan attempted to ground his thought in a complex of assumptions which he called (after Whitman) "Democratic Vista." In part the power imagery is the outgrowth of a Whitmanesque Romanticism that interfuses "power and beauty"; in part it reflects the late nineteenth-century concepts of nature and its determinisms as "power," concepts popularized by Herbert Spencer and fascinating to others, including Theodore Dreiser, in the Chicago Renaissance of the 1890's. Coordinate with the power-imagery is "an image of Man as a vast personality" in which "the individual and the mass become one," together with images of architecture as "action" and of engineering as "reaction." Out of this complex emerges an emphasis on "freedom" as the condition for the exercise of "orderly power," and freedom is to be achieved by "actually *thinking* in terms of mathematics"—of engineering, of art, and of science—growing "as the spirit of man sought freedom in the open." The end result of this coordination of freedom and power was to be "conscious deeds in the open," as reflected in the artistry of Michelangelo, "the living presence of a man who had *done things in the beneficence of power.*"

Stripped of its pumped-up verbiage and its Whitmanesque bombast, Sullivan's position suggests the attempt to achieve a synthesis of the artistic and scientific imaginations—an attempt implicit in his architecture, explicit in the florid poetics of his writing. An unfortunate by-product of the floridity of Sullivan's style and manner was an excess and intemperance in criticism that alienated many of his contemporaries.

*From Chapter XIII, "The Garden City"** [*Chicago*], in THE AUTOBIOGRAPHY OF AN IDEA *(1924)*

The legend has it that a small flame, in shantytown, destroyed the Garden City in two awful nights and days. The high winds did their carrier's work. The Garden City vanished. With it vanished the living story, it had told in pride, of how it came to be. Another story now began—the story of a proud people and their power to create—a people whose motto was "I will"—whose dream was commercial empire. They undertook to do what they willed and what they dreamed. In the midst of the epic of their striving, they were benumbed by the blow of a great financial panic, and when Louis returned from Paris the effect of this blow had not wholly passed—though the time was nearing. The building industry was flat. Finding thus no immediate use for his new-fangled imported education, and irking at the prospect of idleness, he bethought him to see what others might be doing in their lines, and at the same time get the lay of the land, something he had not found time to do during his first visit. Daily he made his twenty miles or more in the course of a systematic reconnaissance on foot. When this adventure had come to its end, he knew every nook and corner of the city and its environs, and had discovered undisturbed all that had formed the prairie setting of the living Garden City, and all that had remained undestroyed.

Curiosity seemed to be Louis's ruling passion; always he was seeking, finding something new, always looking for surprise sensations, always welcoming that which was fresh and gave joy to the sight. He had a skill in deriving joyful thoughts from close observation of what is often called the Commonplace. To him there was nothing commonplace—everything had something to say. Everything suggested it be listened to and interpreted. He had followed the branches of the Chicago River, had located the lovely forest-bordered River des Plaines, and the old-time historic portage. Had

* This was Sullivan's poetic name for Chicago.

read Parkman's vivid narrative of La Salle and the great Northwest, and his wonder stories of Marquette and Joliet, and he shared in mind the hardships of these great pioneers. Thus he came to know the why and wherefore of the city; and again he said: *This is the Place for me!* This remnant scene of ruin is a prophecy!

In a while the pulse of industry began the slow feeble beat of revival, and the interrupted story of imagination and will again renewed its deep refrain in arousing energy. The Garden City had vanished with its living story. That tale could not be twice told; that presence could not be recalled. It had gone forever with the flames. Hence a new story must be told. Naught else than a new story could be told. Not again would the city be the same. It could not be the same—men could not now be what they were. It was the approach of this new story that excited Louis; he would bide his time. He worked briefly now, at intervals, in the office of this or that architect, until he had nearly covered the field. These men were mostly of the elder generation, whose venerable clients clung to them for Auld Lang Syne. They were men of homely makeup, homely ways. Louis found them very human, and enjoyed their shoptalk, which was that of the graduate carpenter. He did not demur because they were not *diplômés* of the Beaux Arts. He preferred them as they were; much of their curious wisdom stuck to him. They were men of their lingering day. To them Louis was a marvel of speed. Indeed, one of the younger of them, who laughed like a goat, remarked to his partner, "That Irish-*man* has ideas!"

He was a caustic joker and a man of brains, this same Frederick Baumann. Educated in Germany to the point of cynicism, he was master of one idea which he embodied in a pamphlet entitled "A Theory of Isolated Pier Foundations," published in 1873. The logic of this essay was so coherent, its common sense so sound, that its simple idea has served as the basis of standard practice continuously since its day. All honor therefore to Frederick Baumann, man of brains, exploiter of a new idea, which he made up out of his head. His vigorous years reached on to ninety-five, and as each one of them passed him by in defile, the world and its people seemed to his sharp, mirthful eye, to grow more and more ridiculous—a conviction that gave him much comfort as his vertebrae began to curve. Louis met him frequently of evenings, at the gymnasium, and liked to talk to him to get his point of view, which he found to be, not bitter, but Mephistophelean. He was most illuminating, bare of delusion, and as time went on Louis came to regard him as a goat-laughing teller of truths out of school—but he, Louis, did not forget.

Reliable textbooks were few in those days. Due to this fact Louis made Trautwine's *Engineers' Pocket Book* his Bible, and spent long hours with it. The engineering journals kept close track of actual current doings, and thus Louis found himself drifting toward the engineering point of view, or state of mind, as he began to discern that the engineers were the only men who could face a problem squarely; who knew a problem when they saw it. Their minds were trained to deal with real things, as far as they knew them, as far as they could ascertain them, while the architectural mind lacked this directness, this simplicity, this singleness of purpose—it had no standard of reference, no bench mark one might say. For he discerned that in truth the science of engineering is a science of *reaction,* while the science of architectural design —were such a science to be presupposed—must be a science of *action.* Thus Louis arranged in his mind the reciprocal values of the primary engineering and the primary architectural thought, and noted the curious antagonism existing between those who professed them. The trouble as he saw it was this: That the architect could not or would not understand the real working of the engineering mind because it was hidden in deadly literal attitude and results, because of the horrors it had brought forth as misbegotten stigmata; while the engineer regarded the architect as a frivolous person of small rule-of-thumb consequence. And · both were largely right; both professions contained small and large minds— mostly small or medium. Nevertheless they were all human beings, and therefore all ridiculous in the Mephistophelean sense of Frederick Baumann.

About this time two great engineering works were under way. One, the triple-arch bridge to cross the Mississippi at St. Louis, Captain Eades, chief engineer; the other, the great cantilever bridge which was to cross the chasm of the Kentucky River, C. Shaler Smith, chief engineer, destined for the use of the Cincinnati Southern Railroad. In these two growing structures Louis's soul became immersed. In them he lived.

Were they not his bridges? Surely they were his bridges. In the pages of the *Railway Gazette* he saw them born, he watched them grow. Week by week he grew with them. Here was romance, here again was man, the great adventurer, daring to think, daring to have faith, daring to do. Here again was to be set forth to view man in his power to create beneficently. Here were two ideas widely differing in kind. Each was emerging from a brain; each was to find realization. One bridge was to cross a great river, to form the portal of a great city, to be sensational and architectonic. The other was to take form in the wilderness, and abide there; a work of science without concession. Louis followed every detail of design, every measurement, every operation as the two works progressed from the sinking of the caissons in the bed of the Mississippi, and the start in the wild of the initial cantilevers from the face of the cliff. He followed each, with the intensity of personal identification, to the finale of each. Every difficulty encountered he felt to be his own; every expedient, every device, he shared in. The chief engineers became his heroes; they loomed above other men. The positive quality of their minds agreed with the aggressive quality of his own. In childhood his idols had been the big strong men who *did* things. Later on he had begun to feel the greater power of men who could *think* things; later the expansive power of men who could *imagine* things; and at last he began to recognize as dominant, the will of the creative dreamer: he who possessed the power of vision needed to harness imagination, to harness the intellect, to make science do his will, to make the emotions serve him—for without emotion nothing.

This steadfast belief in the power of man was an unalloyed childhood instinct, an intuition and a childhood faith which never for a day forsook him, but grew stronger, like an indwelling demon. As day by day passed on, he saw power grow before his eyes, as each unsuspected and new world arose and opened to his wonder eyes; he saw power intensify and expand; and ever grew his wonder at what men could do. He came in a manner to worship man as a being, a presence containing wondrous powers, mysterious hidden powers, powers so varied as to surprise and bewilder him. So that Man, the mysterious, became for him a sort of symbol of that which was deepest, most active in his heart. As months passed and the years went by, as world after world unfolded before him and merged within the larger world, and veil after veil lifted, and illusion after illusion vanished, and the light grew ever steadier, Louis saw power everywhere; and as he grew on through his boyhood, and through the passage to manhood, and to manhood itself, he began to see the powers of nature and the powers of man coalesce in his vision into an IDEA *of power*. Then and only then he became aware that this idea was a *new idea*—a complete reversal and inversion of the commonly accepted intellectual and theological concept of the nature of man.

That IDEA which had its mystical beginning in so small a thing as a child's heart grew and nurtured itself upon that child's varied, consistently continuing and metamorphosing experiences in time and place, as has been most solicitously laid bare to view in detail, in the course of this recital. For it needs a long long time, and a rich soil of life experience, to enable a simple, single idea to grow to maturity and solid strength. A French proverb has it that "Time will not consecrate that in which it has been ignored," while the deep insight of Whitman is set forth in the line, "Nature neither hastens nor delays."*

Louis's interest in engineering as such, and in the two bridges in particular, so captivated his imagination, that he briefly dreamed to be a great bridge engineer. The idea of spanning a void appealed to him as masterful in thought and deed. For he had begun to discern that among men of the past and of his day, there were those who were masters of ideas, and of courage, and that they stood forth solitary, each in a world of his own. But the practical effect of the bridges was to turn Louis's mind from the immediate science of engineering toward science in general, and he set forth, with a new relish, upon a course of reading covering Spencer, Darwin, Huxley, Tyndall, and the Germans, and found a new, an enormous world opening before him, a world whose boundaries seemed destined to be limitless in scope, in content, in diversity. This course of reading was not completed in a month, or a year, or in many years; it still remains on the move.

What Louis noted as uppermost in the scientific mind was

---

* This line is not a direct quote, but it is Whitmanesque. In "Song of Myself" #30:1–2, we find "All truths wait in all things,/They neither hasten their own delivery nor resist it,"; and in "A Song of the Rolling Earth" #1:18, "The earth neither lags nor hastens."

its honest search for stability in truth. Hitherto he had regarded his mathematics as an art; he had not followed far enough to see it as a science. Indeed, he had hitherto regarded every constructive human effort as an art, and to this view he had been held through the consistent unfolding of the Idea. Inevitably this view was to return in time; through the channels of science itself. For that which at once impressed Louis as new to him and vital was what was known as *The Scientific Method*. He saw in it a power of solution he long had fruitlessly been seeking. His key to an outlook took shape in the scientific method of approach to that which lay behind appearances; a relentless method whereby to arrive at the truth by tireless pursuit. He now had in his hands the instrument he wanted. He must learn to use it with a craftsman's skill. For the scentific method was based on exact observation from which, by the inductive system of reasoning, an inference was drawn, an hypothesis framed, to be held tentatively in "suspended judgment" until the gathering of further data might raise it to the dignity of a theory, which theory, if it could stand up under further rigorous testing, would slowly pass into that domain of ordered and accepted knowledge we fondly believe to be truth. Yet science, he foresaw, could not go either fast or far were it not for imagination's glowing light and warmth. By nature it is rigid and prosaic—and Louis early noted that the free spirits within its field were men of vision—masters of imagination, men of courage, great adventurers—men of one big, dominant idea.

[pp. 243–250]

Now Louis felt he had arrived at a point where he had a foothold, where he could make a *beginning* in the open world. Having come into its responsibilities, he would face it boldly. He could now, undisturbed, start on the course of practical experimentation he long had in mind, which was to make an architecture that fitted its functions—a realistic architecture based on well-defined utilitarian needs—that all practical demands of utility should be paramount as basis of planning and design; that no architectural dictum of tradition or superstition or habit should stand in the way. He would brush them all aside, regardless of commentators. For his view, his conviction was this: That the architectural art to be of contemporary immediate value must be *plastic*; all senseless conventional rigidity must be taken out of it; it must intelligently serve—it must not suppress. In this wise the forms under his hand would grow naturally out of the needs and express them frankly, and freshly. This meant in his courageous mind that he would put to the test a formula he had evolved, through long contemplation of living things, namely, that *form follows function,* which would mean, in practice, that architecture might again become a living art, if this formula were but adhered to.

The building business was again under full swing, and a series of important mercantile structures came into the office, each one of which he treated experimentally, feeling his way toward a basic process, a grammar of his own. The immediate problem was increased daylight, the maximum of daylight. This led him to use slender piers, tending toward a masonry and iron combination, the beginnings of a vertical system. This method upset all precedent, and led Louis's contemporaries to regard him as an iconoclast, a revolutionary, which was true enough—yet into the work was slowly infiltrated a corresponding system of artistic expression, which appeared in these structures as novel and to some repellent, in its total disregard of accepted notions. But to all objections Louis turned a deaf ear. If a thousand proclaimed him wrong, the thousand could not change his course. As buildings varying in character came under his hand, he extended to them his system of form and function, and as he did so his conviction increased that architectural manipulation as a homely art or a fine art must be rendered completely plastic to the mind and the hand of the designer; that materials and forms must yield to the mastery of his imagination and his will; through this alone could modern conditions be met and faithfully expressed. This meant the casting aside of all pedantry, of all the artificial teachings of the schools, of the thoughtless acceptance of inane traditions, of puerile habits of uninquiring minds; that all this mess, devoid of a center of gravity of thought, and vacant of sympathy and understanding, must be superseded by a sane philosophy of a living architecture, good for all time, founded on the only possible foundation—Man and his powers. Such philosophy Louis had already developed in broad outline in the course of his many dissatisfactions and

contemplations. He wished now to test it out in the broad
daylight of action, and to perfect its form and content.

[pp. 257–259]

From KINDERGARTEN CHATS *(Revised 1918)*

XII. FUNCTION AND FORM   (1)

You were going to tell me more about language, and you—

No, I was not. I began to tell you something about function
and form, when you interrupted; and that is what I am to do
now.

That is so; we didn't finish, did we?

We can never finish. We may talk for long, and get only
a start; but it will be a right start, I believe. We may, perhaps,
see where the end lies, but it will be and remain like a star in
the sky, unreachable and of unknown distance; or it will be
like life itself, elusive to the last—even in death; or it will be
like a phantom beacon on a phantom stormy sea; or as a
voice, calling, afar in the woods; or, like the shadow of a cloud
upon a cloud, it will glide, diaphanous and imponderable,
floating in the still air of the spirit.

What's that you are talking about?

The interrelation of function and form. It has no beginning,
no ending. It is immeasurably small, immeasurably vast;
inscrutably mobile, infinitely serene; intimately complex yet
simple.

But you surely told me to listen, not to the words, but to
the thought. How can I follow, if you are always thinking
away ahead of the words? You seem to take delight in it.

That is true. I will specify: Now, it stands to reason that a
thing looks like what it is; and, vice versa, it is what it looks
like. I will stop here, to make exception of certain little
straight, brown cankerworms that I have picked from rose-
bushes. They looked like little brown, dead twigs at first.
But speaking generally, outward appearances resemble inner
purposes. For instances: the form oak tree resembles and
expresses the purpose or function oak; the form pine tree
resembles and indicates the function pine; the form horse
resembles and is the logical output of the function horse; the

form spider resembles and is the tangible evidence of the function spider. So the form wave looks like the function wave; the form cloud speaks to us of the function cloud; the form rain indicates the function rain; the form bird tells us of the function bird; the form eagle is the function eagle, made visible; the form beak of that eagle, the function beak of that eagle. And so does the form rosebush authenticate its function rosebush; the form rose branch tells of the function rose branch; the form rosebud, speaks for the function rosebud; the form full-blown rose recites the poem full-blown rose. And so does the form man stand for the function man; the form John Doe means the function John Doe; the form smile makes us aware of the function smile; so, when I say: A man named John Doe smiles—we have a little series of functions and forms which are inseparably related, and yet they seem very casual to us. If I say, John Doe speaks and stretches out his hand, as he smiles, I add a little to the sum of the functions and the forms, but I do not affect their validity or their continuity. If I say, He speaks ungrammatically and with a lisp, I merely modify a little the form your own impressions are taking as you listen; if I say that, as he smiled, and stretched out his hand, and began speaking, with a lisp and ungrammatically, his lip trembled and a tear formed in his eye—are not function and form moving in their rhythm, are you not moving in your rhythm while you listen, am I not moving in my rhythm as I speak? If I add that, as he spoke, he sank into a chair, his hat fell from his relaxing fingers, his face blanched, his eyelids drooped, his head turned a little, have I done more than add to your impression and my sympathy? I have not in reality added or detached; I have not made or unmade; I speak, you listen—John Doe lived. He did not know anything or care anything about form or function; but he lived them both; he disbursed them both as he went along through life. He lived and he died. You and I live and we shall die. But John Doe lived the life of John Doe, not of John Smith: that was his function and such were his forms. And so the form Roman architecture means, if it means anything at all, the function Roman; the form American architecture will mean, if it ever succeeds in meaning anything, American life; the form John-Doe architecture, should there be such an architecture, must mean nothing, if it means not John Doe. I do not lie when I tell you John Doe

26. Louis Sullivan, Wainwright Building (1890–1891), St. Louis, Missouri.

lisped; you do not lie when you listen; he did not lie when he lisped; then why all this lying architecture? Why does John-Doe architecture pretend it is John-Smith architecture? Are we a nation of liars? I think not. That we architects are a sect, a cult of prevaricators, is another matter. And so, in man-made things, the form literature means nothing more or less than the function literature; the form music the function music; the form knife the function knife; the form ax the function ax; the form engine, the function engine. And again, in nature, the form water, the function water; the form rivulet, the function rivulet; the form river, the function river; the form lake, the function lake; the form reeds, the function reeds; the forms fly above the water and bass below the water —their related functions; and so the fisherman in the boat; and so on, and on, and on, and on—unceasingly, endlessly, constantly, eternally—through the range of the physical world —visual, microscopic, and telescopic, the world of the senses, the world of the intellect, the world of the heart, the world of the soul: the physical world of man we believe we know, and the borderland of that world we know not—that world of the silent, immeasurable, creative spirit, of whose infinite function all these things are but the varied manifestations in form, in form more or less tangible, more or less imponderable—a borderland delicate as the dawn of life, grim as fate, human as the smile of a friend—a universe wherein all is function, all is form: a frightful phantasm, driving the mind to despair, or, as we will, a glorious revelation of that power which holds us in an invisible, a benign, a relentless—a wondrous hand.

My goodness! What a light that throws on the bank!

What bank?

You know.

Bank me no banks—that has neither form nor function here—but listen: Like sees and begets its like. That which exists in spirit ever seeks and finds its physical counterpart in form, its visible image; and uncouth thought, an uncouth form; a monstrous thought, a monstrous form; a thought in decadence, a form in decadence; a living thought, a living form. Light means light—a shadow means eclipse. How many shadows do men cast! How many live in shadows! How many walk in darkness! How many struggle in their night! How many wander, all forlorn, in the verge of death's deep valley!

How many are mired in the black pit! How many drag others thereunto! Great is the light that shines. Profound the shadow that Man casts upon his own spirit! Opaque and moribund that man who gives forth, not a light, but a shadow in his daily walk. A dense, material, moving phantom, he, who stands before the sun and puts his art in obscuration! Stand out of my light! Stand out of our light! I say! Platoons of dead men! This is the day when strikes the hour upon high noon, within a cloudless sky! Avast the sun! Avaunt the clay that doth eclipse it! Shall the hour sound, and no man answer cheerily its call? Shall the sun shine and no flower bloom in gladness? Shall the joyous heavens find no answer to their smile, but sullen turbid stares! It cannot be, it shall not be: for of the wilderness I'll make a song of spring that shall dispel its gloomy wintry skies and icy snows, and make awake to sweet rejuvenance the lark, the soaring, singing lark that doth abide within the hearts—of all the young!

That's fine! Although it looked pretty dark at one time, especially for the claymen. Do you often have these fits? If you do, telephone me so that I can get around in time to hear the next one. By the way, what has become of function and form in the shuffle?

I dreamed again. But this time I awake to that of which I dreamed—the charming reality of your own proper person, your wit and your ways. My dream was its own function; the words, its audible form.

Is there then form in everything?

Form in everything and anything, everywhere and at every instant. According to their nature, their function, some forms are definite, some indefinite; some are nebulous, others concrete and sharp; some symmetrical, others purely rhythmical. Some are abstract, others material. Some appeal to the eye, some to the ear, some to the touch, some to the sense of smell, some to any one or all or any combination of these. But all, without fail, stand for relationships between the immaterial and the material, between the subjective and the objective— between the Infinite Spirit and the finite mind. Through our sense we know substantially all that we may know. The imagination, intuition, reason are but exalted forms of the physical senses, as we call them. For Man there is nothing but the physical; what he calls his spirituality is but the most exalted reach of his animalism. Little by little, Man, through his senses, divines the Infinite. His highest thoughts, his most delicate yearnings arise, through an imperceptible birth and growth, from the material sense of touch. From hunger arose the cravings of his soul. From urgent passions have the sweetest vows of his heart arisen. From savage instincts came the force and powers of his mind. All is growth, all is decadence. Functions are born of functions, and in turn, give birth or death to others. Forms emerge from forms, and others arise or descend from these. All are related, interwoven, intermeshed, interconnected, interblended. They exosmose and endosmose. They sway and swirl and mix and drift interminably. They shape, they reform, they dissipate. They respond, correspond, attract, repel, coalesce, disappear, reappear, merge and emerge: slowly or swiftly, gently or with cataclysmic force—from chaos into chaos, from death into life, from life into death, from rest into motion, from motion into rest, from darkness into light, from light into darkness, from sorrow into joy, from joy into sorrow, from purity into foulness, from foulness into purity, from growth into decadence, from decadence into growth. All is form, all is function—ceaselessly unfolding and infolding—and the heart of man unfolds and infolds with them: Man, the one spectator before whom this drama spreads its appalling, its inspiring harmony of drift and splendor, as the centuries toll and toll the flight of broad-pinioned Time, soaring, from eternity to eternity: while the mite sucks the juices of the petal, and the ant industriously wanders here and there and here and there again, the songbird twitters on the bough, the violet gives her perfume sweetly forth in innocence. All is function, all is form, but the fragrance of them is rhythm, the language of them is rhythm: for rhythm is the very wedding march and ceremonial that quickens into song the unison of form and function, or the dirge of their farewell, as they move apart, and pass into the silent watches of that wondrous night we call the past. So goes the story on its endless way.

XIII. FUNCTION AND FORM (2)

It seems to me that I could have gotten a clearer idea of your recent harangue on function and form, if you had used half as many words. Still, I think I catch your meaning after

a fashion. The gist of it is, I take it, behind every form we
see there is a vital something or other which we do not see,
yet which makes itself visible to us in that very form. In other
words, in a state of nature the form exists *because* of the
function, and this something behind the form is neither more
nor less than a manifestation of what you call the infinite
creative spirit, and what I call God. And, allowing for our
differences in education, training, and life associations, so that
we may try to see the same thing in the same way, what you
want me to understand and hold to is, that, just as every form
contains its function, and exists by virtue of it, so every function finds or is engaged in finding its form. And, furthermore,
while this is true of the everyday things we see about us in
nature and in the reflection of nature we call human life, it is
just as true, because it is a universal law, of everything that
the mind can take hold of.

You are "arriving," as we say.

Well, I suppose of course there is some application of this
to architecture?

Well, rather. It applies to everything else, why not to
architecture?

But there must be a definite application of the theory. What
is the application?

Can't you figure it out?

I suppose if we call every building a form—

You strain my nerves—but go on.

I suppose if we call a building a form, then there should be
a function, a purpose, a reason for each building, a definite
explainable relation between the form, the development of
each building, and the causes that bring it into that particular
shape; and that the building, to be good architecture, must,
first of all, clearly correspond with its function, must be its
image, as you would say.

Don't say good architecture, say, merely, architecture; I
will know what you mean.

And that, if a building is properly designed, one should be
able, with a little attention, to read *through* that building to
the *reason* for that building.

Go on.

Well, that's all right for the logical part of it; but where
does the artistic side come in?

No matter about the artistic side of it. Go on with your story.

But—

Never mind the "buts."

Well, then, I suppose if the law is true of the building as a whole, it must hold true of its parts.

That's right.

Consequently each part must so clearly express its function that the function can be read through the part.

Very good. But you might add that if the work is to be organic the function of the part must have the same *quality* as the function of the whole; and the parts, of themselves and by themselves, must have the quality of the mass; must partake of its identity.

What do you mean by organic?

I will tell you, later on.

Then if I am on the right track, I'm going to try to keep on it. It's rather fun to do your own thinking, isn't it?

Yes, it is: and rather good for the health and the happiness. Keep on, and someday you will get the blood to your brain. If the surge is not too sudden, you may yet become a useful citizen.

I overlook your sneer, because I am interested in what I myself am saying. I would observe in passing, however, that you are not any too considerate. But, to go on: If it is true of the parts in a larger sense, then it must be equally true of the details, and in the same sense, isn't it?

In a similar sense, yes.

Why do you say "similar"?

Because I mean "similar." The details are not the same as the parts and the mass; they cannot be. But they can be and should be similar to the parts and to the mass.

Isn't that splitting hairs?

If there were more of such hairsplitting it would be well for our architecture.

Why so? I don't understand.

Because its significance reverts to the *organic quality* which I mentioned to you. There is no limit to the subdivisibility of *organic thinking.*

And what is the difference between logical thinking and organic thinking?

A world of difference. But we haven't come to that yet.

Then, I infer, I can go on and consider my detail as of itself a mass, if I will, and proceed with the regular and systematic subdivision of function with form, as before, and I will always have a similarity, and organic quality—if I can guess what you mean—descending from the mass down to the minutest subdivision of detail. That's interesting, isn't it? The subdivisions and details will descend from the mass like children, grandchildren, and great-grandchildren, and yet, they will be all of the same family.

That's the first enlivening word I've heard you say.

Well, it's catching, you know. I begin to get an inkling now of what you meant by the "voice, calling, afar in the woods." Perhaps, too, some of the little seeds are coming up and will need watering by and by.

Yes, yes. Very good as far as you go. But I wish to warn you that a man might follow the program you have laid down, to the very last detail of details, and yet have, if that were his makeup, a very dry, a very pedantic, a very prosaic result. He might produce a completely logical result, so called, and yet an utterly repellent one—a cold, a vacuous negation of living architecture—a veritable pessimism.

How so?

Simply because logic, scholarship, or taste, or all of them combined, cannot make organic architecture. They may make logical, scholarly, or "tasty" buildings, and that is all. And such structures are either dry, chilling, or futile.

Well then, tell me *now,* in anticipation, what characterizes a real architect?

First of all a poetic imagination; second, a broad sympathy, humane character, common sense, and a thoroughly disciplined mind; third, a perfected technique; and, finally, an abundant and gracious gift of expression.

Then you don't value logic.

It has its excellent uses.

But cannot everything be reduced to the syllogism?

So the textbooks would seem to claim; yet I should not wish to see a rose reduced to syllogism; I fear the result would be mostly syllogism and that poetry would "vanish with the rose." Formal logic cannot successfully deal with the creative process, for the creating function is vital, as its name implies, whereas the syllogism is an abstraction, fascinating as a form of the function, so-called pure reason; yet, when subordinate to inspiration, it has a just and high value. I say there is a logic over and above book logic, namely, the subconscious energy we call imagination. Nevertheless, formal logic has its purpose and its place.

Then you do prize logic?

I surely do. It is a power of the intellect; but it has its limitations. It must not play the tyrant.

By the way; you were to explain the word "organic."

You have a memory—which shows that you are following and, still better, anticipating my argument. I had for the moment overlooked the item. But we will take it up next time, when we may discuss it leisurely.

I think this is great sport.

So do I.

XIV. GROWTH AND DECAY

In seeking now a reasonably solid grasp on the value of the word "organic," we should at the beginning fix in mind the values of the correlated words, "organism," "structure," "function," "growth," "development," "form." All of these words imply the initiating pressure of a living force and a resultant structure or mechanism whereby such invisible force is made manifest and operative. The pressure, we call Function: the resultant, Form. Hence the law of function and form discernible throughout nature.

I have already cautioned you against the fugacious nature of words, their peculiar tendency to transformation in meaning while they retain the same outward form. This is because the form of a word is not itself truly organic; it is arbitrary, and has very little inherent capacity for change in response to a change in significance—especially if the change be a subtle one. Beyond the mechanical changes that the grammarians call declensions, conjugations, compoundings, affixes, suffixes, and so on, words, when written, can be modified or developed in significance only, or nearly so, by association with other words—when they are in rhythmical, organized motion. In speech, the word is rendered more plastic: hence the value of oratory. Statically words have little significance, as you may as-

sure yourself by consulting any dictionary; but, when once
they are treated dynamically and pictorially, their power to
convey thought increases enormously; still, let it always be understood that the powers are not in the words so much as in
the mind and heart of him who uses them as his instrument.
The thought, the feeling, the beauty is not so much in the words
as in what the words suggest, or are caused to suggest, to the
mind of the reader, the hearer; and this power of suggestion,
of evoking responsive imagination, is the power of the artist,
the poet: he who surcharges words.

Some time ago you asked what connection there might be
between words and architecture. There is this immediate and
important connection—that architecture, for the past several
centuries, has suffered from a growing accretion of words:
it is now in fact so overgrown and stifled with words that the
reality has been lost to view. Words and phrases have usurped
the place of function and form. Finally phrase-making has
come to be an accepted substitute for architecture-making.

Now, as we two together are seeking the sense of *things,*
as we are searching out *realities,* let us pronounce now, once
for all, that the architecture we seek is to be a reality in
function and form and that that reality shall unfold within
the progressing clarity of our view.

The architecture that we see today bespeaks lost organic
quality. Like a man once strong but now decrepit, it no longer
functions normally. Hence its form has become abnormal.
It no longer speaks in tones of ringing eloquence as of yore—
it now cries out to the attentive ear with an appalling, inarticulate cry, now muffled, now piercing, but ever the wail of
disorganization, the sigh of dissolution. Its features have a
pallid leer, a rictus. Its eye is lusterless, its ear is dulled, its
vitals atrophied. So moves it wearily on its crutch of scholarship—groping through spectacles of words.

The architecture *we seek* shall be as a man active, alert,
supple, strong, sane. A generative man. A man having five
senses all awake; eyes that fully see, ears that are attuned
to every sound; a man living in his present, knowing and
feeling the vibrancy of that ever-moving moment, with heart
to draw it in and mind to put it out: that incessant, that
portentous birth, that fertile moment which we call Today!
As a man who knows his day, who loves his day, who knows
and loves the exercise of life, who rightly values strength and

kindliness, whose feet are on the earth, whose brain is keyed to the ceaseless song of his kind: who sees the past with kindly eye, who sees the future in a kindling vision: as a man who wills to create: So shall our art be. For to live, wholly to live, is the manifest consummation of existence.

XV. THOUGHT

I am quite a little impressed by what you say concerning our search for realities rather than mere words. It sounds straightforward and penetrating in one sense and illuminating in another. It seems to direct the faculties straight ahead of one, to focus them on something definite, something that I feel sure must exist and must be true. Still, for all that, we must use words, must we not?

Not necessarily. You need words only when you are to communicate with others by that special method called written or spoken language. Music, painting, sculpture, architecture are manifestly wordless forms of communication; so is gesture, so is facial expression. Words, however, are sometimes useful in explaining these and other things; in fact, explanation is one of the chiefest uses of words, if not the most important. By means of words we try to make clear to others our feelings, thoughts, intentions, recollections, and a great number of other things—in short, our mental or emotional attitude at any time on any subject, and for these purposes words are pretty well adapted, especially where purely human relations are concerned. But there is a vast domain lying just beyond the reach of words; and, to express our impressions of it, our insight into it—our contact with that which lies beyond man—the fine arts enter and carry on a form of language, of expression, of communication, of explanation, that lies beyond words. Now architecture as at present practiced is a crude pretense at art. But, believe me, it is truly a fine art when its capabilities are once understood, when its true nature is once known, when its plasticity, its power for eloquence, its dramatic, its lyric resources, its fluency of expression are once grasped by the mind and the heart. No form of expression can excell it in force, beauty, delicacy, subtlety, and versatility when in sympathetic hands.

Take my word for it now, my young friend, and I will try to explain it to you later when you shall have come to understand, through your own inward experiences and the growth of your moral nature, what real thinking and real feeling mean—that there is no state of feeling that may not find its true image in the real, the plastic, the poetic architectural art, that art which I am forced to call the New Architecture.

But in passing I may say that real thinking is better done without words than with them, and creative thinking *must* be done without words. When the mind is actively and vitally at work, for its own creative uses, it has no time for word building: words are too clumsy: you have no time to select and group them. Hence you must think in terms of *images,* of pictures, of states of feeling, of rhythm. The well-trained, well-organized, well-disciplined mind works with remarkable rapidity and with luminous intensity; it will body forth combinations, *in mass,* so complex, so far-reaching that you could not write them down in years. Writing is but the slow, snail-like creeping of words, climbing, laboriously, over a little structure that *resembles* the thought: meanwhile the mind has gone on and on, here and yonder and back and out and back again. Thought is the most rapid agency in the universe. It can travel to Sirius and return in an instant. Nothing is too small for it to grasp, nothing too great. It can go in and out of itself—now objective, now subjective. It can fasten itself most tenaciously on a fact, on an idea; or sublimate and attenuate itself with ethereal space. It will flow like water; it may become as stable as stone. You must familiarize yourself, my boy, with some of the possibilities of that extraordinary agent we call thought. Learn its uses and how to use it. Your test will always be—results; for real thinking brings real results. Thinking is an art, a science of magnificent possibilities. It is like an army with banners, where the horses cry ha! ha! at the sound of the trumpets. After awhile you will instinctively learn to know whether a given man is thinking or mooning. It's a great art, my lad, remember this, it's an inspiring art. I mean the real, fluent, active thinking, not the dull stammering and mumbling of the mind: I mean the mind awake.

Words, after all, are but a momentary utterance of thought. They may be, in that utterance, as beautiful as the song of a bird we hear, but they are not the bird: for the bird is flown, and sings elsewhere another song in the forest, ere the first has become a memory with us. Of all the songs sung in the forest how many do we hear? And the forest sings its own song: how many of us hear it? And the song is of the forest, it is not the forest. So, let your thoughts be at times like the songs we hear not, the song of the singer in the solitudes. Therefore I would take your mind away from words, and bend it to thinking.

Thinking is a philosophy. Many people believe that when they are reading in a book they are of necessity thinking; that when they listen to someone's discourse they are thinking; but it does not necessarily follow. The best that reading and listening can do is to *stimulate* you to think your own thoughts, but, nine times out of ten, you are thinking the other man's thought, not your own. What occurs is like an echo, a reflection; it is not the real thing. Reading is chiefly useful in that it informs you of what the other man is thinking, it puts you in touch with the currents of thought among your fellows, or among those of the past. But you must carefully and watchfully discriminate between pseudothinking and real thinking. Pseudothinking is always imitative, real thinking is always creative. It cannot be otherwise. You cannot create unless you think, and you cannot truly think without creating in thought. Judge our present architecture by this standard and you will be amazed at its poverty of thought, its falsity in expression, its absence of manhood. Moreover, real thinking is always in the *present tense*. You cannot think *in* the past; you can think only *of* the past. You cannot think *in* the future; you can think only *of* the future. By great power of imagination you may think of the past and of the future *almost* in terms of the present: the one is the function of the historian, the other that of the prophet. But *reality* is of, in, by, and for the present, and the present only. Bear this strictly in mind, it is highly important, it must lie at the very root of your new education, for it is with the present only that you are in physical, vital contact, and I have told you that real thought, vital thought, is born of the physical senses. It is in the present, only, that you *really live;* therefore it is in the present, only, that you can *really think.* And in this sense you think organically. Pseudothinking is inorganic. The one is living, the other dead. The present is the *organic moment,* the *living moment.* The past and the future do not exist: the one is dead, the other unborn. The present is that twinkling of an eye that separates death from life, as time moves on: but thought is quicker than the twinkling of an eye.

Bear this all closely in mind, my lad. Do not for a moment suppose that it is hairsplitting. I want you to get at the vital essence of things, and this is vital, it is momentous, it is profoundly significant, for it is of *the search after life*—that search on which the mind of the world has been concentrated, with indefatigable intensity, since the beginning of man as a thinking being. The first thing upon which you must bend your mind is to learn to think seriously, accurately, methodically, persistently, thoroughly, and fearlessly. Never doubt the powers of your own mind, for they are there, waiting for you to discover them, to know them, to use them. You will not learn in the printed books how to think this way, but you will find it in the great open book of the life about you. It is all there waiting for you to discover it, to know it, and to use it. Have no fear, and have no doubt. I tell you it is so. It is only the conventional teacher of architecture who could tell you that you are a dullard by birth and an imbecile by pre-destination. I tell you you were born all right and that you have powers of which you are not aware: every lad has, and might develop them if his parents did not ask him every five minutes how much he is "getting," and if he can't get a "raise" next week. Moneygrubbing will defeat any kind of education.

So, first, learn to think; then learn to act. Learn to think as an architect should think, then act as an honest architect should act. When you think organically you will act organically. Just as soon as your thoughts begin to take on an organic quality, your buildings will begin to take on an organic quality, and thereafter they will grow and develop together. But they will not do this until you have so begun—no, never until then. But do not be ashamed to begin in a small way. Everything begins in a small way. Make sure, only, that it is the right way. Seek to learn something of your own nature—your aptitudes, your powers, your limitations. Strive to increase the powers, to remove the limitations. You cannot hope to know your own powers until you test them with the force of will and the backing of character to overcome obstacles. It is almost folly to talk of the limitations of the mind: leave that to the idlers. I tell you that the limitations of your mind are much farther off than you suppose. I would not waste a moment on you did I not profoundly believe it. The so-called average mind has vastly greater powers, immeasurably greater possibilities of development than is generally supposed. But we need teachers—we need teachers of the right sort. The popular notions on this subject are grotesquely untoward, woefully inadequate. The main thing is to catch the mind young enough, start it right, and train it right. The power of the individual mind is great. It is sheer fiddle-faddle to think otherwise. Those who doubt it are those who have not taken the trouble and will not take the trouble to inquire of the nearest child of tender years. Go to, the subject exasperates me, for I have eyes to see. Think for a moment, think what would be the power and the glory of a people if the individual minds were properly trained, instead of all this disastrous waste and malpractice. Would it not reverse some of the cherished notions of the political economists? But enough of this.

I will start you right, and start you carefully: after that it will be your business to keep right. I will give you the landmarks and the blazings in that country which I have explored alone: but it is the land of promise—and I return to tell you of it, and to point the way.

So don't trouble much about words for the present. They will come into useful play when you shall have thoughts that naturally seek expression in words. But do not misunderstand me. I would not for a moment underrate the study of language, on the contrary, I highly cherish it; I mean only that for the present you are to turn all your faculties toward realities and let the words go. Think your thoughts in terms of your own nature, of your own surroundings, of your own art. Seek toward this end: That architecture, its organic forms, its inorganic materials, may respond to your will, to your persuasion, and become the plastic medium whereby you shall express not word-thoughts but building-thoughts, and the function then will flow to the minutest details of form in orderly sequence, as surely as the sap flows to the tip of the slenderest tendril of a vine—to the tips of the uttermost leaves of the giant forest tree.

But you cannot do this in a day, in a week, in a year. It must be for you a lifework, a long, steady, continuous infolding and unfolding—just as the tree grows and expands year after year. For, as I have quoted to you, "Time will not consecrate that in which she has been ignored"—that so runs the French saying. And to realize a little of what the saying means, "Nature neither hastens nor delays," think on the one hand of the lightning flash, of the speed of thought, and, on the other, of the gradual elevation of a continent, of the revolution of the sun about the earth [*sic*].

You have set me a terrible task. I feel discouraged from attempting it.

Nothing of the sort. The more you think, the more you will delight in thinking; the more you contemplate, the more you will delight in contemplation; the more you act, the more you will delight in action. Little by little I will suggest to you how to think and how to express your thoughts. Meanwhile bear in mind that you are not to think merely *on occasions,* as a sort of ceremonial, but daily, hourly, all the time—it must become your fixed and natural habit of mind. So will your thinking steadily grow in power, clearness, flexibility, and grace; and you will ever thereafter feel what the spirit of independence and self-control truly means.

[pp. 42–55]

Frank Lloyd Wright, from AN AUTOBIOGRAPHY
(New York, 1932), pp. 138–146, 148–149,
151–164.

Frank Lloyd Wright (1869–1959) has been securely
established in reputation as the most creative and original
American architect of the last half-century. His name has
become a familiar and popular synonym for the new architecture, as Einstein's for the new science and Freud's for the
new psychology; even his detractors, legitimate as some of
their attempts to reassess may be, cannot seem to find the
critical weapons to make their criticisms more than occasional.
Wright's versatility, together with the scope and variety of
his output, is reminiscent of the careers of technological innovators such as Bogardus and Edison and of the humanist
career of Thomas Jefferson. It could be said of Wright, as
Bronson Alcott said of Thoreau, that he was "the sole signer
of the declaration [of independence] and a Revolution in
himself . . . ," but this would be to underestimate the context
in which Wright came of age, and it would also be to accept
the image of the lonely and embattled man of the 1920's and
1930's as characterizing his entire career.
Wright left the School of Engineering at the University of
Wisconsin in 1887, just before he had completed his course;
shortly afterward he entered the offices of Adler and Sullivan
in Chicago. He presented himself as a "sympathetic though
critical listener" to Sullivan, his *"Lieber Meister,"* whom he
recognized as an "incorrigible romanticist" for all of Sullivan's "logical inclinations, his uncompromising search for a
principle." In the retrospect of *An Autobiography* Wright
liberally acknowledges his debt to Sullivan's formative influence, but at the same time underdramatizes the creative

freedom afforded by the Chicago Renaissance and over-dramatizes Philistine resistance and the sterile and repressive "prevailing mode" of General Grant Gothic. Wright also underscores the "subconscious" nature of Sullivan's genius—by implication, in contrast with his (Wright's) dedicated attempt at a "conscious" creativity. Wright's view of Sullivan thus stands in slant conflict with Sullivan's view of himself and of his announced goal: "conscious deeds in the open." In this sense Wright's autobiography overlaps his own projected image with the image he projects of Sullivan. The overlap in turn suggests a kinship in their points of view, a kinship somewhat underrated in the reorganizing retrospect of auto-biography.

In style and manner Wright is no less the late nineteenth-century Romantic than Sullivan, though Wright's prose (and pose) are far less florid, poetic, and evocative. Both are preoccupied with nature as, in Wright's phrase, "this urge to growth and its consequences," but where Sullivan emphasizes nature as "power," Wright tends to emphasize nature as moral and human. Sullivan's is the ideal of "freedom" as the condition for the synthesis of man's imaginative powers; Wright's ideal is to keep *the truest and best of which man is capable where man can use it.*" This distinction is perhaps in keeping with the distinction between Sullivan's architectural preoccupation with buildings on a public scale and Wright's (1892–1910) preoccupation with domestic scale. The distinction is reflected in Wright's observation that he was interested in the exceptions to "the rule so broad as to admit of no exceptions," where Sullivan was interested in the "uncompromising search" for that rule. Wright's prose, as a consequence, is more suggestive practically, Sullivan's more evocative poetically; and yet to date Wright's career, both in his architecture and his writing, still seems the career of the exceptional creator and, for all his effort, not the career of the creator-teacher.

From AN AUTOBIOGRAPHY *(1932)*

"BUILDING THE NEW HOUSE"

The first thing to do in building the new house was to get rid of the attic and therefore of the dormer, get rid of the useless "heights" below it. Next, get rid of the unwholesome basement, entirely, yes absolutely—in any house built on the prairie. Instead of lean, brick chimneys, bristling up everywhere to hint at "Judgment" from steep roofs, I could see necessity for one chimney only. A broad generous one, or at most, two, these kept low-down on gently sloping roofs or perhaps flat roofs. The big fireplace in the house below became now a place for a real fire, and justified the great size of this chimney outside. A real fireplace at that time was extraordinary. There were mantels instead. A "mantel" was a marble frame for a few coals. Or it was a piece of wooden furniture with tile stuck in it around a "grate," the whole set slam up against the wall. An insult to comfort. So the *integral* fireplace became an important part of the building itself in the houses I was allowed to build out there on the prairie.

Comforting to see the fire burning deep in the masonry of the house itself.

Taking a human being for my "scale" I brought the whole house down in height to fit a normal one—*ergo,* 5′ 8″ tall, say. Believing in no other scale than the human being I broadened the mass out all I possibly could, brought it down into spaciousness. It has been said that were I three inches taller (I am 5′ 8½″ tall) all my houses would have been quite different in proportion. Perhaps.

House walls were now to be started at the ground on a cement or stone water table that looked like a low platform under the building, and usually was. But the house walls were stopped at the second-story windowsill level, to let the bedrooms come through above in a continuous window series under the broad eaves of a gently sloping, overhanging roof. For in this new house the wall as an impediment to outside

27. Frank Lloyd Wright, Ward Willits House (1902), Highland Park, Illinois.

light and air and beauty was beginning to go. The old wall
had been a part of the box in which only a limited number
of holes were to be punched. It was still this conception of a
wall which was with me when I designed the Winslow house.
But after that my conception began to change.

My sense of wall was not a side of a box. It was enclosure
to afford protection against storm or heat when this was
needed. But it was also increasingly to bring the outside
world into the house, and let the inside of the house go
outside. In this sense I was working toward the elimination of
the wall as a wall to reach the function of a screen, as a
means of opening up space, which, as control of building
materials improved, would finally permit the free use of the
whole space without affecting the soundness of structure.

The climate being what it was, violent in extremes of heat
and cold, damp and dry, dark and bright, I gave broad pro-
tecting roof shelter to the whole, getting back to the original
purpose for which the cornice was designed. The underside
of the roof projections was flat and light in color to create
a glow of reflected light that made upper rooms not dark,
but delightful. The overhangs had double value: shelter and
preservation for the walls of the house as well as diffusion of
reflected light for the upper story, through the "light screens"
that took the place of the walls and were the windows.

And at this time I saw a house primarily as liveable interior
space under ample shelter. I liked the sense of "shelter" in the
look of the building. I still like it.

Then I went after the popular abuses. Eliminated odds and
ends in favor of one material and a single surface as a flat
plane from grade to eaves. I treated these flat planes usually
as simple enclosing screens or else I again made a plain band
around the second story above the windowsills turned up
over onto the ceiling beneath the eaves. This screen band
would be of the same material as the underside of the eaves
themselves, or what architects call the "soffitt."

The planes of the building parallel to the ground were all
stressed—I liked to "stress" them—to grip the whole to
Earth. This parallel plane I called, from the beginning—the
plane of the third dimension. The term came naturally
enough: really a spiritual interpretation of that dimension.

Sometimes I was able to make the enclosing wall screen

below this upper band of the second story—from the second-story windowsill clear down to the ground—a heavy "wain-scot" of fine masonry material resting on the cement or stone "platform" laid on the foundation. I liked the luxury of masonry material, when my clients felt they could afford it.

As a matter of form, too, I liked to see the projecting base or water table of masonry set out over the foundation walls themselves, as a substantial "visible" preparation for the building. I managed this by setting the studs of the walls to the inside of the foundation walls instead of to the outside.

All door and window tops were now brought into line with each other with only comfortable head clearage for the average human being.

Eliminating the sufferers from the "attic" enabled the roof to lie low.

The house began to associate with the ground and become natural to its prairie site.

And would the young man in Architecture believe that this was all "new" then? Yes—not only new, but it was all destructive heresy—or ridiculous eccentricity. Stranger still all somewhat so today. But then it was all so *new* that what prospect I had of ever earning a livelihood by making houses was nearly wrecked. At first, "they" called the houses "dress reform" houses, because society was just then excited about that particular "reform." This simplification looked like some kind of "reform" to the provincials.

Oh, they called the new houses all sort of names that cannot be repeated, but "they" never found a better term for the work unless it was "horizontal Gothic," "temperance Architecture" (with a sneer), and so on. I don't know how I escaped the accusation of another "Renaissance-Japanese" or "Bhutanese" from my complimentary academic contemporaries. Eclectics can imagine only eclecticism.

What I have just described was all on the *outside* of the house. But it was there, chiefly because of what had happened *inside*.

Dwellings of that period were cut up, advisedly and completely, with the grim determination that should go with any "cutting" process. The "interiors" consisted of boxes beside boxes or inside boxes, called *rooms*. All boxes were inside a complicated outside boxing. Each domestic "function" was properly box to box.

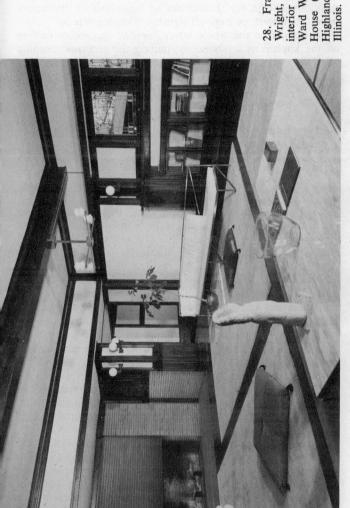

28. Frank Lloyd Wright, interior of Ward Willits House (1902), Highland Park, Illinois.

I could see little sense in this inhibition, this cellular sequestration that implied ancestors familiar with penal institutions, except for the privacy of bedrooms on the upper floor. They were perhaps all right as "sleeping boxes."

So I declared the whole lower floor as one room, cutting off the kitchen as a laboratory, putting the servants' sleeping and living quarters next to the kitchen but semidetached, on the ground floor. Then I screened various portions of the big room for certain domestic purposes, like dining or reading—receiving callers.

There were no plans in existence like these at the time, but my clients were pushed toward these ideas as helpful to a solution of the vexed servant problem. Scores of unnecessary doors disappeared and no end of partition. Both clients and servants liked the new freedom. The house became more free as "space" and more liveable too. Interior spaciousness began to dawn.

Thus an end to the cluttered house. Fewer doors; fewer window holes, though much greater window area; windows and doors lowered to convenient human heights. These changes made, the ceilings of the rooms could be brought down over onto the walls, by way of the horizontal broad bands of plaster on the walls themselves above the windows, colored the same as the room ceilings. This would bring the ceiling surface and color down to the very window tops. The ceilings thus expanded by way of the wall band above the windows gave generous overhead to even the small rooms.

The sense of the whole was broadened, made plastic, too, by this means.

Here entered the important new element of plasticity—as I saw it. And I saw it as indispensable element to the successful use of the machine. The windows would sometimes be wrapped around the building corners as emphasis of plasticity and sense of interior space. I fought for outswinging windows because the casement window associated the house with the out of doors, gave free openings, outward. In other words the so-called "casement" was simple, more human in use and effect, so more natural. If it had not existed I should have invented it. But it was not used at that time in the United States so I lost many clients because I insisted upon it. The client usually wanted the "guillotine" or "double-hung" window in use then. The guillotine was neither simple nor human. It was only expedient. I used it once in the Winslow house and rejected it thereafter forever. Nor at that time did I entirely eliminate the wooden trim. I did make it "plastic," that is to say, light and continuously flowing instead of the prevailing heavy "cut and butt" carpenterwork. No longer did "trim," so called, look like "carpenterwork." The machine could do it all perfectly well as I laid it out, in the search for "quiet." This plastic trim, too, enabled poor workmanship to be concealed. There was need of that trim to conceal much in the way of craftsmanship because machines versus the union had already demoralized the workmen.

The machine resources of the period were so little understood that extensive drawings had to be made merely to show the millman what to leave off. But finally the trim thus became only a single flat narrow, horizontal band running around the room walls at the top of the windows and doors and another one at the floors. Both were connected with narrow vertical thin wood bands that were used to divide the wall surfaces of the whole room smoothly and flatly into color planes folded about the corners—exterior corners or interior corners—and in the trim merely completed the window and door openings in this same plastic sense. When the handling of the interior had thus become wholly plastic instead of structural—a new element, as I have already said, had entered the prairie-house architecture. Strangely enough an element that had not existed in architecture before, if architectural history is to be credited. Not alone in the trim but in numerous ways too tedious to describe in words, this revolutionary sense of the *plastic* whole, began to work more and more intelligently and have fascinating unforeseen consequences. Here was something that began to organize itself. When several houses had been finished, compared with the house of the period there was very little of that house left standing. But that little was left standing up very high indeed. Nearly everyone had endured the house of the period as long as possible, judging by the appreciation of the change. Now all this probably tedious description is intended to indicate in bare outline how thus early there was an ideal of organic simplicity put to work, with historical consequences, in this country.

Let me now put all this in clear outline for you. The

main motives and inclinations were—and I enjoyed them
all . . . and still enjoy them—

*First . . . to reduce the number of necessary parts of the
house or the separate room to a minimum, and make all
come together as free space—so subdivided that light, air,
and vista permeated the whole with a sense of unity.*

*Second . . . to associate the building as whole with its
site by extension and emphasis of the planes parallel to the
ground, but keeping the floors off from the best part of the
site thus leaving that better part for use in connection with
the use of the house. Extended level planes or long narrow
levels were found useful in this connection.*

*Third . . . to eliminate the rooms as boxes and the house
itself as another boxing of the boxes, making all walls enclosing screens; ceilings and floors to flow the enclosing
screen as one large enclosure of space, with minor or subordinate subdivisions only. And also to make all proportions
more liberally human, eliminate waste space in structure, and
make structure more appropriate to material. The whole made
more sensible and liveable.* Liberal *is the best word. Extended
straight lines or streamlines were useful in this.*

*Fourth . . . to get the unwholesome basement up out of
the ground, entirely above it as a low pedestal for the living
portion of the home, making the foundation itself visible as
a low masonry platform on the ground on which the building would stand.*

*Fifth . . . to harmonize all necessary openings to outside
or inside with good human proportions and make them occur
naturally, singly, or in series, in the scheme of the whole
building. Usually they now appeared as light screens—usually
turning the corners—instead of walls, because chiefly the
architecture of the house was expressed in the way these
openings happened to such walls as were grouped about the
rooms anyway. The* room *was now the essential architectural
expression. And there were to be no holes cut in walls anywhere or anyhow as holes are cut in a box, because this was
not in keeping with the ideal of "plastic." Cutting holes
was violence.*

*I saw that the insensate, characterless flat surface, cut
sheer, had geometric possibilities . . . but it has, also, the
limitations of bare geometry. Such negation in itself is some-*

*times restful and continually useful—as a foil—but not as
the side of a box.*

*Sixth . . . to eliminate combinations of different materials
in favor of mono-material so far as possible, and to use no
ornament that did not come out of the nature of materials
or construction to make the whole building clearer and more
expressive as a place to live in and give the conception of
the building appropriate revealing emphasis. Geometrical or
straight lines were natural to the machinery at work in the
building trades then, so the interiors took on this rectilinear
character naturally.*

*Seventh . . . to so incorporate all heating, lighting, plumb-
ing that these mechanical systems became constituent parts
of the building itself. These service features became architectural features. In this attempt the ideal of an organic
architecture was at work.*

*Eighth . . . to incorporate as organic architecture, so far
as possible, furnishings, making them all one with the
building, designing the equipment in simple terms for
machinework. Again straight lines and rectilinear forms. Geometrical.*

*Ninth . . . eliminate the decorator. He was all "appliqué"
and all efflorescence, if not all "period." Inorganic.*

This was all rational so far as the thought of an organic
architecture went. The particular forms this thought took in
the feeling of it all could only be personal to myself.

There was nothing whatever at this time to help make
them what they were.

But, all this seemed to me the most natural thing in the
world and grew up out of the circumstances of the moment.

What the ultimate "forms" may be worth in the long run
is all they are worth.

Now simplicity—organic simplicity—in this early constructive effort I soon found to be a matter of the sympathy
with which such coordination might be effected. Plainness
was not necessarily simplicity. That was evident. Crude
furniture of the Roycroft-Stickley-Mission style, which came
along later, was offensively plain, plain as a barn door—
but never simple in any true sense. Nor, I found, were
merely machine-made things in themselves necessarily simple.

To "think," as the Master used to say, "is to deal in simples."
And that means with an eye single to the altogether. This, I
believe, is the single secret of simplicity: that we may truly
regard nothing at all as simple in itself. I believe that no one
thing in itself is ever so, but must achieve simplicity—as an
artist should use the term—as a perfectly realized part of
some organic whole. Only as a feature or any part becomes
harmonious element in the harmonious whole does it arrive
at the state of simplicity. Any wild flower is truly simple,
but double the same wild flower by cultivation, it ceases to
be so. The scheme of the original is no longer clear. Clarity
of design and perfect significance both are first essentials of
the spontaneous born simplicity of the lilies of the field.
"They toil not, neither do they spin." As contrasted with
Solomon who "toiled and spun" and who, no doubt had
put on himself and had put on his temple properly "composed" everything in the category of good things but the
cookstove. Solomon in his day was probably "fundamentalist"
in his architecture—that is to say, "by book." He had "tastes"
and may have been something of a functioneer.

SIMPLICITY

Five lines where three are enough is stupidity. Nine pounds
where three are sufficient is obesity. But to eliminate expressive words in speaking or writing—words that intensify
or vivify meaning is not simplicity. Nor is similar elimination
in architecture simplicity. It may be, or usually is, stupidity.

In architecture, expressive changes of surface, emphasis of
line and especially textures of material or imaginative pattern may go to make facts more eloquent—forms more
significant.

Elimination, therefore, may be just as meaningless as
elaboration, perhaps more often is so.

To know what to leave out and what to put in; just where
and just how, ah, *that* is to have been educated in knowledge
of SIMPLICITY—toward ultimate Freedom of Expression.

As for objects of art in the house—even in that early day
they were *bêtes noires* of the new simplicity. If well chosen

—well enough in the house, but only if each were properly "digested" by the whole. Antique or modern sculpture, paintings, pottery, might well enough become objectives in the architectural scheme, and I accepted them, aimed at them, assimilated them often. Such precious things may take their places as elements in the design of any house, gracious and good to live with. But such assimilation is difficult. Better to design all as integral features.

I tried to make my clients see that furniture and furnishings not built in as integral features of the building should be designed as attributes of whatever furniture *was* built in and should be seen as a minor part of the building itself even if detached or kept aside to be employed on occasion.

But when the building itself was finished, the old furniture they already possessed usually went in with the clients to await the time when the interior might be completed in this sense. Very few of the houses, therefore, were anything but painful to me after the clients moved in and, helplessly, dragged the horrors of the Old Order along after them.

Soon I found it difficult, anyway, to make some of the furniture in the "abstract." That is, to design it as architecture and make it "human" at the same time—fit for human use. I have been black and blue in some spot, somewhere, almost all my life from too intimate contact with my own early furniture.

Human beings must group, sit or recline, confound them —and they must dine, but dining is much easier to manage and always was a great artistic opportunity. But arrangements for the informality of sitting in comfort singly or in groups still belonging in disarray to the scheme as a whole: *that* is a matter difficult to accomplish.

But it can be done now and should be done because only those attributes of human comfort and convenience should be in order which belong to the whole in this integrated sense. About three fifths of the contents of nearly every home could be given away with good effect to that home. But the things given away might go on to poison some other home. So why not destroy, at once, these undesirable things?

Human use and comfort should not be taxed to pay dividends on any "designer's" idiosyncrasy.

Human use and comfort should have intimate possession of every interior . . . should be felt in every exterior.

Decoration is intended to make Use more charming and Comfort more appropriate or a privilege has been abused.

As these ideals worked away from house to house, finally freedom of floor space and elimination of useless heights worked a miracle in the new dwelling place. A sense of appropriate freedom had changed its whole aspect. The whole became different, but more fit for human habitation, and more natural for its site.

It was impossible to imagine a house once built on these principles somewhere else. An entirely new sense of space values in architecture came home. Architecture taking the road to freedom.

It now appears these new values came into the architecture of the world. New sense of repose in quiet streamline effects arrived. The streamline and the plain surface seen as the flat plane, had then and there some thirty years ago found their way into buildings as we see them in steamships, airplanes and motorcars, although still intimately related to building materials, environment, and the human being.

But, more important than all beside, still rising to greater dignity as an idea as it goes on working, was the ideal of plasticity. That ideal now began to emerge as a means to achieve an organic architecture. (Plasticity may be seen in the expressive flesh covering of the skeleton as contrasted with the articulation of the skeleton itself.) If "form" really "followed function"—as the Master declared—here was direct means of expression to that end. The only true means I could see then or can see now to eliminate the separation and complication of joinery in favor of the flow of expressive continuous surface. Here—by instinct at first all ideas germinate—a principle entered into building that has since gone around the world. In my work this idea of plasticity may now be seen as "continuity."

In architecture, plasticity is the expression of a thought. The thought, taken into structure throughout, will re-create in a badly "jointed," distracted world the entire fabric of human society. This magic word "plastic" was a word that *lieber Meister* Louis Sullivan was himself fond of using in reference to his idea of ornamentation, as distinguished from all other, or applied, ornament. But now, why not the larger application in the structure of the building itself in this sense?

Why a principle working in the part if not living in the whole?

If form really followed function—it did by means of this ideal of plasticity—why not throw away the implications of post or upright and beam or horizontal entirely? Have no beams or columns piling up as "joinery." Nor any cornices. Nor any "features" as *fixtures*. No. Have no appliances of any kind at all, such as pilasters, entablatures, and cornices. Nor put into the building any fixtures whatsoever as "fixtures." Eliminate the separations and separate joints. Classic architecture was fixation-of-the-fixture. Entirely so. Now why not let walls, ceilings, floors become *seen* as component parts of each other, their surfaces flowing into each other to get continuity in the whole, eliminating all constructed features just as Louis Sullivan had eliminated background in his ornament in favor of an integral sense of the whole. Here an ideal began to have consequences. Conceive now that an entire building might grow up out of conditions as a plant grows up out of soil, as free to be itself, to "live its own life according to Nature," as is the tree. Dignified as a tree in the midst of nature.

[pp. 138–146]

THE NATURE OF MATERIALS

From this early ideal of plasticity another ideal came. To be consistent in practice, or indeed if as a principle it was to work out in the field at all, I found that plasticity must have a new sense as well as a science of materials.

The greatest of the materials, steel, glass, ferro, or armored concrete, were new. Had they existed in the ancient order we would never have had anything at all like "classic architecture."

And it may interest you, as it astonished me, to learn that there is nothing in the literature of the civilized world on the nature of materials in this sense. So I began to study the nature of materials, learning to "see" them. I now began to learn to see brick as brick, learned to see wood as wood, and to see concrete or glass or metal each for itself and all as themselves. Strange to say, this required great concentration of imagination. Each material demanded different handling and had possibilities of use peculiar to its own nature. Appropriate designs for one material would not be appropriate at all for another material. At least, not in the light of this ideal of simplicity as *organic plasticity*. Of course, as I could now see, there could be no organic architecture where the nature of materials was ignored or misunderstood. How could there be? Perfect correlation is the first principle of growth. Integration, or even the very word "organic" itself, means that nothing is of value except as it is naturally related to the whole in the direction of some living purpose. My old Master had designed for the old materials all alike; brick, stone, wood, iron wrought or iron cast or plaster— all were grist for his rich imagination with his sentient ornamentation.

To him all materials were only one material in which to weave the stuff of his dreams. I still remember being ashamed of the delight I at first took in thus seeing—thanks to him, too—so plainly around the beloved Master's own practice. But *acting* upon this new train of ideals brought work sharply up against the tools I could find to get the ideas into practical form. What were the tools in use everywhere? Machines— automatic, many of them. Stone or wood-planers, molding shapers, various lathes and power saws, all in commercialized organized mills. Sheetmetal breakers, gigantic presses, shears, molding and stamping machines in the sheetmetal industry, commercialized in "shops." Foundries and rolling mills turned out cast iron and steel in any imaginable shape. The Machine as such had not seemed to interest Louis Sullivan. Perhaps he took it for granted. But what a resource, now, that rolling or drawing or extruding of metal. And more confusion to the old order, concrete mixers, form makers, clay bakers, casters, glassmakers, all organized in trades unions.

The unions themselves were all units in a more or less highly commercialized union in which craftsmanship had no place except as survival for burial: standardization already become inflexible necessity. Standardization was either enemy or friend to the architect. He might choose but, I felt, as he chose he became master and useful or he became a luxury and eventually a parasite. Although not realized then, at all, nor yet completely realized by the architect, machine standardization had already taken the life of handicraft in all its expressions. But for this outworn expression as it appeared in our country as pseudoclassic architecture I had never had any respect and my old Master had less than none. Academic architecture had not troubled me much either before or after I had met him. But the new architecture as an expression of the new order of the machine did begin now to trouble me. If I was to realize new buildings I should have to have new technique. I should have to so design the buildings that they would not only be appropriate to materials, but so the machine that would *have* to make them could make them surpassingly well. But with this ideal of integral order now supreme in mind I would have done nothing less than this, even could I have commanded armies of craftsmen. Because, by now, I had come under the discipline of a great ideal. There is no discipline so severe as the perfect integration of true correlation in any endeavor. But there is no discipline that yields such rich rewards in work, nor any discipline so safe and sure of results. Why should human relations be excepted?

The straight line, the flat plane were limitations until proved benefits by the machine. But steel-in-tension was clearly liberation: steel, the spider. Set the spider spinning his web, to enmesh glass, the perfect clarity to protect internal space.

Lesser ideas flew in flocks, like birds from this fertile central ideal—flying always in the same direction—but further on each occasion for flight until great goals were in sight.

But before telling you about the goals now in sight, some of the reactions to this endeavor, as I met them along the road to Freedom, new thirty years ago but now called modern, might be interesting.

[pp. 148–149]

THE PROTESTANT

The Larkin Building was the first emphatic protest in architecture—yes—it was the first emphatic outstanding protestant against the tide of meaningless elaboration sweeping the United States, as Uncle Dan,* calling it a different name, had prophesied it would. The United States were being swept into one grand rubbish heap of the styles so far as creating an architecture was concerned.

The Larkin Administration Building was a simple cliff of brick hermetically sealed to keep the interior space clear of the poisonous gases in the smoke from the trains that puffed along beside it.

It is perhaps tedious to go into details of this structure here. The story of the Larkin Building might well take its place beside the others, but that story is already so many times written in the various architectural books and journals of Europe, as well as in our own country, that there is no need to write it again.

It is enough to say that, in masonry material—brick and stone—the Larkin Administration Building in terms of the straight line and the flat plane was a genuine expression of power directly applied to purpose in architecture in the sense that the liner, the plane, or the car is so. And fair to say that it had profound influence upon European architecture for this reason.

The character as well as the opportunity for beauty of our own age were both coming clear to me at that time. In fact, I saw then as now that they are one. I saw our own great chance in this sense still going to waste on every side. Rebellious and protestant as I was myself when the Larkin Building came to me, I was conscious also that the only way to succeed as either rebel or protestant was to make architecture genuine and constructive affirmation of the new Order of the Machine Age. And I worked to get that something into the Larkin Building, interested now also in the principle of *articulation* as related to that Order. But

* Daniel H. Burnham (1846–1912), at this period the dean of Chicago architects and a protagonist of the new East Coast classicism.

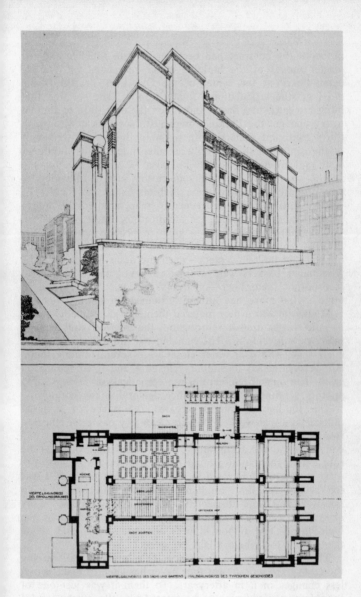

29. Frank Lloyd Wright, drawing of Larkin Building (1904),
Buffalo, New York.

not until the contract had been let to Paul Mueller and the
plaster model of the building stood completed on the big
detail board at the center of the Oak Park drafting room
did I get the articulation I finally wanted. The solution that
hung fire came in a flash. And I took the next train to Buffalo
to try and get the Larkin Company to see that it was worth
thirty thousand dollars more to build the stair towers free
of the central block, not only as independent stair towers for
communication and escape, but also as air intakes for the
ventilating system. It would require this sum to individualize
and properly articulate these features as I saw them.

Mr. Larkin, a kind and generous man, granted the appropriation, and the building as architecture, I felt, was saved.

This entire building was a great fireproof vault: probably
the first really fireproof building. All the furniture was made
in steel and built into place—even the desks and chairs. The
wastepaper baskets were omitted. I never had a chance to
incorporate them later—or design the telephone I had in
mind as the office had already arranged for both.

Magnesite was a new material then. We experimented with
it—and finally used it—throughout the interior. And I made
many new inventions. The hanging partition. The automatic
chair-desk. The wall water closet were several among them.
All were intended to simplify cleaning and make operation
easy. The new architecture was practical or it was only
another sentimentality, to further demoralize the country.

The top-lighted interior created the effect of a great
official family at work in day-lit, clean airy quarters, officered
from the central court. The top story was a restaurant and
conservatory, the ferns and flowers seen from below. The
roof was a recreation ground paved with brick.

The officers appreciated the building in practice but it was
too severe for the "fundamentalist" tastes of the Larkin
family. They were distracted, too, I imagine by so many
experiments, some of which delayed the completion of the
building. A few minor failures annoyed them—and made
them think the whole might be, queer?

They never realized the place their building took in the
thought of the world—for they never hesitated to make senseless changes in it in afteryears. To them it was just one of
their factory buildings—to be treated like the others. And I
suppose from any standpoint available to them, that was all

it was. In architecture they were still voluntary pallbearers for the remains of Thomas Jefferson.

Now Unity Temple came into the studio at Oak Park—let us again say workshop instead of studio.

Several invitations to submit work in competition had come in by this time. But no matter how promising the program or how many promises were made I steadily refused to enter a competition. I have refused ever since.

COMPETITIONS

The world has gained no building worth having by competition because: (1) The jury itself is necessarily a hand-picked average. Some "constituency" must agree upon the "jury." (2) Therefore the first thing this average does as a jury, when "picked," is to go through all the designs and throw out the best ones and the worst ones. This is necessary in order that the average may average upon something average. (3) Therefore any architectural competition will be an average upon an average by averages in behalf of the average. (4) The net result is a building well behind the times before it is begun to be built.

This might seem democratic if mediocrity is the democratic ideal in architecture. No. Competitions are only opportunity for inexperienced youth to air their proficiency with the "project."

Moreover, to further vitiate the objective, every architect entering any competition does so to win the prize. So he sensibly aims his efforts at what he conceives to be the common prejudices and predilections of the "jury."

Invariably the man who does this most accurately wins the competition.

A competition was first thought of for Unity Temple, but the idea abandoned and the commission given to me after much debate among the committee.

Committee decisions, too, are seldom above mediocre unless the committee is "run" by some strong individual. In this case the committee was so "run" by Charles E. Roberts— inventor. He was the strong man in this instance, or Unity Temple would never have been built.

30. Frank Lloyd Wright, The Universalist Church (Unity Temple) (1906), Oak Park, Illinois.

Let us take Unity Temple to pieces in the thought of its architect and see how it came to be the Unity Temple you now see.

DESIGNING UNITY TEMPLE

Had Dr. Johonnot, the Universalist pastor of Unity Church, been Fra Junipero the "style" of Unity Temple would have been predetermined. Had he been Father Latour it would have been Midi-Romanesque. Yes, and perhaps being what he was, he was entitled to the only tradition he knew—that of the little white New England Church, lean spire pointing to heaven—"back East." If sentimentality were sense this might be so.

But the pastor was out of luck. Circumstances brought him to yield himself up "in the cause of architecture." The straight line and the flat plane were to emerge as the cantilever slab.

And to that cause every one who undertakes to read what follows is called upon to yield. It should only be read after studying the plans and perspective of Unity Temple. Constant reference to the plan will be necessary if the matter is to come clear.

Our building committee were all "good men and true." One of them, Charles E. Roberts, a mechanical engineer and inventor, enlightened in creation.

One, enlightened, is leaven enough in any Usonian lump. The struggle . . . it is always a struggle in architecture for the architect where "good men and true" are concerned—began.

First came the philosophy of the building.

Human sensibilities are the strings of the instrument upon which the true artist plays . . . "abstract" . . . ? But why not avoid the symbol, as such? The symbol is too literal. It is become a form of literature in the arts.

Let us abolish, in the art and craft of architecture, literature in any "symbolic" form whatsoever. The sense of inner rhythm, deep planted in human sensibility, lives far above other considerations in art.

Then why the steeple of the little white church? Why *point* to heaven?

I told the committee a story. Did they not know the tale of the holy man who, yearning to see God, climbed up and up the highest mountain—up and up on and to and up the highest relic of a tree there was on the mountain too? Ragged and worn, there he lifted up his eager perspiring face to heaven and called on "God." A voice . . . bidding him get down . . . go back!

Would he really see God's face? Then he should go back, go down there in the valley below where his own people were —there only could *he* look upon God's countenance.

Was not that "finger," the church steeple, pointing on high like the man who climbed on high to see Him? A misleading symbol perhaps. A perversion of sentiment—sentimentality.

Was not the time come now to be more simple, to have more faith in man on his Earth and less anxiety concerning his Heaven about which he could *know* nothing. Concerning this heaven he had never received any testimony from his own senses.

Why not, then, build a temple, not to God in that way— more sentimental than sense—but build a temple to man, appropriate to his uses as a meeting place, in which to study man himself for his God's sake? A modern meeting house and good-time place.

Build a beautiful Room proportioned to this purpose. Make it beautiful in this *simple* sense. A *natural* building for natural Man.

The pastor was a "liberal." His liberality was thus challenged, his reason piqued, and the curiosity of all aroused.

What would such a building be like? They said they could imagine no such thing.

"That's what you came to me for," I ventured. "I can imagine it and will help you create it."

Promising the building committee something tangible to look at soon—I sent them away, they not knowing, quite, whether they were foolish, fooled, or fooling with a fool.

That Room; it began to be that same night.

Enter the realm of architectural ideas.

The first idea—to keep a noble Room in mind, and let the room shape the whole edifice, let the room inside be the architecture outside.

What shape? Well, the answer lay, in what material? There was only one material to choose, as the church funds were $45,000, to "church" 400 people in 1906. Concrete was cheap.

Concrete alone could do it. But even concrete as it was in use at that time meant wood "forms" and some other material than concrete for outside facing. They were in the habit of covering the concrete with brick or stone, plastering and furring the inside of the walls. Plastering the outside would be cheaper than brick or stone but wouldn't stick to concrete in our climate. Why not make the wooden boxes or forms so the concrete could be cast in them as separate blocks and masses, these separate blocks and masses grouped about an interior space in some such way as to preserve this desired sense of the interior space in the appearance of the whole building? And the block-masses be left as themselves with no "facing." That would be cheap and permanent.

Then, how to cover the separate features and concrete masses as well as the sacrosanct space from the extremes of northern weather. What roof?

What had concrete to offer as a cover shelter? The slab—of course. The reinforced slab. Nothing else if the building was to be thoroughbred, meaning built in character out of one material.

Too monumental, all this? Too forthright for my committee I feared. Would a statement so positive as that final slab over the whole seem irreligious to them? Profane in their eyes? Why?

The flat slab was direct. It would be "nobly" simple. The wooden forms or molds in which concrete buildings must at that time be cast were always the chief item of expense, so to repeat the use of a single one as often as possible was desirable, even necessary. Therefore a building all four sides alike looked like the thing. This, in simplest terms, meant a building square in plan. That would make their temple a cube, a noble form.

The slab, too, belonged to the cube by nature. "Credo simplicitas."

That form is most imaginative and "happy" that is most radiant with the "aura" or overtone of superform.

Geometric shapes through human sensibility have thus acquired to some extent human significance as, say, the cube or square, integrity; the circle or sphere, infinity; the straight line, rectitude; if long drawn out . . . repose; the triangle . . . aspiration, etc.

There was no money to spend in working on the concrete mass outside or with it after it was once cast.

Good reason, this, if no other, for getting away from any false facing. Couldn't the surface be qualified in the casting process so this whole matter of veneered "façade" could be omitted with good effect? This was later the cause of much experiment, with what success may be seen.

Then the Temple itself—still in my mind—began to take shape. The site was noisy, by the Lake Street car tracks. Therefore it seemed best to keep the building closed on the three front sides and enter it from a court at the center of the lot.

Unity Temple itself with the thoughts in mind I have just expressed, arrived easily enough, but there was a secular side to Universalist church activities—entertainment—Sunday school, feasts, etc. . . .

To embody these latter with the temple would spoil the simplicity of the room—the noble ROOM—in the service of MAN for the worship of GOD.

So finally I put the space as "Unity House," a long free space to the rear of the lot, as a separate building to be sub-divided by movable screens, on occasion. It thus became a separate building but harmonious with the Temple—the entrance to both to be the connecting link between them. That was that.

To go back to the Temple itself. What kind of "square room"? How effect the cube and best serve the purpose of audience room?

Should the pulpit be put toward the street and let the congregation come in and go out at the rear in the usual disrespectful church fashion so the pastor missed contact with his flock? And the noise of the street cars on Lake Street come in?

No. Why not put the pulpit at the entrance side at the rear of the square Temple entirely cut off from the street and bring the congregation into the room at the sides and on a lower level so those entering would be imperceptible to the audience? This would make the incomers as little a disturbance or challenge to curiosity as possible. This would preserve the quiet and the dignity of the room itself. Out of that thought came the depressed foyer or "cloister" corridor either side leading from the main entrance lobby at the center to the stairs in the near and far corners of the room. Those entering the room in this way could see into the big room but not be seen by those already seated within it.

And when the congregation rose to disperse here was opportunity to move forward toward their pastor and by swinging wide doors open beside the pulpit let the flock pass out by the minister and find themselves directly in the entrance loggia from which they had first come in. They had gone into the depressed entrances at the sides from this same entrance to enter the big room. But it seemed more respectful to let them go out thus toward the pulpit than turn their backs upon their minister to go out as is usual in most churches. This scheme gave the minister's flock to him to greet. Few could escape. The position of the pulpit in relation to the entrance made this reverse movement possible.

So this was done.

The room itself—size determined by comfortable seats with leg room for four hundred people—was built with four interior free-standing posts to carry the overhead structure. These concrete posts were hollow and became free-standing ducts to ensure economic and uniform distribution of heat. The large supporting posts were so set in plan as to form a double tier of alcoves on four sides of this room. Flood these side alcoves with light from above: get a sense of a happy cloudless day into the room. And with this feeling for light the center ceiling between the four great posts became skylight, daylight sifting through between the intersections of concrete beams filtering through amber glass ceiling lights thus the light would, rain or shine, have the warmth of sunlight. Artificial lighting took place there at night as well. This scheme of lighting was integral, gave diffusion and kept the room space clear.

The spacious wardrobes between the depressed foyers either side of the room and under the auditorium itself, were intended to give opportunity to the worshippers to leave their wraps before entering the worshipful room. And this ward-

robe would work as well for the entertainments in the long
room to the rear because it was just off the main entrance
lobby.

The secular hall—Unity House—itself, was tall enough to
have galleries at each side of the central space—convertible
into classroom space.

A long kitchen connected to each end of the secular space
was added to the rear of Unity House for the Temple
"feasts."

The pastor's offices and study came of themselves over the
entrance lobby the connection between the two buildings.
The study thus looked down through swinging windows into
the secular hall—while it was just a step behind the pulpit.

All this seemed in proper order. Seemed natural enough.

Now for proportion—for the "concrete" expression of concrete in this natural arrangement—the ideal of an organic
whole well in mind.

For observe, so far, what has actually taken place is only
reasoned *arrangement*. The "plan" with an eye to an exterior
in the realm of ideas but "felt" in imagination.

First came the philosophy of the thing in the little story
repeated to the trustees. All artistic creation has its own. The
first condition of creation. However, some would smile and
say, "the result of it."

Second there was the general purpose of the whole to
consider in each part: a matter of reasoned arrangement.
This arrangement must be made with a sense of the yet-
unborn whole in the mind, to be blocked out as appropriate
to concrete masses cast in wooden boxes. Holding all this
diversity together in a preconceived direction is really no light
matter but is the condition of creation. Imagination conceives
here the PLAN suitable to the material and the purpose—
seeing the probable—possible form.

Imagination reigns supreme, when now the *form* the whole
will naturally take, must be seen.

And we have arrived at the question of *style*.

But if all this preliminary planning has been well conceived,
that question in the main is settled. The matter may be intensified, made eloquent or modified and quieted. It cannot
much change. Organic is this matter of style now. The
concrete forms of Unity Temple will take the character of

all we have so far done, if all we have so far done is harmonious with the principle we are waking to work. The structure will not put forth its forms as the tree puts forth branches and foliage—if we do not stultify it, do not betray it in some way.

We do not choose the style. Style is what this is now and what we *are*. A thrilling moment this in any architect's experience. He is about to see the countenance of something he is invoking. Out of this sense of order and his love of the beauty of life—something is to be born maybe to live long as a message of hope and joy or a curse to his kind. *His* message he feels. Nonetheless is it "theirs," and rather more. And it is out of love and understanding such as this on the part of an architect that a building is born to bless or curse those it is built to serve.

Bless them if they will see and understand. Curse them and be cursed by them if either they or the architect should fail to understand. . . . This is the faith and the fear in the architect as he makes ready—to draw his design.

In all artists it is the same.

Now comes to brood—to suffer doubt and burn with eagerness. To test bearings—and prove assumed ground by putting all together to definite scale on paper. Preferably small scale at first. Then larger. Finally still larger scale studies of parts.

This pure white sheet of paper! Ready for the logic of the plan.

T-square, triangle, scale—seductive invitation lying upon the spotless surface.

Temptation!

"Boy! Go tell Black Kelly to make a blaze there in the workroom fireplace! Ask Brown-Sadie if it's too late to have baked Bermudas for supper! Then go ask your mother—I shall hear her in here—to play something—Bach preferred, or Beethoven if she prefers."

An aid to creative effort, the open fire. What a friend to the laboring artist, the poetic baked onion. Real encouragement to him is great music.

Yes, and what a poor creature, after all, creation comes

singing through. About like catgut and horsehair in the hands
of Sarasate.*

Night labor at the drafting board is best for intense
creation. It may continue uninterrupted.

Meantime reflections are passing in the mind—"design is
abstraction of nature, elements in purely geometric terms"—
that is what we ought to call pure design? . . . But—nature,
pattern and nature, texture in materials themselves often
approach conventionalization, or the abstract, to such a
degree as to be superlative means ready to the designer's
hand to qualify, stimulate, and enrich his own efforts. . . .
What texture this concrete mass? Why not its own gravel?
How to bring the gravel clean on the surface?

Here was reality. Yes, the "fine thing" is reality. Always
reality?

Realism, the subgeometric, is, however, the abuse of this
fine thing.

Keep the straight lines clean and significant, the flat plane
expressive and clean cut. But let texture of material come
into them.

Reality is spirit . . . essence brooding just behind aspect!

Seize it! And . . . after all, reality *is* supergeometric, casting
a spell or a "charm" over any geometry, as such, in itself.

Yes, it seems to me, that is what it means to be an artist
. . . to seize this essence brooding just behind aspect. These
questionings arising each with its train of thought by the
way, as at work.

It is morning! To bed for a while!

Well, there is Unity Temple at last. Health and soundness
in it, though still far to go.

But here we have penciled on the sheet of paper, in the
main, the plan, section and elevation as in the drawings
illustrated here, all except the exterior of "Unity House," as
the room for secular recreation came to be called.

To establish harmony between these buildings of separate
function proved difficult, utterly exasperating.

Another series of concentrations—lasting hours at a time
for several days. How to keep the noble scale of the temple

* Pablo Martin Meliton de Sarasate (1844–1908), a Spaniard who was
one of the greatest concert violinists in the nineteenth century.

in the design of the subordinate mass of the secular hall and
not falsify the function of that noble mass? The ideal of an
organic architecture is severe discipline for the imagination.
I came to know that full well. And, always, some minor
concordance takes more time, taxes concentration more than
all besides. To vex the architect, this minor element now
becomes a major problem. How many schemes I have thrown
away because some one minor feature would not come true
to form!

Thirty-four studies were necessary to arrive at this as it is
now seen. Unfortunately they are lost with thousands of
others of other buildings. The fruit of similar struggles to
coordinate and perfect them all as organic entities—I wish
I had kept.

Unity House looks easy enough now, for it is right enough.

But this *"harmony of the whole"* where diverse functions
cause diverse masses to occur is no light affair for the architect—nor ever will be if he keeps his ideal high.

Now observe the plans and the elevations, then the model
or photograph of the building. See, now, how all that has
taken place is showing itself *as it is* for what it is.

A new industrial method for the use of a new material is
improved and revealed. Roof slabs—attic walls—screen walls
—posts and glass screens enclose, as architecture, a great
room.

The sense of the room is not only preserved—*it may be
seen as the soul of the design*. Instead of being built into the
heart of a block of sculptured building material, out of sight,
sacrosanct space is merely screened in . . . it comes through
as the living "motif" of the architecture.

The grammar of such style as is seen here is simply and
logically determined by the concrete mass and flat layer
formation of the slab and box construction of the square
room, proportioned according to concrete-nature—or the
nature of the concrete. All is assembled about the coveted
space, now visibly cherished.

Such architectural forms as there are, each to each as all
in all, are cubical in form, to be cast solid in wooden boxes.
But *one* motif may be seen, the "inside" becoming "outside."
The groups of monoliths in their changing phases, square in
character, do not depart from that single IDEA. Here we have
something of the organic integrity in structure out of which

issues character as an aura. The consequence is style. A stylish development of the square becoming the cube.

Understanding Unity Temple one may respect it. It serves its purpose well. It was easy to build. Its harmonies are bold and striking, but genuine in melody. The "square," too positive in statement for current *"taste,"* the straight line and the flat plane uncompromising, yes. But here is an entity again to prove that architecture may, if need be, live again as the nature-of-the-thing in terms of building material. Here is one building rooted in such modern conditions of work, materials, and thought, as prevailed at the time it was built. Single-minded in motif. Faithful in form.

Out of this concentration in labor will come many subsequent studies in refinement—correction of correlation, scale tests for integration. Overcoming difficulties in detail, in the effort to keep all clean and simple as a whole, is continued during the whole process of planning and building.

Many studies in detail yet remain to be made—determine what further may be left out to protect the design. These studies seem never to end, and in this sense, no organic building may ever be "finished." The complete goal of the ideal of organic architecture is never reached. Nor need be. What worthwhile ideal is ever reached?

But, we have enough now on paper to make a perspective drawing to go with the plan for the committee of "good men and true" to see. Usually a committee has only the sketch to consider. But it is impossible to present a "sketch" when working in this method. The building as a whole must be all in order before the "sketch," not after it.

Unity Temple is a complete building on paper, already. There is no "sketch" and there never has been one.

Hardest of an architect's trials, to show his work, first time, to anyone not entirely competent, perhaps unsympathetic.

Putting off the evil contact as long as possible—letting all simmer. The simmering process, too, is valuable. There is seldom enough of it.

What hope to carry all through? The human ground for hope is gone over carefully again and again—wakeful nights. Already the architect begins to fear for the fate of his design. If it is to be much changed he prefers to throw it all away and begin all over again.

No—not much hope except in Mr. Roberts. Why not ask

him to see the design and explain it to him first? This is done. He is delighted. He *understands!* He is himself an inventor. And every project in architecture needs this one intimate friend in order to proceed. Mr. Roberts suggests a model. The model is soon made.

All right; let the committee come now. They do come—all curious. Soon confounded—taking the "show-me" attitude.

At this moment the creative architect is distinctly at disadvantage as compared with his obsequious brother of the "styles." His brother can show his pattern-book of "styles," speak glibly of St. Mark's at Venice or Capella Palatine, impress the no less craven clients by brave show of erudite authorities—abash them.

But the architect with the ideal of an organic architecture at stake can talk only principle and sense. His only appeal must be made to the independent thought and judgment of his client. The client, too, must know how to think from generals to particulars. How rare it is to go into court where that quality of mind is on the bench! This architect has learned to dread the personal idiosyncrasy—offered him three times out of five—substitute for such intelligence.

But, we try and we use all our resources, we two—the inventor and myself—and win a third member of the committee at the first meeting. Including the pastor, there are now four only left in doubt.

One of the four openly hostile—Mr. Skillin. Dr. Johonnot, the pastor, himself impressed but cautious—very—and tactful. He has a glimpse of a new world.

There is hope, distinctly hope, when he makes four as he soon does and the balance of power is with us.

We need three more, but the architect's work is done now. The four will get the others. The pastor is convinced. He will work! So doubt and fears are finally put to sleep—all but Mr. Skillin's. Mr. Skillin is sure the room will be dark—sure the acoustics will be bad. Finally the commission to go ahead is formally given over his dissent and warnings. Usually there is a Mr. Skillin in Usonia on every building project.

Now, who will build the Temple? After weeks of prospecting, no one can be found who wants to try it. Simple enough —yes—that's the trouble. So simple there is nothing at all to gauge it by. Requires too much imagination and initiative to be safe. The only bids available came in double, or more, our utmost limit. No one really wanted to touch it. Contractors are naturally gamblers, but they usually bet on a sure thing—as they see it.

Now Paul Mueller comes to the rescue, reads the scheme like easy-print. Will build it for only a little over their appropriation—and does it. He takes it easily along for nearly a year but he does it. Doesn't lose much on it in the end. It is exciting to him to rescue ideas, to participate in creation. And together we overcame difficulty after difficulty in the field, where an architect's education is never finished.

This building, however, is finished, to be opened on a Sunday.

I do not want to go. Stay at home.

When the church was opened the phone began to ring. Listened to happy contented voices in congratulation. Finally weary, I take little Francie by the hand to go out into the air with her to get away from it all. Enough.

But just as my hat goes on my head, another ring, a voice, Mr. Skillin's voice—"Take back all I said . . . Light everywhere—all pleased."

"Hear well?"

"Yes, see and hear fine—see it all now."

"Glad."

"Goodbye." At last the doubting member was now sincere in praise and a "good sport" besides.

Francie got tossed in the air. She came down with a squeal of delight.

And that is how it was and is and will be.

Now, even though you are interested in architecture this story is more or less tedious and meaningless to you, as you were fairly warned it would be at the beginning, without close study of the plans and photographs as it is read. I have undertaken here, for once, to indicate the process of building on principle to ensure character and achieve style, as near as I can indicate it by taking Unity Temple to pieces. Perhaps I am not the one to try it.

As for the traditional church as modern building! Religion and art are forms of inner experience—growing richer and deeper as the race grows older. We will never lose either. But I believe religious experience is outgrowing the church—not outgrowing religion but outgrowing the church as an institution. Just as architecture has outgrown the Renaissance and for reasons human, scientific, and similar. I cannot see the ancient institutional form of any church building as anything but sentimental, or survival for burial. The Temple as forum and good-time place—beautiful and inspiring as such—yes. A religious edifice raised in the sense of the old ritual? No. I cannot see it at all as living. It is no longer free.

Of course what is most vitally important in all that is to be explained cannot be said at all. It need not be, I think. Here in this searching process may be seen work, as the boys in the studio would crowd around and participate in it. As you too, perhaps, may see certain wheels go around. Certain hints coming through between the lines may help someone who needs help in comprehending what a building really means.

This brief indication of the problem of building out of the man will not clear up the question as to what is style much either. But a little by way of suggestion, I hope.

Man's struggle to illumine creation, is another tragedy.

[pp. 151–164]

Part V: Reaction in America and Epilogue in Europe (1890-1920)

1. Introduction

The "new architecture" in America, as evolved by Richardson, Sullivan, Root, and Wright and championed by Montgomery Schuyler, would not, as Daniel Burnham remarked to Frank Lloyd Wright, "prevail." Its failure to prevail has been described and rationalized in a variety of ways: as a victory for the Philistine hordes over the enlightened few, as the regional victory of East Coast architects and their Beaux Arts point of view over the Chicago School and its western vitality, as a function of the World's Columbian Exposition (Chicago, 1893) and the "classical" façades of its "White City," as a function of John Wellborn Root's death and the breakup of Sullivan's partnership with Adler, and as a massive failure or misdirection of aesthetic education on all levels in this country. And all these reasons have validity as both reasons and symptoms; but they also, taken collectively, emphasize the role of the embattled individual genius in architecture and read as "great-man history." They deemphasize what may have been the more central causal roles of expansionism and of the new wealth—the new and tremendous potential for "conquest" of the environment. If a failure or misdirection of aesthetic education was at fault, it was a fault almost minor in contrast with the economic growth and the capacity for construction that made it possible to publish the failure on such a grand scale.

The new wealth and the new technology made it possible

31. Cass Gilbert, Woolworth Building (1911–1913), New York City.

to transform the environment in ways for which there were virtually no precedents; they also made it possible for individuals to conduct their lives in ways for which there were no precedents. At the same time the growth of historical and cultural self-consciousness in the nineteenth century had radically increased popular feeling in favor of precedents that could be advertised and demonstrated. For example, it is apparent that some of the robber barons literally went shopping in the historical past for a model in imitation of which their lives could be planned; they chose a sentimentalized (Sir Walter Scott) version of the medieval barony—largely because the range of their wealth made *anything* possible, and the barony offered the illusions of form and order. Perhaps central to an understanding of this whole flux in the late nineteenth century is the observation that man can't tolerate excessive freedom and that he will provide for his own imprisonment if he is too radically freed.

In architecture, Richardson's approach seemed "old fashioned" to the *avant-garde* of the 1890's because he had used traditional materials and a traditional structural technology. On the other hand, architects with a Beaux Arts prejudice, even though some of them had been trained in Richardson's office, were rejecting his work as crude and unsophisticated. The new and vital emphasis on materials that was the core of Richardson's approach tended to be overlooked in the rejection of his brick and masonry technology or in the rejection of the bold clarity of his architectural forms. Sullivan's approach, for all of its excellence, enjoyed a success only as long as there was a premium on architectural economy. As soon as surplus wealth made it possible to tolerate the waste of labor and materials in what Giedion has called "commercial classicism" and "Woolworth Gothic," the practical necessity that supported the clarity and relative severity of Sullivan's approach no longer existed. And Frank Lloyd Wright's prairie houses, as indigenously American as they were, were not designed for the Philistine hordes but for the affluent few who were perceptive enough to appreciate them.

Sullivan, echoed by Wright, dramatized the World's Columbian Exposition as the turning point, the historical moment when the forces of reaction accomplished their victory over the architectural revolutionaries. As Sullivan saw them, the forces of reaction were compound: on the one hand, the East Coast architects together with those western architects who felt themselves to be unsophisticated inferiors; on the other hand, the public, miseducated, its taste perverted by the spectacle of the fair. Thus, for Sullivan the fair ushered in an epoch of diseased architecture. Daniel Burnham, Root's partner and Sullivan's Chicago contemporary who was the fair's chief of construction, regarded it as "this victory of peace . . . when so many American artists joined together in loving emulation and created an epoch. . . ." Our verdict on the fair may very well be closer to Sullivan's than to Burnham's, but in the 1890's there was another ingredient involved: the fair's motto was "Not Matter, but Mind," and the fair was advertised (and popularly accepted) as *art,* for once with money no object. Americans had become accustomed to being regarded and criticized as a people more interested in money than in aesthetic values; and the fair was to answer that criticism, to be a demonstration of American aesthetic hunger and an advertisement of an achieved aesthetic maturity. William Dean Howells, novelist and influential literary critic, saw the fair in these terms. For all his emphasis on the necessity for "realism" in fiction and for all of his argument against separating *literature* from life—when he responded to the fair, Howells separated the visual arts from architectural realism as sharply as did any of his contemporaries. In one of his "Letters of an Altrurian Traveller" (September 28, 1893) Howells remarked that "the Fair City is a bit of Altruria." (Altruria was a utopia Howells had created for literary and critical contrast to the far from utopian America of the 1890's.) For Howells, the fair was:

. . . the first great triumph of Altrurian [utopian] principles among this people in a work of peace; in their mighty civil war they were Altrurian enough; . . . but here for the first time in their pitiless economic struggle, their habitual warfare in which they neither give nor ask quarter, and take no prisoners, the interests submitted themselves to the arts, and lent themselves as frankly to the work as if there had never been a question of money in the world.

In a sense, Howell's reaction offers a key to the architectural and aesthetic dilemma of the fair and of the epoch of which the fair was symptom. The basic assumption was that economic values and aesthetic values are sharply antithetical (as, in the fair's motto, matter is to mind). Once this assumption that art is other than the realities of an urban-industrial economy is granted, then it follows that art is something foreign that is added over and above the economic; or, in terms of the popular metaphor, aesthetic values must "conquer" economic values. The assumption also involves the fallacy of judging the product by the motive: the motive of the fair was to sacrifice money in the interests of achieving the higher values of art (it was expected that the fair would lose money); therefore the fair was a triumph of Altrurian principles. In other words, Howells's experience of the fair was not visual experience of its architecture but literary experience of the abstract statement of value that architecture could be read as having symbolized—a statement of social reform. The assumption that aesthetic values are achieved at the expense of economic values also has two corollaries: If it costs more, it must be better aesthetically; and, Any purely utilitarian building (grain elevator, factory, warehouse, office building) is simply not to be regarded as architecture.

This parochial view of art as something expensive and foreign meant, of course, that the conscious art of Richardson, Sullivan, and Wright was limited in its influence, though Berlage in 1912 seems to have assumed a somewhat broader dissemination of Sullivan's and Wright's points of view than they assumed at the time or than contemporary critics usually assume today. The parochial view also meant that all kinds of anonymous structures simply did not catch or inform the eye since nothing was aesthetically valuable that did not so advertise itself. The aesthetic excitement of Paul Bourget's vision of the exuberant energy and growth of Chicago climaxes in his description of the stockyards; the stockyards were apt to strike the American critic as *The Jungle* (Upton Sinclair, 1906), a concentrated image of the "pitiless economic struggle." As an indirect result, the energies of architectural reform were at cross purposes with the energies of social reform as those energies were expressed (1890–1915) in the Progressive Movement.

European response, as represented in this anthology by Bourget, Berlage, and Gropius, was not hampered by the American assumption of a moral antithesis between economic barbarism and artistic refinement. European criticisms are thus closer to Schuyler's position, though not as concerned with the opposition between the new architecture and conspicuous-consumption classicism. The European concern is with the implied contrast and opposition between the new American architecture and what Gropius calls "our European [historical] nostalgia."

The new architecture did not "prevail" overnight in Europe any more than it did in this country. But European interest in the new American architecture did amount to a ferment of excitement. Mies Van Der Rohe recalls the impact and stimulus of an exhibition of Sullivan's work at The Hague in 1910; Wright's work was first published (with considerable acclaim) in Berlin in the same year; Berlage widely praised both Sullivan's and Wright's work in illustrated lectures and articles after his 1911–1912 trip to America; Gropius's response to an American industrial architecture that would not have been considered architecture at all in this country, and Le Corbusier's interest—all these contributed to and reflected a European affirmation of American architectural ideas. It is somewhat ironic that the perceptiveness of the European response to American architecture in this period is not unlike the perceptive reception that English critics had accorded Melville and Whitman in the 1850's (while Melville and Whitman were being roundly condemned as nonwriters by most of their American contemporaries).

European architects, who were already heavily involved by 1910 in the effort to free themselves from Beaux Arts academicism and to realize their own renaissance of clarity, absorbed the American departures and preserved their energies not only in architecture itself but also in new forms of art education, particularly in the Bauhaus. The displacement of the Bauhaus personnel in the 1930's and the emigration of many of them to this country reinfected American architecture with its own virus and gave us new perspectives on the work of Sullivan and Wright and their revolutionary contemporaries. This is not to say that the architectural clock stopped in America in 1910, only to start again under the impact of the Bauhaus in the 1930's. Wright complained bitterly (and justifiably) toward the end of his life that after all he had gone on working and producing, 1910–1940. But in spite of his complaint his work had been in partial eclipse, and his real reputation has derived not only from the qualities of his work but also from an awakened ability to experience and respond to his work, an ability that depends in large part on the reforms in art education which the Bauhaus and its influence accomplished. That that influence spread as rapidly and as deeply as it did in this country would seem to indicate that the American organism was peculiarly susceptible in the 1930's and 1940's to the virus it had so successfully resisted between 1890 and 1910.

2

Montgomery Schuyler, "The 'Sky-Scraper' up to
 Date," THE ARCHITECTURAL RECORD (New
 York, January–March, 1899), Vol. VIII,
 No. 3, pp. 231–257.

Montgomery Schuyler (1843–1914) was a journalist
who developed into the leading architectural critic of his
time. His stance is far more that of the polemicist and reformer than that of Mrs. Van Rensselaer (see pages 438 ff.)
or Harriet Monroe (see pages 464 ff.). In effect his career
was an extended campaign for what he called "the architecture of the future" and against what Eidlitz had deplored as
"the art of covering one thing with another thing to imitate
a third thing, which, if genuine, would not be desirable." His
"Point of View" as announced in the opening pages of his
American Architecture (New York, 1892) was founded on
the critical premise that "the radical defect of modern architecture in general, if not of American architecture in particular, is the estrangement between architecture and building,
between the poetry and the prose." He argues that architects
should "bring their art more into alliance, more into union,
more into identity with the art of building." He saw in that
alliance-union-identity the promise of "a living, a progressive,
a real architecture," and he regarded the Brooklyn Bridge
as its achievement: "one of the noblest monuments of architecture in the world, as it is one of the greatest and most
honorable works of engineering."

32. Printing House Square, New York City, in 1903. *Left to right:* Richard Morris Hunt, Tribune Building; Robert H. Robertson, American Tract Society; George B. Post, Times Building.

Greeley   *Franklin*

The "Sky-Scraper" up to Date

It is strange that the solution of a building problem so new as that presented by the steel-framed tall building should have apparently so largely ceased to be experimental. The American architect is a good deal fonder than his co-worker in other countries of proving all things; he is by no means so much inclined to hold fast that which is good. On the contrary, he is still altogether too much disposed rather to vindicate his own "originality" than to essay the task, at once more modest and more difficult, of "shining with new gracefulness through old forms." Of course his originality will be less crude, and more truly original, in proportion to his education, meaning both his knowledge and his discipline. Nothing can be more depressing than the undertaking to do "something new" by a man who is unaware what has already been done, or who has not learned how it is done. When, within a quarter of a century, the practicable height of commerical buildings has been raised, by successive movements and successive inventions, from five stories to twenty-five, we should expect, given the preference for originality that is born in the American architect, and the absolute necessity for originality that has been thrust upon him by these new mechanical devices, some very wild work, indeed, much wilder than we have had. What nobody could have expected, when the elevator came in to double the practicable height of commercial buildings, and even less when the steel-framed construction came in again to double the height made practicable by the elevator alone, is what has actually happened, and that is a consensus upon a new architectural type. The general treatment of the "sky-scraper" is already conventional, in the sense of being agreed upon. It is nearly as distinct an architectural type as the Greek temple or the Gothic cathedral. The fury of experimentation seems already to have subsided, and the designers to be all working upon recognized lines and executing variations within understood limits. All this is the work of twenty-five years, since the vertical extension made possible by the elevator began to be recognized in building. Nay, it is really the work of ten, since the steel frame came in to supplement the elevator. The elevator doubled the height of office buildings, and the steel-frame doubled it again, and yet there is less of eccentricity and freakishness; more of conformity and homogeneousness, among the twenty-story buildings than there used to be among the five-story buildings.

The first business buildings in which the possibilities of the elevator were recognized were the Tribune Building and the Western Union Building in New York,* which were concurrently under construction twenty-five years ago. They were much more conspicuous and comment-provoking than even the St. Paul and the Park Row† now are, because they were alone and because lower New York then had a skyline, from which they alone, excepting the church spires, were raised and detached. The skyline was "the purple line of humbler roofs," built to the limit as that limit was set by the power of ascension of the unassisted human leg. Through this line of five stories the new monsters protruded in a portentous fashion, and though really they were but of half as many stories again as the older edifices that formed the skyline, they were more distinctive features than the successors which are four and even five times as high as the old-fashioned edifices. Now, New York has no skyline at all. It is all interruptions, of various heights and shapes and sizes, not even peaks in a mountain range, but scattered or huddled towers which have nothing to do with each other or with what is below. A clever British observer says with truth that New York from either river is "hideous and magnificent," for that it "cries aloud of savage and unregulated energy."

It is true that the first two elevator buildings had visible roofs, the one a lofty mansard with three-story dormers, the other a steep wedge, and that they were, therefore, taller than some of their successors which contained more stories, as well as more shapely. But they were in reality timid beginnings. It came soon to be seen that, even with walls of actual masonry, it was profitable to build full twice as many stories

* Tribune Building (1873–1875), Printing House Square, designed by Richard Morris Hunt (1827–1895), see illustration 32. Western Union Building (1874–1875), designed by George B. Post (1837–1913).

† St. Paul (1889–1890), Broadway and Ann Street, designed by George B. Post. Park Row or Syndicate Building (1897–1898), designed by Robert H. Robertson (1849–1919). At the time Schuyler was writing, this was, at 32 stories, the tallest building in the city.

with the elevator as had been practicable without it. Ten or twelve stories became the limit. When the height varied from seven stories to twelve was our period of experimentation in commercial building. There was a great deal of wild work, and some interesting work, but there was no entirely successful work. There was no "convention." Designers were not agreed with each other, and a designer often appeared to be at odds with himself, upon the very data of his artistic problem. They divided their fronts and grouped their stories capriciously and eccentrically. In the face of the new requirements they ignored that primary truths of design were as applicable to ten stories as to three. They would have saved themselves and the people who had to look at their work a grievous trouble by merely reverting to Aristotle and bearing in mind the precept of the father of criticism, that a work of art must have a beginning, a middle, and an end.

The architect who first impressed upon his contemporaries and the public that this precept was applicable to high buildings was a public benefactor. It was from his inculcation of a forgotten truth that the consensus in the design of tall buildings began, of which we everywhere see the results. Confusion became order in his path. I do not undertake to say who it was who first designed a tall front in conformity with this ancient truth, and sharpened Aristotle's wise saw with a modern instance. But I should say that the designer who enforced it most powerfully was the architect of the Union Trust Company's Building on Broadway. He had come from making, in the north front of the Times Building,* a success which was only partial by reason of the indistinctness and confusion of the primary divisions, when he perceived, from a contemplation of the executed work, what was the matter with it, and proceeded, in the design of the Union Trust, to remedy those defects. There is here no confusion about the principal features of the composition nor any doubt about their forming an architectural countenance. The basement is distinctly set off from the superstructure, and this in turn from the crowning feature, the roof and its appendages, and the intermediate stories are plainly intermediate and connect-

* Union Trust Building, 80 Broadway opposite Rector Street, designed by George B. Post (1837–1913); Times Building (1888), now Pace Institute, on Park Row at Printing House Square, also designed by Post. See illustration 32. The Times Tower in Times Square was designed by Cyrus L. W. Eidlitz (1853–1921) and postdates (1902–1904) this article (1899).

ing. The force of the arrangement is independent of the style, a more or less Richardsonian Romanesque, independent of the detail, though this is studied and successful, independent even of the features adopted to carry it out. It does not essentially matter whether the central and chief division be formed by openings running through it, as in the Union Trust, or by rows of small and similar openings, which leave the shaft to assert itself as nearly as may be as an equal and monotonous surface. The essential point is that there should be a triple division, and that the three parts should both assert themselves as parts and combine into a whole.

This is the agreement, the convention, which so many designers of sky-scrapers have adopted that whatever sky-scraper does not conform to it becomes what a contributor of yours is in the habit of calling an "aberration." Let it be noted, however, that aberration is not necessarily a term of reproach. It is, according to the dictionary, "a deviation from the customary structure or type." Such a departure may or may not be justified by its result. If there is less reason in it than in the customary structure, if the deviation seems to come from mere caprice, then the designer has failed to justify it. If, and insofar as it is more reasonable, more expressive, more beautiful, then the designer has justified it and is to be congratulated. Our latest architecture contains in its sky-scrapers examples of both kinds. But let us first consider the more noteworthy of recent tall buildings which conform to the convention. In these the connection is more specific than that of a mere triple division. It is founded upon the analogy of a column, with its division into base, shaft, and capital, and even conforms, as far as may be, to the proportions of the classic column. That is to say, the shaft, the middle division, is much taller and very much plainer than the base or the capital. The plainness of it is as essential to the analogy as the excess. The nearer it comes to being a quite monotonous mass, the more value have the variations and ornaments of the base and the capital to which its plainness is a relief and a foil. It may doubtless be subdivided, so as to be an organic whole within a larger whole. But this subdivision is difficult to manage, for several reasons.

While the inheritance of three thousand years may be taken as a warrant for the primary triple division, which thus passes without challenging inquiry, a subsequent subdivision needs an explanation. To be "rhythmical," this subdivision must itself be triple, and to triply subdivide a member of a triple composition, without thereby confusing the primary division and thus the unity of the work is a difficult feat, of which the success has not been worth the trouble in any example of the tall building known to me. It is, of course, possible to introduce at the bottom and at the top of the shaft a story recalling the transition, in the actual column, to the base and to the capital. This has been done in the Union Trust with success. But the bonding of the shaft itself is recognized in the column as a modern and corrupt interference with classic purity. In the Empire Building,* this bonding has been attempted by means of stories intercalated at equal distances, framed in emphatic moldings, and treated with some separateness, in what we may still call the shaft. The principal front of the Empire, the side, is, however, so fortunate in its extent that its altitude is no longer the principal dimension, and that the analogy of the column is not directly recalled. But even here it seems that the decorative top and the decorative base would be more effective, and the composition clearer, if the central mass had been treated with absolute uniformity. The most that can be said for the intercalated stories is that they do not much interfere with the monotony of the central mass. But they interfere enough, it seems to me, to indicate that the architect did not appreciate the high architectural value of the monotony, in conjunction with the more ornamental parts. Any difference in the treatment of the several stories not only is, but must appear, arbitrary and capricious. By this device, one story is made to differ from another story in importance, whereas it is not only true, but it is known to every believer that above the ground floor, or the ground floor and the first floor, the stories are all alike. In the Washington Life,† it is true, it is the third story which is the quarters of the corporation that is the builder and owner of the edifice, and this fact is properly enough recognized in signalizing the story in question by a somewhat greater ornateness, which, however, by no means amounts to a separateness of treatment. Indeed, nothing is to be gained by cloaking or dissembling

* Empire Building (1896), Broadway and Rector Street, designed by (Francis H.) Kimball and Thompson. See illustration 10.

† Washington Life (1898), Broadway and Liberty Street, designed by Cyrus L. W. Eidlitz.

facts that everybody knows, and such a fact it is that the rentable stories of an office building are all identical in function and equal in dignity. An attempt to disguise this takes away from the architecture in which it is made the excuse of honest utilitarian necessity. The famous plea of the pickpocket is the best the "sky-scraper" can make for itself: "Il faut vivre." It is ill with that "sky-scraper" upon which the magistrate can retort "Je ne vois pas la nécessité."* To that crusher the architect exposes his sky-scraper who makes capricious distinctions between stories that everybody knows serve similar purposes. The St. Paul is laid wide open to it by the presentation of its stories as half stories, and the inclusion of two of them in each apparent story, as is done throughout the "architecturesque" part of the work, the three-sided tower faced with limestone, that occupies the truncated angle, and is crowned by the rich order. Doubtless the doubling of the stories "gives scale," and a swaggering aspect to the structure, and avoids the squareness of the openings that would result from leaving the actual arrangement undisguised. But it is plain even from the architecturesque parts that the facts have been suppressed instead of being expressed. A cellular arrangement as equal and monotonous as that of a honeycomb has been overlaid by an architectural arrangement which has as little as possible to do with it, and deprives it of its one excuse for being, that it is as it must be. "I do not see the necessity," the spectator may and must exclaim. The tall and lanky opening which results from overlaying the real wall with an architectural trellis is no more graceful a form than the nearly square opening which would have ensued if the wall had been let alone. It is true that the orders could not have been applied. But it is very questionable whether the ten orders are as effective as the twenty actual stories would have been. In any case the twenty superposed stories appear alongside, in the parts that are not architecturesque, and put the architecture to an open shame. Not only do we not see the necessity, but we see that there is no necessity, and a caprice like that is fatal to a building which must be justified by its necessity or not at all.

Upon the whole the most successful of the sky-scrapers are those in which the shaft is made nothing of, in which

* "It is necessary to live. . . . I do not see the necessity."

the necessary openings occur at the necessary places, are justified by their necessity, but draw no attention to themselves. They become impressive not as units, but as a series, and this may be a very fine impressiveness. Rectangular holes are not pretty, but ten stories of them all alike are sure of making their effect. In the St. Paul, the unarchitecturesque fronts which the spectator is requested to ignore, but cannot, in which the square holes stand confessed and nothing is done to them, are to one spectator more impressive than the evidently factitious architecture alongside of them. They would be more impressive still if the cornices which mark the arbitrary architectural division of the truncated front were not continued across them to the impairment of the effect of reality that they would produce if they were left alone, and to the interruption of a monotony so often repeated that it would become almost sublime. The question which Lord Melbourne was in the habit of asking his colleagues, when they asked what ground he meant to take on some new political issue, is one which might properly be addressed to a good many designers of sky-scrapers who are solicitous what to do with the main body of their buildings: "Can't you let it alone?"

Of course, a shaft can be effectively variegated without denying either the equality of importance and similarity of purpose between its different stories, or compromising its own importance as an organic part of the building. This may be done, as we shall see hereafter, by the introduction of molded ornament in terra-cotta, which is so plastic that it seems to require ornament, and in which elaborate ornament is so cheap, if it be often repeated, as not to be out of place even in a building of bare utility. It may also be done in color, and that is one of the lessons of the St. James,* on many accounts a very interesting building. It is doubtless a good thing that most of the designers of tall buildings have avoided any contrast of color, and have brought their baked clay as nearly as might be to the tint of their stonework. There is safety in monochrome, and whoso departs from it does so at his peril. But few critical observers of the St. James will be disposed to deny that its designer has vindicated his right to leave this safe refuge. It is a pity, of course, that

* St. James (1897–1898), Broadway and Twenty-sixth Street, designed by Bruce Price (1845–1903).

the emphasis of color should not go with the emphasis of structure, that the weak tint should cover the frame and the strong tint the filling. It is a mistake to introduce recessed courses in a screen of red brick for the sake of the shadows, and then to nullify the shadows by introducing a course of white brick at the bottom of the recess. But the middle part of the St. James is nevertheless effectively relieved of monotony without denying the identity of purpose in its different stories and without confusing the composition.

This successful exception does not invalidate the rule that the shaft is impressive by its extent and its monotony of repetition, and as an interval of plainness and repose between the more elaborate base and the elaborate capital. It is these features which may properly appeal to attention on their own account, as well as on account of their contribution to the total results. The ornament which is meant to be worthy of the closest inspection is naturally given to the base, although the capital is properly the more ornate member. There is a dictum of Ruskin which is rather exceptional among his dicta as being the expression of mere and obvious good sense. Ornament, he says, may be, or must be, in greater effective quantity at the top of a building, but the most exquisite should be kept at the bottom. Accordingly all the designers make their entrances as well worth looking at as they can, and, indeed, it would be a solecism not to signalize the means by which a population mounting into the hundreds gains and leaves its place of daily business. Perhaps the commonest device for giving importance to the entrance is to extend it through two stories. Of course this device in a building of which the primary purpose is to get the maximum of rentable area is illogical as well as wasteful. But it must be owned that the architects who have fined their clients in the rental value of the space in the second story over the entrance, space which might have been rented for a hundred pence and given to the poor owner, get their architectural compensation from the process. The Broadway entrance to the Singer Building* has the air of a burrow, and there is an inadequacy bordering on meanness in the

* Singer Building (1897–1898), Broadway and Liberty Street, designed by Ernest Flagg (1857–1947). This is not Flagg's Small Singer Building (1902–1904), 516–563 Broadway, and still in existence, nor is it his Singer Tower (1906–1908), 140 Broadway, and still in existence.

actual entrance to the Park Row. Many designers who, although on architecture they are bent, have yet a frugal mind, reconcile their conflicting emotions by confining the actual entrance to the ground floor, and still signalizing it by some special treatment of the opening above it, with which the entrance is supposed to be architecturally incorporated. This is the arrangement adopted in the Dun Building,* where, indeed, in the Broadway front, the "feature" is not even over the entrance, and in the longer front of the Singer Building. In the St. Paul it is the sculptured figures which are represented in the act of carrying twenty stories of wall that emphasize the entrance without sacrificing space. In the Washington Life it is the two-story order at the center of the longer front, which is too nearly an engaged order to constitute or represent a portico, and has the air of having been set up against the building. The same thing is true of the much larger and more conspicuous order in front of the New York Life,† an impressive feature in itself which loses much of its impressiveness when it is seen in connection with the building with which it is not architecturally incorporated. The effect of the actually engaged order of the American Surety Building,‡ with the columns in antis behind it is very much better than either of these inadequately projected orders, and is, indeed, about the most successful entrance upon this scheme that any of the tall buildings has to show. Another scheme is that of confining the entrance to the ground story, and surmounting it with a decoration which does not pretend to subserve any other function than that of signalizing it. This is the case with the free-standing circular pediment or panel over the entrance to the Bayard Building,§ and it may be commended as an example to such architects as are quite sure that they can equal the author of that work in the attractiveness of their surface decoration. To other designers it may be said that the most eligible method of giving importance to their entrances seems to be

* Dun Building (1896), Broadway and Reade Street, designed by Harding and Gooch.
† New York Life (1896), Broadway, Catharine Lane, Leonard and Elm streets, designed by McKim, Mead and White.
‡ American Surety Building (1894), Broadway and Pine Street, designed by Bruce Price.
§ Bayard Building (later Condict Building) (1897–1898), 66 Bleecker Street, designed by Louis Sullivan. This building still stands, stripped, however, of its original "cap" and of all its ornament. Cf. illustration 26.

that of running the opening into the second story if they can gain the consent of their owner to that sacrifice.

The entrance is in most cases the chief feature of the basement, of the architectural base. But it is not the only feature —and, indeed, the most effective treatment is that in which the whole substructure becomes a feature. If one is to forego detailed functional expression in favor of abstract architectonics, the height of a commercial building before the elevator came in suggested a height of base which is in agreeable proportion to the "sky-scraper." This suggestion has been acted upon by many designers who have underpinned the shafts of their tall buildings with a four- or five-story building, designed as such and fairly complete in itself. The basement of the Dun Building offers a very fairly successful example of this treatment. The crowning member, including all above the eleventh story, seems distinctly infelicitous, both in proportion and treatment, and the variegation of the shaft sufficient to destroy the effect of repetition, which becomes more impressive in proportion to the extent of the series, without substituting any other. But, granting the author his two-story openings, which may at least conceivably light a lofty apartment with a mezzanine floor, the four-story basement seems to me a very well designed building, a composition fairly complete in itself, and at the same time a fitting preparation for the superstructure. In this latter respect the executed work is a distinct improvement upon the original design, which showed the basement as a five-story building with a quite unmeaning trophy to signalize the entrance which it does not designate, and especially with a continuous balcony which emphatically cuts it off from what is above. The restudy the basement has received has done it a great deal of good. The removal of a story from the lofty openings has made them much more tractable. The omission of the huge window frame of the front is a clear gain. But especially the confinement of the balcony to the center of each front, while continuing its line in a belt along the interval of wall, while it still leaves the basement to assert itself as a feature, also allows it to be allied with the superstructure, and substitutes at the angle the effect of continuity for that interruption.

The effect of the triple arcade in the long front of this basement has been very much amplified and extended in the

long arcade which is the most striking feature of the flank
of the Empire Building. This flank, confronting Trinity
churchyard, and thus having as good an assurance of
permanent visibility from an effective distance as can be had
in New York, offered a very unusual opportunity, of which
it will not be disputed, that, so far as this arcade is concerned, the designers have fully availed themselves. Doubtless the tenants of the floor above the springing may consider
that they have been sacrificed to architecture. But this arcade
of seven openings, on a scale twice that employed elsewhere
in the building or in its neighbors, is really architectural,
really a stately series, with its effective abutment of a much
more solid flank of wall and its effective correspondence in
scale with the order, also embracing two stories, at the top
of the building. It must be now evident how much these two
features, and with them the building, would gain in effect if
the interval between them were an interval as nearly as
might be of complete repose, a repetition twelve times of an
identical design for a story of offices.

But it is the crowning member, the capital, which offers
the greatest opportunity for individuality and variety of
treatment. It is apt to be the only part which is visible from
a distance. Anything like conformity is out of the question.
New York has no skyline, and is not likely to have any, so
long as the estimates of the most profitable height of commercial buildings vary from ten stories to thirty, and as the
law does not intervene to draw the line of altitude. It is
impossible for a designer to conform to what exists, much
less to what may exist after his building is completed. All
that he can do is to make his own building as presentable and
shapely as the conditions will permit. It is maintained by
some critics that a strict adherence to the conditions compels
an architect to stop with the completion of his parallelepiped,
and to forbear a visible roof. Doubtless the flat roof enables
him to fill his honeycomb level to the top with a row of cells
for the working bees. But it does not enable him to give any
form or comeliness to the skyline of his building. The
parallelepiped is not an architectural form, as anybody will
have impressed upon him by looking at the random rows
of parallelepipeds in lower New York from across the East
or the North River. The practical owner may have had some
reason who objected to his architect's design for a steeply

roofed ten-story building, upon the ground that "That's all right on the Rhine, but it ain't business." Nevertheless, he was insisting upon a defacement of the city, which is in great part wanton. For a visible roof will obviously supply additional accommodation at a less cost than that of building "to the limit" all the way up. Few sensitive spectators can have observed from afar the towering mass of the American Surety Building without feeling that the tall shaft needs the crown that would convert it into a campanile. On the other hand, few sensitive spectators can have failed to experience a touch of gratitude to the architect of the American Tract Society* for having enclosed part of that edifice in a picturesque hood, even though the hood be avowedly extraneous to the building, which is visibly enclosed in it and completed without reference to it. The St. Paul has no visible roof, but it has a true crown in the tall order, encrusted with decoration effective from every point from which it can be seen at all, which surmounts the three-fronted tower which the architect has arbitrarily set off as the "architecturesque part" of his building, leaving the architecture of the more shameful parts to take care of itself. This crown is in itself a grateful object, and the more grateful from a point of view from which the edifice it crowns cannot be made out in detail and may be ignored. Of substitutes for a visible roof, in cases where the architect felt bound to build to the limit, vertically and laterally, one of the most successful is the crowning order of the St. James, with an oriel framed in metal in each intercolumniation, and the effect of the whole feature greatly enhanced by its projection from the plane of the wall below. This overhanging of the top is evidently as feasible and legitimate in a steel frame as in a timber frame, in which it has been so often and so effectively employed. It offers an architectural opportunity which it is strange should not have been oftener embraced. In the present instance, it has been done rather timidly, as very likely it had to be. But in a free-standing building, or even in a corner building, it seems that it might sometimes be done more boldly and with a corresponding increase of effectiveness.

The same device is employed, though with even less em-

---

* American Tract Society (1894), Nassau and Spruce streets, designed by Robert H. Robertson. See illustration 32.

phasis, although to an excellent result, in the Washington
Life Building. This building is acclaimed by everybody as
one of the very best of the sky-scrapers, and it owes its
whole effectiveness to the treatment of the capital, to the
introduction and the treatment of a visible roof. The base
is without pretensions, except in the portico of the entrance,
where, as has already been remarked, the practicable projection does not suffice to give it the effect of a portico,
while on the other hand it is not incorporated with the
building. The shaft is reduced to its very simplest expression,
a mere repetition of the openings of the tiers of cells, which
leaves it as nearly as may be a plain shaft. The detail of
the lower stories, successful in scale and careful both in
design and execution, offers nothing striking. But the steep
wedge-shaped roof seems to have been designed "not
laboriously, but luckily." It gives character to the building
below it and makes it a picturesque object equally in a near
and in a distant view. The projection of the order, slight as
it is, is very effective, almost indispensable as a detachment
of the capital. The dormers are exceedingly well designed
in themselves and most effectively relieved against the green-
ish bronze of the tiles, the color of which is one of the chief
successes of the work, from the pictorial point of view. The
widening of the building at the rear gives rise to an unavoidable awkwardness in the roofing, as seen from the south,
the quarter from which the illustration of the Broadway front
is taken. The awkwardness is mitigated as much as possible,
and will disappear when the side comes to be concealed by
another tall building. This contingency is contemplated by
the evidently provisional treatment of the south wall, a treatment which is an unusually judicious compromise between
the conflicting claims of the owner's pocket and the architect's wish to bestow comeliness upon "the more shameful
parts," and to make them presentable so long as they are
visible. Meanwhile, however, the most favorable view of the
Broadway front is that from the northwest, from which the
provisional architecture is not seen, and which the illustrations do not include. Our street architecture offers very
few glimpses so satisfying as that of this wedge of furrowed
bronze, with the single bold dormer, so lucky in scale and
in design, relieved against it. Not less good in its way is the
broad northern flank with the four dormers, and scarcely

less good the west front, which "shines over city and river" standing knee-deep in the lower buildings of the waterfront. If this had been the principal front, the architect would very probably have introduced a single dormer above, to unite and dominate the two, and thus have reproduced the effect so familiar and always so effective in the timberwork of the German Renaissance. The conspicuous roof, with the separate treatment of the upper stories of the wall, emphasized by the order, and the slight expansion which it marks, constitute the capital of the building, and it is plainly a feature with which no equal and uncompromising parallelepiped, built to the limit in all dimensions, can at all compete. . . .

All the buildings thus far mentioned have been designed in general conformity with the convention which enforces not only the Aristotelian triple division, but the more specific analogy of the column. But it should not be forgotten that the assumption of that analogy, convenient as it is, is, after all, only an assumption, and a more or less arbitrary assumption, since it not only does not facilitate, but may even obstruct, the detailed expression in design of structure and of function. That the Aristotelian maxim itself is an assumption, or that the application of it to architecture is arbitrary, not many designers or critics can be prepared to admit. It is not necessary that they should be psychologists, and able to explain in words why a building triply divided should be more "agreeable to the spirit of man" than a building which consists from top to bottom in tiers of similar cells, any more than that they should be able to explain why in fenestration the arithmetic progression 3, 5, and 7 is agreeable. On either point they can safely take an appeal to universal consciousness. *Securus orbis judicabit.** But it is also true that the "sky-scraper" is in fact a series of equal cells, and that the only suggestions for a triple division that inhere in the conditions are the facts that the ground floor has a different destination from that of the floors above, and suggests a distinctive treatment of the bottom, and the fact that a visible roof, or in default of it the necessity for a protective and projecting cornice, compels a distinctive treatment for the top. Almost without exception, the designers of the tall buildings make a further assumption, which is not only

---

* The verdict of the world will be conclusive.

arbitrary but manifestly baseless, and that is that in designing them they are designing buildings of masonry, instead
of merely wrapping skeletons of metal in fire-resisting
material. That basements should be more solid than super-
structures; that arches should have visible abutments; that
walls should "reveal" their thickness: these and many more
of the traditions of masonry have no relevancy at all to the
new construction. If architects make and we allow these
assumptions, we ought not to forget that they are baseless
assumptions, and that the best work done according to them
is not a solution, but an evasion of the problem presented
by the modern office building. That is why an aberration, a
"deviation from the customary structure or type," is not
necessarily condemnable, may, on the contrary, be highly
laudable. It all depends upon whether the departure is a
mere caprice of the designer, or an attempt to come closer
to reason and reality than is possible under the conventional
treatment.

Decidedly an aberration is the Singer Building in lower
Broadway. This scarcely comes within our scope, since the
building is not an example of the skeleton construction, and
rests at the modest ten stories, which seems to be the commercially practicable limit of a structure with real walls.
Considering the enormous costliness of the land on which
it stands, this self-restraint indicates either a very obstinate
or a very facile owner, who may well be astonished at his
own moderation in contenting himself with half the rentable
area he might have had. Commercially, and in spite of the
brand-newness and smartness of its modish Parisian detail,
the Singer Building is a reversion, advantageous as it might
be, on civic grounds, to restrict the height of all commercial
buildings to the height to which its owner has voluntarily
restricted himself. Moderate as this height is in comparison
with the neighbors it has yet seemed excessive to the architect, who has bent his efforts to the task of keeping it down.
This he has done by a triple division, accentuated not only
by horizontal members emphatic to the verge, if not beyond
the verge, of extravagance, but by a change of material in
the different divisions, the lower being a monochrome of
light stone and the middle a field of red brick relieved with
stone. Nay, the principal divisions are so emphasized and
the subordinate divisions so slurred that a ten-story building

presents the appearance of one of three stories, with a corresponding exaggeration of scale. At least until a legal limit is put upon the height of buildings, this is likely to remain unique. But while it does not invite imitation, one has to own that a thing of which it is questionable whether it was worth doing has been unquestionably well done.

Of another deviation from the customary type, the Park Row Building, it is not easy to discern the motive. This structure has the distinction, which is to be hoped it may retain, of the tallest yet, and confronts the next tallest, the St. Paul, across the street, which is more properly an alley. It can scarcely be said to be "by merit raised to that bad eminence," although, like its neighbor, it has the salutary effect of a warning rather than of an example. In each case there are inherent awkwardnesses in the problem which were obviously difficult to surmount, and which have obviously not been surmounted. But the design of the principal front of the Park Row, which in effect comprises the architecture, is noteworthy for its rejection of the convention upon which most of the recent tall buildings have been designed, without substituting for it any scheme that is obviously more rational, or that is even readily apprehensible. Laterally there is an emphatic triple division, into flanking walls kept as plain and solid as the practical requirements will allow, and a more open center, consisting of five superposed orders, not counting the two-story colonnade of the basement. The relation of these orders is by no means felicitous. Some are stilted on pedestals of a story in height, while others stand directly upon the entablatures of those below, without apparent reason. Vertically, there is no clear division. It is not apparent whether the first two stories or the first five constitute the architectural base. The upper five pretty clearly constitute the capital, being occupied by an order more developed than those below, although the cornice that marks them off from what is below is no more important than other horizontal lines which can have no such special significance. The sixteen stories below this cornice may be taken as the shaft, and by looking very hard, it is possible to discern that this is meant to be triply subdivided into a beginning of five stories, containing an order furnished with pedestals, a middle of seven, containing two orders directly superposed, and an end of four, containing another order, while the inter-

mediate divisions are marked by balconies. But the principal
and the subordinate divisions are so nearly equal in emphasis
as to produce uncertainty and confusion, and to excuse the
cursory observer for declaring that the front shows no composition at all. Without going so far as that, it seems safe
to say that the architect would have done better if he had
accepted and abided by the current convention.

Very different is the aberration presented by the Bayard
Building in Bleecker Street. There is nothing capricious in
the general treatment of this structure. It is an attempt, and
a very serious attempt, to found the architecture of a tall
building upon the facts of the case. The actual structure is
left or, rather, is helped, to tell its own story, This is the
thing itself. Nobody who sees the building can help seeing
that. Neither the analogy of the column, nor any other
tradition or convention, is allowed to interfere with the task
of clothing the steel frame in as expressive forms as may
be. There is no attempt to simulate the breadth and massiveness proper to masonry in a frame of metal that is merely
wrapped in masonry for its own protection. The flanking
piers, instead of being broadened to the commercially allowable maximum, are attenuated to the mechanically allowable
minimum. Everywhere the drapery of baked clay is a mere
wrapping, which clings so closely to the frame as to reveal
it, and even to emphasize it. This is true at least of the
uprights, for it seems to me a defect in the general design,
from the designer's own point of view, that it does not take
enough account of the horizontal members. As anybody may
see in a steel cage not yet concealed behind its screens of
masonry, these are as important to the structure as the uprights. In the Bayard they are largely ignored, for the panels
which mark the different floors are apparently mere inser-
tions, answering no structural purpose, and there is no suggestion of any continuous horizontal members, such as, of
course, exist and are even necessary to stability. Mr. Sullivan,
some years ago, wrote a very interesting paper on the aesthetics of the tall building, of which the fundamental position
was that form must follow function, and that "where function does not vary form does not vary." These are propositions
from which nobody who believes that architecture is an art
of expression will dissent, and with which the present writer
heartily agrees. But in applying them to the case in question,

Mr. Sullivan declared that the lower two (or possibly three) stories of a tall office building had a destination so different from that of the superstructure, that a distinguishing treatment for them was not only required but demanded, and that the uppermost story in turn, being in great part devoted to the "circulating system" of the building, should also be differentiated. I remember suggesting to him that it was in fact only the ground floor which could be said to differ in function from its successors and that his inclusion of additional stories may have been inspired by an instinctive desire to obtain a base more proportional, according to our inherited notions of proportion, to a lofty superstructure than a single story could furnish. However that may be, in the Bayard it is the ground floor that is treated as the base. Even the second story "counts in" with the superstructure, to which logically it belongs. In spite of the separate treatment of the ground floor, the continuity of the structure is felt and expressed, even in the design of the capitals, which are plainly not real capitals, spreading to carry a weight of greater area, but mere efflorescences of decoration. It is not a question whether two or three stories would not be more effectively proportional to the superstructure than one. It is a question of fact. The result, whatever else one may think of it, is a sense of reality very different from what we get from the sky-scrapers designed on conventional lines. It puts them to the same sort of shame to which the great roof trusses of the Manufactures Building in Chicago* put the imitative architecture with which they were associated. Not that the gauntness and attenuation of the resulting architecture are in this case altogether agreeable to an eye accustomed to the factitious massiveness of the conventional treatment. But, at the worst, this front recalls Rufus Choate's famous toast to the Chief Justice: "We look upon him as the East Indian upon his wooden idol. We know that he is ugly, but we feel that he is great." We feel that this front is a true and logical exposition of the structure. If we find it ugly notwithstanding, that may be our own fault. If we can find no failure in expressiveness, the architect may retort upon us that it is no uglier than it ought to be.

* Manufactures Building (1893), World's Columbian Exposition, Chicago, designed by George B. Post. The main roof of iron and glass arched an area 1,400 feet long by 385 feet wide. The brilliant engineering of the roof trussing was masked by an elaborate "Corinthian" décor.

Meanwhile the aesthetic, as distinguished from the scientific, attractiveness of the Bayard Building without doubt resides in the decoration which has been lavished upon it, and which is of a quality that no other designer could have commanded. I am unable to agree with Mr. Sturgis's* condemnation of the crowning feature of the building, in a recent number of this magazine, as "most unfortunate." In fact, the upper two stories are internally one story, the upper floor being a gallery surrounding a well extending through both, and lighted from above. Doubtless the arches and the rudimentary tracery are not forms of metallic architecture, but they do not belong to metallic architecture. The arches are in fact of brickwork, faced with terra-cotta, and the thrust of them is visibly, as well as actually, taken up by the tie rods at the springing. The intermediate uprights, the mullions, cease at this level, while the prolongation of the principal uprights is clearly denoted by the winged figures under the cornice. A designer who has adhered so strictly to the unpromising facts of the steel cage through eleven stories is scarcely to be severely blamed for "treating resolution" to this extent in the twelfth. If the building, apart from its wealth of decoration, recalls the works of contemporaneous engineering rather than of historical architecture, that also is "as it must be." The Bayard Building is the nearest approach yet made, in New York, at least, to solving the problem of the sky-scraper. It furnishes a most promising starting point for designers who may insist upon attacking that problem instead of evading it, and resting in compromises and conventions.

* Russell Sturgis (1836–1909) was an architect who studied with Leopold Eidlitz and in Munich. By the 1890's he was recognized as the dean of architectural critics in this country; his criticism appears now to have been more facile, less trenchant than Schuyler's, and somewhat more conservative.

3

Paul Bourget, OUTRE-MER / IMPRESSIONS OF AMERICA (New York, 1895), pp. 114–129, translated from *Outre-Mer / notes sur l'amérique* (Paris, 1894).

Paul Bourget (1852–1935) was a French man of letters: journalist, essayist, poet, and novelist. He is associated with the "passive disillusion" of late nineteenth-century *décadence;* his excitement about Chicago, its architecture and stockyards, the "colossal effort of imagination" it represents, seems somewhat contrary to the reputation he had in the 1890's. The "tower of the auditorium" is the tower of Louis Sullivan's building (see illustration 25), and from it Bourget in 1893 looked out on a Chicago which Sigfried Giedion was later to regard as the birthplace of twentieth-century architecture, "the perfect illustration of American audacity in the direct assault that was made upon its problems."

Chicago in an autumn morning from the tower of the Auditorium.—It is two hundred and seventy feet high, and it crowns and dominates a chaotic cyclopean structure which connects a colossal hotel with a colossal theatre. One's first visit on arriving should be here, in order to get the strongest impression of the enormous city, lying black on the shore of its blue lake.

Last night, when the conductor called out the name of the station at which I was to leave the train, a frightful storm, such as one experiences nowhere but in America, was deluging the whole country with cataracts of water, and between the station and the hotel I could see nothing but the outlines of gigantic buildings hanging, as it were, from a dark sky streaked with lightning, and between them small wooden houses, so frail that it seemed as if the furious wind must scatter their ruins to the four quarters of the tempest-tossed city.

This morning the sky is clear, with a soft, warm clearness, washed clean by the rain. It brings out all the more strikingly the dark coloring of the city, as it is reflected back from the deeper azure of Lake Michigan, plowed with steamboats like a sea. Far as the eye can reach Chicago stretches away, its flat roofs and its smoke—innumerable columns of whitey-gray smoke. They rise straight upward, then stoop to heap themselves into vapory capitals, and at last meet together in a dome above the endless avenues.

It needs but a few minutes for the eyes to become accustomed to the strange scene. Then you discern differences of height among these levels. Those of only six or seven stories seem to be the merest cottages, those of two stories are not to be distinguished from the pavement, while the "buildings" of fourteen, fifteen, twenty stories, uprise like the islands of the Cyclades as seen from the mountains of Negroponte.

A mighty murmur uprises from below like that of no other city. There is an incessant tinkle of locomotive bells, that seem to be sounding in advance the knell of those they are about to crush. They are everywhere, crossing the streets, following the lake shore, passing over the river which rolls its leaden waters under soot-colored bridges, meeting and crossing each other's tracks, pursuing and overtaking one another. Now you distinguish an elevated road, and there, beside the railways on the level of the street, you see other trains on the avenues, three or four cars long, but without locomotive. It is the cable system. And there are steamers lowering their yards and coming to anchor in the harbor.

Yes, the scene is strange even to unreality, when one reminds oneself that this Babel of industry grew out of a tiny frontier post—Fort Dearborn. The Indians surprised it and massacred the garrison about 1812. I am not very far beyond my youth, and yet how many men have I known that were alive then, and how near that date is! In 1871, that is to say, later than the Franco-Prussian War, there was fire writhing around this very place where I am standing this bright morning. The irresistible devouring force of one of the most terrific conflagrations mentioned in history transformed this entire plain into a burning mass which still smoked after many days had passed.

"Where this tower now stands," said my Chicago guide, concluding the epos of that awful event, "you might have stood in a bed of ashes, with not a single house between the lake on your right hand and the river on your left."

I looked from one to the other, the river and the lake, as I heard these words. That month of October, 1871, was more than near to me; it seemed as if I could touch it, as if I were still in it. I could tell the names of the books that I was reading then, the articles that I was writing. I could remember how I spent almost every day. I realized with an almost physical accuracy the length of the years since that date— twenty-two. How few hours that makes, after all! and I leaned again over the balustrade of the tower, gazing down upon this prodigy, stunned with the thought of what men have done!

Men! The word is hardly correct applied to this perplexing city. When you study it more in detail, its aspect reveals so little of the personal will, so little caprice and individuality, in its streets and buildings, that it seems like the work of some impersonal power, irresistible, unconscious, like a force of nature, in whose service man was merely a passive instrument.

This power is nothing else than that business fever which here throbs at will, with an unbridled violence like that of an uncontrollable element. It rushes along these streets, as once before the devouring flame of fire; it quivers; it makes itself visible with an intensity which lends something tragical to this city, and makes it seem like a poem to me.

When, from this overhanging tower, you have gazed down upon this immense volcano of industry and commerce, you go down to look more closely into the details of this exuberant life, this exhaustless stream of activity. You walk along the sidewalks of streets which bear marks of haste—here flag-stones, there asphalt, yonder a mere line of planks crossing a miry swamp. This want of continuity in road material is repeated in the buildings. At one moment you have nothing around you but "buildings." They scale the very heavens with their eighteen and twenty stories. The architect who built them, or, rather, made them by machinery, gave up all thought of colonnades, moldings, classical decorations. He ruthlessly accepted the speculator's inspired conditions—to multiply as much as possible the value of the bit of earth at the base by multiplying the superimposed "offices."

One might think that such a problem would interest no one but an engineer. Nothing of the kind! The simple power of necessity is to a certain degree a principle of beauty; and these structures so plainly manifest this necessity that you feel a strange emotion in contemplating them. It is the first draft of a new sort of art—an art of democracy made by the masses and for the masses, an art of science, where the invariability of natural laws gives to the most unbridled daring the calmness of geometrical figures. The portals of the basements, usually arched as if crushed beneath the weight of the mountain which they support, look like dens of a primitive race, continually receiving and pouring forth a stream of people. You lift your eyes, and you feel that up there behind the perpendicular wall, with its innumerable windows, is a multitude coming and going—crowding the offices that perforate these cliffs of brick and iron, dizzied with the speed of the elevators. You divine, you feel the hot breath of speculation quivering behind these windows. This it is which has fecundated these thousands of square feet of earth, in order that from them may spring up this appalling growth of business palaces, that hide the sun from you and almost shut out the light of day.

Close beside the preposterous, Babel-like building extends a shapeless bit of ground, undefined, bristling, green with a scanty turf, on which a lean cow is feeding. Then follows a succession of little wooden houses, hardly large enough for a single family. Next comes a Gothic church, transformed into a shop, with a sign in great metal characters. Then comes the red and pretentious ruin of some other building burned the other week. Vacant lots, shanties, churches, ruins—speculation will sweep over it all tomorrow, this evening perhaps, and other "buildings" will spring up. But time is needed, and these people have none. These two years past, instead of completing their half-finished city, they have been amusing themselves in building another over yonder, under pretext of their exhibition. It is entirely white, a dream city, with domes like those of Ravenna, colonnades like those at Rome, lagoons like Venice, a fair of the world like Paris.

They have succeeded, and now the most composite, the

most cosmopolitan of human mixtures fill these suburban and elevated railways, these cable cars, coaches, carriages, which overflow upon these unfinished sidewalks before these wildly dissimilar houses. And as at Chicago, it seems that everything and everybody must be larger, more developed, stronger, so from block to block in the middle of these streets are posted, to maintain order, enormous mounted policemen, tall as Pomeranian grenadiers; gigantic human barriers against which break the seething eddies of this multitude. Most of them are Germans; their red faces are unformed as if hewn out with a hatchet, as if hastily blocked out, and their bullock-like necks and shoulders make a striking comment on divers facts of the daily papers, which continually tell of some "hands up" performed in the taverns, the gambling houses, or simply in a carriage, or on the tramway.

"Hands up!" It is the classic command of the western robber, as he enters, revolver in hand, his first business to make sure that you have not yours. How many times has it been uttered in the suburbs of this city, the meeting place of the adventurers of the two worlds? How many times will it yet be uttered? But the spirit of adventure is also the spirit of enterprise, and if the size of the policemen of this surprising city attests the frequency of surprises attempted by these ruffians, it completes its complex physiognomy; different, surely, from every other since the foundation of the world, a mosaic of extreme civilization and almost barbarism, a savage existence only partly discerned through the abruptness of this industrial creation. In short, it is Chicago, a miracle that would confound the dead of seventy years ago, if they were to return to earth and find themselves in this city, now the ninth in the world as to population, which when they were alive had not a single house.

One of the enormous branches of traffic of this city is in meat. The Chicago folk are a little ashamed of it. In earlier days they would talk to you of their packinghouses, with that artless pride which is one of the charms of great parvenus. It is the simplicity natural to an elemental strength, which knows itself strong and loves to exercise itself frankly. They are tired now of hearing their detractors call them the inhabitants of Porkopolis. They find it a grievance that their city is always "identified," as they say here, with that brutal butchery, when it has among its publishing houses one of the vastest marts of books in the world, when its newspapers never let any incident of literature or art pass without investigating it, when it has founded a university at a cost of seven millions of dollars, when it has just gathered together representatives of all forms of belief, at its remarkable Parliament of Religions—a phenomenon unique in the history of human idealism! Chicago aspires to be something more than the distributor of food, although last year a single one of its firms cut up and distributed one million seven hundred and fifty thousand hogs, a million and twenty-five thousand beeves, and six hundred and twenty-five thousand sheep. Its enemies seek to crush it under figures like these, omitting to remember that the Chicago of the abattoirs is also the Chicago of the "White City," the Chicago of a museum which is already incomparable, the Chicago which gave Lincoln to the United States.

On the other hand, these abattoirs furnish material most precious to the foreigner who desires to understand the spirit in which the Americans undertake their great enterprises. A slaughterhouse capable of shipping in twelve months, to the four parts of this immense continent, three millions five hundred thousand dressed cattle is worth the trouble of investigating. Everywhere else the technical details are very difficult to grasp. They are less so here, the directors of these colossal manufactories of roast beef and hams having discovered that the best possible advertisement is to admit the public to witness their processes of working. They have made a visit to their establishments, if not attractive—physical repulsion is too strong for that—at least convenient and thorough. On condition of having your nerves wrung once for all, these are among the places where you shall best see how American ingenuity solves the problems of a prodigiously complicated organization.

I therefore did like other unprejudiced tourists, and visited the "stockyards" and the most celebrated among the "packinghouses," as they are called—cutting-up houses, rather—which is here in operation; the one, indeed, the statistics of whose operations I have but now quoted. This walk through that house of blood will always remain to me one of the most singular memories of my journey. I think, however, that I owe to it a better discernment of the characteristic features of an American business concern. If this is so, I shall have no reason to regret the painful experience.

To reach the "Union Stock Yards," the carriage crosses an immense section of the city, even more incoherent than those which border on the elegant Michigan Avenue. It stops before the railways, to permit the passage of trains running at full speed. It crosses bridges, which immediately after uprear themselves to permit the passage of boats. It passes by hotels which are palaces, and laborers' houses which are hovels. It skirts large plots of ground, where market gardeners are cultivating cabbages amongst heaps of refuse, and others which bear nothing but advertisements. How shall I deny myself the pleasure of copying this one, among a hundred others:

"Louis XIV was crowned King of France at the age of five years (1643). X——'s pepsin had been crowned with success as a remedy for indigestion before it had been publicly known a single year."

The advertising fields give place to more houses, more railways, under a sky black with clouds, or smoke—one hardly knows which—and on both sides of the road begin to appear fenced enclosures, where cattle are penned by the hundred. There are narrow lanes between the fence, with men on horseback riding up and down. These are the buyers, discussing prices with the "cowboys" of the West.

You have read stories of the "ranches." This adventurous prairie life has taken hold upon your imagination. Here you behold its heroes, in threadbare overcoats, slouch hats, and the inevitable collar and cuffs of the American. But for their boots, and their dexterity in guiding their horses by the knees, you would take them for clerks. They are a proof, among many others, of the instinctive disdain of this realistic people for the picturesque in costume. That impression which I had in the park in New York, almost the first day, as of an immense store of ready-made clothes hurrying hither and thither, has never left me. And yet, nothing can be less "common," in the bad sense of the word, than Americans in general, and these western cowboys in particular. Their bodies are too nervous, too lithe, under their cheap clothes. Their countenances, especially, are too intent and too sharply outlined, too decided and too stern.

The carriage stops before a building which, in its massiveness and want of character, is like all other manufactories. My companions and I enter a court, a sort of alley, crowded with packing boxes, carts, and people. A miniature railway passes along it, carrying packing boxes to a waiting train, entirely composed of refrigerator cars, such as I saw so many of as I came to Chicago. Laborers were unloading these packing boxes; others were coming and going, evidently intent upon their respective duties. There was no sign of administrative order, as we conceive it, in this establishment, which was yet so well ordered. But already one of the engineers had led us up a staircase, and we enter an immense hall, reeking with heavy moisture saturated with a strong acrid odor, which seems to seize you by the throat. We are in the department where the hogs are cut up. There are hundreds of men hard at work, whom we have not time so much as to look at. Our güide warns us to stand aside, and before us glides a file of porkers, disemboweled and hung by their hind feet from a rod, along which they slip toward a vaulted opening, where innumerable other such files await them. The rosy flesh, still ruddy with the life that but now animated them, gleams under the electric light that illuminates those depths. We go on, avoiding these strange encounters as best we may, and reach at last, with feet smeared in a sort of bloody mud, a platform whence we can see the initial act of all this labor, which now seems so confused, but which we shall shortly find so simple and easy to understand. There are the pigs, in a sort of pit, alive, grunting and screaming, as if they had a vision of the approach of the horrible machine, from which they can no more escape than a doomed man whose head lies on the guillotine. It is a sort of movable hook, which, being lowered by a man, seizes one of the creatures by the cord which ties its hind legs together. The animal gives a screech, as he hangs, head downward, with quivering snout and a spasmodic agitation of his short fore legs. But already the hook has slid along the iron bar, carrying the hapless victim to a neighboring recess where, as it slips by, a man armed with a long knife cuts its throat, with a slash so well aimed and effective that there is no need to repeat it. The creature utters a more terrific screech, a stream of blood spurts out, jet black and as thick as your arm. The snout quivers more pitifully, the short legs are agitated more franti-

cally, but the death struggle only quickens the motion of the
hook, which glides on to a third attendant.

The latter, with a quick movement, cuts down the animal.
The hook slides back, and the carcass falls into a sort of canal
tank filled with boiling water, in which an automatic rake
works with a quick vibratory motion. In a few seconds it has
caught the creature, turned it over and over, caught it again,
and thrown the scalded carcass to another machine, which in
a few more seconds has shaved it from head to tail. In another second, another hook has descended, and another bar
carries that which, four minutes ago, was a living, suffering
creature, toward that arched opening where, on coming in, I
had seen so many similar relics. It is already the turn of
another to be killed, shaved, and finished off. The operation
is of such lightning quickness that you have no time to realize
its atrocity. You have no time to pity the poor things, no
time to marvel at the cheerfulness with which the butcher—
a redheaded giant, with shoulders broad enough to carry an
ox—goes on with his horrible work.

And yet, even in its lower forms, life is something so mysterious, the death and sufferings, even of a creature of the
humblest order, are something so tragic when, instead of carelessly picturing them you look them thus full in the face, that
all spectators, and they are many, cease to laugh and joke.
For my part, before this coarse slaughterhouse scene I felt
myself seized with an unreasoning sadness, very short but very
intense, as if, for a few minutes, the spirit of Thomas Grain-
dorge had passed before me—the philosophic dealer in salt
pork and oil, so dear to my master, Taine. It suddenly
seemed as if I saw before me existence itself, and all the work
of nature, incarnated in a pitiable symbol. All that I had
often thought of death was as if concrete before my eyes, in
the irresistible clutch of that hook lifting those creatures, as
the overpowering force of destruction which is in the world
will one day seize us all—sages, heroes, artists, as well as
these poor unconscious brutes. I saw them rushing, writhing,
moaning, their death agonies following fast on one another,
as ours follow one another, only a little more rapidly—how
little more, considering how fast time flies, and how small a
part remains for all that must be done! And the way that we
looked in at this ghastly scene, my companions and I, was
in nothing different from the way with which others will one

day look on at our entrance into the great darkness, as on a
picture, a something exterior, whose reality, after all, concerns
only the being who undergoes it!

We went into the department reserved for the cattle. Here
the death struggle is different. No outcry, almost no blood;
no terrified expectation on the creature's part. And the scene
is all the more tragic. The animals are penned by twos, in
stalls like those of a stable, though without the manger. You
see them trying, with their intelligence and their gentleness,
to accommodate themselves to the narrow space. They gazed
with their large, soft eyes—upon whom? The butcher,
standing in a passageway a little above them. This man holds
in his hand a slender bludgeon of steel. He is waiting until
the ox is in the right position. You see him gently, caressingly,
guiding the animal with the tip of his bludgeon. Suddenly he
uplifts it. It falls upon the creature's forehead, and it sinks
down in a lifeless heap.

In an instant a hook has lifted it up, blood pouring from
the mouth and nostrils, its large glassy eyes overshadowed
with a growing darkness, and within another minute another
man has stripped the skin from the breast, letting it hang
down like an apron, has cut open the carcass, and sent it by
the expeditious method of the sliding bar, to take its place
in the refrigerating room. Thousands of them await here the
time for being carried and hung up in other rooms, also of
ice, but on wheels, ready to be dispatched. I see the closing
of the last car of a train on the point of departure. The locomotive whistles and puffs; the bell rings. On what table of
New York or Boston, Philadelphia or Savannah, will at last
appear this meat, fattened on the prairie pasture lands of some
district in some western state, and here prepared in such a
way that the butcher will have merely to cut it into pieces? It
will arrive as fresh, as intact, as if there had not been thousands and thousands of miles between the birth, death, and
dismemberment of the enigmatical and peaceable creature.

If there was nothing but killing to be seen in this manufacture of food, it would hardly be worthwhile to go through
so many bloody scenes for the sake of verifying, in one of its
lower exemplifications, what the philosopher Huxley somewhere magnificently calls "the gladiatorial theory of existence," the severe law that murder is necessary to life. But
this is only a first impression, to experience before passing to

a second, that of the rapidity and ingenuity of the cutting up and packing of this prodigious quantity of perishable meat. I don't know who it was who sportively said that a pig that went to the abattoir at Chicago came out fifteen minutes later in the form of ham, sausages, large and small, hair oil, and binding for a Bible. It is a witty exaggeration, yet hardly overdone, of the rapid and minute labor which we had just seen bestowed upon the beasts killed before our eyes; and the subdividing of this work, its precision, simplicity, quick succession, succeeding in making us forget the necessary but intolerable brutality of the scenes we had been witnessing.

An immense hall is furnished with a succession of counters placed without much order, where each member of the animal is cut apart and utilized without the loss of a bone or a tendon. Here, with a quick, automatic blow, which never misses, a man cuts off first the hams, then the feet, as fast as he can throw them into caldrons, which boil and smoke them before your eyes. Farther along, a hatchet, moved by machinery, is at work making sausage meat, which tubes of all sizes will pour forth in rolls ready for the skins, that are all washed and prepared. The word "garlic," which I see written on a box in German, "Knoblauch," and the accompanying inscription, transports me to the time of the Franco-Prussian War, when each Prussian soldier carried in his sack just such provisions, which had come from this very place. These products of Chicagoan industry will be sent far enough beyond New York!

Elsewhere the head and jowl are cleaned, trimmed, and dressed, to figure in their natural form in the show window of some American or European market. Elsewhere, again, enormous receptacles are being filled with suet which boils and bubbles, and having been cunningly mixed with a certain proportion of cream will be transformed into margarine, refined in an automatic beating machine of which we admired the artful simplicity.

"A workingman invented that," said our guide. "For that matter," he added, "almost all the machines that are used here were either made or improved by the workmen."

These words shed light for us upon all this vast workshop. We understood what these men require of a machine that for them prolongs, multiplies, perfects the acts of men. Once again we felt how much they have become refined in

their processes of work, how they excel in combining with
their personal effort the complication of machinery, and also
how the least among them has a power of initiative, of direct
vision and adjustment.

Seated again in our carriage, and rolling away over the
irregular wooden pavement made of round sections of trees
embedded at pleasure in the mud, we reflected upon what we
had just seen. We tried to discern its intellectual significance,
if we may use this word in reference to such an enterprise.
And why not? We are all agreed that the first characteristic
of this enterprise is the amplitude, or rather the stupendous-
ness, of its conception. For an establishment like this to have,
in a few years, brought up the budget of its employees to five
million five hundred thousand dollars, that is, to more than
twenty-seven millions of francs, its founders must have clearly
perceived the possibilities of an enormous extension of business, and have no less clearly perceived, defined, and determined its practical features.

A colossal effort of imagination on the one hand, and, on
the other, at the service of the imagination, a clear and
carefully estimated understanding of the encompassing reality
—these are the two features everywhere stamped upon the
unparalleled establishment which we have just visited. One of
us pointed out another fact—that the principal practical feature is the railway, reminding us that the locomotive has
always been an implement of general utility in American
hands. By it they revolutionized military art and created a
full-panoplied modern warfare, such as the Germans were
later to practice at our expense. In the great national war of
1860, they first showed what advantage could be taken of
this new means of mobilization. The length of the trains they
sent out during that period has passed into legend. In fact, the
establishment which we have been discussing is only one particular case of that universal use of the railway, which is
itself only a particular illustration of that essentially American
turn of mind—the constant use of new methods.

The entire absence of routine, the daily habit of letting the
fact determine the action, of following it fearlessly to the end
—these characteristics grow out of the other, and this acute
consciousness of the fact also explains that sort of superficial
incoherence in the distribution of labor which we have already
noticed. Extreme clearness, perspicuity of administrative

order, always spring from an *a priori* theory. All societies and all enterprises in which realism, rather than system, rules are constructed by juxtaposition, by series of facts accepted as they arise. But how should the people here have leisure to concern themselves with those small, fine points of administrative order with which our Latin peoples are so much in love? Competition is too strong, too ferocious, almost. There is all of warfare and its breathless audacity back of the enterprises of this country, even of those most firmly established, like this one.

Our guide, who listens to our philosophizing without seeming much to disapprove, tells us that this very year, in order to elude a coalition of speculators in grain, which he explains to us, the head of the house which we have just visited was forced to erect in nineteen days, for the housing of his own wheat, a building three hundred feet square by a hundred high!

"Yes, in nineteen days, working night and day," he said, smiling; "but we Americans like 'hard work.'"

With this almost untranslatable word—to one who has not heard it uttered here—our visit ends. It sums it up and completes it with a terseness worthy of this people of much action and few phrases!

[pp. 114–129]

4

THE WORLD'S COLUMBIAN EXPOSITION (1893):
Harriet Monroe, JOHN WELLBORN ROOT:
ARCHITECT (Boston, 1896), pp. 242–248;
Louis H. Sullivan, THE AUTOBIOGRAPHY OF
AN IDEA (New York, 1924, 1956), pp. 316–
327.

These passages on the exposition are included in this section on "Reaction" because the exposition has become symbolic of turn-of-the-century rejection of what H. P. Berlage called "modern American architecture" in favor of conspicious-consumption classicism. This rejection has been dramatized as a victory of East Coast architects over the architects of the "Chicago School." Sullivan perhaps over-rated the exposition as *cause* since he saw it as a contest between Chicago and the East, won by the East, and since he saw it as the source of the virus that infected public attitudes toward architecture. This emphasis on *cause* over-simplifies what was in actuality *symptom*; the energies of the Chicago School were dissipated not as a result of the exposition but as a result of rapidly expanding affluence in combination with an intensification of national aesthetic self-consciousness (in effect, a cultural inferiority complex). It is misleading to argue that the course of twentieth-century architecture would have been different—if the exposition had been Chicago School and not New York School—if Root had lived to dominate the board of architects, and so on. It would be more accurate to argue that the emergence of the United States as a world power (1890–1920) was reflected in the desire to build eclectic monuments that would over-whelm the competition of European aesthetic history—a

33. Richard Morris Hunt, Administration Building (1893), World's Columbian Exposition, Chicago, Illinois.

desire coupled with the affluence, the economic ability, to make the attempt. In this sense the exposition was not the cause but the symptom of a national perversion of energies and capacities.

The board of architects that designed the exposition praised itself as the greatest assemblage of talent "since the Renaissance." The "White City" the board created was dominated by a riot of buildings in cast iron and "staff,"* molded to look like the permanent monuments of a great renaissance. Decorative excess was the rule, liberally spiced with "classical" sculptures of every hero from Columbus and Leif Ericson to Leatherstocking and Tom Sawyer. Richard Morris Hunt's Administration Building (see illustration 33) struck the keynote of eclectic flamboyance. The central buildings, "The Court of Honor," stood as the New World's boast of its victory over the relatively modest eclecticism of the École des Beaux Arts in particular and of European academicism in general. Sullivan's Transportation Building (see illustration 34) on the periphery stood in color as the only effective architectural counterstatement to this self-conscious white renaissance. Other brief moments in the fair also had their countereffect. A windmill exhibit presented in full scale a panorama of the evolution of the windmill from its crude beginnings to its Plains States' refinement; and various anthropological exhibits were impressive, particularly the Yucatan Ruins, which are reputed to have influenced Wright's Unity Temple design.

Perhaps in retrospect, view books of the exposition are striking not for their depiction of the virus of conspicuous-consumption classicism but for their depiction of the extraordinary exuberance, the expansionist flamboyance of this "fair to end all fairs."

* "Staff" is a mixture of plaster of Paris, with a little cement, glycerin and dextrin, in water. Before it sets, it is as malleable as papier-mâché; when hardened, it looks like marble from a short distance away.

From "Last Days" in Harriet Monroe, JOHN WELLBORN ROOT: ARCHITECT *(1896)*

John Root's conception of the fair differed much from the White City of memory. If he had lived and his ideas had prevailed, the Columbian Exposition would have been a City of Color; a queen arrayed in robes not saintly, as for a bridal, but gorgeous, for a festival. These two ideals are both worthy of honor. One was embodied in delicate beauty, to win the praises of the world; the other vanished when a great man died. For the first I do not need to speak: its noble stateliness made its own appeal. We lived for half a year in the awe and wonder of it, and it lingers in memory, under the sunshine of that gracious summer, as a glimpse into realms unearthly, the chosen abode of perfect souls. For the second I must say my feeble word, remembering the enthusiasm and strength of purpose which this unrealized dream concentrated. That word will be unconvincing, perhaps; because no architectural scheme can be fairly judged until it is completed before men's eyes, and because any disturbance of our memories of the White City will seem a desecration. But the beauty of the lily is no reason why the rose should not also be beautiful. And all the flowers of memory cannot make it impossible that one unrecorded should be as lovely as these. The difficulty lies in the proving. What eye can behold the perished flower, however marvelous? What hand can delineate the Columbian City as its first architect saw it? Mine is powerless to offer more than a few hints showing the rough outline of his conception.

The fundamental point in Root's creed as an architect was sincerity: a building should frankly express its purpose and its material. Thus it would have been impossible for him to design, as the chief buildings of the fair, imitations in staff of marble palaces: these could not express their material; or to adopt a classic motive: this could not express the purpose of a modern American exposition. He wished to admit frankly in the architectural scheme the temporary character of the fair: it should be a great, joyous, luxuriant midsummer efflorescence, born to bloom for an hour and perish—a splendid buoyant thing, flaunting its gay colors between the shifting blues of sky and lake exultantly, prodigally. Edifices built in pursuance of this idea should not give the illusion of weight and permanence: they should be lighter, gayer, more decorative than the solid structures along our streets. To his mind the dominant note in our civilization was its youth, its newness, crudeness: manifestly things were beginning here— beginning with a swift rush and turmoil of creative energies. He wished to show its affluence, its sumptuous conquering enthusiasm. He wished to offer to the older nations a proof of new forces, new ideals, not yet developed and completed, but full of power and prophetic of charm. He wished to express our militant democracy as he felt it, pausing after victory for a song of triumph before taking up its onward march.

Manifestly these turbulent awakening energies could not be presented through any formal and crystallized type of architecture. The classic type, Root was inclined to feel, had attained its ultimate perfection in Greece, and its motives had been restudied and developed through succeeding centuries until they were scarcely capable of a new vitalization which should express the modern purposes. It was a style for the open-air life and the fair blue skies of Athens, not for wind-swept and storm-beaten Chicago. Moreover, it was a monumental style, not suitable for holiday structures built of temporary materials. Among all the tentative sketches of the fair, or portions of it, which Root threw off from day to day during these busy weeks, there is scarcely a trace of a classic motive. On the contrary, there is much that is unconventional or even bizarre, conceived in a lyric mood with delightful freshness and spontaneity. He was much pleased one day when an English artist, trained in the schools, but hospitable to new suggestions, recognized what he was striving for in one of these drawings: "You've got an exuberant barbaric effect there—a kind of an American Kremlin," he said; "lots of color and noise and life."

A vigorous and masterful panorama of ephemeral magnificence—such was the ideal these sketches present. Kremlin and Nishni-Novgorod give suggestions of the turn his mind was taking with regard to form and splendor. This idea of a World's Fair would not have given the nations a Celestial City—it would not have been divine, but it would have been sympathetically and broadly human. Its appeal to the popular imagination would have been, perhaps, the more intimate, potent, and enduring. Root's sketches adopted usually the Romanesque type of arch and column as a form more pliable than the Greek, a form which admitted the use of American species of flower and leaf in ornamentation. The Fisheries Building, which was designed by Mr. Henry Ives Cobb,* was the best example on the grounds of Root's ideas of fair architecture. Its frankly playful use of staff, as a medium whose easy plasticity invited an endless variety of gay detail, would have struck him as honest and poetic; and the delicate, even humorous adaptation of sea forms of animal and plant life would have appealed to his sense of fitness. Such happy imaginings, however, he would have vivified with color instead of freezing them in white. Color was, to his feeling, a necessity in any architectural expression of a great festival. In this opinion he was at one with the Greeks themselves, who added to the creamy translucency of their marble brilliant accents of color. He was outborne also by the instinct of the people, who loved the Court of Honor best, not when the noon sunshine glared on its façades of opaque white, but when the twilight made them luminous with pink and gold and purple, or the Night, flashing her million lamps, clothed them in mysteries of shimmer and shade.

I am convinced that the people would have responded with joy to an intelligent use of color in the treatment of buildings at the great festival, that it would have added a strong element of beauty and gayety, and emphasized the grandeur of noble façades. The Transportation Building, with its beautiful Golden Door, was an interesting experiment in this direction, although Mr. Sullivan's sumptuous orientalism was scarcely given a fair setting as the only strong note of color among many classic façades of changeless white. Problems of outdoor decoration have been studied but little by our decorators, for the best of reasons. Root had much confidence in Mr. William Pretyman's† ideas on this subject, an enthusiast whose Old World studies did not make him reject new ideas. During these months they discussed somewhat this problem of outdoor color, and afterwards, when Mr. Prety-

---

* Henry Ives Cobb (1859–1931), born in Brookline, Mass., educated at M.I.T., had settled in Chicago in the 1880's and was thus one of the western or Chicago architects associated with the fair.

† William Pretyman, a Chicago decorator with a reputation as a colorist, was appointed the fair's "Director of Color." He resigned when the decision was made (apparently behind his back) to have the fair "all perfectly white."

man was appointed Chief of Color for the fair, he experimented in the tinting of staff with thin washes of pure transparent oil colors, believing that opaque paint of the ordinary kind would harden and artificialize the delicate material, and that white especially would destroy its creamy translucency. In these experiments beautiful results were obtained, but Mr. Pretyman resigned his post too early to carry out his ideas, the only example of them on the grounds being the little East India House, that delicate opal set in green. Any one who saw the Fisheries Building, for example, when it was first completed in 1892, and noted the lovely amber tones of the staff melting graciously into the sunlight, could not fail to feel a painful shock when this seductive bloom was hidden forever under the heavier white. Somehow the poetry of the building seemed to have gone out of it.

Root's possible decisions in points of detail are of course a mere matter of conjecture. While he lived all projects were still chaotic, and his mind, as usual, was open to all suggestions. We know only his initial preferences, not his ultimate choice. During these months the scale was still his dominant thought. "He was thinking of the bones as no one else did," says a gentleman familiar with him at this time. "He had dug up his mammoth and set it up while others were wondering how big such an animal could be, and when told of its existence, were opening their eyes without being able to measure its magnitude." Yet he did not neglect the sinews and integument of his giant. During these last weeks of his life he caused experiments with colored tiles and terra-cotta to be carried on at the terra-cotta works; and his accurate mind—a mind which, in the service of clients, hated extravagance and waste—was full of speculations in regard to the availability and cost of this material and of others, such as glass, wood, staff. Staff, which had been used extensively in Paris, was not his preference for large structures, though it might have been his choice eventually for a great deal of the work. He would never have used it in imitation of marble, but he would have appreciated its delightful temptations to gayety of modeling and coloring. Terra-cotta, in rather strong tones, he would undoubtedly have used as extensively as its price would admit. But, whatever the materials, his whole heart was centered upon his hope of an American fair—an architectural scheme which should express exuberantly our young, crude, buoyant civilization, and strike our note at last in the world's art.

I have often wondered whether Root could have carried out his ideas of fair architecture through the board of architects whom he appointed. Remembering his sanguine belief in these ideas, and the persuasive power of the man to inspire others with his own enthusiasm, I think it possible that he might have achieved the impossible with these men trained in the schools and bound by precedents. But it would have been much easier for his fertile mind to design the whole exposition than to get what he wanted out of others. We used to urge that he should strike the keynote of his scheme by taking the Administration Building, but the most magnanimous sense of duty to his profession made him reject the suggestion. The leading American architects should be invited to serve on the advisory board, and this invitation implied an extension of professional courtesy by which their senior member, whom Root recognized as Mr. Richard M. Hunt,* should be requested to design the most important building. It implied, also, I suppose, a certain deference to the will of the majority of this board in regard to the type of architecture which should prevail. And so one may merely surmise what would have happened if Root's fixed purpose of a fair which should express our national life and character, presented to these architects with all his exactness and persuasive power, had met their fixed resolve for the classic. Representatives of four out of the five outside firms came on together from the East for the first conference, appointed to begin on the twelfth of January. On the way they talked over the enterprise which summoned them, and fixed upon the classic type of architecture as the only one in which they could work together harmoniously. This plan the architect-in-chief could scarcely have ratified—could they have accepted his? It is probable that most of the five Chicago architects, judging from the character of their designs for the fair, would have upheld Root. But the ideas he cherished so ardently were never presented to his fellow laborers. On the morning when the first conference began, he was stricken with pneumonia; a day or two before it ended, he died. If he had lived, there

---

* Richard Morris Hunt (1827–1895), financially successful and forthright in his pragmatism, was the dean of the eastern architects and (from the eastern point of view) of American architects.

would have been another battle of Chicago against the East,
new methods against old, our own beauty against the beauty
of the past. For my feeling that the progressive spirit would
have conquered, I have only the precedent of the city's earlier
victories, and my knowledge of Root's power in persuading
men even against their training and preferences.

[pp. 242–248]

From Louis H. Sullivan, THE AUTOBIOGRAPHY OF AN IDEA (1924)

And Chicago rolled on and roared by day and night except
only in its stillest hours toward dawn. There seemed to reside
in its dreams before the dawn during these years something
not wholly material, something in the underlying thoughts of
men that aspired to reach above the general level of intelligence and the raucous hue and cry. At least Louis thought so.
Then, as now, was the great lake with its far horizon, the
sweeping curve of its southern shore, its many moods, which
every day he viewed from his tower windows. And there was
the thought, the seeming presence of the prairies and the far-
flung hinterland. In such momentary trance his childhood
would return to him with its vivid dream of power, a dream
which had now grown to encompass the world; from such
reverie he would perchance awaken to some gossip of Adler,
standing by, concerning the inside story of some of the city's
great men, all of which was grist for Louis's mill, for Adler
was quite literal when he told these anecdotes, and Louis
listened keenly to them, and learned. The two frequently
lunched together. Shoptalk was taboo. But they did not talk
about the coming World's Fair, as authorized by Act of
Congress in 1890. It was deemed fitting by all the people that
the four hundredth anniversary of the discovery of America
by one Christopher Columbus should be celebrated by a great
world exposition, which should spaciously reveal to the last
word the cultural status of the peoples of the earth; and that
the setting for such display should be one of splendor, worthy
of its subject.

Chicago was ripe and ready for such an undertaking. It had
the required enthusiasm and the will. It won out in a contest

34. Louis Sullivan, Transportation Building (1893), World's Columbian Exposition, Chicago, Illinois.

between the cities. The prize was now in hand. It was to be
the city's crowning glory. A superb site on the lake adjoined
the southern section of the city. This site was so to be transformed and embellished by the magic of American prowess,
particularly in its architectural aspects, as to set forth the
genius of the land in that great creative art. It was to be a
dream city, where one might revel in beauty. It was to be
called The White City by the Lake.

Now arose above the horizon the small white cloud. It
came from eastward. It came borne upon the winds of pre-
destination. Who could fancy that a harmless white cloud
might cast a white shadow? Who could forecast the shape of
that shadow? It was here that one man's unbalanced mind
spread a gauze-like pall of fatality. That one man's unconscious stupor in bigness, and in the droll fantasy of hero-
worship, did his best and his worst, according to his lights,
which were dim except the one projector by the harsh light
of which he saw all things illuminated and grown bombas-
tically big in chauvinistic outlines. Here was to be the test of
American culture, and here it failed. Dreamers may dream;
but of what avail the dream if it be but a dream of misinter-
pretation? If the dream, in such a case, rise not in vision far
above the general level of intelligence, and prophesy through
the medium of clear thinking, true interpretation—why
dream at all? Why not rest content as children of Barnum,
easy in the faith that one of "them" is born every minute.
Such in effect was the method adopted in practice while the
phrase-makers tossed their slogans to and fro.

At the beginning it was tentatively assumed that the firm
of Burnham & Root might undertake the work in its entirety.
The idea was sound in principle—one hand, one great work—
a superb revelation of America's potency—an oration, a
portrayal, to arouse that which was hidden, to call it forth
into the light. But the work of ten years cannot be done in
two. It would require two years to grasp and analyze the
problem and effect a synthesis. Less than three years were
available for the initiation and completion of the work entire,
ready for the installation of exhibits. The idea was in consequence dismissed. As a matter of fact there was not an
architect in the land equal to the undertaking. No veteran
mind seasoned to the strategy and tactics involved in a wholly
successful issue. Otherwise there might have arisen a gorgeous
Garden City, reflex of one mind, truly interpreting the aspira-

tions and the heart's desire of the many, every detail carefully considered, every function given its due form, with the sense of humanity at its best, a suffusing atmosphere; and within the Garden City might be built another city to remain and endure as a memorial, within the parkland by the blue waters, oriented toward the rising sun, a token of a covenant of things to be, a symbol of the city's basic significance as off-spring of the prairie, the lake, and the portage.

But "hustle" was the word. Make it big, make it stunning, knock 'em down! The cry was well meant as things go.

So in the fall of 1890 John Root was officially appointed consulting architect, and Daniel Burnham, chief of construction.

Later, with the kindly assistance of Edward T. Jefferey, Chairman of the Committee on Buildings and Grounds, Burnham selected five architects from the East and five from the West, ten in all.* Burnham and Jefferey loved each other dearly. The thought of one was the thought of both, as it were—sometimes. Burnham had believed that he might best serve his country by placing all of the work exclusively with eastern architects; solely, he averred, on account of their surpassing culture. With exquisite delicacy and tact, Jefferey, at a meeting of the committee, persuaded Daniel, come to Judgment, to add the western men to the list of his nominations.

A gathering of these architects took place in February, 1891. After an examination of the site, which by this time was dreary enough in its state of raw upheaval, the company retired for active conference. John Root was not there. In faith he could not come. He had made his rendezvous the month before. Graceland was now his home. Soon above him would be reared a Celtic cross. Louis missed him sadly. Who now would take up the foils he had dropped on his way, from hands that were once so strong? There was none! The shadow of the white cloud had already fallen.

The meeting came to order. Richard Hunt, acknowledged dean of his profession, in the chair, Louis Sullivan acting as secretary. Burnham arose to make his address of welcome.

---

* The eastern firms represented were Frederick Law Olmsted & Co.; McKim, Mead and White; Richard Morris Hunt; and George B. Post, all of New York; and Peabody and Stearns of Boston. The western firms, in addition to Burnham and Root, were Burling and Whitehouse, Jenney and Mundie, Henry Ives Cobb, S. S. Beman, Adler and Sullivan, all of Chicago, and Van Brunt and Howe of Kansas City.

He was not facile on his feet, but it soon became noticeable that he was progressively and grossly apologizing to the eastern men for the presence of their benighted brethren of the West.

Dick Hunt interrupted: "Hell, we haven't come out here on a missionary expedition. Let's get to work." Everyone agreed. Burnham came out of his somnambulistic vagary and joined in. He was keen enough to understand that "Uncle Dick" had done him a needed favor. For Burnham learned slowly but surely, within the limits of his understanding.

A layout was submitted to the board as a basis for discussion. It was rearranged on two axes at right angles. The buildings were disposed accordingly. By an amicable arrangement each architect was given such building as he preferred, after consultation. The meeting then adjourned.

The story of the building of the fair is foreign to the purpose of this narrative, which is to deal with its more serious aspects, implications, and results. Suffice it that Burnham performed in a masterful way, displaying remarkable executive capacity. He became openminded, just, magnanimous. He did his great share.

The work completed, the gates thrown open May 1, 1893, the crowds flowed in from every quarter, continued to flow throughout a fair-weather summer and a serenely beautiful October. Then came the end. The gates were closed.

These crowds were astonished. They beheld what was for them an amazing revelation of the architectural art, of which previously they in comparison had known nothing. To them it was a veritable Apocalypse, a message inspired from on high. Upon it their imagination shaped new ideals. They went away, spreading again over the land, returning to their homes, each one of them carrying in the soul the shadow of the white cloud, each of them permeated by the most subtle and slow-acting of poisons; an imperceptible miasm within the white shadow of a higher culture. A vast multitude, exposed, unprepared, they had not had time nor occasion to become immune to forms of sophistication not their own, to a higher and more dexterously insidious plausibility. Thus they departed joyously, carriers of contagion, unaware that what they had beheld and believed to be truth was to prove, in historic fact, an appalling calamity. For what they saw was not at all what they believed they saw, but an imposition of the spurious upon their eyesight, a naked exhibitionism of charlatanry in the higher feudal and domineering culture, conjoined with expert salesmanship of the materials of decay. Adventitiously, to make the stage setting complete, it happened by way of apparent but unreal contrast that the structure representing the United States Government was of an incredible vulgarity, while the building at the peak of the north axis, stationed there as a symbol of "The Great State of Illinois," matched it as a lewd exhibit of drooling imbecility and political debauchery. The distribution at the northern end of the grounds of many state and foreign headquarters relieved the sense of stark immensity. South of them, and placed on the border of a small lake, stood the Palace of the Arts, the most vitriolic of them all—the most impudently thievish. The landscape work, in its genial distribution of lagoons, wooded islands, lawns, shrubbery, and plantings, did much to soften an otherwise mechanical display; while far in the southeast corner, floating in a small lagoon or harbor, were replicas of the three caravels of Columbus, and on an adjacent artificial mound a representation of the Convent of La Rabida. Otherwhere there was no evidence of Columbus and his daring deed, his sufferings, and his melancholy end. No keynote, no dramatic setting forth of that deed which, recently, has aroused some discussion as to whether the discovery of America had proved to be a blessing or a curse to the world of mankind.

Following the white cloud, even as a companion in iniquity, came the gray cloud. It overwhelmed the land with a pall of desolation. It dropped its blinding bolt. Its hurricane swept away the pyramided paper structures of speculation. Its downpour washed away fancied gains; its raindrops, loaded with a lethal toxin, fell alike upon the unjust and the just, as in retribution, demanding an atonement in human sacrifice. The thunder ceased to roll, the rain became a mist and cleared, the storm subsided, all was still. Overhead hung the gray cloud of panic from horizon to horizon. Slowly it thinned; in time it became translucent, vanished, revealing the white cloud which, in platoons, unseen, had overrun the blue. Now again shone the sun. "Prosperity" awakened from its torpor, rubbed its eyes and prepared for further follies.

It is said that history repeats itself. This is not so. What is mistaken for repetition is the recurrent feudal rhythm of exaltation and despair. Its progressive wavelike movement in action is implicit in the feudal thought, and inevitable, and so long as the feudal thought holds dominion in the minds of men, just so long and no longer will calamity follow upon the appearance of prosperity. The end is insanity, the crumbling and the passing of the race, for life is ever saying to Man: "If you wish to be destroyed I will destroy you." The white cloud is the feudal idea. The gray cloud, the nemesis contained within that idea. The feudal idea is dual, it holds to the concept of good and evil. The democratic idea is single, integral. It holds to the good alone. Its faith lies in the beneficence of its power, in its direct appeal to life. Its vision reveals an inspiring vista of accomplishment. Its common sense recognizes man as by nature sound to the core, and kindly. It as clearly sees, in the feudal scheme, a continuous warfare—as well in so-called times of peace as in sanguinary battle. It views all this as lunacy, for its own word is "kindness." It bases its faith upon the heart in preference to the intellect, though knowing well the power of the latter when controlled. It knows that the intellect, alone, runs amuck, and performs unspeakable cruelties; that the heart alone is divine. For it is the heart that welcomes life and would cherish it, would shield it against the cannibalism of the intellect.

From the height of its Columbian Ecstasy, Chicago drooped and subsided with the rest, in a common sickness, the nausea of overstimulation. This in turn passed, toward the end of the decade, and the old game began again with intensified fury, to come to a sudden halt in 1907. There are those who say this panic was artificial and deliberate, that the battle of the saber-toothed tigers and the mastodons was on.

Meanwhile the virus of the World's Fair, after a period of incubation in the architectural profession and in the population at large, especially the influential, began to show unmistakable signs of the nature of the contagion. There came a violent outbreak of the classic and the Renaissance in the East, which slowly spread westward, contaminating all that it touched, both at its source and outward. The selling campaign of the bogus antique was remarkably well managed through skillful publicity and propaganda, by those who were first to see its commercial possibilities. The market was ripe, made so through the hebetude of the populace, big businessmen, and eminent educators alike. By the time the market had been saturated, all sense of reality was gone. In its place had come deepseated illusions, hallucinations, absence of pupillary reaction to light, absence of knee reaction—symptoms all of progressive cerebral meningitis: The blanketing of the brain. Thus Architecture died in the land of the free and the home of the brave—in a land declaring its fervid democracy, its inventiveness, its resourcefulness, its unique daring, enterprise, and progress. Thus did the virus of a culture, snobbish and alien to the land, perform its work of disintegration; and thus ever works the pallid academic mind, denying the real, exalting the fictitious and the false, incapable of adjusting itself to the flow of living things, to the reality and the pathos of man's follies, to the valiant hope that ever causes him to aspire, and again to aspire; that never lifts a hand in aid because it cannot; that turns its back upon man because that is its tradition; a culture lost in ghostly *mésalliance* with abstractions, when what the world needs is courage, common sense and human sympathy, and a moral standard that is plain, valid, and livable.

The damage wrought by the World's Fair will last for half a century from its date, if not longer. It has penetrated deep into the constitution of the American mind, effecting there lesions significant of dementia.

Meanwhile the architectural generation immediately succeeding the classic and Renaissance merchants are seeking to secure a special immunity from the inroads of common sense, through a process of vaccination with the lymph of every known European style, period, and accident, and to this all-around process, when it breaks out, is to be added the benediction of good taste. Thus we have now the abounding freedom of eclecticism, the winning smile of taste, but no architecture. For Architecture, be it known, is dead. Let us therefore lightly dance upon its grave, strewing roses as we glide. Indeed let us gather, in procession, in the night, in the rain, and make soulful, fluent, epicene orations to the living dead we neuters eulogize.

Surely the profession has made marvelous improvements in trade methods, over the old-fashioned way. There is now a dazzling display of merchandise, all imported, excepting to be sure our own cherished colonial, which maintains our Anglo-Saxon tradition in its purity. We have Tudor for colleges and residences; Roman for banks, and railway stations and libraries—or Greek if you like—some customers prefer the Ionic to the Doric. We have French, English, and Italian

35. McKim, Mead and White, Library (1901–1906), Columbia University, New York City.

Gothic, classic, and Renaissance for churches. In fact we are prepared to satisfy, in any manner of taste. Residences we offer in Italian or Louis Quinze. We make a small charge for alterations and adaptations. Our service we guarantee as exceptional and exclusive. Our importations are direct. We have our own agents abroad. We maintain also a commercial department, in which a selective taste is not so necessary. Its province is to solve engineering problems of all kinds, matters of cost, income, maintenance, taxes, renewals, depreciation, obsolescence; and as well maintenance of contact, sales pressure, sales resistance, flotations, and further matters of the sort. We maintain also an industrial department in which leading critics unite in saying we have made most significant departures in design. These structures however, are apart from our fashionable trade. Our business is founded and maintained on an ideal service, and a part of that service we believe to consist in an elevation of the public taste, a setting forth of the true standards of design, in pure form, a system of education by example, the gradual formation of a background of culture for the masses. In this endeavor we have the generous support of the architectural schools, of the colleges and universities, of men of wealth, and of those whose perspicacity has carried them to the pinnacle of eminence in finance, industry, commerce, education, and statesmanship. Therefore we feel that we are in thorough accord with the spirit of our times as expressed in its activities, in its broad democratic tolerance, and its ever-youthful enthusiasms. It is this sense of solidity, solidarity, and security that makes us bold, inspires us with the high courage to continue in our self-imposed task. We look for our reward solely in the conviction of duty done; our profound belief that we are preparing the way for the coming generation through the power of our example, our counsel, and our teachings, to the end that they may express, better than we ourselves have done, the deep, the sincere, the wholesome aspirations of our people and of our land, as yet not fully articulated by the higher culture, in spite of our best efforts toward that end. This task we are quite aware we must eventually leave to the young who are crowding upon us, and we wish them joy in their great adventure when we relinquish our all.

[pp. 316–327]

5

H. P. Berlage, "NEURERE AMERIKANISCHE ARCHITEKTUR" ("The New American Architecture"), SCHWEIZERISCHE BAUZEITUNG (Zurich, Sept. 14 and 21, 1912), Vol. LX, No. 11, pp. 148–150; No. 12, pp. 165–167. Translated by Lily Boecher.

Hendrick Petrus Berlage (1856–1934) was a Dutch architect and architectural critic. He is noted for his strenuous attempts to free himself from traditional historicism in his own designs and for the energy of his campaign to preach the necessity of that freedom. Berlage's approach to architecture was largely through an emphasis on structure; he argued that the supporting elements in a building should read as supports, and conversely that any element that reads as a support should actually support. His name is often linked with that of the German architect Peter Behrens (1868–1938), whose emphasis was on simple and honest form as Berlage's was on direct and honest structure. Berlage and Behrens are regarded as important early modern architects in Europe. Sigfried Giedion notes in *Space, Time and Architecture*, page 360, that Le Corbusier first became acquainted with Frank Lloyd Wright's work through this article of Berlage's.

The New American Architecture (1912) Travel Impressions of H. P. Berlage, Architect in Amsterdam*

In the usual discussion of American architecture only the so-called "skyscraper" is mentioned. No one seems to pay any attention to anything else that is being built in America. Only the typical American office building is regarded as remarkable —and remarkable primarily for its construction. Everyone talks about the iron framework which is the skeleton of the building—built at the outset to its full height and afterward surrounded by stone construction. No one ever remarks on the possibility of beauty in these buildings; and therefore everyone thinks there is no beauty in them. On the contrary, it is assumed that the beauty of these buildings is in inverse proportion to their height; and the European looks down with the greatest contempt on all that is called American architecture.

However, there is an American architecture of great value, quite apart from the architecture of the skyscrapers, though this does not mean that the skyscrapers cannot also be of great beauty.† The subject of my thesis is the real modern architecture of America—that architecture which is not fashioned in terms of historical style motifs; for, as peculiar as it may sound, the original American office building, in spite of its immense height, is designed in imitation of old

---

* On March 30, 1912, our learned colleague the architect H. P. Berlage gave a lecture to the Zurich Association of Engineers and Architects (*Minutes*, Vol. LIX, p. 208). To oblige us he summarized his lecture in a report that we reproduce here. We wished to give the readers of our magazine the same great pleasure that the colleagues of the Zurich Association had when they listened to Berlage's lecture and saw his slides. We have also added some representative pictures to his report, though we will have to present them in three issues on account of their great number. The time consumed in preparation of the originals and of our plates is the reason for the delay in the publication of this report. For the courtesy of making the plans and photographs available to us we are not only very much obliged to Mr. Berlage but also to the architect Frank Lloyd Wright.

—EDITORS, Schweizersche Bauzeitung

† Cf. *"Reiseeindrücke aus den Vereinigten Staaten von Nordamerika"* (Travel Impressions of the United States of North America), Professor F. Bluntschli, *Schweizersche Bauzeitung*, Vol. XXXVIII, pp. 23 ff., with illustrations.

style motifs. There are some exceptions, particularly in buildings designed by the architect [Louis] Sullivan. The beginning of modern architecture in American dates from the
emergence of [Henry Hobson] Richardson, the well-known
architect of Trinity Church [1873–1877] in Boston, a building
which is greatly admired, and rightly so. The style of this
church is, however, Romanesque and not modern. The Romanesque motifs are not treated freely; the forms, on the
contrary, are exact copies of old designs, and the building as
a whole does not reflect a modern conception. As a result,
after a short time Richardson ceased to be regarded as a
modern architect; and the more so since he used too many
Romanesque details in his secular buildings, even though he
used them with great skill.

Sullivan, a pupil of Richardson's,* is regarded by his followers as the forerunner of modern American architecture,
though he too, under the influence of his teacher, initially
used motifs which were obviously Romanesque. But early in
his career Sullivan freed himself from this influence and tried
to work independently. This independence shows beautifully,
particularly in the skyscraper of moderate height.† In the
"classical" skyscraper one is not aware of the iron
core or skeleton, although it is the main principle of its
construction. In contrast, Sullivan (and this marks him as an
architect with modern feeling) began to let the construction
show; that is, the stone covering followed the iron skeleton.
Sullivan's buildings demonstrate therefore a definitely different
structure in which the "upward tendency" is strongly emphasized. One can see a certain relationship with Gothic principles since here, as in Gothic, the windows are placed between
proportionally small pillars. The horizontal connections, the
windowsills, are recessed, and therefore the vertical tendency
is not disturbed. The pillars dissolve at their tops into figurines
that carry the flat, projecting roof.

Sullivan is, by the way, a good decorative artist; he has

---

* This is, of course, an overstatement of the relationship between Sullivan
and Richardson. There is no evidence that they ever met, though Sullivan
records, in The Autobiography of an Idea, his response to the tower of the
New Brattle Street Church in Boston, and Sullivan's Chicago Opera House
is clearly conceived in terms of Richardson's "red-blooded" influence. See
illustrations 23 and 25.

† This aspect of Berlage's article was illustrated with a photograph of the
Bayard (later Condict) Building on Bleecker Street in New York City. Cf.
illustration 26.

understood how to decorate his buildings with beautiful ornament. From a modern point of view he overdoes it in my opinion; he does not leave one surface plain. He has made, however, a great step forward: the ornaments in themselves have a classical beauty; they are very distinguished, and they are kept subordinate to the construction. I saw a large department store in Chicago which had been built by Sullivan.* This building is also overloaded with ornament, but nevertheless it makes a quiet and distinguished impression.

I also got to see a sketch of a Protestant church,† a design which differed radically from the usual conception of a church building. Sullivan feels that a Protestant church should be nothing more than the ideal community hall where everyone can see and hear the minister from every seat. Protestant churches which are being built at present still suffer almost everywhere because they cling to the old forms of the Catholic church. Sullivan has had the courage to give the interior of his church the form of a half circle and to place the tower above the center of the church, that is to say, right above the pulpit. This seems to me most remarkable because this placement gives the tower a higher ethical significance. The composition of this church may strike us as peculiar, but it looks very original. I can well imagine that Sullivan had to fight for the realization of this design, since I cannot imagine church elders readily agreeing to it.

In my opinion Sullivan's masterwork is a bank which he has recently completed in the small American town of Owatonna, Minnesota [see illustration 36]. A great mind always creates new surprises, and so does Sullivan's. This building does not resemble the above-mentioned building at all. The main hall is a massive block; the outlying, smaller business areas are appended to one side. Sullivan likes brick, which is available in beautiful materials in America. He therefore uses natural stone only for the base or pedestal of this building; and he raises the brick walls up from it. A strong cornice, built out in a collar of brick, finishes off the whole with an emphasis on the horizontal.

The illustration says more than any detailed description

* Carson, Pirie Scott Store (1899, 1903–1904, 1906).
† St. Paul's Methodist Church, Cedar Rapids, Iowa (1910–1912).

36. Louis Sullivan, The Security Bank (1907–1908), Owatonna, Minnesota.

could, and I do not want to expand on it. Everyone who looks carefully at this picture will have to admit that the building makes a great impression in its grandiose bulkiness. If one can imagine the beautiful color of the materials and recognize the beauty of the inlaid terra-cotta ornament, he must come to the conclusion that he stands in the presence of an architectural work of art. This work of art distinguishes itself, as does every other real work of art, by its forcefulness (not to be mistaken for coarseness), and in this case it distinguishes itself still more through its particular originality. There is, as far as I know, nothing comparable to it anywhere in Europe.

I must limit myself and take leave of Sullivan, though I could say much more about him as a poet, as a philosopher, and as an excellent writer.

[Vol. LX, No. 11, pp. 148–150]

Frank Lloyd Wright is a student of Sullivan's and is an architect of very special importance. I do not know whether Sullivan studied in Paris, but Wright is a student of the École des Beaux Arts.* Like Sullivan, Wright has nothing in his design-forms that reminds us of historical styles; his is an absolutely independent architecture. Wright leans on modern European architects more than Sullivan did, and like the modern Europeans, Wright struggles to simplify architectural masses and to treat ornament only as an aside; but his grouping of masses is so original that in the final analysis no European tendency is evident in his work.

Wright's specialty is the design of elegant country houses. He has built many in the vicinity of Chicago. The design of the D. D. Martin House [Buffalo, New York] is typical. The building has only two floors. The ground floor consists of living quarters and a children's playroom. The wall surfaces of this floor are almost uninterrupted by windows. In impressive contrast the upper floor has continuous rows of small windows; all the remaining rooms are in this upper floor. The ground floor lends itself to an organization in extended horizontal sequence since all the rooms open into each other and are also connected by long corridors. The Americans

---

* This is, of course, a reversal of the facts. Sullivan did study at the École; Wright did not. Wright's formal training was in the School of Engineering at the University of Wisconsin.

do not like to separate living areas with doors but prefer occasionally to close the openings with curtains. As a result, the interior affords beautiful views, not only from room to room, but also from the rooms into the halls, toward the staircase, and so on. These effects are heightened because the Americans are adept at decorating their houses with objects of art. Americans are fond of books as well, and often have shoulder-high bookshelves along the walls. Wright also likes flower decorations, and he likes to project out the walls of the ground floor at the height of the windows of the second floor in a way that forms a sort of outside trench in which flowers can be planted. The view from within, out over the flowers, into the garden beyond provides a rare sensation.

The low-pitched roof rests, in an unexpected way, directly on top of the upper floor; many of the rooms on that floor have the roof for a ceiling. This, together with the radically projected eaves, gives the rooms a quiet tone. One can imagine that such a house is extremely attractive. I had the impression of an extraordinary intimacy, and only with great effort could I tear myself away from those rooms. The originality of the rooms can best be described by the word "plastic"—in contrast to European interiors which are flat and two-dimensional. Outwardly as well as inwardly one can recognize an originality in these country houses—an originality that may enable one to talk about a new and native American architecture because there is nothing like it in Europe. Just as the English country house became the model for the European private house, so, no doubt, Wright's country houses will become the models for American private houses. Indeed this is already the case as can be seen in country houses built by many different architects since the beginning of Wright's career.

Some of the details of Wright's designs are particularly charming, for instance: entrances and halls, motifs with which he likes to work and through which he knows how to accomplish decorative effects. Such things are, however, difficult to describe; and since I have to restrict myself, these pictures will have to suffice.*

* This section of Berlage's article was illustrated with the following: D. D. Martin House, Buffalo, New York, general exterior, view of entrance, interior of living room with fireplace, interior of reception room, an exterior of the annex and a ground plan of the group; Coonley House, Riverside, Illinois, interior past the stairway toward the living room, two exteriors; Thomas P.

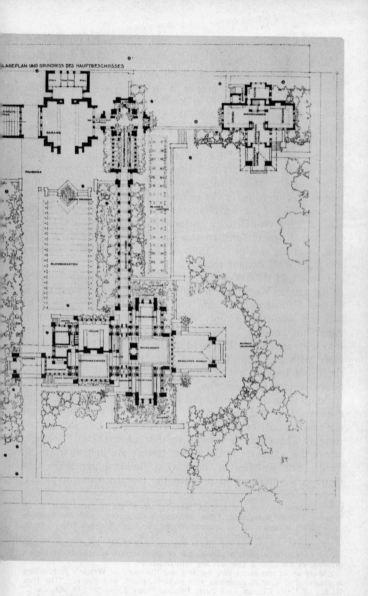

37. Frank Lloyd Wright, plan of D. D. Martin House (1904),
Buffalo, New York.

Wright has also built a church, actually a sort of meeting hall, which again reflects the great originality of his art. The interior of the church proper is designed as a square; the Sunday school is housed in another part of the building.†
Wright has worked here with the same contrasts that he uses in his country houses; he has placed the row of windows high up under the roof of the church; and this placement, together with the solid base of the wall, creates a unified space in the interior. The flat roof is projected out and casts a beautifully decorative shadow. The "plasticity" of this building is imposing in the generosity of its scale, reminiscent of the scale of an Egyptian temple. I have heard that the elders of the church were extreme in their opposition to this building. I can understand this because the elders must have had, as in the case of the Sullivan church, an entirely different image of a Protestant church.‡

I was told that Wright's masterwork is the office building of the Larkin Company in Buffalo, New York. I went to see it, and I must confess that that is not to say enough. The building consists of only one room because the modern American concept is that an office should not be divided into separate rooms. The head of the office works at the same table with his employees, and from his table his view can reach out into the entire forceful space with its various open floors which, like galleries, surround the central hall. The building is made of brick, and it looks like a warehouse from the outside.§ The interior hall has excellent light in spite of the masses of brick which surround the exterior corner towers. The effect is similar to that of the Unity Temple where the staircases in the corner towers are lighted from the inside. The galleries in the Larkin Building get their light through windows set in between the massive exterior pillars.

Hardy House, Racine, Wisconsin, exterior from the garden side; J. B. Wescott House, Springfield, Ohio, exterior from garden; and one example of Wright's influence on his contemporaries, the Emil Rudolph House, Highland Park, Illinois, designed by George W. Maher.

† Berlage's remarks on the Unity Temple, Oak Park, Illinois, were illustrated with a floor plan, a photograph of the exterior of the church and a drawing of the church interior. See illustration 30.

‡ More about this interesting building and the spirit of Wright's architecture is available in a small pamphlet with pictures, plans, and figures: "The New Edifice of Unity Church, Oak Park, Illinois, Frank Lloyd Wright, Architect." Descriptive and historical matter by Dr. Rodney F. Johonnot, Pastor. Published by the New Unity Church Club, June, 1906.—Berlage's note.

§ The Larkin Administration Building (1904) was demolished in 1950.

The building is conceived in terms of contrasts and with very powerful effect. Whatever concept one may have of an office building, particularly here in Europe, there is no office building here with the monumental power of this American one. The material of the interior (as of the exterior) walls is brick which alternates with the concrete ceilings. The detailing is handled naturally and in accordance with Wright's originality, and again it shows his strong creative genius.*

I left convinced that I had seen a great modern work, and I am filled with respect for this master who has been able to create a building which has no equal in Europe. I have tried to give you a brief glimpse of modern American architecture by describing works of the two greatest American architects of our time. Perhaps I have not done justice to others; during my short stay in America many things which might have been worth seeing may have remained unknown to me. Upon the advice of a young colleague of mine who worked in Sullivan's office, I concerned myself primarily with the work of Sullivan and Wright. But in so doing I may say that I have not strayed far from the truth; and my colleague, whose judgment I value highly, is of the same opinion.

Certainly—and I have already had the opportunity of stating this before—Wright has many followers who continue the work in terms of his ideas; and yet these other architects work outside of Wright's direct influence and demonstrate an ability to be independent at the same time that they honor the good principles of the master.

Some of the most interesting recent buildings in America are apartment houses of 10 to 12 or even more floors.† The demand for apartments is even greater in America than it is here in Europe. Because domestic help is so expensive in America, people are forced to live as economically and as simply as possible, and they are forced therefore to build comfortably designed apartments, each with its own kitchen. In Europe, and especially in Germany, there are good recent

* Berlage's remarks on the Larkin Building were illustrated with a photograph of the exterior and three photographs of the interior.

† Berlage illustrated these remarks with a photograph of the exterior and the plan of a typical floor of the Spencer Arms Apartments, Broadway, New York. The floor plan shows three apartments, one 7-room, one 8-room and one 9-room, each with two maid's rooms. Berlage adds: "Note the separate apartments for domestic help off the kitchen and pantry in these apartments. Each of the apartments opens onto the central Public Hall which is serviced by two passenger elevators."

examples by well-known architects of this kind of building. These European buildings are remarkable architecturally; but the conception of the American apartment buildings is at least their equal.

I had occasion to admire the correct principle of the mass effect of these American buildings. All decorations which could damage this effect are avoided. Great wall surfaces are composed in a well-balanced distribution of pedestal, structure, and cap. The windows are cut in without elaborate frames. The brick, which is the material throughout, is beautiful in its color. These simple elements have to accomplish the whole effect and certainly do so.

In the end, this undecorated structural simplicity has become the reigning principle in America, and not just for apartment buildings in particular, but for modern American architecture in general. Shouldn't it be possible to talk now of a relationship between the efforts there and here in Europe? I came back from America convinced that a new architecture is growing and that this architecture already shows striking results. We Europeans certainly have no reason to regard American architecture as inferior. On the contrary, the designs of the best American architects show an originality and an imagination which promise a great evolution in the future. I hope that with this short description I have succeeded in showing the readers of this magazine that American architecture should be accorded the high estimation which it really deserves.

[Vol. LX, No. 12, pp. 165–167]

6

Walter Gropius, "Die Entwicklung moderner In-
dustriebaukunst," from DIE KUNST IN INDUS-
TRIE UND HANDEL/JAHRBUCH DES DEUT-
SCHEN WERKBUNDES (Jena, 1913) pp. 17–
22, translated by Ruth Vollmer.

Walter Gropius (born 1883), as architect, teacher, and
critic, has occupied a position of central importance in
twentieth-century architecture. Before World War I he was
active in the Deutsche Werkbund, a civic association for the
integration of the arts in modern industry and commerce.
The association was made up not only of artists, architects,
and academicians but also of civic and political leaders. At
the close of World War I Gropius established the Bauhaus
at Weimar; the Bauhaus was moved to Dessau in 1925. As
a school, the Bauhaus was an educational projection of the
ideals of the Werkbund—dedicated to the attempt to break
down the arbitrary distinctions between the fine arts on the
one hand and the useful and mechanical arts on the other.
The Bauhaus was closed by the Nazis upon their accession
to power. Gropius and many of his coworkers in the Bauhaus
eventually emigrated to America, where they have been instrumental in reshaping our approach and response to visual
and spatial experience. It should be pointed out, however,
that that reshaping was consonant with the American tradition as that tradition had evolved through the nineteenth
century to its first climax in the work of Sullivan and
Wright. In this sense the influence of Gropius and his Bauhaus
colleagues was not a "foreign intrusion" as much as it was
a reaffirmation and redirection that infused new life into the
Sullivan-Wright tradition and saved that tradition from being

obscured by fine-arts academicism and national aesthetic self-consciousness.

The Development of Modern Industrial Architecture*

In the fields of commerce and industry a desire for beauty of form has made itself felt in addition to the demand for technical and commercial perfection. Not only in the manufacture of commodities but also in the construction of machines, vehicles, and factories which serve bare necessity, aesthetic viewpoints are being taken into consideration— compactness of form, color, and elegance of appearance. Obviously the mere material improvement of a product does not suffice for successful competition in the international market. The technical perfection of an object is universal; therefore an object must be impregnated with a spiritual idea and with aesthetic form if it is to be singled out and favored among the quantity of equal products. Industry is faced with the problem of concerning itself seriously with aesthetic questions. The manufacturer must gradually remove the stain of cheap appearance from his merchandise and imbue it with the noble qualities of handcrafted products, and this must be in addition to the advantages of machine production. Only then will industry's original idea, the substitution of mechanical procedures for handicraft, be realized.

The craftsmen of the past united three laborers in one person—the technician, the merchant, and the artist. As long as the assistance of the artist was regarded as dispensable, machine-made products had to remain inferior substitutes for hand-crafted products. Gradually it has been realized in commercial circles that new values can be brought to industry through the initiative of the artist. And now with improved understanding one can guarantee the artistic quality of the machine product by asking the artist to participate in the designing of the form which is to be mass produced. Hence,

* Gropius illustrated his essay out of his collection of photographs of grain elevators in the Americas and of factories in Detroit and Cincinnati. Gropius recalls that after the photographs had been published he showed them to Le Corbusier in Paris and that Le Corbusier republished them in his book *Vers une Architecture*.

a collaboration between artist, merchant, and technician will ensue; and this collaboration, when organized in a contemporary spirit, can possibly replace the lost facets of individual craft labor. The artist has the capacity to inspire the dead product of the machine; his creative energy will survive as an enzyme in the product. The artist's collaboration is not a luxury, not a fortuitous addition; it must become an indispensable component in the totality of modern industry.

One is still inclined to underestimate the material value and efficacy of the artistic component because it fails to impress the aesthetically inexperienced manufacturer. It does not suffice to hire patternmakers who are supposed to create "Art" for seven to eight hours a day on a meager monthly salary, and then reproduce a thousandfold their dull designs and distribute them all over the world. It is not that easy to obtain an artistically mature design. Just as technical invention and business management need independent minds, the design of new formal expression needs strong artistic power and an artistic personality. The most ingenious artistic ideas are just good enough for mass production if they are to benefit not only the individual but also the general public. It has already been shown by practical experience that it is shortsighted for a manufacturer to economize on design expenses. Leading industrial corporations have proved—and this decides the issue—that in the long run it pays if they concern themselves not only with technical perfection and economic worth but also with the artistic value of a product, designed to carry good taste and a sense of propriety to the masses. In this way the manufacturer reaps the honor of advancing culture, and he also achieves the mercantile equivalent, his profit.

It is understandable that practical-minded men refuse to discuss aesthetics in their field of work until they are forced to do so for economic reasons. In the past decades of technical development there has been no time for aesthetic considerations. Functioning primarily as engineer and merchant, the manufacturer had concerned himself first with practical demands and had found his profit in their fulfillment. He looked upon art, insofar as it entered his horizon, as a private fancy which he kept out of the field of his industrial activity. Today, the leaders of industry know that more than economy and perfect technology are necessary to a role in world trade.

As soon as an industrialist has recognized the advantages
of the artist's participation when successfully utilized, he
will begin to inform the entire field of his profession with
this recognition; he will transfer the artist's participation from
the product, which by nature is the nucleus of his professional
interest, to the place of work. In the past the factory has
been only a necessary evil. One had been content with buildings of hopeless shabbiness. However, increasing prosperity
has produced increasing demand for improvement. Better
lighting, heating, and ventilation were provided first; and now
and then an architect was called in afterward, and with little
understanding he draped the naked forms of utilitarian
structures with silly, nonessential decorations. This procedure
is unfortunately still in favor today. Unsolved points of conflict in the building are covered over, and the real character
of the building is veiled with a mask of borrowed styles which
have nothing in common with the serious nature of the
factory. The dignity of the enterprise suffers from this disguise. The difficulties cannot be solved in so cheap a way.

Instead of a superficial formulation, a real grasp of the
intrinsic problems of this new artistic orientation in architecture is needed: spirit instead of formula, careful artistic
study and planning of basic forms, elimination of ornamental
appendages. It is at the very outset of the planning phase of
a building that the artist has to be called in. Only then can
the artist understand and realize the organizational directives
of his client and make visual the meaning of the manufacturing process and find a dignified expression for the
inner values of the establishment and its methods of labor.
The skillful disposition of the floor plan and a skilled pro-
portioning of the masses of the building lie at the center of
the architect's spiritual endeavor; it is not, as some still
believe, a matter of adding ornamental accessories. We cannot fit a borrowed Rococo or Renaissance style to the concise
severities of our technical and commercial life, its efficient
handling of materials, of financial means, of the labor force,
and of time—because the once noble form used senselessly
becomes a sentimental phrase. The new time demands a
meaning of its own. Clearly conceived form, leaving nothing
to chance, distinct contrasts, an integrated order of the parts,
the rhythmic repetition of equal elements in series, and the
achievement of unity in form and color—all these will, in

correspondence with the energy and economy of our public life, become the aesthetic tools of the modern industrial designer.

These are only directions. They will become integrated architecture, filled with artistic power, only in the hands of a gifted architect. The essentially new character of industrial building ought to be particularly stimulating to the imagination of the artist since there is no traditional form to block his free rein. The less inhibited the development of full originality of form can become, the more advertising power the building will have for its enterprise and the more it will meet the advertising demands of its client, the industrialist. A dignified garment may justifiably be regarded as a promising reflection of the whole character of an enterprise. The artistic beauty of a factory building will certainly be in its impressive outline more fascinating to the public than advertising signs which dull the eye with their obtrusive relentlessness. The living force of an artistic idea will also never lose its effectiveness.

A building which has originated in this way, in a collaboration of client and architect, will have advantages which will pervade the entire organism of a factory. A clear internal arrangement, which is lucidly demonstrated on the outside as well, can considerably simplify the manufacturing process. But also, from a social point of view, it is important that the modern industrial laborer perform his work in well-proportioned rooms instead of in bleak and ugly industrial barracks. The laborer will collaborate more happily in the realization of common values when his place of work obliges his and everyone else's inborn sense of beauty and enlivens the monotony of his mechanical labor. Thus, with increasing contentment, individual workmanship and the efficiency of operation will steadily grow.

There are only isolated areas where industrialists have, in generous foresight, consulted the artistically trained architect at the outset of the erection of their industrial plants, but it seems already that values of unequivocal range will spring from these progressive industrial enterprises. As soon as educated people outside of commercial life learn of these enterprises which pursue ideal goals above the material satisfaction of the masses, the fame of these enterprises spreads rapidly. The first and biggest step in this path was

made by the Allgemeine Elektrizitäts-Gesellschaft [General
Electric Company] in Berlin when they called Peter Behrens*
as artistic consultant for the entire field of their industrial
endeavor. In half a decade this happy association of a
generous organization and a gifted artist has created works
which are at present perhaps the strongest and purest witnesses to this new European concept of building. They
demonstrate the capacity for revaluation and for new creation
of changed or indeed new thoughts on life in our time.
Through the simple means of elementary structure, buildings
of truly classic gesture originated to dominate sovereignly
their environment. The A.E.G. has established monuments
of nobility and power which no one can pass without being
impressed. A.E.G.'s achievement has become a model for
all industry, and one has not had to wait long for successors.
With this increase of interest the right architect and the
matching industrialist are finding each other and getting
together. A few examples of these new factory buildings are:
the Kaffee-Handels-A.-G. in Bremen (architect, H. Wagner),
the Delmenhorster Anker-Linoleum-Fabrik (architect, Stof-
fregen), the Chemischen Fabrik in Luben near Posen (Hans
Poelzig), and some others.† These new factories reveal an
affinity of architectural feeling which eventually will come
to design the natural garment for the vital life form of our
time and sternly reject all romantic remnants of architectural
form as weak falsehoods.

Germany seems to have gained the lead in the field of
artistic factory building in comparison with other European
countries. But in the motherland of industry, in America,
there are industrial complexes whose unknown majesty sur-
passes even the very best of our German buildings of this
kind. The grain elevators of Canada and South America,
the coal bunkers of the big railroads, and the most recent
work halls of the North American industrial corporations
impress one as having a monumental strength that can almost
stand comparison with the buildings of ancient Egypt. They
have an architectural image of such convincing impact that

* Behrens (1868–1938) was a German architect who is regarded as one of
the important early modern architects.
† Among these "others" Gropius might have mentioned his own Fagus
Factory (1910–1911) now under the protection of the West German Government, but in 1913 it was not considered good form for an architect to make
positive statements in print about his own architecture.

the spectator cannot help but grasp the meaning of the building. What these buildings are is self-evident, and their monumental effect cannot be explained as inherent in their physical size. It seems that their designers have retained an independent, healthy, and pure feeling for massive, compact, and integrated forms. Therein lies for us a valuable hint: that we should abandon our respect for our historical nostalgia and any other intellectual considerations which dim our modern European artistic creativity and which obstruct our artistic immediacy.

7

The Chicago Tribune *Competition (1922)*

The five illustrations from the *Chicago Tribune* Competition can stand here as images of the complex of attitudes comprised in American and European responses to the new architecture. In commemoration of its seventy-fifth anniversary the *Chicago Tribune* announced a $100,000 architectural competition for the design of a new Tribune Tower, a tower that would be "an enhancement of civic beauty" and which would "provide . . . a worthy structure, a home that would be an inspiration to [the *Tribune*'s] workers as well as a model for generations of newspaper publishers." Louis Sullivan (who did not enter the competition) hailed "the craving for beauty thus set forth by the *Tribune*" as "high Romance." The competition attracted 263 designs from architects in 23 countries, "a league," as the *Tribune* called it, "for new and bold treatment of the theme of the skyscraper—one that is to make architectural history for generations to come."

The Jury of Award selected as the winner the design of Howells and Hood of New York City (see illustration 38). Second prize went to Eliel Saarinen, whose entry arrived from Finland "at the eleventh hour"; and the jury gave third prize to Holabird and Roche of Chicago (see illustration 40). The jury stated with appropriate national modesty: "One gratifying result of this world competition has been to establish the superiority of American design." The jury noted Saarinen's design as the one European (though small country) exception; Louis Sullivan responded with considerable indignation that Saarinen's design should have won, and suggested, on the basis of what he claimed was inside information, that the jury had consciously decided not to award

38. Howells and Hood, *Chicago Tribune* Building (1924), Chicago, Illinois.

39. *Chicago Tribune* Competition (1922), Plate 197, Walter Gropius and Adolph Meyer, Weimar, Germany.

40. *Chicago Tribune* Competition (1922), Plate 21, Holabird and Roche, Chicago, Illinois.

41. *Chicago Tribune* Competition (1922), Plate 160, Paul Gerhardt, Chicago, Illinois.

42. *Chicago Tribune* Competition (1922), Plate 238, B. Bijvoet
and J. Duiker, Zandvoort, Holland.

first prize to any foreign design. The majority of the American designs given honorable mention are variations of Woolworth Gothic, as are the two American prizewinners; the majority of the European designs given honorable mention are Beaux Arts classicism.

Many of the designs attempt in various and often quite fanciful ways to fool the eye into seeing the skyscraper as small and intimate in scale. Many are attempts to rationalize the skyscraper as a column or an obelisk; one of the most striking is the Egyptian fantasy (see illustration 41). Very few of the designs reflect any awareness of or respect for the Chicago School and its designs of the 1880's and 1890's, and most of the few designs that show any awareness of Sullivan and Wright are European (see illustrations 39, 42). Howells and Hood's prizewinning design extends the Woolworth Gothic tradition in an archaeological direction by concentrating on a vocabulary of decoration derived from a single monument, the so-called Butter Tower at Rouen. Six years later, under the urging of a different patron, Howells and Hood's design for the *Daily News* Building in New York would amount to a reassertion of the skyscraper as skyscraper. The third prize winners, Holabird and Roche, had worked convincingly in the Chicago manner in the early years of the twentieth century, but the somewhat restrained Gothic of their *Tribune* entry is given a further eclectic flourish by the crowning statue, which is apparently Athena treated in quasi-Egyptian fashion.

The European designs of Gropius and Meyer (Weimar, Germany) and of Bijvoet and Duiker (Zandvoort, Holland) are basically European, but they also involve refreshing evidence that the influence of the Chicago School and of Sullivan and Wright was alive in Europe, just as Howells and Hood's next newspaper tower in 1930 was to prove that influence capable of a rebirth in America. The *Tribune* Tower Competition did "make architectural history," but somewhat less directly than had been intended. The avalanche of Gothic and classical forms seems today to have passed into oblivion far more rapidly than the jury with its prizes and honorable mentions would have expected; and yet a few of the designs which the jury overlooked were there as a forecast of the second phase of the architectural revolution that was to come in the 1930's and after. Conspicuous-consumption classicism has not, of course, suffered total defeat. It is still among us in all its 1893 bravado in the Rayburn Building; and new, subtle forms of it are beginning to appear as conspicuous-consumption modern, suggesting that even the new architecture can be subject to the unresolved dilemma posed by the assumed opposition between art and economy.

8

Postscript

In the course of preparing and editing this anthology, I have become more and more interested in what seem to me certain problems in architectural criticism in our own time. One of these problems derives from the fact that most modern buildings, and particularly the skyscraper, are not self-contained. Architectural monuments of the past, whether the Parthenon or Chartres or a medieval monastery or Jefferson's University of Virginia, were relatively self-contained as physical identities, housing all their structures and functions. The modern skyscraper is not self-contained. Without electricity for light and air conditioning and elevators, without steam to heat it and water to cool it and clean it, it would be uninhabitable; without the complex transportation systems that concentrate its workers and without the telephonic and other communications systems that make their work possible, it would be useless. The beautiful proportions of a Lever House or a Seagram Building are only the exposed tip of an iceberg; beneath the surface are the less beautiful proportions of miles of wire and pipe and tunnel, and aboveground, at a distance, other facilities, including power stations with their contribution to air and water pollution. As presently stated, our definitions of what a building is dictate a consideration of unity and proportion in the individual structure; but the skyscraper, quite apart from the social and economic complexes that make it necessary and possible, is only one element of a large physical complex; and if we were to judge its architecture in terms of its containment of that whole larger complex, we should have to alter our evaluations. I do not mean to suggest that we should abandon our focus on the single structure in favor of a focus on city planning but that we should reconsider the assumptions we make about the perimeter of a given building, redefining our answers to the question: Where does the building stop and the environment begin—so that our evaluation of a building is based on a clear notion of the entity we are evaluating.

Another problem in criticism derives from the implicit separation of large-scale or public architecture from small-scale or domestic architecture. Large-scale architecture tends to accept the urban-electronic realities of the contemporary world, but domestic housing has yet to resolve the oppositions between those realities and the insistent desire for more natural-organic sites and forms. We all complain of machine-made "samevilles," and yet as a compromise they result directly from our inability to resolve the urban-agrarian dilemma. In the early years of this century an automobile and a modest house cost about the same amount of money; a comparable house in 1965 costs 10 to 15 times as much; a more than comparable automobile costs the same or less. All the various resistances to prefabrication (conservatism in the building trades, public prejudice against standardization, and so on) are usually cited to explain this lag; and yet the fact remains that we have only singular (and often brilliant and always expensive) architectural solutions for the problem of domestic housing. We do not have an acceptable, repeatable solution that can be reproduced on a large scale; and within the individual house we have yet to realize the spatial flexibility that could be made possible by integrating home machines and appliances with each other and with the whole structure of which they are now indispensable parts.

It strikes me that we have a dilemma not unlike the dilemma that resulted from the nineteenth-century attempt to read architecture as though it were literature: we are still in danger of reading and translating only the surfaces of our architecture, and of accepting the surfaces as the full expression of the whole architectural complex. When we half congratulate ourselves on the architectural revolution of the last sixty years, it might be just as well to hesitate over our own dilemmas and problems.

Bibliography

Most of the works cited in this bibliography are secondary sources, many of them valuable not only for their perspectives and for the information they present but also for their bibliographies of primary and secondary sources.

1. BIBLIOGRAPHIES

Avery Index to Architectural Periodicals, Avery Memorial Library, Columbia University, New York, N.Y.

Hitchcock, Henry-Russell. *American Architectural Books: A List of Books, Portfolios, and Pamphlets on Architecture and Related Subjects, Published in America before 1895,* 3d revised edition. Minneapolis, 1946.

Roos, Frank J., Jr. *Writings on Early American Architecture: An Annotated List of Books and Articles on Architecture Constructed Before 1860 in the Eastern Half of the United States.* Columbus, Ohio, 1943.

Wall, Alexander J. *Books on Architecture Printed in America 1775–1830.* Cambridge, Mass., 1925.

2. GENERAL STUDIES OF ARCHITECTURAL AND CULTURAL HISTORY

Adams, Richard P. "Architecture and the Romantic Tradition: Coleridge to Wright," *American Quarterly,* IX (1957), pp. 46–62.

Andrews, Wayne. *Architecture, Ambition and Americans.* New York, 1955. Contains "A Selected Bibliography," pp. 289–303.

———. *Architecture in America: A Photographic History from the Colonial Period to the Present.* New York, 1960.

Cahill, Holger, and Alfred H. Barr, Jr., eds. *Art in America.* New York, 1939. "Lists and Bibliographies," pp. 153–162.

Coles, William A., and Henry Hope Reed, Jr., eds. *Architecture in America: A Battle of Styles*. New York, 1961. Brief Selected Bibliography, pp. 399–400.

Fitch, James Marston. *American Building: The Forces That Shape It*. Boston, 1948.

———. *Architecture and the Aesthetics of Plenty*. New York, 1961. "Notes," pp. 285–294.

Giedion, Sigfried. *Mechanization Takes Command: A Contribution to Anonymous History*. New York, 1948.

———. *Space, Time and Architecture: The Growth of a New Tradition*. Cambridge, Mass., 1949.

Gowans, Alan. *Images of American Living: Four Centuries of Architecture and Furniture as Cultural Expression*. Chicago, 1964.

Hamlin, Talbot Faulkner. *The American Spirit in Architecture*. New Haven, 1926.

Hitchcock, Henry-Russell. *Architecture: Nineteenth and Twentieth Centuries*. Baltimore, 1958. Selective International Bibliography, pp. 463–472.

———. *Modern Architecture: Romanticism and Reintegration (1750–1929)*. New York, 1929.

Jones, Howard Mumford. *O Strange New World, American Culture: The Formative Years*. New York, 1964. "Reference Notes," pp. 397–449.

Kimball, Sidney Fiske. *American Architecture*. Indianapolis, 1928. "Notes" contain bibliographical references, pp. 231–243.

Kouwenhoven, John A. *Made in America: The Arts in Modern Civilization*. New York, 1948. "List of Sources and References," pp. 271–290.

Larkin, Oliver W. *Art and Life in America*. New York, 1949. "Bibliographical Notes," pp. 483–514; "Supplementary Bibliography," pp. 515–517.

Lynes, Russell. *The Tastemakers*. New York, 1954. Bibliography, pp. 343–347.

McCallum, Ian Robert More. *Architecture, U. S. A*. New York, 1959. Bibliography, pp. 213–216.

Marx, Leo. *The Machine in the Garden: Technology and the Pastoral Ideal in America*. New York, 1964. "Notes" include bibliographical references, pp. 367–384.

Matthiessen, F. O. *American Renaissance: Art and Expression in the Age of Emerson and Whitman*. New York, 1941.

Mumford, Lewis. *The Culture of Cities*. New York, 1938. Bibliography, pp. 497–552.

———. *Roots of Contemporary American Architecture*. New York, 1959.

———. *Sticks and Stones: A Study of American Architecture and Civilization*. New York, 1934.

Neutra, Richard. *Survival Through Design.* New York, 1954.

Pierson, William H., Jr., and Martha Davidson, eds. *Arts of the United States: A Pictorial Survey.* Based on a collection of color slides assembled by the University of Georgia under a grant by Carnegie Corporation of New York. New York, 1960.

Reps, John W. *The Making of Urban America: A History of City Planning in the United States.* Princeton, 1965. Bibliography, pp. 545–562.

Tallmadge, Thomas Eddy. *The Story of Architecture in America.* New York, 1927.

Tunnard, Christopher, *The City of Man.* New York, 1953.

———, and Henry Hope Reed, Jr. *American Skyline.* Boston, 1955.

Zevi, Bruno. *Architecture as Space: How to Look at Architecture.* New York, 1957.

3.   STUDIES RELEVANT TO PART I

Boullée, Étienne Louis. *Treatise on Architecture*, ed. Helen Rosenau. London, 1953.

De Zurko, Edward Robert. *Origins of Functionalist Theory.* New York, 1957. Bibliography, pp. 243–255.

Herrmann, Wolfgang. *Laugier and Eighteenth Century French Theory.* London, 1962.

Kaufmann, Emil. *Architecture in the Age of Reason: Baroque and Post-Baroque in England, Italy, and France.* Cambridge, Mass., 1955.

———. "Three Revolutionary Architects: Boullée, Ledoux, Lequeu," *Transactions of the American Philosophical Society,* New Series, Vol. 42, Part 3. Philadelphia, 1952. Bibliography, p. 559.

Kimball, Sidney Fiske. *Domestic Architecture of the American Colonies and of the Early Republic.* New York, 1922.

Summerson, John Newenham. *Architecture in Britain, 1530–1830.* London, Baltimore, 1953. Bibliography, pp. 349–355.

4.   STUDIES RELEVANT TO PART II

Allston, Washington. *Lectures on Art, and Poems,* ed. Richard Henry Dana, Jr. New York, 1850.

Bode, Carl. *The Anatomy of American Popular Culture, 1840–1861.* Berkeley and Los Angeles, 1959. "A Note on the Sources" includes Bibliography, pp. 277–281.

Early, James. *Romanticism and American Architecture*. New York, 1965.

Frary, Ihna Thayer. *They Built the Capitol*. Richmond, 1940.

――――. *Thomas Jefferson, Architect and Builder*. Richmond, 1931. Bibliography, pp. 131–133.

Gallagher, H. M. Pierce. *Robert Mills, Architect of the Washington Monument, 1781–1855*. New York, 1935.

Gilchrist, Agnes Eleanor. *William Strickland, Architect and Engineer, 1788–1854*. Philadelphia, 1950. Includes bibliographies.

Hamlin, Talbot Faulkner. *Benjamin Henry Latrobe*. New York, 1955.

――――. *Greek Revival Architecture in America: Being an Account of Important Trends in American Architecture and American Life Prior to The War Between the States*. New York, 1944. "Some Articles of Architectural Interest Published in American Periodicals Prior to 1851," Appendix B, pp. 356–382. Bibliography of sectional, contemporary, and modern sources, and views of Greek Revival, pp. 383–409.

Lehmann-Hartleben, Karl. *Thomas Jefferson, American Humanist*. New York, 1947.

Metzger, Charles R. *Emerson and Greenough, Transcendental Pioneers of an American Aesthetic*. Berkeley and Los Angeles, 1954. Bibliography, pp. 149–150.

Morrison, Hugh Sinclair. *Early American Architecture, from the First Colonial Settlements to the National Period*. New York, 1952. Includes bibliographies.

Newton, Roger Hale. *Town and Davis, Architects: Pioneers in American Revivalist Architecture, 1812–1870, Including a Glimpse of Their Times and Their Contemporaries*. New York, 1942.

Place, Charles A. *Charles Bulfinch, Architect and Citizen*. Boston, 1925.

Wright, Nathalia. *Horatio Greenough, the First American Sculptor*. Philadelphia, 1963. "Notes" include bibliographical references, pp. 305–358.

5.   STUDIES RELEVANT TO PART III

Calhoun, Daniel Hovey. *The American Civil Engineer: Origins and Conflict*. Cambridge, Mass., 1960. "Bibliographical Note," pp. 219–237.

Bannister, Turpin C. "Bogardus Revisited," *Journal of the Society of Architectural Historians*, Vol. XV, No. 4 (Dec., 1956), 12–22; Vol. XVI, No. 1, 11–19.

Green, Constance McLaughlin. *Eli Whitney and the Birth of American Technology*. Boston, 1956. "A Note on the Sources," pp. 197–204.

Holbrook, Stewart H. *Machines of Plenty: Pioneering in American Agriculture*. New York, 1955. Bibliography, pp. 239–242.

Kirby, Richard Shelton, and others. *Engineering in History*. New York, 1956. Bibliographies at the end of each chapter.

———, ed. *Inventors and Engineers of Old New Haven*. New Haven, 1939.

Larkin, Oliver W. *Samuel F. B. Morse and American Democratic Art*. Boston, 1954. "A Note on the Sources," pp. 201–203.

Pierson, William Harvey, Jr. "Industrial Architecture in the Berkshires," unpublished doctoral dissertation, Yale University. Williamstown, Mass., 1949.

6. STUDIES RELEVANT TO PART IV

Campbell, William. "Frank Furness, an American Pioneer," *The Architectural Review*, 110 (Nov., 1951), pp. 311–315.

Condit, Carl W. *The Chicago School of Architecture: A History of Commercial and Public Building in the Chicago Area, 1875–1925*. Chicago, 1964. Bibliography, pp. 221–225.

Hitchcock, Henry-Russell. *The Architecture of H. H. Richardson and His Times*. Hamden, Conn., 1961. Bibliography, pp. 337–338.

———. *In the Nature of Materials, 1887–1941, the Buildings of Frank Lloyd Wright*. New York, 1942.

Manson, Grant Carpenter. *Frank Lloyd Wright*. New York, 1958. Bibliography, pp. 219–222.

Morrison, Hugh. *Louis Sullivan, Prophet of Modern Architecture*. New York, 1952. Includes bibliographies.

Mumford, Lewis. *Brown Decades: A Study of the Arts in America, 1865–1895*. New York, 1931. "Sources and Books," pp. 249–258.

Paul, Sherman. *Louis Sullivan, an Architect in American Thought*. Englewood Cliffs, N.J., 1962. "A Bibliography: the Writings of Louis Sullivan," pp. 147–151.

Peisch, Mark L. *The Chicago School of Architecture*. New York, 1965.

Scully, Vincent Joseph, Jr. *Frank Lloyd Wright*. New York, 1960. "Bibliographical Note," pp. 117–118.

———. *The Shingle Style: Architectural Theory and Design from Richardson to the Origins of Wright*. New Haven, 1955. Bibliography, pp. 165–174.

Wijdeveld, Hendricus Theodorius. *The Life-Work of the American Architect, Frank Lloyd Wright*. Santpoort, Holland, 1925.

7. STUDIES RELEVANT TO PART V

Banham, Reynor. *Theory and Design in the First Machine Age*. New York, 1960.

The Columbian World's Fair Atlas. Brooklyn, 1893.

Condit, Carl W. *American Building Art: The Twentieth Century*. New York, 1961. Bibliography, pp. 393–405.

Joedicke, Jürgen. *A History of Modern Architecture,* trans. by James C. Palmes. London, 1959, 1961.

Moore, Charles. *Daniel H. Burnham: Architect, Planner of Cities*. 2 vols. Boston, 1921.

———. *The Life and Times of Charles Follen McKim*. Boston, 1929.

Pehnt, Wolfgang. *Encyclopedia of Modern Architecture*. New York, 1964. Selected bibliography on the history of modern architecture, p. 327; brief bibliographies at the end of individual articles.

Pevsner, Nikolaus. *Pioneers of Modern Design from William Morris to Walter Gropius*. 2d edition, New York, 1949.

Platz, G. A. *Die Baukunst der neuesten Zeit*. Berlin, 1927, 2d edition, 1930.

Richards, James Maude. *An Introduction to Modern Architecture*. 3d revised edition, London, Baltimore, 1956.

Schuyler, Montgomery. *American Architecture and Other Writings,* ed. William H. Jordy and Ralph T. Coe. 2 vols. Cambridge, Mass., 1961. Bibliography, "Schuyler's Architectural Writings Originally Published in Periodicals," pp. 641–653. Abridged, New York, 1964.

Taut, Bruno. *Die neue Baukunst in Europa und Amerika*. Stuttgart, 1929.

Zevi, Bruno. *Storia dell'architettura moderna*. Turin, 1950; 3d, revised, edition, 1955. Contains one of the better bibliographies of modern architecture.